Adolescents Today

SECOND EDITION

JOHN S. DACEY
Boston College

SCOTT, FORESMAN AND COMPANY
Glenview, Illinois
Dallas, TX   Oakland, NJ   Palo Alto, CA   Tucker, GA   London, England

Library of Congress Cataloging in Publication Data

DACEY, JOHN S.
  Adolescents today.

  Includes bibliographies and indexes.
1. Adolescence—Addresses, essays, lectures.
2. Adolescent psychology—Addresses, essays, lectures.
I. Title.
HQ796.D18 1982   305.2'3   81-14616
ISBN 0-673-16023-8   AACR2

To my favorite teenagers in the world,
Julie, Jennifer, and Kristen Dacey,
this book is lovingly dedicated.

Photographs

Page
2:    Joanne Meldrum, photographer.
38:   Joanne Meldrum, photographer.
82:   Stock Boston; Donald Dietz, photographer.
112: Stock Boston; Elizabeth Crews, photographer.
154: Stock Boston; Cary Wolinsky, photographer.
178: Stock Boston; Julie O'Neil, photographer.
204: Stock Boston; Michael Weisbrot, photographer.
236: EKM-Nepenthe; Robert V. Eckert, Jr., photographer.
274: Stock Boston; Franklin Wing, photographer.
308: Stock Boston; David A. Krathwohl, photographer.
344: Stock Boston; Harry Wilks, photographer.
370: Archive Pictures, Inc.; Jill Freedman, photographer.
398: Stock Boston; Charles Gatewood, photographer.
426: Joanne Meldrum, photographer.

Cover photographs:
Upper Right: J. Stuart Edmonson, photographer.
Left Center: Photophile; Tom Tracy, photographer.
Bottom Right: Four By Five, Inc.

ISBN: 0-673-16023-8

1 2 3 4 5 6 7 8-KPF-88 87 86 85 84 83 82 81

Contents

Preface to the First Edition   xiii

Preface to the Second Edition   xv

Acknowledgments   xvi

Part One | **Developmental Patterns** | **1**

Chapter 1 | **The Study of Adolescence**   3

Chapter Highlights   3
Defining Adolescence   5
   Its Beginnings   *5*
   Memorable Incidents of Adolescence   *6*
   The Adolescent Diary   *8*
   Activity: What Were You Like?   *9*
Recapitulation Theory: G. Stanley Hall   11
Psychoanalytic Theory: Sigmund Freud   12
   The Structure of Personality   *13*
   The Stages of Development   *14*
Psychoanalytic Theory: Anna Freud   16
Psychoanalytic Theory: Otto Rank   17
Environmental Theory: Ruth Benedict and Margaret Mead   19
Social Psychology: Robert Havighurst   20
Social Psychology: Erik Erikson   21
Focal Theory: Coleman   27

A Tentative Definition of Adolescence   28
　　Activity: Classmate Maturity Rating   *29*
How to Study Adolescence   29
　　Descriptive Studies   *30*
　　Manipulative Experiments   *30*
　　Naturalistic Experiments   *31*
　　Longitudinal Studies   *31*
　　Cross-Sectional Studies   *32*
　　Longitudinal/Cross-Sectional Studies   *32*
　　A Comparison of Research Techniques   *32*
Summary   33
Questions   35
References   35

Chapter 2　　**The Search for Identity**   **39**
Chapter Highlights   39
Erikson's Identity Crisis   41
　　Activity: Stage of Life Matrix   *42*
Negative Identity   44
The Moratorium of Youth   44
Identity Status   45
　　Activity: Identity Rating   *48*
Vocational Identity   49
　　Parental Influence   *51*
　　The Influence of Sex   *53*
　　Activity: Your Own Vocational Identity   *54*
　　Career Education   *55*
Sexual Identity and Role   57
　　The Influence of Environment   *58*
　　Social Roles of the Sexes   *62*
　　Activity: Sex-Role Stereotype Test   *62*
　　Androgyny   *65*
　　The Future of Androgyny   *68*
　　Activity: Make Your Own Sex Role Test   *70*
Achieving an Identity Today   71
　　Future Shock   *71*
　　The Republic of Technology   *72*
The Achieved Identity   74
Summary   74
Questions   76
References   76

Chapter 3　　**The Onset of Puberty**   **83**
Chapter Highlights   83
Early Studies of Puberty   84
The Human Reproductive System   85

Adolescent Knowledge of Reproduction 85
Activity: How Well Do You Know Your Own Reproductive System? 86
The Female Sexual System 88
The Male Sexual System 89
When Does Puberty Start? 91
Activity: What Was Your First Reaction to Menarche? 92
Activity: What Was Your First Reaction to "Wet Dreams"? 92
Activity: "Sleeping Beauty": A Tale of Menstruation 93
The Effects of Timing on Puberty 94
The Early-Maturing Female: Ann 94
The Average-Maturing Female: Beth 94
The Late-Maturing Female: Cathy 96
The Average Adolescent Girl of One Hundred Years Ago: Dorothy 96
The Early-Maturing Male: Al 96
The Average-Maturing Male: Bob 97
The Late-Maturing Male: Chuck 97
The Average Adolescent Male of One Hundred Years Ago: Dan 98
Normal Age Ranges of Puberty 99
Inappropriate Physical Growth 101
Adolescents' Attitudes Toward Their Bodies 102
Summary 103
Activity: How I Feel About My Body (Female) 104
Activity: How I Feel About My Body (Male) 105
Questions 108
References 109

Chapter 4 **Thinking Style** 113
Chapter Highlights 113
Intellectual Development 114
The Role of Intelligence 115
Stages of Cognitive Development: Piaget 117
Variables in Intellectual Development 120
Stages of Intellectual Development in the College Years 124
Creative Development 127
The Creative Product 127
The Creative Mental Process 128
Activity: Uses for a Brick 130
Creativity, Giftedness, and the IQ 132
Creative Personality Traits 133
Activity: The Two-String Test 134
The Critical Period Hypothesis 135
Obstacles to Creativity 135
Aids to Creativity 137
Activity: Guidelines for Improving Your Own Creativity 138
Intelligence 139
The Measurement of Intelligence 139
Intelligence and Genes 140

Tommy: A Real Problem Child   *141*
Learning Disabilities   142
Nonlinear Thinking   143
   Communications and Thinking Patterns   *143*
   McLuhan's Theory and Adolescent Identity   *145*
   Activity: Freaking Out Grandma   *146*
Summary   147
Questions   148
References   148

Chapter 5   **Moral Judgment   155**
Chapter Highlights   155
Piaget's Theory of Moral Development   157
   The Practice of Rules   *158*
   The Awareness of Rules   *159*
Peck and Havighurst's Theory of Moral Development   160
Kohlberg's Theory of Moral Development   161
   Levels of Moral Judgment   *161*
   Activity: Rank the Characters   *164*
   How Moral Development Occurs   *165*
Morality and Sex Role   166
   Reasons for Differences in Levels of Morality   *166*
   Gilligan's Theory   *166*
Moral Education   168
   Kohlberg's Approach   *168*
   Research on Moral Education   *169*
   The Just Community School   *170*
Problems in and Suggestions for Moral Education   171
Summary   172
Questions   173
References   174

Part 2   **Interactions with the Environment**   **177**

Chapter 6   **The Changing American Family   179**
Chapter Highlights   179
The Changing Status of the American Family   180
   The End of the Extended Family   *180*
   Divorce   *181*
   Working Mothers and Nurturing Fathers   *181*
   Families and the Courts   *182*
   Parental Attitudes   *183*
   The Change from Primary to Secondary Group Status   *184*
The Effects on Adolescents of the Changing Status of the Family   184

The Loss of Functions   *184*
Activity: Your Family's Values   *185*
Fewer Adult Models   *186*
The Increase in Age-Related Activities   *187*
The New Individualism   *187*
Inappropriate Family Patterns   *188*
Momism: A Special Case   *188*
The Generation Gap   *189*
Activity: The Mini-Generation Gap   *190*
The Effects of Birth Order   191
Activity: Are You What Your Birth Order Has Made You?   *192*
Coping with Change   194
Ginott's Advice to Parents   *194*
Alternatives to the Traditional Family   *195*
Activity: My Family Tree   *196*
Summary   198
Questions   199
References   199

Chapter 7

Relationships with Peers   205
Chapter Highlights   205
Adolescent Subcultures   206
The Origin of Subcultures   207
The Psychogenic Model   *207*
The Culture Transmission Model   *207*
The Behavioristic Model   *207*
Elements of the Adolescent Subculture   208
Propinquity   *208*
Unique Values and Norms   *208*
Peer Group Identity   *209*
Charismatic Leadership   *209*
Desire for Autonomy   *210*
Special Channels of Communication   *210*
Proliferation of Group Languages   *211*
Activity: The Crowds in My College Class   *213*
Concern for the Underdog   *213*
Developmental Patterns of Peer Groups   214
Types of Associations   *214*
Stages of Development   *215*
Activity: The Crowds in My High School   *217*
Purposes of the Peer Group   218
Activity: Adolescent Perceptions of Peer Groups   *219*
When Peer Relations Fail   219
Effects of the School Setting on Peer Interactions   220
Evaluating Interactions in the Classroom   221
Activity: The Sociogram   *222*

Improving Peer Group Communications   223
   Communications Games   *224*
   The Language of Acceptance   *228*
Summary   230
Questions   232
References   232

Chapter 8   **Love and Sex**   **237**
Chapter Highlights   237
The Meaning of Love   238
Sexuality   239
   The Sexual Revolution   *240*
   Stages of Sexuality   *241*
Autosexual Behavior   241
Homosexual Behavior   243
   Myths About Homosexuals   *243*
   Causes of Homosexuality   *244*
   Societal Attitudes   *245*
   Activity: An Interview with a Group of Lesbians   *246*
   Activity: An Interview with a Group of Male Homosexuals   *247*
Heterosexual Behavior   249
Motivations for Sexual Behavior   253
Sexual Values   254
The Unmarried Teenage Parent   255
   Trends in Behavior   *256*
   Race Differences   *257*
   Causes of Adolescent Pregnancy   *258*
   The Adolescent Parent   *259*
Sex Education   261
   Sex Education and the Schools   *262*
The Demythologizing of Love   265
   Activity: Musical Values   *265*
Summary   267
Questions   268
References   269

Chapter 9   **The Schools**   **275**
Chapter Highlights   275
The Crisis in the Schools   277
   "Civil War" in the High Schools   *277*
   "Technical Deficiencies" of the High School   *279*
   Activity: What Would You Do?   *280*
How Academically Effective Are the Schools?   281
   Lower Validity of the SAT   *282*
   Changing Educational Goals   *282*
   Activity: A Fly on the Wall   *283*

Improving the Schools: "Small and Simple"   284
Improving the Schools: Back to Basics   284
    Activity: Should You Really Have a High School Diploma?   *286*
Improving the Schools: Conflict Negotiation   287
Improving the Schools: Discipline Management   288
    Kindsvatter's Method   *289*
    Glasser's Method   *290*
    Johnson's Method   *291*
Improving the Schools: Comprehensive Education   292
    Recommendations of the National Panel   *292*
    Experiential Learning   *292*
Improving the Schools: The Outward Bound Approach   294
Improving the Schools: The Walkabout Approach   295
Alternative Schools   296
    Alternative vs. Conventional Schools   *296*
    Three Alternative Schools   *297*
    Activity: How Would You Change Your Teachers?   *300*
Summary   302
Questions   304
References   304

Chapter 10   **Substance Abuse**   **309**
Chapter Highlights   309
Some Definitions   310
    Activity: What Do You Know About Drugs?   *313*
Soft Drugs   316
    Marijuana   *317*
    Activity: Reasons for Using Marijuana   *317*
    Cocaine   *318*
    Tobacco   *318*
    Alcohol   *319*
    Activity: Talking to Teenagers About Drinking   *319*
Hard Drugs   320
    Hallucinogens—Psychedelics   *320*
    Narcotics   *321*
    Stimulants   *321*
    Sedatives   *322*
Stages of Substance Abuse   322
    Drugs and Sex   *324*
    Ethnic Group and Abuse   *325*
    Activity: Do Your Own Study of Drug Use   *328*
    Crime and Abuse   *330*
Drug Use and Personal Relationships   331
Alternatives to Drug Abuse   331
Improving School Climate   335
    Activity: School Climate Survey   *336*

Summary 337
Questions 338
References 339

Chapter 11   **Mental Disturbance, Death, and Disease** 345

Chapter Highlights 345
Mental Disturbance Among Adolescents 347
  Types of Mental Disorder *348*
  Defense Mechanisms *349*
  Activity: The Best Defense—A Good Defense Mechanism? *349*
The Crisis of Death 350
Suicide 353
  Causes of Suicide *354*
  Story: My Attempts at Suicide *358*
  The Special Case of the College Student *359*
  Treatment and Prevention *359*
Disease and Disability 361
  Incidence *361*
  Community Health Services for Adolescents and Their Families *362*
  Activity: How Is Your Mental/Physical Health? *364*
Summary 365
Questions 366
References 366

Chapter 12   **Delinquent Behavior** 371

Chapter Highlights 371
The Nonaggressive Status Offender 372
  The Runaway *372*
  The Prostitute *373*
The Juvenile Delinquent 374
  Activity: Juvenile Crime in Your Town *375*
  Social Class and Delinquency *378*
  Personality and Delinquency *379*
  The Inadequate Family *381*
  Activity: Delinquent Activities of Friends *382*
  Long-Term Implications of Delinquent Behavior *383*
Gangs 384
  Gangs and Social Class *384*
  Characteristics of Gang Joiners *385*
The Treatment of Delinquency 385
  The Behaviorist Approach *385*
  The Psychotherapeutic Approach *387*
  Halfway Houses *388*
  The Ecological Approach *389*
  Outward Bound *390*
  The Diversion Program *392*
  Activity: My Own Crime History *392*

Summary   393
Questions   395
References   395

Chapter 13   **Values**   399
Chapter Highlights   399
Raths' and Simon's Theory of Values   400
Religious Values   401
  Activity: How Religious Are You?   *402*
  Cultural Influences   *403*
  Participation and Belief   *404*
  The Family's Influence on Religion   *404*
  Religious Education   *405*
  Stages of Religious Growth   *405*
  The Conversion and Confirmation Experience   *407*
  Religious Revival   *407*
The Effect of the Media on Values   408
  The Media and Aggressiveness   *409*
  Television and Other Values   *409*
The Effect of Music on Values   412
The Acquisition of Values   414
Values Clarification Techniques   414
  Activity: Things I Like to Do   *415*
  Values Clarification Strategies   *416*
  An Evaluation of Values Clarification   *419*
A Comparison of Values Clarification and Moral Education   419
Summary   420
Questions   421
References   422

Chapter 14   **Adolescence Past, Present, and Future**   427
Chapter Highlights   427
Adolescence Past   428
Adolescence Present   429
Adolescence Future   431
  New Ways of Dealing with Adolescents   *431*
  New Ways of Understanding Adolescents   *432*
Advice of Experts to Beginners   434
  Honesty   *435*
  Sense of Humor   *435*
  Tolerance   *436*
  Clarity in Setting Limits   *436*
  Paying Attention to the Withdrawn Child   *437*
  Clarifying Values—Yours and Theirs   *437*
  Communications Skills   *438*
Summary   438

Questions   439
References   439

Appendix A: The Survey   440

Appendix B: An Evaluation of Birth Control Techniques   453

Appendix C: Services Available to Youth in Most

Medium-to-Large Cities   457

Glossary   460

Name Index   469

Subject Index   477

Preface
to the First Edition

Adolescents Today is designed for use in adolescent psychology courses at the introductory level. Most of the data it reports has been drawn from recent psychological research, although information gleaned from sociology, anthropology, education, and popular literature has also been included where appropriate. Theoretically, it is oriented toward the work of Erik Erikson, although a number of other approaches are explained and evaluated.

Current problems in adolescent life are emphasized. Among these are violence in the schools, sex roles and morality, declining family life, new educational practices, unwed parenthood, the switch from political to vocational interests, concerns over emotional disturbance and suicide, drug and alcohol abuse, and changing patterns in the relationships between youth and the rest of society.

The book is organized in two sections. Part 1 (Chapters 1 through 5) first defines adolescence and then describes the developmental patterns associated with identity, puberty, thought, and moral judgment. Part 2 (Chapters 6 through 14) treats the influences of the environment, beginning with the inner circle of the family and extending outward and upward to the complex world of values formation.

Each chapter is introduced by chapter highlights, which give a topical outline of the chapter, and a list of key terms and concepts and important people. Within each chapter are activities, whose aim is to increase the reader's empathy for teenagers and insight into his or her own adolescent years. Throughout the book is a feature called "Would You Agree?" that presents differing views of research findings or controversial theories. The objective of this feature is to engage the reader in a thoughtful consideration of opposing theories and interpretations. My own views are expressed as "A Personal Note" or "A Personal Opinion."

Each chapter ends with a summary, questions, a list of cited references, and a list of additional references. The latter is a bibliography of over 1000 books and articles on adolescence, most of them published within the last few years.

The results of a recent survey of over 100 persons currently working with adolescents is presented in Appendix A. Conducted by the author, the study asked these practitioners fifty questions about the youth with whom they work. Thus, it provides more recent data than that available in other published research. Respondents were selected in order to obtain numerous viewpoints in terms of region, age, size of town, and normality of the youth reported on. The survey resulted in a number of interesting and surprising insights into current teenage attitudes and behavior. Two additional appendixes are Appendix B, an evaluation of birth control techniques, and Appendix C, services available to youth in most medium-to-large cities. A glossary of terms concludes the text.

As Chapter 14 makes clear, I believe that it is especially hard to be an adolescent in these times of expanding options and never-ending change. This book was written not only to provide up-to-date information on the many aspects of teenage life, but also to offer suggestions to those who work with adolescents on helping make adolescent lives happier and more meaningful.

John S. Dacey

Preface
to the Second Edition

In the three years since *Adolescents Today* was published, the theories and research on adolescent behavior have undergone some important changes. Almost 200 new books and articles have been consulted, and in most cases, these findings were reviewed for this new edition. There are new or revised sections on the areas of the androgynous sex role, cognitive development (especially the theories of Flavell and Perry), moral development, family status, contraception, teenage pregnancy, venereal disease, drug abuse and prevention, and suicide. There are additional suggestions for the practitioner in several places. Finally, the survey of professionals working with adolescents in the field has been updated for this edition. On the basis of considerable advice, almost all of the pedagogical features of the first edition have been maintained in this edition.

I felt three years ago, and I still do today, that these are particularly difficult times to be an adolescent. As I said in that preface, this book was written not only to provide up-to-date information on the many aspects of teenage life, but also to offer suggestions to those who work with adolescents on helping make their lives happier and more meaningful. I have had considerable help in attempting to make this edition more effective at achieving these two goals, and I sincerely hope that it will prove to be so.

John S. Dacey
Lexington, MA

Acknowledgments

I would like to thank a number of my fellow professors who have used this book in their classes, and who have kindly made suggestions as to how this edition could be improved:

Leander Abbott, Cayuga Community College, Auburn, New York;

Charlotte Ferguson, Benedict College, Columbia, South Carolina;

Dyan Harper, Southern Illinois University, Carbondale, Illinois;

Janice King, Northern Nevada Community College, Elko, Nevada; and

Alan Krasnoff, University of Missouri, St. Louis, Missouri.

Ann Sibley typed the revisions to this edition, and as with the first edition, generally oversaw its completion.

Nancy Carter and Chris Jennison, editors at Scott, Foresman, and copyeditor LaDonna Wallace, were invariably helpful. Dr. Jane Hamilton worked closely with me on the changes for this edition and made many valuable contributions for which I am grateful.

part 1

Developmental Patterns

In this book a great number of generalizations are made about a very large number of people—the over 30 million teenagers living in the United States in the early 1980s. Certainly not everything written in the pages that follow will apply to every one of them, nor even to all the subgroups to which they belong. Nevertheless, such generalizations can be extremely helpful to those who are or are planning to work with adolescents today. They provide the basis for differentiating between typical and atypical, or normal and deviant, behavior. They also provide the basis for educated guesses on how to deal with a wide range of behaviors.

Some generalizations concern behaviors or traits whose development is clearly influenced by our genetic inheritance. These characteristics are a part of our nature at birth, although some are not manifested until later in life (such as the physical changes of puberty). Other traits, for example, the ethical values we hold, result entirely from our interactions with the environment.

Part 1 examines the first type, developmental traits, in several contexts. Following the first chapter on various approaches to the study of adolescence, we look at the development of identity, puberty, thinking, and morality, and the various genetic and environmental factors contributing to it. Part 2 studies the effect of social institutions (such as schools and the family) and cultural forces (such as sex role values) on the developing adolescent.

Chapter One

The Study of Adolescence

Chapter Highlights

Defining Adolescence
  Its Beginnings
  Memorable Incidents of Adolescence
  The Adolescent Diary
  What Were You Like?
Recapitulation Theory: G. Stanley Hall
Psychoanalytic Theory: Sigmund Freud
  The Structure of Personality
  The Stages of Development
  Would You Agree?
Psychoanalytic Theory: Anna Freud
Psychoanalytic Theory: Otto Rank
Environmental Theory: Ruth Benedict and
      Margaret Mead
Social Psychology: Robert Havighurst
Social Psychology: Erik Erikson
Classmate Maturity Rating
A Tentative Definition of Adolescence
  Focal Theory: Coleman
How to Study Adolescence
  Descriptive Studies
  Manipulative Experiments
  Naturalistic Experiments
  Longitudinal Studies
  Cross-Sectional Studies
  Longitudinal Cross-Sectional Studies
  A Comparison of Research Techniques
Summary

Key Terms and Concepts

evolution
catharsis
anthropoid
sensory-motor skills
storm and stress
libido
id
ego
superego
defense mechanisms
authority figures
erogenous zones
stimulation
Oedipal conflict
latency
developmental tasks
identity crisis
moratorium
repudiation
identity confusion
focal theory
descriptive studies
manipulative experiments
naturalistic experiments
longitudinal studies
cross-sectional studies

Important People

G. Stanley Hall
Sigmund Freud
Anna Freud
Otto Rank
Ruth Benedict
Margaret Mead
Robert Havighurst
Erik Erikson
John Coleman

These are the best years of your life! You'd better enjoy them now, because before you know it, you'll be weighted down with adult responsibilities!

Most middle-aged persons today can remember, when they were young, hearing similar words spoken by their parents, especially in answer to their complaints of life's difficulties. It used to be a common belief that adolescence was carefree, but it is not so common any more. In fact, some believe that adolescence has become the *worst* period in one's life (Warshaw, 1978).

Others say it always has been a difficult time. The Greek philosopher Socrates complained in the fifth century B.C. that

> *Our youth now love luxury. They have bad manners, contempt for authority; they show disrespect for their elders and love chatter in place of exercise. They no longer rise when others enter the room. They contradict their parents, chatter before company, gobble up their food, and tyrannize their teachers.*

Most large dictionaries, after having defined a "teen" as a person from eleven to nineteen years old, also give this definition of the word: "teen (tēn), n. Injury; misery, affliction; grief." Taken from Middle English, this definition is now obsolete. But the above observation, made two-and-one-half thousand years ago, has a familiar ring. Critical as it is, many adults would find it too mild for adolescents today. They point to the startling increases in the use of alcohol and drugs, the commissions of theft, vandalism, and assaults, and the contempt for authority on the part of many youth as evidence that things have never been worse.

Are adolescents becoming more of an affliction to society? Is it harder to be

4

an adolescent than it used to be? If so, can we understand why? Can anything be done? Such questions are heard more and more often. But before we can answer them, we must try to define adolescence.

DEFINING ADOLESCENCE

Its Beginnings

At what point does adolescence begin? Many suggestions have been offered:

- When girls begin to menstruate; when boys have their first ejaculation.
- When the level of adult hormones rises sharply in the bloodstream.
- When they first think about dating.
- When their pubic hair begins to grow.
- When girls are 10 years old; when boys are 11½.
- When an interest in the opposite sex begins.
- When girls develop breasts.
- When they pass the initiation rites set up by society; for example, in the Catholic Church, confirmation; in the Jewish faith, bar mitzvah and bas mitzvah.
- When they become unexpectedly moody.
- When children turn 13.
- When they form exclusive social cliques.
- When they think about being independent of their parents.
- When they worry about the way their bodies look.
- When they enter seventh grade.
- When they can determine the rightness of an action, independent of their own selfish needs.
- When their friends' opinions influence them more than what their parents think.
- When they begin to wonder who they really are.

Although there is at least a grain of truth in each of these statements, they don't help us much in defining adolescence. For example, although most would agree that menstruation is an important event in the lives of women, it really isn't a good criterion for the start of adolescence. First menstruation (called menarche) can occur at any time from 8 to 16 years of age. We would not call the menstruating 8-year-old an adolescent, but we would certainly call the nonmenstruating 16-year-old one.

Another approach to defining this period of life is to examine the major events that occur during it. Below are some vignettes from the lives of individuals who were asked to "tell of an incident from your adolescence which you believe most typifies it."

Memorable Incidents of Adolescence

Betty, age 22 *I remember getting caught by my mother with one of my girl friends in the closet. We were 11. Well, we were exploring each other's bodies—juvenile adolescent masturbating, I guess you'd call it. My mother just freaked out. She screamed, "What are you doing?" It was embarrassing. We denied everything, and her whole reaction to the thing finally was to give me a pamphlet put out by the Tampax Company on "Your Growing Years." She wouldn't talk about it, though. She didn't punish me—I don't think she even told my father about it. I guess this must be just our secret.*

Mary, age 49 *My life was dull when I was a teenager. I was 19 when my daughter was born in 1949. I ran away from home—that I will admit to.*

I remember that in high school I made myself an outfit in sewing class: a pair of shorts and a middy top. That's when I was thin; I looked jazzy. I went to the beach with my girlfriend Jean. Jimmy, the guy I was going with at the time, called my parents' house and found out where I was. I was sitting on the beach smoking a cigarette when Jimmy came up from behind me and pulled the cigarette right out of my mouth. He said, "Don't you ever, ever! Don't you ever, ever act this way!" I should have married him. He tried to do a lot for me. I should have married him, but I played him along and I did him a lot of dirt.

Glenn, age 35 *In my home town, there were two distinct sections—the upper-middle-class WASPs and the lower-middle-class immigrants from Eastern Europe. At our high school, the two groups never mixed. I belonged to the first group and regularly dated a girl from it.*

One Friday in my junior year, a bunch of us were riding in a bus to a nearby university to see a play. I was riding with my girlfriend, and across the aisle sat Elaine, a gorgeous Polish girl whom I had often admired from afar. To my surprise, she kept looking at me in a flirting way.

We got to the play half an hour early. While we were waiting, Elaine came up to me and asked if I would like to see a special place she knew of. It turned out to be a lovely garden. We stayed there talking for some time and were late for the play. The teacher yelled at us, but at least we got to sit together.

Throwing caution to the winds, I rode home on the bus with her. She turned out to be much less shy than I had thought. We had a pretty heavy necking session, and as we neared home, a powerful orgasm swept over me. I was amazed and confused, because I didn't think that could happen unless you touched yourself. When I got off the bus, I was ecstatic. This ended abruptly when my girlfriend came over to me. She glanced at me, and though I couldn't be sure, I thought she could tell what had happened. She started to speak, but tears filled her eyes, and she quickly turned and left.

I didn't sleep that night. I soon learned the real cost of the ride. My friends were furious at me, and obviously Elaine's friends had gotten to her, because she never spoke to me again. My girlfriend did speak to me, but only to tell me what a rat I was and to get out of her life. Adolescence is a part of my life which I have no desire to relive!

Clare, age 19   The summer of eighth grade my friend Judi and I were working on painting and redoing the CYO room in my parish. It was a very big deal because we were associating with high school people on almost equal terms. I liked this boy, Ross, who was a sophomore. He was a wrestler during school and worked outdoors during the summer, so he had a tanned, muscular body. I was 14, and he appealed to me enormously.
One day the other people who were working on the place left and we were alone. He asked me to massage his back, so I did that. I loved the feel of his body. He kissed me, and we ended up lying on a couch all afternoon. He taught me to French kiss and to neck and make "hickies" in an almost formal, teacher-to-student manner. I loved it. I went home with a hicky on my neck, made sure that all my friends knew about it and who put it there, and it was fun going through all the effort it took to hide it from my mother.

Eddie, age 19   I was 14 when I first did a crime. Me and a friend were going to bust into this house, because he saw where the lady hid the back door key, but then he chickened out. I went in at two in the morning, and I was hardly even scared. I went into the bedroom and I remember I was excited to hear the people breathing. I grabbed all the stuff on the dresser and knocked over the lamp. The man jumped out of bed and grabbed me — he was strong as hell. I thought I had it, but then I bit him hard on the arm and he let go. I beat it fast. I still held on to the jewelry, but when I took it to a guy the next day, he said it was all cheap junk. I still don't know if it was or not. I been in some trouble since then, but never again for busting into houses!

Sue, age 27   From grades seven through twelve, Linda Albert was my physical education teacher. I felt a very embarrassing infatuation toward her. I felt guilty because I did, in fact, love this woman. All my behavior was designed to please her. I spent my entire energies perfecting my technique on the parallel bars, and fantasized about the look in her eyes when I was spotlighted on the "big night."

She got married during my freshman year of high school. I remember a feeling of immense loss and jealousy. I started to doubt my own sexuality and its "normalcy." I never fantasized about sleeping with her, but her touch on my shoulder increased my heartbeat threefold. It was a reality that I never admitted to others, for fear of ridicule, and one that I pretty much denied to myself, for fear of recognizing myself as a homosexual.

I often left her anonymous notes to brighten her day. I felt incredible excitement when I was picked to present her with a pewter water pitcher from the class of '68. Of course it's different now — she's Linda, not Mrs. Albert. I recognize her womanhood and my womanhood, and I feel comfortable about the love that exists.

Jennifer, age 33   *The incident I remember most vividly happened when I was in the eleventh grade. I guess every school has its arch-radicals, and ours were Dan and Dolores, who went together. They were constantly making statements that infuriated everyone. We were together one night at a friend's house, and they were lecturing us about United States foreign policy. Everyone was making fun of their ideas, most particularly my boyfriend Bob and me. Dolores had said something, I don't remember what now, and I made a sarcastic remark that made everyone laugh uproariously. She and Dan were very angry and stormed out of the gathering.*

The next morning I was awakened at seven by a phone call from Dolores's mother screaming at me, "What have you people done to them?" Her voice was shrill with hysteria, and it took me several minutes to realize what she was saying. Dan and Dolores were dead. They had been found in Dan's car, parked in Dolores's garage. The garage door was closed and the running engine had asphyxiated them. It slowly became clear that Dolores's mother felt that I had somehow caused her daughter's death.

The next day, the official story was put out by her parents: The couple had been talking in the car, left the motor running to keep warm (it was winter), and they had fallen asleep and died there. I remember staring at Dolores's calm face as she lay in the casket, dressed in a lovely pink gown. I didn't know then and I don't know now whether her death was the result of a suicide pact or an accident, but the guilt that I felt that day is with me still!

When we examine some of the major themes of adolescence in these episodes — sex, guilt, loyalty, parental conflict, friendship, confused values — and the emotional intensity with which they are experienced, we can begin to shape a definition of adolescence.

The Adolescent Diary

Perhaps the most revealing way to gain insight into adolescent thinking is to read a teenager's diary. Here is an excerpt from the diary of Debbie, age 14.

Now I think I should say something about my life as a teenager so far this year. My life centers around me and school. The only thing that keeps me going is my boyfriend Dick. He makes all the despising of my parents, friends, schoolwork, and self worth it.

First my family. Probably of all the people in the world I know, I get along best with my sister. She has a terrific personality, whereas I don't, and she'll always listen to what I have to say. In general, I hate my mother. This, I feel, is only natural since she is the main force standing in the way of my social life. My mother is a warm, intelligent lady, but I'm a rat and I hate her.

Religion has little place in my life. As much as I hate to admit it, I think Jesus is a phoney, set up by men only to scare men into being slaves of the church. Eventually I think he will be denounced.

My theory is: Have faith in yourself. If that fails, people. If that fails, God.

If you can't believe in anything, then you are dead as a person. God is the why of what exists.

In the ninth grade there are about fifteen different cliques. We're labelled the intellectuals, which is a laugh because we're about the least intellectual people in the state. We spend hours on end talking about gossip, lives, the Beatles, and each other. We spend days doing handstands and walking around town.

One can clearly see, even in this brief excerpt, the contradictions and confusions of feeling that are often present in adolescent thought. However, as a general approach to defining the adolescent experience, the diary is limited in usefulness.

What Were You Like?

Below are some questions about your personality which you might enjoy answering. Pretend you are in the eighth grade. Let your mind drift back to that time, and imagine yourself sitting in your favorite classroom. Look around the room and see who is sitting there. Try to answer these questions as you would have then.

A. Are the following statements true or false?

1. Most of the other kids in the class are stronger than I am.   T   F
2. I am about as intelligent as anybody in this classroom.   T   F
3. I am certainly not one of the teacher's favorite students.   T   F
4. Most people would say I am above average in athletic ability.   T   F
5. I am probably one of the more attractive students in this class.   T   F
6. I am one of the shortest of the kids here.   T   F
7. I would say that I am more mature than most of my friends.   T   F
8. I am more popular than most of my classmates.   T   F
9. I am very moody and I seem to get upset easily.   T   F
10. I am unhappy with several of my physical traits.   T   F

B. In the following multiple-choice statements, choose the one that best fits you.

1. My knowledge of sex is
   a. practically nonexistent.
   b. much less than the other kids'.
   c. about the same as the other kids'.
   d. much greater than the other kids'.

2. At parties and dances, I am known as
   a. a real wallflower.
   b. shy, except with my close friends.
   c. outgoing.
   d. the life of the party.

3. I would describe my relationship with my parents as
   a. very loving; we really understand each other.
   b. friendly, but we sometimes have unpleasant fights.
   c. stormy about half the time.
   d. we are usually so angry at each other that we hardly talk at all.

4. My interest in my school work is
   a. high.
   b. moderate.
   c. low.
   d. nonexistent.

5. Thoughts about death and physical illness:
   a. I am plagued with such thoughts.
   b. I frequently have such thoughts and they bother me from time to time.
   c. I don't think very much about such things.
   d. I don't recall thinking about these problems at all.

C. Fill in the blanks in the following sentences:

1. The thing I would change most about my life is _____.
2. My best friend is _____.
3. My deepest secret is _____.
4. My fondest memory is _____.
5. The thing of which I am most ashamed is _____.

D. Rank the following characteristics in the order in which they are true of you. Put a 1 in front of the characteristic that best describes you; put a 2 in front of your second most typical trait, and so on.

_____ Eager-beaver student   _____ Handsome/pretty
_____ Sports enthusiast   _____ Kind and generous
_____ Boy/girl crazy   _____ A loyal friend
_____ Introspective   _____ Well mannered
_____ Humorous   _____ Reliable

A more formal approach to examining the meaning of adolescence is to look at the theories offered by psychologists, sociologists, and anthropologists.

RECAPITULATION THEORY: G. STANLEY HALL

G. Stanley Hall (1844–1924) is known as the father of adolescent psychology. Building upon Charles Darwin's ideas about **evolution,** * Hall constructed a psychological theory of human development, published in two volumes and entitled *Adolescence* (1904).

Hall believed the now-discredited idea that each person's biological development passes through the same series of stages that characterized the evolutionary development of the species. He further elaborated this idea by assuming that each person recapitulates the cultural development of the human race. Hall thought that all development is determined by physiological (i.e., genetic) factors. Development occurs in an unchangeable, universal pattern, and the effects of the environment are minimal. For example, Hall argued that some socially unacceptable behavior in children, such as fighting and stealing, is inevitable. He urged parents to be lenient and permissive, assuring them that children must have this **catharsis,** and that when they reached the later developmental stages, these behaviors would simply drop out of existence.

Hall posited four periods of development of equal duration, which he felt correspond to the four stages of development of our species: animal, **anthropoid,** half-barbarian, and civilized.

Infancy: birth–4 years. In this stage children recapitulate the animal stage in which mental development is quite primitive. Sensory development is the most important aspect of this period, together with the development of **sensory-motor skills.**

Childhood: 4–8 years. Hunting and fishing, using toy weapons, and exploring caves and other hiding places are common activities of childhood. Language and social interaction begin to develop rapidly, as they did during the nomadic period of the human race.

Youth: 8–12 years. This period corresponds to the more settled life of the agricultural world of several thousand years ago. This is the time when children are willing to practice and to discipline themselves; this is when routine training and drills are the most appropriate — especially for language and mathematics.

Adolescence: 12–25 years. **Storm and stress** typify human history for the past 2000 years, as well as youth. Adolescence is a new birth, for now the higher and more completely human traits are born.

Hall made a major point of the "contradicting tendencies" of adolescence — the experience of violent mood swings — which he felt tended to make youth more human. Some of the turbulent variations he noted are

- Energy and enthusiasm vs. indifference and boredom
- Gaiety and laughter vs. gloom and melancholy
- Vanity and boastfulness vs. humiliation and bashfulness

*Terms that appear in boldface in the text are defined in the glossary at the back of the book.

- Idealistic altruism vs. selfishness
- Sensitivity vs. callousness
- Tenderness vs. cruelty

Hall felt that the development of most human beings stopped short of this fourth stage, in which appreciation of music and art and the higher tendencies are achieved. Most people seemed fixated at the third stage, in the dull routine of work. A social reformer, Hall believed that adolescence is the only period in which we have any hope of improving our species. He felt that placing teenagers in enriched environments would improve their genes, which their children would then inherit. Hence we could become a race of "superanthropoids."

In recapitulation theory, we have an interesting but quite inaccurate picture of human social development. Most psychologists today believe Hall tried to force reality to fit an outmoded conception of evolutionary development. His theory is considered wrong for several reasons: While it may have described children of the early 1900s with some accuracy, it does not coincide with our knowledge of them today. It most particularly does not present a true picture of adolescence. Although the majority of youth in his time may not have had much appreciation for civilized culture, this was clearly due not to genetic imperfections, but to such factors as having been forced to leave school to work on the farm. In addition, Hall's belief in the genetic transmission of acquired (improved) characteristics is scientifically false. Since Hall looked only at American culture, and since most individuals in that culture did develop similarly, he mistakenly thought that genes were responsible for this similarity. Later study of other cultures has shown wide differences in developmental patterns.

A far more refined description of human growth tendencies, though one which also emphasizes genetic control, is that of Sigmund Freud.

PSYCHOANALYTIC THEORY: SIGMUND FREUD

Sigmund Freud (1856–1939) was a highly original thinker whose ideas were elaborated over the course of a long and productive life. The inevitable inconsistencies of his thought that resulted, plus his new psychological vocabulary and formal style of writing have contributed to a misunderstanding of his ideas by many today. Nevertheless, his ideas have made a tremendous contribution to the psychology of adolescence.

Like Hall, Freud paid close attention to the ideas of Charles Darwin. He too saw life as a series of fixed stages of development mediated almost entirely by biologically determined forces. These forces, therefore, he mistakenly thought of as universal and not subject to cultural differences. He seriously questioned the idea of free will.

Freud felt that just as there is physical energy in our bodies, there is psychic energy that motivates our choices. Psychic energy is channeled and redirected throughout our system through the mechanism he called the **libido.** The uses of this energy depend both on the instincts with which we are born and on our early experiences, mainly those from birth through five years of age.

The Structure of Personality

Freud suggested there are three structures of the human personality. These are the **id, ego,** and the **superego.** The only structure with which we are born is the id. Incorporating all of our basic drives and energies, the id operates on the pleasure principle. The pleasure principle drives us to try to obtain whatever we want, whenever we want it. In this early stage of our life, we are not able to make sharp distinctions between the real and the imaginary. A newborn infant is completely incapable of adjusting its own desires to the needs of the real world, because it can't perceive the boundary between self and nonself.

From the moment of birth, the world begins to teach us the facts of reality. The development of this awareness of reality takes place with the development of our ego, which operates not on the pleasure principle but on the reality principle ("You get what you want when you get it!"). It is the job of the ego to mediate between the blind desires of the id and the demands of the external world. The ego also defends our sensitive personalities from the sometimes harsh reality of the world. It does this by means of a psychic censor, which uses **defense mechanisms** for our protection. (The function of defense mechanisms will be discussed in detail in Chapter 11.)

The third and final structure of the human personality to develop is the superego. This is similar to the traditional idea of conscience, with one important difference. Freud's superego consists of nothing but the moral teachings of the culture in which we are raised. He rejects the religious belief that our conscience is made up of cultural teachings plus an innate understanding of right and wrong. The superego begins to develop during the second year of life, and has as its main function the restriction of the unbridled demands of the id. At this time, the ego begins developing its main function, that of mediating between the contradictory demands of the id and the superego. Human beings, Freud believed, are doomed to constant internal conflict between these two forces, and only if they develop strong egos are they able to avoid mental illness.

The superego develops not as the result of an understanding of the way the world really is, but rather as a result of the idealistic teachings of our parents, teachers, clergy, and others, who tell us what they think we ought to believe. One of the major problems during adolescence arises from the sense of betrayal young people feel if they see that these moral teachers have taught them to believe in ideals which they themselves do not practice. The greater the discrepancy between what adults have professed and what they actually do, the greater the feeling of betrayal on the part of teenagers, and the more strongly they reject their earlier identification with these moral teachers. To the extent that **authority figures** have become confused and conflicted about their own values, as some suggest is the case today, we can expect adolescent resentment of adults to be greater today than it used to be.

The Stages of Development

Freud believed that the ways in which the id, ego, and superego develop depend very much on the ways in which the young child's sexuality develops. He argued that the stages of sexual development coincide with the pleasure center that is dominant at a particular age, that is, the organ of the most intense sensual gratification. For example, at birth, the child's major pleasure center is his mouth. These pleasure centers (or as Freud called them, **erogenous zones**) need an appropriate amount of stimulation. Too much or too little **stimulation** can cause the person to become fixated at that stage, thus hampering development at the later stages. Freud designated five stages of development (the first three being the most important):

The oral stage: birth–1½ years. Nursing, eating, and talking are the main gratifications during this period. A child who is overstimulated (given too much) at this stage may become intensely interested in sucking, eating, and drinking (the passive oral substage). This fixation can continue into adulthood, causing a dependency on cigarettes or a need to constantly chatter. If understimulated, the child may learn to enjoy the biting and screaming that was originally a response to frustration (the oral-sadistic substage). In later life this tendency may be carried out, for example, in making bitingly sarcastic remarks.

The anal stage: 1½–3 years. Toilet training is the main activity in this period of anal gratification. Because of understimulation (too little attention to their toilet training), children may learn to hold back excretions in order to please their parents or displease them (the anal-retentive substage). In later life, they may be stingy misers or uncooperative, irritable persons. Because of overstimulation, children may become too giving in order to please their parents (the anal-expulsive substage). Later, they may be the kind of persons who "would give you the shirt off their back," and is never able to save money.

The phallic stage: 3–5 years. Development of the genital focus of sexual interest begins. (It should be noted here that Freud conceived of sexual pleasure quite broadly, including all erogenous feelings in his definition.) In the phallic substage (3–4 years) children learn to understand and enjoy their bodies through manipulating their genitals. Freud argued that they should not be punished for masturbating. Their later ability to interact sexually with other persons depends on the way their parents react to early masturbation. If parents make too much of an issue of masturbation, it is likely to become fixated in children's minds, and they may either become compulsive masturbators or feel a repulsion for sex altogether.

The Oedipal substage: 4–5 years. Freud's term *Oedipal substage* refers to that period when children become physically interested in gaining love and physical affection from the parent of the opposite sex. (Oedipus was the king in Greek drama who unwittingly slew his father and later married his mother.) Although children of both sexes are thought to have an equally strong interest in their parents, it is much more acceptable in most Western cultures for girls to have love feelings toward their fathers than for boys to have love feelings toward their mothers. When a boy begins to show his physical feelings for his mother, this is often the signal for an angry response from the father. Statements such as "I don't want that kid sleeping with you!" or "I don't like to see him tied to your apron strings!" quickly teach the son that his behavior is unacceptable. The boy then develops a strong attachment to the father partly out of fear that he might be punished if he does not. Daughters, on the other hand, are not nearly so criticized for their affectionate attitude toward their fathers. Sometimes mothers are not too happy about it, but they seldom object to their daughter jumping on her father's lap and hugging and kissing him. The female Oedipus complex, which Freud called the Electra complex, therefore tends not to be resolved at this time. (Today psychologists refer to **Oedipal conflict** to characterize both.)

The latency stage: 5–12 years. Freud believed that the sexual impulses "go to sleep" during the years from 5 to 12, hence they are in a **latency** stage. When sexual interests recede, children become increasingly active physically. They enjoy playing with age mates of their own sex and seem to have little interest in children of the opposite sex. Freud explained that girls seem to be somewhat more interested in boys than the reverse because of their relatively unresolved Oedipal feelings.

The puberty stage: 12 years and up. Puberty is marked by the reemergence of strong Oedipal feelings. With the onset of changing hormonal balances and the accompanying strengthening of sexual interest, adolescents undergo an unconscious increase in desire for the parent of the opposite sex. Boys remain largely unaware of these desires because of the earlier resolution of the conflict. They therefore go about trying to select girls as love objects who remind them of their mothers. Of course, boys must avoid girls who remind them too much of their mothers, because such girls are also taboo. Freud has hinted that if a boy's Oedipal conflict is resolved at too great a psychic cost, he may be so afraid of any mother substitute that he may become homosexual.

Girls, who have not as yet resolved their Oedipal feelings, experience strong sexual interest in their fathers, which causes conflict because of our strong taboos against incest. The problem is often complicated by the fact that the father also has stirrings of physical interest in his daughter at this time. These feelings are usually unconscious (although probation officials report that one-third of all female offenders have been sexually assaulted by their fathers). The father not only sees his teenage daughter as an image of his wife at her youthful best, but also sees himself again at his own youthful best. The conflict he feels over this attraction, coupled with his daughter's conflicting feelings, would lead us to expect a period of difficult relationship between fathers and daughters when the daughters are between 13 and 15 years old. Indeed, this does seem to be the case. Freud also suggested that if the daughter's Oedipal feelings are too strongly resolved at this time, she may become a lesbian.

Freud was mistaken about the results of an overly strong resolution of the Oedipal conflict. If a boy is made to fear an attachment to women, he may either become homosexual, or he may go in the opposite direction and become the "macho" he-man type, who seems to be the very opposite of the homosexual. The he-man, however, only appears to have a strong interest in women. In reality he only wants to dominate them, preferring the company of other males for such typically masculine activities as boxing matches and hunting trips. His attitudes are similar to those of at least some female-hating homosexuals, although the he-man would undoubtedly deny this vehemently.

The same situation is true of women. The apparent opposite of the lesbian is the "Southern belle" type. She seems to be entranced by men, but if her behavior is looked at more closely, she is really a manipulator of men. She dislikes and distrusts men, and has much more in common with women. It appears that if one is to have a successful heterosexual adjustment, it is necessary to transfer one's sexual feelings towards one's parent to another person of the same sex as the parent, rather than reject these feelings altogether.

In summary, Freud viewed puberty as that period in which the instinctual drives of the id come into (sometimes violent) conflict with the social drives of the superego. The ego is seen as the beleaguered middleman who has the unenviable job of mediating between these powerful and opposite forces. Later theorists have argued that Freud placed too little confidence in the ability of the ego to bring about resolutions of the conflict. They believe that when circumstances foster the growth of a healthy ego, the period of adolescence can be much less stormy and stressful than Freud thought it had to be. One of these theorists was Freud's daughter Anna.

PSYCHOANALYTIC THEORY: ANNA FREUD

A trained psychoanalyst like her father, Anna Freud (1895–   ) believes that his definition of adolescence was too sketchy. She suggests that because Freud was so involved with his discovery that sexuality begins not at puberty but in early infancy, he overemphasized the importance of that earlier stage in the total developmental picture. Anna Freud has spent the major part of her professional life trying to extend and modify psychoanalytic theory as applied to adolescence.

Anna Freud sees the major problem of adolescence as being the restoration of the delicate balance between the ego and the id, which is established during latency and disrupted by puberty. Latency, she feels, is the time when children adopt the moral values and principles of the people with whom they identify. Childhood fears are replaced with internalized feelings of guilt which are learned during this period. The id is controlled during latency by the strength of the superego. At puberty, however, the force of the id becomes much greater, and the delicate balance is destroyed.

The problems brought about by this internal conflict cause the adolescent to regress to earlier stages of development. A renewed Oedipal conflict brings about fears that are entirely unconscious and often produce intense anxiety. Therefore the unconscious defenses of the ego tend to multiply rapidly, most especially the typical ones of repression, denial, and compensation (see Chapter 11). The problem, of course, is that the use of these defense mechanisms causes new stresses within the individual and tends to further increase the level of anxiety.

Anna Freud described two additional adolescent defense mechanisms: asceticism, in which, as a defense against the sexual, "sinful" drives of youth, the teenager frequently becomes extremely religious and devoted to God; and intellectualization, in which the adolescent defends against emotionality of all kinds by becoming extremely intellectual and logical about life.

Among Anna Freud's other contributions are her studies of stressful relationships between children and parents (Chapter 6), and of deviant children (Chapter 11).

PSYCHOANALYTIC THEORY: OTTO RANK

A pupil of Sigmund Freud's, Otto Rank (1884–1939) expanded the concept of ego into his "guilt-will" theory. He argued that human beings are born with no real will of their own, but rather behave solely on the basis of inborn instincts. However, as we interact with the environment, we begin to differentiate ourselves from others and notice and want a variety of things. In other words, we begin to develop an individual will. The differences in how and what one wants is a major distinction among people.

The development of the will is primarily dependent on the reaction of the child's parents. Rank (1945) thought that parents react to the newly developing will of their child either with complete disdain and negativism, or with acceptance and appreciation, or with a mixture of the two. The results of these three reactions cause three types of personality to develop:

The acquiesor. In the great majority of cases, Rank felt, the reaction of the parent to the child's newly developing will is rejection and ridicule. When parents behave this way, the following sequence of events may occur. Children interpret their parents' rejection of their desires as a rejection of themselves, and become afraid that they are going to lose their parents' love. These feelings of shame and guilt quickly make them withdraw what they will in order to be in accord with their parents' desires. Then they will not lose their love — their greatest need at this vulnerable early age. Before very long children come to anticipate what their parents will or will not want. This process quickly becomes unconscious. Children start to want what they think their parents will want, thereby reducing the possibility of conflict between their own will and that of their parents. They become "acquiesors." Most of us, Rank suggests, are acquiesors. That is, we think we know what we want, but our desires are really controlled by the wills of others. Our unconscious and almost instantaneous assessment of what our parents and other powerful figures will want us to want determines what we will do.

The conflicted person. In this case, the parents sometimes react negatively to their child's desires, but on other occasions are perfectly willing to go along with them. Rank believed that this promotes deep conflicts within the child and is the source of virtually all neurosis. With enough repetition of this sequence, the child becomes extremely hesitant and lacking in self-confidence. Sometimes the child dares to exhibit his true feelings, but always with the sense that he may or may not be rejected for them. This type of child tends to grow up with a sense that life is frustrating and inconsistent.

The creative child. Relatively few parents seem to value the developing will of their children. Rank suggested that those parents who do value this developing will always go along with the will of their children, unless the desires of the child violate the rights of others or endanger their own safety.

Rank believed that children who are brought up this way are the only ones who develop a sense of the legitimacy of their ideas. They are capable of questioning long-standing conventions. They dare to take a fresh look at every situation, because their parents have encouraged them to believe their will is an appropriate and acceptable thing to have. They are the only children who will ever be creative, because they are the only ones who dare to rely more on their own judgment than others'. The acquiesor and the conflicted person cannot face the criticism that might come from taking an unpopular stand.

What happens to these three personality types when they reach adolescence? It is a quite different story for each.

For Rank as for Anna Freud and Sigmund Freud, the early teens are dominated by the raging competition between internal and external forces. For acquiesors, the conflict is soon resolved. The internal drives are subjugated and repressed, and external forces win out readily. Acquiesors can be reasonably happy because they force themselves to respond to their "duties" and rationalize their desirability.

Conflicted persons continue to be dominated by the demands of the inner and outer worlds. As a result of continuous conflict, they become adults with inferiority feelings and neurotic symptoms.

Creative persons are able to remove themselves from the domination of both their internal and external needs. Rank suggests they are able to harmonize the demands of both worlds and grow into self-assured and powerful adults.

ENVIRONMENTAL THEORY:
RUTH BENEDICT AND MARGARET MEAD

In the early decades of this century, while the theories of the psychoanalytic school were gaining considerable attention, anthropologists had only begun to study so-called primitive tribes. Not until the 1920s and '30s did this research result in serious publication. When it did, however, it was accompanied by a serious attack on the psychoanalytic position. Anthropologists were finding that behaviors on which psychoanalysts based their position simply did not exist in other cultures. For example, 10-year-olds in some cultures are much more sexually active than in the United States. If human behavior differs from culture to culture, then clearly the idea that development is biologically determined cannot be right. These anthropologists, most notably Ruth Benedict (1887–1948) and Margaret Mead (1901–1978) argued that the behavior of the individual depends to a great extent on the environment in which he or she is raised.

The major difference between Western technological societies and undeveloped, isolated societies was a difference in the *continuity* of psychosocial development. The anthropologists saw development in industrialized societies as highly discontinuous. In America, children are expected to act like children until a certain period of time when, quite abruptly, they are expected to begin to act like adults. In the more "primitive" cultures, this process is much more gradual and less disruptive. Benedict (1950, 1954) specified three major areas in which cultural conditioning is continuous in primitive societies and discontinuous in Western societies:

Sexual role. Children in our society, at least until recently, were ignorant of the specifics of sexual behavior. They knew little about sexual intercourse, childbirth, breast feeding, menstruation, and the like. Then, on their wedding nights, they were expected to perform as sexually knowledgeable adults. As many older married people will tell you, this seldom happened.

Responsibility. In our society, children are allowed (even encouraged) to be somewhat irresponsible. However, the moment they leave home, get a job, or get married, they are expected to be totally responsible for their behavior. One seldom asks advice of one's parents after one has "flown the nest."

Dominance. Young people are expected to switch from a totally submissive role as children living in the homes of their parents to a totally dominant role, as themselves the parents of babies, often in less than a year. When living with parents, they are expected to follow directions. Then, if they get married and have a baby right away, they are expected to assume the totally dominant role of controlling the life of their own child.

These abrupt changes, occurring as they do without adequate preparation during the adolescent period, put a great strain on the life of the individual. As a preparation for adult life, Mead has suggested that we allow our youth to engage in "trial marriages" (see Chapter 8) in which teenagers are allowed to live and sleep together and to practice sexual intercourse with the benefit of birth control.

Although persuasive, this cultural view has been criticized on several grounds. As Muuss (1975) has pointed out:

Culture is more homogeneous in primitive societies; one can expect greater similarities in the behavior of adolescents, since they have limited opportunities to make choices. Their behavior can be predicted more easily than that of youths in a modern Western city whose individual differences would be greater because of (1) heterogeneity of culture, (2) rapidity of cultural change, and (3) diversified cultural and hereditary background (p. 107).

Thus, whereas psychoanalysis sees individual development as determined by biological factors, anthropology sees it as determined by environmental factors. Both agree, however, that individual development is almost entirely the result of factors not under the individual's control. Each person is the result of either biological or cultural inheritance.

SOCIAL PSYCHOLOGY: ROBERT HAVIGHURST

By the 1950s, two major new theories developed as a reaction to the determinism of psychoanalysis and the environmentalists. Robert Havighurst (1900–   ), a social psychologist at the University of Chicago, became the spokesperson of one of them. He suggested that there are specific **developmental tasks** at each stage of life, which lie midway between the needs of the individual and the ends of society. He defined these tasks as skills, knowledge, functions, and attitudes that are needed by an individual in order to succeed in life. As with Freudian theory, the inability to successfully negotiate any particular stage interferes with success at all succeeding stages.

Havighurst believes strongly in the idea that maturation interacts with the environment to produce the individual's personality, a position with which almost all psychologists would agree today. For any particular task, there is a period in our lives during which mastery of the task is easiest and most appropriate. An attempt to master a particular task too soon cannot succeed. Inability to master the task at the most appropriate time does not mean that it can not be mastered later, but that is much more difficult.

Havighurst suggests that developmental tasks differ from culture to culture, and some tasks differ more than others. The degree to which a developmental task depends on biological factors limits the amount of its cultural variation. For example, the need to have sexual relationships with others is deeply rooted in our biological nature. Therefore we see little cultural variation in the sex drive. Other aspects of our social relationships, such as dating, are much less connected to biological development, and we see great cultural variation in dating patterns.

Havighurst (1951) describes nine developmental tasks for the adolescent period, which he defines as being approximately between the ages of 12 to 18:

1. Accepting one's physique and accepting a masculine or feminine role.

2. New relations with age mates of both sexes.
3. Emotional independence of parents and other adults.
4. Achieving assurance of economic independence.
5. Selecting and preparing for an occupation.
6. Developing intellectual skills and concepts necessary for civic competence.
7. Desiring and achieving socially responsible behavior.
8. Preparing for marriage and family life.
9. Building conscious values in harmony with an adequate scientific world-picture.

Although written over a quarter-century ago, Havighurst's list holds up rather well today. Research has lent considerable support to Havighurst's theory, and educators and therapists have found his ideas useful.

SOCIAL PSYCHOLOGY: ERIK ERIKSON

Harvard psychologist Erik Erikson's (1902–   ) *Psycho-Social Theory of Human Development* (1967) is an amazingly perceptive and at times poetically beautiful description of the course of human life. Erikson's view of human development derives from extensive study of people living in an impressive variety of cultures—Germany, India, the Sioux of South Dakota, the Yuroks of California, and wealthy adolescents in the Northeastern United States, and from intensive studies of such historical figures as Mahatma Gandhi and Martin Luther. Like Havighurst, he sees human development as the interaction between hereditary and environmental influences.

According to Erikson, human life progresses through a series of eight stages. Each of these stages is marked by a crisis that needs to be resolved by the individual for growth to occur. Erikson uses the term crisis in a medical sense, as an acute period during illness, at the end of which the patient will take a turn for the worse or better. At each life stage, the individual is pressured by internal needs and external demands of society to make a major change in a new direction.

The ages at which people go through each of the stages vary, but the sequence of the stages is fixed; that is, it is necessary to have experienced each crisis before proceeding to the next. Inadequate resolution of the crisis at any stage hinders development at all succeeding stages, unless special help is received. When, for internal or external reasons, a person is unable to resolve a crisis at any of the stages, Erikson suggests that "a deep rage is aroused comparable to that of an animal driven into a corner" (p. 68). Previously unresolved personal crises undoubtedly explain much of the criminal behavior of youth.

It is important to note that Erikson's description of the eight stages of life is a picture of the ideal, and that no one ever completes the stages perfectly.

Basic trust vs. mistrust: birth–1½ years. In the first stage, which is by far the most important, a sense of basic trust should develop. For Erikson, *trust* has an unusually broad meaning. The trusting infant is one who is learning what to expect in his or her world. It is not so much that the world is a safe and happy place, but rather that it is an orderly, predictable place. There are causes and effects that one can learn to anticipate. For Erikson, then, trust might well include knowledge that one will be spanked regularly for disobeying rules.

If the infant is to grow into a person who is trusting and trustworthy, it is essential that a great deal of regularity exist in its early environment. The child needs variation, but this variation should occur in a regular order that the child can learn to anticipate. For example, the soft music of an FM radio can provide regular changes in sound level. So does the movement of the colorful toy birds hanging over a child's crib. The recurring attentions of a caring person who is not overtaxed by other responsibilities is an example of regularity of the most important type.

Some children born in poverty begin life with irregular and inadequate care. The crucial factor seems to be the anxiety and insecurity bred by poverty that affect the family and other relationships so important to the development of trust. When a child's world is so unreliable, we can expect mistrust and hostility, which under certain circumstances can develop into antisocial, even criminal, behavior.

Of course, most poor people do not become criminals, but if one does, our penal system is likely to destroy what trust may be left, especially if the wrong-doer is an adolescent. Consider this statement of a fourteen-year-old girl whom we'll call Caroline, an inmate in a "school" for delinquent girls:

Locked up. Going on my third day. In a freezing cold room. You sleep in there. Look at four walls. They don't give you nothing but one blanket. The bed is just a rubber mattress and a wooden block for it to go on. A little window with chicken wire. And a pail. And a door and nothing else but four walls. They let you out three times a day for a few minutes and they don't let you speak to nobody. They got nothing in here. You're not even supposed to have a book to read. It's freezing. It's an icebox. One blanket. One . . . You feel like you want to scream. You feel like you're in a madhouse. There's no need of putting kids in solitary confinement. I see no need of it at all. I wouldn't put a dead dog in this room. I wouldn't . . . I don't know. You can't really describe this place unless you're here. You've got to live here before you can really tell. They should send a real good kid here, you know, one that people would believe and have her come to live here for about a week. Or two, three weeks, you know. Then let her report back everything! Tell the people. Just let that person describe this. I know the State Senate is investigating this place and I hope they tear it down because it needs to be torn down. But I don't think the Senate is really going to do anything because it's going to take a lot of people to close this place, to tear it down.

TABLE 1-1
ERIK ERIKSON'S THEORY OF DEVELOPMENT

Stage	Age	Psychosocial Crisis
1	Infancy 0-1½	Trust vs. Mistrust
2	Early Childhood 1½-3	Autonomy vs. Shame, Doubt
3	Play Age 3-5	Initiative vs. Guilt
4	School Age 5-12	Industry vs. Inferiority
5	Adolescence 12-18	Identity and Repudiation vs. Identity Confusion
6	Young Adult 18-25	Intimacy and Solidarity vs. Isolation
7	Adulthood 25-65	Generativity vs. Self-Absorption
8	Maturity 65+	Integrity vs. Despair

Source: Erikson, 1967, p. 273.

Caroline is talking about her solitary confinement at the school. She was placed there in 1970 because she ran away from home three times. Her alcoholic mother signed a warrant for her arrest, and the judge had her jailed "to teach her a lesson." This school was closed a few years ago, but it is still far too typical of society's reactions to even slight deviations on the part of adolescents. There are many differences between this girl and the "good girl" whom she refers to, but the major difference is one of basic trust. Caroline doesn't believe that people will find her trustworthy, and by providing her experiences such as this, we are insuring that she will not be.

Each of the life crises involves a conflict between two opposing characteristics (see Table 1-1). Erikson suggests that successful resolution of each crisis should favor the first of the two characteristics, although its opposite must also exist to some degree. Although we should help infants develop into basically trusting persons, the totally trusting person would be continually in danger of being duped because of unrealistic expectations of others. An appropriate level of mistrust is healthy, especially if not learned too soon in life.

Autonomy vs. shame and doubt: 1½-3 years. When children become 1½ years old, they should move into the second stage, characterized by the crisis of autonomy versus shame and doubt. This is the time when they begin to gain control over their bodies and is the usual age at which toilet training is begun.

Erikson agrees with other psychoanalysts in believing that toilet training has far more important consequences in one's life than control of one's bowels. The sources of generosity and creativity lie in those experiences surrounding body exploration. If children are encouraged to explore their bodies and environment, a level of self-confidence develops. If, on the other hand, they are regularly reprimanded for their inability to control excretion, they come to doubt themselves. They become ashamed and afraid to test themselves. Although some self-doubt is appropriate, self-control should be fostered at this stage.

Initiative vs. guilt: 3–5 years. The third crisis, initiative versus guilt, begins when children are about 3 years old. Building on the ability to control themselves, children now learn to have some influence over others in the family and to successfully manipulate their surroundings. If their parents and others make them feel incompetent, however, they develop a generalized feeling of guilt about themselves. In the autonomy stage they can be made to feel ashamed by others; in this stage, they learn to make themselves feel ashamed.

Freud suggests the child's superego, or conscience, now emerges, and family members become models of proper behavior. If these models are capable, achieving people, the child will tend to develop a sense of personal initiative. If they are not, a deep and generalized sense of guilt will rob the child of the strength needed to deal with the crises ahead.

Industry vs. inferiority: 5–12 years. The fourth stage corresponds closely with the elementary school years. Now the task is to go beyond imitating ideal models and to learn the elementary technology of the culture. Children expand their horizons beyond the family and begin to explore the neighborhood. Their play becomes more purposeful, and they seek knowledge in order to complete the tasks that they set for themselves.

A sense of accomplishment in making and building should prevail. If it does not, children may develop a lasting sense of inferiority. Here we begin to see clearly the effects of inadequate resolution of earlier crises. As Erikson puts it, the child may not be able to be industrious because he may "still want his mother more than he wants knowledge." He suggests that the typical American elementary school, staffed almost entirely by women, can make it difficult for children (especially boys) to make the break from home and mother. Under these circumstances, children may learn to view their productivity merely as a way to please their teacher (the mother substitute), and not as something good for its own sake. Children may perform in order to be "good little workers" and "good little helpers," and fail to develop the satisfaction of pleasing themselves with their own industry.

Identity and repudiation vs. identity confusion: 12–18 years. Clearly this fifth stage is of the greatest importance for our study of adolescence. It is described briefly here, so that you can see how it fits into the total life cycle, and in greater detail in Chapter 2.

The main task of the adolescent is to achieve a state of identity. Erikson, who originated the term **identity crisis,** uses the word in a special way. In addition to thinking of identity as the general picture one has of oneself, Erikson refers to it as a state toward which one strives. If one were in a state of identity, the various aspects of one's self images would be in agreement with each other; they would be identical. Ideally, a person in the state of identity would have no internal conflicts whatsoever. An example of conflicted identity would be a person who, having decided to quit smoking, at first feels very proud of the decision. However, as the need for a cigarette increases, the person's pleasure center comes into conflict with his rational self. An internal battle between his id and superego ensues, and he becomes visibly upset and irritable. A person in a state of identity would not have such a conflict. The several aspects of his personality would have identical attitudes towards smoking; he would either smoke without guilt feelings or he would not smoke. Identity also requires concurrence between the individual's sense of himself and the views that other people have of him. In this way his inner being is confirmed by those about him.

This calm, purposeful, strong-willed human being hardly reminds us of the average adolescent. Erikson sees adolescence as a period of **moratorium** — a "time out" period in which the adolescent experiments with a variety of identities, without having to assume the responsibility for the consequences of any particular one. We allow adolescents this moratorium so that they can try out a number of ways of being, the better to come to their own particular identity. The moratorium period does not exist in primitive societies. Some have suggested that only Western industrial societies can afford the luxury of a moratorium. Others say that only because the values in Western industrial societies are so conflicted do adolescents *need* a moratorium.

Repudiation of choices is another essential aspect of reaching personal identity. In any choice of identity, the selection we make means that we have repudiated all the other possibilities, at least for the present. When youths cannot achieve identity, when **identity confusion** ensues, it is because they refuse or are unable to make choices. As Biff, the son in Arthur Miller's *Death of a Salesman,* says, "I just can't take hold, Mom, I can't take hold of some kind of life!" Biff sees himself as many different people; he sometimes acts one way in one situation and the opposite way in another — a hypocrite. Because he refuses to make choices and shies away from commitments, there is no cohesiveness in his personality. He is aware of this lack, but is unable to do anything about it.

Erikson suggests that identity confusion is far more likely in a democratic society because there are so many choices. In a totalitarian society, youths are usually given an identity, which they are forced to accept. Erikson points to the Hitler Youth Corps of Nazi Germany in the 1930s as a successful example of a national effort backed by intense propaganda to get all the adolescents in the country to identify with the same set of values and attitudes. In democratic societies, where more emphasis is placed on individual decision making, choices abound, and some children may feel threatened by this overabundance. Nevertheless, a variety of choices is essential to the formation of a well-integrated personal identity.

Intimacy vs. isolation: 18–25 years. The next three stages, which define adulthood, are summarized here so that their relationship with the adolescent stage can be seen. In the sixth stage, intimacy with others should develop. Erikson is speaking here of far more than sexual intimacy. He is talking about the essential ability to relate one's deepest hopes and fears to another person and to accept another's need for intimacy in turn.

Each of us is entirely alone, in the sense that no one else can ever experience life exactly the way we do. We are imprisoned in our own bodies, and unable to be certain that our senses experience the same events in the same way as another's. Only if we become intimate with another are we able to understand and have confidence in ourselves. During this time of life our identity may be fulfilled through the loving validation of the person with whom we have dared to be intimate (see Chapter 8).

Generativity vs. stagnation: 25–65 years. Generativity means the ability to be useful to ourselves and to society. As in the industry stage, the goal here is to be productive and creative. However, productivity in the industry stage is a means of obtaining recognition and material reward. In the generativity stage, one's productivity is aimed at generating a sense of personal fulfillment. Thus, the act of being productive is itself rewarding, regardless of whether recognition or reward results.

Although this stage can provide great satisfaction to those who reach it, several theorists (for example, Roazen, 1976) have suggested that the majority of adults never do. Many males appear to become fixed in the industry stage, doing their work merely to obtain the social symbols of success — a big car, a fancy house, a color televison. Women, they suggest, may become fixed in the identity stage, confused and conflicted about their proper role in life. They rarely achieve intimacy and therefore rarely reach the stage of generativity.

When people fail in generativity they begin to stagnate, to become bored and self-indulgent, unable to contribute to society's welfare. Such adults often act as though they were their own only child.

Integrity vs. disgust and despair: 65 years and up. To the extent that one has been successful in resolving the first seven crises, one will achieve a sense of personal integrity. Adults who have a sense of integrity accept their lives as having been well spent. They feel a kinship with people of other cultures and of previous and future generations. They have a sense of having helped to create a more dignified life for humankind. They have gained wisdom.

When people look back over their lives and feel they have made the wrong decisions or, more commonly, that they have too frequently failed to make any decision at all, they see life as lacking integration. They feel despair at the impossibility of "having just one more chance to make things right." They often hide their terror of death by appearing contemptuous of humanity in general, and those of their own religion or race in particular. They feel disgust with themselves.

Summarizing his theory, Erikson (1959) says,

We are now working toward, and fighting for, a world in which the harvest of democracy may be reached. But if we want to make the world safe for democracy, we must first make democracy safe for the healthy child. In order to ban autocracy, exploitation, and the inequality in the world, we must realize that the first inequality in life is that of child and adult. Human childhood is long, so that parents and schools may have time to accept the child's personality and trust and keep it to be disciplined and human in the best sense known to us. This long childhood exposes the child to grave anxieties and to a lasting sense of insecurity which, if unduly and senselessly intensified, persists in the adult in the form of vague anxiety—anxiety which, in turn, contributes specifically to the tension of personal, political, and even international life. This long childhood exposes adults to the temptation of thoughtlessly and often cruelly exploiting the child's dependence by making him pay for the psychological debts owed to us by others, by making him the victim of tensions which we will not, or dare not, correct in ourselves or in our surroundings. We have learned not to stunt a child's growing body with child labor; we must now learn not to break his growing spirit by making him the victim of our anxieties.

If we will only learn to let live, the plan for growth is all there (p. 157).

FOCAL THEORY: JOHN COLEMAN

Obviously, defining adolescence is no easy task. Probably the major single impediment is the widespread disagreement on exactly how difficult adolescence is for adolescents themselves. This can be seen as an overriding issue in the theories just described. At one extreme are those theorists who believe that adolescence should be a time of considerable disruption because of the abrupt and extreme changes that are going on in the various spheres of the adolescent's life. This is known as "classical" theory. At the other extreme are teenagers themselves, who give considerable support for the idea that adolescence is a fairly ordinary period of life. This is referred to as the "empirical" theory. Although each position has its strong proponents, clearly both positions cannot be true. Clinical/developmental psychologist John Coleman (1980) offers a compromise view, which he calls **focal theory.**

Coleman studied the attitudes of 800 boys and girls (100 each at ages 11, 13, 15, and 17) on a wide variety of topics. His questions included the areas of self-image, being alone, heterosexual relationships, parental relationships, friendships, and large group situations. He found that although each of these areas is of concern to some adolescents at all age levels, each peaks at a decidedly different time.

For example, conflict with parents was of concern to less than 20 percent of 11-year-old boys, whereas 60 percent of 17-year-old boys expressed a problem with it. Less than one-fifth of the 11-year-old boys studied had fears of rejection from their peer group, but over half worried about this at 15 years old. By 17 this concerned only about one-third. Almost 40 percent of the 11-year-old males suffered anxiety over heterosexual relationships. This dropped steadily to 10 percent by the time they were 17.

On the basis of his data and his observations in clinical practice, Coleman suggests that adolescents tend to restrict themselves to being upset about one issue at a time. As he puts it,

> *Adolescence is not an either/or phenomenon, but, as the evidence shows, is a period in the life cycle which contains difficulties; and where stress is experienced, though of a minor rather than a major nature. There is conflict with parents, over mundane domestic issues, rather than over fundamental values. Many young people experience feelings of unhappiness but on the whole these go unnoticed by parents or teachers. Adolescents do worry over their future identities as they become older, but these worries rarely cause an identity crisis (1980, p. 7).*

Figure 1–1 is a representation of Coleman's focal model. Each of the stages in the model is a different issue or relationship which is of most importance to the adolescent at that age. Thus it can be seen that in the major aspects of adolescent life, most issues are relatively well resolved. Even when two issues are in conflict, adolescents tend to suppress one so that they can tackle one issue at a time.

Although focal theory is intended to explain the ups and downs of life for the great majority of adolescents, Coleman does recognize that there are those for whom it does not apply. For example, the late maturer may well find that because conflicts over such issues as sexuality, puberty, and growth spurt have been delayed, they hit all at once. For this person, adolescence is, at least for a while, a period of "storm and stress."

What are the major issues that arise in the course of adolescence? How many of them are there? At what ages do each of them peak? Do they peak at the same age for boys and girls? How long does one issue take before the next issue is attacked? Focal theory may be accurate, but it does not yet answer these important questions. More research is clearly needed on a number of questions. Nevertheless, we are at a stage where a tentative definition of adolescence can be presented.

A TENTATIVE DEFINITION OF ADOLESCENCE

The adolescent is any person, usually between the ages of 11 and 19, who has clearly started the search for a personal identity. In this process, the person examines many of the philosophical, psychological, social, and physical options which are available. The adolescent tries out numerous self-images and behaviors and accepts or rejects them. However, not until there is at least a sense of self-acceptance can adolescence end. A person has successfully achieved the goals of

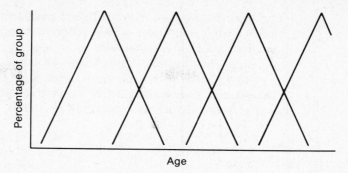

Figure 1-1   A Graphic Representation of Coleman's Focal Theory

Source: Adapted from Coleman, 1978.

adolescence only when he or she is able to engage in a truly intimate relationship with another.

In summary, adolescence is a period of rapid personal development beginning at puberty and ending at adulthood, at which time most people have achieved employment, a relatively permanent relationship with another person, or both (Abbott, 1981).

Classmate Maturity Rating

One of the ways to examine adolescence is to think about it in terms of people we know. Consider the members of your high school graduating class. It will help if you have a copy of your high school yearbook, opened to the pictures of the members of your class.

Rate the people in the class, whether you know them well or not, as having been childish for their age, a typical adolescent, or already an adult. In some cases you may find this difficult, but do your best to rate as many members of the class as you can.

How would the members of that class have rated you? Show your ratings to someone else who graduated with you, and see whether they agree with your judgments. Having completed your rating, ask yourself what criteria you used in making your ratings. Could you give a definition of adolescence now?

HOW TO STUDY ADOLESCENCE

The study of adolescence as a critical period in human development began only at the turn of the century. Led by Clark University psychologist G. Stanley Hall

(1904), this early theorizing was based mainly on what is now called "armchair speculation," as in those days psychologists had little experimental data about youth on which they could rely.

Today we use many approaches to understanding human behavior. Each has its strengths and weaknesses; none is completely reliable. Grinder (1978) describes six basic techniques: **descriptive studies, manipulative experiments, naturalistic experiments, longitudinal studies, cross-sectional studies,** and a combination of the last two.

Descriptive Studies

These are the most common studies of adolescence, and probably the most useful. Most are numerically descriptive: how many 12-year-olds think the government is doing a good job, versus 17-year-olds; how much money the average 14-year-old has to spend per week; how many teenage pregnant girls were or were not using birth control; how happily or unhappily the average 16-year-old boy views his sex life. In addition to asking their opinions, some studies describe adolescents simply by counting the number and types of their behaviors. A second type, case studies, observes a few individual youths in great detail, in order to make generalizations about the majority of youth.

An example of the case study approach is Roll's and Miller's (1978) "Adolescent Males' Feeling of Being Understood by Their Fathers as Revealed Through Clinical Interviews." They studied twenty boys who felt they were understood by their fathers and twenty who felt they were not. Although both groups of fathers were equally strict, the first group was seen as fair in their punishment, while the second was not.

Descriptive studies have the advantage of generating a great deal of data, but because the data describe events at a single point in time, their sequence cannot be considered in the analysis, and causes and effects cannot be determined.

Manipulative Experiments

In the quest for the *causes* of behavior, psychologists have designed many experiments. In these, they attempt to keep all variables (all the factors that can affect a particular outcome) constant except one, which they vary systematically. If there are differences in the results of the experiment, they can be attributed to the manipulated variable.

Flomenhaft's (1974) study, "Outcome of Treatment for Adolescents," used this approach. He randomly selected 150 patients in need of psychiatric care to be treated in a hospital setting. Another 150 such patients received care outside the hospital. The inpatients received an average of forty-five days' care, compared to an average of twenty-five for the outpatients. In spite of the difference in type and amount of treatment, he found no differences between the two groups on his measure of getting well. (This is a strong argument for outpatient care, which is less expensive and disruptive to the adolescent's life.)

But there are problems with manipulative experiments. How do you know your results are reliable? Was the treatment similar to normal treatment conditions? Do subjects see themselves as special (because you picked them) and thus react atypically? For these reasons, researchers often rely on naturalistic experiments.

Naturalistic Experiments

In these experiments, the researcher acts solely as an observer and does as little as possible to disturb the environment. "Nature" performs the experiment, and the researcher acts as a recorder of the results. This technique is frequently used in studies of personality, where laboratory conditions would most likely alter behavior. Educator Phillip Jackson (1968) used this approach when he spent an entire year sitting daily in several classrooms. The students became so used to his presence that he was able to observe their behavior with what probably was unprecedented accuracy.

The main problems with this technique are that it requires great patience and objectivity, and it is impossible to meet the strict requirements of a true scientific experiment.

Longitudinal Studies

The methods described above have the weakness of making observations at only one point in time. The longitudinal study, which makes several observations of the same individuals at periodic intervals, can answer important questions the others cannot, such as determining the long-term effects of learning on behavior, the stability of habits and intelligence, and the factors involved in memory. An example is the research of Nettleton and Cline (1975). They measured the attitudes toward dating, sex, and birth control of 700 unwed mothers. Attitudes were assessed at the time of delivery and two years later. They found surprisingly little change over the two-year period (see Chapter 8).

However, there are many problems with longitudinal research. It is expensive and often hard to maintain because of changes in availability of researchers and subjects. Changes in the environment can also distort the results. For example, if you began in 1960 to study changes in political attitudes of youth from ten to twenty years of age, you would probably have concluded that adolescents become more and more radical as they grow older. But the war in Vietnam would surely have had much to do with this finding. The results of the same study done between 1970 and 1980 would probably not show this radicalizing trend.

Another type of longitudinal research, retrospective studies, in which subjects are asked what they remember or believe to have happened, are also prone to the distortions of time. For example,

> parental reminiscences of child-rearing include what actually happened, what they have read about raising children, what they wish might have happened; and what they want the investigator to think about them as parents. Parental practices are also often modified during a child's development, and parents may forget which practices they used with which child (Grinder, 1978, p. 12).

Cross-Sectional Studies

This method compares individuals of various ages at the same point in time, in order to investigate the effects of maturation. For example, if you want to know how creative thinking changes or grows during adolescence, you could administer creativity tests to groups of 11-, 13-, 15-, 17-, and 19-year-olds, and check on the differences of the average scores of the five groups.

Savin-Williams' study (1977) examined the attitudes toward the figure of Jesus Christ among 274 10- and 16-year-olds to see how age affects feelings about religious subjects. He concluded that there is a less favorable attitude among those 16, but found that "the trend is less of an open rebellion or rejection of traditional images of Jesus with age than a questioning or a doubting" (p. 366).

There is a problem with this method, too. Although the effects of cultural change can be minimized by careful selection, it is possible that the differences you find may be due to differences in individual makeup, rather than maturation.

Longitudinal Cross-Sectional Studies

When a cross-sectional study is done at several points in time with a single group of individuals (such as administering creativity tests to one group at different ages), the problems mentioned above are eliminated. This type of research is complicated and expensive.

Bengston and Starr (1975) have suggested five variables that are responsible for differences among individuals and which can best be studied through this combined technique: chronological age; inherited traits; life-cycle effects; the period effect (some dramatic event that affects people for the rest of their lives); and ideological consciousness (some individuals come to think of themselves as a special group, as did many youth during the 1968 Democratic Convention).

A Comparison of Research Techniques

How do we evaluate the various methods of research? Techniques for studying human behavior may be compared on the basis of a number of criteria. Two of the most significant are the degree to which the variables in the study can be

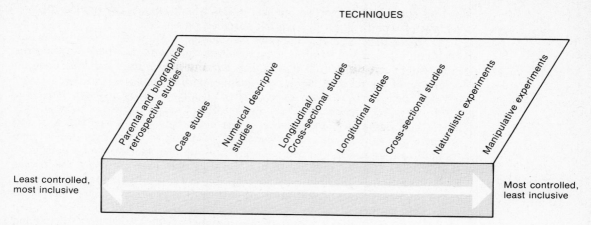

*Figure 1–2 A Comparison of Research Techniques**

controlled and the degree to which the researcher may be certain that *all* factors relevant to the study are included. Under most circumstances, the more control, the greater is the likelihood of identifying causes and effects. Unfortunately, the more controlled a study is, the less likely are important but unanticipated factors to be revealed. The case-study method is more likely to include unanticipated factors, but is often too inclusive. Comparing biographical data is often impossible due to differences in the way individuals respond. Control *that* variation by the use of a questionnaire, and you are no doubt masking relevant responses again. The important thing is to tailor the method to the research problem and be aware of the limitations of the approach one chooses. Figure 1–2 compares techniques in terms of degree of control and inclusivity.

SUMMARY

Six methods for studying adolescence scientifically are: (1) case studies, in-depth descriptions of the lives of individuals; (2) cross-sectional studies, the measurement of change in groups of individuals of different ages in order to determine the effect of age; (3) longitudinal studies, the measurement of change in a group of individuals over time to determine the effects of age; (4) manipulative experiments, research in which the experimenter manipulates a variable such as an instructional technique in order to discover the effects on some group of individuals; (5) naturalistic experiments, in which the investigator measures the effect on some group of persons of some naturally caused change in their environment;

*The positions on the continuum represent what is generally the case; like most generalizations, there are significant exceptions.

and (6) numerical descriptive studies, research that studies the number or percentage of a particular trait from the specified population.

Each of these scientific methods has strengths and weaknesses. In evaluating them, two criteria are of most importance: the degree to which the variables in the study can be controlled, and the degree to which the researcher may be certain all of the relevant factors are included in the study.

G. Stanley Hall, known as the father of adolescent psychology, based his 1904 work, *Adolescence,* on ideas distilled from Charles Darwin's theory of evolution. Hall designated adolescence as the years between 12 and 25, a period characterized by "contradicting tendencies" — violent mood swings — which contributed to the process of making youth more human. Hall applied a version of recapitulation theory to adolescence, holding that each person's life passes through the same series of stages as those that occurred during the entire history of the human species. Freud believed that the Oedipal and Electra complexes recur with hormonal change during adolescence. He held that the primary goal of adolescence is to seek opposite-sex parent substitutes, without identifying those substitutes too closely with the parent (in which case homosexuality is likely to result).

Anna Freud sought to expand upon her father's treatment of the adolescent period. She saw the major issue of adolescence as the restoration of the delicate balance between the ego and the id, which is established during latency and disrupted in the early phase of puberty.

The psychoanalytic theory advanced by Otto Rank centers around three basic personality types: acquiesors, conflicted persons, and creative ones. Like both Freuds, Rank believed that the early teens are dominated by raging competition between internal and external forces. He believed that acquiesors resolve this competition by settling for a reasonably happy acceptance of their "duties," while the conflicted person would be likely to have inferiority feelings and neurotic symptoms, intensified by the ordeal of the tug between the internal and external forces. The creative types, said Rank, are equipped with the ability to achieve a harmony between the forces and to rise above the negative aspects of the competition.

Ruth Benedict and Margaret Mead have contributed a cultural theory of personality development. The thrust of their approach is that cultural variations play a great role in determining an individual's make-up. Both contended that adolescents in Western industrial societies are placed under more intense stress than those in agricultural societies because of the abrupt role switches expected of them.

Robert Havighurst's social psychological theory describes nine developmental tasks for the adolescent period, which he saw as extending from ages 12 to 18: (1) accepting one's physique and accepting a masculine or feminine role; (2) new relations with age mates of both sexes; (3) emotional independence of parents and other adults; (4) achieving assurance of economic independence; (5) selecting and preparing for an occupation; (6) developing intellectual skills and concepts necessary for civic competence; (7) desiring and achieving socially responsible behavior; (8) preparing for marriage and family life; and (9) building conscious values in harmony with an adequate scientific world picture.

Erik Erikson identifies eight stages of life, each of which consists of a crisis to be resolved. These are: 0 to 1½ years, trust vs. mistrust; 1½ to 3 years, autonomy vs. shame and doubt; 3 to 5 years, initiative vs. guilt; 5 to 12 years, industry vs. inferiority; 12 to 18, identity and repudiation vs. confusion; 18 to 25 years, intimacy and solidarity vs. isolation; 25 to 65, generativity vs. self-absorption; and over 65, integrity vs. despair.

Questions

1. What is adolescence?
2. Why study adolescence?
3. When does adolescence begin?
4. Whose description of adolescence is best, and why?
5. What are the stages in human development?
6. Why do these stages always follow the same order?
7. What happens in the case of fixation?
8. What are the methods of studying adolescence?

References

Abbott, L. T.   Suggested in personal communication, January 22, 1981.

Benedict, R.   *Patterns of culture.* New York: New American Library, 1950.

Benedict, R.   "Continuities and discontinuities in cultural conditioning." In W. E. Martin & C. B. Stendler (Eds.), *Readings in child development.* New York: Harcourt, Brace, 1954.

Bengston, V. L., & Starr, J. M.   "Contrast and consensus: A generational analysis of youth in the 1950's." In R. J. Havighurst & P. H. Dreyer (Eds.), *Youth—seventy-fourth yearbook of the N.S.S.E.* Chicago: University of Chicago Press, 1975.

Coleman, J. C.   "Current contradictions in adolescent theory." *Journal of youth and adolescence, 7*(1), 1978, 1–11.

Dacey, J.   "A school where kids swing from the trees." *Learning,* December 1976, *5*(4), 68–72.

Erikson, E.   *Childhood and society.* New York: Norton, 1950.

Erikson, E.   "Identity and the life cycle: selected papers." *Psychological Issues Monograph* (Series I, No. 1). New York: International Universities Press, 1959.

Erikson, E.   *Psycho-social theory of human development.* New York: Norton, 1967.

Erikson, E.   *Identity: Youth and crisis.* New York: Norton, 1968.

Evans, R.   *Dialogue with Erik Erikson.* New York: Harper & Row, 1967.

Flomenhaft, K.   "Outcome of treatment of adolescents." *Adolescence,* Spring 1974, *11*(33), 57–66.

Freud, Anna.   "Adolescence." In A. E. Winder & D. L. Angus (Eds.), *Adolescence: contemporary studies.* New York: American Book, 1968.

Freud, S.   *New introductory lectures on psychoanalysis* (W. J. H. Sprott, trans.). New York: Norton, 1933.

Freud, S.   *A general introduction to psychoanalysis* (J. Riviere, trans.). New York: Permabooks, 1953.

Grinder, R.   *Adolescence.* New York: Wiley, 1978.

Hall, G. S.   *Adolescence* (2 vols.). New York: Appleton, 1904.

Havighurst, R. J.   *Developmental tasks and education.* New York: Longmans, Green, 1951.

Jackson, P. *Life in classrooms*. New York: Holt, Rinehart, & Winston, 1968.

Keniston, K. "Prologue: youth as a stage of life." In R. J. Havighurst & P. H. Dreyer (Eds.), *Youth*. Chicago: University of Chicago Press, 1975.

Mead, M. *Culture and commitment: A study of the generation gap*. New York: Doubleday, 1970.

Mead, M. "Mental health in a changing culture." *Mental health,* 1972, *56*(3), 6–8.

Morris, W. (Ed.). *The American heritage dictionary*. Boston: Houghton Mifflin, 1971.

Muuss, R. *Theories of adolescence* (3rd ed.). New York: Random House, 1975.

Nettleton, C., & Cline, D. W. "Dating patterns, sexual relationships, and use of contraceptives by 700 unwed mothers during a two-year period following delivery." *Adolescence,* Spring 1975, *10*(37), 45–58.

Rank, O. *Will therapy and truth and reality*. New York: Knopf, 1945.

Roazen, P. *Erik H. Erikson: The power and limits of a vision*. New York: Free Press, 1976.

Roll, S., & Miller, L. "Adolescent males' feelings of being understood by their fathers as revealed through clinical interviews." *Adolescence,* Spring 1978, *13*(49), 83–94.

Savin-Williams, R. C. "Age and sex differences in the adolescent image of Jesus." *Adolescence,* Fall 1977, *12*(47), 353–366.

Warshaw, M. "Adolescent psychology viewed from the kitchen." *Phi Delta Kappan,* February 6, 1978, 390–392.

Additional References

Committee on Adolescence, Group for the Advancement of Psychiatry. *Normal adolescence.* New York: Scribner's, 1968.

Cottle, T. J. "On studying the young." *Journal of youth and adolescence,* 1972, *1*(1), 3–11.

Darwin, C. R. *The origin of species by means of natural selection.* London: Murray, 1859.

Erikson, E. *Young man Luther.* New York: Norton, 1958.

Freud, S. *The basic writings of Sigmund Freud* (A. Brill, Ed.). New York: Modern Library, 1938.

Grinder, R. E. "Epilogue: Two models for the study of youth—1944 versus 1975." In R. J. Havighurst & P. H. Dreyer (Eds.), *Youth.* Chicago: University of Chicago Press, 1975.

Kubie, L. S. "Introduction." In R. M. Jones, *An application of psychoanalysis to education.* Springfield, Ill.: Charles C. Thomas, 1960.

Mead, M. *Sex and temperament in three primitive societies.* New York: New American Library, 1935.

Chapter Two

The Search for Identity

Chapter Highlights

Erikson's Identity Crisis
  Stage of Life Matrix
Negative Identity
The Moratorium of Youth
Identity Status
  Identity Rating
Vocational Identity
  Parental Influence
  The Influence of Sex
  Your Own Vocational Identity
  Career Education
Sexual Identity and Role
  The Influence of Environment
  Social Roles of the Sexes
  Sex-Role Stereotype Test
  Androgyny
  The Future of Androgyny
Achieving an Identity Today
  Future Shock
  The Republic of Technology
The Achieved Identity
Summary

Key Terms and Concepts

identity
negative identity
premature foreclosure
identity status
identity confusion
identity foreclosure
identity moratorium
identity achievement
vocational identity
sexual identity
sexual role
career education
transsexual
sex-role orientation
sex-role preference
sex-role adaptation
hermaphrodite
chromosome
anaclitic identification
stereotypes
androgyny
future shock
new obsolescence
new convergence

Important People

Erik Erikson
James Marcia
Sandra Bem

"Who are you?" said the caterpillar. Alice replied rather shyly, "I—I hardly know, sir, just at present—at least I know who I was when I got up this morning, but I must have changed several times since then."
—Lewis Carroll, Alice in Wonderland

The adolescent's effort to discover and create an identity is the most important task of this period of life. Whether or not this quest results in an actual crisis, as Erikson suggests, is a matter of debate.

Goethals and Klos (1976) argue that if the crisis exists at all, it comes only at the end of adolescence:

> *It is our opinion that college students do not typically have a firm sense of identity and typically have not undergone an identity crisis. College students seem to be in the process of identity seeking, and experience identity crisis toward the end of senior year and in their early post-college experience. A male or female's disillusionment with their job experience or graduate study, a female's disappointment at being at home with small children is often the jolt that makes them ask what their education was for, and why they are not as delighted with their lives as they had been led to believe they would be (p. 129).*

Adolescent psychologist Manaster (1977) concurs:

> *An identity crisis may be normative at Harvard, and among such persons as George Bernard Shaw, Martin Luther, and St. Augustine. It is not so with the common man—those persons who are not cognitively equipped and/or socially encouraged to have an identity crisis (p. 120).*

University of Michigan researchers (Bachman, O'Malley, and Johnston, 1978) have been studying changes in the attitudes and goals of 2,000 male adolescents for the past ten years. They have concluded that contrary to the view "of adolescence as a period of great turbulence and stress, we found a good deal of consistence along dimensions of attitudes, aspirations, and self-concept." Few of their subjects gave any evidence of having experienced an identity crisis.

Erikson, who himself had an extensive and rather difficult identity crisis in his youth, supposed that "My friends will insist that I needed to name this crisis in everybody else in order to really come to terms with it" (1975, p. 26).

Crisis or no, it is undoubtedly true that most adolescents undergo many doubts about their identity, and that the search for identity is usually difficult. The following pages will explore the processes of identity formation in some depth.

ERIKSON'S IDENTITY CRISIS

Erikson's own identity crisis is an example of the process in the extreme. Although its origins lie partly in the shadows, and he has said little about them, two researchers (Berman, 1975; Roazen, 1976) claim to have pieced the story together. Erikson was born in Frankfurt-am-Main, Germany, in 1902. His mother, whose maiden name was Abrahamsen, was a native of Copenhagen, Denmark. His father was also a native of Denmark, but we do not know his name. His mother was Jewish. It is not clear whether his parents were ever married, but it is known that his father deserted his mother before he was born. He was three years old when his mother married Dr. Theodor Homburger, who adopted him. His stepfather was also Jewish, and was president of the Frankfurt synagogue. The religious component of Erikson's background led to later conflict. In the synagogue he was referred to as a *goy* (a non-Jewish outsider) apparently because, being Danish, he was thought to be Christian. Equally unpleasant, among his schoolmates he was mocked for being a Jew.

The second major conflict in his life concerned his vocation. In his twenties, he studied art, and in 1928 was teaching art at a school near Vienna. There he met his wife-to-be, Joan Serson, an American student who was in psychoanalysis as part of her training as an analyst. Through her he became interested in this science, and during the next year, after considerable doubt, he left art and teaching and underwent analysis himself. In 1930 they were married. By 1933, she had convinced him that he must leave Austria (anti-Semitism was on the rise in Hitler's Germany), and so they left for Denmark. He was unable to establish himself as a psychologist there, and they came to the United States, eventually settling in Boston. It is interesting to note Erikson's suggestion that highly creative people tend not to complete their identity crises until they are thirty. Erikson himself was just about thirty when he began his work in the United States. He published several articles on psychoanalysis under the name of Erik Homburger, but when he became a naturalized citizen of the United States, he decided to change his name to Erikson. Was his new name an acknowledgement of his admiration for the Danish discoverer of America? Or was it the choice of his young son, who thought of himself as Erik's son? Both suggestions have been made. At about this time he became increasingly interested in Christianity and is today a devout adherent.

We have in Erikson an individual who went through an intense identity crisis, which was resolved by the creation of a brand-new person with a new name, religion, and occupation. His theory of human development is no doubt colored to some extent by these experiences. At the same time, the intensity and degree of his identity crisis have made him extremely sensitive to the problems that all adolescents go through. Erikson's explanation of personality development in the adolescent has gained wide acceptance among psychologists today.

Stage of Life Matrix

Let's examine the patterns that occur when we look at the lives of real people. Suppose we identify eight people whose stages of life correspond to the appropriate ages of Erikson's theory. If we were to put this data on a matrix of the life stages, it would look like this: (You may wish to reread the description of these stages in Chapter 1.)

Name	0–1½	1½–3	3–5	5–12	12–18	18–25	25–65	65+
Tim	Trust							
Gayle		Autonomy						
Jim			Initiative					
Ron				Industry				
Eustace					Identity			
Grace						Intimacy		
Peg							Generativity	
Sidney								Integrity

As you can see, if life were ideal, all data would fall somewhere along the diagonal leading from the upper left to the lower right corner of the matrix. In fact, it does not work that way. In a study that I and my students conducted, we rated almost 700 persons in all age groups according to the eight stages. The matrix looked like this:

	0–1½	1½–3	3–5	5–12	12–18	18–25	25–65	65+
Trust	28	12	14	21	16	3	4	1
Autonomy		32	11	13	9	4	3	2
Initiative			37	21	18	14	12	5
Industry				51	36	21	25	11
Identity				11	41	26	38	11
Intimacy					12	54	43	15
Generativity						12	38	14
Integrity								29

These ratings are a matter of our judgment, but they are probably fairly accurate. Life, it appears, is less orderly than theory. However, if you look closely at the numbers (only those between the lines conform to the theory), you will see a rather clear pattern, one that does not depart so much from the ideal matrix above.

It is also noteworthy that while many were at lower stages than would be hoped for in ideal development (for example, 71 persons over 1½ years still lacked basic trust), only a few were ahead of their expected stage (12 were in the intimacy stage at 12–18 years).

Try filling in the matrix below with the names of several of your acquaintances, making sure you have one or an equal number in each age group. Write their stage under their corresponding group. What pattern is revealed? How do your ratings compare with those of others who also know the people you chose?

Name	0–1½	1½–3	3–5	5–12	12–18	18–25	25–65	65+

NEGATIVE IDENTITY

While most adolescents do not go through changes as great as Erikson's, many take on what he calls a **negative identity**. A person with negative identity adopts one pattern of behavior because he is rebelling against demands that he follow an opposite pattern. An example is the boy who joins a gang of shoplifters, not because he wants to steal, but because he doubts his masculinity and seeks to prove that he is not a coward through the dangerous act of theft. Another example is the sexually permissive girl who is punishing her mother for trying to keep unreasonably strict control over her. Sex is not her goal; proving that she is no longer her mother's baby is.

In his psychohistorical biography of German religious leader Martin Luther (1483–1546), called *Young Man Luther* (1958), Erikson paints a sombre picture of negative identity.

Luther's greatness as a leader, says Erikson, was partly built on the enormous anger and unresolved conflict he experienced in his late teens. Luther's decision to become a monk and enter the monastery was the assumption of a negative identity. The choice expressed his rejection of fifteenth-century society rather than his devotion to Catholicism. Luther indulged in further contrariness by trying to be a better monk than anyone else. Luther's strong internal conflict is illustrated by the story of Luther falling into a nervous fit while performing in the choir. As he fell to the ground, he is said to have cried out, "It isn't me!" Many other incidents also indicate he couldn't accept being who he was.

Erikson believes that Luther had an extended identity crisis. His monkhood was used as the time and place for working out a positive identity. As his identity evolved, Luther devoted himself without reluctance to God and turned all his fury against the Pope, fomenting the Protestant religious upheaval. Like Erikson, Luther's identity crisis was not resolved until he reached thirty.

THE MORATORIUM OF YOUTH

Youth is an age marked by instability and noted for its lack of conviction in selecting friends, occupation, and other values. Erikson insists that indecision is an essential part of the moratorium of youth. Tolerance of it leads to a positive identity and **premature foreclosure** of the moratorium may lead to great loss. The adolescent who makes his choices too early usually comes to regret them, and is especially vulnerable to identity confusion in later life.

Erikson suggests that such religious initiation ceremonies as Catholic confirmation and Jewish bar mitzvah may tend to limit the young, forcing them into a narrow, negative identity. This is done by dogmatically spelling out the specific behaviors expected by adults. On the other hand, such ceremonies can suggest to the youth that the adult community now has more confidence in his ability to make decisions. The effect depends on the explanation of the goals of the ceremony.

Although some youth tend to be overly idealistic, Erikson believes that idealism is an essential aspect of identity strength. In the young person's search for a person or an idea to be true to, he is building a commitment to an ideology that will help him unify his personal values. He needs ideals in order to avoid the disintegration of personality that is the basis of most forms of mental illness.

Sidney Jouard (1971) suggests that identity confusion results in "dispiritation." He likens the various aspects of the human psyche to the cogs of a machine. When the cogs do not fit together well, the person loses personal strength and integrity and becomes dispirited. When, on the other hand, "all systems are go," the personality becomes coordinated, one feels at peace with oneself, and "inspiritation" occurs.

It is inspiritation toward which Erikson sees the adolescent striving, but which he can only reach as the result of temporary, partial disorganizations of his inner self. When we see an adolescent showing neurotic or even psychotic symptoms, it is often because he is in the midst of testing the foundation of his life (see Chapter 11). He should not be treated in the same way as a younger or older person with the same symptoms of mental illness. The chances for recovery are far greater at this stage.

IDENTITY STATUS

Erikson's ideas on adolescence have generated considerable research on identity formation in recent years. The leader in this field is James Marcia (1966, 1967, 1968), a psychologist at the State University of New York at Buffalo who has made a major contribution to our understanding through his research on **identity status**. (See Table 2–1.)

Marcia believes that there are two essential factors in the attainment of a mature identity. First, the person must undergo several *crises* in choosing among life's alternatives, such as a crisis of religious belief. Second, he must finally come to a *commitment,* an investment of himself, in his choices.

Since a person may or may not have gone through the crisis of choice and made a commitment to his choices, there are four possible positions, or statuses, for him to be in.

Status 1. **Identity confusion**: no crisis has been experienced and no commitments have been made.

Status 2. **Identity foreclosure**: no crisis has been experienced, but the person has come to commitments, usually forced on him by his parents.

Status 3. **Identity moratorium**: considerable crisis is being experienced, but no commitments are yet made.

Status 4. **Identity achievement**: numerous crises have been experienced and resolved, and relatively permanent commitments have been made.

TABLE 2–1
SUMMARY OF RESEARCH FINDINGS ON MARCIA'S FOUR IDENTITY STATUSES

Status 1. Identity Confusion*	Status 2. Foreclosure
The individual in the state of identity confusion	The individual in the state of foreclosure
1. May be the "playboy" type; doesn't care what others do as long as he's allowed to do what he wants.	1. Appears superficially like the identity-achieved person (status four).
2. May be the "cop-out" type; avoids crises and confrontation by escaping through drugs and self-delusion.	2. Has not really considered other goals and values, accepting the ones which were given to him.
3. May be the "personality disintegration" type; becomes so disoriented that he may fall into schizophrenia or attempt suicide.	3. Frequently explains his choices on the basis that they will be pleasing to his parents.
4. Tends to be an opportunist.	4. Takes great satisfaction in pleasing others, especially those he looks up to.
5. Is extremely interested in what others think and will adopt the attitude of those he is currently impressed by. Frequently has deep feelings of guilt and rejection.	5. Has the most rigid personality.
6. Is too willing to change his opinions about himself. Found to be the most willing to accept incorrect personality sketches about himself.	6. Has the greatest interest in maintaining traditions.
7. Has the most problems with interpersonal relationships.	7. Is most bound by his habits.
8. Even though he is as intelligent as others, tends to enroll in the easiest college majors.	8. Carefully avoids conflict situations.
9. Is the most likely to role play in different situations.	9. Shows the greatest respect for authority and enjoys being told precisely what to do.
10. Has a father who is more controlling than those in any of the three other categories.	10. May have the highest level of aspiration, even in the face of failures.
11. Demonstrates the least amount of basic trust.	11. Evaluates himself most critically.
	12. Is least flexible in his judgments.
	13. Has the lowest ratings in anxiety.
	14. Has the highest self-esteem ratings, if a woman.
	15. Has the most favorable attitude toward education.
	16. Has a father who is neither too harsh nor too lenient, but who is very effective at control.
	17. Is most likely to set unrealistic goals for himself.
	18. Overidentifies with his peer group and his heroes.

*Research findings here are somewhat contradictory.

Unlike Erikson's eight stages, which follow each other in an unchangeable sequence, Marcia's identity statuses are not necessarily sequential. The only prerequisite for the identity achievement status is the moratorium condition.

TABLE 2–1 (continued)

Status 3. Moratorium	Status 4. Identity Achievement
The individual in the state of moratorium	The individual in the state of identity achievement
1. Has many unresolved questions.	1. Has the strongest ego.
2. "Plays the field" with the opposite sex.	2. Is the most stable and mature in his behavior.
3. Is very much an experimentalist.	3. Is most accepting of himself.
4. Frequently changes his mind about his values.	4. May or may not have values similar to his parents, but whatever values he has are strongly held.
5. Likes to be an extremist, at least temporarily.	5. Has a stable self-definition.
6. Frequently is concerned about his own mental health.	6. Is the most willing to act on the basis of his values.
7. Tends to become involved in "changing the system."	7. Is capable of real intimacy with others.
8. Often thinks of himself as a phony because he is aware of his conflicts.	8. Is the most aware and accepting of his own limitations.
9. Is the least willing to be influenced or controlled by others.	9. Scores the highest when given tasks under stress.
10. Is the least cooperative with those who would give him help.	10. Sets more realistic goals for himself than others.
11. Is the least predictable in his activities.	11. Is the best able to evaluate himself.
12. Scores the highest on anxiety tests.	12. Is the most flexible when interacting with others.
13. Is the least confident in his choice of a college major, the least confident in the use of education in general.	13. Is the most consistent in his judgment, regardless of the opinions of others involved.
14. Has parents who are the most permissive.	14. Rates lowest in discrepancy between self-perception and the perception others have of him.
15. Is the most critical of the "establishment."	15. Is most effective in interpersonal interaction.
	16. Has a father who tends to be relaxed and encouraging rather than controlling.

Note: The above findings are summarized from the review of the literature by Muuss (1975).

Measurement of change in identity status has been done in several ways. Marcia (1967) has described his method as follows:

Identity statuses are established by means of a thirty-minute, semistructured interview. All interviews follow the same outline, although deviations from the standard form are permitted in order to explore some areas more thoroughly. In most cases, the criteria for ending an interview are a completion of the prescribed questions as well as some feeling of certainty on the interviewer's part that the individual has provided enough information to be categorized. Interviews are tape-recorded and then replayed for judging: hence, each interview is heard at least twice (p. 119).

The questions in the interview concerned the person's attitude toward his vocation, personal value system, sexual attitudes, and religious beliefs. Later, this approach specifically focused on the individual's sexual attitudes. Schenkel and Marcia (1972) discussed with college women their attitudes toward premarital intercourse. The students were rated not on their approval or disapproval of premarital intercourse, but on whether they had experienced a crisis of choice and, if so, whether they had now come to be committed to their position.

Both Marcia and Freedman (1970) and Constantinople (1969) have found that college students tend to move from identity confusion to identity achievement across their four years of college. Constantinople also found that there was an average tendency to move toward identity achievement even within the course of a school year.

Identity Rating

Try Marcia's four-point scale on people you know. Choose ten friends and write their names in the spaces below. Put the number of the identity status you choose for each person after his or her name. Do the rating quickly, without thinking about it too much—this tends to make the rating more accurate.

	Name	Rating
1.		
2.		
3.		
4.		
5.		
6.		
7.		
8.		

9. _____   _____

10. _____   _____

Notice how many of your ratings fall into each category. Were most of them in the fourth category, identity achievement? If so, was this because most of the friends you chose for this activity have an achieved identity, or perhaps because you unconsciously choose them on that basis? Have most adults achieved identity? Have you?

There are many aspects of identity, some of which will be treated in later chapters. The two factors most closely linked to overall identity status, **vocational identity**, and **sexual identity** and **role**, are discussed in the following sections.

VOCATIONAL IDENTITY

Historically, a person's definition of himself has been closely bound up with his work. With only a few exceptions, all adult members of society are expected to contribute to it by their labor. Only in the twentieth century, however, have individuals had much choice in vocations. With the advent of the technological revolution in the seventeenth and eighteenth centuries, the number of choices began to expand. A view of the adolescent employment status today may be seen in Table 2–2.

A major change in the last few decades has been the growing importance of leisure-time activity in one's total identity. Today, many individuals devote as little energy as possible to their jobs in order to commit themselves to their hobbies and avocations. As Erikson (1968) points out, however, the jobs that people choose still play a major role in their representation of themselves to society. Rice (1975) suggests four major considerations in the choice of a vocation:

1. *Service.* Some individuals feel that meeting the needs of others or in some way bettering society is the major criterion for the choice of a job.

2. *Practicality.* Others look to find a job which will "pay off." They consider geographical areas where the job opportunities are greatest, and seek jobs where the chance of earning money is the highest.

3. *Prestige.* A third group chooses vocations they think will enhance their esteem in the eyes of parents and other significant people. Service or money is of minor, if any, importance.

4. *No rational choice.* This group chooses jobs on the basis of whatever comes along first and is likely to provide some economic independence.

TABLE 2–2
EMPLOYMENT STATUS OF THE ADOLESCENT POPULATION BY RACE

Employment status and race	Both sexes, 16–19 years (1980)
TOTAL	
Total noninstitutional population	16,549
Total labor force	9,549
Percent of population	57.7
Civilian labor force	9,242
Employed	7,603
Agriculture	380
Nonagricultural industries	7,223
Unemployed	1,640
Percent of labor force	17.7
Not in labor force	7,000
WHITE	
Total noninstitutional population	13,920
Total labor force	8,464
Percent of population	60.8
Civilian labor force	8,233
Employed	6,955
Agriculture	358
Nonagricultural industries	6,597
Unemployed	1,278
Percent of labor force	15.5
Not in labor force	5,456
BLACK AND OTHER	
Total noninstitutional population	2,629
Total labor force	1,085
Percent of population	41.3
Civilian labor force	1,009
Employed	648
Agriculture	22
Nonagricultural industries	626
Unemployed	361
Percent of labor force	35.8
Not in labor force	1,544

Source: *Employment and Earnings*, March 1981.

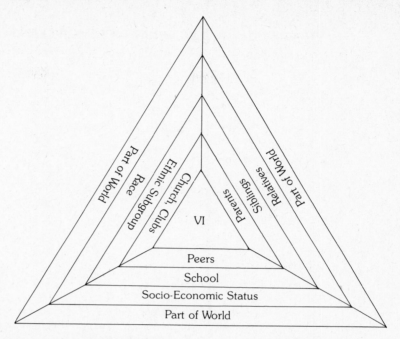

Figure 2–1   *Environmental Influences on Vocational Identity*

Among the factors influencing vocational choice are intelligence, special talents, physical capacity, race, ethnic group, sex, amount of education, role models, needs and interests, current economic conditions, and geographical location. (Figure 2–1 represents one way to look at the many influences on vocational identity.) Another factor that influences job choice for many is federal law governing the jobs teens may hold and the conditions under which they may hold them. Table 2–3 lists the main types of jobs for teens and their availability to youth of various ages. However, two factors seem to play by far the greatest role: parental influence and sex.

Parental Influence

Of the many studies of parental influence on vocational choice, two are especially noteworthy. Kandel and Lesser (1969) found that while the suggestions of friends are important to vocational choice, the influence of parents (and most particularly of mothers) is approximately twice as great as that of peer groups.

The ways in which parents are able to influence the vocational choices of

TABLE 2–3
FEDERAL LAW CONCERNING JOBS FOR TEENS

Job Type	13 or less	14	15	16	17	18
Deliver newspapers	•	•	•	•	•	•
Acting	•	•	•	•	•	•
Work for parents— nonfarm	•	•	•	•	•	•
Pump gas*		•	•	•	•	•
Bag groceries*		•	•	•	•	•
Wash dishes*		•	•	•	•	•
Nonhazardous farm job outside school hours		•	•	•	•	•
Hazardous farm job				•	•	•
Other nonhazardous jobs				•	•	•
Any job for any hours						•

*No more than 3 hours per school day, 40 hours per week, 18 weeks per school year, between 7 A.M. and 7 P.M.
Note: This table summarized from a review of the literature appearing in "Teenage Jobs" (1977).

their children have been described by Rice (1975), who suggests that parents influence their children's vocational choices:

1. Through strongly suggesting interests and activities from the time children are very young by such means as providing certain play materials and reinforcing hobbies and interests.

2. By providing apprenticeship training. Sometimes, especially in the case of boys, a parent will teach the child an occupation.

3. Through turning over the family business to the children, making it easier to decide where their best economic opportunities lie.

4. By providing role models for their children to follow. Although this is a more subtle approach to influencing vocational choice, it is often the most effective. If the child feels admiration for his parents, then the vocational choices they advocate strongly direct the child's choices.

5. Through ordering or limiting the choices of their children. Many vocational choices require parental assistance or economic help. If the parent exerts strong pressure on the child to follow a particular direction, there may be little else the child can do.

6. By exhorting the child to pursue a socioeconomic status as high or higher than that of the parents. Parents have traditionally wanted their children to do as well or better than they have. In recent times, one has seen this tendency exaggerated in parents who as children went through the economic depression of the 1930s. The fears of economic loss they experienced are often a strong incentive for their children to try to gain some stability and safety above and beyond that which the parents were able to achieve.

The Influence of Sex

Boys and girls experience a differential effect of sex role on their vocational choices. These influences come from a variety of sources and are sometimes decidedly negative.

Influences on the male. Rogers (1977) points to the following five influences on boys' vocational choices:

1. Parents are much more likely to try to pressure their son into a premature vocational choice than they are their daughters.
2. Parents are more likely to emphasize status and salary in influencing a boy's choice.
3. Although males may have more choices of occupations than females, they frequently do not have the information they need to make good choices. Most females seem to have even less.
4. Jobs that involve physical and mental hazards are more often chosen by men than women. These jobs may be acceptable in one's early years, but be too strenuous for later years.
5. Men are usually forced to consider their role as a family provider in making a job selection. This may cause them to subordinate their own personal satisfaction to consideration of economic questions.

Influences on the female. A number of researchers (Rice, 1975; Manaster, 1977; Rogers, 1977) have reviewed the even greater difficulties women face in making vocational choices:

1. Girls receive little orientation toward job selection. Both in school and from parents, the whole question of jobs for women has been given less emphasis than for men.
2. Most of the jobs available to women are of a poorer status and provide less economic remuneration than for men.
3. The options open to women are considerably more restricted than for men. As Gottlieb and Bell (1975) point out, the major jobs open to women are schoolteacher, guidance counselor, social worker, nurse, or health professional.

4. Women are more influenced by what they think men will accept as a woman's job than vice versa.

5. Women are more concerned about what society in general will consider a feminine job than are men (Harmon, 1971).

6. Girls have fewer opportunities for training in high school than boys. As Neill (1974) discovered in one city's vocational schools, boys were able to choose from ten different trade areas, whereas girls had only the choice among four.

7. Women often think that they must wait and see what kind of husband they choose before they make a vocational and residential choice.

8. Perhaps the most important problem for women is that many feel they must take into account the effect of their vocational choice on their future family. Since women have been educated to seek the meaning of their lives in the intimacy of a marriage and the nurturing of children, the entire question of working is often fraught with conflict.

Your Own Vocational Identity

By this stage in your life, you have probably chosen a vocation, or at least have a pretty good idea of what it will be. However, there were undoubtedly times when you thought you were going to do something else. Think back to your early adolescence and try to recollect what other vocational choices you considered. You may want to ask your parents or friends to help you remember, because the choices we decide not to make are often repressed. List five choices you thought about but rejected in the spaces below.

1. _____

2. _____

3. _____

4. _____

5. _____

Now write in the vocation you expect to enter when you complete your education.

6. _____

Do you see any pattern in these six vocations? Do they fit any of Rice's four categories of vocational motivation (service, practicality, prestige, no rational choice)? Do you feel that one of these four categories is clearly better than any of the others?

Who has had the most influence on your vocational choice?

_____

Who would you say has had the second most influence on this choice?

_____

Who would be the person most likely to be able to persuade you to change your mind about your vocation?

_____

Career Education

Career education, which is the attempt of the school to improve the validity of vocational choice of its students and their satisfaction with those choices, is one of the most significant innovations in education today. It is not entirely new; counselors have tried to assist in vocational choice for many decades. The major change has been the introduction of career education into every phase of the curriculum, with participation on the part of all teachers in all subjects at all grade levels.

Many educators believe that the schools have not fulfilled one of their primary roles — preparing young people for the future. Kenneth Hoyt, former U.S. Assistant Commissioner of Education, has identified ten problems in our schools which career education addresses. His position on these problems has been officially adopted by the U.S. Office of Education.

1. Too many persons leaving our educational system are deficient in the basic academic skills, as well as self-understanding and work attitudes, required for adaptability in today's rapidly changing society.

2. Too many students fail to see meaningful relationships between what they are being asked to learn in school and what they will do when they leave the educational system. This is true both of those who complete their schooling and those who drop out of the educational system.

3. American education, as currently structured, best meets the educational needs of that minority of persons who will become college graduates and neglects needs of the majority of students who will never graduate college.

4. American education has not kept pace with the rapidity of change in the postindustrial occupational society. As a result, when worker qualifications are compared with job requirements, we find overeducated and undereducated workers are present in large numbers. Both the boredom of the over-

educated worker and the frustration of the undereducated worker have contributed to growing worker alienation in the total occupational society.

5. The growing need for, and presence of, women in the work force has not been adequately reflected in either the educational or the career options given to girls enrolled in our educational system.

6. The growing need for continuing education of adults is not being adequately met by our system of public education.

7. Insufficient attention has been given to encouraging the development of skills through learning opportunities outside the structure of formal education.

8. The general public, including both parents and the business-industry-labor community, has not been given an adequate role in the formulation of educational policy.

9. American education as currently structured does not adequately meet the needs of minority and economically disadvantaged persons in our society.

10. Post-high school education has given insufficient emphasis to educational programs at the subbaccalaureate degree level.

The federal government is currently sponsoring a wide variety of career education programs. These programs (U.S. Office of Education, 1975) all have in common one set of learner outcomes: Career education should seek to produce persons who are

1. Competent in the basic academic skills required for adaptability in our rapidly changing society.

2. Equipped with good work habits.

3. Capable of choosing, and who have chosen, a personally meaningful set of work values that leave them with a desire to work.

4. Equipped with career decision-making skills, job-hunting skills, and job-getting skills.

5. Equipped with vocational personal skills at a level that will allow them to gain entry into, and attain a degree of success in, occupational society.

6. Equipped with career decisions they have made based on the widest possible set of data concerning themselves and their educational-vocational opportunities.

7. Aware of means available to them for continuing education once they have completed formal schooling.

8. Successful in being placed in a paid occupation, in further education, or a vocation that is consistent with their current career education.

9. Successful in incorporating work values into their total personal values structure in such a way that they are able to produce what, for them, is a desirable life-style.

There is not space to describe all of the emerging innovations in career education. Clearly, today's teachers are finding themselves involved in helping their students achieve a vocational identity in ways undreamed of when they themselves were students.

SEXUAL IDENTITY AND ROLE

Woman may be said to be an inferior man. — Aristotle.

Although this statement is obviously absurd, its underlying attitude is still widespread. People today are far less willing to admit to a belief in female inferiority, but many still act as though it were so. However, the influence of the women's movement, as well as of science and other forms of social change, is profoundly affecting the way we view sexual identity and sexual role.

First, we must make a distinction between sex identity and sex role. Sex identity results from those physical characteristics and behaviors that are part of our biological inheritance and that characterize us as males or females. An example of a sex-linked physical characteristic is the penis and testes of the male. A corresponding behavior is the erection of the penis when stimulated. Sex role, on the other hand, results partly from genetic makeup and partly from the specific traits that are in fashion at any one time and in any one culture. For example, it seems that females are able to express their emotions through crying more easily than males, although there is no known genetic cause for this behavior.

It is possible for a person to accept his or her sex identity but to reject his or her sex role. Jan Morris (1974), the British author, spent most of her life as the successful journalist, James Morris. She accepted the fact that she had a male sex identity, but deeply resented having to perform the male sex role. She always felt that inside she was really a woman. The **transsexual** operation that changed her from male to female caused many problems in her life, but she says she is infinitely happier to have her body match her feelings about her sex role.

Sex role itself has three aspects:

1. **Sex-role orientation.** Individuals differ as to how confident they feel about their sex identity. Males often have a weaker sex-role orientation than females. (This will be discussed later in the chapter.)

2. **Sex-role preference.** Some individuals have no doubts about their sex identity, but may feel unhappy about their sex role, as did Jan Morris.

3. **Sex-role adaptation.** This is defined by whether other people judge individual behavior as masculine or feminine.

It seems clear that while sex roles may be modified by differing cultural expectations, sex identity is fixed rather early in a person's development. John Money and his associates at Johns Hopkins University believe there is a critical period for the development of sex identity, which starts at about 18 months and ends at about four years. Once sex identity has been established, it is very difficult to change (Money and Ehrhardt, 1972).

Once culture has had the opportunity to influence the child's sex identity, it is unlikely to change, even when biological changes occur. Even in such extreme changes of **chromosome** failure as gynecomastia (breast growth in the male) and hirsutism (abnormal body hair in girls), sex identity is not affected. In almost all cases, adolescents desperately want medical treatment so they can keep their sex identities.

The Influence of Environment

How does the environment affect a person's sex role? The process appears to go something like this: (1) Children learn, usually before their second birthday, that they are male or female. They are shown the major differences between the sexes, and are told that they should try to be like the people of their own sex. (2) They observe people of their sex and imitate as much of their behavior as they can. (3) They are reinforced by praise and love for their successes in imitating these behaviors. This process continues throughout their childhood, reaching its peak in adolescence.

> *The girl must now cease playing football, the all-boy gang is kid stuff now. Boys and girls will be constantly and consistently reminded that they are male or female and must behave as such if they are to escape social penalties. The complementary relationship of the sexes is reflected throughout the orientation of teenage society. At dances, the boy leads; the girl follows. He must ask her for a date, though perhaps she has inveigled him into asking her. It means that the polarity of sex roles reaches its zenith (Rogers, 1977, p. 337).*

Sigmund Freud uses the term **anaclitic identification** in describing how sex identity develops. Both boys and girls identify most strongly with their mother in the first two years, because they see her as their source of nourishment. Boys later have to repudiate this identification and learn to identify with their fathers. This change starts at about the second year and leaves boys forever insecure about their gender, Freud thought. This accounts for the striving of the adolescent male to prove he is a man. Boys who have had a weak or absent father seem to have the greatest need to prove their masculinity. It does seem true in our society that girls have less question about their sex identity than boys; they seem not to have to demonstrate their femininity with such vehemence.

Psychologists have identified six major environmental determinants of sex role. These are parents, the absence of the father, siblings, schools, peers, and the mass media.

Parents.   It should come as no surprise that children who identify with their own sex have parents whom they perceive as warm and powerful. Warm, positive father-son relationships (Payne and Mussen, 1956) and mother-daughter relationships (Mischel, 1970) lead to the strongest sex identity. Interestingly, most studies have found the father to have the greater influence on the development of the sex role of both boys and girls. Johnson (1963) found that fathers who view themselves as masculine and who have positive regard for their wives reinforce femininity in their daughters and masculinity in their sons. On the other hand, fathers who are seen by their children as ineffectual promote serious conflicts in sex role identification. If the father is permissive (Stein and Bayley, 1973), aggression, assertiveness, and independence, which are seen to be masculine behaviors, are more likely to develop in both males and females.

These findings have led Kilpatrick (1976) to warn that parents who actively discourage the development of separate sex roles actually may be doing harm to their children:

> This does not mean that the father ought to be autocratic and ironfisted; merely that he ought to be careful, if only for the sake of his son's masculinity, of relinquishing the traditional role of decision-maker and limit-setter. Playing such a role, need not, of course, exclude the father from adopting certain aspects of the feminine role such as nurturance and affection. It does little good for the father to be dominant if he is not also warm and supportive. If he is merely a powerful and feared oppressor, it is unlikely that his children will be able to identify with him at all (p. 13).

Father absence.   We have a good deal of information about the effects of father absence, because in the great majority of one-parent families it is the father who is gone. It is apparent that father absence has a far greater effect on males than on females; also, the greatest effect occurs in the early years (Kilpatrick, 1976), as would be predicted by Money's critical-period hypothesis. Other studies of the effects of father absence during the Second World War (Nelson and Maccoby, 1966) found that the sons of absent fathers had a far more feminine pattern of characteristics when they entered college than sons whose fathers had been present. However, Douvan and Adelson (1966) found that if mothers whose husbands are absent try to reinforce masculine behavior, and if they encourage adult males to participate in the lives of their sons, these negative effects can be greatly reduced.

The effect of the father's absence on the female sex role is less, but it does exist. A fascinating study by Hetherington (1972) looked at the behavior of three groups of teenage girls: those whose fathers were present, those whose fathers were absent because of divorce, and those whose fathers were absent because of death. Daughters of the divorcés were overtly sexual, dated early, and had little trouble relating to boys. Daughters whose fathers had died showed the opposite behavior, being very shy and uncomfortable around boys. The behavior of girls whose fathers were present fell in the middle range of these extremes.

Siblings.   The presence of older brothers or sisters in a family has an influence on the sex role of the younger sibling, but not as much as one might think.

Brim (1958) found that girls who had older brothers exhibited more masculine behavior than girls who had older sisters, but at the same time, there was little difference in the feminine characteristics of the two groups of girls, pointing up that decidedly masculine and feminine traits are not mutually exclusive in individual behavior. Sutton-Smith and Rosenberg (1965) came to the same conclusions for college students. Wohlford (1971) found that the effects of older brothers and sisters are greater when the father is absent than when the father is present.

Schools.   Schools have a powerful influence on the development of sex identity, and until recently clearly have been guilty of encouraging an inferior sex role for women through the differential treatment of females in textbooks, course requirements, school and classroom structure, through treatment by teachers and counselors, and even through such subtle means as the sex distribution of staff. Although the women's movement began to renew itself more than twenty years ago, recent studies have shown our schools changing their orientation toward sex role and identity very slowly.

Numerous studies document the sexist attitudes of teachers and counselors (Broverman, et al., 1970; Fagot and Patterson, 1969; Kellogg, 1969; Naffziger, 1971). In fairness, however, it should be noted that even when educators have seriously tried to modify children's sex-role behavior, it has proven to be a difficult task. In several Boston schools (Tavris, 1975), a six-week program to alter children's perception of their sex roles was conducted in the kindergarten, fifth, and ninth grades. Although girls were able to make a change in their attitudes to female sex roles, with ninth-grade girls changing the most, boys in all three grades were extremely resistant to attitude change. Tavris concluded that boys seem to like the idea that women are better off in the home serving their husbands, and they feel uncomfortable with any alteration in traditional patterns of role behavior.

Other studies (Minuchin, 1965; McCracken, 1973) have found that in classrooms where an individualized flexible curriculum is maintained, and where children are encouraged to follow their own interests as much as possible, the children have less rigid attitudes toward sex roles.

One of the results of the women's movement, especially for younger women, has been a greatly increased participation in school sports, and most interestingly, in physical contact sports that until recently were the sole domain of men. Government support through Title XI has been crucial. Rohrbaugh (1979) has reviewed recent studies to see what effects participation in these sports has had on women.

The findings seem very much to support the goals of the liberation movement. First of all, there has been a considerable concern that women participating in these sports will become "masculinized" (that they will start to take on characteristics of males). A number of studies have shown that they do not develop huge muscles or "tough attitudes." Rohrbaugh suggests that the "muscle myth" is precisely that. More importantly, women athletes were found not only to be healthier and more energetic, but to have higher images of themselves. In almost every case studied, there was a distinct increase in self-esteem and self-confidence as a result of participating in a vigorous sport.

Rohrbaugh looked at many aspects of the effects of sports on women, and found them to be almost totally positive. She concludes that:

> *The feminist's attitudes about 'physicality' and defying sex role norms essentially reverses the usual arguments about whether sports 'masculinize' women. The feminists are implying that they do — and that that is a good thing. For defiance builds strength. And who's to say what will happen, as more and more women begin to feel the strength of their bodies — and hence the courage of their convictions (p. 42).*

Peers.   The adolescent's own peer group has always been rigidly conventional in terms of social expectations. In 1961, Coleman found that the major requirements for popularity and social leadership in high school were athletic accomplishment for boys and physical beauty for girls. There has been some change in these attitudes since Coleman did his study. Youths are not so rigid as they used to be in terms of sex role; intellectual qualities are no longer thought to be unfeminine; and male superiority, at least at the college level, seems to be giving way to the ideal of companionship between equals (Komarovsky, 1973). Boys and girls are forming friendships at earlier ages than they used to and are developing richer intersex relationships than formerly (Berger, et al., 1972).

However, there is some question that values have really changed all that much.

> *I doubt that there are very fundamental changes in the values that adolescent subcultures attach to traditional roles. A recent incident in my own university is one illustration. The male students in one of the large dormitories set up a table in the dining room, from which they held up a sign "rating the appearance of each female who walked into the dining room on a scale of one to ten." A minority of females were outraged, but large numbers who heard this was happening rushed back to their rooms, changed their clothes, and combed their hair before entering the dining room (Stein, 1976, pp. 249–250).*

Mass media.   Commercial television programing has continually reinforced sex-role stereotypes. The detective or police programs that have dominated television during the late 1970s are filled with he-men who typically use violence to overcome problems. Of the thirty-seven "cop" shows on the air recently, only three starred women, and in these, two of the heroines were successful as police officers by virtue of their looks rather than their brains. Newspaper and magazine advertisements portray men as voices of authority, competent in judging the worth of a product, while women are used as background sex objects. In many, the woman's role is to smile adoringly at the man who has decided to use product A, the implication being that if the reader also uses this product, he will be able to have sex with beautiful women. With few exceptions, the Saturday lineup of TV cartoons watched by so many younger children also show women in an inferior status. As Howe (1971) points out, children are constantly bombarded by such biased words as *mankind, brotherhood,* and *manhood.* He suggests that few children understand these terms as referring to males and females equally. An important research report, *The Television Image of Women* (1975), states that although women now constitute 40 percent of the work force, their professional status is practically ignored on television. Women are addressed in commercials in two main categories: beauty aids and underwear, and care and maintenance of home and family.

In many schools today teachers and students in English courses have begun analyzing the sexist overtones of television programs and commercials; hopefully this sensitization will reduce the effect of television sex stereotypes on children.

Social Roles of the Sexes

This section considers three aspects of the social roles of the sexes: sex-role **stereotypes**, the function of sex roles, and the concept of **androgyny**.

Sex-role stereotypes. There are a number of stereotypes common in our culture that assign behavior as typically either male or female. Some of them are clearly true, some are clearly false, and some we are not sure about. Test your knowledge of sex-role stereotypes (see below), and then look at Table 2–4. This table lists the most typical stereotypes that differentiate females from males, which the research literature classifies as well-founded, unfounded, or debatable.

Sex-Role Stereotype Test

In what ways are males and females really different? There are many stereotypes about sex roles; some are accurate, some are not. Extensive recent research has helped establish the truth about these traits. Check the following statements true or false to learn your "chauvinist" rating (remember, women can be chauvinists, too).

Compared to males, the average female in the United States

	True	False
1. Is more suggestible.	—	—
2. Is more social.	—	—
3. Has greater verbal ability.	—	—
4. Is smarter.	—	—
5. Is less aggressive.	—	—
6. Is better at rote learning and simple repetitive tasks.	—	—
7. Has less ability to process high level mental tasks.	—	—
8. Is less analytic, more intuitive.	—	—
9. Has less math ability.	—	—

10. Is more auditory.   —   —
11. Lacks achievement motivation.   —   —
12. Fears success.   —   —
(Answers are on the following page.)

It is interesting to note that of the well-founded stereotypical differences between women and men, listed in Table 2–4, the only personality trait listed is aggressiveness. There are many other stereotypes about personality differences, but research does not support these. It is also interesting that although women fear success more than men, it is not because they don't care about achievement.

Erikson's ideas about the biological determinants of male and female sex roles come from his studies of early adolescents (1963). In a series of experiments, he tossed wooden blocks on a table and asked each child to make something with them. Girls, he found, tend to make low structures like the rooms of a house. Having finished these structures, the girls then use other blocks as furni-

TABLE 2–4
STEREOTYPES OF THE DIFFERENCES BETWEEN FEMALES AND MALES*

Females differ from males in that females are . . .

Well-founded	Unfounded	Debatable
Higher in verbal ability	More social	More fearful, timid, and anxious
Lower in visual-spatial ability	More suggestible	Lower in activity level
Weaker in mathematical ability	Higher in self-esteem	Less competitive and more cooperative
Less aggressive	Better at rote learning	Less dominant
More afraid to be successful, especially in mixed sex competition, but less so for black females than for white females	Better at simple repetitive tasks	More compliant
	Poorer at higher level cognitive processing	More nurturant
More easily able to maintain their sex role identity	Less analytical	More maternal
	More affected by environment	
	Less affected by environment	
	Lower in achievement motivation	
	More auditory, but less visual	

*Most of these findings come from an excellent review of the literature, *The Psychology of Sex Differences,* by Maccoby and Jacklin (1974).

Answers to the Sex-Role Stereotype Test

1. F	7. F
2. F	8. F
3. T	9. T
4. F	10. F
5. T	11. F
6. F	12. T

ture, which they move around in the spaces of the rooms. Boys, on the other hand, tend to build towers, which, after completion, they usually destroy. Erikson makes the analogy between the roomlike structures of the girls and their possession of a womb, and the towerlike structure of the boys and their possession of a penis. He feels that these differences account for greater aggressive behavior in males. Penis and tower alike are seen as thrusting symbols of power. He also suggests that differences in biological function cause the differences we see in male and female mental illness. Males get sick when they are unable to express the anger and hostility resulting from their natural aggressive tendencies. Females, on the other hand, suffer from a lifelong fear of being left empty, or more simply, a fear of being left alone. Women have a natural desire to fill up the womb within them, and if they are unable or unwilling to bear children, they become prone to mental illness.

Erikson's ideas have been severely criticized by representatives of the women's movement, notably Kate Millett and Gloria Steinem, who say that, like most psychoanalysts, Erikson mistakes learned behavior for biology. In response, Erikson argues that the pervasive anger of many feminists stems from their unconscious fear of being possessed by their own bodies, rather than owning them by choice and using them with deliberation. Although he has frequently espoused complete economic equality between men and women, Erikson continues to insist that genital differences are the cause of important psychological differences. In this he certainly does maintain close ties with the psychoanalytic tradition.

Although the women's movement has launched strong attacks on unfair stereotyping, sex-role stereotypes appear to be remarkably persistent (Bieliauskas, 1974; Ponzo and Strowig, 1973; Rosenkranz, et al., 1968; Williams, et al., 1975). It is not just men who seem reluctant to change their attitudes toward women's status; many women are also ambivalent toward a new view of their role (Jesser, 1974, "A Happy and Traditional Home," 1974). Komarovsky (1973) found that 85 percent of a sample of Illinois teenage females said that they wanted to be taken care of by men. Although the attitudes of many women have become more liberal, the change is by no means great.

At least for the second half of the 1970s, the original women's liberation movement seems to have lost its momentum, having been replaced by a "new feminism" . . . Such feminists lack sympathy with the formal liberation movement. Instead, their feminism applies to women who want to be women in the traditional sense, but insist on their social and economic rights (Rogers, 1977, p. 351).

The function of sex roles.   Some sociologists (for example, Parsons, 1955) have argued that because traditional sex roles are functional within the family, they are therefore necessary in the broader society. Stein (1976) disagrees:

Obviously in traditional terms, males are expected to perform instrumental functions; females to perform expressive functions. A number of questions have been raised about this formulation even within the traditional family structure. First, instrumental and expressive activities are not mutually exclusive. One may do both. Second, many of the managerial activities of a modern housewife are instrumental—managing a budget, buying clothes and objects for the home, organizing several sets of carpools, piano lessons, dental appointments, and the myriad of other activities in which the modern children are involved. Finally, a division of activities and differences of operating may not promote husband-wife relationships because they involve few shared interests (p. 252).

Stein believes that research clearly indicates the dysfunction of sharply different sex roles for males and females in the following three areas:

1. *Self-esteem.* Males who have confidence in their own masculinity are also higher in self-esteem than males who have a low sense of masculinity, but females who have a high sense of femininity do *not* necessarily feel a high sense of self-esteem (Connell and Johnson, 1970; Sears, 1970).

2. *Anxiety and emotional problems.* Girls are generally more anxious than boys, and there is more anxiety in highly feminine girls than in other females (Webb, 1963).

3. *Achievement.* Although females with a relatively strong sex identity perform better in many kinds of tasks than other females, in terms of creativity people who are able to combine characteristics of the opposite sex with attributes of their own sex are most likely to be creative (Stein and Bayley, 1973).

Androgyny

Sex roles in America today are not very healthy, according to researcher Sandra Bem (1975). She says that highly masculine males tend to have better psychological adjustment than other males during their adolescent years, but when they become adults, they tend to be victims of high anxiety and neuroticism and to experience low self-acceptance. The picture is not much better for females. Highly feminine females also tend to have considerable anxiety and suffer from low self-esteem.

In addition, Bem points out, traditional sex typing necessarily forces people to restrict their range of behavior. Men should never do "women's work," and women should never enter the "men's world."

Bem believes that we would all be much better off if we were more androgynous. This word comes from the Greek "andro" for male, and "gyne" for female; it refers to a person who is able to act like a "typical male" in situations where that is appropriate and like a "typical female" where that is appropriate. To find out whether androgyny really exists, Bem first developed an up-to-date sex role test. Through a somewhat complicated procedure, she developed the *Bem Sex Role Inventory* (BSRI). This test was administered to over 155 undergraduate students. She found that approximately 50 percent of those tested adhere to "appropriate" sex roles. About 15 percent showed themselves to be *cross-sex-typed;* that is, most of the items they choose on the BSRI would normally be chosen by persons of the opposite sex. The remaining 35 percent were androgynous.

Having established this, the question remained whether or not the actual behavior of persons categorized as traditional, cross-sex-typed, and androgynous would fit their test responses. To check the validity of the BSRI (i.e., to determine whether her test was accurate), Bem developed a series of well-designed experiments. As representative behaviors, she chose two masculine characteristics (independence and assertiveness), and one feminine characteristic (responsiveness to another living creature). These characteristics were chosen as being "the very best of what masculinity and femininity have come to stand for" (p. 61).

Independence. To study the independence of her subjects, she seated them in a booth equipped with microphones and earphones. They were then shown a series of cartoons which they were to rate from high to low on the basis of humor. Before the subjects made their ratings, they heard what seemed to be four students in other booths turning in their ratings. Actually these "other students" were really voices preprogrammed on tapes. The cartoons had been judged previously on the basis of humor. The people on the tapes always ranked low humor cartoons as very funny, and vice versa. Therefore, if the real respondents said what they were really thinking, they would almost always be going against those who had spoken before them. To do so would show considerable independence of judgment.

Bem found that only 33 percent of the feminine women were independent (above the mean for all students). This is as compared to 70 percent of the masculine and androgynous students. Thus her hypothesis was supported.

Assertiveness. In this experiment, students were called on the telephone and given an unreasonable request: that they spend two hours filling out a questionnaire about insurance policies. The students were not asked *if* they would do it; they were merely asked what time they would be available. Therefore, it would take a certain amount of assertiveness to refuse to participate.

Two-thirds of the feminine women said that they found it very difficult to refuse to participate in this experiment. Only 28 percent of the androgynous students and the masculine men had difficulty telling the caller that they would not participate. This finding supports Bem's theory.

Responsiveness. In the first part of this experiment, students were brought into a room and told that the experimenter wanted to see how different activities would affect their moods. A six-week-old kitten was left in the room with them. Through a secret viewing window, the subjects were watched, and the number of times that they touched or petted the kitten was counted as an index of responsiveness to another living creature.

In a second version of the experiment, other subjects were put in the same room and allowed to either play with the kitten, read magazines, work puzzles or a maze, or just sit there. In this experiment, the amount of time that students played with the kitten was measured.

Only nine percent of the masculine students were interested in playing with the kitten. One-half of the other students were responsive to it. Interestingly, and contrary to Bem's expectations, only one-third of the feminine women were responsive to the kitten, but two-thirds of the androgynous women played with it.

Two additional experiments were conducted to measure responsiveness. In a third study, undergraduates were told that the reaction of babies to them as strangers was being tested. Actually Bem and her associates were measuring the students' reactions to the baby. Each student was left alone with an infant for ten minutes, and the number of times that he or she talked to the baby, smiled at it, or picked it up were recorded.

Only twenty-one percent of the highly masculine men spent time responding to the baby, compared to 50 percent of the other students. Most of the feminine women did respond warmly to the baby, but none more so than the androgynous women.

Finally, an experiment was conducted in which students believed they were being observed in a study of acquaintanceship. They came to the study in pairs, and each pair drew lots so that one would be a "talker," and the other would be a "listener." Unknown to the listener, the drawing was rigged so that all of the talkers were Bem's confederates. These confederates spouted a long list of personal problems which they recited from a memorized script. The listener's behavior was measured in terms of the number of responsive gestures and statements they made to the talkers' problems. Once again, the masculine men were seen to be least responsive. As compared to 60 percent of all students, only 14 percent of them showed a strong sympathy and concern for the talker. This time, the feminine women reacted more strongly than everyone including the androgynous women. Again, these studies lend strong support to the existence of the androgynous sex role.

Rigidity vs. flexibility in sex roles.   As a follow-up to the above studies, Bem and her colleague, Ellen Lenney, conducted experiments to test the rigidity of sex roles.

In an ingenious approach, they told students that they wanted to photograph them making choices. They then asked the students to choose one each of thirty pairs of activities that had a pay level beside each of the items. Some of the pairs included a masculine activity (one example was oiling a hinge) and a feminine activity (preparing a baby bottle). Some of the activities matched male or female type activities against neutral activities.

There were two sets of this instrument. On the male form, the female activity always paid most. The opposite was true for the female form.

They found that many individuals regularly chose the lower paying activity, rather than choose an activity that was higher paying, but characteristic of the opposite sex. Seventy-one percent of the students who strongly affiliated with their own sex type turned down the better paying choice, as compared to only 42 percent of the androgynous students.

Bem and Lenney then brought the students back for a second session. Each was asked to perform three male tasks, three female tasks, and three neutral tasks while they were being photographed. At the completion, the subjects were asked to indicate on a series of scales how they felt about doing each of the activities. Those who identified most highly with their own sex felt much worse than the androgynous people about doing a task which did not fit their sex. They were much more likely than androgynous people to say that they "felt less attractive and likable, more nervous and peculiar, less masculine or feminine, and didn't particularly enjoy the experience" (p. 62).

On the basis of these studies, Bem concludes that rigid sex roles are costly to our personalities, because of the conflict that results and the energy necessary to deal with the stress such conflicts bring about. She argues that the androgynous sex role is far more functional because it allows us to do whatever we feel is really appropriate, regardless of whether the situation is "masculine" or "feminine."

The Future of Androgyny

The objectives of androgyny are twofold:

Situational behavior.   To cry, to be assertive, to hug — whatever the situation calls for, whatever behavior would be appropriate for one sex, that behavior should also be appropriate for the other. Decisions as to what to do should be up to the individual, without regard to his or her sex.

Vocational choice.   People should be able to choose a vocation on the basis of ability and interest, without regard to sex role. A male should be able to be a dental hygienist, a manicurist, even a "mother"; a woman should be able to be a crane operator, a bank president, even a "father." Interest and ability, not gender, should predominate in the decision.

Komarovsky (1976), discussing the results of her study of college students' attitudes and reviewing the results of several others, indicates that among the educated, at least, acceptance of androgynous sex roles is very high. College men and women in general agree that women should have an equal opportunity to attain any job, and that they should be paid equal to men for equal jobs. But there is one serious problem: the majority of males and a high percentage of females agree that women should be the *child rearers* in our society.

Further evidence comes from a study (Komarovsky, 1976) of a nationwide sample of young adult women. In that study, over three-fourths agreed that "it is better for everyone involved if the man is the achiever outside the home and the woman takes care of the home and family."

In her study of college males, Komarovsky (1976) found that quite a few of them "perceived (and felt relieved thereby) that the withdrawal from work during childbearing would so handicap a woman that she would be unlikely to *excel her husband in occupational success and earnings*" (italics mine) (p. 250).

Most of the males in this study reported experiencing serious role conflicts in their interactions with women. Komarovsky states that:

The overwhelming majority of the seniors attributed the strains in relationships with women to personal inadequacies. In this the men were similar to women in the 1950's, when only a minority of women recognized the social roots of their frustrations. This recognition, on the part of men, will be slower in coming than in the case of women. The very reforms that might alleviate the strains experienced by the seniors inevitably entail yielding some power and privileges, and few possessors of power can be expected to yield it lightly. Only a few seniors acknowledged that the rewards of power and privilege hardly compensated them for the pressures and obligations of masculinity. The vast majority would not wish to change places with the weaker sex (p. 248).

Is it foolish to hope that males and females can come to treat each other more openly, more intimately, and more equitably than they do at present? Is the "battle of the sexes" inevitable? Komarovsky thinks not, and offers a number of suggestions which should help to alleviate the situation:

- Fathers, in particular, should offer more expressive and emotional parenting than they do at present. This would serve as a model to young males that it is all right to exhibit their affective side by expressing their feelings.

- Conversely, mothers who competently perform a job and assert themselves in family and other decisions also provide effective role models to their children, especially their daughters.

- As Maccoby and Jacklin (see above) discovered in their review of the literature, "Both men and women take a tougher stand toward children of their own sex." Therefore, adults of both sexes should take part in the rearing of their children, so that children experience the special benefits of interacting with the parent of the opposite sex.

- The status of part-time work should be upgraded. For example, colleges and schools should be willing to grant tenure to part-time employees who spend the other part of their time in the homemaking role.

- Paternity leaves should be granted to fathers, as well as maternity leaves to mothers.

- "Child enrichment centers" should be established. These should be easily accessible, of high quality, and available to all economic classes.

- New housing and neighborhood patterns should be encouraged, so that child-rearing families can form closer and more cooperative ties. The role of parenting, fulfilled by both males and females, should receive a higher status and recognition as a highly skilled contribution to society.

- Single status and childlessness in marriage should also be treated with greater respect than at present.

- "Symmetrical role allocation in marriage" should be encouraged. That is, all of the jobs of childrearing and homemaking should be shared by *both* marriage partners, so that they will be more empathetic with each others' problems and successes.

Komarovsky, who is the author of several well-known books on marriage and the family, believes that it would be naive indeed to expect that these innovations will come quickly or easily. In fact, she believes that the achievement of androgynous sex roles will demand a restructuring of our society, a reorganization "in a far more profound way, in my opinion, than would be necessary, for example, to solve the problems of the Black minority in the U.S." (p. 249). The alternative is to accept a growing degree of conflict and confrontation between the sexes — a disheartening prospect indeed.

Make Your Own Sex Role Test

The specific behaviors that make up sex roles frequently change, with some behaviors going out of fashion and others coming in. Until recently, for example, "I prefer a shower to a bath" was a good item. Women almost always chose a bath, presumably because it is luxurious and soothing, while men chose a shower, possibly because it is speedy and efficient. No one really knows why, but it doesn't matter a great deal. The purpose of a sex role test is to measure how much individuals subscribe to the various aspects of society's current view of their sex, and this test item did well in discriminating between males and females. In general, a person is highly feminine (whether a man or woman) if they respond to the items in the way that females usually respond.

Thus any valid sex role test must be regularly updated. How good are you at choosing valid items, that is, those that discriminate well between the sexes? Try writing a 10 to 20 item test and try it out on your friends. It might be fun to set up a competition between several test writers. The effectiveness or validity of an item can be scored by counting the number of responses of each sex to it. The greater the difference, the better the item.

To get you started, here are several items you might include:

Yes   No

- I like to cook fancy dishes.
- I am interested in electronics.
- *Playboy* is well worth its price.
- People usually don't care enough about each other.

ACHIEVING AN IDENTITY TODAY

Many believe that it has never been harder to reach a state of identity than today, and that because of what sociologist Alvin Toffler (1970) calls **future shock**, the problem will get worse.

Future Shock

If the last 50,000 years of man's existence were divided into lifetimes of approximately 62 years each, there have been about 800 such lifetimes. Of these 800, fully 650 were spent in caves. Only during the last 70 lifetimes has it been possible to communicate effectively from one lifetime to another — as writing made it possible to do. Only during the last six lifetimes did masses of men ever see a printed word. Only during the last four has it been possible to measure time with any precision. Only in the last two has anyone anywhere used an electric motor. And the overwhelming majority of all the material goods we use in daily life today have been developed within the present, the 800th, lifetime (p. 148).

The amount of change we must deal with in our daily lives has been increasing geometrically. Toffler believes that future shock is a result of having to cope with too much change in too short a period of time and will cause many of us to become disorganized and even mentally ill. He compares it to culture shock — the feeling we may get on arriving in a foreign country for the first time. Nothing seems the same. The language, customs, and scenery are different. We become disoriented and anxious. But in the back of our minds we know that if this discomfort becomes too great, we can hop on a plane and go back to the safety of our own culture. With future shock, there is no going home.

Orson Welles called future shock the "premature arrival of the future." We have only to look at our own grandparents to observe its effects. We see their irritation and bewilderment: "Everything is changing. No one cares about traditions. Nothing is the same any more." We ourselves are harassed by the myriad choices we must make. Commercials insist that we keep up with the latest. We live in a throw-away society. We find ourselves constantly changing everything, not only our possessions, but even our friends. We make many more friends than our grandparents did; our friendships endure for shorter periods of time and are of a shallower nature.

Our mobility is also threatening the basic solidarity of our families, creating a "new race of nomads." Family solidarity is subjected to other new strains. Instead of the familiar family structure of father, mother, children, and some relatives, we find a whole new set of alternatives, new relationships, new types of community. We see people living together in untraditional ways, as unmarried lovers, in group marriages, in homosexual marriages.

Toffler's main point is that the *rate* of change in our daily lives has different implications for our identities, and is often a more crucial factor in our well being, than the *direction* of change. There are three major aspects of the rate of change, each of which is rapidly increasing:

1. *Transience.* There is a decrease in the permanence of things and people in our lives.

2. *Novelty.* The dissimilarity of new situations in our lives from old situations is greater than it used to be.

3. *Diversity.* Changes differ not only in how quickly they come and how different they are from the past, but also in how many kinds there are. The stability in people's lives that once made for less diversity of change has been greatly eroded.

Toffler warns that future shock may lead many individuals to develop "fluid identities," changes of personality according to one's perception of the desires of others. Such a person has a whole "series of selves" he can call on, depending on the situation. This usually causes one's sense of reality to deteriorate, the first step on the way to mental illness (see Chapter 11). What is real, and what can one believe in? The mental health of adolescents depends on the answers they find.

The Republic of Technology

In his brilliant bicentennial essay for *Time* magazine (Jan. 19, 1977), historian Daniel Boorstin analyzes the problem of identity from another viewpoint. Referring to the western world today as the "Republic of Technology," he points to two major problems. First is the problem of the **new obsolescence**. Throughout most of history, he states, day-to-day continuity was the norm. Changes in peoples' lives were always a matter of news. In the Republic of Technology, quick obsolescence has become the rule. Rapidly developing nations are speedily destroying their inheritance; and while it takes centuries or even millenia to build civilizations, the renovation of an "underdeveloped" nation can be accomplished in mere decades. Boorstin calls the second problem the **new convergence**. Due to technology, the differences between peoples of the world are swiftly diminishing. Boorstin suggests that

> *each forward step in modern technology tends to reduce the difference between the older categories of experience. Take, for example, the once elementary distinction between transportation and communication; between moving the person and moving the message . . . With the increasing congestion of city traffic, with the parking problems and the length of holding patterns over airports, a television screen becomes a superior way of getting there. So when it comes to public events, often you are now more there when you are here than when you are there! (p. 37).*

Both the new obsolescence and the new convergence are the results of the special characteristics of technology. They are described below.

1. Technology invents needs and exports problems. At the time of its introduction, there was no public demand for the cigarette. Our desire for this product is almost totally the result of advertising. Technology has a way of multiplying the unnecessary.

2. Technology creates momentum that is irreversible. Nothing can be uninvented. This fact may seem unimportant, but consider the result of the increased demands brought about by technology and advertising. Boorstin argues that we have now come to the point where we are rapidly depleting the resources of the world in order to manufacture things that are basically unessential but exist because of need creation. Once we grow accustomed to the use of some product, we become extremely reluctant to give it up.

3. Technology assimilates. Communications technology has accomplished what years of revolution and philosophical thought were unable to accomplish — a kind of equality of experience. Through the wonders of television, people with very little money can experience, if indirectly, all the things that were once only the province of the rich.

4. Technology insulates and isolates. At the same time that technology brings us closer together, it also separates us. Boorstin gives as an example the difference between people traveling on a long stagecoach journey, whose only diversion was conversation, and a flight on a 747, where everyone is fastened to his seat and has his eyes and ears glued to the movie screen.

5. Technology uproots. This characteristic is most responsible for future shock. We are now able to go places and do things undreamed of in the past century, and these changes are redesigning the very nature of life. Jet lag and the disintegration of the nuclear family are both examples of technological disruption.

Boorstin asks,

Will we be able to continue to enrich our lives with ancient and durable treasures, enjoy our inheritance from our nation's founders, while the winds of obsolescence blow about us, while we enjoy the delights of ever-wider sharing? Will we be able to share the exploring spirit, reach for the unknown, enjoy the multiplication of our wants, live in a world whose rhetoric is advertising, its standard of living has become its morality—yet avoid the delusions of utopia, a life within satisfying limits? (p. 38).

THE ACHIEVED IDENTITY

If a person is able to steer his way through the troubled waters of today's world, what kind of person is he likely to be? When asked what the psychologically healthy adult should be able to do, Freud said, "*Leiben und arbeiten,*" to love and to work. Erikson has quoted his teacher's maxim many times, but his own description is considerably more extensive. Roazen (1976) summarizes Erikson's description of the mature adult as a person who

- Is tolerant of himself and those who interact with him.
- Has the capacity to make informed choices.
- Has the courage to stand alone.
- Is able to achieve mastery in the tasks he undertakes.
- Has the vision to open up new realities.
- Is able to weather the conflicts he faces.
- Has the capacity to do well, according to the standards of those who are significant to him.
- Elaborates one of his dominant abilities (for example, his math ability) into a full-time occupation.
- Is able to be childlike, and is most human when he is at play.

How does one achieve the goals of maturity? A difficult question, surely; but in recent years social scientists have learned quite a bit about growing up successfully and how we can help others do it. Much of the information presented in the following chapters concerns this new knowledge.

SUMMARY

The process of achieving an identity is thought to be marked by an identity crisis, which occurs in adolescence or, as some believe, in early adulthood. Erik Erikson, who first used the term *identity crisis*, is used as a case study in the search for identity, and his "crisis," through which he achieved a new name, religion, and occupation, is presented.

An unusual deviation from the identity process is known as "negative" identity. A person with a negative identity adopts one pattern of behavior because he is rebelling against demands that he follow an opposite pattern. Martin Luther's struggle with the Catholic Church is an example.

There are four types of identity status: (1) identity confusion—a situation in which no crisis has been experienced by the adolescent and no commitments have been made; (2) identity foreclosure—a status in which no crisis has been experienced, but the person has come to commitments, often forced on him by his parents; (3) identity moratorium—a status in which considerable crisis has been experienced, but no commitments have yet been made; and (4) identity achievement—a status in which numerous crises have been experienced, and also relatively permanent commitments have been made.

Two of the most significant aspects of identity are vocational and sexual. A person's choice of work plays a critical role in the definition of self. Today vocational identity is influenced by the fact that work takes up less of one's time and leisure activities more. Four criteria for choosing a vocation are: (1) service, in which the person attempts to meet the needs of his job through meeting the needs of others; (2) practicality, in which the person tries to choose a job that will pay off the best; (3) prestige, in which a vocation is chosen that results in the greatest praise from parents and other significant people; and (4) no rational choice, in which a job is chosen on the basis of its being the first opportunity presented to the individual. Vocational choice is strongly influenced by one's parents and one's sex. The schools have played an increasing role in vocational choice through programs of career education.

The second important aspect of identity is sexual role. Three aspects of sex role are: (1) sex-role orientation, differences among individuals as to how confident they feel about their sex identity; (2) sex-role preference, whether or not the individual is happy about the sex role he has; and (3) sex-role adaptation, how other people see the individual behaving in his sex role.

Sex role differs from sex identity in that one's role is defined by how one acts in the presence of others, while sex identity means how a person feels inside about the sex into which he or she was born.

The environment has a significant effect on both sex identity and sex role. Sex identity appears to be fixed in the child at an early age. Sex role is more fluid, can change throughout the person's life, and has varied in different periods in history. Identity is learned through imitation. The child imitates the parent or others of his own sex, and is reinforced for successful imitation of appropriate behavior.

Both boys and girls identify mainly with their mothers during the first two years. Girls continue this identification, but in order to achieve male identity boys must learn to identify with their fathers. This takes place about the second year and, according to Freud, leaves boys forever insecure about their gender.

Six major environmental determinants of sex role are parents, absence of the father, siblings, schools, peers, and the mass media. It has been found that females are higher in verbal ability and lower in spatial ability, weaker in mathematical ability, less aggressive, more afraid to be successful, and more easily able to maintain their sex-role identity. It is interesting to note that the only personality trait that differentiates males and females is aggressiveness.

There is disagreement as to whether sex roles are functional within the family and necessary for society, or dysfunctional. Sharply differentiated sex roles may cause problems in self-esteem and emotional health. People who are not restricted to behaving only in masculine and feminine ways are called "androgynous." Androgynous individuals may come to define a new standard of psychological health.

The difficulty of achieving a state of identity may worsen because of what sociologist Toffler has described as "future shock." Future shock results from too much change in too short a period of time. The increase in impermanence, novelty, and diversity within society may lead people to develop fluid identities in which personalities are changed according to the perceptions of the desires of others. The "series of selves" that results from this adaptation could cause deterioration of one's sense of reality.

Historian Boorstin describes "the new obsolescence," in which cultural traditions that have taken centuries to evolve are abandoned for renovation and modern technology, and "the new convergence," in which the differences between peoples of the world are diminishing through a common technology. These phenomena can also make identity achievement difficult.

People who have achieved identity are characterized as being tolerant of themselves and others, able to achieve mastery in the tasks they undertake, able to cope with new realities as well as conflicts, having the capacity to make informed choices and to use their dominant abilities in a full-time occupation, and, most especially, having the capacity to play.

Questions

1. What is an identity crisis? A negative identity?
2. What are four types of identity states?
3. How are vocational and sexual identities formed?
4. Why is it difficult to achieve the state of identity today?
5. What are the characteristics of the person who has achieved identity?

References

Bachman, J. G., O'Malley, P. M., & Johnston, J.   *Adolescence to adulthood: change and stability in the lives of young men.* Ann Arbor, Mich.: Institute for Social Research, 1978.

Bauer,R., & Stein, G.   "Sex counseling on campus: short-term treatment techniques." *American journal of orthopsychiatry,* 1973, *43*(5), 824–839.

Bem, S. L.   "Androgyny vs. the light little lives of fluffy women and chesty men." *Psychology today,* 1975, *9*(4), 58–59; 61–62.

Berger, A. S., Gagnon, J. H., & Simon, W.   "Gender role expectations among adolescents." Paper presented to the American Sociological Association, New Orleans, August 1972.

Berman, M.   "Review of 'life history and the historical movement' by Erik Erikson." *New York Times magazine,* March 30, 1975.

Bieliauskas, V.   "A new look at 'masculine protest'." *Journal of individual psychology,* 1974, *30,* 92–97.

Boorstin, D. "Tomorrow: the republic of technology." *Time,* January 17, 1977, 36–38.

Brim, O. G. "Family structure and sex role learning by children: a further analysis of Helen Koch's data." *Sociometry,* 1958, *21,* 1–16.

Broverman, I., Broverman, D., Clarkson, F., Rosenkrantz, P., & Vogel, S. "Sex-role stereotypes and clinical judgments of mental health." *Journal of consulting and clinical psychology,* 1970, *34,* 1–7.

Bureau of Labor Statistics. "Jobs for which apprenticeships are available." Washington, D.C.: U.S. Department of Labor, 1976.

Coleman, J. *The adolescent society.* New York: Free Press, 1961.

Connell, D. M., & Johnson, J. E. "Relationship between sex-role identification and self-esteem." *Developmental psychology,* 1970, *3,* 268.

Constantinople, A. "An Eriksonian measure of personality development in college students." *Developmental psychology,* 1969, *1,* 357–372.

Douvan, E., & Adelson, J. *The adolescent experience.* New York: Wiley, 1966.

Employment and Earnings. Washington, D.C.: U.S. Dept. of Labor, Bureau of Labor Statistics, January, 1981.

Erikson, E. *Young man Luther: a study in psychoanalysis and history.* New York: Norton, 1958.

Erikson, E. *Childhood and society* (2nd ed.). New York: Norton, 1963.

Erikson, E. *Identity: Youth and crisis.* New York: Norton, 1968.

Erikson, E. *Gandhi's truth: on the origins of militant nonviolence.* New York: Norton, 1969.

Erikson, E. *Life, history, and the historical moment.* New York: Norton, 1975.

Evans, R. *Dialogues with Erik Erikson.* New York: Harper & Row, 1967.

Fagot, B. I., & Patterson, G. R. "An *in Vivo* analysis of reinforcing contingencies for sex-role behaviors." *Developmental psychology,* 1969, *1,* 563–568.

Goethals, G. W., & Klos, D. S. *Experiencing youth* (2nd ed.). Boston: Little, Brown, 1976.

Gottlieb, D., & Bell, M. "Work expectations and work realities: a study of graduating college seniors." *Youth and society,* 1975, *7*(1), 69–83.

"A happy and traditional home is still the goal, but a happy home doesn't have to contain children." *Psychology today,* 1974, *7*(12), 102.

Harmon, L. W. "The childhood and adolescent career plans of college women." *Journal of vocational behavior,* 1971, *1*(1), 45–56.

Hetherington, E. M. "Effects of father absence on personality development in adolescent daughters." *Developmental psychology,* 1972, *1*(3), 313–326.

Hetherington, E. M. "Girls without fathers." *Psychology today,* 1973, *6*(9), 47–52.

Howe, F. "Sexual stereotypes start early." *Saturday review,* October 16, 1971, 76–82.

Jesser, C. J. "A dim light on the way to Damascus: selective feminism among college women." *Youth and society,* 1974, *6*(1), 49–62.

Johnson, M. M. "Sex-role learning in the nuclear family." *Child development,* 1963, *134,* 319–333.

Jouard, S. *The transparent self.* New York: Van Nostrand-Reinhold, 1971.

Kandel, D., & Lesser, G. "Parental and peer influences on educational plans of adolescents." *American sociological review,* 1969, *34,* 213–223.

Kellogg, R. "A direct approach to sex-role identification of school-related objects." *Psychological reports,* 1969, *24*(3), 839–841.

Kilpatrick, W. K. "Identity: Continuity, fidelity, and future shock." *Adolescence,* Summer 1974, *9*(34), 285–288. (a)

Kilpatrick, W. K. "Identity, youth, and the dissolution of culture." *Adolescence,* Fall 1974, *9*(35), 407–412. (b)

Kilpatrick, W. K. "Boy, girl, or person." *Boston College bridge magazine,* Winter 1976, *39*(2), 9–15.

Komarovsky, M. "Cultural contradictions and sex roles: The masculine case." *American journal of sociology,* 1973, *78,* 873–884.

Maccoby, E., & Jacklin, C. "What we know and don't know about sex differences." *Psychology today,* 1974, *8*(7), 109–112.

Manaster, G. *Adolescent development and the life tasks.* Boston: Allyn & Bacon, 1977.

Marcia, J. E. "Development and validation of ego identity status." *Journal of personality and social psychology,* 1966, *3,* 551–558.

Marcia, J. E. "Ego identity status: relationship to change in self-esteem, general maladjustment and authoritarianism." *Journal of personality,* 1967, *35,* 118–133.

Marcia, J. E. "The case history of a construct: ego identity status." In E. Vinacke (Ed.), *Readings in general psychology.* New York: Van Nostrand-Reinhold, 1968.

Marcia, J. E., & Freedman, M. L. "Ego identity status in college women." *Journal of personality,* 1970, *38,* 249–263.

Marland, S. P. "Career education: For and against." *School review, 1973, 82*(1), 57–66.

McCracken, J. H. "Sex typing of reading by boys attending all male classes." *Developmental psychology,* 1973, *8,* 1–48.

Minuchin, P. "Sex-role concepts and sex typing in childhood as a function of school and home environments." *Child development,* 1965, *36*(4), 1033–1048.

Mischel, W. "Sex typing and socialization." In P. H. Mussen (Ed.), *Carmichael's manual of child psychology.* New York: Wiley, 1970.

Money, J., & Ehrhardt, A. *Man and woman/boy and girl.* New York: New American Library, 1972.

Morris, J. "Conundrum." *Ms. magazine,* July, 1974, 57–64.

Muuss, R. *Theories of adolescence.* New York: Random House, 1975.

Naffziger, K. "A survey of counselor educators and other selected professionals." Unpublished dissertation, University of Oregon, 1971.

Neill, G. "Women's liberation expected to reach locker room soon." *Phi Delta Kappan,* 1974, *55*(9), 643–644.

Nelson, E. A., & Maccoby, E. E. "The relationship between social development and differential abilities on the scholastic aptitude test." *Merrill-Palmer quarterly,* 1966, *12* (4), 269–284.

Newman, P., & Newman, B. "Early adolescence and its conflict: group identity versus alienation." *Adolescence,* Summer 1976, *11*(42), 261–273.

Parsons, T. "Family structure and the socialization of the child." In T. Parsons & R. F. Bales (Eds.), *Family socialization and interaction process.* Glencoe, Ill.: Free Press, 1955.

Payne, D. E., & Mussen, P. H. "Parent-child relations and father identification among adolescent boys." *Journal of abnormal and social psychology,* 1956, *52,* 358–362.

Ponzo, Z., & Strowig, R. "Relations among self-role identity and selected intellectual and non-intellectual factors for high school freshmen and seniors." *Journal of educational research,* 1973, *67*(3), 137–141.

Rice, F. P. *The adolescent.* Boston: Allyn & Bacon, 1975.

Roazen, P. *Erik H. Erikson.* New York: Free Press, 1976.

Roe, A. "Early determinants of vocational choice." *Journal of counseling psychology,* 1959, *4,* 212–217.

Rogers, D. *The psychology of adolescence.* Englewood Cliffs, N.J.: Prentice-Hall, 1977.

Rohrbaugh, J. Femininity on the line. *Psychology Today,* August, 1979, *13*(3), 30–42.

Rosenkrantz, P., et al.   "Sex-role stereotypes and self-concepts of college students." *Journal of consulting and clinical psychology,* 1968, *32*(3), 282–295.

Schenkel, S., & Marcia, J. E.   "Attitudes toward premarital intercourse in determining ego identity status in college women." *Journal of personality,* 1972, *40*(3), 472–482.

Sears, R. R.   "Relation of early socialization experiences to self-concept." *Child development,* 1970, *41,* 267–290.

Simon, W., Berger, A. S., & Gagnon, J. H.   "Beyond anxiety and fantasy: the coital experiences of college youth." *Journal of youth and adolescence,* 1972, *1*(3), 203–222.

Stein, A. H.   "Sex role development." In J. F. Adams (Ed.), *Understanding adolescence* (3rd. ed.). Boston: Allyn & Bacon, 1976.

Stein, A. H., & Bayley, M. M.   "The socialization of achievement orientation in females." *Psychological bulletin,* 1973, *80,* 345–366.

Sutton-Smith, B., & Rosenberg, B. G.   "Age changes in the effects of ordinal position on sex-role identification." *Journal of genetic psychology,* 1965, *107*(1), 61–73.

Tavris, C.   "Male supremacy is on the way out. It was just a phase in the evolution of culture." *Psychology today,* 1975, *8*(8), 61–69.

"Teenage jobs." *Parade,* June 5, 1977, 6.

"The television image of women." *Intellect,* 1975, *103*(2363), 424–425.

Toffler, A.   *Future shock.* New York: Random House, 1970.

U.S. Office of Education.   "An introduction to career education." Washington, D.C.: Department of Health, Education, and Welfare, 1975.

Webb, A.   "Sex role preference and adjustment in early adolescence." *Child development,* 1963, *34,* 609–618.

Williams, J., Bennett., S., & Best, D.   "Awareness and expression of sex stereotypes in young children." *Developmental psychology,* 1975, *11*(5), 635–642.

Wohlford, P., Santrock, J. W., Berger, S. E., & Liberman, D.   "Older brother's influence on sex-typed, aggressive and dependent behavior." *Developmental psychology,* 1971, *4,* 124–134.

Additional References

Barinbaum, L.   "Identity crisis in adolescence: the problem of an adopted girl." *Adolescence,* Winter 1974, *9*(36), 547–554.

Berdie, R. F.   "Interests, occupation, and personality." *Intellect,* 1975, *103*(2363), 300–302.

Broverman, I., Vogel, S., Broverman, D., Clarkson, F., & Rosenkrantz, P.   "Sex-role stereotypes: a current appraisal." *Journal of social issues,* 1972, *28,* 59–72.

Clark, C.   "White-collar kids in blue-collar jobs." *Money,* 1976, *5*(2), 32–36.

Cvetkovich, G., Grote, B., Lieberman, E. J., & Miller, W.   "Sex-role development and teenage fertility-related behavior," *Adolescence,* Summer 1978, *13*(50).

Dellas, M., & Gaier, E. L.   "The self and adolescent identity in women: options and implications." *Adolescence,* Fall 1975, *10*(39), 399–408.

Donovan, J. M.   "Identity status and interpersonal style." *Journal of youth and adolescence,* 1975, *4*(1), 37–55.

Donovan, J. M.   "Identity status: its relationship to Rorschach performance and to daily life patterns." *Adolescence,* Spring 1975, *10*(37), 29–44.

Erikson, E.   *Identity and the life cycle: selected papers.* New York: Norton, 1959.

Erikson, E.   *Insight and responsibility: lectures on the ethical implications of psychoanalytic insight.* New York: Norton, 1964.

Erikson, E.   *Dimensions of a new identity: the 1973 Jefferson lectures in the humanities.* New York: Norton, 1974.

Gartner, A., & Riessman, F.   "Is there a new work ethic?" *American journal of orthopsychiatry,* 1974, *44*(4), 563–567.

Greenberger, E., & Sorensen, A. B.   "Toward a concept of psychosocial maturity." *Journal of youth and adolescence,* 1974, *3*(4), 329–358.

Harper, L. V., & Sanders, K. M.   "Preschool children's use of space: Sex differences in outdoor play." *Developmental psychology,* 1975, *11*(1), 119.

Healey, Gary W., & DeBlassie, R. R.   "A Comparison of Negro, Anglo, and Spanish-American adolescents' self concepts." *Adolescence,* Spring 1974, *9*(33), 15–24.

Hetherington, E. M.   "Effects of paternal absence on sex-typed behaviors in Negro and white preadolescent males." *Journal of personality and social psychology,* 4, 1966, 87–91.

Keniston, K.   "Youth: a new stage of life." *The American scholar,* Autumn 1970, *39,* 631–654.

Keniston, K.   "The tasks of adolescence." In *Developmental psychology today.* Del Mar, Calif.: CRM, 1971.

Kinsey, A., et. al.   *Sexual behavior in the human male.* Philadelphia: Saunders, 1948.

McDonald, G. W.   "A reconsideration of the concept 'sex-role identification' in adolescent and family research." *Adolescence,* Summer 1978, *13*(50).

Mead, M.   "The primitive child." In C. Murchison (Ed.), *Handbook of child psychology* (2nd. ed.). 1933.

Mead, M.   *Male and female.* New York: Morrow, 1949.

Mead, M.   "The young adult." In E. Ginsburg (Ed.), *Values and ideals of American youth.* New York: Columbia University Press, 1961.

Newman, P. R., & Newman, B. M.   "Identity formation and the college experience." *Adolescence,* Summer 1978, *13*(50).

Polsby, G. K.   "Unmarried parenthood: potential for growth." *Adolescence,* Summer 1974, *9*(34), 273-284.

Protinsky, H. O., Jr.,   "Eriksonian ego identity in adolescents." *Adolescence,* Fall 1975, *10*(39), 428-432.

Ramsdell, E. A., & Gaier, E. L.   "Identity and reality reflected in adolescent fiction: the early sixties and the early seventies." *Adolescence,* Winter 1974, *9*(36), 577-592.

Schenkel, S.   "Relationship among ego identity status, field-independence, and traditional femininity." *Journal of youth and adolescence,* 1975, *4*(1), 73-82.

Smith, D., Taylor, R., & Werblud, M.   "Make it happen: a guide to developing school volunteer programs." Newton, Mass.: The Korda Project, 1977.

Williams, R., & Oliver, S.   "The students' guide to volunteering." Newton, Mass.: The Korda Project, 1977.

Williams, R., & Oliver, S.   "The coordinators' guide to student volunteering." Newton, Mass.: The Korda Project, 1977.

Chapter Three

The Onset of Puberty

Chapter Highlights

Early Studies of Puberty
The Human Reproductive System
Adolescent Knowledge of Reproduction
How Well Do You Know Your Own Reproductive System?
The Female Sexual System
The Male Sexual System
When Does Puberty Start?
What Was Your First Reaction to Menarche?
What Was Your First Reaction to "Wet Dreams"?
"Sleeping Beauty": A Tale of Menstruation
The Effects of Timing on Puberty
The Early-Maturing Female: Ann
The Average-Maturing Female: Beth
The Late-Maturing Female: Cathy
The Average Adolescent Female of One Hundred Years Ago: Dorothy
The Early-Maturing Male: Al
The Average-Maturing Male: Bob
The Late-Maturing Male: Chuck
The Average Adolescent Male of One Hundred Years Ago: Dan
Normal Age Ranges of Puberty
Inappropriate Physical Growth

Adolescent Attitudes Toward Their Bodies
How I Feel About My Body (Female)
How I Feel About My Body (Male)
Summary

Key Terms and Concepts

puberty
sex education
hormonal balance
skeletal growth
maximum growth spurt
menarche
nocturnal emissions
normal range of development
motor development
maturation
maturity
hormone therapy
psychosocial dwarfism

Gretchen, my friend, got her period. I'm so jealous, God. I hate myself for being so jealous, but I am. I wish you'd help me just a little. Nancy's sure she's going to get it soon, too. And if I'm last, I don't know what I'll do. Oh please, God. I just want to be normal.
—Judy Blume, Are You There, God? It's Me, Margaret.

Since the development of written language, people have been describing the abrupt physical and emotional changes of puberty. However, the scientific study of puberty started only at the turn of the century when, with the advent of child labor laws, teenagers were increasingly withheld from the work force to continue in school. Teachers and psychologists were far more interested in the way children developed than were the factory owners who had governed the lives of so many teenagers in the previous century.

EARLY STUDIES OF PUBERTY

The girls are clearly beginning to look like young ladies, while the boys with whom they have thus far played on scarcely equal terms now seem hopelessly stranded in childhood. This year or more of manifest physical superiority of the girl, with its attendant development of womanly attitudes and interests, accounts in part for the tendency of many boys in the early teens to be averse to the society of girls. They accuse them of being soft and foolish, and they suspect the girls' whispering and titterings of being laden with unfavorable comments regarding themselves (King, 1914, p. 13).

This quaint and somewhat condescending description of the differences between males and females is typical of many of the adolescent theorists of this time (e.g., Bourne, 1913; Burnham, 1911; King, 1912, 1914; Smedley, 1899–1900). Understandably, these writers had far less data available than we do today, and there was a large subjective component to their opinions.

For example, King (1914) stated that for girls, puberty peaks at 12, and for boys, at 13. He based this opinion on the fact that in Boston in 1913 there were fewer deaths per thousand among 12-year-old girls and 13-year-old boys than for any other female and male age group, respectively. Because relatively few died at these ages, King argued that this was when "vital force" was highest, and thus was an indication of the onset of puberty. This is an interesting but highly dubious hypothesis. For one thing, the age at which the death rate is lowest changes from year to year and from place to place. Biological factors such as the timing of puberty are now known to be less variable than death rate.

This is not to say that empirical research was lacking at the time, or that knowledge of the effects of the environment on development was all guesswork. For instance, Boas's (1911) studies of the relationship between socioeconomic factors and the time of onset of puberty (the poorer the child, the later the puberty, on the average) continue to be borne out today (Rank, et al., 1967; Tanner, 1970).

Nevertheless, personal opinions and biases seem more prevalent in these early writings than in modern textbooks. King (1914, p. 25) suggested that the major causes of delayed puberty were "excessive social interests, parties, clubs, etc., with their attendant interference with regular habits of rest and sleep" and that the *second* major cause of delayed puberty was "an excess of physical work," an indication of the enormous split in life-styles between children of the wealthy and the poor.

THE HUMAN REPRODUCTIVE SYSTEM

Much more is known today about the various aspects of puberty. We know more about the organs of our reproductive systems and how these organs function together. We know a good deal about how the sexual system changes as the child approaches adulthood. And we are learning how to present this knowledge to adolescents effectively.

——— ADOLESCENT KNOWLEDGE OF REPRODUCTION ———

At one residential center for delinquent adolescent males, female college seniors were invited to participate in a discussion of sexuality. At first the questions were taken from cards the boys had prepared, but soon there was a more open exchange of ideas. One boy asked exactly where various organs are located, and one of the girls demonstrated by pointing to her body. When another asked what a Tampax looked like, a real one was passed from hand to hand. (The boys were quite puzzled until the girls realized they had forgotten to remove the paper wrapper!) The session was so successful that several more were held.

Unfortunately, new techniques and materials in **sex education** are not being given much of a chance these days. Sex education courses are actually on the wane. Hence, the sex information "underground" is still functioning. In this process, 14-year-olds teach 12-year-olds how sex works:

"Babies come out of their mothers' breasts — the nipples open up to let them out."

"You get a girl pregnant if you put your tongue in her mouth while kissing."

"The two weeks after a girl's period is her 'safe' time."

"If you masturbate too much, hair will grow on your palms, and eventually you'll go crazy."

"Most girls really don't like sex, but they can't help getting excited if you rub the backs of their necks."

"If you don't have at least one orgasm per month, your penis will shrivel up and fall off."

"Once your penis goes into a girl's vagina, she can hold it in as long as she wants to."

The 14-year-olds become 16-year-olds and learn that their information is wrong, but they do not go back to the younger children and correct it. The latter become the new 14-year-olds, who tell the new 12-year-olds the same wrong information. And so it goes.

The underground system of sex education will end only when schools are allowed to teach about sex. It will continue as long as these programs start only in junior high school (seventh grade). Most teachers and psychologists feel that young teenagers tend to repress sexual learning because it embarrasses them. Ideally such programs should start in kindergarten.

How well do you know your own reproductive system? Take the test below, then read the following sections on the female and male sexual systems.

How Well Do You Know Your Own Reproductive System?

Most of us seem to think we understand the workings of sex and reproduction well enough, yet when asked to define the various parts of our sexual system, we don't do very well. How high would you rate your knowledge?

If you would like to learn how much you really know (and this knowledge is important, if only because adolescents may ask you questions about it), take this test. Put an M in the first column after each male sex organ, an F after each female sex organ, or M/F if it is both. To make this test a little more interesting (and accurate), put a 1 in the second column if you are not at all sure of your answer, a 2 if you are somewhat confident, and a 3 if you feel certain you're right. The correct answers may be found by examining Figures 3-1 and 3-2. For each correct answer, enter your confidence number in the score column. If wrong, enter a minus and the confidence number. Total the plus and minus scores and subtract the latter from the former.

	M, F, M/F	Confidence 1, 2, 3	Score
Glans penis	_____	_____	_____
Prostate	_____	_____	_____
Ovary	_____	_____	_____
Vas deferens	_____	_____	_____
Bartholin's glands	_____	_____	_____
Labia minora	_____	_____	_____
Cervix	_____	_____	_____
Mons pubis (mons vereris)	_____	_____	_____
Cowper's glands	_____	_____	_____
Urethra	_____	_____	_____
Ureter	_____	_____	_____
Fimbriae	_____	_____	_____
Fallopian tubes	_____	_____	_____
Clitoris	_____	_____	_____
Hymen	_____	_____	_____
Testes	_____	_____	_____
Scrotum	_____	_____	_____
Foreskin	_____	_____	_____
Epididymis	_____	_____	_____
Vulva	_____	_____	_____
Ova	_____	_____	_____
Pituitary gland	_____	_____	_____
Labia majora	_____	_____	_____
Uterus	_____	_____	_____
		Total score	_____

This test has been given to groups of sophomores and graduate students. The possible score is 72. The sophomores, whose mean age is 18, averaged 55 on the test. The graduates, whose mean age is 27, averaged 38.

The Female Sexual System

The parts of the female sexual system are defined below and are illustrated in Figure 3–1.

Ova: the female reproductive cells stored in the ovaries. These eggs are fertilized by the male sperm. Girls are born with 200,000 to 400,000 follicles, each of which holds an ovum. At puberty, only 10,000 remain, but this is much more than sufficient for a woman's reproductive life. Since one egg ripens approximately every twenty-eight days from her midteens to her late forties, a woman releases less than 500 ova during her lifetime.

Ovaries: glands which release one ovum each month. They also produce the hormones estrogen and progesterone, which play an important part in the menstrual cycle and pregnancy.

Bartholin's glands: a pair of glands located on either side of the vagina. These glands provide a fluid during sexual excitation that acts as a lubricant in intercourse.

Labia minora: the two smaller inner lips of the vaginal opening.

Labia majora: the larger outer lips of the vaginal opening.

Cervix: the opening to the uterus located at the inner end of the vagina.

Uterus: the hollow organ (also called womb) in which the fertilized egg must implant itself for a viable pregnancy to occur. The egg attaches itself to the lining of the uterus from which the unborn baby draws nourishment as it matures during the nine months prior to birth.

Mons pubis or *mons veneris:* the outer area just above the vagina which becomes larger during adolescence and on which the first pubic hairs appear.

Urethra: a canal leading from the bladder to the external opening through which urine is excreted.

Ureter: a tube connecting the kidneys with the bladder.

Fimbriae: hairlike structures located at the opening of the oviduct that help move the ovum down the Fallopian tube to the uterus.

Fallopian tubes: conduct the ova from the ovary to the uterus. A fertilized egg that becomes lodged in the Fallopian tubes, called a Fallopian pregnancy, cannot develop normally and if not surgically removed will cause the tube to rupture.

Clitoris: comparable to the male penis. Both organs are extremely similar in the first few months of life, becoming differentiated only as sexual determination takes place. The clitoris is the source of maximum sexual stimulation and becomes erect through sexual excitement. It is above the vaginal opening, between the labia minora.

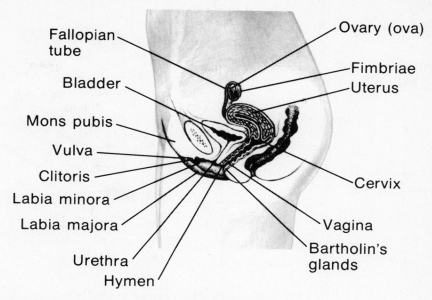

Fallopian tube

Bladder

Mons pubis

Vulva

Clitoris

Labia minora

Labia majora

Urethra

Hymen

Ovary (ova)

Fimbriae

Uterus

Cervix

Vagina

Bartholin's glands

Figure 3–1   *The Female Reproductive System*

Hymen: a flap of tissue which partially covers the vagina in virgins.

Vulva: the external genital organs of the female.

Pituitary gland: the "master" gland located in the lower part of the brain. It controls sexual maturation and monthly menstruation.

The Male Sexual System

The parts of the male sexual system are defined below and are illustrated in Figure 3–2.

Glans penis: the tip or head of the penis.

Foreskin: a flap of loose skin that surrounds the glans penis at birth, often removed by surgery called circumcision.

Testes: the two oval sex glands suspended in the scrotum that produce sperm. Sperm are the gene cells that fertilize the ova. They are equipped with a tail-like structure, which enables them to move about through a swimming motion. After being ejaculated from the penis into the vagina, they attempt to swim through the cervix into the uterus and into the Fallopian tubes where fertilization takes place. If one penetrates an egg, conception of a human being occurs. Although the testes regularly produce millions of sperm, the odds against any particular sperm penetrating an egg are enormous. The testes also produce testosterone, the male hormone that affects other aspects of sexual development.

Epididymis: a small organ attached to each testes. It is a storage place for newly produced sperm.

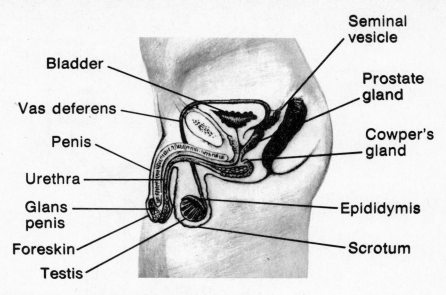

Bladder

Vas deferens

Penis

Urethra

Glans
penis

Foreskin

Testis

Seminal
vesicle

Prostate
gland

Cowper's
gland

Epididymis

Scrotum

Figure 3–2 *The Male Reproductive System*

Scrotum: the sac of skin located just below the penis, in which the testes and epididymis are located.

Vas deferens: a pair of tubes which lead from the epididymis up to the prostate. They carry the sperm when the male is sexually aroused and about to ejaculate.

Prostate glands: produce a milky alkaline substance known as semen. In the prostate the sperm are mixed with the semen to give them greater mobility.

Cowper's glands: are located next to the prostate glands. Their job is to secrete a fluid that changes the chemical balance in the urethra from an acidic to an alkaline base. This fluid proceeds up through the urethra in the penis where it is ejaculated during sexual excitement just before the sperm-laden semen. About a quarter of the time, sperm also may be found in this solution, sometimes called preseminal fluid. Therefore, even if the male withdraws his penis before he ejaculates, it is possible for him to deposit some sperm in the vagina, which may cause pregnancy.

Urethra: a canal that connects the bladder with the opening of the penis. It is also the path taken by the preseminal fluid and sperm during ejaculation.

Ureter: a tube connecting each of the kidneys with the bladder.

Pituitary gland: the master gland controlling sexual characteristics. In the male it controls the production of sperm, release of the male hormone testosterone (and thus the appearance of secondary sexual characteristics such as the growth of hair and voice change), and sexual excitement.

TABLE 3–1
THE SEQUENCE OF PHYSIOLOGICAL CHANGE IN MALES AND FEMALES

Females

Change in **hormonal balance.**
The beginning of rapid **skeletal growth.**
The beginning of breast development.
Straight pigmented pubic hair.
Maximum growth spurt (when growth is at its fastest rate).
The appearance of kinky pigmented pubic hair.
Menarche (first menstruation).
The appearance of hair on the forearms and underarms.

Males

Change in hormonal balance.
The beginning of skeletal growth.
The enlargement of the genitals.
The appearance of straight, pigmented pubic hair.
Early voice changes (voice "cracks").
First ejaculations (wet dreams, **nocturnal emissions**).
The appearance of kinky, pigmented pubic hair.
Maximum growth spurt.
The appearance of downy facial hair.
The appearance of hair on the chest and underarms.
Late voice change.
Coarse pigmented facial hair.

Note: This table is adapted from Muuss (1975).

WHEN DOES PUBERTY START?

Is there any one physiological event that marks the beginning of adolescence? The sequence of bodily changes in puberty is surprisingly constant. This holds true whether puberty starts early or late and regardless of the culture in which the child is reared. Table 3–1 lists the sequences of physiological change.

Which of these physical events in the life of the adolescent might we choose as the actual beginning of puberty? Change in hormonal balance is first, but its beginning is difficult to pinpoint. Skeletal growth, genital growth, pubic hair, breast development, voice change, growth spurt—all are inconvenient to measure. Some have suggested that menarche is the major turning point for girls, but many women do not recall menarche as a particularly significant event. Sometimes the first ejaculation is suggested as the beginning of adolescent puberty for males, but this too is often a little remembered (and possibly repressed) event.

What Was Your First Reaction to Menarche?

(Typical Responses of College Women)

"I felt grateful. It meant I was normal. There was always that chance that I'd be the last one to get it, or not get it until I was 17."

"I was scared and embarrassed, mostly embarrassed. I felt like everyone who looked at me could tell I was wearing one of those awful Kotex pads!"

"I was terrified that my mother would tell my father and he'd tell my brothers. He would only tell them so they'd be more understanding, but I knew they'd only make fun of me."

"I just didn't want to think about it. It was 'the curse.' "

"All I could think of was what I would feel if someone saw me buying sanitary napkins at the drugstore."

"I laughed. I don't know why. I just thought it was funny."

"My mother and my school had prepared me for it, and although it was a surprise, it was kind of exciting to feel like I was a woman."

"When it happened, my mother called my older sister, my aunt, a female friend of hers, and me together in our den. She said, 'I have an announcement to make. We are all women here.' Everyone knew what she meant, and it was like a celebration. It made me feel really proud!"

"When I finally got it (I was 14), my mother told my father, who came to me and said, 'I hear you got your period, Judy. Congratulations.' Then he shook hands with me. I thought I would *die* with embarrassment!"

"My mother must have neglected to tell me the whole story in advance (I was only 11), because when I got it, I said, 'Well, I certainly am glad *that's* over with!'—thinking it only happened once!"

What Was Your First Reaction to "Wet Dreams"?

(Typical Responses of College Men)

"I don't remember."

"I remember thinking, 'Anything that feels this good must be a sin.' Sure enough, a friend told me he asked a priest, and was told that if you want it to happen, that's a mortal sin. I really hated that guy for telling me!"

"I was really embarrassed. I couldn't think of a way to keep my mother from seeing it on my sheets."

"I thought it was strange, but my older brother said it was normal and after that it was no big deal."

"I enjoyed it, although I was sort of curious about why it was happening."

"I thought they were fun! I didn't feel any anxiety, but I wondered what my mother must have thought."

"They made me very anxious, and I just wished they would stop!"

"Sleeping Beauty": A Tale of Menstruation

Once upon a time Sleeping Beauty was born, and her parents, the King and Queen, invited fairies to her christening. These good fairies endowed her with beauty, grace, health, and other fine qualities. Unexpectedly, a jealous, evil fairy came to the christening. She uttered a dreadful curse: Sleeping Beauty would prick her finger on the distaff of a spinning wheel and bleed to death. One of the good fairies was able to change this threat of death into one hundred years' sleep. The King tried to prevent the curse from taking effect; he removed all the distaffs from the kingdom. While her parents were away, Sleeping Beauty at the age of 15 discovered a locked chamber. She walked into the room and saw an old woman who was spinning. Sleeping Beauty was fascinated by the spinning wheel, touched it, and pricked her finger on the distaff. She fell into a deep sleep for one hundred years until she was awakened by the kiss of her lover, Prince Charming.

The famous child psychologist Bruno Bettelheim (1976) believes that fairy tales such as "Sleeping Beauty" profoundly instruct us about the emotional turmoils of childhood and adolescence. In the Sleeping Beauty story, all of the parents' attempts to prevent their child's sexual awakening fail, because such aspects of sexuality as menstruation are inevitable. Bettelheim believes that the dreadful "curse" which causes bleeding is symbolic of menstruation, and turns out to be a blessing in disguise for Sleeping Beauty. After her long withdrawal into a deathlike sleep, she is awakened by Prince Charming. During her hundred years of inward-turning contemplation, Sleeping Beauty was struggling to attain the physical and emotional maturity she needs to be ready for love and marriage to Prince Charming.

Can you think of other fairy tales that are symbolic stories of adolescence?

Given our understanding of the physiology of adolescents and differences in individual psychology and culture, we would have to conclude that there is no single event marking the onset of puberty but rather a complex of events whose effects may be sudden or gradual.

THE EFFECTS OF TIMING ON PUBERTY

In a general sense, the onset of puberty affects all adolescents in the same way. However, the *age* at which these changes begin has some very specific effects on the adolescent's life. (Figure 3–3 illustrates how twelve-year-old adolescents can differ greatly in their stage of physiological development — and did so even many years ago!) In this section, eight adolescents, four males and four females, are compared in order to illustrate the differences that often occur among children even though they are all in the **normal range of development.** Each adolescent is 14 years old. The first female and male are early maturers, the second are average maturers, and the third, late maturers. They all fall within the typical range of all adolescents. The fourth female and male are representative of the average adolescent of one hundred years ago.

The Early-Maturing Female: Ann

At 5 feet, 5 inches, and 130 pounds, Ann is considerably bigger than her age mates. Her growth accelerated when she was 8 years old, and by the time she was 10½, her maximum growth spurt crested. She is still growing taller but at a slower rate. Her **motor development** (coordination and strength) had its greatest rate of increase two years ago. She is stronger than her age mates, but her strength and coordination have reached their maximum.

She started menstruating three years ago, at age 11, and her breasts are already in the secondary (adult) stage. Her pubic and underarm hair are also at an adult stage.

Ann is conflicted about the way her body looks. She feels conspicuous and vulnerable because she stands out in a crowd of her friends. Her greater interest in boys, and their response, often causes conflicts with other girls. They envy the interest the boys show in her more mature figure. She often has negative feelings about herself because she is "different." Even though other girls tend to avoid her now, her early **maturation** will become an asset to her in later adolescence. Nevertheless, she may experience some difficulties; she may find herself in situations (such as with drugs, sex, or drinking) for which she is not yet ready. She also will not always find it easy to find a boy tall enough to dance with.

In summary, we can say that while Ann is experiencing difficulties with her early **maturity,** she will begin to feel better about herself as she approaches 16.

The Average-Maturing Female: Beth

Although Beth is also 14, she is different in almost *every* way from Ann. She represents the typical adolescent today in the sense of the averageness of her

Figure 3–3   *Comparison of Male and Female Growth (King, 1914)*

measurements and physical change. It is clear that there is no such person as an "average" adolescent from the standpoint of personality and behavior.

Beth is 5 feet, 3 inches tall, and weighs 120 pounds. She reached her maximum growth two years ago, and is also starting to slow down. She is presently at the peak of her motor development.

Her breasts are at the primary breast stage; she is beginning to need a bra, or thinks she does. She started menstruating two years ago. She has adult pubic hair, and her underarm hair is beginning to appear.

She feels reasonably happy about her body, and most but not all of her relationships with her peers are reasonably satisfying. Although she does have some occasional emotional problems, they are not related to her physical development as much as are Ann's.

The Late-Maturing Female: Cathy

Cathy is at the lower end of the normal range of physical development for a 14-year-old girl. She is only 4 feet, 8 inches tall, weighs 100 pounds, and is just beginning her growth spurt. She is not too happy about this, as she feels that the other girls have advantages in relationships with boys.

Cathy's breasts are at the bud stage; her nipples and encircling areolae are beginning to protrude, but she is otherwise flat-chested. She has just begun menstruation. Pubic hair growth has started, but as yet no hair has appeared under her arms.

Other girls tend to feel sorry for her, but they also look down on her. She is more dependent and childlike than the others. She feels a growing dislike for her body, and she is becoming more and more introverted and self-rejecting because of it. At this stage her immaturity is not a great disability; at least she is more mature than some boys her age. As she reaches later adolescence, her under-developed figure may be a more serious source of unhappiness for her if she accepts conventional standards of sexual desirability.

The Average Adolescent Female of One Hundred Years Ago: Dorothy

Although records of adolescent physical development of one hundred years ago are less than adequate, we can be fairly certain of some aspects of it. Dorothy, who was typical for her time, was physically much like Cathy is now. At 4 feet, 7 inches, she was one inch shorter, and at 85 pounds, she weighed 15 pounds less than Cathy. At age 14, Dorothy would still have had four years to go before her peak of motor development, and she would not have started to menstruate for another year. In all the other physical ways she looked a great deal like Cathy. The major difference between the two girls is that while Cathy is unhappy about her body's appearance, Dorothy, who was perfectly typical, felt reasonably good about hers.

The Early-Maturing Male: Al

Al finds that at 5 feet, 8 inches tall, he towers over his 14-year-old boyfriends. He reached his maximum growth spurt approximately two years ago and weighs 150 pounds. He is now about two years before the peak of his motor development. His coordination and strength are rapidly increasing, but contrary to the popular myth, he is not growing clumsier. As adolescents reach their peak of motor development, they usually handle their bodies better, although adults expect them to have numerous accidents. It is true that when one's arms grow an inch longer in less than a year, one's hand-eye coordination suffers somewhat. However, the idea of the gangling, inept adolescent is more myth than fact.

Al's sexual development is also well ahead of that of his age mates. He already has adult pubic hair, and hair has started to grow on his chest and underarms. He began having nocturnal emissions almost two years ago, and since then the size of his genitals has increased almost 100 percent.

Because our society tends to judge male maturity on the basis of physique and stature, Al's larger size has advantages for him. He is pleased with his looks, although once in a while it bothers him that someone treats him as though he were 17 or 18 years old. Nevertheless, he uses the advantages of his early maturity whenever possible.

His friends tend to look up to him and to consider him a leader. Because size and coordination enable athletic superiority, and because success in school sports has long meant popularity, he has the most positive self-concept of all the adolescents described here, including the females. He has a good psychological adjustment, although he is sometimes vain, and is the most confident and responsible of this group. He engages in more social activities than the others, which also occasionally gets him into trouble, because he is not psychologically ready for some of the social activities in which he is permitted to participate.

The Average-Maturing Male: Bob

Interestingly, Bob is exactly the same height as his "average" counterpart, Beth, at 5 feet, 3 inches tall. He outweighs her by 10 pounds, at 130 pounds. He is currently in the midst of his maximum growth spurt, and is four years away from reaching the peak of his coordination and strength.

His sexual development began about a year ago with the start of nocturnal emissions, and he is just now starting to grow pubic hair. As yet he has no hair on his chest or under his arms. However, his genitals have reached 80 percent of their adult size.

Bob gets along well with his age mates. He is reasonably happy with the way his body has developed so far, although there are some activities that he wishes he could excel in. Most of the attributes that he aspires to are already possessed by Al, whom he envies. This causes few problems, as Bob still has every reason to hope his body will develop into his ideal physical image.

The Late-Maturing Male: Chuck

Chuck is also similar in stature to his counterpart, Cathy. They are both 4 feet, 8 inches tall, although at 90 pounds, Chuck is 10 pounds lighter than Cathy. He is as yet a year-and-a-half away from his maximum growth spurt, and must wait six years before his motor development will peak.

Chuck's sexual development is also lagging behind those of the other two boys. His genitals are 50 percent larger than they were two years ago, but as yet he has no pubic, chest, or underarm hair. He has not yet experienced nocturnal emissions, although these are about to begin.

He is the least happy with his body of the adolescents described here. His voice has not yet changed, he is considerably less strong and coordinated than

**TABLE 3–2
A COMPARISON OF THE PHYSICAL DEVELOPMENT OF EIGHT
ADOLESCENTS**

| | Females | | | | Males | | | |
	Ann	Beth	Cathy	Dorothy	Al	Bob	Chuck	Dan
Height	5'5"	5'3"	4'8"	4'7"	5'8"	5'3"	4'8"	4'7"
Weight	130 lbs.	120 lbs.	100 lbs.	85 lbs.	150 lbs.	130 lbs.	90 lbs.	90 lbs.
Hair	Adult pubic, underarm	Adult pubic, starting underarm	Starting pubic, no underarm	Starting pubic, no underarm	Adult pubic, starting chest, underarm	Starting pubic, no chest, underarm	Not yet started	Not yet started
Motor development, coordination and strength	Two years after peak	At peak	Two years before peak	Four years before peak	Two years before peak	Four years before peak	Six years before peak	Eight years before peak (inferred)
Maximum growth spurt	Four years ago	Two years ago	Just starting	Not yet started	Two years ago	Now	Not yet started	Not yet started

Note: This table is a summary of the following research sources: Damon, et al., 1969; Muuss, 1970; Poppleton and Brown, 1966; Tanner, 1961, 1962, 1963, 1968(a) and (b); Boas, 1911; Bourne, 1913; King, 1912, 1914; and Smedley, 1899–1900.

the other boys, and he is much smaller than they. They tend to treat him as a scapegoat and often ridicule him. He chooses to interact with boys who are younger than himself, and is attracted to activities in which mental rather than physical prowess is important, such as chess and band. He avoids girls, almost all of whom are more physically mature than he. This lack of heterosexual experience may later affect his self-concept.

Chuck lacks confidence in himself and tends to be dependent on others. He was of almost average size in grammar school, and now feels he has lost prestige. He frequently does things to gain the attention of others, but these actions seldom bring him the acclaim he craves. Probably as a result, he is more irritable and restless than the others, and engages in more types of compensating behaviors.

The Average Adolescent Male of One Hundred Years Ago: Dan

At 4 feet, 7 inches, Dan was shorter than Chuck by one inch, and weighed the same, 90 pounds. He trailed Chuck in sexual development by two years, and, at age 14, his genitals have increased only 20 percent in size.

TABLE 3–3

A COMPARISON OF THE DEVELOPMENT OF SEX-RELATED FEATURES OF EIGHT ADOLESCENTS

	Females				Males			
	Ann	Beth	Cathy	Dorothy	Al	Bob	Chuck	Dan
Genitals	Definite increase in size, but not carefully measured				100% increase in size	80% increase in size	50% increase in size	20% increase in size (inferred)
Breasts	Secondary breast stage	Primary breast stage	Bud stage	stage				
Menstrua-tion	Started three years ago	Started two years ago	Just starting	Won't start for one year				
Nocturnal emissions					Started two years ago	Started one year ago	Just starting	?

Note: This table is a summary of the following research sources: Damon, et al, 1969; Faust, 1960; King, 1914; and Tanner, 1962, 1970.

However, the major difference between Chuck and Dan lies in self-satisfaction; while Chuck is extremely unhappy about the way he is developing, Dan was as happy as Bob is now because he was quite average, for that time. Although we cannot know what his relationship with his peers was like or how he viewed himself, we can guess that these would have been quite similar to Bob's.

The effects of the timing of the onset of puberty on these eight adolescents are summarized in Tables 3–2, 3–3, and 3–4.

NORMAL AGE RANGES OF PUBERTY

The above descriptions illustrate the great variability in adolescent growth and the variability with which adolescents respond to growth. It should be kept in mind, however, that self-image and peer relationships are not entirely determined by physique. "Average-sized" adolescents do not always lead a charmed life, and many late and early maturers are quite comfortable with themselves. Adolescents who have clarified their values and set their own standards are not likely to be overly affected by pubertal changes or the peer approval or disapproval brought about by them.

The small size of Dorothy and Dan, who were average teenagers one hun-

TABLE 3–4
A COMPARISON OF THE REACTIONS OF EIGHT ADOLESCENTS TO THE TIMING OF THE DEVELOPMENT OF THEIR PHYSICAL AND SEX-RELATED FEATURES

| | Females | | | |
	Ann	Beth	Cathy	Dorothy
Body image	Conflicted	Happy	Unhappy	Happy
Relationship with peers	Other girls say she's boy crazy, avoid her	Independent of physiology	Other girls pity, look down on her	?
View of self	Feels conspicuous and vulnerable, conflicts because of earlier interest in boys, often self-rejecting because "different," self-image improves later	Reacts more to psychological and less to physical factors than do late or early maturers	Is more dependent and childlike, shows a growing dislike of her body, is becoming introverted and self-rejecting	?

| | Males | | | |
	Al	Bob	Chuck	Dan
Body image	Very happy	Happy	Unhappy	Happy
Relationship with peers	Leader—looked up to by others	Independent of physiology	Treated as scapegoat, ridiculed	?
View of self	Positive self-concept, high physiological adjustment, most confident and responsible, engages in more social activities, may have problem because of high expectations of him by others	Depends more on psychological and less on physical factors than for late or early maturers	Lacks confidence, tends to be dependent on others, seeks attention, is more irritable and restless, many compensating behaviors	?

Note: This table is a summary of the following research sources: Bourne, 1913; Clifford, 1971; Douglas and Ross, 1964; Faust, 1960; Frisk, et al., 1966; Jones and Mussen, 1958; Mussen and Jones, 1957; Peskin, 1973; and Peskin and Livson, 1972.

dred years ago, is part of the phenomenon called the "secular trend." Adolescents have been entering puberty sooner and growing taller and heavier over the

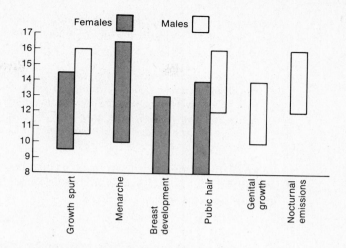

Figure 3–4   *Normal Age Ranges of Puberty*

Note: This figure is a summary of the research of Tanner (1970) and Marshall and Tanner (1970).

centuries. An example is the earlier onset of menstruation—three years earlier on the average than one hundred years ago. This trend has been irregular, and there is good reason to believe that it will level off within the next century (Tanner, 1970; Eichorn, 1970). It now appears that there are limits beyond which improved nutrition and health are likely to have little or no effects. There is also the possibility that, with increased environmental pollution and overpopulation, the secular trend may reverse itself.

Figure 3–4 details the age ranges considered normal for development. Adolescents who experience these changes earlier or later than the age ranges indicated may have no medical problem, but it is probably a good idea to consult a doctor. If a glandular imbalance exists, the doctor can usually remedy this problem with little difficulty.

INAPPROPRIATE PHYSICAL GROWTH

Inappropriate physical development, while rare, will be described briefly here. The two major types are gynecomastia, male breast growth, and virilism, the development of several masculine traits in the girl, including hirsutism (facial and chest hair) and voice deepening. Both conditions can usually be reversed with **hormone therapy** (Money and Ehrhardt, 1972).

Another problem that occasionally occurs is **psychosocial dwarfism,** in which puberty is so delayed that the teenager looks like a seven- or eight-year-old child. This condition is the result of an extremely negative environment. In one case, the child had been severely beaten by his mother and by his six brothers and sisters, who were themselves beaten if they refused to participate. He was found naked in a closet, the door of which had been nailed shut. His doctor described his situation:

> In the manner typical for victims of the battered child syndrome, this particular sixteen-year-old boy fits the formula of being forced to suffer punishment by way of atonement for his parents' own shortcomings and transgressions. In particular, the stepmother may have been pathologically destroying in him, by proxy, an image of what she could not tolerate in herself, namely, her own illegitimacy (Money and Wolff, 1974, p. 128).

Removal to a positive environment usually helps the child recover some, but seldom all, of his lost growth and development. The earlier this is done, the greater the recovery.

ADOLESCENTS' ATTITUDES TOWARD THEIR BODIES

Curiously, there is little recent research on the topic of adolescents' feelings about their own bodies (Clifford, 1971; Faust, 1960). The results of these studies are somewhat conflicting and now rather out of date. Therefore, with the help of some colleagues, the following questionnaire was developed and administered to 135 college freshmen who came from fifteen different states. The results of this survey follow, but first perhaps you might like to respond to it yourself.

In looking at the results of the freshman body-image study (Tables 3–5 and 3–6), we see that the majority of both men and women believe their bodies to be average. This is not surprising, because most people are average, by definition. Somewhat more men than women were willing to admit that they were smaller in overall size, but almost half the women in the study thought they were smaller than average in their bust size. It is unlikely that this is true, so this finding is probably more indicative of the sensitivity about possessing small breasts that has been created by our culture. There is reason to believe these attitudes are changing.

With the tremendous emphasis on slimness (especially female) in the media today, we could expect even those with average bodies to be dissatisfied, and they are. A considerably larger number of women were dissatisfied with their bodies than were men. Whether this is because women are more willing to admit they feel unhappy about their bodies or because they really do is impossible to say. Women were most concerned about their weight and legs. Yet, although 55 percent of the women felt bad about their weight, 70 percent of them thought their weight was average; 55 percent were dissatisfied with their legs, but 80 percent thought that their legs were average. Women were also bothered about the quality of their skin and about their figures in general. Perhaps not so surprising was the finding for female sports ability. Whereas 85 percent of the women thought that their ability was average, over a third of them felt bad about their ability. This is no doubt a reflection of the increased interest and support for sports activities among women. One further finding among the women that should be noted is the very high percentage who felt good about their eyes and faces. Perhaps self-acceptance is more crucial here.

Men expressed more satisfaction with their body features. Surprisingly, what bothered men most was the quality of their hair; almost one-third said that they felt bad about their hair. Four other characteristics disturbed one-fourth of the freshmen men: their physiques, the amount of hair on their faces, the quality of their voices, and their overall looks. A high percentage of this sample felt they were bigger, larger, or better than average compared to others. The majority of women and the high majority of men said that they felt good about most aspects of their bodies. It is possible that these freshmen were not expressing their true feelings. It is also possible that college students actually are superior to others in their physical attributes. Terman (see Chapter 4) found that those who were superior intellectually also tended to be superior in other aspects of their development. If this is true, then it is not surprising to find that college students feel relatively good about their bodies.

SUMMARY

Puberty is a period marked by abrupt physical and emotional changes whose onset may occur over a range of time.

Scientific studies of puberty began around the turn of this century, when adolescence began to be seen as an independent and unique phase in development. Early researchers had very little data on puberty, and much of what they had was anecdotal or conjectural in nature.

In recent years, our knowledge of the human reproductive system and organ function has helped us gain better understanding of sexual changes from childhood to adulthood. Sequences of bodily changes in puberty are constant whether they start early or late, and regardless of the culture in which the person is raised. In females, the sequence is (1) change in hormonal balance, (2) beginning of skeletal growth, (3) beginning of breast development, (4) appearance of straight pigmented pubic hair, (5) maximum growth spurt, (6) appearance of kinky, pigmented pubic hair, (7) first menstruation, and (8) appearance of hair on the forearms and underarms. In males the sequence is (1) change in hormonal balance, (2) beginning of skeletal growth, (3) the enlargement of genitals, (4) the appearance of straight pigmented pubic hair, (5) early voice change, (6) first ejaculation, (7) appearance of kinky, pigmented pubic hair, (8) maximum growth spurt, (9) appearance of downy facial hair, (10) appearance of hair on chest and underarms, (11) late voice change, and (12) coarse pigmented facial hair (Muuss, 1975).

Generally speaking, the onset of puberty affects all adolescents in the same way, in that all experience similar physiological developments. However, the age at which puberty occurs can have different effects on self-concept and relation-

How I Feel About My Body (Female)

My age _____ My height _____ My weight _____ My waist _____ inches

	Compared to Others			How I Feel About It		
	Bigger, larger than average	Average	Smaller, less than average	Good	Bad	Neither
1. My height	_____	_____	_____	_____	_____	_____
2. My weight	_____	_____	_____	_____	_____	_____
3. My bust	_____	_____	_____	_____	_____	_____
4. My hips	_____	_____	_____	_____	_____	_____
5. My legs	_____	_____	_____	_____	_____	_____
6. My nose	_____	_____	_____	_____	_____	_____
	Better than average	Average	Less than average	Good	Bad	Neither
7. The quality of my hair	_____	_____	_____	_____	_____	_____
8. The beauty of my eyes	_____	_____	_____	_____	_____	_____
9. My face in general	_____	_____	_____	_____	_____	_____
10. My figure in general	_____	_____	_____	_____	_____	_____
11. My clothes	_____	_____	_____	_____	_____	_____
12. My cleanliness	_____	_____	_____	_____	_____	_____
13. My posture	_____	_____	_____	_____	_____	_____
14. My sports ability	_____	_____	_____	_____	_____	_____
15. How coordinated I am	_____	_____	_____	_____	_____	_____
16. The quality of my skin	_____	_____	_____	_____	_____	_____
17. My strength	_____	_____	_____	_____	_____	_____
18. My teeth	_____	_____	_____	_____	_____	_____
19. My overall looks	_____	_____	_____	_____	_____	_____

How I Feel About My Body (Male)

My age _____ My height _____ My weight _____ My waist _____ inches

	Compared to Others			How I Feel About It		
	Bigger, larger than average	Average	Smaller, less than average	Good	Bad	Neither
1. My height	_____	_____	_____	_____	_____	_____
2. My weight	_____	_____	_____	_____	_____	_____
3. My nose	_____	_____	_____	_____	_____	_____
4. My penis	_____	_____	_____	_____	_____	_____
5. The amount of hair on my face	_____	_____	_____	_____	_____	_____
6. The amount of hair on my body	_____	_____	_____	_____	_____	_____

	Better than Average	Average	Less than Average	Good	Bad	Neither
7. My teeth	_____	_____	_____	_____	_____	_____
8. The quality of my hair	_____	_____	_____	_____	_____	_____
9. My eyes	_____	_____	_____	_____	_____	_____
10. My face in general	_____	_____	_____	_____	_____	_____
11. My strength	_____	_____	_____	_____	_____	_____
12. My physique (build)	_____	_____	_____	_____	_____	_____
13. My voice	_____	_____	_____	_____	_____	_____
14. My chest	_____	_____	_____	_____	_____	_____
15. My clothes	_____	_____	_____	_____	_____	_____
16. My cleanliness	_____	_____	_____	_____	_____	_____
17. My sports ability	_____	_____	_____	_____	_____	_____
18. How coordinated I am	_____	_____	_____	_____	_____	_____
19. The quality of my skin	_____	_____	_____	_____	_____	_____
20. My overall looks	_____	_____	_____	_____	_____	_____

TABLE 3–5
FINDINGS FOR THE FRESHMAN BODY-IMAGE STUDY: FEMALES

	Compared to Others			How I Feel About It		
	Bigger, larger than average	Average	Smaller, less than average	Good	Bad	Neither
1. My height	10*	75	15	65	10	25
2. My weight	15	70	15	45	55	0
3. My bust	5	50	45	45	15	40
4. My hips	25	65	10	35	35	30
5. My legs	15	80	5	30	55	15
6. My nose	5	90	5	55	5	40
	Better than average	Average	Less than average	Good	Bad	Neither
7. The quality of my hair	50	50	0	75	5	20
8. The beauty of my eyes	60	40	0	80	0	20
9. My face in general	45	50	5	85	0	15
10. My figure in general	40	45	15	35	35	30
11. My clothes	55	45	0	65	5	30
12. My cleanliness	65	35	0	70	5	25
13. My posture	15	70	15	40	20	40
14. My sports ability	10	85	5	40	35	25
15. How coordinated I am	35	65	0	40	25	35
16. The quality of my skin	15	80	5	40	35	25
17. My strength	35	65	0	45	15	40
18. My teeth	55	40	5	75	10	15
19. My overall looks	45	50	5	45	10	45

* Rounded to the nearest five percent.

ship with others. Some adolescents mature early, some late; most mature with their peers, and each group experiences a different sense of self-concept.

At 14, the early-maturing female would be around 5 feet, 5 inches tall and weigh 130 pounds. Her breasts are at the secondary stage and she began menstruation three years ago. She is often conflicted about her physical development because she feels she stands out among her peers. Her early interest in boys makes her feel conspicuous and vulnerable. Despite her negative image of herself, early maturation becomes an asset to her in later adolescent life.

TABLE 3–6
FINDINGS FOR THE FRESHMAN BODY-IMAGE STUDY: MALES

	Compared to Others			How I Feel About It		
	Bigger, larger than average	Average	Smaller, less than average	Good	Bad	Neither
1. My height	50*	25	25	75	0	25
2. My weight	25	50	25	70	15	15
3. My nose	15	85	0	70	15	15
4. My penis	15	70	15	60	15	25
5. The amount of hair on my face	15	60	25	50	25	25
6. The amount of hair on my body	0	85	15	30	15	55
	Better than average	Average	Less than average	Good	Bad	Neither
7. My teeth	50	35	15	70	15	15
8. The quality of my hair	25	50	25	30	30	40
9. My eyes	35	50	15	60	15	25
10. My face in general	50	50	0	90	10	0
11. My strength	35	65	0	60	15	25
12. My physique (build)	35	65	0	60	25	15
13. My voice	15	60	25	50	25	25
14. My chest	25	60	15	60	15	25
15. My clothes	25	75	0	70	0	30
16. My cleanliness	50	50	0	100	0	0
17. My sports ability	40	40	20	85	0	15
18. How coordinated I am	65	35	0	100	0	0
19. The quality of my skin	35	40	25	70	15	15
20. My overall looks	40	40	20	75	25	0

*Rounded to the nearest five percent.

An average-maturing female of the same age would be 5 feet, 3 inches tall and weigh 120 pounds. Her breast development is in the primary stage and she started menstruating two years ago. She is reasonably happy about herself and her emotional problems are not linked with her physical development, as they are with her early- or late-maturing peers.

A late-maturing female of 14 would be 4 feet, 8 inches tall and weigh 100 pounds. Her breast development is in the bud stage and she has just started menstruation. She is unhappy about her physical development and is more child-like in behavior than her peers. Her friends tend to pity and look down on her. Her dislike of her body may make her introverted and self-rejecting.

An average 14-year-old female adolescent one hundred years ago was very much like the late maturer of today, though she was perfectly normal. Thus, she was happy about herself physically. She would not have menstruated for another year and would not have reached her peak of motor development for four years.

At 14, the early-maturing male would be 5 feet, 8 inches tall and weigh 150 pounds. He is very happy about his development and he is looked up to by others. He has a very positive self-concept and is confident of himself. He engages in more social activities than his peers, but may get into trouble because of his psychological immaturity and the high expectations others have of him because of his physical maturity.

An average-maturing male would be 5 feet, 3 inches tall and weigh 130 pounds. He is quite happy about himself and may look up to the early maturer for the ideal physical image he hopes to develop into. It will be four more years until his motor development peaks.

A late-maturing male of 14 would be 4 feet, 8 inches tall and weigh 90 pounds. He is unhappy about himself and is often ridiculed by his peers. He lacks confidence, tends to be more dependent on others, and is often irritable and restless because of his unsuccessful attempts to gain acclaim.

An average male adolescent one hundred years ago was also like the late maturer of today. Although he would have waited eight more years until his peak of motor development, he was probably quite happy about himself because he did not differ physically from his peers.

Adolescents have been entering puberty sooner and growing larger over the centuries. This is called "secular trend," and it is expected to level off within the next century.

Fortunately, inappropriate forms of physical growth are rare. One is gynecomastia, the growth of breasts by males; the other is virilism, the development of masculine traits in females. Psychosocial dwarfism is another inappropriate growth which seems to be the result of an extremely negative environment. Removal from a negative to a positive environment seems to help, but normal development is seldom attained.

Questions

1. What changes occur during puberty?
2. What are the effects of these changes?
3. What are the physical effects of the early and late onsets of puberty?
4. What are the emotional results of early- and late-starting puberty?
5. How do the typical female and male adolescents feel about their bodies?

References

Bettelheim, B. *The uses of enchantment.* New York: Knopf, 1976.

Blume, J. *Are you there, God? It's me, Margaret.* New York: Bradbury, 1970.

Boas, F. "Growth." In H. Kiddle (Ed.), *A cyclopedia of education.* New York: E. Steiger, 1911.

Bourne, R. S. *Youth and life.* Boston: Little, Brown, 1913.

Burnham, W. H. "Hygiene of adolescence." In H. Kiddle (Ed.), *A cyclopedia of education.* New York: E. Steiger, 1911.

Clifford, E. "Body satisfaction in adolescence." *Perceptional motor skills,* 1971, *33,* 119–125.

Damon, A., Damon, S. T., Reed, R. B., & Valadian, I. "Age at menarche of mothers and daughters, with a note on accuracy of recall." *Human biology,* 1969, *41,* 161–175.

Douglas, J. W. B., & Ross, J. N. "Age of puberty related to educational ability, attainment, and school leaving age." *Journal of child psychology and psychiatry,* 1964, *5,* 185–196.

Douvan, E. "Sex differences in the opportunities, demands, and development of youth." In R. J. Havighurst & P. H. Dreyer (Eds.), *Youth.* Chicago: National Society for the Study of Education, 1975.

Eichorn, D. H. "Physiological development." In P. H. Mussen (Ed.), *Carmichael's manual of child psychology.* (Vol. 1, 3rd ed.) New York: Wiley, 1970.

Faust, M. S. "Developmental maturity as a determinant in prestige in adolescent girls." *Child development,* 1960, *31,* 173–184.

Frisk, M., Tenhunen, T., Widholm, O., & Hortling, H. "Psychological problems in adolescents showing advanced or delayed physical maturation." *Adolescence,* 1966, *1* (2), 126–140.

Jones, M. C., & Mussen, P. H. "Self-conceptions, motivations, and interpersonal attitudes of early and late maturing girls." *Child development,* 1958, *29,* 491–501.

King, I. *Social aspects of education.* New York: Bobbs-Merrill, 1912.

King, I. *The high school age.* Indianapolis: Bobbs-Merrill, 1914.

Marshall, W. A., & Tanner, J. M. "Variations in the pattern of pubertal changes in boys." *Archives of dissertations on children,* 1970, *45,* 13.

Money, J., & Ehrhardt, A. *Man vs. woman/boy vs. girl.* New York: New American Library, 1972.

Money, J., & Wolff, G. "Late puberty, retarded growth, and reversible hyposematotropinism (psychosocial dwarfism)." *Adolescence,* Spring 1974, *9*(33), 121–134.

Mussen, P. H., & Jones, M. C. "Self-conceptions, motivations, and interpersonal attitudes of late and early maturing boys." *Child development,* 1957, *28,* 243–256.

Muuss, R. E. "Adolescent development and the secular trend." *Adolescence,* 1970, *5*(19), 267–284.

Muuss, R. E. *Theories of adolescence* (3rd ed.). New York: Random House, 1975.

Naffziger, C. C., & Naffziger, K. "Development of sex role stereotypes." *Family coordinator,* 1974, *23*(3), 251–258.

Peskin, H. "Influence of the developmental schedule of puberty on learning and ego functioning." *Journal of youth and adolescence,* 1973, *2*(4), 273–290.

Peskin, H., & Livson, N. "Pre- and post-pubertal personality and adult psychologic functioning." *Seminars in psychiatry,* 1972, *4*(4), 343–353.

Poppleton, P. K., & Brown, P. E. "The secular trend in puberty: has stability been achieved?" *British journal of educational psychology,* 1966, *36,* 97–101.

Rank, J. L., Schumsky, D. A., & Witt, M. T. "Heights, weights, and obesity in urban school children." *Child development,* 1967, *38,* 515–530.

Smedley, F. W.   *Report of the child study and pedagogic investigation.* Chicago: Chicago public schools, 1899-1900.
Tanner, J. M.   *Educational and physical growth.* London: University Press, 1961.
Tanner, J. M.   *Growth at adolescence* (2nd ed.). Oxford: Blackwell, 1962.
Tanner, J. M.   "The regulation of human growth." *Child development,* 1963, *34,* 817-848.
Tanner, J. M.   "Earlier maturation in man." *Scientific American,* 1968, *218,* 21-27.(a)
Tanner, J. M.   "Growth of bone, muscle, and fat during childhood and adolescence." In G. A. Lodge (Ed.), *Growth and development of mammals.* London: Butterworth, 1968.(b)
Tanner, J. M.   "Physical growth." In P. H. Mussen (Ed.), *Carmichael's manual of child psychology* (Vol. 1, 3rd ed.). New York: Wiley, 1970.
Tavris, C.   "Male supremacy is on the way out. It was just a phase in the evolution of culture." *Psychology today,* 1975, *8*(8), 61-69.
"The television image of woman." *Intellect,* 1975, *103*(2365), 424-425.

Additional References

Allen, C. D., & Eicher, J. B.   "Adolescent girls' acceptance and rejection based on appearance." *Adolescence,* 1973, *8*(29), 125-138.
Angrist, S. S.   "The study of sex roles." *Journal of social issues.* 1969, *25*(1), 215-232.
Horn, P.   "The myth of the ugly feminist. Guess who believes it?" *Psychology today,* 1975, *9*(6), 39; 122.
Lerner, R. M.   *Concepts and theories of human development.* Reading, Mass.: Addison-Wesley, 1976.
Lerner, R. M., & Karabenick, S. A.   "Physical attractiveness, body attitudes, and self-concept in late adolescents." *Journal of youth and adolescence,* 1974, *3,* 307-316.
Lerner, R. M., & Korn, S. J.   "The development of body build stereotypes in males." *Child development,* 1972, *43,* 912-920.

Lerner, R. M., Orlos, J., & Knapp, J. "Physical attractiveness, physical effectiveness, and self-concept in late adolescents." *Adolescence,* Fall 1976, *11*(43), 313–326.

Lorenz, K. "Genetic decay." *Intellectual digest,* 1974, *4*(8), 23–30.

Maccoby, E. "Sex differentiation during childhood." *Catalog of selected documents in psychology,* Nov. 1976, *9,* 97.

Maccoby, E. E., & Jacklin, C. N. "What we know and don't know about sex differences." *Psychology today,* 1974, *8*(7), 109–112.

Matis, J. "Adolescent sexuality and societal change." *American journal of psychotherapy,* July 1976, *30,* 433–440.

Money, J. "Differentiation of gender identity." *Catalog of selected documents in psychology,* Nov. 1976, *6,* 93.

Nesselroade, J., & Baltes, P. B. "Adolescent personality development and historical change: 1970–1972." *Monographs of the society for research in child development,* 1974, *39*(1), (Serial No. 154).

Peterson, A. "Physical androgyny and cognitive functioning in adolescents." *Developmental psychology,* Nov. 1976, *12*(6), 524–533.

Roberts, J., & Ludford, J. "Skin conditions in youths 12–17, United States." *Vital and health statistics* (DHEW). Rockville, Md., August 1976.

Romar, N. "The motive to avoid success and its effects on performance of school-age males and females." *Developmental psychology,* 1975, *11*(6), 689–699.

Schwartz, M., & Baden, M. A. "Female adolescent self-concept: An examination of the relative influence of peers and adults." *Youth and society,* 1973, *5*(1), 115–128.

"Sex differences a myth?" *APA monitor,* 1975, *6*(3), 10.

Stattieri, J. R. "Body build and behavioral expectancies in young females." *Developmental psychology,* 1972, *6,* 125–127.

Stempfel, R. S. "The question of sex hormone therapy in cases of delayed puberty." *Journal of pediatrics,* 1967, *70*(6), 1023–1024.

Chapter Four

Thinking Style

Chapter Highlights

Intellectual Development
  The Role of Intelligence
  Stages of Cognitive Development
  Variables in Intellectual/Ethical Development
  Stages of Intellectual/Ethical Development in
    the College Years
Creative Development
  The Creative Product
  The Creative Mental Process
  Uses for a Brick
Creativity, Giftedness, and the IQ
  Creative Personality Traits
  The Two-String Test
  The Critical Period Hypothesis
  Obstacles to Creativity
  Aids to Creativity
  Guidelines for Improving Your Own Creativity
Intelligence
  The Measurement of Intelligence
  Intelligence and Genes
  Tommy: A Real Problem Child
Learning Disabilities
Nonlinear Thinking
  Communications and Thinking Patterns
  McLuhan's Theory and Adolescent Identity
  Freaking Out Grandma
Summary

Key Terms and Concepts

thinking style
abstract thought
intellect
adaptations
mental structures
reflexes
schema
operations
organization
assimilation
accommodation
equilibrium
sensorimotor stage
preoperational stage
concrete operational stage
formal operational stage
object constancy
reversibility
conservation
hypothetical deductive reasoning
inversion
compensation
information processing strategy
consolidation
solidification

dualism
relativism
commitment
empirico-induction
hypothetico-deduction
unusualness
appropriateness
transformation
condensation
associationism
structuralism
remote associations
critical period
intelligence

Intelligence Quotient (IQ)
linear thinking
print-oriented people
nonlinear thinking
neotribal people

Important People

Jean Piaget
Marshall McLuhan
Sarnoff Mednick
William Perry
John Flavell

A friend of mine showed me this book, My Secret Garden. *It was about different people's fantasies. Reading it, it suddenly occurred to me that you could create a whole new world just in your head! I don't know why I hadn't thought of it before, but the idea excited me terrifically. I began lying in bed on weekend mornings till 11 or 12 o'clock making up "my secret world." I went to fabulous new places. I met friends who were always kind and cooperative. And of course I fell in love with a guy like you wouldn't believe!*

—Susan, a tenth-grade student

The impressive physical and social changes that occur during adolescence tend to obscure the fact that profound changes in **thinking style** are also taking place. In adolescence, thinking ability reaches its full potential. The increased capacity for **abstract thought** enables the adolescent to formulate problems, to devise solutions, to judge experience, to reconsider values. The evolution of abstract thought is both exciting and disconcerting.

What causes the flowering of abstract thinking in adolescence? Why does it reach a higher level in some than in others? In order to answer these questions, we must look at how the intellect itself develops.

INTELLECTUAL DEVELOPMENT

The foremost contributor to the study of intellectual development in children is Jean Piaget. Beginning his scholarly career at 11(!), Piaget soon published numerous papers on birds, shellfish, and other topics of natural history. As a result, the diligent Swiss was offered the curator's position at the Geneva Natural History Museum. He was only 15 at the time and turned it down to finish high school. He received his Ph.D. in biology at the age of 21. Since then he wrote more than fifty books. He clearly possessed more than his share of intelligence.

Piaget began his research on cognitive development in 1920 when he took a position in the Binet Laboratory in Paris. He was given the task of standardizing a French version of an English-language test of reasoning ability, which enabled him to observe how children responded to the questions. He discovered that while there were similarities in the wrong answers given by each age group, there were differences in why wrong answers were given. For example, 5-year-olds would give a wrong answer for one reason, whereas older age groups gave the same wrong answer for other reasons. This discovery led Piaget to the idea that children of different age groups have different thinking patterns. Prior to 1920, little research had been done on the nature of intelligence. Most scientists believed that children were miniature adults who used adult thinking methods, but used them poorly. They felt that as information was poured into the child, mental maturity gradually developed. Piaget discovered that specific thinking abilities must be acquired before the child's intellect could fully mature; information alone is not enough. Furthermore, he observed that these mental abilities develop in stages, each one preparing the way for the development of the next.

The Role of Intelligence

Piaget's background in biology formed the basis for his view of intelligence. If you have ever seen an episode of "The Undersea World of Jacques Cousteau," you have probably been amazed by the way ocean dwellers biologically adapt themselves to their particular environments. The puffer fish swells to twice its size when threatened by an enemy. The anglerfish uses its dorsal fin as bait to lure smaller fish to its mouth. Nature is filled with examples of superb **adaptations** of animals to their environments. But nature has not fitted people to any specific environment. It has equipped them to adapt to most environments through the gift of intelligence. Like the swelling of the puffer fish, human intellect seemed to Piaget to be another of nature's examples of biological adaptation.

The adaptive mechanism of intelligence matures through the growth of increasingly more effective **mental structures.** These structures can best be defined as the blueprints that equip us to affect our environment. They are the tools of adaptation.

At birth, all interaction with the environment is a reflection of the environment. When a specific event (a stimulus) occurs, infants react automatically to it. Sucking and crying are examples of these **reflexes.**

Soon after birth, reflexes are transformed into elementary mental structures, which Piaget called **schema.** Schema are organized patterns of behavior that infants use to interact with the environment. Infants develop schema for looking, for grasping, for placing objects in their mouths, and so on. As infants grow older and begin to encounter more elements of their world, basic schema are combined and rearranged into even more efficient structures. By the time children reach seven, higher forms of psychological structures are developing. These structures are called **operations.**

According to Piaget, adult thinking is composed of numerous operations which enable the individual to manipulate the environment. Operations are mental, internalized actions. They are similar to programs in a computer. Programs enable the computer to manipulate the data fed into it in various ways. For example, both computers and mental operations can be programmed to calculate the average score of a group of tests.

When we remark that a person looks different, we have made a mental comparison with the way he or she looked previously. We have performed the operation of comparison with the data we have collected from the environment. Another mental operation is picturing new combinations of objects. When you want to rearrange the furniture in your room, you can first imagine various combinations of the furniture, adopting and discarding numerous arrangements, without leaving your chair. Our adaptive tools, then, evolve from reflexes to schema and finally to operations, which are our adult thoughts.

In addition to reflexes, the infant has at birth two basic tendencies or drives that affect intellectual functioning throughout his or her lifetime. They are **organization** and **adaptation**, and they govern the way we use our schema to adjust to the demands of the environment.

Organization. Our innate tendency to organize causes us to combine our schema more efficiently. The elementary schema of the infant are combined and reorganized to produce a coordinated system of higher-order mental structures. Each time a new schema is acquired, it is integrated into existing schema. Consider children learning to throw a ball. They may understand the various parts of a good throw, but they will not throw the ball well until they have integrated these parts to a smooth and efficient movement. The better organized this movement is, the more successful they are likely to be.

Adaptation. The second tendency inherent in all human beings is to adapt to the environment. Adaptation consists of two complementary processes: **assimilation** and **accommodation.** We assimilate when we perceive the environment in a way that fits our existing schema. We accommodate when we modify our schema to meet the demands of the environment. Let us consider these essential processes in some detail.

We try to assimilate as much as possible because it is easier — that is, it uses less energy — than accommodation. It is easier to see situations, events, and objects as something we understand and can work with. When asked to describe an unfamiliar object, we say: "It looks like an orange," or "It's hard like a rock." To make these comparisons, we perceive the object in a way that fits what we know. We look for similarities. If an object or idea makes sense to us or is meaningful, it is because we can assimilate it into existing structures. Similarly,

of them mentally to suit the structures for reading in your mind.
you are able to read these words, because you alter your perception

You may have physically assimilated the above idea by turning this book around — by rearranging the environment. When we mentally alter what we see, we *recognize* or rethink it and thus assimilate it.

Does –...- - ..-.. 88 * * * 8 --'"? To answer this question written in code, you would have to learn the key. In doing so, you would be acquiring a *new* schema, which would become integrated with existing schema of language. This is called accommodation. Let us suppose that you are required to break this code. On examination, you first may find some similarity with Morse or some other familiar code — you would assimilate it. Thus, the process of assimilation forms a basis for accommodation. The educated guess you make to help you break the code is accommodation.

All mental activity uses assimilation and accommodation. An effective intellect must balance these processes. A person who is incapable of assimilation, such as a mentally retarded person, does not have the capacity to take advantage of his previous experiences. A person who is incapable of accommodation is largely unresponsive to his environment. The rigid schizophrenic is an example.

Stages of Cognitive Development: Piaget

Schema grow out of inherited reflexes through assimilation and accommodation and become integrated into more complex structures because of the tendency to organize. This process takes place in stages, beginning at birth and usually ending in the latter part of adolescence. Piaget likened intellectual development to the gradual assembly of a large building. The parts of the building are continually adjusted throughout its construction so that they contribute to the stability of the whole.

Mental structures become not only more complex but also more flexible, enabling us to cope with more elements of the environment. Piaget says that humans continually strive to create a state of **equilibrium** between themselves and the world. Ideally this means having the right schema for each of the demands the world places on us. Of course, this perfection is never achieved, but the tendency toward equilibrium urges us through the stages of development.

Mental growth takes place in four stages, each one laying the foundation for the next. They are: the **sensorimotor stage** (birth to 2 years); the **preoperational stage** (2 to 7 years); the **concrete operational stage** (7 to 11 years); and the **formal operational stage** (11 years and up). These are approximate ages at which children begin and end a stage.

The sensorimotor stage (birth–2 years).   At birth, mental operations are nonexistent. Infants manipulate the environment through reflex action in response to physical needs such as pain and hunger. Sucking is an example. Soon these reflexes develop into more complex habits, and infants become aware of the relationship between their actions and their effects on the environment.

Infants are egocentric at birth; they do not experience the external world as separate from themselves. The existence of objects in the environment of infants is entirely dependent on their sensory perception of them. When an object is removed from their sight or touch, they do not search for it. They act as though it no longer exists. As the sensorimotor stage proceeds, infants develop **object constancy,** the awareness that objects exist independent of their perception.

The preoperational stage (2–7 years).   Until this stage, children's intellectual tools consisted of the ability to use their senses and to interact with the world through movement. When children learn to talk, they acquire the ability to symbolically represent objects. Consider the statement, "I want a cookie." To make this demand, children must be aware that cookies exist as a class of objects. They must also have acquired the verbal symbol *cookie* and connected feelings of hunger with the symbol for an object that will satisfy it. Now that they have symbols to represent objects in their world, they can manipulate these objects mentally. Now they can think.

Language development brings with it a new form of self-centeredness or egocentricity. The equilibrium achieved in the sensorimotor stage is upset once again. Children are able to use symbols, but do not understand that words are only representatives of objects. If you ask a 3-year-old to tell you what a ball is, he is quick to respond, "It's a ball," thinking that the properties of a ball, its roundness and its bounciness, are expressed by the word itself.

Children at this stage also lack the ability to engage in a discussion. Instead they partake in what Piaget calls collective monologues. If you observe a group of 3-year-olds talking, you may notice that most of them don't talk *to* each other so much as *next to* each other. Preoperational children believe that everyone else thinks as they do.

Preoperational thinking uses a different logic, called transductive; children at this stage reason from particular to particular rather than from general to particular (deductive) or particular to general (inductive). For example, Piaget's daughter Jacqueline reasoned that it was not afternoon because she had not yet had her nap.

The concrete operational stage (7–11 years).   As children learn to cope with the new discoveries that accompany language, they attempt to create a new equilibrium between themselves and the world around them. This is achieved partly through experiencing the differences between themselves and others; they become less self-centered.

School-age children are concerned with order. If you watch a group of children playing, you will observe that they make play systematic by creating an orderly set of rules on which all must agree. Decisions about rules can only be made when the viewpoints of others are considered. Behavior at this stage becomes social and cooperative.

Children now become concerned with *why* things happen. The intuitive thinking style of the preoperational stage is replaced by elementary logic, as operations begin to develop which enable children to form more complex mental actions on concrete elements of their world.

Logical thinking requires that one have an understanding of the physical properties of the world. When asked, "Which is heavier, a pound of feathers or a pound of lead?" the correct answer depends on one's understanding of the concept of density in relation to measurement. Preoperational children cannot understand that the weight is the same regardless of the density of the objects. The operations necessary for this understanding are developed in the concrete operational stage.

There are a number of processes involved in logical thinking. The first is **reversibility.** Piaget illustrates this concept with the following example. A child is shown two tall glasses of the same size filled with equal amounts of water. When asked which has more water, the child replies that they have the same amount. When the contents of one of the glasses is poured into a wider, shorter container, and the question is repeated, the preoperational child will say, "The tall glass has more." The concrete operational child will maintain that they are still equal; he is able to mentally pour the water from the short, wide container back into the tall glass, and thus realize that the amount of water does not change because the shape of its container has changed.

Another process of logical thought is **conservation.** What happens when a cube of sugar is dropped into a glass of water? The preoperational child thinks that the sugar has disappeared when it dissolves. The concrete operational child understands that the sugar has merely changed form; he is able mentally to conserve the substance.

The classification of objects and events develops in this stage. At about 7, children learn to arrange objects in order by length and size, and later by weight and volume. They can group objects and events in larger categories based on common properties such as rain, snow, and sunshine into the category of weather.

When children acquire these operations, they become able to logically solve problems by the use of elementary deductive reasoning. However, their thinking style still needs refinement. Ask the 11-year-old, "How would things be different if we had no thumbs?" and he is likely to respond, "But we *do* have thumbs!" The concrete operational child does not consider possibilities that are not real. The tools of thought are assembled, but still need the refinement that takes place in the formal operations stage.

The formal operational stage (11 years and up).   In adolescence, one's thinking style takes wing. Changes in thinking style are fundamental to personality and moral development.

Formal operations expand thought to the abstract. Reality is represented by mental symbols that can be manipulated, as data is represented by electromagnetic code that can be programmed in the computer. The mental operations that take place in the concrete operational stage involve only objects that can be physically acted on.

The adolescent is capable of forming conclusions based on hypothetical possibilities. Answering the question, "What would things be like if we had no thumbs?" involves mentally picturing a hypothetical hand with no thumbs. This "mental hand" is contrasted with the reality of a real hand and various conclusions produced.

Thinking in the formal stage becomes much more orderly and systematic. Most 9-year-olds would be unable to answer the question, "If Jane's hair is darker than Susan's, and Susan's hair is darker than Mary's, whose hair is darkest?" Although a 9-year-old is capable of "ranking" the children by darkness of hair, he or she is unable to manipulate facts concerning imaginary people; but, if given dolls with different colored hair, the child would have no trouble with the solution.

Adolescents are able to perform operations on ideas they create mentally. When asked, "What will the world be like in ten years?" adolescents might think, "We may have no oil." Having started with that thought, they can form a system of possibilities based on their original assumptions. This is **hypothetical deductive reasoning,** or reflection. Reality is looked at from different angles; its shape is altered as if it were passed through a prism; then it is put back together in a new form — a new idea.

When most adolescents reach the apex of this fourth stage is debatable. Higgins-Trenk and Gaite (1971) found that no more than half of the 17-year-olds they studied had reached it. Arlin (1975) suggests that there are really two substages of the formal operational stage. The first, reached in early adolescence, is the ability to solve abstract problems. The second, reached later if at all, is the sensitivity to the existence of problems; he calls it the "problem-finding" stage.

Variables in Intellectual Development

Psychologist John Flavell (1977), on the basis of his own studies and his review of the literature, has suggested that there are seven aspects of the transition from childhood to adolescent and adult thinking. These seven aspects are considered in the sections below, from the standpoint of an imaginary adolescent situation.

Let us imagine the following scenario. The local television station has decided to sponsor a new program called "Young Women Today." It has already hired a 24-year-old woman to host the show, a person who has had considerable experience in the talk-show format. In addition, they want to hire a 17-year-old high school girl as an assistant host. This has been announced at the local high school. Because the employers are sure that many female students will apply for this job, they have designed a simple application form. With it, they hope to identify the better candidates whom they will interview more extensively. On this application form, the applicants are to describe two characteristics that would make them an especially good choice for the assistant's job.

Here are Flavell's seven aspects of the childhood-adolescent cognitive transition, analyzed from the standpoint of this scenario:

The real versus the possible.   As was mentioned above, for Piaget (1973), probably the most important cognitive change from childhood to adolescence has to do with the growing ability of the adolescent to imagine possible and even impossible situations. Elementary school children tend to approach problems by examining the data firsthand, and attempt to make guesses about the solution to the problem on the basis of the first piece of information they happen to look at. As Flavell suggests, the child has "an earthbound, concrete, practical-minded sort of problem approach, one that persistently fixates on the perceptible and inferable reality there in front of him" (p. 103). The preliminary approach is a series of guesses as to what the information available can mean.

This is no longer the case for 17-year-old Ellen, who would very much like to get the television show job. As it happens, she is the daughter of an unemployed actor. She wonders whether this is a fact she should mention. She thinks that it may help her, both that her father has been in show business, and that her family could use the money. On the other hand, she suspects that the television people might think that if her father has been unsuccessful in show business, she may be too. Whereas a nine-year-old child might put this fact down on the application, hoping that it might make some difference, Ellen tries to think of all the possible ramifications of this piece of information before choosing whether to select it as one of her two relevant pieces of information.

Ellen is obviously a formal operational thinker. For her, as Flavell would describe it, "reality is seen as that particular portion of the much wider world of possibility which happens to exist and hold true in a given problem situation" (p. 103).

Empirico-inductive versus hypothetico-deductive methods.   A further major difference between concrete and formal operational thinkers is in their *method* of problem solving. Younger children use an **empirico-inductive** approach, that is, they are likely to look at available facts and try to induce some generalization from them. Adolescents, on the other hand, are likely to use **hypothetico-deductive** reasoning, to hypothesize about the situation and then deduce from it what the facts *should be* if the hypothesis were true. Adolescents tend to look at what might be, in two senses: they attempt to discover several possibilities in a situation before starting to investigate it empirically. Then they try to imagine the possible outcomes of each possibility.

Whereas the younger child might be satisfied with simply putting down two possible characteristics on the application, Ellen is likely to think of what the ramifications are for each of a number of possible characteristics that she might put down. For example, she might hypothesize that if the station has a reputation for being concerned with poor people, they would be sympathetic with the fact that her father is out of work and needs a job. On the other hand, if the station has a reputation for fierce competition, it might look negatively on this information, thinking that perhaps her whole family are "losers."

Intra-propositional versus inter-propositional thinking.   Elementary school-aged children, especially older ones, may well be able to think of a number of possible outcomes that would result from a single choice. It is only in later adolescence, for the most part, that they are able to think of the ramifications of *combinations* of propositions.

In Ellen's case, for example, she may decide that her father's unemployment may hurt her, but she may balance this by stating that she herself has maintained a paper route successfully for the past four years.

Inter-propositional thinking can become infinitely more complex than intra-propositional thinking. Logicians (students of logical thinking) have discovered many aspects of the interrelationships which can occur between sets of propositions. They are concerned with the conjunction between ideas, with the necessary implications of assertions, with the sufficiency of the explanations of causation, and so forth. These complexities usually become part of the repertoire of thinkers as they develop into adulthood.

An important aspect of this complexity is the ability to think logically about statements which may have no relationship to reality whatsoever. As Flavell states, "formal operational thinkers understand that logical arguments have a disembodied, passionless life of their own, at least in principle" (p. 106). Most persons find thinking about abstract concepts — for example, the laws of trigonometry — more difficult than thinking about the construction of a table, but the laws of logic are no different in either case. During adolescence and adulthood, the person becomes aware of this.

Combinations and permutations.   Because concrete operational thinkers look at propositions only one way at a time, they are often unable to imagine all of the possible combinations or permutations of a set of data. During adolescence, the thinker becomes able to realize that systematically generating combinations (A with B, A with C, B with C, etc.) can aid in thoroughly examining the possible solutions of a problem.

It is entirely likely that Ellen would sit down and draw up a list of all good characteristics before even starting to decide which of these would be best to put on her application. To improve her creativity, she might write all of these characteristics on separate sheets of paper, put them in a hat, and draw them out in pairs to see if she comes across a pair which she thinks will be unusually appealing. Without such a technique, she might never have thought of that particular pair.

Inversion and compensation.   Suppose you have before you two containers with an equal amount of water in each, hanging evenly from each side of a balance scale. Obviously, if a cup of water is added to the container on the right, it will sink to a level lower than the container on the left. If you were asked to make the containers even again, you would probably recognize that it could be done in one of two ways, withdraw a cup of water from the container on the right (**inversion**), or add a cup of water to the container on the left (**compensation**). Concrete operational thinkers are likely to think of one or the other of these solutions, but not both. They usually will not recognize that there is more than one possible way to solve the problem. Having solved it one way, they are no longer willing to tend to the task. Because formal operational thinkers are able to imagine both inversion and compensation as being useful in solving a problem, they have a better chance of coming up with a more fruitful solution.

Ellen would have been using compensation if she had mentioned her newspaper job to balance her father's unemployment. She might have been using inversion if she had simply left out the fact that her father was unemployed.

Information processing strategies.   Older thinkers are not only more likely to have a large array of problem-solving strategies, but are also more likely to attempt to devise a plan to use this array. Such a plan is an **information-processing strategy.**

Flavell points to the game of "Twenty Questions" as an example of this difference. In this game, the problem solver is given twenty questions of the yes-or-no type to solve a problem. For example, if the problem is to guess what person the questioner is thinking of, an excellent question would be, "Is the person alive?" This eliminates a tremendous number of possibilities. Other questions such as "Is the person a woman?" or "Is the person an adult?" are examples of this effective problem-solving strategy. Concrete operational problem solvers are more likely to name twenty particular individuals and thus (unless they are lucky) lose the game.

Ellen has the problem of attempting to discover what major criteria the television people have in mind in selecting their talk show host. She might go to several individuals in the community who could have some knowledge about those criteria. Furthermore, she might use a good strategy in asking questions of those informed persons. At any rate, to the extent that she has reached the formal operations stage, she is much more likely to do so.

Consolidation and solidification.   The changes from childhood to adulthood mentioned so far have been qualitative. There are also two quantitative aspects of this transition. The mental gains that are being made are slowly consolidated. Not only are the improved problem-solving techniques learned, but they are employed in a wider variety of situations, and with greater skill. The various aspects of formal operational thinking interact with each other and produce a quantum leap in thinking ability at this time. Furthermore, these gains seem to be solidified. That is, the thinker is more certain and confident in the use of the newly gained mental skills, and is more likely to use them in new situations.

If Ellen were, let us say, twelve years old instead of seventeen, she may have tried some of the tactics that she has used in getting this job, but she might very well have given up quickly and just put down any two traits which seemed acceptable to her. It is her greater experience with these thinking styles which gives her the motivation to persevere at the task.

How far does the average adolescent in this country go toward the achievement of these seven aspects suggested by Flavell? Have all adults reached full and complete formal operations? The truth is, we don't know. We do have some tentative information, however.

Higgins-Trenk and Gaite (1971) found that no more than half the seventeen-year-olds they studied had attained formal operation. Martorano (1974) found a gradual increase in this type of reasoning from eleven through eighteen years, but discovered that a considerable number of the eighteen-year-olds were often unable to complete tasks calling for formal operations.

The question of the criteria as to when a person has reached formal operations is important. For example, Henle (1962) and Wason and Johnson-Laird (1972) discovered that even well-educated adults are susceptible to a large variety of errors in reasoning problems. Arlin (1975) suggests that this may be because there are really two substages of the formal operations stage. The first, which is usually reached in early adolescence, is the ability to solve abstract problems when presented by someone else. The second stage, which may not be reached at all, is the sensitivity to the existence of problems. Arlin calls this the "problem-finding" stage, and suggests that although it is an equally important aspect of formal operations, many adults have not entered it.

In an extensive review of Piagetian-type experiments with adolescents, Neimark (1975) concludes that:

> Logical reasoning, as reflected in consistent performance across a broad class of instances, does not appear until adolescence, and even at that age is by no means a universal attainment of all adolescents (p. 570).

Stages of Intellectual/Ethical Development in the College Years

Harvard psychologist William Perry (1968, 1970, 1981) studied the intellectual and ethical development (see Chapter 5 also) of several hundred students aged seventeen to twenty-two who were enrolled at Harvard during the years 1954 to 1963. These students responded to several checklists on their educational views, and were interviewed extensively on the basis of their responses. The results of these studies led Perry to suggest a sequence of intellectual and ethical development which typically occurs during these years. This sequence consists of nine positions, which indicate progress from belief in absolute authority to the recognition that one must make commitments and be responsible for one's own beliefs.

Perry's nine stages are divided into three broader categories, as follows:

I. *Dualism* ("Things are either absolutely right or absolutely wrong").

Position 1: The world is viewed in such polar terms as we versus others, right versus wrong, and good versus bad. If an answer is right, it is absolutely right. We get right answers by going to authorities who have absolute knowledge.

Position 2: A student recognizes that uncertainty exists, but ascribes it to poorly qualified authorities. Sometimes individuals can learn the truth for themselves.

Position 3: Diversity and uncertainty are now acceptable, but considered temporary because the authorities do not know what the answers are. The student becomes puzzled as to what the standards should be in these cases.

II.   *Relativism* ("Anything can be right or wrong depending on the situation; all views are equally right").

Position 4a: The student realizes that uncertainty and diversity of opinion are often extensive, and recognizes that this is a legitimate status. Now he or she believes that "anyone has a right to an opinion." It is now possible for two authorities to disagree with each other without either of them being wrong.

Position 4b: Sometimes the authorities (such as college professors) are not talking about right answers. Rather, they want students to think for themselves, supporting their opinions with data.

Position 5: The student recognizes that all knowledge and values (including even those of an authority) exist in some context. It is therefore relative to the context. The student also recognizes that simple right and wrong are relatively rare, and even they exist in a specific context.

Position 6: The student apprehends that because we live in a relativistic world, it is necessary to make some sort of personal commitment to an idea or concept, as opposed to looking for an authority to follow.

III.   *Commitment* ("Based on the available evidence and my understanding of my own values, I have come to new beliefs").

Position 7: The student begins to choose the commitments that he or she will make in specific areas.

Position 8: Having begun to make commitments, the student experiences the implications of those commitments, and explores the various issues of responsibility involved.

Position 9: The student's personal identity is affirmed through the various commitments made. There is a recognition of the necessity for balancing commitments, and the understanding that one can have responsibilities which are expressed through a daily life-style. Perry (1981) describes this stage as follows: "This is how life will be. I will be wholehearted while tentative, fight for my values yet respect others, believe my deepest values right yet be ready to learn. I see that I shall be retracing this whole journey over and over — but, I hope, more wisely."

Some students move through these stages in a smooth and regular fashion; others, however, are delayed or deflected in one of three ways:

Temporizing: Some students remain in one position a year or more exploring its implications, hesitating to make any further progress.

Escape: Some students use opportunities for detachment, especially those offered in Positions 4 and 5, to refuse responsibility from making any commitments. Since everyone's opinion is "equally right," the student believes that no commitments need be made, and thus escapes from the dilemma.

Retreat: Sometimes, conflicted by the confrontation and uncertainties of the middle positions, students retreat to earlier dualistic positions.

There has been considerable research on Perry's theory (Blake, 1976; Broughton, 1975; Knefelkamp, 1974; Knefelkamp and Slepitza, 1976; Kurfiss, 1975; Meyer, 1975; Perry, 1968 a and b, 1970, 1981; Stephenson and Hunt, 1977; Widick, 1975; and Widick, Knefelkamp and Parker, 1975). These studies have been reviewed by King (1977). Although there have been a number of complaints about the research design of some of these studies, which detracts from the confidence we might otherwise have in Perry's scheme, major criticism has been of a more philosophical nature.

Boyd (1972), Broughton (1975), and Heffernan (1971) have argued that Perry's theory confuses cognition with aspects of personality and morality. Heffernan argues that Positions 1 through 5 have to do mainly with intellectual meaning, and that Positions 6 through 9 address "ways of establishing identity, finding personal stability in the chaos of relativism, orienting oneself through acts or series of commitments, and refining a meaningful life-style" (p. 9). Broughton agrees, but says that the division comes between Positions 6 and 7. Boyd believes that interaction between the two realms occurs throughout Perry's theory.

Kurfiss (1975) argues that far from confusing these areas, Perry has performed a valuable service in attempting to bridge them. She says that he is aware of what he is doing here, and cites the title of his 1970 book, *Forms of Intellect and Ethical Development in the College Years*, as evidence of this awareness.

In response to many of the criticisms of Perry's scheme, Kitchener & King (in press) have described a seven-stage theory of developing justifications of beliefs. Their theory is called Reflective Judgment, and is based on the work not only of Perry, but also of Harvey, Hunt, and Schroder (1961), and Broughton (1975). They have developed a semistructured interview and a scoring scheme that assesses developing philosophical assumptions and the ways in which students at different educational levels use evidence and authorities to justify beliefs. To date eleven studies using the same instrument to assess Reflective Judgment level have been completed (Brabeck, et al., 1981). Perry's scheme and the Reflective Judgment theory are major examples of attempts to theoretically describe and empirically investigate the nature of mature intellectual development.

The development of abstract thought gives the adolescent a new power and a new joy. In the ability to think about thinking is the beginning of creativity.

CREATIVE DEVELOPMENT

> *This is the story about a very curious cat named Kat. One day Kat was wandering in the woods where he came upon a big house made of fish. Without thinking, he ate much of that house. The next morning when he woke up he had grown considerably larger. Even as he walked down the street he was getting bigger. Finally he got bigger than any building ever made. He walked up to the Empire State Building in New York City and accidentally crushed it. The people had to think of a way to stop him, so they made this great iron box which made the cat curious. He finally got inside it, but it was too heavy to get him out of again. . . . There he lived for the rest of his life. But he was still curious until his death, which was 6,820,000 years later. They buried him in the state of Rhode Island, and I mean the whole state — Jerry, a seventh-grade student*

The restless imagination, the daring exaggeration, the disdain for triteness that this story demonstrates — all are signs that its young author has great creative potential. With the right kind of encouragement, with the considerable knowledge we now have about how to foster creativity, this boy could develop his talents to his own and society's great benefit.

Before discussing ways of developing creativity, we must first describe this elusive characteristic. The next sections consider the three main areas of creative thinking: the *product* resulting from the creative effort, the mental *process* that produces it, and the *personality* traits of the creative person.

The Creative Product

Although most people agree that creativity cannot be defined as a logical or a mechanical process, they disagree as to the best ways to define it. History is replete with the misjudgments of the masses — and the critics — as to how creative a product is. The search for unbiased criteria has been elusive.

A unique approach to setting criteria for creativity has been to specify the typical reactions people have to products that are almost universally accepted as creative (Jackson and Messick, 1965). Table 4–1 describes four criteria that can be used to judge creative products: **unusualness, appropriateness, transformation,** and **condensation,** along with the specific judgmental standards and emotional responses that go with each of these criteria. The first criterion, unusualness, is an obvious aspect of creativity. It is judged by comparing the product being judged to existing norms for such a product. If the product is really unusual, the almost instantaneous response of the judge will be surprise. In Salvador Dali's painting, "The Crucifixion," Christ is seen as though the viewer were looking down on him from atop a tall stepladder. People frequently gasp when they first see the painting.

TABLE 4–1
CRITERIA FOR JUDGING CREATIVE PRODUCTS

Product Properties	Judgmental Standards	Emotional Responses of Judges
Unusualness	Norms	Surprise
Appropriateness	Context	Satisfaction
Transformation	Constraints	Stimulation
Condensation	Summary power	Savoring

Note: This table adapted from P. W. Jackson and S. Messick (1965).

Appropriateness, the second criterion, is necessary so that we exclude from our definition a product that is unusual, but that is not related to an accepted purpose. (Contrast the gibberish of a mentally deranged person with a sonnet of Shakespeare's.) Appropriateness takes its meaning from and can only be judged within a particular context. When a product has a distinct appropriateness, it generates a feeling of intense satisfaction in the observer. People find Handel's *Messiah* to be unusually satisfying music because of its ability to uplift them spiritually; its form expresses its purpose.

In any field of human activity, there are rules and constraints within which people must operate. The creative person somehow is able to transform these constraints to create a new approach or product. One judges this transformation in terms of the constraints imposed upon the creator. Beethoven's music is considered unusually creative because he was able to produce new forms while obeying the stringent constraints placed on the composition of classical music. When a product demonstrates unique transformation, judges react by feeling greatly stimulated.

Condensation, the final criterion, refers to the simplicity of a product. A highly creative product has the ability to summarize complex elements into a simple, pure unity. Condensation is evident not only in poetry, drama, and music, but also in science. Many mathematical and physical formulas are creative condensations—for example, Einstein's $E = MC^2$. By condensing complex facts about the universe, it helps us understand how it works. When a product demonstrates condensation, we wish to savor the results; we want to hear our favorite piece of music over and over, or return again and again to look at a great painting.

The Creative Mental Process

There are two theories as to how the mind of a creative person works: **associationism,** in which creative people are thought to bring various parts of problems together in new and imaginative ways, and **structuralism,** in which creative people are believed to deal with whole problems, restructuring them in their entirety.

Associationism.   The major proponent of this school of thought is psychologist Sarnoff Mednick (1963). He believes that creativity is the process by which ideas already in the mind are associated in unusual, original, and useful combinations. Every idea we have in our mind is associated with some of our other ideas, and the associations belonging to a particular idea are arranged in lists. Those associations at the top of the list are closely linked to the idea; as we move down the list, the associations become weaker and come to mind less quickly. Table 4–2 gives an example of an idea and the strength of its associations. Ten is the highest rating, indicating that the ideas "ride" and "fun" are closely associated to "bike."

If you were asked to say the first thing that comes into your mind when hearing the word *black,* you would probably say "white." *White* is a strong associate of the concept *black. Shoes* might also come to mind, but it would be lower on the list of associations to *black* for most people.

When the average person thinks about solving a problem, he casts about in his mind for associations that could serve as solutions to his problem. Usually the first idea that seems applicable to the problem is accepted. Mednick argues that creative people are those who go further down the list, searching for more unusual but higher-quality associations to solve their problems. It is these so-called remote associations that produce creative products. The poet Marianne Moore put remote associations together in a pleasing new way when she wrote, "The lion's ferocious chrysanthemum head." Although this billowy flower is seldom

TABLE 4–2
SAMPLE ASSOCIATIONS TO THE WORD *BIKE*,
ACCORDING TO STRENGTH OF ASSOCIATION

Strength Rating	Bike
10	Ride, fun
9	Transportation, red
8	Ten-speed, fast
7	
6	Old County Road
5	
4	Mary and Bob
3	
2	
1	Athletic supporter

Uses for a Brick

In a five-minute period write down all the uses you can think of for a brick. The scoring for this test of your hypothetical creative ability appears on page 131. You will be scored not only for the number of uses you think of, but also on how different they are from each other and on their originality. For example, using a brick to build a house is acceptable, but using a brick to catch worms (you leave a brick on the ground, and when you come back two weeks later to pick it up, there will be worms under it) is a much more original idea.

Scoring for the "Uses for a Brick" Test

To score this test, give yourself one point for each use for a brick listed within the five-minute period. Then give yourself one point for all uses that fall into a different category from the others. For example, if you said building a house, building a fence, and building a fireplace, you may give yourself only one point. These uses of a brick all fall into the single category of building. You can also score this test for originality by comparing your responses to those of other members of your class. Give yourself five points for each of your uses that no one else in the class thought of. A total score of 25 or above indicates a high level of hypothetical creative ability.

---

associated with ferocity, the apparent contradiction is appealing — it makes us see lions in a new and startling way.

Some people have very short lists of ideas that are strongly associated with each; they can produce only a few associations. These people are often rigid and dogmatic in their beliefs and tend to produce little that is creative. Others have longer lists of less tightly associated ideas; they are less committed to getting "the one right answer," and are not so threatened by being wrong. They have the flexibility that allows the mental search for remote associations. Some of their freely associated ideas may be silly, but some might produce really creative combinations. Most people fall somewhere between these extremes.

Mednick suggests that "familiarity breeds rigidity." The more we know about a subject, the less likely we are to be creative about it. We willingly accept the laws and principles in a particular area and no longer question them after we have dealt with them for a long time. This may be the reason that theoretical physicists and master chess players are said to have passed their prime after age 35. Einstein, for example, was only 19 when he developed his theory of relativity. Unfortunately, only a few are able to resist the growing rigidity of age. Persons who have been highly creative in their advanced years such as Piaget, Stravinsky, Picasso, and Maugham are extremely rare.

Structuralism. Michael Wertheimer, the major explicator of the structuralist position, disagrees that creativity consists only of associating ideas in new and different ways (Torrance, 1969). The creative musician does not write notes on a paper in hopes of getting new associations. Rather, he gets a half-formed idea of the *finished piece* of music and then works backward to complete his idea. He develops an overview of the entire structure and then rearranges its parts.

Creative solutions, the structuralists argue, are often obtained by changing one's point of reference. This can happen when we change the position from which we view a scene or problem, or as our needs change. Imagine that you are looking into a display window of a clothing store. The brightly colored dresses stand out in the foreground; the pastel curtains behind them are not so prominent; and we don't notice at all that the window dresser has left part of a sandwich on the floor. However, suppose we look at that store window when we are extremely hungry. The sandwich will leap out in the foreground more clearly than anything else in the window. Wertheimer argues that getting a new point of view on the whole of a problem, rather than rearranging its parts, is more likely to produce creativity.

CREATIVITY, GIFTEDNESS, AND THE IQ

As Feldman (1979) has pointed out, there have been many studies of "giftedness," but only a few of the exceptionally creative, highly productive person. He believes that this unfortunate situation is mainly the fault of "the foremost figure in the study of the gifted," Lewis M. Terman. Terman is well known for his research on 1,000 California children whose IQ's in the early 1920s were 135 or higher. Terman believed these children to be the geniuses of the future, a label he kept for them as he studied their development over the decades. His was a powerful investigation, and one which has been followed by scholars and popular writers alike.

Precisely because of the notoriety of this research, Feldman argues, we have come to accept a *quantitative* definition of genius, and a somewhat low one (135) at that. Feldman notes that the Encyclopedia Britannica now differentiates two basic definitions of genius: the numerical one fostered by Terman; and the concept as first described by Sir Francis Galton, "creative ability of an exceptionally high order as demonstrated by actual achievement."

Feldman says that genius, as defined by IQ, really only refers to precociousness — doing what others are able to do but at a younger age. Prodigiousness (as in child prodigy) has also come to be thought of as precociousness, but it originally referred to someone who was *qualitatively* different in ability from the rest of us. This is a different concept from that of simply being able to do things sooner. Further, prodigiousness calls for a highly improbable concurrence of high talent and an environment that is ready and open to creativity. If such youthful prodigies as Mozart in music or Fischer in chess had been born two thousand years earlier, they may well have grown up much more normally. In fact, if Einstein has been born *fifty* years earlier, he might have done nothing special — particularly since he did not even speak well until he was five!

So if prodigies are more than just quicker at learning, what is it that truly distinguishes them? On the basis of his intensive study of three prodigies, Feldman urges that

> *Perhaps the most striking quality in the children in our study as well as other cases is the passion with which excellence is pursued. Commitment*

*and tenacity and joy in achievement are perhaps the best signs that a coinci-
dence has occurred among child, field, and moment in evolutionary time.
No event is more likely to predict that a truly remarkable, creative contribution will eventually occur (1979, p. 351).*

Thus *personality* variables seem to be at least as important as the intellect in high
creative achievement. Let us turn now to a consideration of these variables.

Creative Personality Traits

A number of studies (reviewed in Dacey, 1976) have compared highly creative
and average people in terms of their personalities. They suggest that creative
people

- Are more aware of the existence of problems.
- Have greater flexibility when presented with problems.
- Have a somewhat greater tendency toward emotional disturbance, but also
  have more self-control to deal with this tendency.
- Are able to be both analytical and intuitive in their thinking.
- Are able to think both convergently — the ability to solve problems that have
  only one correct answer — and divergently — the ability to solve problems that
  have many possible answers.
- Demonstrate a greater determination and perseverance.
- Have a higher-than-average intelligence, but do not often measure in the "ge-
  nius" range.
- Seem to have a need for disorder, which allows them to get greater satisfac-
  tions by bringing order to a chaotic situation.
- Are more open to experience and less defensive about accepting new
  information.
- See themselves as responsible for most of what happens to them.
- Enjoy being playful and childlike; have the ability to toy with the
  environment.
- Engage more frequently in solitary activities, especially as children.
- Are able to delay gratification for longer periods of time.
- Are more likely to question the status quo.
- Are more independent of the judgment of others.
- As a woman, is more likely to be masculine than other women; as a man, is
  more likely to be feminine than other men.
- Are more spontaneous and less inhibited.

- Are less frightened by the unknown, the mysterious, and the puzzling, and are often positively attracted to them.
- Are less afraid of their own impulses and hidden emotions.

Creative adolescents have been described as follows. They

- Like to do their own planning, make their own decisions, and need the least training and experience in self-guidance.
- Do not like to work with others, and prefer their own judgment of their work to the judgment of others. They therefore seldom ask other students or their teachers for opinions.
- Take a hopeful outlook when presented with complex difficult tasks.
- Have the most ideas when a chance to express individual opinion is presented. These ideas frequently invoke the ridicule of others.
- Are most likely to stand their ground in the face of criticism.
- Are the most resourceful when unusual circumstances arise.
- Can tolerate uncertainty and ambiguity better than others.
- Are not necessarily the "smartest" or "best" students.

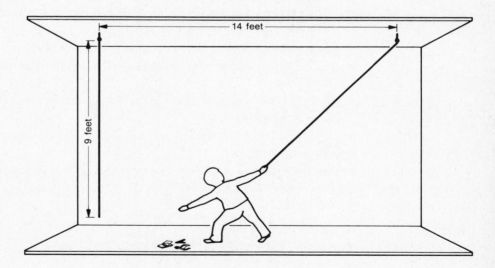

Figure 4–1 The Two String Test How can the person in this picture reach the second string in order to tie the two strings together? Each string is almost 9 feet long. They are permanently attached to the ceiling of the room 14 feet apart. To help solve this problem, the person may use either a mousetrap or a wooden spring-type clothespin. Neither of these is long enough so that it could be used to reach the other string. The explanation appears on page 136.

In their compositions, creative youth typically

- Show an imaginative use of many different words.
- Are more flexible; for example, in a narrative they use more situations, characters, and settings. Rather than taking one clearly defined train of thought and pursuing it to its logical conclusion, creative students tend to switch the main focus quickly and easily, and often go off on tangents.
- Tend to elaborate on the topic assigned, taking a much broader connotation of it to begin with, and then proceeding to embellish even that.
- Are more original. (This is the *most important* characteristic. The others need not be evidenced, but this one must be.) Their ideas are qualitatively different from the average students'. A teacher might react to the creative child's work in this way: "I know what most of the kids will do with the topic, but I never know what to expect from this one!"

The Critical Period Hypothesis

A number of theorists, notably those of the psychoanalytic school (Sigmund Freud, Otto Rank, and Alfred Adler), have argued that creativity manifests itself very early in life, usually by age 5. It is fostered by proper levels of stimulation (Freud) and parental approval of the child's developing will (Rank). People are either creative or not, depending on their early childhood experiences and subconscious processes; trying to develop a person's creativity after this time will prove fruitless.

However, there is evidence that creativity *can* be increased later in life. Several researchers (Torrance, 1969; Guilford, 1962; Ripple and Dacey, 1969) believe that there is a second **critical period** in life, adolescence, when creativity is open to enrichment; since creativity is so much a matter of one's self-concept and motivation, and since adolescence is a period in which self-concept is being defined, creativity may be fostered during this period. Ripple and Dacey (1969) studied the relationships between ten personality characteristics and verbal creativity. They found these characteristics and creativity to be considerably less stable during adolescence than they are for younger or older populations; thus, the relationships are also in a state of flux. Assuming that this instability is due to the teenager's need to reexamine and redefine his or her personality traits, they designed programmed instruction in creative thinking based on this need, and significantly raised the scores of the majority of eighth-graders in their study. Hence, it seems clear that the adolescent is open to changes in creative thinking.

Obstacles to Creativity

We may agree that creativity is a valuable trait and should be fostered, but how? Educator Ralph Hallman (1967) has listed a number of obstacles and aids to creativity. Several persistent obstacles to creativity are:

Solution to the Two-String Test (and Some Thoughts on Creative Imagination)

The correct answer to the Two-String Test is that either object can be used to solve the problem. You simply attach either the mousetrap or the clothespin to the string, swing it away from yourself, run over and grab the other string, then return to the center and catch the weighted string as it swings back. The strings can then easily be tied together.

As you can see from looking at the picture, you can only walk about 8 feet toward one string while holding the other in your hand. Since the distance between the strings is 14 feet, there are still 6 feet to go. Almost no one is tall enough to reach out with one hand, one foot, or either of the objects to be able to reach the other string.

One of my graduate students did produce a different solution. When a class was asked for volunteers to solve the problem, a nun came forward. After studying the problem for a moment, she decided that neither the mousetrap nor the clothespin would work. She reached under the apron of her habit and took out an enormous set of rosary beads. Holding one string in her hand, she walked out as far as she could toward the other, swung the rosary beads over her head, and easily snagged the other string!

A number of interesting results have regularly occurred with this test. Almost all sixth-graders and 80 percent of eighth-graders are able to solve the problem within the fifteen minutes allowed. Only half of my undergraduates ever solve it, and almost no graduate students do! Apparently, the more education one has, the less capable one is of creative problem solving.

The main problem is "functional fixity." The longer we are in school, the more we come to accept the conventional uses of objects. An example of functional fixity is the mousetrap solution proposed by a graduate student. He decided that he would first catch mice with the trap until he got one that was not seriously injured. He would then make a pet of it and train it to run over to the other piece of string and bring it to him. This is an imaginative idea, but it would not solve the problem, since a mouse cannot bring the string very far without leaving the ground. The student was unable to perceive a mousetrap outside of its usual function. Sixth-graders have no trouble at all thinking of a mousetrap as a weight.

There are also sex differences. Females are usually only one-half as successful as males in solving the problem at any age level. Many women say they are incapable of handling this type of problem. One student suggested that since women have less training in mechanics, they naturally do less well. Another student, a married woman, said that she frequently encounters problems in her daily housework that require using things in ways other than they are normally intended, and that other women do also. Her husband, on the contrary, is reluctant to do a job unless he has all the appropriate tools. She suggested that men get much less practice than women in using things in alternative ways.

A major reason women generally do less well than men on problem-solving tasks is because of the anticreative attitudes they learn from their parents and from female elementary school teachers. Of course, female children today are less rigidly molded than previously. To the extent that real changes in sex roles are coming about, we can happily anticipate a much larger creative contribution from women.

1. *Pressures to conform.* The pressure on the individual to follow standardized routines and inflexible rules is probably the major inhibitor. Authoritarian parents and teachers who demand order are responsible for the demise of a great deal of creative talent.

2. *Ridicule of unusual ideas.* This destroys one's feelings of worth and makes one defensive and compulsive.

3. *An excessive quest for success and the rewards it brings.* An overconcern with material success is often the result of trying to meet the standards and demands of others in order to obtain the rewards they have to give. In the long run, this distorts one's view of reality and robs one of the strength of character to be creative.

4. *Intolerance of a playful attitude.* Innovation calls for playing around with ideas, a willingness to fantasize and make believe, and a healthy disrespect for accepted concepts. Often the creative person is seen as childlike and silly and his activity as wasteful, but these are only appearances. As Hallman remarks, "Creativity is profound fun."

Aids to Creativity

Parents and teachers can help teenagers to be more creative, but not with traditional authoritarian methods. While specific techniques can now be described, thanks to some imaginative research, attitude remains the most important factor. Hallman suggests these approaches as aids to creativity:

1. *Provide for self-initiated learning.* Most people find it hard to encourage adolescents to initiate and direct their own learning. After all, this is certainly not the way the majority of adults were taught. Many adults fear that if children are given greater freedom to explore reality on their own, they will learn wrong things or will not learn the right things in the proper sequence. Yet learning "the right facts" is less important than learning how to learn. Adult encouragement of adolescent experimentation and imagination is vital to creative growth.

2. *Encourage overlearning.* Only when people make themselves fully familiar with a particular situation can they detach themselves enough to get an original view of it. This does *not* mean becoming so familiar with a situation that no alternatives to it can be imagined.

3. *Defer judgment.* Encourage adolescents to make wild guesses, to juggle improbable relationships, to take intellectual risks, to take a chance on appearing ridiculous. Don't block unusual ideas by overstating what is required, or by providing correct answers too quickly.

4. *Promote intellectual flexibility.* Creativity calls for shifting points-of-view, dreaming up new uses for things, and imagining as many possible solutions to a particular problem as possible.

5. *Encourage self-evaluation.* A person who comes up with a creative idea is a minority of one. Many ideas were rejected for years before people began to realize their worth. Galileo's proof that the earth is not the center of the universe is an example. Creative people must know their own minds and be relatively independent of the judgment of others. To become good judges of their own thinking, youth must be given ample opportunity to practice such judgments.

6. *Ask lots of open-ended questions.* One extensive study showed that 90 percent of the time the average teacher asks questions to which there can be only one right answer, which the teacher already knows. Questions that pique curiosity and allow many possible right answers were asked only 10 percent of the time.

7. *Assist the person to cope with frustration and failure.* Thomas Edison tried more than 2000 combinations of metal before he found just the right kind for the electric element in his first light bulb.

Guidelines for Improving Your Own Creativity

Here are some suggestions (Dacey, 1976) that should make *you,* as well as the adolescents you work with, more creative problem solvers:

- Avoid the "filtering out" process that blocks problems from awareness. Become more sensitive to problems by looking for them.

- Never accept the first solution you think of. Generate a number of possible solutions, then select the best from among them.

- Be aware of your own defensiveness concerning the problem. When you feel threatened by a problem, you are less likely to think of creative solutions to it.

- Get feedback on your solution from others who are less personally involved.

- Try to think of what solutions someone else might think of to your problem.

- Mentally test out opposites to your solutions. When a group of engineers tried to think of ways to dispose of smashed auto glass, someone suggested trying to find uses for it instead. Fiberglass was the result!

- Give your ideas a chance to incubate. Successful problem solvers report that they frequently put a problem away for a while and later on the solution comes to them full blown. It is clear that they have been thinking about the problem on a subconscious level, which is often superior to a conscious, logical approach.

- Diagram your thinking. Sometimes ideas seem to fork, like the branches on a tree; one idea produces two more, each of which produces two more, and so on. Diagramming will let you follow each possible branch to its completion.

- Be self-confident. Many ideas die because the person who conceived them thinks they *might* be silly. Women have been especially vulnerable here.

- Think about the general aspects of a problem before getting to its specifics.

- Restate the problem several different ways.
- Become an "idea jotter." A notebook of ideas can prove surprisingly useful.
- Divide a problem, then solve its various parts.

Really good ideas frequently require some personal risk on the part of the problem solver. In this we are like the turtle, who can never move forward until he sticks his neck out.

INTELLIGENCE

It was a very curious thing. When I was about thirteen, my father's intelligence started to drop. His mental abilities continued to decline until I reached twenty-one, when these abilities began miraculously to improve. Mark Twain, Pudd'nhead Wilson.

Many adolescents make the same observation about their parents' thinking abilities, but the observation actually has much more to do with a change in adolescents' self-concept than with any change in their parents' intelligence. As their own ability matures, they overestimate it and devalue their parents' intelligence accordingly. This misjudgment is only one of many that are frequently made about intelligence.

The Measurement of Intelligence

The measurement of intelligence has a relatively short history. It began in the early 1900s in France as a response to the Ministry of Education's decision to provide mentally retarded children with a different type of education. Alfred Binet developed a test to identify these children; it is the great-grandparent of today's IQ **(Intelligence Quotient)** test.

Everybody believes he knows what IQ is, but not many understand what the IQ test really measures. All IQ tests are actually composed of a series of subtests; some have as few as five subtests, others have more. Each subtest attempts to measure an aspect of mental functioning. Not all kinds of mental functioning are measured by IQ tests, however. For example, arithmetic reasoning and verbal association are measured, but social abilities and self-knowledge are almost never included. IQ tests only try to measure cognitive abilities, which are regularly used in the classroom. Although the tests can predict academic success with a fair degree of accuracy in white, middle-class American schools (which is what they are designed to do), they are often erroneously used as a measure of intelligence. IQ tests are presumed to measure only innate ability (those capacities with which we were born), but clearly previous learning is involved to some extent.

Another major problem of IQ tests is that teachers and others who use them often consider only total scores in their estimate of children's abilities. Let's take the popular Wechsler Adult Intelligence Scale (1955). If we were to give the six subtests to two 16-year-olds, they might get these subscores:

Subtests	Roger	Jean
Information	10	25
Comprehension	10	0
Arithmetic	5	0
Digit span	10	25
Similarities	5	0
Vocabulary	10	0
	50	50

Each got the same raw score, 50, which was the number of answers they got right. If we look at the test manual, we find that the average mental age of children who score 50 on this test is 16. (These averages are based on thousands of scores.) When we know a person's mental and chronological age, we can compute his or her IQ by using the formula

$$IQ = \frac{\text{mental age}}{\text{chronological age}} \times 100$$

Thus, both Roger's and Jean's IQ $= \frac{16}{16} \times 100 = 100$.

Their IQ of 100 is exactly average; they are at the precise intelligence level that we would expect of the typical 16-year-old.

The problem is that they aren't at all like each other! Roger is average in all of the six areas tested by the Wechsler. Jean, on the other hand, is a genius on information and digit span, but severely retarded in comprehension, arithmetic, similarities, and vocabulary. Such extreme scores as Jean's are unlikely; Roger's are much more common. However, both sets of scores are possible, and they demonstrate how children who have the same IQ can be quite different from each other in intellectual abilities.

Intelligence and Genes

The question of how much of one's intelligence as measured by IQ is the result of inherited ability and how much of learning is a difficult one, which has caused considerable controversy. One argument has been over the assignment of reasons to explain the difference in the average IQ's of black and white Americans; blacks test on an average 15 IQ points lower than whites. Professor Arthur Jensen of Stanford University reviewed a large number of studies on the correlation of IQ's of identical twins raised apart and together, adopted children and their parents, and other groups. On the basis of this review, he concluded that genetic inheritance accounts for four-fifths of intelligence. Since genetic factors cannot be changed, at least at present, Jensen argued that there is little that can be done to reduce this difference between the races. In some states, his findings have been used as the basis for reducing our commitment to equal opportunities in education.

There are a number of problems with Jensen's review. For example, only white twins were studied, and interventions were begun only after three to four years of life (Dacey, 1976). Jensen's position has been further weakened by the results of a study done by Scarr and Weinberg (1976). They looked at the intelligence scores of black children adopted by middle-class white parents during the 1960s. By examining the education and occupation levels of the biological parents of the children, they were able to determine that the children could be expected to have an average IQ of about 90. The actual IQ's of the children, however, averaged 106. Although the adopting parents had higher IQ's and socioeconomic status than the biological parents, we cannot be sure that this environmental influence was the cause of the higher IQ's of the children. However, no other explanation seems to account for these results as well. Even more revealing was the researchers' finding that "the earlier the child was placed, the fewer disruptions in his life, and the better care in the first few years of life, the higher his later IQ score was likely to be." This study offers strong evidence that intellectual ability is responsive to stimulation, especially if it comes early enough.

Tommy: A Real Problem Child

This is a story about a real boy named Tommy who was born in 1847. By the time he was ten years old, a neighbor described him as "a real troublemaker who would surely wind up in jail." His clothes were unkempt and dirty. His health was poor and he suffered frequent bouts of viral infections. He had an unusually large head and a smaller than average body.

His teachers stated that the quality of his schoolwork was generally poor. He especially had a great deal of trouble with spelling and rote learning. He cared little for reading or writing, and consistently expressed negative attitudes toward school.

He frequently interrupted his class by what his teachers called "asking foolish questions." They found him excessively rude, and complained that he could not resist playing practical jokes on his classmates.

When he was nine, he set fire to his house. When asked why he did it, he said, "Because I wanted to see what the flames would do." He was given a severe beating by his father, while many of his neighbors watched with satisfaction.

He was always getting in some kind of trouble. Once he knocked a beehive down with a stick, causing it to land near a group of people, many of whom were stung by the bees. He ruined a pair of trousers by sitting on a dozen eggs in an attempt to hatch them himself. He encouraged some of his playmates to swallow some gaseous chemicals to "see if human beings could be made to fly." Neighbors cited frequent explosions coming from the basement of his house, caused by his playing with chemicals which he readily obtained from his mother.

From the age of ten on, Tommy no longer attended school. He stayed at home in the custody of his mother, a former schoolteacher, who decided she could better educate him herself. This plan greatly upset his father, who felt that strong discipline and obedience training was what the youth really needed. He and his wife frequently fought over Tommy's behavior.

Far from ending up in jail, Tommy went on to become one of the most imaginative and creatively productive persons in human history. Can you guess who he is? (The answer* appears on the bottom of the following page.)

LEARNING DISABILITIES

Although some children have difficulty learning because of a general low level of intelligence, others have specific learning disabilities. The National Advisory Committee on Handicapped Children (1968) defines learning disabilities this way:

> Children with special learning disabilities exhibit a disorder in one or more of the basic psychological processes involved in understanding or using spoken or written language. These may be manifested in disorders of listening, thinking, talking, reading, writing, spelling, or arithmetic. They include conditions which have been referred to as perceptual handicaps, brain injury, minimal brain dysfunction, dyslexia, developmental aphasia, etc. They do not include learning problems which are due primarily to visual, hearing or motor handicaps, to mental retardation, emotional disturbance or to environmental disadvantage.

Learning-disabled children have average or above-average intelligence, but are unable to keep up with their classmates. They may be clumsy or awkward, with poor eye-hand coordination and possibly some speech defect. They usually have a short attention span and are easily distracted; they may be hyperactive or hypoactive.

Teachers who have learning-disabled children in their classrooms can help in several ways (Afrow, 1977). First, teachers can learn all they can about learning disabilities and what causes them in order to better inform the parents of their children's needs. They can then work closely with parents to solve attention and homework difficulties. If the children are given individualized instruction at their level, they will have a better chance of completing assignments at school or at home. Most important is to provide as much affection and positive ego-support as possible, keeping the success rate high and the failure rate low.

Johnson and Myklebust (1967) found the prevalence of learning disabilities to be around 7 to 8 percent of the public school population, while the National Advisory Committee on Handicapped Children (1968) reported it to be between 1 and 3 percent of the public school population. The difference between these two sets of figures is due to the lack of standardized criteria that would allow us to determine the actual number of learning-disabled children.

A recent study on learning disabilities in the United States found that only 975 secondary schools have learning disabilities programs. Only 9 percent of the total school districts in the United States provide special facilities for secondary school-age learning-disabled children (Scranton and Downs, 1975). They reported that

> *Perhaps most neglected is the area of secondary learning disability programs. Introductory disability texts often contain references to exemplary elementary school programs and/or techniques used within the elementary school. These texts however, contain little or no mention of the "adolescent," "junior high" or "secondary level" learning disabled child. The exceptions to this are few and far between. The lack of information in this area illustrates the fact that much more work is needed at the secondary level for the learning-disabled student (p. 126).*

NONLINEAR THINKING

Some psychologists believe that there is another type of change in adolescent thinking which has been occurring only in the last few decades. If they are correct in their observations, the implications are literally mind-boggling.

Marshall McLuhan, founder of the Center for Culture and Technology at the University of Toronto, argues that the thinking patterns of the current generation of adolescents differ markedly from those of their elders because of the enormous influence of the new forms of communication media on youth. The differences in thinking patterns are believed to be so deep as to have created not just a generation gap, but a generation chasm, so wide as to make effective communications between the generations almost impossible.

Communications and Thinking Patterns

McLuhan's major premise is that the means by which we take in information controls how we think about that information. Thus, communications media define to a great extent the thinking patterns that we develop. There have been three periods in the human history of communication. The first period was characterized largely by face-to-face interactions and ended around the middle of the fifteenth century with Gutenberg's invention of the printing press. In the second period, 1450 to the early 1900s, the main communications medium was the

*Thomas Alva Edison

printed word. The third period, which we are in now, is characterized by electronic media. Print is becoming less and less important as the telephone, telegraph, phonograph, radio, movies, television, and satellite communications become ever more crucial in our daily lives.

Each type of media emphasizes one or more senses and deemphasizes others. Whereas personal interaction employs virtually all of the senses, print narrows the focus to the eyes alone. This drastic deemphasizing of the other senses, according to McLuhan, has a striking impact on the way we think.

Print makes us think in a "linear" fashion. To communicate by the printed word, we must first break down the object or event about which we wish to communicate into its component parts. If we were describing a battle, we would take the information as it comes to us and put it into a logical time sequence. This may not be the way that we heard about the battle, but we would reorganize our information so that it "makes sense."

> Once a culture uses such a media for a few centuries, it begins to see the world in a one-thing-at-a-time, abstract, linear, fragmented, sequential way. And it shapes its organizations and schools according to the same premises. The form of print has become the form of thought. The medium has become the message (Culkin, 1966, p. 8).

Kilpatrick (1971) compares McLuhan's view of print to the factory assembly line. In our mass production system, everything is arranged in an unchanging order. The product is broken down into its components, and each specialized person helps assemble the whole. There is nothing emotional about an assembly line — it is an entirely rational operation. Logic was used to organize it, logic is used to keep it going. The feelings of the workers along the line are of little consequence to the total effort.

Linear thinking flowered in the late eighteenth and early nineteenth centuries, the Age of Reason. This was the height of the intellectual movement, in which scientific discovery and rational philosophy had great influence on people's minds, and in which the emotions were suppressed so as to be as logical as possible in all decision making. It was the effects of extreme rationality that Freud was to note in neurotic behavior.

Print-oriented people were more easily able to remain emotionally aloof from the circumstances of their times. Virtually all information about the world came through print, usually some considerable time after events had occurred. People could read with detachment about the hideous wars and famines of the 1800s and 1900s. This ability to avoid emotional involvement in the lives of others was the result of emphasizing one sense, vision, to the exclusion of all the others. By using mostly the eyes, and mostly for reading, it was possible to view the world in a sequential, categorical way. Self-centered individualism was encouraged because print, as compared to electronic media, isolates one from the feelings and problems of others.

Early in the twentieth century, the monopoly of print was finally broken. Electronic media extend all of our senses, but especially hearing. Most of our information comes to us, largely through television, in a random and frequently illogical order — in bits and pieces out of which we must make our own sense. It is not organized for us, as in books, magazines, and newspapers. In this stage, we return to nonlinear thinking and face-to-face communications. The difference is that now almost instantaneous personal contact of people throughout the world is possible. We have returned to group-oriented behavior, and are much more concerned with other human beings than we have been in the past 500 years.

The person living in this new age now belongs to what McLuhan calls the "global village." Electronic media have put us into instant, personal contact with each other. It is no longer possible for us to read about tragedies such as the Nazi atrocities or the Vietnamese war without feeling personally involved. As **neotribal people,** we see ourselves as an integral part of a much larger society than did print-oriented people. We are more inclined to live in the present and to feel free to give expression to our feelings. McLuhan says that we are "bound into a seamless web of kinship and interdependence with our fellow residents on this planet." Table 4–3 summarizes McLuhan's theory.

McLuhan's Theory and Adolescent Identity

With considerable insight, Kilpatrick (1971) has described the expected effects of the "global village" age on modern adolescents. With retribalization, the struggle for identity will become muted as the group seeks to impose its standards on the individual. The trend to identity foreclosure (see Chapter 2) will increase. Sociologist Edgar Friedenberg (1965) has argued that adolescence itself is vanishing because of the lack of internal struggle. He believes that high schools have come to

TABLE 4–3
McLUHAN'S THEORY OF COMMUNICATION AND CULTURE

Tribal Villages (Prehistory–1451)	Print-Oriented People (1451–1900s)	Neotribal People— Nonlinear Thinking (1900–?)
Media nonexistent Face-to-face contact	Printed media Contact through reading	Electronic media Personal contact through technology
Nonlinear thinking, nonrational	Linear thinking, rational	Nonlinear thinking, rational-nonrational
Sensual, use of all senses	Antisensual, emphasis on vision	Sensual, use of all senses
Nonsequential information input	Sequential information input	Nonsequential information input
Group-oriented, "other-directed"	Self-oriented, "inner-directed"	Group-oriented, "inner-other directed"
Home manufacture; humans as craftspeople	Assembly lines; humans as automatons	Computer automation; people as inventors

Freaking Out Grandma

In the spaces below, list as many activities as you can which, if you did them in your grandmother's presence, would make her very upset. They should be activities you regularly do, rather than ones that you would do just to disturb her.

1. _____

2. _____

3. _____

4. _____

5. _____

6. _____

7. _____

8. _____

9. _____

10. _____

Were you able to think of many activities that would bother your grandmother? What do these activities have in common with each other? Would your friends list similar activities to the ones you put down? What does this exercise tell you about McLuhan's theory?

accept only those who conform to the accepted standards, and are beginning more and more to punish individualism itself. At the same time that the pressures of conformity are increasing, so also is the tightness of the teenage subculture, which excludes and actively rejects understanding by adults. It is difficult for adolescents to form their own identity without adult models; it is even harder for them to gain an identity independent of the pressures of their peers.

Adolescence used to be thought of as the time when children become more future-oriented. Plans for the future were formed, and parents worried about the 18-year-old who had no career goal. Today, planning for the future is increasingly unpopular. The absence of a future orientation, together with an almost total commitment to the teen culture, makes maturity harder than ever to achieve.

There may be one bright spot in all of this. There is at least the possibility that today's "neotribal" adolescents will, when they become parents, treat their own adolescent children with more respect and understanding because the difference in thinking processes between their two generations will be less. It is also possible that scarcity of jobs and the "back to basics" movement of the late 1970s reintroduced print-orientation to some extent, thus narrowing the generation gap. It does seem that the intergenerational conflicts of the 1960s are not as severe today. At any rate, it is clear that the full implications of McLuhan's view of nonlinear thinking have yet to be seen.

SUMMARY

Adolescence is a complex process of growth and change. Because biological and social changes are so much the focus of attention, changes in the adolescent's thinking style often go unnoticed. Yet it is during adolescence that thinking ability reaches its highest level — the level of abstract thought.

To understand how abstract thought develops, we have to know more about the intellect itself. Jean Piaget theorized that the human intellect is another of nature's examples of biological adaptation; thus, the adaptive mechanism of intelligence matures through the growth of increasingly more effective mental structures.

Mental structures develop from birth as reflexes. Through assimilation and accommodation, they form schema (organized patterns of behavior). Because of an inherent tendency to organize, these schema combine and rearrange themselves into larger psychological structures called operations (internalized actions), which are adult thoughts.

This process of mental growth takes place through four developmental stages: sensorimotor, preoperational, concrete operational, and formal operational. Each stage lays the groundwork for the next, preparing for the emergence of abstract thought in the adolescent.

Adolescence is also a critical period for creative development. Creative products are judged by the criteria of unusualness, appropriateness, transformation, and condensation.

There are two schools of thought as to the nature of the creative process: associationism and structuralism. Associationism defines creativity as the process by which ideas already in the mind are associated by unusual, original, and useful combinations; structuralism assumes that the creative person gets an overview of the entire structure and imaginatively rearranges its parts through changing his or her point of reference.

As adolescents' intelligence develops, their perceptions and often their entire thinking styles change markedly. The IQ test is frequently used to measure intelligence, but since this test only measures ability to do well in white, middle-class schools, its use frequently leads to serious misconceptions.

A new type of thinking pattern seems to be emerging, particularly among adolescents — nonlinear thinking. Marshall McLuhan argues that our thinking patterns are defined by the dominant mode of communication in a culture. Adults tend to think in a logical linear manner because they are print oriented. Adolescents are more oriented toward electronic media, particularly television, which results in nonlogical intuitive thought, lack of future orientation, and a "live for today" attitude. This absence of future orientation, combined with a total commitment to a teen culture, complicates the thinking process and makes maturity more difficult than ever to achieve.

Questions

1. What are the stages of cognitive development?
2. In what ways is adolescence a special period for the development of creativity?
3. In what ways do changes in thinking occur?
4. How does the measurement of intelligence affect educational practice?
5. Of what importance is nonlinear thinking?

References

Afrow, M. "Criteria of learning disabilities." Unpublished paper, Peabody, Mass. Peabody Schools, 1978.

Arlin, P. K. "Cognitive development in adulthood: a fifth stage?" *Developmental psychology*, 1975. *11*(5), 602–606.

Blake, L. A measure of developmental change: a cross-sectional study. Paper presented at the annual meeting of the American Psychological Association, Washington, D.C., 1976.

Boyd, D. Some thoughts on a comparison of Perry and Kohlberg. Unpublished manuscript, Harvard University, 1972.

Brabeck, M. The relationship between critical thinking skills and the development of reflective judgment. Unpublished doctoral dissertation, University of Minnesota, 1980.

Brabeck, M., King, P., Kitchener, K., Mines, R., Welfel, E. Learning to make judgments: how students defend what they believe. A presentation made at the annual meeting of the American College Personnel Association, Cincinnati, 1981.

Broughton, J. The development of natural epistemology in adolescence and early adulthood. Unpublished doctoral dissertation, Harvard University, 1975.

Clemens, S. "Pudd'nhead Wilson and those extraordinary twins." In *The writings of Mark Twain* (Vol. 14). New York: Harper, 1907–1919.

Coleman, J. S. *The adolescent society.* Glencoe: Free Press, 1971.

Culkin, J. "Education in a post-literate world." *Media and methods*, November 1966, pp. 6–9.

Dacey, J. *New ways to learn.* Stamford, Conn.: Greylock, 1976.

Dacey, J. S., & Ripple, R. E. "The facilitation of problem solving and verbal creativity by exposure to programmed instruction." *Psychology in the schools*, July 1967, *4*(3), 240–245.

Feldman, D. "The mysterious case of extreme giftedness." In Passow, A. H. (Ed.). *The gifted and the talented: Their education and development.* Chicago: University of Chicago Press (NSSE), 1979.

Flavell, J. *Cognitive development.* Englewood Cliffs, N.J.: Prentice-Hall, 1972.

Friedenberg, E. S.   *The vanishing adolescent.* New York: Delta, 1959.

Friedenberg, E. S.   *Coming of age in America.* New York: Vintage, 1965.

Guilford, J. P. "Factors that aid and hinder creativity." *Teachers' college record,* 1962, *63,* 391.

Hallman, R.   "Techniques of creative teaching." *Journal of creative behavior,* July 1967, *1*(3), 325–330.

Harvey, D., Hunt, D., and Schroder, H.   *Conceptual systems and personality organization.* New York: Wiley, 1961.

Heffernan, J.   Identity formation, identity orientations and sex differences related to college environment features: a comparative study of conventional and innovative undergraduate programs. Unpublished doctoral dissertation, University of Michigan, 1971.

Henle, M.   "On the relationship between logic and thinking." *Psychological review,* 1962, *69,* 366–378.

Higgins-Trenk, A., & Gaite, A. J. H.   "Elusiveness of formal operational thought in adolescents." *Proceedings of the 79th Annual Convention of the American Psychological Association,* 1971.

Jackson, P. W., & Messick, S.   "The person, the product, and the response: conceptual problems in the assessment of creativity." *Journal of personality,* 1965, *33*(3), 309–329.

Johnson, D., & Myklebust, H.   *Learning disabilities: educational principles and practices.* New York: Grune & Stratton, 1967.

Kilpatrick, W. K.   "McLuhan: Implications for adolescence." *Adolescence,* Summer 1971, *6,* 235–258.

King, P.   The development of reflective judgment and formal operational thinking in adolescents and young adults. Unpublished doctoral dissertation, University of Minnesota, 1977.

King, P.   William Perry's theory of intellectual and ethical development. *Applying new developmental findings.* Knefelkamp, L., Widick, C., Parker, C., et al., Jossey-Bass, Inc., San Francisco, 1978.

King, P., and Parker, C.   Assessing intellectual development in the college years. A report of the instructional improvement project, 1976–1977. Unpublished manuscript, University of Minnesota, 1978.

Kitchener, K.   Intellectual development in late adolescents and young adults: reflective judgment and verbal reasoning. Unpublished doctoral dissertation, University of Minnesota, 1977.

Kitchener, K., and King, P.   Reflective judgment: concepts of justification and their relationship to age and education. Journal of applied developmental psychology, in press.

Knefelkamp, L.   Developmental instruction: fostering the intellectual and personal growth of college students. Unpublished doctoral dissertation, University of Minnesota, 1974.

Knefelkamp, L., and Sleptiza, R.   "A cognitive-developmental model of career development—an adaptation of the Perry scheme." *The counseling psychologist,* 1976, *6,* (3), 53–58.

Kurfiss, J.   Late adolescent development: a structural epistemological perspective. Unpublished doctoral dissertation, University of Washington, 1975.

Lawson, J.   The relationship between graduate education and the development of reflective judgment: a function of age or educational experience. Unpublished doctoral dissertation, University of Minnesota, 1980.

Martorano, S. C.   The development of formal operational thought. Unpublished doctoral dissertation, Rutgers University, 1974.

May, R.   *The courage to create.* New York: Norton, 1975.

McLuhan, M. *The Gutenberg galaxy*. New York: Signet, 1962.

Mednick, S. "Research creativity in psychology graduate students." *Journal of consulting psychology*, 1963, *27*(3), 265–266.

Mednick, S., & Mednick, M. "An associative interpretation of the creative process." In C. W. Taylor (Ed.), *Widening horizons in creativity*. New York: Wiley, 1964.

Meyer, P. Intellectual development of college students as measured by analysis of religious content. Unpublished doctoral dissertation, University of Minnesota, 1975.

Mines, R. An investigation of the developmental levels of reflective judgment and associated critical thinking skills. Unpublished doctoral dissertation, University of Iowa, 1980.

National Advisory Committee on Handicapped Children. *Special education for handicapped children*. Washington, D.C.: Department of Health, Education, and Welfare, 1968.

Neimark, E. D. "Longitudinal development of formal operations thought." *Genetic psychology monographs*, 1975, *91*, 171–225.

Perry, W. Cognitive and ethical growth. In Chickering, A. (Ed.), *The modern American college*. San Francisco: Jossey-Bass, 1981.

Perry, W. Forms of intellectual and ethical development in the college years. New York: Holt, Rinehart and Winston, 1968a.

Perry, W. Patterns of development in thought and values of students in a liberal arts college: a validation of a scheme. U.S. Dept. of Health, Education, and Welfare, Office of Education, Bureau of Research, Final report, April, 1968b.

Ripple, R., & Dacey, J. "Relationships of some adolescent characteristics and verbal creativity." *Psychology in the schools*, July 1969, *6*(3), 321–324.

Scarr, S. "Environment, heredity, and intelligence: the IQ argument." *Science*, 1971, *174*, 1223–1228.

Scarr, S., & Weinberg, W. "IQ test performance of black children adopted by white families." *American psychologist*, October 1976, *31*(10), 726–740.

Scranton, T., & Downs, M. "Learning disabilities in the U.S." *Journal of Learning Disabilities*, 1975, *8*(6), 394–399.

Stephenson, B., and Hunt, C. Intellectual and ethical development: a dualistic curriculum intervention for college students. *The counseling psychologist*, 1977, *6*(4), 39–42.

Strange, C., and King, P. Intellectual development and its relationship to maturation during the college years. *Journal of applied developmental psychology*, in press.

Teilhard de Chardin, P. *Phenomenon of man*. (Bernard Wall, trans.). New York: Harper, 1959.

Terman, L. M. "The discovery and encouragement of exceptional talent." *American psychologist*, 1954, *9*, 221–230.

Torrance, E. P. *Creativity*. Belmont, Calif.: Fearon, 1969.

Updike, J. *The centaur*. Greenwich, Conn.: Fawcett, 1965.

Updike, J. *Rabbit redux*. Greenwich, Conn.: Fawcett, 1973.

Updike, J. *A month of Sundays*. Greenwich, Conn.: Fawcett, 1975.

Updike, J. *Rabbit, run*. Greenwich, Conn.: Fawcett, 1976.

Wason, P. C., and Johnson-Laird, P. N. *Psychology of reasoning: structure and content*. Cambridge, Mass.: Harvard University Press, 1972.

Wechsler, D. *Adult intelligence scale*. Los Angeles: Psychological Corporation, 1955.

Welfel, E. The development of reflective judgment. Its relationship to year in college, academic major, and satisfaction with major among college students. Unpublished doctoral dissertation, University of Minnesota, 1979.

Widick, C. An evaluation of developmental instruction in a university setting. Unpublished doctoral dissertation, University of Minnesota, 1975.

Widick, C., Knefelkamp, L., and Parker, C. The counselor as a developmental instructor. *Counselor education and supervision*, 1975, *14*, 286–296.

Wood, P. An analysis of the structural relationships between two tests of critical thinking and reflective judgment. Unpublished masters thesis, University of Iowa, 1980.

Additional References

Abney, C. "A comparative study of creative thinking ability in three student groups at the University of Arkansas as measured by the remote associations test." *Dissertation abstracts international,* 1970, *30*, 2717a.

Berzonsky, M. D. "Formal reasoning in adolescence: an alternative view." *Adolescence,* Summer 1978, *13*(50), 279–290.

Benedict, R. *Patterns of culture.* Boston: Houghton Mifflin, 1959.

Bickham, S. "The educational implications of Arthur Jensen's research." *Intellect,* 1974, *103*(2361), 161–164.

"Big change in adolescent reading." *Intellect,* 1975, *104*(2367), 8.

Davis, G. A. "Teaching for creativity: Some guiding lights." *Journal of research and development in education,* 1971, *4*(3), 29–34.

Fitzgerald, J. M., Nesselroade, J. R., & Baltes, P. B. "Emergence of adult intellectual structure." *Developmental psychology,* 1973, *9*(1), 114–119.

Flavell, J. H. *The developmental psychology of Jean Piaget.* Princeton, N.J.: Van Nostrand, 1963.

Gall, M., & Mendelsohn, G. "Effects of facilitating techniques and subject-experimenter interaction on creative problem solving." *Journal of personality and social psychology,* 1967, *5*, 211–16.

Ginsburg, H., & Opper, S. *Piaget's theory of intellectual development.* Englewood Cliffs, N.J.: Prentice-Hall, 1969.

Gowan, D., & Torrance, P. *Creativity: its educational implications.* New York: Wiley, 1967.

Hall, G. S. *The contents of children's minds on entering school.* New York: E. L. Kellogg, 1893.

Inhelder, B., & Piaget, J. *The growth of logical thinking from childhood to adolescence.* New York: Basic Books, 1958.

Jensen, A. "How much can we boost I.Q. and scholastic achievement?" *Harvard educational review, 39, 1*(1969), 1–123.

Jensen, A. "The differences are real." *Psychology today,* December 1973, *7*, 80–84.

Keillor, J. "The effects of experimentally induced consciousness expansion and conscious control upon intellectual functioning." *Dissertation abstracts international,* 1971, *31*-B, 4339.

Lewis, R. W. "Implosions of knowledge." *Intellect,* 1974, *102*(2357), 428–429.

Martindale, C. "What makes creative people different." *Psychology today,* July 1975, *9*(2), 44.

McLuhan, M. *Understanding media.* New York: McGraw-Hill, 1964.

McLuhan, M., & Fiore, Q. *The medium is the message.* New York: Bantam, 1967.

Mendelsohn, G., & Griswold, B. "Assessed creative potential, vocabulary level, and sex as predictors of the use of incidental cues in verbal problem solving." *Journal of personality and social psychology,* 1966, *4*, 423–31.

Ohnmacht, F., & McMorris, R. "Creativity as a function of field independence and dogmatism." *Journal of psychology,* 1971, *79*, 165–68.

Piaget, J. *Six psychological studies.* New York: Random House, 1967.

Piaget, J. *The psychology of the child.* New York: Basic Books, 1969.

Piaget, J. *The psychology of intelligence.* Totawa, N.J.: Littlefield, Adams, 1973.

Pringle, M. K., & Varma, V. P. *Advances in educational psychology.* New York: Harper & Row, 1974.

Ross, R. J. "The empirical status of the formal operations." *Adolescence,* Fall 1974, *9*(35), 413–420.

Siegler, R. S., Liebert, D. E., & Liebert, R. M. "Inhelder and Piaget's pendulum problem: teaching preadolescents to act as scientists." *Developmental psychology,* 1973, *9*(1), 97–101.

Trachtman, L. E. "Creative people, creative times." *Journal of creative behavior,* 1975, *9*(1), 35–50.

Ward, W. C., Kogan, N., & Pankove, E. "Incentive effects in children's creativity." *Child development,* 1972, *43,* 669–676.

Witkin, H. A., Goodenough, D. R., & Karp, S. A. "Stability of cognitive style from childhood to young adulthood." *Journal of personality and social psychology,* 1967, *7*(3), 291–300.

Chapter Five

Moral Judgment

Chapter Highlights

Piaget's Theory of Moral Development
   The Practice of Rules
   A Personal Note
   The Awareness of Rules
Peck and Havighurst's Theory of Moral
   Development
Kohlberg's Theory of Moral
   Development
   Levels of Moral Judgment
   How Moral Development Occurs
Morality and Sex Role
   Reasons for Differences in Levels of
     Morality
   Gilligan's Theory
   Would You Agree?
   Rank the Characters
Moral Education
   Kohlberg's Approach
   Research on Moral Education
   The Just Community School
   Problems in and Suggestions for
     Moral Education
Summary

Key Terms and Concepts

ethical development
conditioning
pluralism
codification
autonomy
fixated
preconventional morality
conventional morality
postconventional morality
Milgram electric shock
   obedience test
principle of justice
cultural mores
moral maturity score
Just Community School

Important People

Jean Piaget
Lawrence Kohlberg
R. H. Peck
Robert Havighurst
Carol Gilligan

"Become a politician? Not me! They're all a pack of liars and crooks. Even businessmen are more moral than they are!"
— *Julie, a ninth-grade student*

It is popular in some circles today to compare the morals of Americans with those of the Romans as their empire was dying. Some suggest that our high crime rate, the political dishonesty exemplified by the Watergate scandal, and the cynical attitudes of our disaffected youth are evidence that the country is becoming morally bankrupt. They lay a great deal of the responsibility for this sad situation on the doorstep of our schools.

Is morality the proper concern of the schools? Those who think so say that the ability of the family and the church to provide for the **ethical development** of children has been so seriously weakened that if the schools do not take over this job, it simply will not be done.

Character development was once the *primary* goal of education. In colonial America, schools were usually operated by religious groups. The schoolmistress and master were counted on to foster good character in students, even if they chose to use force, which they frequently did. Up to the 1900s, there was little disagreement on the meaning of good character. There were theological differences, but almost all adults embraced similar ethical beliefs and reinforced each other in teaching these beliefs to the young.

Early in this century, this unanimity began to weaken. The waves of immigration, the swelling population of cities, and the change from an agricultural to an industrialized society played a major part in the disintegration of this accord. The competing claims of the many different cultural and religious groups in our "melting pot" society meant a retreat from the public espousal of a single set of moral beliefs. The separation of church and state meant that public schools had to scrupulously avoid teaching religion. Teachers were ordered to avoid moralizing, propagandizing, and indoctrinating students in ethical beliefs. The part played by schools in moral development dwindled. In the 1950s, Madalyn Murray O'Hair won her Supreme Court case against compulsory prayer in public school, and the last vestige of religion was removed from educational life.

156

It is interesting to note that in the Soviet Union, the trend over the last seventy-five years has been the reverse. *Vospitania* (moral education) has had a growing role in Soviet education, fostered by the ideological belief that good character can be **conditioned** through the careful reinforcement of appropriate behavior. As Russian psychologist T. P. Repin, writing in *From Zero to Seven (Ot Nolya Do Semi,* 1967) says, "Moral education should begin very early, before the child completes his first year and before he can understand the nature of adult explanation. If conditioning is well done, understanding will come later" (p. 154).

In this century, America has become more and more **pluralistic**; that is, many ethical positions coexist peacefully here. Not many would wish for a singular, state-imposed morality such as exists in many communist countries. However, there is a growing belief that our moral standards are deteriorating. For example, in a recent survey of University of Pennsylvania students, one-third admitted that they cheated on tests when they could (Swift, 1977). Accordingly, there has been renewed interest in having our schools foster at least basic ethical attitudes in the young. When the National Education Association recently asked teachers across the country in what subject areas they wanted help, moral education was the third most frequently mentioned area (Washington, 1977).

A second reason for a renewed desire for moral education is growth of our knowledge of how moral judgment develops and how to foster that development. Psychologists Jean Piaget, Lawrence Kohlberg, R. H. Peck, and Robert Havighurst have made significant contributions to this field. The following sections describe their theories of moral development.

PIAGET'S THEORY OF MORAL DEVELOPMENT

Jean Piaget, best known for his theory of cognitive development (see Chapter 4), has also received widespread acclaim for his ideas on the moral development of the child. Piaget (1932:1948) defines morality as "the understanding of and adherence to rules through one's own volition." He has studied moral behavior by observing children play the game of marbles. Marbles, as you probably know, calls for each player to roll a marble from behind a line into a two-foot wide circle. Each player places one of his marbles in the circle. Any marbles the shooter is able to knock out of the area belong to him. When there are no longer any marbles in the circle, each player must put in another marble. This social situation provides a good chance to watch the development of morality, since children of most ages and in many different countries play the game and are able to talk about their understanding of its rules.

Piaget suggests that we can look at the development of morality in two ways: the way children actually practice the rules and the degree of their awareness of those rules. This distinction is made because children are often able to follow rules without being able to verbalize them.

The Practice of Rules

The four stages of rule practice suggested by Piaget are as follows:

Stage one: the individual stage (up to 3 years). In this period the mechanics of the game begin to be understood by children; they realize that there is regularity in the world and that this regularity may be seen in games. The rules of the game tend to be ritualized. Once the ritual is mastered, children often want to go on to other games.

However, children at this stage have no sense of "oughtness" about the rules. They imitate older children and have no inner awareness that the rules are necessary to play the game. The game itself is not a social activity and is often played alone. Enjoyment is derived only by imitation of the movements of the game.

Stage two: the egocentric stage (4–7 years). Now one can see the beginnings of responsibility to follow the rules, although children may continue not only to misunderstand the rules, but to play with different sets of rules. For example, they do not necessarily take turns, nor do they collect their winnings. They rarely object if there is more than one winner. The major change at this stage, however, is the awareness that it is important to play the game with other children. Players are beginning to enjoy the social interaction, but their own desires are uppermost. whole of child

Stage three: the cooperation stage (8–11 years). By now children have strong concerns for the definition of the rules, which are fixed and common for all players. Manual dexterity in the play of the game is secondary to winning. Even if luck plays a part, the child cares more about winning than about playing well. Cooperation is essential at this stage, but it is still largely a matter of necessity. The main thing is to rigidly follow the rules and to insure no one deviates from them.

Stage four: the codification of the rules (12 years and up). The change that takes place at this stage is of great importance to teachers and others who work with adolescents. Children's mental functioning takes a sharp new direction; they become able to reason hypothetically and abstractly. They can ask, for example, what would happen if it were to rain up instead of down, a question that earlier would be considered ridiculous. They are able to imagine a large variety of possibilities in any situation.

A PERSONAL NOTE

When I was in junior high school I recall getting together with some friends to play the game of blackjack, or Twenty-One. This game is quite simple but has a lot of variations. We began discussing and writing down our agreements as to what would happen if any of the many contingencies were to occur. For three afternoons in a row we discussed the rules, and the discussions were so enjoyable that we never did play the game. We were clearly at the codification stage.

Teachers and others working with adolescents should be aware of this strong need. If teenagers have a role in making the rules, they are far more likely to obey them.

Children at this stage become deeply interested in the reasons behind the rules and can more readily imagine different and perhaps better rules for the game of marbles. They become more consistent in their practice of the game because of their new interest in the **codification** of rules in general. Adolescents take great pleasure in anticipating all possible cases in a game and in developing rules to cover any of those possibilities.

The Awareness of Rules

At any of these stages, children may or may not be consciously aware of the rules they are following. Piaget suggests that there are three stages in the development of the consciousness of rules.

Stage one: individualism (up to 5 years). As children learn to play a game, they usually know that some things are allowed and some forbidden. They also have the sense that these strictures apply all the time. But this is the extent of their awareness of regulations in play. They are primarily interested in doing whatever they want to do, and if that fits well with their playmates' interests, fine; if not, that's fine too.

Stage two: heteronomy (6–9 years). Piaget asked the children three questions: "Can the rules be changed?" "Have the rules always been the same?" and "How did the rules begin?"

He discovered that children in this age group have exaggerated respect for the sanctity of rules. Most are firmly convinced that rules in general have been handed down from authority figures like fathers or sometimes from a politician or religious leader. Children are aware that rules can change, but believe that it is solely in the power of one of these authorities to change them.

Piaget correlates this stage with the development of the child's superego. Children now identify strongly with those in authority; some see rules as sacred and absolutely unchangeable. Their sense of themselves is closely tied with their sense of the adults in their family and society. Just as mystics cannot differentiate between their ideas and those that they believe to be God's, children at this stage cannot distinguish between their own (often mistaken) interpretations of the rules and rules which actually have been imposed from above.

Stage three: autonomy (10–12 years). Now the dictates of adults and older children are left behind, and the rules become the tools of the player. Players may suggest rules at any time, and if these changes are accepted by all the players, then the game may be altered accordingly.

Piaget believes that the tendency toward **autonomy** and a strong desire for
codification of rules

codification of the rules are natural outgrowths of children's maturation. Thus, he sees biological evidence that democracy is more natural than dictatorship. At this stage, there is a natural equality among all participants. Obviously some ideas are considered more reasonable than others, and an individual counts on the group to recognize these differences. He or she also expects the group players to prohibit unfair innovations, because these would make the game less a matter of skill than it should be. There is a strong sense that each person, whether a good player or not, is entitled to one vote, and that the group has every right to make changes in the governance of the game they are playing.

Now adolescents realize that the generations before them have also made changes to rules. They can understand, for example, that the game of marbles was probably invented hundreds of years earlier by children playing with rounded pebbles, and that the rules of the game must have been continuously modified over time.

For Piaget, the development of morality is closely linked to the development of intellectual ability. Thus, good character is largely a matter of good *thinking*. Peck and Havighurst (1960) have argued that *personality* plays an even more important role in the development of character.

PECK AND HAVIGHURST'S THEORY OF MORAL DEVELOPMENT

R. H. Peck and R. J. Havighurst (1960), two educational researchers, investigated moral development by looking at the attitudes and traits individuals show in their relationships to other people. Their main source of information came from their subjects' opinions of each other; these subjects ranged in age from 10 to 17.

Peck and Havighurst were able to describe five types of motivation for ethical behavior, which appeared to represent definite stages in moral development and occurred in sequential order. However, it is possible for behavior to become fixed at one stage; an adult could be stuck at stage one (although an infant cannot be at stage five). These stages are described below.

Stage one: amoral type. People in this stage are completely egocentric, caring only about gratifying their own wishes. They tend to be disorganized and unhappy, and have relatively little control over their impulses. They often have strong but subconscious guilt feelings and act with hostility toward themselves and others.

Stage two: expedient type. Although giving an appearance of considerate behavior, these people are really quite selfish. They are able to fit into society more easily than the amoral type, but only because they fear punishment. Their conscience is weak, and they tend to be greedy and corrupt.

Stage three: conforming type. People in stage three act in a moral way, but only because of their strong desire to conform to group norms. They are followers who seek to avoid public disapproval, and are stable to the extent that the society in which they live is stable. Like stage-two people, they are submissive to authority and are considered "other-directed." Such persons have strong superegos and suffer greatly from the constant harassment of their consciences. Peck and Havighurst suggest that most people's moral development stops at this stage; thus, conformity is the most common motivation for moral behavior.

Stage four: irrational-conscientious type. These people conform to their own standards of right and wrong rather than to the group code. However, irrational-conscientious people respond rigidly to the dictates of conscience and are therefore difficult to live with. They are willing to do the unpopular thing with complete confidence in their own moral standards. Their main goal is to live an irreproachable life.

Stage five: rational-altruistic type. The main motivation of people in this stage is concern for the welfare of others. They are capable of taking a realistic look at the needs of others without imposing their own biases. They have what James Marcia calls an "achieved identity," and because of this are able to be strong leaders and benefactors.

Peck and Havighurst (1960) believe that most people tend to become **fixated** at one of these stages fairly early in their lives, and it becomes their operational base of moral behavior.

> *As the children were studied from age 10 to 17, each individual tended to show a predictable, stable pattern of moral character. Many of their overt actions changed, of course, as they grew older, learned new social and intellectual skills, and developed through puberty. However, each child appeared to maintain very persistently his deeply held feelings and attitudes toward life, and the modes of reacting which we call his character structures (p. 155).*

Piaget and Peck and Havighurst see one's level of morality as relatively unchangeable after the childhood years. Harvard psychologist Lawrence Kohlberg disagrees; while his ideas on moral development borrow heavily from Piaget, he believes that both the above theories are too rigid. Kohlberg feels that if the appropriate instructional techniques are used, people can be helped to raise their level of moral judgment. Because so much of his research has been done with adolescents, his work is of particular relevance.

KOHLBERG'S THEORY OF MORAL DEVELOPMENT

Levels of Moral Judgment

In one of his early investigations of moral development, Kohlberg (1963) studied the moral judgments of 72 boys, ages 10, 13, and 16. He presented them with fictional dilemmas in which the main character wants to help a needful person but would have to break a law to do so. Each boy was asked to justify one of two outcomes: either an act in which the law was broken but the person was helped, or an act in which the help was withheld but no law was broken. Kohlberg did not care which of the two choices the boys made, but was interested rather in the rationale they gave for their choice. After examining the different rationales, he felt he could describe six different levels of moral judgment. The first two levels he calls **preconventional morality** because at both the individual acts in an amoral way. Preconventional morality is similar to Piaget's stage-one (individual) morality and Peck and Havighurst's stage-one (amoral) and stage-two (expedient) types of morality.

At the second two levels the individual conforms to traditional morality, so Kohlberg refers to them as **conventional morality.** They compare to Piaget's stage-two (egocentric) and stage-three (cooperation) morality and Peck and Havighurst's stage-three (conforming) and stage-four (irrational) types of morality. Kohlberg's last two levels have in common the fact that they stem from the individual's own moral principles, so he labels them **postconventional.** They compare to Piaget's stage-four (codification) and Peck and Havighurst's stage-five (rational-altruistic) moral types. A summary of these comparisons appears in Table 5–1.

Kohlberg's six levels are described in Table 5–2, with an example of a moral dilemma which illustrates each different level of resolution.

Most young children and most delinquents are at levels one and two. Most adults are at levels three and four. Kohlberg estimates that 20 to 25 percent of American adults are at the postconventional levels (five and six), with only 5 to 10 percent ever reaching level six. However, since his studies have turned up very few level-six adolescents, Kohlberg treats levels five and six together (Lickona, 1977). Table 5–2 summarizes these findings.

At the lower levels people act to avoid punishment; at the higher ones, they act to avoid self-condemnation. Conduct, therefore, is correlated with beliefs,

TABLE 5–1
COMPARISON OF THREE THEORIES OF MORAL DEVELOPMENT

Piaget	Peck and Havighurst	Kohlberg
1. Individual	1. Amoral	1. Obedience, punishment
2. Egocentric	2. Expedient	2. Instrumental hedonism
3. Cooperation	3. Conforming	3. Good boy/Good girl
4. Codification	4. Irrational-conscientious	4. Authority and social order
	5. Rational-conscientious	5. Contractual-legalistic
		6. Universal ethics

TABLE 5–2
KOHLBERG'S LEVELS OF MORAL JUDGMENT

The dilemma: Al, age 14, sees his brother Jimmy, age 10, steal money from their mother's purse. Should Al tell Mom what Jimmy did?

Preconventional Morality
Level One: obedience and punishment. Child is self-centered, has strict pleasure-pain orientation. *Al:* "I wouldn't tell Mom—Jimmy would only get even with me later. It's better not to get involved."

Level Two: naive instrumental hedonism. Trade-offs and deals are made, but only if the child sees something in it for himself. Need satisfaction is still uppermost, but an awareness of the value of reciprocity has begun. *Al:* "It's better if I don't tell. I do bad things sometimes and I wouldn't want Jimmy squealing on me."

Conventional Morality
Level Three: good-boy morality. Child is eager for approval of others. Wants to maintain good relations. *Al:* "It's better to tell on him. Otherwise, Mom might think I was in on it."

Level Four: authority and social order. Child now seeks approval of society in general, but has rigid ideas as to what rules are; "Law and Order" mentality. *Al:* "I have no choice but to tell. Stealing just isn't right."

Postconventional morality
Level Five: contractual legalistic. Child makes contracts and tries hard to keep them; attempts to keep from violating the will or rights of others, believes in the common good. *Al:* "I'll try to persuade Jimmy to put the money back. If he won't, I'll tell. I hate to do it, but that money belongs to Mom, and he shouldn't have taken it."

Level Six: universal ethics, individual conscience. Obedience to social rules, except where they can be shown to contradict universal justice; the principles of pacifism, conscientious objection, and civil disobedience fall into this category. *Al:* "The most important thing is that Jimmy comes to see he's being unfair to Mom. Telling on him won't help out. I'm going to try to show him why he's wrong, then I'll help him earn money to pay Mom back without her knowing."

Source: From "How to Encourage Moral Development," by L. Kohlberg in *Learning* (March 1977), pp. 36–44.

Figure 5–1   **The Average Grade in School when Kohlberg's Levels Prevail**

Level	K	1	2	3	4	5	6	7	8	9	10	11	12
1													
2													
3													
4													
5*													

*No more than 25 percent ever reach level five.
Note: This figure is summarized from the findings of Lickona (1977).

with the reasons for the conduct differing greatly at the various levels. Higher-level subjects are much less likely to cheat, for example, because they find cheating inconsistent with their self-perceptions rather than because they fear punishment. Krebs (1967) found that whereas 70 percent of preconventional subjects cheated on a test, 55 percent of conventional subjects cheated, and only 15 percent of postconventional subjects cheated.

In one interesting experiment, the **Milgram electric shock obedience test** (Turiel, 1974) was used to investigate the willingness of persons at the six levels to inflict pain on others. The subjects were told to administer shocks of from 15 to 450 volts to a "learner" in order to get him to learn a task quickly. The "learner" was actually a collaborator who was not really shocked but who put on a convincing performance. Prior to the experiment, each subject was rated as to morality level. A majority of postconventional subjects refused to participate, quit when the victim expressed pain, or said they wanted to quit but felt obligated to fulfill their agreement. The majority of the subjects at the other moral levels willingly continued the experiment.

Kohlberg found that about 50 percent of an individual's statements about a moral dilemma fell into one dominant level, and the rest into the two adjacent levels; the level remained fairly constant regardless of the content of the dilemma. The same levels are also found in other cultures; the sequence of development is the same, although the speed of development is faster and is more likely to proceed to higher levels in some cultures than in others (Kohlberg, 1975).

Kohlberg avoids specifying any ages in connection with his levels. As Piaget and Peck and Havighurst, he believes that any of these levels can be present in adults and that persons can become fixated at any of the levels. Also, these levels are invariably sequential; that is, persons cannot get to a higher level without having moved sequentially through the lower levels.

Rank the Characters

Below is a list of characters in books and plays. For those with which you are familiar, enter the Kohlberg level of moral development that you think best describes the character. The answers could form a good subject for debate. Compare your answers with your classmates'. My answers appear on page 168.

Kohlberg Level

1. Captain Ahab in *Moby Dick*   _____

2. Jo March in *Little Women*   _____

3. Stanley Kowalski in *A Streetcar Named Desire*   _____

4. Holden Caulfield in *The Catcher in the Rye*   _____

5. Madame Defarge in *A Tale of Two Cities*   _____

6. Hamlet in *Hamlet*

     7. Lady Macbeth in *Macbeth*

     8. Clyde Barrow in *Bonnie and Clyde*

     9. Tom Sawyer in *The Adventures of Huckleberry Finn*

    10. Alex in *A Clockwork Orange*

    11. Eliza Doolittle in *My Fair Lady*

    12. Melanie in *Gone With the Wind*

How Moral Development Occurs

What motivates change from a lower to a higher level? Kohlberg suggests three possibilities. The first is that the young child develops a set of beliefs about morality based on the ideals of the adults around him. This set of beliefs the Freudians call the superego. If the child's superego is strong, he will gradually rise to the highest levels of morality. However, it has proved difficult to validate this theory through research.

The second explanation of moral development is religiously oriented. Moral behavior is a response to one's conscience—a combination of learned values and the innate ability to discern right from wrong. When the child's learning is compatible with his conscience, he will tend to be "good." If his teachings have not been "proper," he will have a tendency to be "bad," but he still is responsible for his actions because of the innate part of his conscience. Like the superego theory, there does not seem to be much research evidence for this position.

For Kohlberg, like Piaget, conscience is largely a matter of decision-making ability. He believes that such factors as intelligence, self-esteem, and the ability to delay gratification (also called willpower) are likely to play a major role in the level of morality that the individual has achieved. The knowledge of consequences of one's acts will also play a large part. Philosophical beliefs and personality characteristics, especially in children, Kohlberg argues, tend to have only a minor effect on morality.

The third possibility for moral development (also in agreement with Piaget) is that there is a genetic factor in human morality. The **principle of justice** refers to our inherited potential to recognize when we are being fair or unfair with each other—a concept similar to the religious position. The principle of justice states that all human beings are basically equal in value and that fairness in human interrelations is essential. It is a basic part of our nature and exists universally. Rules (such as traffic regulations) vary from culture to culture, but the principle of justice is the same in all cultures. Unless social forces block it from operating, justice is the natural result of social coexistence, a position similar to Piaget's that democracy is the natural state of human beings.

MORALITY AND SEX ROLE

Is there a difference between males and females in levels of morality? Yes, according to research reviewed by Kohlberg (1970). Whereas the average male reaches level four (law and order), the typical female develops no higher than level three (good girl/good boy).

Reasons for Differences in Levels of Morality

The reasons for this discrepancy in levels of morality of men and women have recently been investigated by Kohlberg's Harvard colleague Carol Gilligan (1977). She believes Kohlberg's theory penalizes women for their greater sensitivity to what others think. She summarizes the situation: "Herein lies the paradox, for the very traits that have traditionally defined the 'goodness' of women, their care and sensitivity to the needs of others, are those that mark them as deficient in moral development" (1977, p. 484). Many psychologists, most of them male, have suggested that women worry too much about the opinions of others and thus lack the objectivity and independence of judgment to make high-level moral decisions. Sigmund Freud indicted the female superego: "Their [women's] superego is never so inexorable, so impersonal, so independent of its emotional origins as we require it to be in men" (Freud, 1933, p. 257). Kohlberg (1971) ascribes the difference to the greater practice males are given in moral problem solving.

Gilligan (1977), on the other hand, believes that the problem lies with male bias inherent in Kohlberg's theory itself: "As long as the categories by which [moral] development is assessed are derived within a male perspective from male research data, divergence from the masculine standard can be seen only as a failure of development" (p. 490). This bias, as she sees it, is the exaggeration of societal goals and the underestimation of interpersonal relations. For example, even if a man were cold and unempathetic toward his children, he would receive a level-six rating so long as he were capable of reasoning on the basis of universal ethics.

Gilligan's Theory

Gilligan argues that in addition to male bias, Kohlberg's scoring system is suspect because it is based only on responses to hypothetical examples. In her research, she has studied moral development by examining the reasoning of women contemplating an abortion, clearly a serious and difficult moral decision. Her lengthy interviews lead her to conclude there are three distinct levels of female moral development, with a specific period of transition between each.

1. *Individual survival.* At this primary level, the person's concern is strictly for herself. The woman about to have an abortion justifies it by saying, "I just don't want a baby, that's all. That would not be good for me now."

2. *Self-sacrifice.* As a result of the first transition, which often occurs during adolescence, the woman moves from selfishness to self-sacrifice. A sense of responsibility and concern for others now dominates her thinking. Even if she wants to have the child, a woman might abort it because "it would not be a good life for the baby, and its father wants me to get rid of it." Gilligan feels that in the lives of most women, men make all the important decisions. Because they have no power anyway, such women justify their position by exalting a life of sacrifice to those who do have power.

3. *Nonviolence.* In the second transition, which for many never takes place, women come to recognize their powerlessness as being more a matter of attitude than of necessity. Such a woman learns to "verify her capacity for independent judgment and the legitimacy of her own point of view" (p. 502). Her moral decisions now include her own needs as well as those of others. Now the criterion is to be nonviolent, to cause as little hurt to self and others as possible. Such decisions are more difficult than those made at the first two levels because they are more complex, but they are also more realistic.

──────────── WOULD YOU AGREE? ────────────

In many ways, Gilligan's position is not so different from Kohlberg's. Her first stage, individual survival, is essentially the same as preconventional morality; self-sacrifice is similar to the conventional stage, and the independence of judgment and concern for all at Gilligan's nonviolent level corresponds closely to postconventional morality.

However, she is correct in criticizing Kohlberg's principle of justice as being too intellectual and unconcerned for human weakness. After all, it has been men, presumably in pursuit of justice, who have kept the nations of the world intermittently at war for most of human history. Pursuit of the principle of nonviolence would never have permitted this vast destruction.

In his fascinating book, *Disappearance* (1951), Phillip Wylie imagines a situation in which all the women in the world disappear from the perception of men, and at the same time, women cannot perceive any men. Wylie then describes what happens in the two unisexual worlds. The men of the various nations quickly fall to blaming each other for the disappearance, war breaks out, and nuclear obliteration follows. Women, on the other hand, hold an international conference, discuss the disappearance and other conflicts, and work their way through to a worldwide nonaggression pact.

Do you think this is a likely scenario? What might some others be?

───────────────────────────────────────

Gilligan cites Erikson's description (1969) of Mahatma Gandhi's private life as an example of the difficulty of this highest level. Venerated for his almost saintly belief in nonviolent resistance to evil, Gandhi was nonetheless often cruel to his wife and close friends when they deviated even slightly from his prescriptions for their behavior. Gilligan suggests that

> *the blind willingness to sacrifice people to the truth, however, has always been the danger of an ethics abstracted from life. This willingness links Gandhi to the biblical Abraham, who was prepared to sacrifice the life of his son in order to demonstrate the integrity and supremacy of his faith. Both men, in the limitations of their fatherhood, stand in implicit contrast to the woman who comes before Solomon and verifies her motherhood by relinquishing truth in order to save the life of her child (p. 515).*

Gilligan does not say that woman's morality is better than man's, nor is it in any way inferior; in its developmental process and in its fruition, she believes, it is distinctly different.

Answers to "Rank the Characters"

		Kohlberg Level
1.	Captain Ahab	5
2.	Jo March	3
3.	Stanley Kowalski	2
4.	Holden Caulfield	4
5.	Madame Defarge	1
6.	Hamlet	5-6
7.	Lady Macbeth	2
8.	Clyde Barrow	1
9.	Tom Sawyer	2
10.	Alex	1
11.	Eliza Doolittle	3
12.	Melanie	5

MORAL EDUCATION

Kohlberg's Approach

The old techniques of moral education were largely limited to the teacher's lectures and exhortations to "be good." They never were very effective. Kohlberg and his coworkers (1975) have implemented a new approach to moral education which relies on the universal principle of justice rather than on **cultural mores**. It attempts to upgrade moral understanding and behavior through personal experiences rather than through indoctrination of a specific moral code. Finally, it is based on carefully researched psychological data rather than on philosophical speculations.

The approach defines moral education as the stimulation of the next step of development through (1) arousal of moral conflict through presentation of relevant problems, and (2) suggestion of solutions to the problem which are one level above the child's present moral level. Kohlberg believes that most children want to function at the highest level of moral reasoning they can comprehend. This is usually one level above the child's dominant level. That is, they can comprehend a level higher than their current level of moral behavior, but they need to have this higher level explained to them before they actually operate at it. Children will not understand reasoning too far above their own level, and reasoning at lower levels, while understood, is rejected.

Research on Moral Education

Although there have been numerous studies of moral education, they tend to contradict each other. In some cases, they contradict themselves. A good example is the study of Kohlberg and Blatt (1972), who investigated the effects of a twelve-week guided discussion program of moral conflicts upon students' moral reasoning. A first study was conducted with 11- and 12-year old Jewish students in a religion class. A second study was done with sixth- and tenth-grade lower-middle class whites and lower-class blacks. In both studies, comparable groups of children not in the program were also tested. Before and after the program, each student's level of moral reasoning was assessed by interviewing the student and rating his response to moral dilemmas, and then his **moral maturity scores** were compared. The religion students' scores increased an average of 66 points (two-thirds of a stage). Over 60 percent of the students moved up one full stage or more. In the second study, the discussion experience also led to a significant increase in moral judgment; however, the change was less dramatic. The average pretest to posttest change was 34 points (one-third of a stage), and 19 percent of the students showed an upward movement of one full stage or more. In both studies the changes in moral reasoning were found to be relatively enduring one year later. Students not in the program changed little. These findings are consistent with Kohlberg's theory. But did the students in the program *behave* more morally?

This was evaluated through Hartshorne and May's (1928) experimental honesty measures. Before and after the discussion programs, these measures were administered to evaluate the students' willingness to cheat. In the first study, there was no positive effect of the moral discussion program on resistance to cheating on the tests. In the second study, there was actually a slight *increase* in the percentage of students willing to cheat after being in the program.

How can this increase in level of moral judgment, but apparent decrease in moral behavior, be explained? First of all, cheating on experimental tests may not be an accurate measure of moral behavior. Cheating on tests is qualitatively different from serious moral conflicts. On the other hand, cheating behavior is related to the levels of moral reasoning children have achieved (Krebs, 1967).

Thus, there are some indications that Kohlberg's method works, and others that it does not. Perhaps our ability to *measure* changes in moral reasoning and behavior is not as advanced as theory and instructional strategy. Also it is likely that further refinements in techniques of moral education will be needed before we can hope to effectively improve moral judgment and behavior. One such attempt is the Just Community School.

The Just Community School

Kohlberg's theories of moral education have been implemented in the **Just Community School** in Cambridge, Massachusetts (Wasserman, 1976), near Harvard University. The founders of the school have attempted to develop moral reasoning by creating a school that is perceived as fair and just by the students and staff. The government of the school is a participatory democracy, much like that described in A. S. Neill's *Summerhill* (1960). "Direct democracy has proved successful in making realistic rules, enforcing them through a student process, and establishing a sense of community and positive morale," says Bill Ford, a teacher at the school.

In other alternative schools, participatory democracy has often failed because it is perceived as a humanitarian frill rather than a central educational goal. Students often become bored when they are required to attend lengthy complicated meetings about scheduling and other administrative matters. Student councils in traditional high schools also often fail to provide effective moral experience for students. Most student councils are not truly democratic and do not have significant decision-making powers.

Just Community School was developed in July 1974, when a group of parents, teachers, and students asked the Cambridge School Committee to establish a new alternative school within Cambridge High School. Just Community has sixty-five students who are from diverse backgrounds (academically gifted and learning-disabled students, children of professional and working-class parents, black and white students). The government of the school is democratic, with each student and teacher having the same rights and voting power. All major school rules are determined in weekly community meetings. Major issues include drug use, "hooking" (cutting school), grading, behavior disturbances, race relations within the school curriculum, stealing, and decision-making procedures. Members of the community determine the consequences for violations of community rules. During community meetings proposals are discussed and parliamentary procedure is used.

Weekly small group sessions are also held, during which community problems are discussed and proposals drafted. The small groups encourage greater personal involvement in moral discussions. According to Ford, these sessions also expose students to higher-level moral reasoning.

The school's English and history curricula use moral discussions as an exploratory tool. Classes read and discuss current problems in America, role-taking and communication, and issues of law and justice in the school and the wider society. One topic studied is the problem of authority. One class read *Antigone* and *Inherit the Wind* and saw the films *If* and *Attica*. Another class explored the moral issues in forced busing. The students read historical court decisions and studied desegregation problems in Boston. Students discussed such questions as: "Do courts have the right to rule on this issue?" "Is this a case for community control?" "What is the real issue?"

On the basis of extensive research on this approach, Reimer concludes that:

The discussion of moral dilemmas is still the most effective means of attaining the single goal of promoting student moral judgment. However, for those aiming for the more complex goals of promoting the application of moral reasoning to the life of the school, the Just Community approach may prove most promising (1981, p. 487).

PROBLEMS IN AND SUGGESTIONS FOR MORAL EDUCATION

Researcher Thomas Lickona (1977) supports Kohlberg's approach to moral education, but describes several problems that teachers should be aware of: (1) It is often difficult for teachers to diagnose a child's stage of functioning (Kohlberg's followers use a 200-page manual, or employ Kohlberg-trained judges to determine moral judgment level); (2) children may operate at several different stages. Focusing on the child's dominant stage of reasoning can limit a teacher's perception of the many facets of a child's moral personality. Teachers may miss "positive moral flashes" (when a child shows sympathetic emotional responses above his current level of reasoning); (3) teachers should not assume a direct link between age and stage; and (4) there should be only one moral curriculum in a classroom. Lickona urges teachers to get involved in Kohlberg's approach to moral education. He describes two examples of teacher behavior to illustrate its value.

When a student yelled at his teacher that she was a "son-of-a-bitchin' whore," she quickly marched him to the principal's office and demanded his expulsion from school. The principal complied. Lickona suggests that the young man got a lesson in level-one reasoning: to avoid punishment and to "act" respectful.

Another teacher's response to verbal abuse was to explain to the youth that his words had so hurt her feelings that, for the time being, she could not even talk to him. Surprised at not being more severely punished, he reflected for a while and then apologized. He received a lesson in the need for mutual respect and cooperation between people.

Table 5–3 presents some suggestions for promoting moral growth.

TABLE 5–3
SUGGESTIONS FOR PROMOTING MORAL GROWTH IN THE CLASSROOM

1. Focus on establishing the classroom as a community where the participants will live and learn together in an atmosphere of respect and security.

2. Provide opportunities for the children to have a voice in establishing the rules of the classroom.

3. Choose punishments that relate to the offense, stressing where possible the effect of the child's action on the group.

4. Make distinctions between criticism of academic work and criticism of behavior, and between rules for the good order of the school and rules affecting justice and human relations.

5. Provide opportunities for peer group work.

6. In stories and discussions of everyday experience, help the children to consider the feelings of other real or fictional persons.

7. Role-play experiences from daily life, events that lead to disappointments, tensions, fights, joys, in order to provide opportunities for the pupils to see the event from perspectives other than their own.

8. Discuss with the class what they consider fair and unfair classroom procedures and relationships.

9. Frequently take time to listen to each student's responses to questions of moral judgment, and stimulate discussions that will provoke higher-stage reasoning, using literature, film, and life experiences.

10. Avoid making judgments about moral development on the basis of behavior. People at six different stages might perform the same action, but for different reasons.

Source: From *Moral Development: A Guide to Piaget and Kohlberg,* by Ronald Duska and Mariellen Whelan, 1975. Reprinted by permission of Paulist Press.

SUMMARY

Is morality the proper concern of our schools? This question has become of considerable concern to educators, both because there is a growing belief that the moral fiber of American youth is deteriorating, and also because we have a greater knowledge of how moral judgment develops and can be fostered. The prime movers in terms of moral developmental theory have been Jean Piaget, R. H. Peck and Robert Havighurst, and Lawrence Kohlberg.

Piaget studied the development of morality by observing Swiss children play the game of marbles. He suggests that we can look at the development of morality in two ways: the way children actually practice the rules and the degree of their awareness of those rules. Piaget has suggested four stages in the practice of rules. They are: up through age 3, the individual stage; ages 4 through 7, the egocentric stage; ages 8 through 11, the cooperation stage; and age 12 and up, the codification of rules stage. Piaget believed that there are three developmental stages in the awareness of rules. They are: up through age 5, individualism; ages 6 through 9, heteronomy; and ages 10 through 12, autonomy.

Peck and Havighurst investigated moral development by looking at the attitudes and traits that individuals show in their relationship to other people. They suggest that morality develops in five stages: (1) amoral; (2) expedient; (3) conforming; (4) irrational-conscientious; and (5) rational-altruistic.

Kohlberg has completed numerous studies of the development of morality, almost all of which have been of teenage boys. He suggests that there are three stages of moral development: preconventional, conventional, and postconventional. Each of his stages is divided into two levels: at the preconventional stage, the levels are obedience and punishment and instrumental hedonism. At the conventional stage, the levels are good-boy/good-girl and authority and social order. The postconventional levels are contractual-legalistic and universal ethics.

One of Kohlberg's major contributions to the field of morality is his conclusion that morality develops largely in the same way that cognition develops. This is in opposition to Freud's theory that morality is a function of the superego and also the position of many religions that morality is an innate characteristic. Kohlberg believes that such factors as intelligence, self-esteem, and the ability to delay gratification (also called willpower) play a major role in the level of morality that an individual is likely to achieve.

Kohlberg's theory is also based on the idea that all human beings have an innate sense of justice. Thus, the development of morality may be seen as an ever-increasing willingness to conform to the dictates of the principle of justice.

Psychologist Carol Gilligan has suggested that women's morality develops in a different way from that of men. Women, she suggests, are more concerned with interpersonal relationships than they are with abstractions like Kohlberg's principle of justice. Thus, she sees female morality developing in phases: self-interest, self-sacrifice, and a concern for nonviolence.

Kohlberg and his coworkers have done numerous experiments on teaching moral thinking. He argues that moral education follows a two-step process. First, it is necessary to arouse a moral conflict through the presentation of relevant problems. Then it is necessary to suggest solutions to the problem that are one level above the child's present moral level. Kohlberg believes that most children want to function at the highest level of moral reasoning they can comprehend, and this is usually one level above their present level. Research on this approach to moral education has indicated some success for the technique.

An actual application of Kohlberg's principles are being tested in an alternative high school known as the Just Community School. In this school the solution of moral problems is the center of the daily curriculum.

Researcher Thomas Lickona has criticized Kohlberg's approach in the following terms: it is often difficult for a teacher to diagnose a child's level of moral functioning; children often operate at several different stages simultaneously; and, it is difficult to have several moral curricula operating in the classroom at one time.

Questions

1. What is moral development?
2. What are Piaget's stages of moral development?

3. What are Peck and Havighurst's stages of moral development?
4. What are Kohlberg's levels of moral judgment?
5. What are the differences among the three theories? What are their similarities?
6. Are male and female morality different?
7. What are the difficulties in trying to teach morality?

References

Blatt, M.   Experimental studies in moral education using a developmental approach. Unpublished Ph.D. dissertation, University of Chicago, 1959.

Duska, R., & Whelan, M.   *Moral development: a guide to Piaget and Kohlberg.* New York: Paulist/Newman Press, 1975.

Erikson, E.   *Gandhi's truth: on the origins of militant nonviolence.* New York: Norton, 1969.

Freud, S.   *New introductory lectures on psychoanalysis* (W. J. H. Sprott, trans.). New York: Norton, 1933.

Gilligan, C.   "In a different voice: women's conception of the self and morality." *Harvard educational review,* 1977, *47*(4), 481–517.

Hartshorne, H., & May, M. A.   *Studies in service and self-control* (Vol. 2). New York: Macmillan, 1928.

Kohlberg, L.   "The development of children's orientations toward a moral order." *Vita humana,* 1963, *6,* 11–33.

Kohlberg, L.   "Development of moral character and moral ideology." In M. L. Hoffman & L. W. Hoffman (Eds.), *Review of child development research.* New York: Russell Sage Foundation, 1964.

Kohlberg, L.   "Moral and religious education and the public schools: a developmental view." In T. R. Sizer (Ed.), *Religion and public education.* Boston: Houghton Mifflin, 1967.

Kohlberg, L.   "Stage and sequence: the cognitive-developmental approach to socialization." In D. A. Goslin (Ed.), *Handbook of socialization theory and research.* Chicago: Rand McNally, 1969.

Kohlberg, L.   "Moral development and the education of adolescents." In R. F. Purnell (Ed.), *Adolescents and the American high school.* New York: Holt, Rinehart & Winston, 1970.

Kohlberg, L.   "Understanding the hidden curriculum." *Learning,* December 1972, *1*(2), 10–14.

Kohlberg, L.   "The cognitive-developmental approach to moral education." *Phi Delta Kappan,* 1975, *56*(10), 610–677.

Kohlberg, L., & Blatt, M.   "The effects of classroom discussion on level of moral development." In L. Kohlberg & E. Turiel (Eds.), *Recent research in moral development.* New York: Holt, Rinehart & Winston, 1972.

Kohlberg, L., & Gilligan, C.   "The adolescent as a philosopher." In J. Kagan & R. Coles (Eds.), *Twelve to sixteen: early adolescence.* New York: W. W. Norton, 1972.

Kohlberg, L., & Kramer, R.   "Continuities and discontinuities in childhood and adult moral development." *Human development,* 1969, *12,* 93–120.

Krebs, R.   "Some relations between moral judgment attention and resistance to temptation." Unpublished Ph.D. dissertation, University of Chicago, 1967.

Lickona, T.   "How to encourage moral development." *Learning,* March, 1977, *5*(7), 36–44.

Milgram, S.   "Behavioral study of obedience." *Journal of abnormal and social psychology,* 1963, *67,* 371–378.

Milgram, S. "Some conditions of obedience and disobedience to authority." *Human relations,* 1965, *18,* 67–76.

Neill, A. S. *Summerhill.* New York: Hart, 1960.

Peck, R. H., & Havighurst, R. J. *The psychology of character development.* New York: Wiley, 1960.

Piaget, J. *The moral judgment of the child.* Glencoe, Ill.: Free Press, 1948. (Originally published 1932, London: Routledge & Kegan Paul.)

Reimer, J. "Moral education: The Just Community approach." *Phi Delta Kappan,* March, 1981, 485–487.

Repin, T. P. *From zero to seven (Ot Nolya Do Semi).* Moscow, 1967.

Swift, P. "Student cheating." *Parade,* May 7, 1977.

Turiel, E. "An experimental test of the sequentiality of developmental stages in the child's moral judgments." *Journal of personality and social psychology,* 1966, *3,* 611–618.

Turiel, E. "Conflict and transition in adolescent moral development." *Child development,* 1974, *45,* 14–29.

Washington, B. "A move to teach moral values in schools." *Boston globe,* July 18, 1977.

Wasserman, E. "Implementing Kohlberg's 'just community concept' in an alternative high school." *Social education,* April 1976, 203–207.

Wylie, P. *Disappearance.* New York: Rinehart, 1951.

Additional References

Adams, D. "Building moral dilemma activities." *Learning,* March 1977, *5*(7), 44.

Bricher, D. C. "Moral education and teacher neutrality." *School review,* 1972, *80*(4), 619–627.

Etzioni, A. "Do as I say, not as I do." *New York Times magazine,* September 26, 1976, 44.

Galbraith, R., & Jones, T. M. *Moral reasoning: a teacher's handbook for adapting Kohlberg to the classroom.* Minneapolis: Greenhaven Press, 1976.

Hall, R., & Davis, J. *Moral education in theory and practice.* New York: Prometheus Books, 1975.

Kuhmerker, L. (Ed.). *Moral education forum.* New York: Hunter College, 1976.

Lasseigne, M. W. "A study of peer and adult influence on moral beliefs of adolescents." *Adolescence,* Summer 1975, *10*(38), 227–230.

Leming, J. S. "Moral reasoning, sense of control, and social-political activism among adolescents." *Adolescence,* Winter, 1974, *9*(36), 507–528.

Lickona, T. (Ed.). *Moral development and behavior: theory, research, and social issues.* Holt, Rinehart, & Winston, 1976.

Mitchell, J. J. "Moral growth during adolescence." *Adolescence,* Summer 1975, *10*(38), 221–226.

Mitchell, J. J. "Moral dilemmas of early adolescence." *Adolescence,* Fall 1975, *10*(39), 442–446.

Rubin, K. H., & Schneider, F. W. "The relationship between moral judgment, egocentricism, and altruistic behavior." *Child development,* 1973, *44*(3), 661–665.

Sullivan, E. *Moral learning: findings, issues and questions.* New York: Paulist/Newman Press, 1975.

Tapp, J. L., & Kohlberg, L. "Developing senses of law and legal justice." *Journal of social issues,* 1971, *27,* 65–91.

Weinrich, H. "The structure of moral reason." *Journal of youth and adolescence,* 1974, *3*(2), 135–143.

part 2

Interactions with the Environment

The patterns of human development that are genetic in origin have been relatively unchanged over the years. Conversely, the impact of the environment has radically altered behavior. The degree of change in our culture has probably never been greater than in the twentieth century, and the last two decades have been peak periods of variation.

In Part 2, we consider how adolescent behavior is influenced by eight aspects of the cultural environment: the family, peer groups and subcultures, love and sexual relationships, schools, drug use and abuse, mental and physical health, delinquency, and value patterns. In general, the results of our analysis are less than encouraging.

Yet the situation is far from hopeless. In each chapter, suggestions for coping with current problems are made. I hope these suggestions will prove useful in practice, and more important, that they will serve as springboards for new and creative insights. Readers who attempt their own solutions will not only understand the material better, but they may also produce new ideas that society badly needs.

Chapter Six

The Changing American Family

Chapter Highlights

The Changing Status of the American Family
  The End of the Extended Family
  Divorce
  Working Mothers and Nurturing
    Fathers
  Families and the Courts
  Parental Attitudes
  The Change from Primary to Secondary Group
    Status
  Your Family's Values
The Effects on Adolescents of the Changing Status
  of the Family
  The Loss of Functions
  Fewer Adult Models
  The Increase in Age-Related Activities
  The New Individualism
  Inappropriate Family Patterns
  Momism: A Special Case
  The Generation Gap
  The Mini-Generation Gap
The Effects of Birth Order
  Are You What Your Birth Order Has Made You?
Coping with Change
  Ginott's Advice to Parents
  My Family Tree
  Alternatives to the Traditional Family
Summary

Key Terms and Concepts

extended family
nuclear family
incorrigible child
emancipated minor
primary groups
secondary groups
cofigurative culture
momism
cultural lag
mini-generation gap
birth order
other-borns
center-of-the-world status
duplication theory
commune
open marriage
swinging
companionship marriage

Important People

Urie Bronfenbrenner
Kenneth Keniston
Haim Ginott

*Mr. Hackett sank into his seat at the supper table with a deep-drawn
sigh, as he glanced from one to another of his seven hearty growing
children, who with hungry eyes and ill-concealed patience, were waiting
for the preliminary grace. Mr. Hackett had repeated these words three
times a day ever since his marriage, as had his father before him.*
—Saybrook, 1869, p. 1.

O f all the changes in American society in recent years, those affecting the
American family have probably been the most extensive. And perhaps nothing has had a greater effect on adolescents than alterations in family living patterns. This chapter looks at the current status of the American family, investi-
gates the effects of family changes on adolescents, and makes suggestions as to
how these changes can be coped with more readily.

THE CHANGING STATUS OF THE AMERICAN FAMILY

If youth are revolting, as some suggest, is the current situation so different from
the past? Jencks and Reismann (1967) and Aries (1962) think not. What is different is that before the twentieth century, young people seldom challenged the
legitimacy of their elders' control over them.

> *In the twentieth century, on the other hand, the increasing separatism of
> teenage culture and the massing together of very large numbers of people
> of identical age and social conditions have gradually led to a new atmo-
> sphere in which the basic legitimacy of adult authority has been increasingly
> called into question (Jencks and Reismann, 1967, p. 86).*

This major shift in attitude is a direct result of the new status of the American
family.

The End of the Extended Family

The **extended family** that was characteristic of American society in the last
century consisted of a mother, a father, their children, some relatives, or additional members of the household such as a hired helper, a maid, or a boarder.

Since 1850 there has been a steady trend away from the extended family toward the **nuclear family**, limited to a mother, a father, and (fewer) children.

Most remaining houses in the older neighborhoods of American cities are very large, not so much because labor and building materials were cheaper a hundred years ago, but because of family size. In 1850, for example, the average size of the American household, including both relatives and nonrelatives, was eight; that is, half of the households in the United States had more than eight people living in them. Today the average household size is 2.3 people, and this figure is continually dropping. Much of this change is the result of the move from farms (90 percent of all families were rural in 1850) to cities, in order to take advantage of the opportunities provided by the industrial-technological revolution. Birth rates declined as the economic necessity for child farm labor diminished. In our sprawling cities, the effects of overcrowding and the high cost of raising a family have been factors in lower birth rates. In the past decade, few commodities have more steeply increased in price than housing, heat, and food. Unfortunately, poor and minority families have always had the most children and are least able to afford them (Lefrancois, 1976).

Divorce

We have experienced a dizzying climb in the divorce rate in our country in recent years. The present estimated rate is about 40 percent for the United States as a whole, and in some sections of the country, notably California, the divorce rate has soared to over 70 percent (Woodward, 1978). For those who have children, the rate (based on Census bureau statistics) will be even higher; about 45 percent will divorce before the children reach 18 (Levine, 1978).

Largely as a result of divorce, over one-sixth of all children in the United States live with only one parent, natural or otherwise. In these families, the head of the household is usually a woman, and she almost always works full time. This change has been astonishingly abrupt. In 1960, 75 percent of nonwhite children and 92 percent of white children lived in two-parent homes (Sudia, 1973). By 1970, these figures had changed to 64 percent and 90 percent, respectively. In 1976, *one out of every three* children did not live with both natural parents (Sebald, 1977).

Working Mothers and Nurturing Fathers

Fifty percent of the women who have school-age children are now employed, at least part time (Bronfenbrenner, 1977). Of those who have children under three years of age, one-third are working. Bronfenbrenner and others have warned of a serious negative impact on these children, but Hoffman (1974) conducted a careful investigation of the differences between the children of working and nonworking mothers and was unable to find any significant effects. Although current research is inconclusive about the effects of working mothers on children, it is likely many factors are involved, for example, whether or not the mother enjoys working. If she does, she may compensate her children for her absence by her greater satisfaction with life. If she doesn't, she may feel that her family ought to compensate her.

In some Israeli kibbutzim (small agricultural villages), both parents in every family work all day. The children are cared for by trained professionals. Most observers (such as Bettelheim, 1969; Long, Henderson, and Platt, 1973) have noted that the high quality of parent-child interaction during nonworking hours more than makes up for maternal absence. The presence of excellent maternal substitutes in many American homes such as grandparents and older babysitters probably also alleviates negative effects. However, such substitutes are often unavailable, and lack of an adult presence undoubtedly contributes to teenage social misbehavior.

Although most fathers still work full time, many are beginning to take an increasing role in the training and caretaking of children, at least in upper- and middle-class families. This change is strongly supported by teenagers today. In one study of university men (McIntyre, Nass, and Battistone, 1974), 88 percent rated the role of father as important as the role of mother, and almost as many believed that husbands should help their wives with child care and housework. Some scientists, looking at the social relationships of lower mammals, have argued that it is unnatural for males to be involved in nurturing children ("Why You Do What You Do," 1977), but others believe that humans' greater cultural adaptability and lesser dependence on biological instincts allow them greater flexibility in their relationships. Bronfenbrenner (1977) has observed a number of societies where men play a large role in child care, in which they are as effective as women.

Families and the Courts

Until recently, children were under the legal jurisdiction of their parents until they reached the age of at least 18, and in some cases 21. Recent state and Supreme Court decisions have redefined the rights of youth in many ways. In almost all states now, teenagers may get medical attention without securing the permission of their parents, and in many states, this medical attention extends to birth control, drug addiction, mental disorders, abortion, and the treatment of contagious diseases. In some states, teenagers may also refuse medical attention such as abortions, even if their parents insist on it. Not all approve of the current emphasis on children's rights. Baumrind (1974) has argued it has encouraged self-centered behavior, and suggests that courts need to pay more attention to responsibilities of youth as well as to their rights.

Although parents have a legal obligation to support their children (unless they are penniless), in a number of states they can escape this responsibility by going to court and declaring their child, almost always an adolescent, **incorrigible** or uncontrollable (Eagan, 1976). If the judge agrees, the child becomes a ward of the state and can be placed in reform school until 21. The increase in runaways is one reason why more and more parents are turning to the courts to govern their teenagers (see Chapter 12).

In some states, a new category of **emancipated minor** has been created to include those adolescents who are under the legal age, but are self-supporting. The status category is ambiguous. Parents lose some but not all of their rights of control over the child, but often what control is retained has yet to be worked out. In some states emancipated minors can be prosecuted by their parents for promiscuity if they are found living with a person of the opposite sex.

Parental Attitudes

Responsibility and control.   Beginning with Freud, many have argued that parental strictness is the cause of much adolescent neurosis. Parents have been urged to be more permissive with their children and at the same time have been made to feel more responsible for their psychological well being. The widespread acceptance of psychological responsibility, coupled with an ever-lengthening period of financial responsibility for their children's education, has made the job of being a parent considerably more difficult (Vincent, 1972).

Troubled by unsettling changes in social patterns, adults have increasingly sought advice on parenting from newspaper columnists, authors of books and magazine articles, and family counselors. According to psychologist Kenneth Keniston (1977), these "experts" are contributing to the problems of the family by giving contradictory advice. For example, while child psychoanalysts advise parents to pay close attention to their children's fantasies, fears, and dreams, behaviorists urge they ignore these and reward desired behavior. Most advice-givers appear to assume that parents are almost totally responsible for their children's development.

Salzman (1973) thinks that parents' feeling more responsible has had the negative effect of making them less and less willing to relinquish parental control, which they may attempt to maintain past the age of adolescence. They fear to grant their child independence because if the child misuses it, the parents may appear to be at fault.

Identification with adolescent values.   Perhaps for the first time in history, we see parents imitating the values and behaviors of their children, perhaps as an attempt to adapt to the times, perhaps because they are not sure of their own values. Gunter and Moore (1975) have suggested that parents often see their children as their only link to the fast-changing world. In an attempt to be "with it," they adopt the dances, music, language, and even drug habits of their children. Note, for example, the popularity of the Beatles among middle-aged people during the early 1970s, following by a few years their children's infatuation with this group. This trend clearly has contributed to the decrease of influence of adults on teenagers today. In one sense, it is natural that there be a relationship between parental and teenage values, because they often have in common their self-doubts over their identity. "Adolescence arrives at a rather unhandy time for some parents. It comes at a time when middle-age parents are asking 'Who am I, what have I accomplished, where am I now, and what does the future hold for me?' " (Rice, 1978, p. 399).

The Change from Primary to Secondary Group Status

Sociologists differentiate between **primary groups** and **secondary groups** in the social life of human beings. The primary group is one in which there is "intimate face-to-face interaction and spontaneous cooperation. It is primary in that it is instrumental in generating the social nature of the individual" (Sebald, 1977, p. 155). Secondary groups are less permanent, involve more casual contacts between the members, generate less deep sentiment, and have less of an impact on the basic values of the members. The families of many teenagers are dropping from a primary to a secondary group status, and most often the new group that takes over primary status in the teenager's life is the peer group. While this is inevitable—and healthy—if it happens too early the benefits of association with the older members of one's family are lost. Bronfenbrenner (1970) puts it succinctly: "[Children] should not grow up associating only with other children because they haven't much to give each other" (p. 37).

THE EFFECTS ON ADOLESCENTS OF THE CHANGING STATUS OF THE FAMILY*

The Loss of Functions

In 1850 the American family fulfilled six major functions: economic-productive, educational, religious, recreational, medical, and affectional. Today the first five are taken over by the factory and office, schools, the church or synagogue, commercial institutions, and the doctor's office and hospital. It appears that the family has been left to provide but one single function—affection for its members.

One hundred years ago, parents and children needed each other more than now, for three major reasons (Coleman, 1961).

Vocational instruction. For both males and females, the parent of the same sex taught them their adult jobs. Most men were farmers and most women,

---

*For many of the ideas in this section, the author is indebted to sociologist H. Sebald of Arizona State University. His theories may be read in greater detail in his *Adolescence: A Social Psychological Analysis,* 2nd ed. (Englewood Cliffs, N.J.: Prentice-Hall, 1977).

Your Family's Values

In the spaces provided below, write the three things you think your mother would say she values most about your family and the three things she dislikes most about it. Do the same for your father, brothers, and sisters. Then write or call each and ask them their answers to these questions. The comparison between what they say and what you thought they would say should provide a good index of how well you understand each of them.

Relative	Things Most Valued	Things Most Disliked
Mother	1. _____ 2. _____ 3. _____	1. _____ 2. _____ 3. _____
Father	1. _____ 2. _____ 3. _____	1. _____ 2. _____ 3. _____
Brother	1. _____ 2. _____ 3. _____	1. _____ 2. _____ 3. _____
Sister	1. _____ 2. _____ 3. _____	1. _____ 2. _____ 3. _____
Brother	1. _____ 2. _____ 3. _____	1. _____ 2. _____ 3. _____
Sister	1. _____ 2. _____ 3. _____	1. _____ 2. _____ 3. _____

housewives. Parents knew all the secrets of work, secrets passed on from genera-tion to generation. Today, nearly 100 percent of men work at jobs different from their fathers, and an increasing percentage of women are not primarily house-wives like their mothers.

Economic value.   Adolescents were a vital economic asset on the farm; without children, the farmer would have had to hire others to help him. Work was a source of pride to the children. It was immediately and abundantly clear that they were important to the family. Today, instead of being an economic asset, most children are an economic burden on the family's resources.

Social stability.   When families almost never moved from their home-towns, parents were a crucial source of information about how to live in the town, knowing all the intricacies of small-town social relationships. One depended on one's parents to know what to do. Today, when the average family moves three times in the first ten years of its existence, and the average American moves every five years, the adults are as much strangers in a new place as the children. In fact, with Dad driving out of the neighborhood to work and Mom to the store or her own work, the children may well know the neighborhood better than they do.

The constant migration to new places in which the elders are as much strangers as the young, and the development of new forms of technology in which the elders are not expert has resulted in what Margaret Mead (1970) refers to as **cofigurative culture.** This is a culture in which the model for the young is the behavior of their own contemporaries.

Fewer Adult Models

Bronfenbrenner (1977) suggests that the ideal home situation for a child of any age is to be around one adult who is affectionate and uncritical and another, more objective adult who decidedly is not. This situation was more likely to exist in earlier times when members of the household included parents, other rela-tives, and nonrelatives. In Steinbeck's *The Red Pony* (1966), the boy has a father who criticizes practically all of his behavior, and a hired man who supplies the support and perspective that the boy needs to view reality more clearly. With fathers away from the home and mothers increasingly away, teenagers seldom experience this ideal situation.

And with parents absent so much, teenagers are not only not told what to do; they also get very little chance to watch what adults do. The absence of relevant adult models has become a serious problem. One sociologist, Barrington Moore (1960), has even suggested that we abandon the family and replace it with a more modern equivalent because we can no longer afford to have teenagers growing up with inadequate or absent adult models. The practice of having pro-fessionals play a large role as parent substitutes, as in Israel and Russia, is becom-ing more popular in many other countries.

The Increase in Age-Related Activities

The change from family to peer group influence has been accelerated by the specialization of the entertainment industry and the media. Both participatory entertainment such as sports and spectator entertainment such as television are more and more aimed at specific age groups. Therefore, everyone, teenagers included, tend to prefer to watch or participate in recreational activities only with members of their own age group.

Television has been especially powerful in this changeover. When teenagers reach 18, they typically will have watched twice as many hours of television as they will have spent in the classroom. These activities isolate teenagers more and more from adults, who spend less time watching television, and force them to rely on friends for security and values orientation.

Bronfenbrenner (1977) found that as teenagers depend more on their friends, they are more likely to view their parents as lacking in affection and not very firm in discipline; they also show greater pessimism about the future, rank lower in responsibility and leadership, and are more likely to engage in antisocial behavior.

On the other hand, we should remember that the shift in allegiance from family to friends is a natural one. Teenagers need the support of their peer group in order to try out new values, to gain skills in problem solving, and to develop their own identities. Furthermore, as they begin to realize that adults have special privileges because of their independence, they naturally want to imitate this independence, even if it means rebelling against parental rules. There has been considerable debate in recent years as to whether rebelliousness is a necessary part of growing up. Most researchers have come to the conclusion that adolescence need not be (and usually is not) a period of extreme turmoil. When teenagers realize that they can count on the support and love of parents who are willing to let go, they make the transition to independence with relative ease.

The New Individualism

One of the clearest effects of the change in family structure has been a new emphasis on satisfying personal needs and desires over loyalty to other members of the family. If the family does not suit the needs of the individual, he or she may leave. Almost a half-million teenagers run away from home every year. The divorce rate shows that many adults, discontented with their family lives, also leave. Many of the elderly are forced to leave when their needs interfere with those of other family members. The media have assisted this trend toward individualism, according to Bronfenbrenner (1977), by depicting the American family as either "a farce, a fairy tale, or a fight," and often as elements of all three.

The major effects of divorce on adolescents (Sorosky, 1977) are four: a sense of rejection and a fear of abandonment; an increased disruption of the typical adolescent conflicts; a fear that his or her own marriage will be a failure (a reasonable fear because children of divorced couples *are* more likely to suffer marriage difficulties); and a *sense* of confusion and disillusionment about life. Sorosky (1977) urges that

> even though [parents] are unable to resolve the hostility that exists between them, they must make every effort to avoid using their children as pawns and to treat them as individuals with personal needs and concerns. What these youngsters are looking for, more than anything else, is a reestablishment of "generation boundaries" in which they can relate to their parents as authority figures, not friends. The parents, including stepparents, must work together, as best they can, to provide loving support as well as firm limits and controls. This will enable their adolescents to continue growing toward individualization; acceptance, expression, and control of aggressive and sexual impulses; identity formation; security in the peer world and a healthy, positive attitude toward the future (p. 134).

Nevertheless, the new individualism has not made Americans wish to abandon marriage and the family (note the high remarriage rate), but rather has led to a search for the skills necessary to maintain good interpersonal relationships. As Sebald (1977) puts it, "Such skills are called for by the abandonment of safe but rigid roles and the adoption of a highly individualistic style that requires sensitivity and increased amounts of communication, and constantly new interpretations of new interactional relations" (p. 145).

Another reflection of the new individualism is the change from status ascription to status achievement. In earlier times, the individual's place in society was defined by his family's; that is, his status was ascribed by the status of his parents. If the young man's father was a lawyer, it was extremely unlikely that he would become a farmer, or vice versa. Today, in most cases, one must achieve one's *own* status in society. This new individualism could produce a family in which the father was a salesman in a department store, the mother a lawyer, their daughter a surgeon, and their son an unemployed artist.

Inappropriate Family Patterns

Jenkins (1969), who has done research on destructiveness among adolescents, has discovered three patterns of family organization leading to negative development, which include the extremes of overcontrol (repression and rejection) and undercontrol (negligence). Table 6–1 summarizes the factors in inappropriate family patterns. Although these patterns cannot be said to be common, there is reason to believe that they are becoming more typical as a result of family disintegration.

Momism: A Special Case

The term **momism** was first coined by Philip Wylie in his best-selling book, *Generation of Vipers* (1942), and has been expanded considerably by Sebald

TABLE 6-1
FACTORS IN INAPPROPRIATE FAMILY PATTERNS

Parenting Style	Result	Position of Child in Family	Number of Children in Family	Typical Parental Marital Situation
Repression of child's desires	Anxious, inhibited child	Youngest	2–3	Natural parents
Rejection of child in general (especially maternal)	Unsocialized, aggressive child	Not youngest	4 or more	Mother, stepfather, or father, stepmother
Negligence, disinterest	Delinquent behavior	Not youngest	4 or more	Mother, stepfather

Note: This table is a summary of the findings of Jenkins (1969).

(1976). Momism refers to the tendency of some mothers to use their children, typically their sons, to gratify their own neurotic needs and anxieties. The mother most vulnerable to this problem is the "half-liberated American female," the person who has been made to feel guilty about "only being a housewife." To justify not following a career, she must become the perfect mother of perfect children, and to achieve this she asserts control of her children by creating dependence and then threatening to withdraw emotional support.

Momism can only flourish when the father is absent, away a good deal, or an extremely ineffectual person. Boys are more vulnerable to momism than girls. The male, lacking an effective model for his behavior, is confused and disoriented, and therefore more dependent upon his mother.

Sebald summarizes the typical "Mom" as someone who (1) is middle class, (2) is more educated than most and has read a good deal about "scientific child-rearing," (3) uses mothering as evidence of her personal competence, (4) has no husband or one who is only peripherally involved with the family, (5) has a son whom she uses to assuage her feelings of being deprived, and (6) has mastered the "giving and withdrawing love" technique.

What are the effects of momism? The son who has been subjected to this neurotic pattern tends to be (1) unable to make decisions, (2) subject to feelings of inferiority, (3) subject to high levels of anxiety, (4) unusually irresponsible, and (5) subject to high levels of narcissism and egocentricism.

The Generation Gap

Although many have written about the psychological, sociological, and philosophical gap between the generations (Margaret Mead has called it more of a chasm than a gap), the best summary comes to us from Sebald (1977), who suggests there are several steps in the process. Parents, he believes, suffer from a never-ending **cultural lag;** they are always behind their children in knowing "the latest" — that is, the latest information, which includes the latest trends and language important to youth. Because parents are ignorant of this special information, adolescents tend to generalize that their parents are basically ignorant. When parents nevertheless insist on being in authority over their children, their children see this claim as irrational.

Using this complaint, which often appears to be valid, youth are in an advantageous position to manipulate the older generation. Angry at being made to feel inferior to adults, teenagers do their best to make adults feel inferior, too, and of late they have been rather successful. This situation "goads intergenerational dissonance to soaring heights."

Adults tend to react by being either permissive or authoritarian, two reactions that appear to take turns as the prevailing national mood toward adolescence. Confronted with inconsistency, teenagers react by taking advantage during the permissive periods and with sullen contrariness during the authoritarian periods.

Some say that events of recent years, such as the end of the Vietnamese war and high unemployment, are narrowing the generation gap because these are problems that affect all generations. Whether or not this is true, it is safe to say that the problem of faulty communications between age groups is serious, and it appears that it will be for some time to come.

The Mini-Generation Gap

The term *generation gap* refers to the significant difference in values held by members of one generation from those held by members of the next generation. This difference has existed for many years. Lately, however, there appear to be growing differences in values even between those who are much closer in age, so fast is our world changing. For example, college professors are beginning to note that the thinking of freshmen is less and less like that of seniors.

Here is an exercise in examining this **mini-generation gap.** Contact a person currently in junior high school (a high school student will do, but not as well). Plan a personal interview if possible or one by letter or phone if not. Before the interview, briefly write down your view of the morality of each of the behaviors below. Then note what the younger person thinks and compare the two. Is there a mini-generation gap?

Behavior	Your View	Younger Person's View
1. Cheating on a test.	_____	_____
2. Stealing small sum from your mother's purse.	_____	_____
3. Stealing over $5.	_____	_____

4. Stealing inexpensive items
    from a store.

    _____   _____

5. Driving 10 miles per hour
    over the speed limit.

    _____   _____

6. Lying about your age in a
    bar.

    _____   _____

7. Using a contraceptive
    device.

    _____   _____

8. Having intercourse with
    more than one person.

    _____   _____

9. Giving an untrue excuse
    when you don't want to do
    something.

    _____   _____

THE EFFECTS OF BIRTH ORDER

So far in this chapter, we have been discussing the relationship between adolescents and their parents. It is clear, however, that the relationships among adolescents and their brothers and sisters also have a decided effect on personality development. One researcher, Toman (1970), has gone so far as to suggest that "birth order rules all." Although this may be an overstatement, **birth order** certainly does make a considerable difference to personality. The most significant differences appear to be between firstborn children and those born later (called **other-borns**). Differences in personality between second- and third-borns, middle- and last-borns, and so on are much less striking. This goes against popular beliefs (such as that last-borns are usually more selfish), but when we consider possible reasons for differences between first- and other-borns, the finding is not surprising. The most widely held theory suggests that firstborns, of all children, have the unique perception of themselves as the center of their world until, with the birth of a sibling, they lose that favored position. It is natural that the firstborn, the only child to experience the undivided attention of parents and relatives, should become egocentric. It is also natural that this child should greatly resent the loss of unique status. If the change is traumatic, the firstborn's sense of basic trust will be damaged. Children without siblings have the firstborn's center-of-the-world status, but don't experience its loss. We would therefore expect to find the effects of the firstborn's status to be mixed, and we do.

Are You What Your Birth Order Has Made You?

In the spaces below, list five of your personality characteristics that you feel are the most admirable and the five that are the least admirable. Ask several friends or relatives what they think these characteristics are in themselves, and compare your list to theirs.

Most Admirable Characteristics	Least Admirable Characteristics
1._____	1._____
2._____	2._____
3._____	3._____
4._____	4._____
5._____	5._____

How well does the description in the text of persons with your birth order fit your description of yourself? If it does not, why not? The most complete description is of firstborns. If you are not a firstborn, how well do you think the description fits your oldest brother or sister? Do you believe that "birth order rules all"?

Firstborns differ from other-borns in that they tend to be

1. More anxious. They worry a lot. There is some evidence that firstborns are more likely to become neurotic (develop phobias and obsessions), but *less* likely to become psychotic.

2. More interested in social approval. This may explain the relative absence of psychosis (psychotics are generally antisocial).

3. More sensitive to the feelings of others. They are more empathetic, but often less sympathetic, than other-borns.

4. More successful economically.

5. Less successful emotionally. MacDonald (1965) found firstborns to be poorer marriage risks. He found happiness in marriage to be ordered, from high to low, as follows:
   a. Other-born male to other-born female.
   b. Firstborn male to other-born female.
   c. Other-born male to firstborn female.
   d. Firstborn male to firstborn female.

6. More creative.

7. **More intelligent.** This is probably due to the greater attention received in the first year of life. There is also some evidence that the mother's hormonal pattern is permanently altered by the birth of the first child, which might affect the intelligence of children born later.

8. **More likely found in the ranks of eminent people.** For example, Lefrancois (1976) reports that of the first twenty-three astronauts to travel in space, twenty-one were firstborns, one had one brother who died in infancy, and one was thirteen years younger than his brother.

9. **Better achievers in school at all levels.**

10. **More reflective, less impulsive.**

11. **Stronger in conscience and more moral in behavior.** Some think this is the result of the stricter discipline firstborns receive, especially from the father.

12. **Finally, firstborns feel they are "different."** And, as the above indicates, they are. This frequently causes them to vacillate between egotism and self-rejection, which in turn results in a loss of self-confidence.

The differences attributed to firstborns may be due to factors other than place in the family. Many eminent people are born to families that are smaller and better educated and their achievement may be the result of educational and cultural advantages rather than birth order (Fortes, 1974; Schooler, 1974; Thompson, 1974). Toman (1970) thinks that in addition to one's place in the family, the sex of his or her siblings makes a big difference in a person's relationships to others in later life.

> *My research has led me to formulate the* **duplication theory**; *the kinds of persons one chooses as a spouse, friends, partner and such, will be determined partially by the kinds of persons he has lived with longest and most intimately. All new relationships to some degree* duplicate *the old ones. The more complete the duplication, the greater the chance that the relationship will last and be happy (p. 45).*

Perhaps the marital happiness ratings suggested by MacDonald are too simplistic. As Toman explains it,

> *Suppose that the older brother of a sister marries the younger sister of a brother. They are getting in marriage precisely the peer relation that they had at home. He is used to a girl his junior, and she to a boy her senior. There should be no conflict over their dominant rights. . . . The worst of all possible matches, roughly speaking, would be the youngest brother of brothers and the youngest sister of sisters. Each would find it difficult to accept the other sex, and there would be constant conflict over dependency needs (p. 45).*

Toman suggests that the following traits tend to characterize each of these types of persons:

- Older brother of brothers: aggressive, assertive, a leader.
- Youngest brother of brothers: capricious, willful, daring, but irritating.
- Oldest brother of sisters: a true ladies' man, a responsible worker, and a good father.
- Younger brother of sisters: girls adore him, love to take care of him. He is somewhat irresponsible and dependent on others for his needs.
- Oldest sister of sisters: dominant, assertive, bossy, self-confident, creative.
- Youngest sister of sisters: charming, adventurous, enthusiastic, willful.
- Oldest sister of brothers: practical, concrete, a good sport and popular with others.
- Youngest sister of brothers: feminine, tactful, submissive but not subservient, an excellent companion.
- Others: a mixture of these traits.

COPING WITH CHANGE

Ginott's Advice to Parents

The late psychologist Haim Ginott was extremely popular for the straightforward advice he gave parents on how to deal with their children. In his best-selling book, *Between Parent and Teenager* (1969), he lists fifteen suggestions for helping parents get along better with teenagers. They are also useful for teachers and others who work with adolescents.

1. Accept the adolescent's restlessness and discontent.
2. Don't try to be *too* understanding. Most particularly, don't say "I know exactly how you feel." No one wants to be so transparent, so simple, when they believe themselves to be so complex, so mysterious, and so inscrutable.
3. Differentiate between acceptance and approval.
4. Don't emulate the teenager's language and conduct.
5. Don't "collect thorns." It is often too threatening to a teenager to have to cope with his personal faults. It does little good to "fling his flaws in his face."
6. Don't "step on corns." All teenagers suspect that they have not really left their childhood yet and therefore are very sensitive to being treated like a baby.
7. Don't invite dependence. The wise parent is sympathetic to his child's growth, tries to make himself dispensable, and resists the desire to intervene too often.

8. Don't hurry to correct facts. "Truth without compassion can destroy love."

9. Don't violate the teenager's privacy.

10. Try to avoid preaching and the use of clichés.

11. Most particularly, try not to lecture.

12. Don't label the teenager in his presence.

13. Don't use reverse psychology. Avoid statements like, "You probably won't be able to do this."

14. Try not to send contradictory messages. For example, don't say things like, "I hope you have a very good time — of course, I won't be able to sleep until you get back."

15. Don't futurize. No one can be sure what his future will bring. If you predict your teenager's future, you may be creating a self-fulfilling prophecy.

Alternatives to the Traditional Family

Because of the considerable discontent that many experience today with traditional family structure and roles, two types of alternatives are being tried out on a wide scale. One is communal living and the other involves experimentation within the structure of marriage.

The commune.   The move to the **commune** has been mainly a young people's movement, which began in the early 1960s and reached a peak around 1970. Groups of families sharing basic community tasks appear to have numerous advantages (Eiduson, 1974). Among these are the greater numbers of people in the commune family that allow for a greater variety of relationships, a greater interest in the education of each other and the children, a greater involvement of fathers with their children, and more relaxed child-rearing practices in which brutality and child-battering are extremely rare.

Still, the success rate of the commune has been low. There are still many in existence, but the great majority have failed, and there are far fewer communes today than there were ten years ago. Perhaps, for many "a commune is really an attempt to run away from basic developmental tasks, an excuse to avoid responsibilities, and a confusion between reality and utopia ... Maybe the fact that youthful communes have an extremely short life span and an exasperatingly high turnover of members bespeaks the pseudo-solution that these alternatives represent" (Sebald, 1977). Many communes seem to have failed precisely because of the good-heartedness of the people who founded them. As one commune founder complained, "There were too many empty people who had come to fill themselves, sapping our energies, needing to be taken care of, and giving nothing at all" (Gardener, 1973).

Experiments within marriage.   Probably far more widespread have been experimental innovations within marriage itself. The **open marriage**, in which

My Family Tree

In the boxes below, list the following information about your family: A, name of your relative; B, number of children; C, main place of residence; D, highest level of education; E, age at marriage; F, occupation; and G, some other fact of your choosing. Can you detect any patterns of change over the generations, such as fewer children, later age at marriage, occupational level, and the like?

A. _____

B. _____

C. _____

D. _____

E. _____

F. _____

G. _____

Maternal Greatgrandparents

A. _____   A. _____

B. _____   B. _____

C. _____   C. _____

D. _____   D. _____

E. _____   E. _____

F. _____   F. _____

G. _____   G. _____

Paternal Greatgrandparents

A. _____   A. _____

B. _____   B. _____

C. _____   C. _____

D. _____   D. _____

E. _____   E. _____

F. _____   F. _____

G. _____   G. _____

Paternal Grandparents

A. _____

B. _____

C. _____

D. _____

E. _____

F. _____

G. _____

Father

A. _____

B. _____

C. _____

D. _____

E. _____

F. _____

G. _____

Maternal Grandparents

A. _____

B. _____

C. _____

D. _____

E. _____

F. _____

G. _____

Mother

A. _____

B. _____

C. _____

D. _____

E. _____

F. _____

G. _____

partners publicly allow each other to have love and sometimes sexual relationships with others, has been tried by some. **Swinging**, in which couples get together with other couples specifically for sexual intimacy, has also gained some popularity. But both of these innovations are still restricted to a very small minority of married people. Far more common today is the **companionship marriage**, in which both of the partners try for equity, flexibility, and a deep sense of intimacy in their relationship (Mace and Mace, 1975). Confrontations, marriage encounters, and sexual therapy are ways in which partners in companionship marriages have attempted to improve the quality of their relationships.

It appears that the marriage relationship in some form is here to stay for the foreseeable future. But it also seems clear that the traditional family, in which the husband made most of the decisions, the wife accepted them, and the couple was devoted not to each other but to their children, is becoming a thing of the past.

Living together. In her well-designed study of cohabitation at Cornell University, Macklin (1974) found that the number of unmarried couples living together is increasing steadily, and mainly for one simple reason: students do not see any reason not to. Of the several explanations offered by the students she interviewed, by far the most common was, "It's more convenient." It seems likely that many will continue to find it convenient, at least until they decide they want to have children together.

Like the companionship marriage, cohabitation usually results in an even distribution of responsibilities between partners. In most cases, finances are separate. These arrangements appear to have made cohabitation increasingly popular with newly divorced 25- to 45-year-olds, too.

Both cohabitation and companionship marriage are becoming more acceptable to society in general. Whether either will prove to foster the relatively permanent commitment we expect of partners in the traditional family remains to be seen.

SUMMARY

Today American families are smaller, serve fewer functions, and are less stable than they were one hundred years ago when most families lived on farms. Since 1850 extended families and large households have been replaced by smaller nuclear families composed of parents (or a parent) and their children. Today the divorce rate is 45 percent, and one-sixth of all children in the United States live in single-parent homes. In 1850 the American family fulfilled six major functions: (1) economic-productive, (2) educational, (3) religious, (4) recreational, (5) medical, and (6) affectional. Today only the last function is performed by the family to any great degree. In the past the pleasures of parenthood were augmented by the economic assistance they received from their children. Today parents have an ever-lengthening period of financial responsibility for their children.

Because families fulfill few functions and because of the absence from home of working mothers, families may be shifting from a primary to secondary group status. Cofigurative cultural changes in societal attitudes and government policy have made the job of being a parent more difficult than ever. The acceptance of psychological theories of child development has increased the emotional responsibilities of parenting.

One especially difficult problem in parenting is "momism." In this case, the mother (or occasionally the father) uses her children to gratify a neurotic need to be a perfect parent. Doubtful of the importance of motherhood in a liberated world, and yet unwilling to seek other satisfactions (such as a career), this mother strives to make her children faultless extensions of herself. By carefully extending and then withholding her love, she forces her children, and most especially her oldest son, into pathological dependence on her.

The generation gap has contributed to family disunity; it is the result of a cultural lag between parental knowledge and perceptions and the latest information affecting their young.

There appear to be numerous effects resulting from one's order of birth in the family. By far the most significant differences lie between firstborns and the other siblings in a family; those traits that characterize first-borns are higher anxiety, intelligence, sensitivity, need for social approval, creativity, economic success, reflectivity, and level of morality.

A number of alternatives to the traditional American family structure have arisen. Two which grew in popularity in the 1960s, the commune and the "open" marriage, now seem to be on the decline. The companionship marriage, in which the partners seek equity, flexibility, and deep intimacy, is now gaining. The traditional family, with the father as sole authority, seems destined for considerable renovation.

Questions

1. What has caused the decline of the extended family?
2. What impact has the sharing of responsibilities by mother and father had on the home? What has been the impact of the divorce rate?
3. What were the major functions the family fulfilled in the past? What are they today?
4. Why has there been a change in adult role models in recent years?
5. What is your opinion of television's impact on the American family?
6. Define "status ascription" and "status achievement."
7. Do you think the generation gap will widen or narrow? Why?
8. Do you think any of the alternatives to the traditional family will be successful? Why?

References

Aries, P.   *Centuries of childhood.* New York: Vintage Press, 1962.
Bettelheim, B.   *The children of the dream.* New York: Macmillan, 1969.

Bronfenbrenner, U. *Two worlds of childhood: U.S. and U.S.S.R.* New York: Russell Sage Foundation, 1970.

Bronfenbrenner, U. "Nobody home: the erosion of the American family." *Psychology today,* May 1977, *10*(12), 40.

Coleman, J. S. *The adolescent society.* Glencoe, Ill.: Free Press, 1961.

Eagan, A. B. *Why am I so miserable if these are the best years of my life?* Boston: Lippincott, 1976.

Eiduson, B. T. "Looking at children in emergent family styles." *Children today,* 1974, *3*(4), 2-6.

Fortes, M. "The first born." *Journal of child psychology and psychiatry,* 1974, *15*(2), 81-104.

Gardener, J. "Communal living: economic survival and family life." In G. E. Streib (Ed.), *Changing family adaptation and diversity.* Reading, Mass.: Addison-Wesley, 1973.

Ginott, H. G. *Between parent and teenager.* New York: Macmillan, 1969.

Gunter, B. G., & Moore, H. A. "Youth, leisure, and post-industrial society: implications for the family." *Family coordinator,* 1975, *24*(2), 199-207.

Hoffman, L. W. "Effects of maternal employment on the child: a review of the research." *Developmental psychology,* 1974, *10*(2), 204-228.

Jencks, C., & Riesman, D. "The war between the generations." *Teachers college record,* 1967, *69*(1), 1-21.

Jenkins, R. "The varieties of children's behavioral problems and family dynamics." *American journal of psychiatry,* 1969, *24,* 1440-1445.

Keniston, K., & The Carnegie Council on Children. *All our children: the American family under pressure.* New York: Harcourt, Brace, Jovanovich, 1977.

Lefrancois, G. *Adolescents.* Belmont, Calif.: Wadsworth, 1976.

Levine, J. "Real kids versus the average family." *Psychology Today,* June 1978, 14-15.

Long, B. H., Henderson, E. H., & Platt, L. "Self-other orientations of Israeli adolescents." *Developmental psychology,* 1973, *8*(2), 300-308.

Mace, D. R., & Mace, V. C. "Marriage enrichment: wave of the future?" *The family coordinator,* April 1975, *24,* 133.

Macklin, E. D. "Cohabitation in college: going very steady." *Psychology today,* November 1974, *8*(6), 53-58.

McIntire, W. G., Nass, G. D., & Battistone, D. L. "Female misperception of male parenting attitudes and expectancies." *Youth and society,* 1974, *6*(1), 104-112.

Mead, M. *Culture and commitment: A study of the generation gap.* New York: Doubleday, 1970.

Mondale, W. F. "The family in trouble." *Psychology today,* May 1977, *10*(12), 9.

Moore, B. "Thoughts on the future of the family." In M. R. Stein, A. J. Vidich, & D. M. White (Eds.), *Identity and anxiety.* Glencoe, Ill.: Free Press, 1960.

Rice, F. P. *The adolescent.* Boston: Allyn & Bacon, 1978.

Ryor, J. "How social change has changed our schools." Washington, D.C.: National Educational Association Newsletter, October 1977.

Salzman, L. "Adolescence: epoch or disease?" *Adolescence,* 1973, *8*(30), 247-256.

Saybrook, E. L. *Sabrina Hackett.* Boston: Lothrop, 1869.

Schooler, J. C. (Ed.). Book review of *Current issues in adolescent psychiatry.* New York: Brunner/Mazel, 1973. *Journal of youth and adolescence,* 1974, *3*(3), 261.

Sebald, H. *Momism: the silent disease of America.* Chicago: Nelson-Hall, 1976.

Sebald, H. *Adolescence: a social psychological analysis* (2nd ed.). Englewood Cliffs, N.J.: Prentice-Hall, 1977.

Sorosky, A. D. "The psychological effects of divorce on adolescents." *Adolescence,* Spring 1977, *12*(45), 123-136.

Steinbeck, J.   "The red pony." In *The long valley.* New York: Viking, 1966.

Sudia, C. E.   "An updating and comment on the United States scene." *Family coordinator,* 1973, *22*(3), 309–311.

Thompson, V. D.   "Family size: implicit policies and assumed psychological outcomes." *Journal of social issues,* 1974, *30*(4), 93–124.

Toman, W.   "Birth order rules all." *Psychology today,* December 1970, pp. 45–49; 68–69.

Vincent, C. E.   "An open letter to the 'caught generation'." *Family coordinator,* 1972, *21*(2), 143–150.

"Why you do what you do."   *Time,* August 1, 1977, pp. 54–63.

Woodward, K.   "Saving the family." *Newsweek,* May 15, 1978.

Wylie, P.   *Generation of vipers.* New York: Rinehart, 1942.

Additional References

Adilman, Philip H.   "Mary Ann and mother: an adolescent's turmoil to individuate." *Adolescence,* Summer 1974, *9*(34), 199–220.

"The American family: future uncertain."   *Time,* December 28, 1970.

Balswick, J. O., & Macredes, C.   "Parental stimulus for adolescent rebellion." *Adolescence,* Summer 1975, *10*(38), 253–266.

Baran, A., Sorosky, A. D., & Pannor, R.   "Secret adoption records: the dilemma of our adoptees." *Psychology today,* 1975, *9*(7), 38–42; 96–99.

Bem, S. L.   "Androgyny vs. the light little lives of fluffy women and chesty men." *Psychology today,* 1975, *9*(4), 58–59; 61–62.

Berger, B., Hackett, B., & Millar, R. M.   "The communal family." *Family coordinator,* 1972, *21*(4), 419–427.

Bengston, V. L., & Starr, J. M.   "Contrast and consensus: a generational analysis of youth in the 1970's." In R. J. Havighurst & P. H. Dreyer (Eds.), *Youth.* Chicago: University of Chicago Press, 1975.

Bettelheim, B.   "The problem of generations." In E. Erikson, *The challenge of youth.* New York: Anchor Books, 1965.

Bush, S.   "A family program that really works." *Psychology today,* May 1977, *10*(12), 48.

Coles, R., & Woodward, K.   "The cold tough world of the affluent family." *Psychology today,* 1975, *9*(6), 67–70; 74–77, 133.

Cottle, T. J.   "Low income youth." In R. J. Havighurst & P. H. Dreyer (Eds.), *Youth.* Chicago: University of Chicago Press, 1975.

Curtis, R. L., Jr.   "Adolescent orientations toward parents and peers: variations by sex, age, and socioeconomic status." *Adolescence,* Winter 1975, *10*(40), 483–494.

Dreyer, P. H.   "Sex, sex roles, and marriage among youth in the 1970's." In R. J. Havighurst & P. H. Dreyer (Eds.), *Youth.* Chicago: University of Chicago Press, 1975.

"Drive for rights of children."   *U.S. News,* 1974, *77*(6), 42–44.

Floyd, H. H., Jr., & South, D. R.   "Dilemma of youth: the choice of parents or peers as a frame of reference for behavior." *Journal of marriage and the family,* 1972, *34*(4), 627–634.

Frank, I., & Frank, R. K.   "The management of adolescent crisis in family practice." *Adolescence,* Spring 1975, *10*(37), 25–28.

Gallagher, B. J.   "An empirical analysis of attitude differences between three kin-related generations." *Youth and society,* 1974, *5*(3), 327–349.

Ginott, H.   *Teacher and child.* New York: Macmillan, 1972.

Gray, D. F., & Gaier, E. L. "The congruency of adolescent self-perceptions with those of parents and best friends." *Adolescence,* Summer 1974, *9*(34), 299.

"A happy and traditional home is still the goal, but a happy home doesn't have to contain children." *Psychology today,* 1974, *7*(12), 102.

Kirp, D. "Student classification, public policy, and the courts." *Harvard educational review,* 1974, *44*(1), 7–52.

Kotler, T. "Characteristics and correlates of parent-son interactions." *Genetic psychology monographs,* 1975, *91*, 121–168.

Lambert, T. A. "Generations and change: toward a theory of generations as a force in historical process." *Youth and society,* 1972, *4*(1), 21–45.

Larson, L. E. "The influence of parents and peers during adolescence: the situation hypothesis revisited." *Journal of marriage and the family,* 1972, *34*(1), 67–74.

Larson, L. E. "System and subsystem perception of family roles." *Journal of marriage and the family,* 1974, *36*(1), 123–138.

Larson, L. E. "An examination of the salience hierarchy during adolescence: the influence of the family." *Adolescence,* 1974, *9*(35), 317–332.

Laufer, R. S., & Bengtson, V. L. "Generations, aging, and social stratification: on the development of generational units." *Journal of social issues,* 1974, *30*(3), 181–205.

LeMasters, E. E. *Parents in modern America* (Rev. ed.). Homewood, Ill.: Dorsey Press, 1974.

Lerner, R. M., & Knapp, J. P. "Actual and perceived intrafamilial attitudes of late adolescents and their parents." *Journal of youth and adolescence,* 1975, *4*(1), 17–36.

Lurie, E. E. "Sex and stage differences in perceptions of marital and family relationships." *Journal of marriage and the family,* 1974, *36*(2), 260–269.

Marotz-Baden, R., & Tallman, I. *Adolescence,* Summer 1978, *13*(50), 251–268.

McBride, A. B. *Growth and development of mothers.* New York: Harper & Row, 1973.

Meyers, J. H., & Zegans, S. L. "Adolescents perceive their psychotherapy." *Psychiatry,* 1975, *38*(1), 11–22.

Mondale, W. A. "Family impact statement: A response from the U.S. Senate." *School review,* 1974, *83*(1), 11–14.

Orloff, H., & Weinstock, A. "A comparison of parent and adolescent attitude factor structures." *Adolescence,* Summer 1975, *10*(38), 201–206.

Peterson, E. T., & Kung, P. R. "Parental control over adolescents according to family size." *Adolescence,* Fall 1975, *10*(39), 419–427.

Rosenblatt, P. C., & Skoogberg, E. L. "Birth order in cross-cultural perspective." *Developmental psychology,* 1974, *10*(1), 48–54.

Rutter, M. *Maternal deprivation, reassessed.* Baltimore: Penguin Books, 1972.

Statistical abstract of the United States. Washington, D.C.: Bureau of the Census, 1975.

Stinnett, N., Farris, J. A., & Walters, J. "Parent-child relationships of male and female high school students." *The journal of genetic psychology,* 1974, *125*, 99–106.

Stuart, I. R., & Abt, L. E. (Eds.). *Children of separation and divorce.* New York: Grossman, 1972.

Swanson, R. B., Massey, R. H., & Payne, I. R. "Ordinal position, family size, and personal adjustment." *Journal of psychology,* 1972, *81*, 53–58.

Walter, W., & Stinnett, N. "Parent-child relationships: a decade review of research." *Journal of marriage and the family,* 1971, *33*(1), 70–111.

Whitehurst, R. N. "Some comparisons of conventional and counterculture families." *Family coordinator,* 1972, *21*(4), 395–401.

Yost, E. D., & Adamak, R. J.   "Parent-child interaction and changing family values: a multivariate analysis." *Journal of marriage and the family,* 1974, *36*(1), 115–121.

Zellermayer, J., & Marcus, J.   "Kibbutz adolescence: relevance to personality development theory." *Journal of youth and adolescence,* 1972, *1*(2), 143–153.

Chapter Seven

Relationships with Peers

Chapter Highlights

Adolescent Subcultures
The Origin of Subcultures
  The Psychogenic Model
  The Culture Transmission Model
  The Behavioristic Model
Elements of the Adolescent Subculture
  Propinquity
  Unique Values and Norms
  Peer Group Identity
  Charismatic Leadership
  Desire for Autonomy
  Special Channels of Communication
  Proliferation of Group Languages
  The Crowds in My College Class
  Concern for the Underdog
Developmental Patterns of Peer Groups
  Types of Associations
  Stages of Development
  The Crowds in My High School
Purposes of the Peer Group
  *Adolescent Perceptions of Peer
    Groups*
When Peer Relations Fail
Effects of the School Setting on Peer
  Interactions
Evaluating Interactions in the Classroom
  The Sociogram

Improving Peer Group Communications
  Communications Games
  The Language of Acceptance
Summary

Key Terms and Concepts

subcultures
psychogenic
culture transmission
behavioristic theory
positive reinforcement
negative reinforcement
inconsistent conditioning
peer groups
cliques
clubs
gangs
crowds
networks
isolates
socioeconomic status
racial composition
sociogram
language of acceptance
"I" message
no-lose method

Important Person

Thomas Gordon

With the expansion in the 1960s came a set of distinctive patterns of activity associated with youth. . . . These patterns include a style of dress, from high involvement with the new fashions to studied rejection of the accepted norms of appropriate dress. They include new forms of music, and sometimes associated with it, drug use. They include small intense subgroups, with contacts ranging from religious and mystical to political activity.

—President's Panel on Youth, 1974, p. 165.

The word *culture* means a social blueprint for behavior. Within a culture, there may be one or more subcultures, each of which, although operating partly from the master blueprint, has its own distinctive patterns of behavior. The United States probably is composed of more subcultures than any other country in the history of the world, both ethnic (Italian, Irish) and racial (black, Puerto Rican, Indian).

ADOLESCENT SUBCULTURES

In the decade following World War I, a spirit of liberality and experimentation prevailed. Many saw that the young "flappers" of the 1920s had unconventional and even rebellious attitudes toward adulthood, but no one suggested that they had a culture all their own. It was not until the 1950s that social scientists began to suspect that young people were creating significant new subcultures. Among the earliest and most antagonistic to the cultural mainstream were the "beatniks" and the Hell's Angels.

During the 1960s there was a debate among social scientists over whether adolescents in general were forming their own distinctive subcultures. Many felt that the high visibility of the more defiant youth was making a false case for the significance of differences between teenagers and adults (Douvan and Adelson, 1966; Douvan and Gold, 1966; Elkin, 1955; Hill and Aldous, 1969). Even in the 1970s some authors have argued that the youth culture exists more in theory than in fact (Bandura, 1972; Davis, 1971; Larson, 1972; Schwartz and Baden, 1973; Stein, Soskin, and Korchin, 1974; Thomas, 1971). Stein, Soskin, and Korchin (1974) found that most teenagers have a strong sense of trust in adults over 30 years old, especially caretaking adults. Larson (1972) found that the desires of parents were more often complied with than those of peers, at least among the fourth-, ninth-, and twelfth-graders he studied.

There were some (Coleman, 1961; Green, 1968; Williams, 1960) who began to argue for the existence of a separate teenage subculture during the 1960s. By the 1970s, the majority shared this view (Coleman, 1974; Lefrancois, 1976; Manaster, 1977; Rogers, 1977; Sebald, 1977). Most agree not only that an adolescent subculture exists, but that adolescents are differentiating themselves from adults more thoroughly than ever.

THE ORIGIN OF SUBCULTURES

How do subcultures get started? Why are there so many of them? There have been three major attempts to explain the origin of subcultures: the **psychogenic**, the **culture transmission**, and the **behavioristic theories** (Sebald, 1977).

The Psychogenic Model

A subculture arises when a large number of people have a similar problem of adjustment, which causes them to get together to deal with the problem and help each other resolve it. Modern teenagers receive a much less practical and more abstract introduction to life than formerly. They see the world as complex and ambiguous; it is unclear how they fit in and what they ought to be doing. Many try to escape from ambiguity into a world which they create with other teenagers. In the past, this way of creating an identity was used almost solely by delinquent youngsters who were unable to find a respected place in society. Today, escape or avoidance of reality is becoming a much more common reaction to personal difficulty.

The Culture Transmission Model

A new subculture arises as an imitation of the subculture of the previous generation. This takes place through a learning process by which younger teenagers model themselves after those in their twenties. Magazines, movies, and television programs aimed at teenagers have been effective mechanisms for perpetuating the so-called teenage subculture. Thus, though new forms of behavior may *seem* to evolve, in actuality most are only imitations of the solutions older people found for their problems when they were teenagers. Not surprisingly, this model argues that teenagers today are really not all that different from those of previous decades.

The Behavioristic Model

This model sees subcultures starting out as a result of a series of trial-and-error behaviors, which are reinforced if they work. It is like the psychogenic model in that a new group is formed by people with similar problems. It differs in that the psychogenic model views behavior as creative and innovative, whereas the behavioristic model sees peer group members behaving the way they do because they have no other choice.

According to behaviorism, teenagers experience adults as "aversive stimuli"; that is, it is painful to interact with adults because in clashes over values adults almost always win. In an attempt to escape from aversive stimuli, adolescents try out different behaviors with each other. They receive both **positive reinforcement** (their interactions with their peers make them feel better about themselves) and **negative reinforcement** (the pain they experience in interacting with adults stops as a result of their noninteraction with the adult world).

Another factor that tends to perpetuate the youth subculture is **inconsistent conditioning**. For example, teenagers are expected to be responsible for their spending, but on the other hand, they have to get parental permission for all but the smallest purchases because they are not legally responsible for their debts. Probably the most painful example of inconsistent conditioning, and one which fortunately no longer exists, was the situation in which they were asked to fight and possibly die for their country, but were not allowed to vote and help influence their country's policies.

Which of these models best explains the origins of the youth subculture? Each offers insights, but the behavioristic model seems to explain adolescent behavior more precisely than the others and thus is most useful.

ELEMENTS OF THE ADOLESCENT SUBCULTURE

Whether they have similar or different origins, from other subcultures, the teenage subculture clearly has a number of common elements; these are described below.*

Propinquity

An obvious but often overlooked factor in the adolescent subculture is that the members of a group live near and know each other prior to joining the group. Gold and Douvan (1969) have suggested that physical closeness is the single most important factor in the makeup of teenage groups.

Unique Values and Norms

All groups have in common the attempt to overcome limitations that would have been placed on the members if they had not belonged to the group (Block and

---

*Many of the ideas presented in this section are drawn from *Youth: Transition to Adulthood,* Report on the Panel on Youth of the President's Science Advisory Committee, James S. Coleman, ed. (Chicago: University of Chicago Press, 1974).

Langman, 1974). Whatever the underlying reason for the group — race, age, politics, ethnic background — its members see a clear advantage in joining with others of similar values. In the teen years, being dominated by adults creates a major motivation for banding together.

There are some important sex differences in peer group values (Smart and Smart, 1973). Girls seek satisfaction of a wider variety of emotional needs in their friendships than boys do, but tend to seek just a few close friends. Girls value loyalty, trustworthiness, and emotional support most of all. Boys, on the other hand, seek friendships that help them assert their independence and resist adult control.

Peer Group Identity

The youth subculture tends to force its members into a deeper involvement with each other. Because teenagers spend so little time with, and derive so little influence from, those older and younger than themselves, they have only each other to look to as models. Today, those under 20 make up a much larger percentage of the population than formerly, and they continue their education for a much longer period. As a result, they spend much more time with other youth and much less time with adults.

A proposal by Newman and Newman (1976) recognizes the growing importance of this factor of group inward-lookingness. They suggest that we divide Erikson's identity stage into two stages: early adolescence (ages 13 through 17) called the group identity versus alienation stage, and later adolescence (ages 18 through 22) called the individual identity versus role defusion stage, recognizing that it is also necessary that one identify with a group or groups in order to achieve a well-resolved personal identity. Although the self-analysis characteristic of peer group membership may bring about considerable confusion, it may be a temporarily desirable situation (Kilpatrick, 1974) in that it prevents youth resolving their identity too soon. The teenage peer group is seen as a relatively safe place for adolescents to take a long look at themselves, prior to deciding what kind of adult they wish to be.

Charismatic Leadership

The peer group almost always revolves around a leader. Whether explicitly or implicitly, leadership is required to coordinate and control the decision-making process within the group. English (1962) suggests that a leader must demonstrate at least four characteristics.

Visibility. Leaders must behave in such a way that they stand out from other members of the group.

Superiority. In the past, athletic ability was the chief means of achieving superiority among boys (Coleman, 1961). The criterion of female superiority was less clear. For both groups, the index of superiority is becoming broader. Now, in addition to physical prowess, teenagers may demonstrate superiority through their good looks, social abilities, or clothes. Intellectual ability still counts for little among teenagers.

Self-confidence. It is not enough to have superior qualities; many teenagers are unable to use their above-average abilities because of their unwillingness to believe they have them. They doubt themselves because they doubt the veracity of their senses. Leadership requires self-confidence to put superiority to work.

Social sensitivity. Effective leadership requires an awareness of the needs of followers, a clear perception of their reactions to leadership behavior, and the ability to adjust this behavior according to their reactions.

The role of leader is usually a prestigious position, especially among teenagers. Adolescents especially need the proof of popularity that leadership gives. Just as *every* group has its leader, *every* school has its "leading crowd." Membership in the leading crowd is almost as desirable as being the leader of one's clique, club, or gang.

Desire for Autonomy

Most subcultures are formed because their members feel themselves inferior to the other members of the main culture. Since they cannot dominate the main culture, the subculture members generally wish to be left alone. Many black leaders today say that they no longer desire integration into white society; they ask rather to gain autonomy from the rule of the white world. They wish to be accepted as a subculture.

Thus it is with the teenager subcultures, some groups of which have had phenomenal success in gaining autonomy from the adult world in the last two decades (such as the hippie movement). Some groups have been the advance guard of such previously forbidden activities as drug use. Many teenagers view with admiration the rejection of authority in its many forms by "courageous" subculture leaders — actions that tend to increase the autonomy and isolation of their subculture.

Special Channels of Communication

Not only do the mass media play a great role in the overall communications between human beings today; there has also been a proliferation of the number of channels of communication that appeal specifically to subcultures. In recent years, movies, television, newspapers, and AM and FM radio stations have increasingly catered to teen interests. Some radio and television programs and special interest newspapers have been organized and controlled by older teenagers themselves. The media have opened up access to a new youth market for specialized goods and services, which is of considerable economic importance due to the phenomenal growth of teenagers' personal funds.

Proliferation of Group Languages

One of the best ways to achieve autonomy from other groups is to speak a language that members of the other groups cannot understand. Many a parent has experienced the frustration of trying to keep up with teenage terminology. Special group or clique languages are termed *argot, group lingo, jargon,* or *slang,* and are marked by the variety and richness of their vocabulary. The following paragraphs give some examples of adolescent jargon in one high school.

> *Hey man, let's go cruisin' and drain some frosties. We'll pull a chirper right in front of the pigs, then do quarters in a wicked rat race with some Bondo!*

As Schwartz and Merten (1967) point out, the language of the adolescent clique reflects and reinforces a distinctive world view. Leona (1978) studied the clique language in one suburban high school in the Northeast. He discovered three main crowds or groups at the high school, each made up of a number of cliques, and two cliques which were independent of the three crowds. Examples of the language used by the cliques are given here, not as definitive terms — clique language changes rapidly and differs from school to school — but rather as examples of the diversity of world views existing within one high school.

One of the most obvious crowds is the "jocks," those who are good at athletics. Although jocks are mostly males, lately a number of females have joined the group. Jocks are easily discernible by their letter sweaters, the choice of one particular brand of sneakers, their use of last names or nicknames for each other, and their short hair. Jocks drink a lot, mostly beer, and almost never smoke marijuana. Examples of their clique language are

Cals: calisthenics.

Psyched: getting excited in order to play well in an athletic event.

Hurting: the other team is winning at the moment.

Cheap shot: hurting a member of the other team in an unfair way.

Get it in gear: hurry up, run faster.

Losing the family jewels: suffering an injury to the genitals.

Going guzzling, getting buzzed: going drinking.

Having an ego problem: being snobbish.

The second major crowd at the school is the "motorheads." These are students, mostly males, who spend a great deal of their time working on their cars and talking about car engines. Females also belong to this group, but only as subordinate associates of the males. Motorheads are notable for their leather jackets (although they are not "bikies" — those interested in motorcycles), their low academic grades, and unwashed or unusual hair styles. (Some may be bald except for a strip of hair down the center of their heads — the so-called Mohawk cut.) Terms in the motorhead language are

A cool head: one who knows a lot about engines.

Cruising: driving around town.

Frosties: cans of beer.

A fix-or-repair-daily: a Ford car.

A Bondo: a dented car repaired with a plastic body filler named Bondo.

Riding the gun: sitting in the passenger's seat.

Getting it on, peeling out, shoving the pedal to the metal: accelerating very quickly.

Pull a chirper, popping the clutch: letting the clutch out quickly while pressing the accelerator.

Quarters: racing for a quarter of mile.

Rat race: Two cars attempting to pass each other on a narrow road.

A third crowd is the "flea bags," a group of male and female students who use drugs regularly, the most popular by far being marijuana. Flea bags are easily recognizable by their denim pants and shirts, their long, unkempt hair, and their frequent absences from class. Some examples of their argot are

Joints, j's, bones: marijuana cigarettes.

Stogie: a large marijuana cigarette.

Taking a hit, toking: smoking a marijuana cigarette.

Getting baked, wasted, high, spaced, stoned, tripped out: feeling the effects of smoking a lot of marijuana.

Bakathon: a marijuana party.

Straight: someone who does not smoke marijuana.

Shot gun: smoking in pairs, with one person putting a joint in his mouth backwards and blowing the smoke into his partner's mouth.

Bong pipe, hookah: another way of smoking, in which the smoke is drawn through water before being inhaled.

Roach: the last part of a marijuana cigarette.

Bummer: an unfortunate situation.

Weirdo: anyone who is against the flea bags.

A favorite song of this group, sung to the tune of "Row, row, row your boat," goes like this: "Roll, roll, roll a joint, take a sip of wine. Take a toke, blow the smoke, and blow your frigging mind!"

One small clique which generally has nothing to do with these crowds is known as the "chewers." This is a group of male students who chew tobacco during and after school. Their favorite activities are sporting events, talking on citizens' band radios, and listening to country and western music. A few examples of their lingo are

Scumbugs, scuzbags: females they do not like.

Minkya, you're all set: a sarcastic criticism of each other.

A fourth group identified by Leona was the "brains," a small group interested in intellectual pursuits. They contemptuously denied having a special language.

The largest group at the school was the "in-betweens," who claimed membership in no particular group. Interestingly, almost all the students Leona interviewed said they were in-betweens, even those who looked as though they belonged to a group and knew its language thoroughly. Apparently a love of individuality still lives!

The Crowds in My College Class

Are you aware of distinct crowds in your class at college? How would you describe them? Does each have its own lingo? See if you can fill in the spaces below.

Crowd: _____

Key phrases: _____

_____

_____

Crowd: _____

Key phrases: _____

_____

_____

Crowd: _____

Key phrases: _____

_____

_____

Now compare your list with those of others in your class who have completed this activity. Do your answers agree? Would you describe the crowds in your high school in the same way?

Concern for the Underdog

The deep concern for the interests of others less fortunate than themselves reached a peak among adolescents in the idealistic years of the late 1960s. Although weakened now by worry over finding suitable employment, concern for the underdog is still strong among American youth. The concern is partly an outgrowth of idealistic values, but also derives from adolescent antagonism toward material achievement and the competitive spirit. Because they are at a political and economic disadvantage relative to the adult world, they tend to be sympathetic to others who are seen as disadvantaged.

> *This was not always so. In the past, the central institutions of society were families, not work organizations, and the "outsiders" in society were those of all ages who belonged to families that were outsiders. Young and old from lower classes were outsiders and united in their alienation; young and old from middle and upper class were insiders and united in their support for the existing system (President's Panel on Youth, 1974, p. 174).*

DEVELOPMENTAL PATTERNS OF PEER GROUPS

Within the adolescent subculture, individuals form themselves into a variety of **peer groups**. Such groups exist at all ages, but seem most important during the teen years, when the need for support and approval by age mates is at a peak. The development of peer relationships follows a discernible pattern, beginning as loose attachments and becoming stronger as the child grows older. A number of levels can be discerned.

Types of Associations

Associates. In the early years of school, before friendships develop, children have associations with each other which are short-term and ephemeral. These associations allow them to practice social interactions and learn the give-and-take that forms the basis for more organized relationships.

Friends. In the middle of elementary school, children form relationships that are more lasting. They are based on mutual interests and give children a deeper understanding of others around them. In these friendships, children discover the benefits that can be derived from discussing their conflicts with someone else. Although such early friendships are almost always between individuals of the same sex, discussions among larger groups of children help make the transition to opposite-sex friendships.

Cliques. **Cliques** can start as early as the third grade, but they are more typically formed in grades five and six. They consist of small groups of three to eight individuals who more or less consciously exclude others from their tight friendship. As with friendships, mutuality of interests is more assumed than discussed, but are somewhat more conscious in the clique.

Clubs.   **Clubs** are cliques with a formal organization. Here the membership is agreed on and the specific goals of the group are stated explicitly.

Gangs.   Like the club, the **gang** has a specified membership. Its goals are usually more or less explicit, and members are expected to cooperate with each other in achieving these goals. Unlike clubs, gangs disdain the specific organization of rules and rely more on the day-to-day judgment of the leadership to decide what the gang will do. The question of gang life in adolescent society has again become of considerable importance, and it is treated in greater detail in Chapter 12.

Crowds.   **Crowds** are loosely knit groups, usually made up of several cliques. Although the crowd is less organized than the club or gang, most adolescents know who is and is not part of a particular crowd. Crowds do not have regular meetings; their members interact mostly at social functions. Their larger numbers make for more diversity of interests and goals than the smaller peer groups.

Networks.   A **network** is an association among several clubs, gangs, or crowds. It is usually formed to promote communication between people of similar interests. The network almost always covers a large geographic area. The Boy Scouts, fan clubs, and ham radio organizations are all adolescent networks. While many networks are set up for cooperative purposes, other exist to foster competition, such as associations of math clubs and science fairs, as well as the informal network between gangs in a particular city.

The pattern of organization of these various types of peer relationships ranges from informal (associations, friendships, cliques) to formal (gangs, clubs) back to informal (crowds, networks) as they get larger in size. This pattern appears to progress through a series of stages that depend on the age of the teenagers involved.

Stages of Development

Dexter Dunphy, an Australian psychologist, spent three years intensively observing adolescent peer groupings. His research yielded a theory of the developmental stages in the ways adolescents relate to each other (Figure 7–1). Although derived from observations of Australian youths, his findings appear to fit well with observations of peer groups of the more technologically advanced societies. It may be that peer group development is universal.

Dunphy (1963) suggests there are five stages in the development of peer groups across the adolescent years.

1. *Precrowd stage.* Males and females interact with each other in cliques isolated by sex. There is little or no interaction between the sexes.

LATE ADOLESCENCE

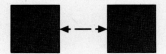

Stage 5: Beginning of crowd disintegration.
Loosely associated groups of couples.

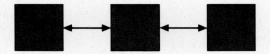

Stage 4: The fully developed crowd.
Heterosexual cliques in close association.

Stage 3: The crowd in structural transition.
Unisexual cliques with upper status
members forming a heterosexual clique.

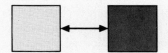

Stage 2: The beginning of the crowd.
Unisexual cliques in group-to-group interaction.

Stage 1: Pre-crowd stage.
Isolated unisexual cliques.

EARLY ADOLESCENCE

Boys   Girls   Boys and Girls

Figure 7–1   Stages of Group Development in Adolescence

From D. C. Dunphy, "The Social Structure of Urban Adolescent Peer Groups," *Sociometry: A Journal of Research in Social Psychology,* Vol. 26, 1963, pp. 235–236.

The Crowds in My High School

Can you remember what the major crowds in your high school were? Did each have its own special language? Try to list these in the spaces below.

Crowd: _____

Key phrases: _____

_____

_____

Crowd: _____

Key phrases: _____

_____

_____

Crowd: _____

Key phrases: _____

_____

_____

Now compare your list with others who have completed this activity. Were their lists like or unlike yours? Would your answers be different if you were attending your high school today?

2. *Beginning of the crowd.* Male and female cliques interact, but rarely male and female individuals. Such contact is considered daring and is often superficially antagonistic.

3. *Structural transition of the crowd.* For the first time, heterosexual cliques are formed. Upper-status members of the unisexual cliques make these first groupings, and dating begins.

4. *The fully developed crowd.* Now heterosexual crowds are formed with identities of their own. Small cliques are also maintained, but they are heterosexual and exist within the structure of the crowd.

5. *Crowd disintegration.* Membership in the crowd gradually becomes less important. This stage usually begins as graduation from high school draws near. Loosely associated groups of couples take the place of the crowd.

Dunphy believes that crowds are of such great importance to their members, especially during the middle of adolescence, because they serve the vital function of providing support while individuals learn heterosexual roles. Interaction with the opposite sex is fraught with dangers in the beginning, and the crowd offers a relatively safe testing ground for experimenting with these new roles.

PURPOSES OF THE PEER GROUP

If you were to ask most teenagers why they have joined a particular clique, club, or gang, they would probably tell you it is because they like the people in the group, or they like the kind of things the group is doing. Actually, there are many other purposes fulfilled by membership in a peer group. Rogers (1977) has summarized a number of these:

The "radar" function. One peer group function is to help the members find out how well they are doing in life. Adolescents can try out some behaviors by "bouncing" them off their peers who act as a radar screen. They then receive a message back as to how well others feel they are performing, and can alter their behavior accordingly.

Replacement for father. Although many, perhaps most, teenagers try to repudiate their father's authority during adolescence, the need for a father figure remains. The group leader often replaces one's father during the transition toward independence.

Support for independence. Closely related is the need for support from others while struggling against parental authority. Most adolescents need to learn to assert themselves, which often gives them strong guilt feelings and fear that their parents will reject them. Mutual support can be relied on among those who have similar concerns.

Ego building. Adolescence is a time of confusion as to who one is. At this low ebb of self-confidence, the peer group often serves the purpose of making one feel at least minimally good about oneself.

Psychic attachment. All human beings experience a deep need for psychological closeness and intimacy with others. In the past, this need was met largely by one's family. Today one's peers, especially in adolescence, have largely taken over this role.

Values orientation. We like to think we select our values by carefully considering how we feel about things and coming to our own conclusions as to what we shall believe (see Chapter 13). In fact, if we were forced to make up our minds about most things without any outside information, we would find it very difficult indeed. The peer group serves as a setting for the discussion of values, so that one has a better chance of seeing a wide range of options and making better choices.

Status setting. All societies have their hierarchy of status, in fact, several of them. Each of us needs to know something about how others regard us in the hierarchy of life. The peer group allows adolescents to learn more about how dominant and subordinate they are, thus giving them a better image of how they appear to others.

Negative identity. Often, youth join groups not so much because they believe in the goals of the group, but because they want to demonstrate their antagonism toward someone else. For example, a person whose parents overcontrol him may join an unruly gang even though he dislikes the occasional violence the group engages in. Nevertheless, he may view membership in the group as proof that he is more independent than his parents believe he is.

The avoidance of adult requirements. When the requirements of the peer group conflict with the requirements of adult society, the latter may be shunted aside. For example, teachers may insist that their students spend a considerable amount of time on homework; being a member of the basketball team may make it difficult to schedule both homework and practice sessions. Therefore, belonging to the basketball team may serve the purpose of excusing the teenager, at least to himself, from doing the homework that he didn't want to do anyway.

Adolescent Perceptions of Peer Groups

How aware are teenagers of the peer groups they themselves belong to? How well can they articulate their feelings about these groups? Ask several adolescents which groups in their school they think they belong to. They will probably mention only the formal organizations they have consciously joined. Then ask them to name any informal groups which they have become members of without really trying. Finally, ask them if they can think of any slang words which are only used in one of the groups they have mentioned.

The results of these interviews may surprise you!

WHEN PEER RELATIONS FAIL

Some teenagers are more dependent upon peer group relations than others: younger adolescents, those in the upper-middle class and the lower class, those who are not working, minority group members, prepubescent males, and postpubescent females (Floyd and South, 1972; Foner, 1974; Sexton, 1970; Wieder and Zimmerman, 1974). For these, the inability to relate successfully to their peers has particularly dire effects. As Conger (1973) says, "Having bad friends is better than having no friends at all." Isolated teenagers are much more likely to lack self-confidence and to overconform to peer values, both of which tend to make them even more likely to be rejected. They are also more prone to mental illness and delinquent behavior (Rogers, 1977).

Many isolated teenagers try to pretend they would rather be alone. This causes even further difficulties.

> For example, the pressure to conform often conflicts with intimacy needs because part of our cultural image of the superyouth is one who is aloof, detached, and beyond the petty inconvenience of deep emotion. Consequently, youth who present an image of cool detachment find this pattern so highly reinforcing that they have trouble abandoning it in favor of genuinely intimate relationships. The more a society (whether it be the youth society or the dominant society) reinforces customs which stress surface appearance and role-playing habits, the greater difficulty its citizens encounter in their attempts to gratify intimacy needs (Mitchell, 1976, pp. 279–80).

Social **isolates** are also more likely to be underachievers. Doing reasonably well in school (at least "C" level) is important in most cliques today (Damico, 1975). The isolate, not being influenced by clique behavior, is less likely to see academic achievement as useful.

EFFECTS OF THE SCHOOL SETTING ON PEER INTERACTIONS

Characteristics of the school environment have important effects on student interactions, among them socioeconomic status and racial composition of the student body, size of the school, school architecture, and degree of formality in the use of school space.

A number of studies (Boyle, 1966; Herriot and St. John, 1966; Liddle, 1962) have found that the higher the **socioeconomic status**, the more likely the students are to attend college and to stay in school until graduation. Lower-class students are also more likely to remain in school when most of the students at the school are of middle or upper-class socioeconomic status.

The racial composition of the school greatly affects the involvement the students feel in the school (Gottlieb and Tenhouten, 1965). When they are few in number, black students tend to be less willing to participate in academic and extracurricular events, apparently because they feel they are less likely to gain the rewards available from school participation. However, if the proportion of black students increases and they become a majority in the school, they become as involved in the school's activities as the former white majority.

The degree of social participation among students is also related to school size. Students in small schools participate more actively in all aspects of the school than do students in large schools (Barker and Gump, 1964). Large schools are more likely to separate the academic and the vocationally oriented students, which further decreases social interactions (Myrick and Marx, 1968). The same effect occurs when new schools are organized in several buildings.

Perhaps the most significant influence of schools on social interaction is the degree of formality demanded by school authorities of social behavior in various school settings. Newman (1976), using the Environmental Assessment Questionnaire, compared seven settings in two different high schools: the cafeteria, the school office, the counselor's office, study halls, the auditorium, the athletic fields, and the restrooms. One school encouraged socializing among faculty and students in these spaces; the other school insisted they be used for limited, formal purposes and in a quiet, orderly manner. Newman concluded that

> *the informal interactions between adults and students in the school (first) serve to communicate the expectations and norms of the larger community with respect to community participation, career choice, religious values, political ideology, etc. . . . Schools that provide the opportunity for informal interactions with adults facilitate the young person's ability to interact with people in positions of authority (p. 415).*

EVALUATING INTERACTIONS IN THE CLASSROOM

Social interactions in the classroom have considerable impact on learning. The class that is divided into small cliques, the class that has many isolated students, makes a poor environment for learning. The age of the students affects social groupings, junior high school students being more likely to develop cliques and strongly adhere to their rules than younger or older students. Teachers can discover these patterns in the classroom and use the information to facilitate learning.

One method of plotting social interactions is the **sociogram**, a schematic drawing that details the groupings in a classroom at any particular time. Figure 7–2 is a diagram of the social interactions done in one classroom. Students were given 3 x 5 cards and asked to put their name on one side. On the other side, they were asked to list up to three students in the class whom they considered to be their "good friends." If they did not feel that anyone in the class was a good friend of theirs, they could leave the card blank. The circles indicate girls, and the squares, boys. The arrows between circles and squares indicate choices each student made. Arrows in both directions indicate mutual choice.

Before reading about how a teacher can use a sociogram, try to answer the questions below about the sociogram of Figure 7–2. Suggested answers to these questions also appear below.

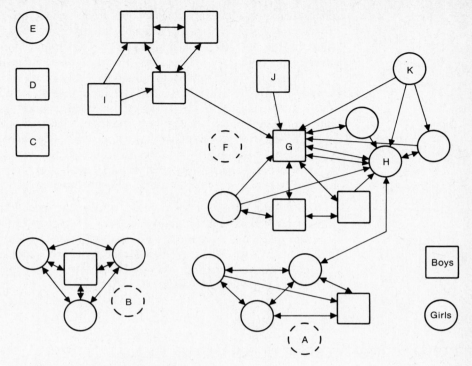

Figure 7–2   *The Sociogram*

The Sociogram: Questions

1. At which grade level do you think this class is?

2. What predictions can you make for the relationships among the students in cliques A and B?

3. What conclusions would you draw about students C, D, and E?

4. How many isolates are there in this class?

5. Which of the cliques in this class is the leading one?

6. If you were to form discussion groups for this class, which students would you be likely to put in one group?

7. For this sociogram, students were asked to say which students they considered to be good friends. What other questions might usefully be asked?

8. What conclusions would you draw about the learning environment of a classroom such as this?

The Sociogram: Answers

1. This is a seventh-grade class, which is indicated by the fact that the class is divided almost entirely into cliques, and that the membership of each clique is primarily either male or female.

2. You can expect some friction and possibly hurt feelings among the girls in groups A and B. It is unlikely, especially in a seventh-grade class, that children of one sex who compete for the friendship of someone of the other sex are likely to maintain their own friendships for very long, and in fact they didn't.

3. These students are clearly isolates. No one picked them and they did not pick anyone else. Student C is Puerto Rican, and students D and E are Chinese. Each of these students recently joined the class and is bused to the school from another neighborhood. It is easy to understand why no other students have picked them yet, as this is a white, middle-class school. It is also typical that they have not picked each other. When a student has a characteristic that makes him or her an isolate from the rest of the class, the student is unlikely to pick another who has the same "negative" characteristic.

4. There are six isolates. Students C, D, and E are isolates; students I, J, and K also are isolates because, even though they have picked others, no one has picked them.

5. Clique F, the members of which are most often picked by students outside the clique, is the leading one.

6. Each of the discussion groups should include at least one of the isolates, as well as at least one of the most popular students. Students G and H, who were chosen most often by other members of the class, are the ones who can best afford to befriend an isolate and to help him or her become accepted by the group.

7. Some other questions might be: "Which students do you most like to work with?" "Which students do you admire the most?" "Which students does the teacher like best?" "Which students would you least like to work with?"

8. It is unlikely that there is a spirit of cooperation in a classroom that is so uncohesive and sharply divided as this one is. Learning in such a class must be especially difficult for the isolates, who have little chance of becoming accepted into the existing cliques. The teacher can have a considerable effect on this situation. The classroom in which the students feel psychologically safe is one in which the most effective learning is likely to take place. When a teacher establishes groupings that foster the breakdown of social isolation, and when the teacher is open to the contributions of the students, an atmosphere conducive to learning is created. Then, joining together in cliques for protection from perceived threats in the classroom is not necessary.

IMPROVING PEER GROUP COMMUNICATIONS

Two major communications problems in peer groups are faulty communications among adolescent members and faulty communications among adolescents and the adults who interact with them. Below are suggestions for remedying them.

Communications Games

Fear and mistrust are often the basis for the existence of peer groups; organizations spring up as an attempt to defend the vulnerable egos of the teenagers who belong to them. Adolescents often have difficulty being honest with each other about their feelings. More importantly, they frequently miscommunicate because their language is imprecise and variable.

One of the ways to help adolescents communicate better is through games. Karen Krupor's useful *Communication Games* (1973) has many suggestions for helping teachers improve communication among their students. Several adaptations of activities from her book are suggested here.

I see A.   This game tests students' observation skills and helps them express their feelings more openly. The class splits into two groups, each sitting opposite the other. It is best if each group is made up of approximately the same number of boys and girls. One at a time, each member of the first group picks out a member of the opposite group and says, "I see A [something about that person] and I like it." For example, the first person might say "I see Bill smiling, and I like it." The second group repeats the exercise.

Other statements that can be useful in this exercise are

"I see A, and I don't like it."

"I see A and it makes me feel B."

"I see A, and I sense that you are feeling B."

"I see A, and I think that you should do B about it. How do you feel about that?"

"I have noticed A about person B. How many others of you in our group have also noticed B?"

Identity card.   Students receive large cards on which they write their answer to one or more of the following questions.

In one word, what is

Your favorite activity?

Your most serious fault?

The thing you are proudest of?

The thing that most frightens you?

Your favorite person?

Your favorite food?

The thing that makes you the most sad?

Questions similar to these may also be used.

Students then exchange cards with as many other students as possible and ask each other questions about their responses. One variation of this game calls for students to guess what others would say about them in response to these questions.

K-D game. An activity that helps show students the importance of giving clear messages in their communications is the K-D game. Each student is requested to choose a partner and place themselves back to back, one partner (A) facing the walls of the classroom and the other (B) facing the center. Partner A is given the loose pieces of a puzzle cut from the letter K, as in Figure 7–3. He is told that it is a letter of the alphabet, but is not told which letter. Partner B is given a picture of the completed K puzzle and has the task of trying to tell partner A what to do with his pieces in order to put the pieces together. Partner A may not ask any questions or in any other way communicate with partner B.

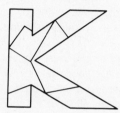

Figure 7–3   The K Puzzle

After five minutes, the partners are instructed that they may both talk, but they must still remain back to back and not look at each other. When one pair has completed the puzzle, they are allowed to walk around the room and observe the other teams. At the end of ten minutes, the game is stopped and discussion of what went on follows. The teacher asks those who completed the puzzle why they think they were successful, starting with the pair who finished first. Then those who were unsuccessful are asked to suggest reasons why they failed.

Now the partners switch positions. Partner B gets the loose pieces of the D puzzle (Figure 7–4), and partner A is given a picture of the complete puzzle. The game then follows the same procedure as before.

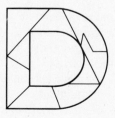

Figure 7–4   The D Puzzle

The teams will probably finish more quickly this time. The teacher may want to wait until all teams have been successful so that everyone feels good about the game. The pattern of the ensuing discussion is the same.

The tinker toy game. This is another game that emphasizes the importance of being accurate and specific in communications. A large set of tinker toys is separated into three piles, so that each has the same set of parts as the other two. The piles are then placed in envelopes.

The class is divided into four teams: Team A is known as the "makers"; teams B and C are the "copiers"; and team D is the "observers." Team A goes out into the hall or some other separate place with one of the sets of tinker toys. They are given five minutes to make something with their set — they may make anything they like. They are also told they are going to have to describe what they have made to teams B and C, so they should decide who will do the describing and how.

Teams B and C also get a set of the tinker toys, which they take to opposite corners of the room. They have the task of building the same object as team A from information provided by messengers from each team, who bring back information from team A. The messengers are allowed to go out to the hallway to talk to the team A information-giver, but they may not see the structure team A has made. Members of team D act as observers of the communications of all three groups.

Team A gives the messengers from teams B and C one piece of information at a time. The messengers return to tell their team what to do, and as soon as they have passed on the information, go back to team A to get a new piece of information. Only verbal information may be used; no body signals are allowed. After ten to fifteen minutes, the messengers may not only pick up information, but may relay questions from their teams. After another ten to fifteen minutes, team A brings the structure it has made into the room, and teams B and C compare what they have made to what team A was trying to tell them to make. It is almost inevitable that the copiers' structure will be quite different from team A's, and considerable amount of laughter will result. Team D, the observers, now contribute their evaluation, and make suggestions about how the groups might have communicated better. If time permits, teams can switch roles and try the whole activity again.

Communications patterns. This game is designed to demonstrate the effects of various physical communications arrangements on group achievement. Although each group supposedly has an equal chance to win, the group in pattern B is more likely to be successful than groups in the other patterns. Each group has five members, with extra students used as referees. They are then arranged in seating patterns A, B, or C (see Figure 7–5), and are told to remain in these patterns throughout the course of the game.

The purpose is for each member of the group to complete one of five puzzles (see Figure 7–6).

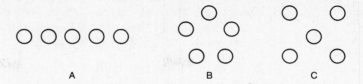

A   B   C

Figure 7–5   Communications Patterns

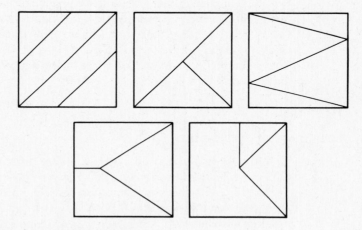

Figure 7–6   Puzzle Squares

The pieces for the five puzzles should be cut out of plain cardboard, according to the pattern shown in Figure 7–6. The pieces are then shuffled so that they are thoroughly mixed; then they are dealt out to the group one at a time. Since there are seventeen pieces, three members get three pieces and two members get four pieces. The task is to pass the pieces among members without talking or using hand signals until each member has completed one square. Each member must accept the piece handed to him by another member. When a team has finished all five squares, they are declared the winners. No one is allowed to speak during the game.

The communications within each group must follow these rules:

1. *Pattern A.* Participants in this straight line pattern can only pass pieces to the person on their left or right. The chairs should be set far enough apart so that persons at each end of the line have difficulty seeing each other's puzzle.

2. *Pattern B.* In this pentagon pattern, members may pass pieces to any other person in the group.

3. *Pattern C.* In this wheel pattern, pieces may only be passed to another person by first handing them to the person in the center, who then may pass them to any other member of the group.

In almost all cases, the pattern B group, which has open communication between all members, will finish first. Pattern C usually comes in second, followed by pattern A. Sometimes pattern A finishes before pattern C because the person in the center of the pattern is not astute enough to facilitate finishing the puzzles.

The discussion that follows this game should encourage students to express their feelings, such as their distress at seeing that some other member needs a piece, but not being able to give it to him, or the frustrations of persons in Pattern C who see those in Pattern B being able to freely pass pieces and feel this is unfair. They can then compare their reactions to this game to real communications patterns in life.

The Language of Acceptance

In his two highly effective books, *Parent Effectiveness Training* (1972) and *Teacher Effectiveness Training* (1975), psychologist Thomas Gordon describes a technique of effective communication between adults and children called the **language of acceptance**. Its purpose is to help adults show their acceptance of children's feelings and desires, for only when people feel truly accepted are they free to move ahead in their developmental tasks.

Gordon feels that most teachers normally use an autocratic language with students. Almost all responses that teachers make to students fall into one of twelve categories. These categories are

- Ordering, directing, commanding.
- Warning, admonishing, threatening.
- Exhorting, moralizing, preaching.
- Advising, giving solutions or suggestions.
- Lecturing, teaching, giving logical arguments.
- Judging, criticizing, disagreeing, blaming.
- Praising, agreeing.
- Name-calling, ridiculing, shaming.
- Interpreting, analyzing, diagnosing.
- Reassuring, sympathizing, supporting, consoling.

- Probing, questioning, interrogating.
- Withdrawing, distracting, humoring, diverting.

Most of these responses are unhelpful and often destructive.

The language of acceptance has been used by many teachers in recent years and the results have been consistently gratifying. The techniques are as follows.

Listen actively. The adult shows that he is attending carefully to what the teenager is saying and does not interrupt him. Even when the adolescent has stopped talking, the adult remains silent because new information may be forthcoming. The adult can show acceptance of the remarks by saying, "uh huh," "yes," or by nodding, thus demonstrating that he desires the youngster to continue speaking.

Restate the youngster's statements. Often the adult can be helpful to the teenager's understanding of him- or herself by restating what has been expressed from a different perspective. For example, if a ninth-grader says, "I hate my mother because she's an alcoholic," the adult might say, "It makes you feel unhappy because you think your mother drinks too much, doesn't it?" By recognizing the unhappiness behind the expressed hatred and by taking the label "alcoholic," which is permanent and negative, and turning it into a temporary problem, the adult can make the teenager see himself and the problem in a new light. He is also removing the self-critical label, "son of an alcoholic," from the youngster, thus showing his acceptance of him.

Use "I" messages. Sometimes when an adult has a problem, he states it as though it were the youngster's problem. For example, "You students always act in a rude way" might be translated, "I feel unhappy because you are making a lot of noise." In the second statement, the adult admits that *he* is the one who has the problem, but because he does, the youngster may soon have one too. This is an **I message.** The goal here is to get both the parties to work with each other to solve the problem so that neither of them suffers from it.

Try the "no-lose" method. A communications technique worked out by Gordon to help resolve conflict is called the **no-lose method.** It involves six steps to be followed in order.

Step 1: Identify and define the conflict. The language of acceptance is helpful here. Frequently children are unable to say what is bothering them because they fear the consequences of mentioning the difficulty. Even when the adult doesn't like what he hears, he must keep an open mind and attempt to get at the real problem.

Step 2: Generate possible alternative solutions. The problem-solving guidelines mentioned in Chapter 4 are useful here.

Step 3: Evaluate as many alternative solutions as possible.

Step 4: Select the best solution from the alternatives.

Step 5: Work out ways of implementing the solution which was selected.

Step 6: After trying out the solution, evaluate how well it has worked.

Adults can enhance the no-lose method by employing active listening and I-messages whenever possible. The combination has been demonstrated to improve communications and cohesiveness in adult-adolescent relationships.

Gordon (1972) has summed up his attitude toward improving communications with teenagers in a statement called "Credo for My Relationships with Youth." In part, he says:

> *You and I are in a relationship that I value and want to keep. Yet each of us is a separate person with his own unique needs and the right to try to meet those needs. I will try to be genuinely accepting of your behavior when you are trying to meet your needs or when you are having problems meeting your needs.*
>
> *When you share your problems, I will try to listen acceptingly and understandingly in a way that will facilitate your finding your own solutions rather than depending on mine. When you have a problem because my behavior is interfering with your meeting your needs, I will listen and then try to modify my behavior, if I can.*
>
> *However, when your behavior interferes with my meeting my own needs, thus causing me to feel unaccepting of you, I will share my problem with you and tell you as openly and honestly as I can exactly how I am feeling, trusting that you respect my needs enough to listen and then try to modify your behavior (p. 305).*

Those who adopt this attitude will usually achieve successful relationships with others, he believes.

SUMMARY

Most sociologists and psychologists agree that adolescents are differentiating themselves from adults more thoroughly than ever. Subcultures can be identified by their distinctive patterns of behavior. Within a culture, which is defined as a blueprint for behavior, there may be one or more subcultures operating partly on the code of the master blueprint and partly on the code of the subculture itself.

There are three major theories of the origin of subcultures. The psychogenic theory is that a large number of people who have a similar problem of adjustment get together and try to deal with the problem and help each other resolve it. The culture transmission theory proposes that new subcultures get started as imitations of subcultures of the previous generation. This implies that teenagers today are not all that different from those of previous decades. Behavioristic theory states that subcultures are the result of trial-and-error behaviors, which are reinforced if they are successful. The behavioristic model seems to offer the most useful explanation.

A number of elements that teenage subcultures have in common are: (1) propinquity; (2) inward-lookingness; (3) psychic attachment; (4) charismatic leadership; (5) desire for autonomy; (6) control of channels of communication; (7) changes in clothing styles and fads; (8) proliferation of group languages; (9) concern for the underdog; and (10) interest in change.

Adolescents form themselves into peer groups because the need for support and approval by age mates is at a peak during this time of life. Peer relationships follow patterns that begin as loose associations and become stronger and more inclusive as the child grows older. The levels of peer group associations are: (1) associates; (2) friends; (3) cliques; (4) clubs; (5) gangs; (6) crowds; and (7) networks.

The organization of these types of peer relationships exists on a continuum from extremely formal to extremely informal, progressing through a series of styles that depend on the age of the teenagers involved.

Dunphy's theory of developmental stages of peer relations is as follows: Stage one is the precrowd stage, in which there are isolated unisexual cliques. Stage two is the beginning of the crowd, in which the unisexual cliques begin to include group-to-group interaction. In stage three, the crowd is in structural transition. The upper-status members of the unisexual cliques form a heterosexual clique. Stage four is the fully developed crowd with the heterosexual cliques in close association. In stage five, the beginning of crowd disintegration occurs and more loosely associated groups of couples start to form, a pattern carried into adulthood.

There are a number of functions of the teenage peer group: (1) the radar function (testing out behavior and getting feedback); (2) replacement for father; (3) support for rebellion; (4) ego building; (5) values orientation; (6) status setting; (7) negative identity; and (8) the avoidance of adult requirements.

For adolescents who are particularly vulnerable, the inability to relate successfully to peers has dire effects, such as mental illness or delinquency. Cliques have a strong influence on over- and underachieving. Studies on the effects of the school setting on peer interactions show that the higher the socioeconomic status, the more likely the students are to attend college and to stay in school to graduate. Large schools are more likely to separate the academic and the vocationally oriented students, and this decreases the interactions between the groups. The most relevant aspect of schools in terms of social interaction is the degree of formality that school authorities demand in various school settings. Teachers can have a considerable impact on peer interactions; an effective means of discovering these patterns in the classroom is the sociogram.

Teachers and others can improve peer group communications by using a variety of game techniques. One technique of effective communication between adolescents and adults is "the language of acceptance." Its purpose is to help adults show their acceptance of a youngster's feelings and desires so that the child can then feel free to move ahead and improve his effectiveness in life. Acceptance can be enhanced by active listening, restating the youngster's statements, and using "I" messages. A communication technique for the resolution of conflict is the "no-lose" method.

Questions

1. What is a subculture? What causes subcultures to form?
2. What are the positive and the negative aspects of teen subcultures?
3. What are the characteristics that an adolescent leader must have?
4. What are the different types of peer groups?
5. Why is the peer group so important to an adolescent?
6. As a teacher, what phrases would you use as the "language of acceptance?"

References

Bandura, A.   "The stormy decade: fact or fiction." In D. Rogers (Ed.), *Issues in adolescent psychology.* New York: Appleton-Century-Crofts, 1972.

Barker, R. G., & Gump, P.   *Big school, small school.* Stanford, Calif.: Stanford University Press, 1964.

Block, R., & Langman, L.   "Youth and work: the diffusion of 'countercultural' values." *Youth and society,* 1974, *5*(4), 411–432.

Boyle, H. P.   "The effects of high school on students' aspirations." *American journal of sociology,* 1966, *71,* 628–639.

Coleman, J. S.   *The adolescent society.* New York: Free Press, 1961.

Coleman, J. S.   "Comments on responses to youth: transition to adulthood." *School review,* 1974, *83*(1), 139–144.

Conger, J.   *Adolescence and youth.* New York: Harper & Row, 1973.

Damico, S. B.   "The effects of clique membership upon academic achievement." *Adolescence,* Spring, 1975, *10*(37), 93–100.

Davis, G. A.   "Teaching for creativity: some guiding lights." *Journal of research and development in education,* 1971, *4*(3), 29–34.

Douvan, E., & Adelson, J.   *The adolescent experience.* New York: Wiley, 1966.

Douvan, E., & Gold, H.   "Model patterns of American adolescence." In L. Hoffman & M. Hoffman (Eds.), *Review of child development research, 2.* New York: Russell Sage Foundation, 1966.

Dunphy, D. C.   "The social structure of urban adolescent peer groups." *Sociometry,* 1963, *26,* 230–246.

Elkin, F., & Westley, W. A.   "The myth of adolescent culture." *American sociological review,* December 1955, *20,* 680–684.

English, H. B.   *Dynamics of child development.* New York: Holt, Rinehart, & Winston, 1962.

Floyd, H. H., Jr., & South, D. R.   "Dilemma of youth: the choice of parents or peers as a frame of reference for behavior." *Journal of marriage and the family,* 1972, *34*(4), 627–634.

Foner, A.   "The polity." In M. Riley, M. Johnson, & A. Foner (Eds.), *Aging and society.* New York: Russell Sage Foundation, 1974.

Gold, M., & Douvan, E.   *Adolescent development: readings in research and theory.* Boston: Allyn & Bacon, 1969.

Gordon, T.   *Parent effectiveness training.* New York: Wyden, 1972.

Gordon, T.   *Teacher effectiveness training.* New York: Wyden, 1975.

Gottlieb, D., & Tenhouten, W.   "Racial composition and the social system of three high schools." *Journal of marriage and the family,* 1965, *27,* 204–212.

Green, A. W.   *Sociology.* New York: McGraw-Hill, 1968.

Herriot, R. W., & St. John, N. H.   *Social class and the urban school.* New York: Wiley, 1949.

Hill, R., & Aldous, J., Jr.   "Socialization for marriage and parenthood." In D. Goslin (Ed.), *Handbook of socialization theory and research.* Chicago: Rand McNally, 1969.

Kilpatrick, W.   "Identity, youth, and the dissolution of culture." *Adolescence,* 1974, *9*(35), 407–412.

Krupor, K.   *Communication games.* Glencoe, Ill.: Free Press, 1973.

Larson, L. G.   "The influence of parents and peers during adolescence: the situation hypothesis revisited." *Journal of marriage and the family,* 1972, *34*(1), 67–74.

Lefrancois, G.   *Adolescents.* Belmont, Calif.: Wadsworth, 1976.

Leona, M.   "Clique language in one suburban high school." Unpublished paper, Boston College, Chestnut Hill, Mass., 1978.

Liddle, G. P.   "Psychological factors involved in dropping out of school." *The high school journal,* 1962, *45,* 276–280.

Manaster, G.   *Adolescent development and the life tasks.* Boston: Allyn & Bacon, 1977.

Myrick, R., & Marx, B. S.   "An exploratory study of the relationship between high school building design and student learning." U.S. Department of Health, Education, and Welfare, No. 5–8006, 1968.

Newman, P.   "Social settings and their significance for adolescent development." *Adolescence,* 1976, *11*(43), 405–418.

Newman, P. R., & Newman, B. M.   "Early adolescence and its conflict: group identity versus alienation." *Adolescence,* 1976, *11*(42), 261–273.

Panel on Youth,   President's Science Advisory Committee. Washington, D.C.: U.S. Government Printing Office (HEW), 1974.

Rogers, D.   *The psychology of adolescence* (3rd ed.). Englewood Cliffs, N.J.: Prentice-Hall, 1977.

Schwartz, M., & Baden, M. A.   "Female adolescent self-concept: an examination of the relative influence of peers and adults." *Youth and society,* 1973, *5*(1), 115–128.

Schwartz, G., & Merten, D.   "The language of adolescence: an anthropological approach to the youth culture." *American journal of sociology,* 1967, *72*(5), 453–468.

Sebald, H.   *Adolescence* (2nd. ed.). Englewood Cliffs, N.J.: Prentice-Hall, 1977.

Sexton, P.   "How the American boy is feminized." *Psychology today,* 1970, *3*(8), 23–29.

Smart, M. S., & Smart, R. C.   *Adolescents: development and relationships.* New York: Macmillan, 1973.

Stein, K. B., Sosken, W. F., & Korchin, S. J. "Interpersonal trust and disaffected high school youth." *Journal of youth and adolescence,* 1974, *3*(4), 281–292.

Thomas, L. E. "Family correlates of student political activism." *Developmental psychology,* March 1971, *4,* 206–214.

Wieder, D. L., & Zimmerman, D. A. "Generational experience and the development of freak culture." *Journal of social issues,* 1974, *30*(2), 137–161.

Williams, R. M., Jr. *American society: a sociological interpretation.* New York: Knopf, 1960.

Additional References

Adeniran, T. "Youth culture in transition: Nigerian youth in the 1970's." *Youth and society,* 1975, *6*(4), 481–494.

Askov, W. H., LaVoie, J. C., & Grinder, R. E. "Social responsibility and interests in school and youth culture." *Adolescence,* 1975, *10*(38), 175–186.

Baizerman, M. "Toward analysis of the relations among the youth counterculture, telephone hotlines, and anonymity." *Journal of youth and adolescence,* 1974, *3*(4), 293–306.

Brake, M. "The skinheads: an English working-class subculture." *Youth and society,* 1974, *6*(2), 179–200.

Block, R., & Langman, L. "Youth and work: the diffusion of 'countercultural' values." *Youth and society,* 1974, *5*(4), 411–432.

Brown, J. W. "The values and norms of the expressive student subculture." *Youth and society,* 1973, *4*(4), 483–498.

Buff, S. "Greasers, dupers, and hippies: three responses in the adult world." In J. M. Starr (Ed.), *Social structure and social personality.* Boston: Little, Brown, 1974.

Carroll, J. W. "Transcendence and mystery in the youth counterculture." *Journal for the scientific study of religion,* 1973, *42,* 361–375.

Curtis, R. L., Jr. "Adolescent orientations toward parents and peers: variations by sex, age, and socioeconomic status." *Adolescence,* Winter, 1975, *10*(40), 483–494.

Fendrich, J. M. "Activists ten years later: a test of generational unit continuity." *Journal of special issues,* 1974, *30*(3), 95–118.

Gifford, V. D., & Colston, D. H. "Group influences on the decisions of selected secondary school students." *Adolescence,* Fall, 1975, *10*(39), 369–372.

Gutmann, D. "The new mythologies and premature aging in the youth culture." *Journal of youth and adolescence,* 1973, *2*(2), 139–155.

Harrison, C. W., Rawls, J., & Rawls, D. "Differences between leaders and nonleaders in six- to eleven-year-old children." *Journal of social psychology,* 1971, *74,* 269–272.

Havighurst, R. J. "Youth in social institutions." In R. J. Havighurst & P. H. Dreyer (Eds.), *Youth.* Chicago: University of Chicago Press, 1975.

Holtz, J. A. "The 'low-riders': portrait of an urban youth subculture." *Youth and society,* 1975, *6*(4), 495–508.

Iaconetta, R. G. "Adolescent-adult interaction and peer-group involvement." *Adolescence,* Fall 1975, *10*(39), 327–336.

Johnson, D. W., & Johnson, R. T. *Learning together and alone: cooperation, competition, and individualization.* Englewood Cliffs, N.J. Prentice-Hall, 1975.

Marsland, D., & Perry, M. "Variations in 'adolescent societies': exploratory analysis of the orientations of young people." *Youth and society,* 1973, *5*(1), 61–83.

Newman, B. M.   "Characteristics of interpersonal behavior among adolescent boys."
Journal of youth and adolescence, 1975, 4(2), 145–153.

Noe, F. P., & Elifson, K. W.   "The pleasures of youth: parent and peer compliance
toward discretionary time." *Journal of youth and adolescence,* March, 1976, pp. 37–
58.

Swift, P.   "Keeping up with youth." *Parade,* September 3, 1972.

Chapter Eight

Love and Sex

Chapter Highlights

The Meaning of Love
Sexuality
  The Sexual Revolution
  Stages of Sexuality
Autosexual Behavior
  Would You Agree?
  Homosexual Behavior
  Myths About Homosexuals
  Causes of Homosexuality
  Societal Attitudes
  Would You Agree?
  An Interview with a Group of
    Lesbians
  An Interview with a Group of Male
    Homosexuals
  Would You Agree?
Heterosexual Behavior
  A Caution about Sexual Activity Research
  Research on Sexual Experience
Motivations for Sexual Behavior
Sexual Values
The Unmarried Teenage Parent
  Trends in Behavior

Race Differences
Causes of Adolescent Pregnancy
The Adolescent Parent
Sex Education
  Sex Education and the Schools
The Demythologizing of Love
  Musical Values
  A Personal Position
Summary

Key Terms and Concepts

feedback
validated
sexual revolution
premarriage relationships
autosexuality
homosexuality
heterosexuality
learning theory

Important People

Erich Fromm
Isadore Rubin

There is a . . . confusion between the initial experience of "falling" in love, and the permanent state of being in love, or as we might better say, of "standing" in love.

—Erich Fromm, 1956, p. 37.

A dolescents desire love, but what they most often experience is infatuation. Fromm makes the distinction between the ephemeral nature of intimacy initiated by sexual attraction and the permanent nature of the love relationship. Adolescents are often infatuated with the idea of love, based more often on fantasies derived from TV and the movies than on reality. But beneath this surface emotion lies a deep need to be found physically attractive and capable — in short, lovable — by others.

THE MEANING OF LOVE

It is easy to say what love isn't, difficult to say what it is. Few have done a better job of defining love than Erich Fromm in his wonderful book, *The Art of Loving* (1956).

Fromm's conception of love starts with the basic need of human beings to receive **feedback** from the environment. Anyone who has ever hallucinated or in some other way has had tricks played on him by his senses realizes how unpleasant and sometimes dangerous it is to misperceive reality. We must have information from the world around us, and to check on its accuracy we must make thousands of comparisons each day of our various sense impressions.

Most of these checks are unconscious. For example, you probably did not notice that the cover of this book was smooth, slightly cool, and its corners sharp. If it had felt bumpy, hot, and round-edged, however, you would have noticed its composition right away. Our minds are constantly making "reality checks," of which we are seldom aware, as though we regularly need to reassure ourselves that our senses are working, that everything is as expected.

238

As important as the confirmation of our sense perceptions is to our equanimity, how much more so is confidence in our innermost feelings. When a person doubts the validity of these, there is a feeling of depression and a disintegration of identity.

How can we gain confidence in our inner self? Fromm suggests this can only be achieved by revealing our inner self to another person who accepts that self. It is not enough for the other to say, "Oh, it's fine that you feel that way," but the person must prove that he or she really understands and values our feelings by sharing part of themselves. Only through the intimacy and acceptance fostered by such a relationship can our most personal self be **validated**. And this last word is the key: when another person truly validates us, we feel love. When they do it regularly, we are "in love" with them.

Are adolescents capable of love as we have defined it? Probably only a few. The ability to be intimate with another requires many experiences of interactions that help one achieve confidence in one's identity. Most adolescents are deeply involved with discovering who they are or want to be. They dare not reveal too much of themselves to others until they can believe that that self is acceptable. Thus, most avoid the long-term commitment of love.

Sex is a different story.

SEXUALITY

If a boy in an unguarded moment tries to entice you to masturbatic experiments, he insults you. Strike him at once and beat him as long as you can stand, etc. Forgive him in your mind, but never speak to him again. If he is the best fighter and beats you, take it as in a good cause. If a man scoundrel suggests indecent things, slug him with a stick or a stone or anything else at hand. Give him a scar that all may see; and if you are arrested, tell the judge all, and he will approve your act, even if it is not lawful. If a villain shows you a filthy book or picture, snatch it; and give it to the first policeman you meet, and help him to find the wretch. If a vile woman invites you, and perhaps tells a plausible story of her downfall, you cannot strike her; but think of a glittering, poisonous snake. She is a degenerate and probably diseased, and even a touch may poison you and your children.

This advice was given to teenagers in 1905 by psychologist G. S. Hall. Today, we smile at its tone of moral indignation. There are few aspects of human behavior that have changed more in this century than sex. Until recently, the popular belief was that, "They're talking more about sex now, but not doing anything more about it!" This may have been true in the first half of this century, but no longer. There have been several causes of the so-called **sexual revolution**.

The Sexual Revolution

Adolescents, seeing their elders flounder in a sea of confused values, began more and more to consult each other on important matters like sex. A far-sighted sociologist, Edgar Freidenberg, saw as early as the late fifties the beginning of this change. He described the genesis of these new attitudes in *The Vanishing Adolescent* (1959). While it has always been the nature of adolescents to revolt against the adult community, adults used to be united in their resistance to it. Now, possibly for the first time in history, adult domination of youthful values has faltered.

The yearning for love and world peace, perennially scorned by the more cynical adults, began in the 1960s to flourish. Adults came to the disconcerting realization that they were beginning to admire and even emulate the values of their adolescent children. As the spirit of "love among brothers and sisters" grew, so did its natural consequence, sex. And a great many adults were no longer sure this was wrong.

Although most teenagers are not ready for mature love, sexual feelings are unavoidable, and for many they are frightening in the extreme. Now come some of the most difficult decisions of life: "Shall I be 'fast' or 'slow'?" "Shall I be heterosexual or homosexual?" "Shall I enjoy my body or strictly discipline it?" To deal with new sexual feelings, the adolescent frequently resorts to defense mechanisms such as asceticism — deceiving oneself that one has no sexual desires — and intellectualization — subjecting one's emotions to the discipline of reason.

The conflict over intimacy and the need for sexual expression foster the distinction adolescents make between love and sex. A major and most difficult task of maturing is to break down this distinction. Many are never able to do it.

Adults help preserve the separation adolescents make between loving and making love. In addition, adults have wanted adolescents to refrain from sex until they are married and working. There is considerable evidence that despite this pressure, today's teenagers are much more free about sex, but are holding off on love commitments. And sexual freedom seems to reflect a more general ease and openness in social behavior. The practice of couple dating seems to be giving way to group dating, in which a number of friends get together to participate in some social event, and only pair off toward the end of the evening, if then.

Margaret Mead (1970), the well-known anthropologist, recommended that teenagers participate in premarriage relationships, in which they would be permitted to live and have sex relations with each other unfettered by the usual legal and social expectations of marriage (but with the understanding that they would practice birth control). Instead of sneaking off to make love in the back seat of a car, a boy might be invited to live in his girlfriend's room, or vice versa, with their parents' consent. Mead suggested that, surreptitiously, trial marriages are already taking place in rapidly growing numbers, and that everyone would be better off if this practice were openly recognized. Teenagers in particular would benefit from the understanding and counsel of adults while practicing these relationships.

Stages of Sexuality

Given that there are new patterns in sexual behavior, can we also expect feelings of love to develop differently? Most psychologists believe that love feelings develop in three steps: love of one's self (**autosexuality**), love of members of one's own sex (**homosexuality**), and love of members of the opposite sex (**heterosexuality**). These stages appear to be natural, although some argue that it is as natural to stay at the second stage as to go on to the third. As we will see, a growing number of adolescents *are* choosing to stay at the homosexual stage.

In the autosexual stage, the child becomes aware of himself or herself as a source of sexual pleasure and consciously experiments with masturbation. The autosexual stage begins at about 2 years of age and continues until the child is about 6 or 7, although in some children it lasts for a considerably longer period of time.

When the child enters kindergarten, the homosexual phase comes to the fore. For most children from the ages of 7 till about 13, best friends, the ones with whom he or she dares to be intimate, are people of the same sex. Feelings become especially intense in the years between 10 and 12 when young people enter puberty and feel a growing need to confide in others. It is only natural that they are more trusting with members of their own sex who share their experiences. Although these relationships are rarely physical, studies (Elias and Gebhardt, 1969; Pomeroy, 1969) report that about one-third of all males and females have experienced sexual play with a member of the same sex at least once during their adolescence. It appears that in most cases such behavior results from curiosity rather than latent homosexuality of the adult variety, however.

The great majority of teenagers move into the third stage, heterosexuality, at about 13 or 14 years, with girls preceding boys by about a year. These three phases are discussed below.

AUTOSEXUAL BEHAVIOR

From the moment we were born we all began making ourselves feel good by touching and playing with our bodies. Some of these experiences were explicitly sexual. From our parents and, later, our schools and churches many of us learned that we were not to continue this pleasurable touching. Some of us heeded their messages and some of us did not. But by the time we were teenagers, whether we masturbated or not, most of us thought it was bad (Boston Women's Health Book Collective, 1976, p. 47).

Masturbation is probably universal to human sexual experience. Although most people still consider it an embarrassing topic, it has always been a recognized aspect of sexuality, legitimate or not. Kinsey, in his 1948 study of male sexuality, found that 97 percent of all males masturbate; among women, approximately two-thirds have masturbated to orgasm by the time they reach 16 (Gagnon and Simon, 1969). Most four- to five-year-olds masturbate, are chastised for it, and stop, then start again at an average age of 14 (Masters and Johnson, 1966). If masturbation is so popular, why has it been considered such a problem?

For one reason, it is believed that the Bible forbids it. Dranoff (1974) points out that the Latin word *masturbari* means "to pollute oneself." For generations, people have taken as a prohibition the passage in Genesis 38:8, in which Onan is slain by the Lord because "he spilled his seed upon the ground." Dranoff argues that Onan was not slain by the Lord for masturbating, but because he refused to follow His directive to mate with his brother's wife. However, the wording of the passage is sufficiently vague that many generations have believed God specifically forbids masturbation.

In addition to the biblical restrictions, for centuries the medical belief was that masturbation causes disease. In 1760, Tissot asserted that a common consequence of masturbation is "locomotor ataxia and early insanity." There are many myths about masturbation—it causes one to go mad, it causes hair to grow on one's palms, it causes one to reject sex with anyone else. There is no research evidence for any intrinsic bad effects of masturbation. In fact, the American Psychoanalytic Association has stated that it should not be considered the sole cause of any particular psychiatric problem (Marcus, 1962).

Another form of autosexual behavior, gang masturbation, has been studied by Verville (1967), who believes this practice is fairly common among 13- to 15-year-old boys. Often, he says, one boy shows the others how masturbation is done, and then the others imitate it. He suggests that gang masturbation can be beneficial to individuals by encouraging a stronger sense of self-confidence through the group's cohesion, but warns that this cohesion has led some masturbation groups to expand their activities to include stealing and vandalism.

Although most psychiatrists feel that there is no intrinsic harm in masturbation and believe it to be a normal healthy way for adolescents to discharge their sexual drive, some teens (mainly boys) feel such a sense of shame, guilt, and fear that they develop the "excessive masturbation" syndrome. In this case, masturbation is practiced even though the child feels very bad about it. These feelings are reinforced by solitude and fantasy, which leads to a debilitating sense of self-condemnation.

WOULD YOU AGREE?

A concerned parent once wondered how she could stop her five-year-old son from masturbating. Asked why she thought it necessary, she said, "For God's sake, if I don't show him it's wrong, he'll probably wind up doing it on a bus someday!" The boy is likely to have such an extreme need to masturbate only if his mother manages to exaggerate its fascination to him through her constant insistence that he stop.

Most psychiatrists argue that masturbation in childhood is not only normal but helpful in forming a positive sexual attitude. It cannot be obsessive at four, so it should be ignored at that age.

It can be obsessive at 14, and if the parent suspects this to be the case, a doctor should be consulted. But this is rare and probably wouldn't arise at all if parents realized how *unnatural* it is to deny sexual release to adolescents until they marry. When masturbation is accepted as neither perverted nor uncommon, few problems are likely to arise.

HOMOSEXUAL BEHAVIOR

Estimates of the number of male Americans who are homosexuals range from 4 percent (Pomeroy, 1969) to 13 percent ("Gays on the March," 1975). These and other sources estimate lesbians to be about 3 percent of the population. Pomeroy (1969) also found that 37 percent of all adult males and almost that many females have had at least one overt homosexual experience. Many gay people feel that the statistics are underestimated because so few gays are willing to admit their sexual preference for fear of repercussions.

Whatever the total figure, there seems to be considerable evidence that the number of homosexuals is growing. Even though the percentages are fairly small, the question of homosexuality is an important one for adolescent psychology, if only because so many adolescents wonder whether or not they *might* be homosexual. Whenever teenagers have difficulty in their relationships with the opposite sex, they are likely to wonder, and usually worry, if they may be homosexuals. Thus, the research on this topic is presented at some length here.

Myths About Homosexuals

Homosexuality is the most misunderstood aspect of sexual behavior. Historically, it has been surrounded by a number of myths:

- Male homosexuals are sissies and will never get involved in a fight.
- Boys with frail physiques and girls with muscular physiques have a strong tendency to become homosexuals.
- Homosexuality results from a psychiatric disorder, usually caused by a hormone imbalance.
- Homosexual men have overprotective mothers and rejecting, inept fathers; in lesbians, the reverse is true.

- Homosexuals frequently attempt to seduce young children; since they cannot give birth to children themselves, this is the only way they can replenish their ranks.

- You can always tell the homosexual male because he "swishes" like a woman when he walks; looks at his fingernails with his fingers pointing away rather than toward himself; uses his hands in an effeminate way, with "limp wrists"; usually talks with a lisp; and crosses his legs like a woman.

- You can always tell a female homosexual because she has unusually short cropped hair; refuses to wear a dress; hates all men; is unusually aggressive; and crosses her legs like a man.

Although these beliefs are widely held, there is no psychological or other evidence of their validity ("Gays on the March," 1975; Hooker and Chance, 1975). Among the most difficult stereotypes confronting homosexuals is the belief that they are "sick." For twenty-three years, until the end of 1973, the American Psychological Association (APA) listed homosexuality among its categories of mental illness. In its decision to exclude homosexuality from that category, the APA Board of Trustees argued that because it cannot be said that homosexuality regularly causes emotional distress or is regularly associated with impairment of social functioning, it does not meet the criteria of a mental illness. However, shortly after this pronouncement, a conservative wing of the APA was able to insist that a category called "Sexual Orientation Disturbance" be established for those people, homosexual or otherwise, who suffer anxieties from the sexual choices they have made.

Causes of Homosexuality

There have been a number of suggestions as to why people become homosexuals. The majority of Americans no longer assume homosexuality is an innate disease (Gallup, 1977). Most now believe it to be the effect of family relationships and social environment.

The two most popular theories are the psychoanalytic and the learning theory positions. Freud suggested that if the child's first sexual feelings about the parent of the opposite sex are strongly punished, the child may identify with the same-sex parent and develop a permanent homosexual orientation. Because researchers have noted many cases in which the father's suppression of the homosexual's Oedipal feelings was not particularly strong, this theory is not held in much regard today.

Learning theory offers another explanation:

The reigning theory among sex researchers is that homosexuality, like heterosexuality, is "learned behavior"—the product of subtle interaction of the child and the significant people around him. Only birds and lower mammals are rigidly programmed to mate with the opposite sex. The higher one goes

*on the mammalian scale, the more the organism is under the sway of learn-
ing rather than inherited factors. But that does not really mean anything
either. Scientists do not yet know how an individual creates a heterosexual
or homosexual value system ("Gays on the March," 1975, p. 37).*

Agreeing that homosexuality is not a mental illness, one psychologist said,
"I'm not going to jump on the opposite bandwagon either and assert that we are
all bisexual, and homosexuality is perfectly normal and healthy. How can we
possibly know at this early stage in the game?" (Malinovich, 1977, p. 86).

Societal Attitudes

Although society is less antagonistic toward homosexuality than it was a decade
ago, there are still strong feelings that homosexuality is either a sin or an illness
or both.

Americans rate homosexuals the group most discriminated against, followed
by blacks, Puerto Ricans, Mexican-Americans, women, and Jews (Harris, 1977).
However, an average of 48 percent also feel that homosexuals should be barred
from a wide variety of jobs, such as camp counsellor (63 percent), school principal (58 percent), teacher (55 percent), and clergyman (50 percent).

———————————————— **WOULD YOU AGREE?** ————————————————

Society's attitudes toward homosexuals depends very much on its *need for children* at any particular time in history. For example, there is almost no mention of
homosexuality in the historical record of early America, a time when the birth of
children was absolutely essential to the continued existence of the community. It
may be that homosexuality was considered so shameful it was never mentioned,
but more probably it was almost nonexistent because of the pressure for childbearing. As America's population need declined, homosexuality became somewhat more prevalent, and was viewed as a crime rather than a sin. With a
further decline in the need for children, homosexuality was reduced to the less
serious category of mental illness. Today, it is no longer officially listed as a
psychiatric illness, and if the United States were to become severely overpopu-
lated, it might even be encouraged. However, if we experienced an unacceptable
population decline, our attitude toward homosexuality would retrace its steps
through these phases.

Many otherwise tolerant people think that homosexuals ought to keep their
sexual preference a secret, so as not to offend those around them. As Abbott
and Love (1974), in their extensive study of lesbianism, said:

Any declaration of the truth about a lesbian's sexuality is regarded by soci-

ety as advertising, broadcasting, or flaunting. What people think should re-main a hidden part of her nature. People see no logic in the lesbian's proclaiming her sexuality, since she could very well remain silent and enjoy all the benefits of the system. One man said, "If I commit adultery, I don't tell people at the office." This is a totally spurious comparison, since adul-tery in no way alters his male identity, but may strengthen it. His social and sexual identity is safely lodged in his heterosexual marriage. His marriage is approved of; by some, his adultery is too. The lesbian, on the other hand, who does not mention her sexuality, is merely in the no-man's land of the single woman, merely with a socio-sexual identity; worse, she is forced to inhabit one not her own (p. 145).

Most of the data we have on homosexuality comes from questionnaire sur-veys and pertains only to specific behaviors. In an attempt to better understand the *feelings* of homosexuals, especially in connection with adolescents, I inter-viewed a group of lesbians and a group of male homosexuals. Some responses to the interview questions are given in the following sections.

An Interview with a Group of Lesbians

How has being a lesbian changed your life?

"Almost everything seems to have changed. Even my relationships with men have become better since I 'came out' [the announcement of one's homosexuality], be-cause I know where I'm coming from. I am not afraid of any ulterior motive, because I know with men the possibility of a sexual attraction isn't there any more. They find it much easier to talk to me because they can sense from me that I'm not expecting anything, so they don't have to prove anything to me."

"I used to be bored by the competition for getting boys. I don't choose to compete."

"I no longer think there's something wrong with me. Sexuality is a big part of every person's body. I have never been able to have intercourse or orgasm with a man. At first, I thought, 'I'm frigid—there's something wrong with me,' but with a woman, it's totally different. It's definitely physical and not just my emotional hangup. I feel much better about myself."

What are some of the problems of being a lesbian?

"We don't know what our parents are going to think. How are they going to be able to say, 'Yes, my daughter is a lesbian'? You're assuming that your parents will come to the realization, but lots of times they just avoid it."

"Meeting other lesbians is a problem. How do you go about meeting other les-bians? You can't just go up to someone and ask them if they are one."

What advice would you give to those who are working with adolescent lesbians or those who think they might be?

"The first thing, don't assume that a person, including an adolescent, is straight or gay. For example, during my first year in college, I was doing career counseling, and I ended up with a 14-year-old homosexual boy. In fact, he was the son of a friend of mine. My reaction was, 'This kid needs counseling!' Little did I know that a year later I was going to be in the same category. My advice is, don't assume you know the sexuality of a person. Don't think of him or her as sick. Everyone should just find out for himself."

"I don't think it's possible for a heterosexual counselor to really help an adolescent who's trying to figure out whether or not he's homosexual or she's a lesbian. That person needs a homosexual who has come out, who has survived and is making it. I don't think a straight person could in any way make it easier. A person can say, 'O.K., I understand, I accept you,' but that's not what the kid needs. He or she needs someone to say, 'I know, I've been there, you're not alone, I feel the same way.' What everyone needs is to know that the world isn't only one way."

"Adolescent lesbians are going through all these crazy feelings. We don't understand these feelings, because it's not talked about. We can't really read about it, because there isn't any information in textbooks. Where do you turn? You just go through it all by yourself and hope that you're not too strange. I felt like I was really different from my friends. If anything, I felt good, or maybe even superior, because they were always waiting by the phone for a boy to call twenty-four hours a day, whereas I never got into that. I just couldn't care less about those things. You should let adolescents know that it's O.K. to be what they are."

An Interview with a Group of Male Homosexuals

How has being a homosexual changed your life?
"It's made me take better care of my appearance. People I know who are straight and married kind of let themselves go. In a heterosexual relationship, girls try to make themselves look as attractive as possible, but the burden is not on the straight man. Once he's married, he just doesn't care how he looks."

"I think it has made me more sensitive to the feelings of other people."

What kind of problems has being a homosexual caused you?
"Sometimes you really feel isolated. People say in a million different ways, 'Don't tell me—I know you're gay—but don't tell me, because if I hear it from you, I won't know what to do, or what to say to you.' "

"I think the lack of having any role models creates a lot of problems. You think, 'I'm the only one in the whole world who's like this, what am I going to do about it?' When you finally realize there are a few more like you, it's a relief."

"I remember when I was in high school and first sorted out where I was heading, I felt very much alone, and I didn't know that it is something that is all right. I didn't know that there are many other people who are just like me. I did discover another boy in my senior year who was gay and who had respect for me. That was the first time I knew I was not alone. Before that it was really tough."

"Even though I realized in high school that I was attracted to men, I thought, 'I'll straighten out some day and get married and have a family.' In my early twenties, I tried to get some reading material on it—some psychology books. When I read about it I was embarrassed, and thought that of course I would outgrow it some day. Well, I haven't outgrown it, but I feel like I'm fine."

What advice would you give to someone who is working with an adolescent homosexual, or someone who thinks he might be?

"If someone were to come up to me and say, 'I'm a leprechaun,' and if I don't know what one is except for some really weird things that I've heard about them, I might be terrified. Even if I didn't know anything about him, I would be afraid. It is just because this is something new, and I don't understand. That is the way people act toward homosexuals. People who do understand homosexuality know that we are not really so strange or dangerous."

"I would say to an adolescent, 'It's O.K., if that's how you feel. You're still young. Don't assume that you're gay just because you're fond of other men. Just because you find other men attractive, don't be afraid of being gay, either.' "

"The English and social studies teachers should talk about homosexuality. Many books and poems have been edited to cover up the fact that they were written by homosexuals. Teachers should tell the kids to go to the library and find the original poem or story and read it and really appreciate it. When the students have come to understand the problem, the teacher should say, 'This poem was written by one man about another.' It would really knock them out!"

WOULD YOU AGREE?

Homosexuals frequently report that their lives are far from easy. There is the fear of exposure, and the pain of ridicule and discrimination that follow it. There is the coldness of many homosexuals, who prefer the temporary excitement of the hunt in gay bars to the commitment of a loving relationship. There are the self-doubts which many homosexuals suffer. And there is the *especially* hard life of the "chicken" (gay teenager), who is often used by the "chicken hawks" (adult homosexuals who prefer teenagers) solely for sexual pleasure.

It is a life-style with many difficult adjustments. For this reason, most gays are not eager to convert others to it. The stereotype of the homosexual as child-seducer is completely unfair. Therefore, laws barring homosexuals from any jobs should be struck down as unconstitutional. More importantly, the straight world should stop treating gays as though they are all ill. Some people may become homosexual because of emotional disturbance, but this is true only of a minority. What is needed is the increased empathy with which we are beginning to treat other oppressed groups.

HETEROSEXUAL BEHAVIOR

Diepold and Young (1979) reviewed twenty studies completed during the 36-year period between the 1940s and the 1970s to discover trends and patterns. One of their more important findings was that most of this research did not lend itself to comparison and integration because of differing methodologies. Jurich (1979) also criticized much of the research on teenage sexuality, claiming that most research tends to search for a single variable or combination of variables that provides an overriding motivation in premarital sexual decisions. His study revealed that there was a highly complex interrelationship among many variables, such as demographic characteristics, environment, and levels of cognitive-moral development, that influenced premarital sexual standards.

Nevertheless, Diepold and Young (1979) were able to discern some trends. One overall conclusion is that since the 1940s, females have gradually but steadily closed the gap between the sexes in sexual activity. They report the following generalizations about specific interpersonal activities among adolescents:

- Almost all teenagers have dated at least once by the age of 18 to 19.
- Most adolescents have participated in kissing by middle adolescence.
- Evidence suggests that both males and females are beginning petting activity at an earlier age nowadays than 30 years ago. About 60 percent have participated by age 16, and 80 to 90 percent by age 19.
- There appears to have been no marked changes in masturbation during the past 30 years for either sex. Almost all males masturbate to orgasm during their teens. This usually begins around the time puberty is reached; boys who reach puberty earlier begin masturbating earlier. About 80 percent of female adolescents have masturbated by age 14, and over 90 percent by age 18.
- There is evidence to suggest that there has been a considerable change in premarital coitus behavior over the studied time period. The 18-year-old male in the 1970s has had experience comparable to a 19-year-old male in the 1940s. The main increase has been in female participation over the years. While the ratio of males to females reporting involvement in intercourse was three to one in the 1940s, it was practically one to one in the 1970s for teenagers 16 years old or over.
- The overall incidence of homosexual contacts during adolescence is not very great and declines with age.

- Some interesting changes were noted regarding birth control during the studied time period. In the 1940s there was less information available; the most common methods of contraception were condoms, withdrawal, and the rhythm method. In the 1970s much more information was available to adolescents, but many studies reveal that most adolescents use no method of birth control, especially during their first few months of sexual experience.

One of the most extensive series of studies has been done by Zelnick and Kantner (1980) for the Alan Gutmacher Institute. They conducted two surveys with 15- to 19-year-old teenagers, one in 1971 and one in 1976. Some of their major findings include the following:

- On the average, there was an increase in premarital intercourse among these teenagers from 27 percent in 1971 to 35 percent in 1976.
- By age 19, 56 percent of the girls had had intercourse, as compared to 46 percent in 1971.
- Although blacks continue to have a higher average prevalence of sexual experience than whites (63 percent compared to 31 percent), the rise for white females was twice as great as for blacks during this period.
- The median age at first intercourse declined over the five-year period by about four months for both blacks and whites.
- The most common place at which teenagers have sex is the home of the boy (41.6 percent), followed by a relative or friend's home (21 percent), the girl's home (16.3 percent), and the automobile (10 percent).
- Although a larger number of teenagers had experienced intercourse in 1976, many were experiencing it with less frequency. While two-fifths of the surveyed sample had not experienced intercourse in the month prior to the interview in 1971, this number had increased to 50 percent by 1976.
- The male partner at first intercourse tends to be two to three years older than the female.

Dignan and Anspaugh (1978) conducted a study to determine whether adolescents whose attitude toward sexuality is permissive are different from those whose attitude is not permissive. They found that the group classified as low in permissiveness was much more homogeneous than the highly permissive group. There were certain determinants that these researchers found could be used to predict high versus low permissiveness. Sexual intercourse within the last year, and age at first intercourse were two such variables. That is, permissiveness can be predicted with quite a high degree of accuracy by recent experience with intercourse and young age at first intercourse. The less permissive adolescents also tended to be regular church attenders, of the same religion as their parents, and from intact families. There were also more females than males in the low permissive group. Interestingly, knowledge of human sexuality was found to have no relation to level of permissiveness.

Abernathy et al. (1979) also measured sexual attitudes and behavior among adolescents. They compared college students from urban, suburban, and rural areas and found that some interesting differences do exist among these groups. A direct relationship appears to exist between sexual permissiveness and degree of urbanization; rural teenagers are the most conservative, those from cities are the most liberal. However, both male and female adolescents from city environments were less willing than the others to grant women the same sexual freedom as men. The suburban females were found to have the highest rates of promiscuous behavior, but were not the most permissive. These authors conclude that there is only a moderate relationship between sexual attitude and behavior, that permissiveness is neither unidimensional nor a simple function of degree of urbanization.

College students' participation in premarital sex has been examined from several viewpoints by Murstein and Holden (1979). The researchers collected information on philosophy of sex, relationship with parents, physical attractiveness, religious feelings, involvement with drugs, commitment to last sexual partner, and attitudes toward marriage and the women's liberation movement.

In this study, 75 percent of the females and 83 percent of the males reported that they engaged in premarital sex. Females were found to be more committed to their partners than were males. Among the females, the following variables were found to affect the probability of participation in premarital sex: relationship with parents, physical attractiveness, religious feeling, and drug involvement. For males, only drug involvement was found to be related to premarital experience.

One of the societal changes that seems to have affected adolescent sexuality most strongly is maternal employment. Hansson et al. (1981) conducted a study to determine whether maternal employment is associated with teenage sexual attitudes and behaviors and therefore increases the likelihood of pregnancy. They found that those girls whose mothers are employed outside the home have a greater tendency to begin sexual relations before the age of 19. They show less concern regarding the risk of unintended pregnancy and score lower in practical knowledge of contraception. This is consistent with earlier reports that daughters whose mothers work tend to be more outgoing and independent.

Sexual harassment and abuse during adolescence has been studied by Herold et al. (1979). These researchers surveyed young women in college and found that nearly 85 percent of them say they have been victims of a sexual offense. Offenses ranged from obscene phone calls (61 percent) and sexual molestation (44 percent) to attempted rape (16 percent) and rape (1 percent). Most of these offenses were discussed with friends. Very few were reported to parents, police, social workers, or other authorities.

Brown (1979) has studied prostitution among teenage girls. She finds that some of the common childhood experiences that occur in girls who later become adolescent prostitutes include alienation from family, parental abuse, low level or failure in education, many changes in family and home life, and dismal job prospects. Entrance into prostitution is motivated by desire for financial enterprise, adventure, delinquent associates, institutionalization, anger and hostility either towards oneself or towards men, sexual promiscuity, and drug abuse. A young girl may also find prostitution a way to gain attention, affection, importance, and the achievement of goals.

Surprisingly, Brown learned that juvenile girls are more seriously punished when arrested for prostitution than are boys. As a matter of fact, these girls often receive harsher treatment than do boys who commit more serious crimes. Girls' correctional facilities are generally more rigid, the fences are higher, and the confinement cells smaller than are boys' facilities.

Wagner (1980) finds that sexuality is integrated into adolescents' concept of self—regardless of their personal experience or knowledge. She states that the search for personal identity is the primary goal of adolescence. Wagner summarizes the current status of research-based knowledge in certain aspects of adolescent sexuality:

Knowledge about sexuality.   There is some evidence to indicate that teenagers who receive sex information from their parents or someone important to them behave more conservatively and responsibly. Males and females are about equally informed, but neither group is well informed. Peers and books are the most common sources of information.

Attitudes, values, and standards.   Current research reveals a trend towards change in sexual mores among the young. In general, permissiveness with affection is emerging as the most popular standard. Adolescent sexuality appears to be as much affected by social change and historical events as by separation and identity formation.

Homosexuality.   Most homosexual contact during adolescence is part of a developmental interlude and will not develop into adult homosexual behavior. It happens more among boys than girls, and usually occurs during early adolescence.

Male-female differences.   Differences in heterosexual specific practices are more evident in younger than in older adolescence. There is tremendous variability among adolescents in terms of specific sexual practices. More advanced types of sexual behavior (such as petting and intercourse) are occurring at earlier and earlier ages. While there has been a decline in male promiscuity, there has been an increase in female permissiveness.

Social context of sexual learning.   By and large, sexuality is learned through experience rather than reading, lectures, or similar ways.

Wagner concludes that each new sexual experience provides the adolescent with opportunities to test autonomous behavior in a conflict situation. She states that societal changes in attitudes, standards, and behavior have all been reflected in sexuality among adolescents.

MOTIVATIONS FOR SEXUAL BEHAVIOR

Most people disregard or repress their sexuality only at their peril. It is true that the sex drive, unlike other instinctual drives like hunger and thirst, can be thwarted without causing death. Some persons are able to practice complete celibacy without apparent harmful effect to their personalities. The great majority, however, become highly irritable when their sexual needs are not met in some way. Sebald (1977),* adapting the ideas of Mitchell, suggests six motives for sexuality:

1. *The need for intimacy.* This need often conflicts with others such as independence and self-protection, but if unmet, it can cause intense depression (see Chapter 11). Traditionally, sexual interaction took place only when two people had achieved intimacy. Today, many youth believe that sexuality can help bring about a sense of intimacy.

2. *The need for belonging.* Most people have a strong need to identify with group behavior. The leaders of an adolescent peer group, usually the more mature members, tend to engage in sex first. They offer a powerful model for the others, who wish to emulate their behavior. Adolescents often date and go steady not so much because they sincerely like their partner as because it is the expected thing to do. Although dating and going steady are no longer expected, sex certainly is.

3. *The desire for power.* Both sexes have a need for control, sometimes expressed in the behaviors of male domination and female manipulation. Its more mature form is the feeling of personal importance that each partner can get from giving the other satisfaction in lovemaking.

4. *The desire for submission.* Submission is the complementary need to power. Just as we sometimes like to have control, we also like to have the feeling of being taken care of. In Eric Berne's terms, the "parent" in us has the desire for power, and the "child" in us has the desire for submission.

5. *Curiosity.* When people's other needs are reasonably well taken care of, they have a desire to explore their environment and their capabilities in relation to it. It is natural, therefore, for healthy adolescents to want to find out more about their new sexual feelings and to learn what directions their feelings can take.

6. *The desire for passion and ecstasy.* The Greek word *ekstasis* means "to be outside of oneself." Medical researchers have suggested that people occasionally need to experience transcendence, the feeling of getting outside of and rising above themselves — in other words, a "high." Sebald suggests that there are three benefits deriving from sexual passion: intense self-awareness,

*From Hans Sebald, *Adolescence: A Social Psychological Analysis,* 2nd ed., © 1977, pp. 130–131. By permission of Prentice-Hall, Inc.

intense awareness of the other person, and confirmation of the other person as someone who is intensely important to you.

I would suggest a seventh reason for sexuality:

7. *Socially approved playfulness.* Society equates playfulness with being irresponsible and foolish. Yet all of us who are no longer children seem to feel the need for going back to that relaxed and happy period. Sexual play can be a situation where we can act silly, use baby talk, and just fool around with our partners. This kind of activity can leave us better prepared to go back to the heavy burdens of adult responsibility.

SEXUAL VALUES

Although the motives for sexual behavior are fairly constant, American values and attitudes toward sex have varied considerably. Sociologist Isadore Rubin (1965) has suggested that Americans hold any of six different value positions:

1. *Traditional asceticism.* Sex is a necessary evil, only to be allowed in marriage and strictly for the purpose of procreation. This view is a feature of religious dogma. Adolescents taught this value think of sex as dirty and frequently have problems accepting the sexual aspect of marriage.

2. *Enlightened asceticism.* Although not considered evil, sex is a somewhat dangerous activity that must be carefully controlled. People are encouraged to master their sexual feelings and to allow them to be expressed only under carefully specified conditions.

3. *Humanistic liberalism.* The goodness or badness of sexual activity is determined by the effect it has on the relationship of the people who engage in it. According to the "situational ethics" that some liberals endorse, any kind of sex would be all right as long as the consequences justify it. Sex among teenagers is acceptable, but only if the teenagers are unusually mature and able to handle the consequences of their behavior.

4. *Humanistic radicalism.* Complete sexual freedom is favored, but only after careful education. No type of sexual activity is considered wrong in itself, so long as physical and emotional damage is not likely to result.

5. *Fun morality. Playboy,* the men's magazine, typifies the point of view that the main motivation for sex is fun. People should be encouraged to engage in sex as much as they like, with no restrictions except that no one is physically abused.

6. *Sexual anarchy.* This philosophy is similar to fun morality, except that it advocates no restrictions on any type of sexual behavior. Sodomy, fetishes,

sadism, masochism, necrophilia — all are considered appropriate expressions of sexuality if the people involved feel they are.

All six sexual values are held by recognizable groups in the United States. None seems to enjoy majority status. There appears to be a growing laissez-faire attitude: "As long as no one interferes with my beliefs, I won't interfere with theirs." This may be one reason why there has been such an increase in pregnancies among unmarried women, especially adolescent girls.

THE UNMARRIED TEENAGE PARENT

"You're pregnant," the doctor said, "and you have some decisions to make. I suggest you don't wait too long to decide what you'll do. It's already been seven weeks, and time is running out!"

"Look, it just can't be true!" I replied. I was trying to convince myself that the doctor was lying. It wasn't supposed to be like this! I was tired of the bitter quarrel I had been having with the clinic doctor. I resented him with every passion. How could I let myself be seen like this?

I had been fearing this answer. I suppose I knew the truth all along, but I really didn't want to face it. I didn't want an abortion, that much I was sure of. Besides, where would I get the money?

For ages now, I had been thinking my period would come any day. Now the truth was in the open! I walked out of the office and headed aimlessly down the street. I looked around and saw only ugliness. I thought about God and how even He had deserted me. It all hurt so much.

"How could this have happened to me?" I thought. "Good girls don't get pregnant!" All of the things my mother had told me were lies. According to her, only the "fast" girls got pregnant. The ones who stayed out late and hung around with boys. I wasn't part of that category!

I looked down at my stuffed belly and thought about my family. Would they be understanding this time? After all, they had plans for my future. They would be destroyed by the news.

"I'm not a tramp," I said to myself. "Then again, I'm only 16 and who would believe that Arthur and I really are in love?"

The feelings of this unmarried girl are all too typical. Children born of these pregnancies have it even harder. Harvard biological anthropologist Melvin Konner (1977) sums it up:

As maternal age drops from age 20, mortality risk for mother and child rise sharply as does the probability of birth defects. Offspring of adolescent mothers, if they survive, are more likely to have impaired intellectual functioning. Poverty, divorce, inept parenting, child neglect, and child abuse are all more frequent in teenage parents (p. 38).

What are the teenagers like who become unmarried parents? The images of the fast and easy girl and sex-obsessed boy are surely false. Most of these couples have had substantial relationships prior to the pregnancy, usually for at least six months. The idea that unmarried parents are usually from the lower socioeconomic class and from one-parent families is also an untrue generalization.

The unmarried mother may be black or white, Protestant, Jewish, or Catholic, have grade eight or college education, be of low or high socioeconomic status, live with both parents or neither, have a firm or nonexistent attachment to the father of the child, use contraceptives or fail to do so. No single profile emerges. We can predict with assurance though, that the teenaged unwed mother will be the least capable of dealing with the situation and that her problem will have to be dealt with by some group in society. She will, in all likelihood, lack the physical, social, emotional, intellectual, and economic resources necessary to carry her through the present illegitimate pregnancy and to help her avoid subsequent ones (Juhasz, 1974, p. 267).

The picture of the unmarried father is quite similar. Although these boys tend to be more immature and inexperienced than others, the idea that they usually run out on their pregnant girlfriends is not a fair one. In fact, well over half of unmarried fathers either marry or continue to have some close relationship with the young mother.

Trends in Behavior

Adolescents in the United States have rates of pregnancy that are among the world's highest, especially inner city adolescents (Bierman and Bierman, 1978; Bruce, 1978; Colletta, 1980; Moore, et al., 1979; McKenry et al., 1979; Silber, 1980; *Teenage Pregnancy*, 1978). Ten percent of American adolescents get pregnant, and six percent of them give birth each year. Of these, one-third give birth out of wedlock, one-third conceive before marriage, and one-third conceive after marriage (McKenry, et al., 1979). In one project, researchers interviewed 1000 thirty-year-olds and found that 10 percent of the men and 31 percent of the women had had a child during adolescence (Russ-Eft et al., 1979).

Even though the birthrate in the United States in general is declining, adolescents are delivering more babies. As a matter of fact, the birthrate among girls below the age of 18 has increased by 75 percent in the last decade (McKenry et al., 1979; Tietze, 1978).

A group of researchers from Johns Hopkins University have conducted a number of surveys for the Alan Gutmacher Institute. They collected and reported data in 1971, 1976, and 1979 to determine and evaluate trends in adolescent sexuality, pregnancy, and contraception (Zelnick and Kantner, 1972, 1977a and b, 1980; and Zelnick, et al., 1979). In the 1976 survey they found that by the age of 17, one in 10 American teenage girls has been pregnant at least once, and by the age of 19 one quarter of them have been pregnant. They also found that one-fifth of all first time pregnancies occurred within the first month of sexual activity and one-half occurred during the first six months of sexual activity. Seventy percent of the first pregnancies in these teenagers were premaritally conceived. Recent estimates indicate that four out of ten 14-year-old girls will be or will have been pregnant by the time they reach age 20!

Race Differences

Many of the studies have shown that there are distinct differences between black and white teenagers in sexual behavior, pregnancy, and the outcomes of such pregnancies. Black teenagers begin sexual experimentation at an earlier age than do white teenagers (Zelnick and Kantner, 1980). The Johns Hopkins University studies determined that blacks are more likely to get pregnant than whites during adolescence, but the gap between the two races has been lessening during the last decade. Unmarried first pregnancies among whites had risen by about one-third between the 1971 survey and the 1976 survey, but there had been no change among blacks.

One study (Thompson, 1980) compared whites and blacks on their beliefs, perceptions, and decisions related to having children. Black teenagers, both males and females, felt more strongly that having children promotes greater marital success, approval from others, and personal security. They also expressed stronger beliefs that couples should have as many children as they wish. Black males, more than females, placed a high value on having children, but black females felt exposed to stronger social pressures to have children.

The Zelnick and Kantner surveys found distinct differences in the outcomes of black versus white teenage pregnancies, which may reflect some of the philosophical differences described above. Not only do black adolescents seem to abort fewer of their pregnancies, but also they may not report abortions at the same rate white teenagers do (Zelnick and Kantner, 1977a). They found that in 1976 white teenagers had 27 percent live births as compared to 76 percent among blacks. Induced abortions accounted for 45 percent of the outcomes of white pregnancies as compared to eight percent for the blacks. Stillbirths and miscarriages account for the rest of the pregnancies. Marriage after a premarital pregnancy among blacks occurred less often than among whites, both in the 1971 and the 1976 survey.

Regardless of marital status, there is a higher incidence of adolescent parenting among blacks than among whites (Russ-Eft et al., 1979). Zelnick and Kantner's survey revealed that only six percent of black infants were living apart from their adolescent mothers in 1976; this was similar to the pattern in 1971. More than 18 percent of the infants of white mothers were put up for adoption in 1976, and other arrangements such as care by the infant's grandmother or other relatives and friends occurred more often among whites than among blacks.

In an extensive review of the recent literature on adolescent pregnancy, McKenry et al. (1979) make an important point about racial differences. They find that while studies of low income nonwhite girls tend to focus on social factors, studies of white, middle-class girls tend to search for psychological explanations for the pregnancies and their outcomes. It is important to remember that while there do appear to be racial and social class differences reported in the research, some of these differences may have more to do with the researchers than with the teenagers themselves.

Causes of Adolescent Pregnancy

Why do so many adolescents get pregnant? McKenry et al. (1979) state that many factors combine to create the situation. They divide the causes into four major categories: physiological, psychological, social, and cognitive abilities.

Physiological: It is presently possible for girls to get pregnant at a younger age because of improvements in the general health among Americans. Menarche occurs at an earlier age than in the past (see Chapter 3). The American Academy of Pediatrics Committee on Adolescence has learned that the fertility rate among girls under 15 years of age has been rising rapidly (1979). Improved nutrition and health care have also contributed to an increase in the potential for young girls to become pregnant (Waltz and Benjamin, 1980).

Psychological: McKenry et al. (1979) state that sometimes pregnancy is the result of a teenager's conscious or unconscious desire to get pregnant. These researchers found that the psychoanalytic model is preeminent in psychological explanations of adolescent pregnancy. Ego strength and family relationships are the most commonly cited reasons. Low ego strength or a low sense of personal worth is said to lead to sexual acting out or use of sex as an escape. Highly dependent girls with a great need for affection and those experiencing social or psychological stress are more likely to become pregnant. Also, girls with an external locus of control are more likely to get pregnant.

Family situations or problems which have been linked to the incidence of adolescent pregnancy include the following: closeness to father, lack of closeness to mother, generally unstable family relationships, father absence accompanied by resentment of the mother, and feelings of rootlessness (McKenry et al., 1979).

Social: Poverty influences the pregnancy rate; insufficient economic and social resources may lead to pregnancy (McKenry et al., 1979). Pressure from peers and the influence of the media are also social precursors to pregnancy during adolescence.

Cognitive Abilities: Another major cause concerns young girls' lack of the knowledge and maturity required to prevent unwanted conceptions. One must possess the cognitive ability to foresee the consequences of sexual activity. Epstein (1979) indicates that some teenagers believe they are too young to become pregnant or that their sexual encounters are too infrequent. A United States Government report (*Teenage Pregnancy,* 1978) indicated that one teen in four did not know it was possible to become pregnant during a single act of intercourse. Others are unable to relate risks of pregnancy to their menstrual cycles or are too menstrually irregular to use such information properly.

Despite organized efforts to improve sex education and to provide information about contraception at an earlier age, many teenagers remain ignorant about the risks of becoming pregnant. One study determined that 68 percent of the girls and 80 percent of the boys interviewed had not learned facts about birth control (Bruce, 1978).

The Zelnick and Kantner surveys determined that in 1976 less than 25 percent of the teenagers who got pregnant had intended to do so. But only one-fifth of these had used contraception. Many teenagers try to act responsibly but there are many obstacles. Many cannot talk to their parents about sex and lack other sources for information.

McKenry et al. (1979) believe that a young girl's maturity, in relationship to avoiding pregnancy, must manifest itself in several ways. She must have self-control; she must be able to foresee the consequences of her behavior; she must believe she can get pregnant; and she must acknowledge her sexuality to doctors or clinic personnel in order to acquire birth control information.

The Adolescent Parent

One report (*Teenage Pregnancy,* 1978) states that teenagers often bring inadequate skills to the job of parenting. Evidence indicates that children born to unmarried parents are three and a half times more likely to become victims of child abuse than the average child.

The McKenry et al. (1979) review of the literature revealed that adolescents often have a negative parenting style. They have little knowledge of normal child development and unrealistic early developmental and behavioral expectations. Adolescent mothers are more impatient, irritable, insensitive, and inclined to use physical punishment. They also exhibit less verbal interaction with their babies than do older mothers. A mother's ability to care for and nurture her children is directly related to her level of maturity. Various stages of her infant's development may lead to fantasies, conflicts, and anxieties within the adolescent mother herself.

In general, having a child in the teen years is not beneficial to the child or the young mother, but there are exceptions. The oft-cited statistics conceal the rare but existent adolescent mothers who are able to become not only effective parents, but also functional and contributing members of their communities.

The teenage father.   Very few studies have been conducted to learn about adolescent fathers. The teenage father is left out of most special programs dealing with adolescent pregnancy and parenthood, including counseling programs (*Teenage Pregnancy,* 1978). This inattention to males is closely related to cultural attitudes that accept sexual behavior among boys but label pregnant girls socially deviant.

One study did seek to learn more about unmarried adolescent fathers. Hendricks (1980) investigated the problems faced by black teenage fathers and their sources of social support. All of the subjects in this study were employed high school graduates. Four percent of them had sisters who were unwed mothers, 35 percent had brothers who were unwed fathers, and 25 percent of them had been born out of wedlock themselves.

Most of the subjects claimed that they enjoyed life, had happy family relations, and liked school. While the researcher found no single problem as the dominant theme among these teenage fathers, the subjects did describe themselves as enduring a wide range of stressful experiences.

In this study, Hendricks sought to determine where black unmarried fathers could go for social support, advice, and coping strategies. His survey revealed that 95 percent of the subjects relied on their families, especially their mothers, for such support. Friends were categorically rejected as lacking expertise, and most were seen as likely to give misleading advice. Community resources such as clergymen and school teachers were likewise rejected. Social services agencies got mixed results; none of the subjects felt they would *seek out* such services, but 95 percent said they would use the services if offered to them.

The specific areas these boys said they would like help with include parenting skills, sex education, job training, and placement services.

The teenage mother. Dresen (1976) offers five suggestions to adolescent girls faced with single parenthood:

1. Differentiate between what you think you *should* do and what you *want* to do. Then, assuming that it doesn't harm anyone else, do what you really *want* to do. You will be far more content.

2. Reach out to people for help when you need it. Talking about ambivalent feelings and fears with others helps put thoughts in proper perspective. Self-help groups such as Parents Without Partners are available in most larger cities. You can gain support by listening to what others in similar situations have done.

3. Engage in some thoughtful and long-range planning about jobs and careers, insurance, and savings plans. Perhaps a return to school should be considered (although a fairly high percentage of schools still forbid teenage mothers to return to their halls).

4. Line up a number of sources that will be helpful to you as a mother; for example, reliable baby sitters, day-care programs, medical clinics, and so forth. Be prepared in case of any emergency.

5. Increase your knowledge about contraception and human sexuality.

Until recently, the situation of unwed parents has been markedly bleak. Juhasz (1974), however, sees a more hopeful future:

With more comprehensive education on human sexuality, with increasing knowledge and acceptance of contraception, and with better understanding of the unwed family constellation, it should be possible to decrease the number of unwanted children. It should also be possible to better prepare par-

ents of those children who are wanted. In addition, it should facilitate effective counseling and assistance for the young parents and their families. Finally, this should increase the likelihood that all who are involved can have happy, healthy, and useful futures (p. 271).

In the achievement of this goal, sex education is clearly the key.

SEX EDUCATION

It is hard to overestimate the need for sex education. The Harvard-based Project on Human Sexual Development has sponsored a series of studies, workshops, and programs to learn more about how teenagers understand sexuality. In one eleven-month study, the investigators interviewed almost 1500 parents to determine the patterns of communication with regard to the issues of sexuality (Roberts et al., 1978). Some of the major findings are summarized here:

- Most parents want their children to be informed about all aspects of sexuality by the time they reach adolescence.
- Most parents want to clarify their own attitudes toward sexuality.
- Less than 15 percent of the parents surveyed said they had never mentioned any aspect of erotic love or its consequences to their children.
- Less than 50 percent of the parents with daughters between the ages of nine and eleven had talked with their children about menstruation.
- Less than 15 percent of the parents had mentioned intercourse or masturbation to their children.
- Less than one percent of the mothers and less than two percent of the fathers had ever mentioned "wet dreams."
- Less than five percent of the respondents had ever mentioned contraception to their children, although a majority of them wanted their children to know about contraception.
- Seventy-five percent of the mothers and 50 percent of the fathers had discussed pregnancy and childbirth with their children, but in a very simplistic manner.

The study also found that communication concerning sexuality is considered by most parents to be the mother's responsibility. Most of the parents in the survey said they wanted their children to know more about their bodies and their sexuality than they did when they were growing up. However, the majority clearly discouraged their children's inquiries about erotic behavior. Many felt uncomfortable with such discussions, especially if they had grown up in a household devoid of communication about sexuality. Even in those families where children's questions are answered, most parents feel that one-time explanations are enough.

The researchers call this common practice the "innoculation theory" (one "shot" will do the job), and they feel it can seriously limit a child's learning. The types of information, the style, and the detail with which they are presented all should change as the child grows. Most people need to be exposed to new information several times, as well as think about it, discuss it, and question it before they can truly understand it.

Two studies focused on communication between mothers and daughters about sexuality (Fox, 1979; Fox and Inazu, 1978). These surveys revealed that 20 percent of the mothers had never told their daughters about menstruation, 50 percent had not discussed the father's role in reproduction, and 68 percent had never talked about any aspect of birth control! These investigators determined that menstruation, dating, and boys are the most commonly talked about sexuality topics between mothers and daughters, while sexual intercourse and birth control are the least discussed.

Walters et al. (1979) conducted a study to determine what American adolescents actually know and do not know about sexuality. They found that while most adolescents understand that pregnancy results from intercourse, many do not understand when. In fact many teenagers erroneously believe that conception occurs near mensus and that midcycle is the safest time to have intercourse. These investigators found that *fewer* than 50 percent of their sample knew the following facts of sexuality:

- Higher rates of infant and mother mortality occur among teenage mothers.
- It is not always easy to tell if a person has a venereal disease.
- X-rays during pregnancy can cause fetal defects.
- There is a relationship between prenatal care and a baby's health.
- It is impossible to be totally sure when a woman cannot get pregnant (Walters et al., 1979).

Dickenson (1978) reviewed the major sources of sex information used by teenagers in 1964 and then again in 1974. He found that at both times parents were the preferred source for most adolescents. However, there was a general change from parents to friends, especially among males. That is, more teenagers in 1974 relied on their friends instead of their parents for information than did in 1964. He also found that youths desire better communication with their parents but feel that avenues are not open to them. Dickenson feels that since so many adolescents are beginning to rely on their peers, school-based sex education must be designed to assure that more of these peers are exposed to adequate and accurate sex information.

Sex Education and the Schools

Can sexuality be adequately taught in the schools? A report issued by the Project on Human Sexual Development (Roberts and Holt, 1979) examines some of the societal factors that stand in opposition to adequate sex education for American youth. The authors state that contemporary American society still has no clear, conscious, coherent policy toward educating young people about sexuality. Many of our laws and social mores are based on assumptions about sexuality, and these assumptions constitute a de facto national policy. Examples of these assumptions are the denial of the existence of sexuality during childhood, and the feeling that people are sexual only during the reproductive period of their lives.

Many communities have turned to the schools for a solution to the problems of sexual ignorance and misinformation among children and adolescents. In 1905, the Organization of the American Society for a Sanity and Moral Prophylaxis was established, marking the beginnings of school-based sex education. The organization's major goal was social hygiene and the elimination of venereal diseases. Up to the 1950s, most school programs concentrated on the control of venereal disease and reproductive biology. In the 1950s, sex education programs began to introduce human development and relationships. In the 1960s, the focus on sex education changed with the establishment of federal programs, such as the Sex Information and Education Council of the United States, and professional groups, such as the American Association of Sex Educators, Counselors, and Therapists (Roberts and Holt, 1979).

There are many models, structures, and forms that sex education programs can take, ranging from single lectures on specific topics to full kindergarten through high school curricula covering all aspects of sexuality. In some programs, nonschool personnel such as doctors or nurses deliver isolated lectures. In the unit-of-study model, sexuality is included as a unit in an appropriate course, such as science or health. Some school systems offer a specific course taught by a special educator. When sex education is integrated into the entire curriculum, sexual issues are treated as they arise naturally from the study of science, social studies, health, the arts, or other course subjects (Roberts and Holt, 1979).

Much controversy still exists as school systems and communities try to determine which model best suits the needs of the students, the wishes of the parents, and the ability of the school system. Yarber (1979) compared sex education in the family to that in schools from the viewpoints of students, parents, teachers, and principals at four different grade levels: third, sixth, ninth, and twelfth grades. Surprisingly, he found that very few differences existed among the groups. All groups supported sex education and felt it should take place in school. Teachers and principals felt that more emphasis should occur at the secondary than at the elementary level. The only significant difference found was between parents and students at the twelfth grade level. Parents, more than students, favored more sex education in school!

In order to learn more about the relationship between sex education and sexual behavior, Dembo and Lundell (1979) explored some of the major reasons for the limited contraceptive use among sexually active adolescents. They state that three intertwining aspects of adolescence contribute to the lack of contraception: lack of information, cognitive-emotional development, and acceptance of sexuality. Many sexually active teenagers are not emotionally or cognitively ready to accept their sexuality enough to allow them to plan for sexual activity. Many feel unprepared to make sexual decisions.

These aspects of adolescence have implications for sex education. Dembo and Lundell (1979) claim that programs should consist of an educational rather than an informational approach. For example, programs that allow for exploration of emotional and physical concerns, help in developing a sense of moral responsibility, and preparations for sexual decision making should be included, according to these authors. This necessitates a highly personalized and individual approach, and the collection of attitudinal and informational data on participants before developing a program.

Unfortunately, few such programs now exist. For example, Spanier (1978) found no real relationship between participation in a sex education course used in public schools and premarital sexual behavior. This study determined that there was no significant difference between the sexual behavior of those who had attended the course and those who had not. There was no more distinction found among different teachers or courses taken in different school years. This study is evidence that truly effective sex education programs may not yet have been designed.

The blame appears to fall in three areas: text inadequacy, student characteristics, and teacher preparedness. Rubenstein et al. (1977) found that students' top 10 interests in sex — venereal disease, birth control, sexual intercourse, love, pregnancy, enjoyment of sex, abortion, sex offenses, guilt about sex, and prostitution — are covered inadequately or not at all in the 31 sex education textbooks they examined. Further, most of the books had a moralizing tone, and the more they moralized, the less they dealt adequately with the student interests. Herold and Benson (1979) learned that many secondary teachers feel student traits often make sex instruction difficult. They pointed primarily to large differences in student maturity, knowledge, values, and reluctance to discuss the topics as major hindrances. Finally, Ryan and Dunn (1979) discovered that teacher preparation is most inadequate, and the majority of prospective teachers interviewed preferred that medical or other specialized personnel handle such instruction. It seems clear that unless a change in attitude in sex education in the schools takes place, we can expect a growing rate of unwanted pregnancies, abortions, and venereal disease. If the prohibition of legal abortions and the interuterine device (IUD) occurs, as advocated by powerful groups such as the Moral Majority, the impact on these areas will be explosive indeed!

So far, this chapter has primarily considered the changing scene of adolescent sexual behavior. Not surprisingly, there have been changes at least as important in the ways teenagers feel and express love. The next section discusses these.

THE DEMYTHOLOGIZING OF LOVE

Psychologist William Kilpatrick (1974) believes that our attitudes toward love have taken a radically different twist. Love has become less romantic and more openly sexual, less oriented toward the future and more toward the present. There is evidence supporting this view from a number of sources.

Song titles, for example, indicate a sharp change in theme. The themes of the past, such as "I Don't Want to Live Without You," "I Only Have Eyes for You," and "You're the One Girl for Me," have been replaced by "Reasons," "Fifty Ways to Leave Your Lover," and "We've Got Tonight."

Musical Values

In the spaces below, name the ten songs you think are currently the most popular. In the second column, place an L if the theme is mainly about romantic love, an S if it is about sex, and an O if neither. Is Kilpatrick right?

Theme:
L or S

1. _____ _____

2. _____ _____

3. _____ _____

4. _____ _____

5. _____ _____

6. _____ _____

7. _____ _____

8. _____ _____

9. _____ _____

10. _____ _____

In movies, too, we see a change in the popular point of view. *Casablanca*, with its theme of undying devotion, would not likely be made today. A much more common theme is "boy meets girl, they sleep together, they leave each other." Even the love stories that do exist, such as *Star Wars* and *Raiders of the Lost Ark*, are space fantasies.

The romantic ideal of eternal love between two people flowered in the Middle Ages with its code of chivalry and remained the dominant literary mode until the 1960s. The one major variation in the romantic love story is its ending. There have been many notable stories of tragic love affairs, such as *Romeo and Juliet*. The impossibility of attaining the romantic ideal is admirably expressed, as you might expect, by Shakespeare in his sixty-fourth sonnet:

> *Ruin hath taught me thus to ruminate,*
> *That time will come and take my love away.*
> *This thought is as a death which cannot choose*
> *But weep to have that which it fears to lose.*

Rollo May (1975) has also expressed the dilemma of the romantic ideal: "We may look at an autumn tree so beautiful in its brilliant colors that we feel like weeping; or we may hear music so lovely that we are overcome with sadness. The craven thought then creeps into our consciousness that maybe it would have been better not to have seen the tree at all, not to have heard the music" (p. 19).

Kilpatrick (1974) suggests that romantic love requires four conditions for its existence:

1. *An orientation to the future.* Central to the concept of romance is the idea of waiting till the perfect person comes along. If one saves oneself for that perfect person, one will be able to achieve perfect satisfaction. Think of the "old-maid aunt" who was jilted by her one true love early in her youth and has never been able to love another. Such a person would get very little sympathy from teenagers today.

2. *A belief in scarcity.* If one believes that suitable lovers are scarce, or even that there is only one "right one," then love and its sexual expression are given a very high premium. There were popular stories in the Middle Ages in which a man loved a woman so much that he didn't dare ask her to marry him, for fear she might turn him down. Thus, he spent his life worshiping her from afar. Today's generation has a more relaxed definition of "suitable lover."

3. *A sharp distinction between the sexes.* Gender typically has been viewed not as a continuum but as existing at opposite poles. "As the sexes come to live closer together, to know each other better, and as the psychic distance between them closes, the possibilities for romantic love which thrives on separation and distance and unreal perceptions decrease" (p. 28).

4. *An individualistic rather than a communal outlook.* Feelings of conquest and possessiveness and jealousy are integral parts of romance. There is the sense of "just the two of us against the world," which has been traditionally reinforced by the values of competition and success. Many young people today have rejected individualism for the more communal outlook. Urban and rural communes, giant rock concerts, encounter and sensitivity groups, child care

centers, the liturgical movement in many churches, food co-ops, and community action groups are examples of this communal spirit. With the competition for grades and jobs in the late 1970s, some youth may be wavering in their allegiance to communal values, but for the moment it continues to be quite strong.

Kilpatrick believes that the demythologizing of romantic love is a good omen, and that the move away from the romantic ideal will benefit us all: "There is also a tradition in the west that teaches that at the deepest level we are all one, that the nature of love is to spread and unite, not confine and restrict, and that in true love for one another there is love for all human beings" (p. 29).

A PERSONAL POSITION

In changing times, it is hard to evaluate change. Only in retrospect can we hope to have any certainty about its benefits. In the meantime, there is the real danger of future shock, the psychological malady resulting from too much change all at once (see Chapter 2).

Adolescents, having no clear models on which to base their values, are even more susceptible than adults to disorientation. It is especially hard for them these days to make their sexual and love lives meaningful and manageable.

What can those of us who would help them do? Most important, I think, is to help them avoid feeling guilty over their inability to make sense out of this aspect of their lives. The more we understand the multiple forces that cause sexual and love conflicts, the more empathetic and helpful we can be to the adolescents with whom we work.

SUMMARY

For most teenagers, learning the relationship between love and sex is a difficult lesson. Love is defined as the intimacy that is built up when two people validate the innermost feelings of each other. Adolescents, most of whom are struggling with their identity, find it difficult to dare to be really intimate with other people. Therefore, sexual activity leads to both positive and negative feelings for them; the drives of puberty attract them to sex, but the intimacy that it brings about is threatening.

Sexuality develops in three stages during adolescence: autosexuality, love of oneself; homosexuality, love of members of one's own sex; and heterosexuality, love of members of the opposite sex.

In the autosexual stage, children become aware of their bodies. Experimentation with masturbation begins early, at about 4 or 5, and the stage continues until the child is about 7 years old. When the child enters kindergarten, the second phase begins. During their elementary school years, children usually become close friends with others of the same sex. These relationships become especially intense in the years between 10 and 12; young people experience many changes and feel a need to confide in someone; it is natural that they are more trusting of members of their own sex. Some children continue the homosexual stage into adulthood. The vast majority of teenagers move into the third stage, heterosexuality, between 13 and 14, with girls preceding boys by about a year.

There are a number of suggested motivations for sexual behavior: the need for intimacy; the need for belonging; the desire for power; the desire for submission; curiosity; the desire for passion and ecstasy; and socially approved playfulness. Also suggested are six categories of sexual values: traditional asceticism; enlightened asceticism; humanistic liberalism; humanistic radicalism; fun morality; and sexual anarchy.

One of the newest and fastest growing problems in adolescence today is illegitimate births. In 1977, almost one out of every ten female teenagers became pregnant. Of these pregnancies, 30 percent ended in abortion, 20 percent resulted in illegitimate births, 30 percent were among married teenagers, and 10 percent were quickly legitimized by a hasty marriage. The images of the fast and easy girl and the sex-obsessed boy are unrealistic. Most of the couples who experienced a pregnancy had substantial relationships prior to the pregnancy.

Sex education in this country is seriously inadequate at present. Of all the teenage girls who became pregnant in 1977, 90 percent said that they did not want to become pregnant, but only 30 percent used birth control of any kind. While many of these teenagers were aware of birth control techniques, they had negative attitudes toward them for a variety of reasons.

Just as societal attitudes toward sexuality are changing rapidly, psychologist Kilpatrick suggests that our attitudes toward love in the 1970s have taken a radically different twist. He believes that love is now much more openly sexual and oriented toward the present rather than the future, and thus less romantic. The idea of romantic love requires four conditions for its existence, according to Kilpatrick: an orientation toward the future; belief in scarcity; sharp distinction between the sexes; and an individualistic rather than a communal outlook. Each of these conditions is becoming rare.

Questions

1. According to Fromm's theory, why is it difficult for adolescents to know the true meaning of love?
2. What are the three stages in the development of love?
3. What has been society's reaction to homosexuals? How is it changing?
4. Has there been a sexual revolution, and if so, what are its causes?
5. What are motives for sexual activity?
6. What are the reasons, now that birth control is so available, for so many unwed teenaged parents?
7. What is the present situation of sex education in the schools?
8. What are the reasons why romantic love has given way to sexual openness?

References

Abbott, S., & Love, B. *Sappho was a right-on woman.* New York: Stein & Day, 1974.

Abernathy, T. I., Robinson, J. Balswick, & King, K. "A comparison of the sexual attitudes and behavior of rural, suburban, and urban adolescents." *Adolescence,* 1979, 14, (54)289-295.

Antonousky, H., Shoham, I., Kavenaki, S., Lancet, M., & Modan, B. "Gender differences in patterns of adolescent sexual behavior."*Journal of youth & adolescence,* 1980, 9(2), 127-141.

Berg, M., Taylor, B., Edwards, L., & Hakansa, E. "Prenatal care for pregnant adolescents in public high school." *Journal of school health,* Jan. 1979, 32-35.

Bierman, B., & Bierman, J. *Parenting a toddler; problems encountered by adolescent mothers,* 1978, *ERIC* document 190249, microfiche edition.

Boston Women's Health Book Collective (2nd ed.). *Our bodies, ourselves.* New York: Simon & Schuster, 1976.

Brown, M., "Teenage prostitution." *Adolescence,* 1979, 14(56), 665-680.

Bruce, J. *Adolescent sexuality and childbearing: a different perspective,* 1978, *ERIC* document 170629.

Campbell, B. K., & Barnlund, D. C. "Communication patterns and problems of pregnancy." *American journal of orthopsychiatry,* January 1977, 47(1), 106-111.

Chilman, C. *Adolescent sexuality in a changing American society.* Nov. 1974, 194-247.

Colletta, N., et al. *Support systems used by adolescent mothers: who helps and what difference it makes.* April 1980, *ERIC* document 187432.

Committee on adolescence. "American academy of pediatrics statement on teenage pregnancy." *Pediatrics,* 1979, 63(5), 795-797.

Cowing, D. E. "Sexual behavior in college students." *American journal of orthopsychiatry,* 1975, 45(2), 284-285.

Dacey, J. S. "Survey of sexual practices of college freshmen." Unpublished study, Boston College, 1978.

Dembo, M., & Lundell, B. "Factors affecting adolescent contraception practices: implications for sex education." *Adolescence,* 1979, 14(56), 657-664.

Dickenson, G. "Adolescent sex information sources: 1964-1975." *Adolescence,* 1978, 13 (52), 653-658.

Diepold, J., & Young, R. "Empirical studies of adolescent sexual behavior: a critical review." *Adolescence, 14*(53), 1979, 45-64.

Dignan, M., & Anspaugh, D. "Permissiveness and premarital sexual activity: behavior correlates of attitudinal differences." *Adolescence,* 1978, 13(52), 703-711.

Dranoff, S. M. "Masturbation and the male adolescent." *Adolescence,* Summer 1974, 9(34), 169-176.

Dresen, S. "Adjusting to single parenting." *American journal of nursing,* 1976, 76(8) 31-39.

Eiduson, B. T. "Looking at children in emergent family styles." *Children today,* 1974, 3(4) 2-6.

Elias, J., & Gebhardt, P. "Sexuality and sexual learning in childhood." *Phi Delta Kappan,* 1969, 1, 401-405.

Epstein, A. *Pregnant teenagers' knowledge of infant development.* March 1979, *ERIC* document 176875.

Feldman, S., & Nash, S. "Changes in responsiveness to babies during adolescence." *Child development,* 1979, 50, 942-949.

Flomenhaft, K. "Outcome of treatment for adolescents." *Adolescence,* Spring 1974, 9(33), 57-66.

Foreman, J. "Sex education: once bitter issue almost dead." *Boston globe,* April 24, 1977, 40.

Fox, G. "The family's influence on adolescent sexual behavior." *Children today,* May–June 1979, 21.

Fox, G., & Inazu, J. *Talking about sex: patterns of mother-daughter communication.* Detroit, MI, 1978.

Freidenberg, E. Z. *The vanishing adolescent.* New York: Random House, 1959.

Fromm, E. *The art of loving.* New York: Harper & Row, 1956.

Gagnon, J. H., & Simon, W. "They're going to learn on the street anyway." *Psychology today,* 1969, *3*(2), 46 ff.

Gallup, G. "Gallup poll." *Boston globe,* July 18, 1977, 16.

"Gays on the march." *Time,* September 8, 1975, 32–43.

Godenne, G. D. "Sex and today's youth." *Adolescence,* Spring 1974, *9*(33), 67–72.

Group for the advancement of psychiatry. *Power and authority in adolescence,* May 1978, *10.*

Hall, G. S. *Adolescence.* New York: Appleton, 1905.

Hansson, R., O'Connor, M., Jones, W., & Blocker, T. "Maternal employment and adolescent sexual behavior." *Journal of youth and adolescence,* 1981, *10*(1), 55–60.

Harris, L. "Harris survey." *Boston globe,* July 18, 1977, 16.

Hendricks, L. "Unwed adolescent fathers: problems they face and their sources of social support." *Adolescence,* Winter 1980, *XV*(60), 861–869.

Herold, E., Mantle, D., & Zemitis, O. "A study of sexual offenses against females." *Adolescence,* 1979, *14* (53), 65–72.

Herold, E., & Benson, R. "Problems of teaching sex education—a survey of Ontario secondary schools." *Family coordinator,* April 1979, 199–203.

Hooker, E., & Chance, P. "Facts that liberated the gay community." *Psychology today,* 1975, *9*(7), 52–55; 101.

Jekel, J., & Forbush, J. "Service needs of adolescent parents." *Journal of school health,* Nov. 1979, 527–530.

Jersild, A. T. *The psychology of adolescence* (2nd ed). New York: Macmillan, 1963.

Josselyn, I. M. "The unmarried mother." In Ralph Slovento (Ed.), *Sexual behavior and the law.* Springfield, Ill.: Charles C. Thomas, 1965, 356–378.

Juhasz, A. M. "The unmarried adolescent parent." *Adolescence,* Summer 1974, *9*(34), 263–272.

Jurich, A. "Differential determinants of premarital sexual standards among college students." *Adolescence,* 1979, *14*(56), 797–810.

Kantner, J., & Zelnick, M. "Contraception and pregnancy: experience of young married women in the United States." *Family planning perspectives,* 1973, *5,* 11–35.

Kaplan, H., Smith, P., & Pokorny, A. "Psychosocial antecedents of unwed motherhood among indigent adolescents." *Journal of youth and adolescence,* 1979, *8*(2), 181–207.

Kilpatrick, W. K. "The demythologizing of love." *Adolescence,* Spring 1974, *9*(33), 25–30.

Kohner, M. "Adolescent pregnancy." *New York times,* October 11, 1977, 38.

Kournany, R., Martin, J., & Armstrong, S. "Sex experimentation by adolescents while babysitting." *Adolescence,* 1979, *14*(54), 283–288.

Lowery, P. "Unwanted pregnancy: why?" *Harvard crimson,* August 3, 1971.

Macklin, E. D. "Heterosexual cohabitation among unmarried college students." *Family coordinator,* 1972, *21*(4), 463–472.

Magid, T., Gross, B., & Shuman, B. "Preparing pregnant teenagers for parenthood." *Family coordinator,* July 1979, 359.

Malinovich, M. "An opinion." *Mademoiselle,* April 1977, 84.

Marcus, I. "Masturbation." *Journal of American psychoanalytic institute,* 1962, *10,* 91–101.

Masters, W., & Johnson, V. *Human sexual response.* Boston: Little, Brown, 1966.

May, R. *The courage to create.* New York: Bantam, 1975.

McKenry, P., Walters, L., & Johnson, C. "Adolescent pregnancy: a review of the literature." *Family coordinator,* Jan. 1979, 17–29.

Mead, M. *Culture and commitment: a study of the generation gap.* New York: Doubleday, 1970.

Moore, K., Jofferth, S., & Wertheimer, I. "Teenage motherhood." *Children today,* Sept. 1979, 12–16.

Murstein, B., & Holden, C. "Sexual behavior and correlates among college students." *Adolescence,* 1979, *14*(56), 625–639.

Polsby, G. K. "Unmarried parenthood: potential for growth." *Adolescence,* Summer 1974, *9*(34), 272–284.

Pomeroy, W. B. "Homosexuality." In R. E. Weitze (Ed.), *The same sex.* Philadelphia: Pilgrim Press, 1969.

Reichlt, P. *The influence of contraception on adolescent sexual behavior.* Oct. 1978, *ERIC* document 165967.

Roberts, E., & Holt, S. *Sexuality and social policy: project on human sexual development.* Harvard University: Population Education, Inc., 1979.

Roberts, E., Kline, D. & Gagon, J. *Family life and sexual learning: project on human sexual development.* Harvard University: Population Education, Inc., 1978.

Rogel, M., Zuehike, M., Petersen, A., Tobin-Richards, M., & Shelton, M. "Contraceptive behavior in adolescence: a decision-making perspective." *Journal of youth and adolescence,* 1980, *9*(6), 491–506.

Rosen, R. "Adolescent pregnancy decision-making: are parents important?" *Adolescence,* Spring 1980, *XV*(57), 43–54.

Rubenstein, J., Watson, F., & Rubenstein, H. "An analysis of sex education books for adolescents by means of adolescents' sexual interests." *Adolescence,* 1977, *12*(47), 293–311.

Rubin, I. "Transition in sex values—implications for the education of adolescents." *Journal of marriage and the family,* May 1965, *27,* 185–189.

Russ-Eft, D., Springer, M., & Beever, A. "Antecedents of adolescent parenthood and consequences at age 30." *Family coordinator,* April 1979, 173–178.

Ryan, I., & Dunn, P. "Sex education from prospective teachers' view poses a dilemma." *Journal of school health,* Dec. 1979, 573–575.

Sebald, H. *Adolescence.* Englewood Cliffs, N.J.: Prentice-Hall, 1977.

"Sex and the single San Francisco girl." *Boston globe,* Aug. 11, 1977, 16.

Shearer, L. "Children bearing children." *Parade,* June 5, 1977, 4.

Shenker, I., & Schildkraut, M. "Physical and emotional health in youth." In R. Havighurst & P. Dreyer (Eds.), *Youth.* Chicago: National Society for the Study of Education, 1975.

Shirreffs, J., & Dezelsky, T. "Adolescent perceptions of sex education needs: 1972–1978." *Journal of school health,* June 1979, 343–346.

Silber, T. "Values relating to abortion as expressed by the inner city adolescent girl—report of a physician's experience." *Adolescence,* Spring 1980, *XV*(57), 183–189.

Sklar, J., & Berkov, B. "The American birth rate: evidence of a coming rise." *Science,* 1974, *189,* 693–700.

Sorensen, R. C. *Adolescent sexuality in contemporary America.* New York: World, 1973.

Spanier, G. "Sex education and premarital sexual behavior among American college students." *Adolescence,* 1978, *13*(52), 659–674.

Tatelbaum, R., Adams, B., Kash, C., McAnarney, E., Roghmann, K., Coulter, M., Charnay, E., & Plume, M. "Management of teenage pregnancies in three different health care settings." *Adolescence,* Winter 1978, *XIII*(52), 713.

Teenage pregnancy: a workshop guide. U.S. Government Printing Office, Washington, D.C.: 1978.

Thompson, K.   "A comparison of black and white adolescents' beliefs about having children." *Journal of marriage and the family,* Feb. 1980, *8*(2), 133–139.

Tietze, M.   *Adolescent parenthood,* 1978, *ERIC* document 160214.

Vener, A. M., Stewart, C. S., & Hager, D. L.   "The sexual behavior of adolescents in middle America: generational and American-British comparisons." *Journal of marriage and the family,* 1972, *34,* 696–705.

Verville, E.   *Behavior problems of children.* Philadelphia: Saunders, 1967.

Wagner, C.   "Sexuality of American adolescents." *Adolescence,* 1980, *15*(59), 567–580.

Walters, J., McKenry, P, & Walters, L.   "Adolescents' knowledge of childbearing." *Family coordinator,* April 1979, 163–171.

Waltz, G., & Benjamin, L.   *Adolescent pregnancy and parenthood* July 1980, *ERIC* document 184528.

Wuerger, M. K.   "The young adult, stepping into parenthood." *American journal of nursing,* August 1976, *76*(8).

Yarber, W.   "New directions in venereal disease education." *Family coordinator,* April 1978, 121–125.

Yarber, W.   "Instructional emphasis in family life and sex education: viewpoints of students, parents, teachers, and principals at four grade levels." *Journal of school health,* May 1979, 263–265.

Zelnick, M., & Kantner, J.   "First pregnancies to women aged 15–19: 1976 and 1971." In R. Muuss (Ed.), *Adolescent behavior and society: a book of readings.* New York: Random House, 1980.

Zelnick, M., & Kantner, J. E.   "The resolution of teenage first pregnancies." *Family planning perspectives,* 1977a, *6*(2) 74–80.

Zelnick, M., & Kantner, J.   "Sexual and contraceptive experience of young unmarried women in the U.S., 1976 and 1971." *Family planning perspectives,* 1977b, *9*(2).

Zelnick, M., & Kantner, J. E.   *National survey for the commission on population growth and the American future.* Washington, D.C.: U.S. Government Printing Office, 1972.

Zelnick, M., Young, K., & Kantner, J.   "Probabilities of intercourse and conception among U.S. teenage women, 1971 and 1976." *Family planning perspectives,* May/June 1979.

Additional References

Arnold, S., & Hoffman, A.   "Chicago planned parenthood's teen scene: a sociological study for participants." *Adolescence,* Fall 1974, *9*(35), 371–390.

Collins, J. K.   "Adolescent dating intimacy: norms and peer expectations." *Journal of youth and adolescence,* 1974, *3*(4), 317–328.

Curtis, R. L., Jr.   "Adolescent orientations toward parents and peers: variations by sex, age, and socioeconomic status." *Adolescence,* Winter 1975, *10*(40), 483–494.

Ewer, P. A., & Gibbs, J. O.   "School returns among pregnant adolescents." *Journal of youth and adolescence,* 1976, *5*(2), 221–229.

Fischman, S.   "The pregnancy-resolution: decisions of unwed adolescents." *Nursing clinic N.A.,* 1975, *10,* 217–227.

Fischman, S. H.   "Delivery or abortion in inner-city adolescents." *American journal of orthopsychiatry,* 1977, *47*(1), Ja.

"Gay activism in colleges."   *Intellect,* 1974, *103*(2360), 77.

Gerson, A.   "Promiscuity as a function of the mother-daughter relationship." *Psychological reports,* 1976, *38,* 113–114.

Goldman, A., Murphy, R., & Babikian, H.   "Group therapy in obstetric management of pregnant adolescents." *New York State journal of medicine,* 1973, *73,* 407–411.

Goldsmith, S., et al.   "Teenagers, sex, and contraception." *Family planning perspectives,* 1972, *4,* 32–38.

Green, R.   "Children's quest for sexual identity." *Psychology today,* 1974, *7*(9), 45–47.

Hall, G. S.   *Adolescence: its psychology and its relations to physiology, anthropology, sociology, sex, crime, religion, and education.* New York: Appleton, 1904.

Hatcher, S. L. M.   "The adolescent experience of pregnancy and abortion: a developmental analysis." *Journal of youth and adolescence,* 1973, *2*(1), 53–102.

Herold, E. S.   "Stages of date selection: a reconciliation of divergent findings on campus values in dating." *Adolescence,* Spring 1974, *9*(33), 113–120.

Jackson, D. W.   "The meaning of dating from the role perspective of non-dating preadolescent." *Adolescence,* Spring 1975, *10*(37), 123–126.

Johnson, C. L.   "Attitudes toward premarital sex and family planning for single-never-pregnant teenage girls." *Adolescence,* Summer 1974, *9*(34), 255–262.

Johnson, C. L.   "Adolescent pregnancy: intervention into the poverty cycle." *Adolescence,* Fall 1974, *9*(35), 391–406.

Kantner, J., & Zelnick, M.   "Sexual experience of young unmarried women in the United States." *Family planning perspectives,* 1972, *4,* 9–18.

Lyness, J. L., Lipitz, M. E., & Davis, K. E.   "Living together: an alternative to marriage." *Journal of marriage and the family,* 1972, *34*(2), 305–311.

Menken, J.   "The health and social consequences of teenage childbearing." *Family planning perspectives,* 1972, *4,* 45–53.

Moerk, E. L.   "Preadolescents' conceptions of children." *Journal of youth and adolescence,* 1974, *3*(3), 217–229.

Nettleton, C. A., & Cline, D. W.   "Dating patterns, sexual relationships and use of contraceptives of 700 unwed mothers during a two-year period following delivery." *Adolescence,* Spring 1975, *10*(37), 45–58.

Offer, D.   "Attitudes toward sexuality in a group of 1500 middle-class teenagers." *Journal of youth and adolescence,* 1972, *1*(1), 81–90.

Osofsky, H. J., Osofsky, J. D., Kendall, N., & Rajan, R.   "Adolescents as mothers: an interdisciplinary approach to a complex problem." *Journal of youth and adolescence,* 1973, *2*(3), 233–249.

Place, D. M.   "The dating experience for adolescent girls." *Adolescence,* Summer 1975, *10*(38), 157–174.

Presser, H. B.   "Early motherhood: ignorance or bliss?" *Family planning perspectives,* 1974, *6,* 8–14.

Rogers, D.   *The psychology of adolescence* (3rd ed.). Englewood Cliffs, N.J.: Prentice-Hall, 1977.

Scheck, D. C., & Emerick, R.   "The young male adolescent's perception of early child-rearing behavior: the differential effects of socioeconomic status and family size." *Sociometry,* 1976, *39*(1), 39–52.

Simmons, R. G., & Rosenberg, F.   "Sex, sex roles, and self-image." *Journal of youth and adolescence,* 1975, *4*(3), 229–258.

Sklar, J., & Berkov, B.   "Teenage family formation in post-war America." *Family planning perspectives, 6,* 80–90.

Spanier, G. B.   "Sexualization and premarital sexual behavior." *Family coordinator,* 1975, *24*(1), 33–41.

Sugar, M.   "At-risk factors for the adolescent mother and her infant." *Journal of youth and adolescence, 5*(3), 251–270.

"Survey of college freshmen."   *Intellect,* 1974, *102*(2358), 482.

Chapter Nine

The Schools

Chapter Highlights

The Crisis in the Schools
  "Civil War" in the High Schools
  "Technical Deficiencies" of the High School
  What Would You Do?
How Academically Effective Are the Schools?
  Lower Validity of the SAT
  Changing Educational Goals
  A Fly on the Wall
Improving the Schools: "Small and Simple"
Improving the Schools: Back to Basics
  *Should You Really Have a High School
    Diploma?*
Improving the Schools: Conflict Negotiation
Improving the Schools: Discipline Management
  Kindsvatter's Method
  Glasser's Method
  Johnson's Method
Improving the Schools: Comprehensive Education
  Recommendations of the National Panel
  Experiential Learning
Improving the Schools: The Outward Bound
  Approach
Improving the Schools: The Walkabout Approach
Alternative Schools
  Alternative vs. Conventional Schools
  Three Alternative Schools
  How Would You Change Your Teachers?
  A Personal Position
Summary

Key Terms and Concepts

open campus
constitutional rights
corporal punishment
instructional modes
paraprofessionals
individualization
behavior modification
school phobia
in-school suspension room
comprehensive high school
comprehensive education
experiential learning
volunteerism
Outward Bound
walkabout
nontraditional schools
voucher system

Important People

John DeCecco
I.K. Richards
James Coleman
Edward Wynne
Richard Kindsvatter
William Glasser
Christopher Johnson
Maurice Gibbons

*As we enter the third century [of public schools] we are obviously facing
grave problems in American education, but we have in the past
confronted such challenges and have succeeded in producing a public
education system with a breadth and depth unmatched in the history of
the world. Indeed, it seems that the very strengths of the system are
forged through the experience of overcoming numerous obstacles.*
                                                    —Senator Birch Bayh, 1978.

In 1900 the American high school served less than 10 percent of the adult
population; by 1940 it was over 50 percent. This phenomenal rate of growth
has continued; today high schools are serving more than 90 percent of teenagers
(over eighteen million students) and graduating 75 percent. In contrast, the percentage of adolescents in secondary schools in western Europe ranges from 4 to
20 percent (National Panel on Adolescent Education, 1976).

According to the U.S. Census Bureau, the average American goes to school
four years longer today than in the 1940s. These educational gains apply to both
sexes, all regions of the country, blacks and whites, and to cities and suburbs.
Today's 20-year-olds have attended school for an average of almost thirteen
years, compared to people over 65, who had an average of only nine years of
school (Sebald, 1977).

This rate of growth has strained the resources of American education
(Williams, 1981). However, the past few years have seen an abrupt decrease in
the rate of growth and this is causing widespread changes in staff and relocation
of students. These difficulties have occurred primarily in the elementary schools
and junior high schools, but in the 1980s, the high schools will also be experiencing such disruptions. In the years from 1962 to 1972 the number of children in
elementary schools increased by 3 percent, those in secondary schools by 28
percent, and those in higher education by 41 percent. U.S. Census Bureau predictions indicate that from 1972 to 1982, the number of children in elementary
school will *decrease* by 11 percent, those in secondary schools by 14 percent,
and those entering higher education will increase by only 6 percent. This is not
because of a decrease in the percentage of individuals going to school, but because so many fewer babies are being born. Actually a slightly higher percentage
of students (77 percent) is expected to graduate from high school in 1983 (U.S.
Dept. of Health, Education, and Welfare, 1975).

THE CRISIS IN THE SCHOOLS

There has been no lack of criticism of our secondary schools in the past two decades. Starting with the blistering indictments of Friedenberg (1959) and Goodman (1960), many have concluded that however well the schools may have served teenagers in the past, their needs are no longer being met; in fact, the junior and senior high schools are actually harmful in their effects. Is the situation really as critical as these authors suggest?

Two unusually comprehensive studies completed in the mid-'70s answer with a resounding "Yes!" DeCecco and Richards (1975) investigated the situation in American high schools for one-and-a-half years, during which time they interviewed 8000 students and 1200 school personnel. The second study, conducted by the National Panel on High Schools and Adolescent Education, was authorized by the U.S. Office of Education in 1972 and completed in 1976. The panel was composed of twelve well-known educators and researchers and two high school students. The findings of both studies are described below.

"Civil War" in the High Schools

America's high schools are drifting toward a kind of anarchy, and faster than most people realize. Too many schools are angry places in which every rule is questioned and conflict is the norm; where students can act in defiance that is astonishing in its destructive effect, where the authorities are beginning to react with strict punishments, armed hallway guards and other forms of repression. These troubles are not confined to the inner city—there is no room for complacency in suburbia (DeCecco and Richards, 1975, p. 51).

DeCecco and Richards called the situation in our high schools nothing less than a "civil war," citing the following facts:

- The cost of vandalism is over $500 million a year, about the same amount spent on textbooks.
- During the five years preceding their study, assaults on teachers increased by 77 percent, causing a total of 70,000 serious accidents in 1975.
- Assaults on students by other students rose 85 percent.
- Robberies of both teachers and students rose 36 percent.
- Rapes and attempted rapes were up by 40 percent.
- Homicides increased 18 percent.
- The number of weapons confiscated was up 54 percent.

Their findings were reinforced by a 1978 study conducted by the National Institute of Education ("The ABC's of Violence," 1978), which estimated that *one out of every nine secondary school students will have something stolen in a typical month. One out of eighty will be attacked during the same period. Among the nation's one million secondary school teachers, 5200 will be attacked—one-fifth of them seriously—in any given month, while about 6000 will be robbed. Vandalism, meanwhile, will cost schools as much as $600 million a year (p. 73).*

The prevailing atmosphere in the 757 school districts studied by DeCecco and Richards was tension and anger. Students expressed their anger by defiance of authority, tardiness and absence, disrupting classroom teaching, and vandalism and robbery. Teachers' anger surfaced in repressive methods to regain silence and order, and in expelling students for minor infractions. School officials showed their anger through unfair enforcement of rules, siding with one ethnic group against another, making themselves unavailable for meetings and blaming both students and teachers for problems in the school.

DeCecco and Richards point to a number of sources of conflict within schools.

Status differences. Although students can create considerable disruptions in the school, they nevertheless have much less status than do school authorities. These differences in status cause frequent power struggles between the two groups.

Fear and distrust. This is often generated when students from diverse backgrounds come together. Misunderstanding and ignorance of the feelings of racial and ethnic groups inevitably cause friction.

The school's role as custodian of the young. Children have little choice but to go to school, and they often resent this fact. At a time when their energies are at their highest, schools frequently restrain them in narrow boundaries of time, space, and information.

The school's role as political socializer. Schools are expected to help students become responsible citizens who will support and actively participate in democratic processes. However, most students have had little experience with responsibility, and are given little chance to exercise it. The average high school is hardly an example of democracy in action. The schools need to give the appearance that everything is under control; schoolteachers, and more especially, administrators depend for their jobs on at least the appearance of tranquility and order within the school. Therefore, when a problem does arise, school authorities tend to impose a solution rather than cope with the difficulty of inviting student participation in a solution.

The tendency of teachers to spend less and less time with students outside of class. This is closely related to the question of violence. Teachers' self-imposed isolation means that they know their students less well, and brings about increasing communication problems. The presence of hall guards and occasionally of armed police causes some students to feel that since they are being treated as prison inmates, they might as well act like them. Many schools have adopted

open campus policies, one result of which has been that teachers and administrators have less of an idea of what is actually going on outside of class. The researchers frequently found that the crowded halls of the schools were scenes of fights and a "brisk traffic in drugs and sex."

DeCecco and Richards believe that many school problems are mishandled because the faculty lacks knowledge of students' legal rights. A number of U.S. Supreme Court decisions have redefined students' rights in schools in recent years. In the 1969 *Tinker* case, it was established that students have the same **constitutional rights** in school as they would have outside it. In *Goss* vs. *Lopez,* 1975, the Court ruled that "the student must be given oral or written notice of charges against him, and if he denies them, an explanation of the evidence the authorities have and an opportunity to present his version." In *Wood* vs. *Strickland,* 1975, the Court decided that students who have been treated illegally may sue school officials for damages. The U.S. Congress in 1974 passed a law that information that could damage a student's chances for getting a job may be released only with his parents' consent. The Court's most recent ruling, that **corporal punishment** is constitutional (Flygare, 1978), will probably also add to the conflict over the exact status of the teenager in school.

"Technical Deficiencies" of the High School

The second major study, completed by the National Panel in 1976, finds the situation less critical but still serious. It places the blame for problems not on administrators, teachers, or students, but on "technical deficiencies" in the system: "The Panel rejects the widely held opinion that the high schools are citadels of reaction and are led and staffed by reactionary groups hostile and resistant to change" (National Panel, 1976, p. 3).

The Panel discovered the following major problems in its study of high schools:

Most schools are too big to be managed effectively. Large size tends to make them inflexible in adapting to newer instructional forms and procedures. The recent history of efforts to deploy teachers in different **instructional modes** (such as team-teaching, use of **paraprofessionals,** modules, and mini-schools) demonstrates the institutional rigidity inherent to bigness: the priorities of management must override the interest of clients. It was originally believed that in bringing students together, the school had to be big so that numerous curricula could be offered. Bigness, however, has not provided for greater **individualization** of curricula.

In prolonging education, we have greatly delayed learning what it means to have adult responsibilities and values. The rites of passage that have traditionally signaled the beginning of adult status (for example, getting a full-time job and managing one's own money) are now often delayed until the early twenties. This delayed independence often causes frustration among today's adolescents.

The approach of the typical high school is still mostly appropriate for imma-

*ture children, although teenagers are maturing earlier than they did when high
schools were begun over 70 years ago.* "The schools baby-sit, at a very high cost
during the day, for the nation's nighttime baby-sitters" (p. 5).

*Differences among the teenagers coming within its walls are too great for
the high school to handle.* The attempts to create mini-schools, schools without
walls, open schools, alternative schools, optimal programs, internships, parallel
courses, independent study, preschools, apprenticeships, and action learning all
indicate an almost desperate attempt to diversify programs offered by the school
to handle these great differences. Diversification is simply making the high school
unmanageable.

There is a considerable gap between the classroom study of citizenship, and
life on a job. The Panel calls for closer linkages between vocational and citizenship education. There has been very little federal support for out-of-school programs; most of the federal efforts have been placed at the elementary school
level. What secondary school support there has been has gone to vocational
education alone, based on the idea that vocational education will help students
get into jobs quicker and more easily. However, recent studies (National Panel,
1976) have shown that graduates of vocational schools tend not to be employed
in the field of their training, and that they do not increase the chances of these
youth finding work. Numerous studies have shown that many adolescents would
like to be working at least part time, but the schools provide an effective means
of keeping them off the job market. Some critics have even suggested that this is
the major purpose of the high school.

*High schools are governed directly or indirectly by nonpolitical school com-
mittees and boards of education that nonetheless sometimes have to deal with
the political issues of the community, such as race relations.* The tendency of
administrators is to avoid conflict between the school board and the community.
The Panel gives high praise to the typical school administrator whose dealings
with the complex forces of the community and the school committee heap conflicting responsibilities on him or her.

*The schools have been asked and have been willing to take on increasing
responsibility for the total education of children, a responsibility shared in the
past with family, church, and local agencies.*

In summary, the Panel found that while teachers and administrators are
struggling mightily with school problems, it seems unlikely they will have any
success until our whole approach to education itself is revamped.

What Would You Do?

You are a junior high school teacher. You need to use the bathroom, and rather
than go down two floors to the men's room, you slip into the boys' room. You have
been in there a few minutes when two students walk in. Without having seen you,
one offers to sell the other a half-ounce of marijuana. What should you do about it?

1. Jump out and grab the marijuana and the money. Tell them that you will confiscate these goods, but that you will tell no one of what is going on. Then leave the boys' room.

2. Wait for the boys to leave and then report both of them to the principal.

3. Take them to their class and let the other kids decide what should happen to them.

4. Confront them, and ask them what they think should be done.

5. Tell the guidance counselor.

6. Call their parents.

7. Confiscate the marijuana, scare them with threats, but let them go.

8. Wait till they leave, then leave yourself. Do nothing.

My Answer to the Marijuana-Sale Dilemma

Most of the options offered to this dilemma involve a strictly *adult* resolution of it. Whether you believe the action of the two students immoral or not, none of these options offer much hope that the two will gain a deeper insight into the ramifications of their behavior.

This, I think, is one of the most important purposes of school. Much of the best education occurs outside the classroom (see Chapters 10 and 13). If you follow option four (have them consider what *they* think should be done), there is the chance that they will develop a truly satisfactory resolution, and one that you and the other authorities might not have thought of. Even if they do not, there is a good likelihood they will have gained a clearer understanding of the implications of their behavior.

The preceding criticisms have dealt mainly with the effects of schools on students' personality and behavior. But the primary avowed purpose of secondary schools has always been *intellectual* development. How well have our schools done here?

HOW ACADEMICALLY EFFECTIVE ARE THE SCHOOLS?

In terms of scholastic performance, it appears that schools are not as effective as they used to be. The national average for the Scholastic Aptitude Test (SAT), which used to predict the student's ability to do college-level work, has been dropping since 1969. Although the causes of this problem are complicated, two major factors seem to be at work: the SAT scores may no longer reflect learning ability as well as they used to, and the schools may no longer be emphasizing cognitive learning as much as they used to.

Lower Validity of the SAT

There are several reasons why the SAT may be less valid today than formerly. First, the SAT used to play a critical role in a college's decision to accept or reject a student. Students usually took the test in their junior year, then retook it in their senior year, hoping that practice would increase their scores; usually this was the case. Today, when the SAT is only one of several measures used to determine college acceptance, many students no longer retake the test in their senior year. The absence of the higher senior scores has caused the national average to drop.

Second, although the purpose of the SAT is to test ability, careful preparation can improve one's score as much as 50 to 100 points. Now that students are aware of the score's lessened importance, they apparently don't prepare as carefully as they used to.

Finally, more students are now applying to colleges than ten years ago. Thus, a larger number take the SAT and a greater percentage of lower-ability students are being tested. This too tends to drop the national average of SAT scores.

Changing Educational Goals

We also have reason to believe that the goals of the schools have changed in the last ten years; the learning items on the SAT have not.

Math scores have been dropping rapidly, perhaps because of a change in goals. Although teachers have been putting more emphasis on understanding and comprehension of mathematics, the test still largely measures computational skills.

Parents and educators are most concerned with the decline in writing ability, especially grammar usage and spelling. This decline has been blamed almost solely on English teachers who, some have alleged, have neglected basic skills while emphasizing writing and oral forms of communication. The remedy, many critics believe, is to assign more reading (the best spur to good writing) as well as drills in spelling and grammar.

Marshall McLuhan (see Chapter 4) thinks otherwise. He argues that the days of avid readers and eloquent writers are nearing an end, regardless of what schools try to do. The effects of the electronic media on the current generation have been to make spoken language and visual information much more important than reading and writing. Educators should understand this unavoidable trend, and help teenagers move toward the improvement of their interpersonal skills.

Educational goals have proliferated as junior and senior high schools have taken over responsibility for a number of areas of life that were not part of their charge in previous years. Research has been done on the role of the schools in such diverse areas as changing female self-concept through athletics (Snyder and

Kiblin, 1977); learning disabilities (Hampton, 1974); the behavior modification of social behavior (Arwood, Williams, and Long, 1974; Wagner and Brietmeyer, 1975; Jensen, 1975); interpersonal relationships (Spencer, 1976; Kobak, 1977); and the rapidly increasing problem of **school phobia** (LeUnes and Siemsgluez, 1977).

Wynne (1978) suggests that schools have been forced to change some of their goals because the disorientation and permissiveness of American society have altered adolescent attitudes in many negative ways. He believes that the following attitudes are most to blame for sidetracking education from its traditional purposes: (1) less willingness to accept deferred gratification; (2) loneliness and the anger and resentment that go with it; (3) ineptness in talking to strangers and adults; (4) inability and exploitiveness in personal relations; (5) low level of loyalty and increased disaffection for society; (6) fear of serious commitment; and (7) greater willingness to hurt others.

There have been numerous other changes in society which helped to multiply the goals of schools. Porter (1978) argues that since 1950, the following changes have been of most significance: (1) the movement toward equality for minorities; (2) the campaign for equity for women; (3) the efforts to educate all the handicapped; (4) lowering the age of majority to 18; and (5) the growth of pervasive influence of television (p. 19).

Whatever may be behind changes in educational goals, there is nearly universal agreement that they have changed, and not for the better. Widespread dissatisfaction has spawned numerous proposals for improvements to the schools. In the sections below, some of these are described.

A Fly on the Wall

One of the best ways to understand adolescents is to seek opportunities to observe them *before* you begin to work with them. A good way to observe without in turn being observed is to be a "fly on the wall" during class intervals in some high school. It is better not to observe in your own high school, because memory and nostalgia may distort your impressions. Select a high school (or several) different in as many ways as possible from the one you went to. Wear the same kind of clothes as the students. Station yourself with some books under your arm either on the first floor of the high school or the top floor. These are usually the places where most of the real action takes place. Be as inconspicuous as possible. After observing for a while, try to answer the following questions:

1. What are the dominant themes of the discussions you hear going on around you?

2. Do the students dress differently from the way you did when you were in high school? What are the functions of the different styles of dress? What are they trying to say through their clothing?

3. Do you notice any illicit behavior?

4. Do the students seem to be moving or hanging around in cliques, or are their associations more random?

5. Are there interactions between students and teachers during these periods?

6. How do you feel about what you see? Is it a pleasant atmosphere? A healthy one?

IMPROVING THE SCHOOLS: "SMALL AND SIMPLE"

Although he believes that schools cannot be expected to remedy the ills of society, educator Edward Wynne (1978) does think they can be a real force in improving society's functioning. His recommendations are summarized in Table 9–1. Most of these changes, it will be noted, involve a return to the types of schools that we used to have thirty or forty years ago. Wynne believes society was more cohesive then partly because of smaller and simpler forms of social organization, and that we can gain much by returning to these forms.

A number of educators (Tyack, 1978; Pacheco, 1978; Coleman, 1978; Porter, 1978), disagree with Wynne, believing that our society has changed so much in recent years that attempting to return schools to their former status will not have the desired effect of unity and cohesion. Pacheco quotes sociologist Emil Durkheim:

> This is to ascribe to education a power it lacks. [Education] is only the image and reflection of society. It imitates and reproduces the latter in abbreviated form: it does not create it. Education is healthy when people themselves are in a healthy state, but it becomes corrupt with them, being unable to modify itself. If the moral environment is affected, since the teachers themselves dwell in it, they cannot avoid being influenced; how then should they impress on their pupils a different orientation from what they have received? Each new generation is reared by its predecessor; the latter must therefore improve in order to improve its successor (p. 318).

Thus, many educators believe that only improvements in society can improve schools, and not the reverse.

IMPROVING THE SCHOOLS: BACK TO BASICS

Another group of educators believes that, while it is not advisable to attempt to return to school organization of the past, we should return to our earlier goal: teaching basic skills. Thomas Massey (1978), Chairman of the Education Committee of the National Conference of State Legislatures, states:

TABLE 9–1
DESIRABLE SCHOOL CHANGES

School Change	External Evidence of Change
Less reliance on technology	Less use of busing, television, computers, national exams, elaborate lab and sports equipment.
Fewer ties to typical urban and suburban patterns	Neighborhood schools; schools that discourage family geographic mobility; schools that encourage more long-term enrollment (K–8 versus K–6).
Lower economic costs, especially to general public	Students and families doing in-school chores and fund raising to lower school costs; decline in average number of years of school attendance.
Less bureaucracy	Greater authority given to building principal; teacher salaries and advancement dependent on less formal criteria; more genuine school decentralization; less subject specialization by teachers; more personalized grading of students.
Smaller educational units	Smaller school buildings or the division of schools in larger buildings into genuine subschools.
Less rationality and individualism	More emphasis on school spirit, character development, honor codes, extracurricular activities, service, good discipline, and patriotism.
Greater parental control	Increasing proportion of public and/or private schools that closely reflect the perspectives of average parents (that is, the majority that is most worried about discipline as compared to other, better organized groups tied to the status quo); emphasis on voucher systems, direct fees from parents, and other devices to heighten impact of parent values.

Source: Edward Wynne, "Desirable School Changes," *Phi Delta Kappan* (January 1978), p. 314.

Emphasis (overemphasis, I believe) on individual legal rights, allegations of discrimination, improper discipline procedures, and educational malpractice has taken much of education out of the classroom and into the courtroom. Indeed, the public schools are having to deal with a number of problems they did not have to treat in the past — because we have expected them to rectify the failings of society and the family (p. 320).

It is clear that we need to improve instruction in basic reading, writing, and mathematics skills. Almost no one questions that the 3 R's are essential. Many school systems have been devising programs to assure that students have at least minimal competency in arithmetic, spelling, writing, and reading.

A leader in this area has been the Denver Public Schools. This system has instituted a series of citywide tests to measure the competencies of students' basic skills. The same set of tests are repeated (in different forms) at all four grades of high school; thus, a student could conceivably graduate after the ninth grade. A senior who is not able to pass the tests gets no diploma for high school. Instead he is granted a "Certificate of Attendance." The city uses the tests not only to measure whether the competencies have been met upon graduation, but also to assist students in achieving these skills. The students who do not pass at the ninth-grade level are given individualized instructional prescriptions, and so on. By the time they are at the end of their senior year, virtually all will pass. The tests also help teachers improve the way they teach. The rates of failure have been dropping ever since the tests were started some years ago, and is now down to 2 percent of the senior class. Those who complete high school with a certificate of attendance may take the tests later in order to gain a high school diploma.

Five years ago, only six states had enacted minimal competency requirements (Schab, 1978). Now about two thirds of the states have such a requirement (Gorth and Perkins, 1980), and it appears that some form of the plan will soon be national.

Should You Really Have a High School Diploma?

Could you pass the Proficiency and Review Test of the Denver high schools? Below are multiple-choice questions similar to those given on the Denver test. Circle the letter of the correct answer. If you answer at least two right in every section, you would pass the test.

Numerical Proficiency

Add the following sets of numbers.

1.   979   A.   2568
        668   B.   2668
        434   C.   2669
        587   D.   2569
                                E.   none of the above

2.   7 1/5   F.   19
        4 3/10   G.   19 5/17
        7 1/2   H.   19 9/10
                                I.   20
                                J.   none of the above

3.   32.58 + 0.103 =   K.   .03371
                                L.   3.271
                                M.   32.683
                                N.   32.71
                                O.   none of the above

Spelling Proficiency

Check the letter of the word you think is misspelled, if any.

4.   A.   touch
      B.   message
      C.   athelete
      D.   excited
      E.   none of the above

5.   F.   cabanet
      G.   chocolate
      H.   yourself
      I.   unknown
      J.   none of the above

6.   K.   blizzard
      L.   button
      M.   elavated
      N.   ignorant
      O.   none of the above

Language Proficiency

Mark each line below with: P if the punctuation is in error; C if the capitalization is in error; G if the grammar is in error; or N if there is no error.

7.   Do you know anyone who has
8.   ever gone to a flea market! Our
9.   High School will have one on Saturday.

Answers: 1.·B; 2.·F; 3.·M; 4.·C; 5.·F; 6.·M; 7.·N; 8.·P; 9.·C.

There are those, and their numbers are growing, who believe that it is already too late to "save" the public schools. They feel that busing, tax cuts, and declining standards make it necessary to open private schools designed to provide strict drilling in the basics. Most of these schools have rigid and highly exclusive entrance requirements. Although in its infancy, this movement seems destined for explosive growth during the 1980s.

IMPROVING THE SCHOOLS: CONFLICT NEGOTIATION

DeCecco and Richards suggest that the way to handle most of the conflicts in today's high schools is through formal negotiation. There are three basic steps in the process.

1. Each party to a conflict must state its version of issues involved. Parties in conflict may be one student against another, a student against a teacher or administrator, or one group against another.

2. All parties must agree on a common, written statement of the issues to be negotiated.

3. Bargaining now takes place in order to reach agreement between the parties. All negotiations should include a written notification of charges, the opportunity to answer charges (with the right that counsel be present) and the opportunity to suggest solutions. When there is unequal status between the parties, it may be necessary to have mediation by a third party. The final agreement should include written plans to carry out the negotiated settlement.

DeCecco and Richards agree that such negotiations could take an enormous amount of school time and generate high emotions. But negotiation of conflict could bring about some of the most important learning that can take place in school—a deeper understanding of democratic concepts and a sense of civic responsibility. The specific benefits of negotiations are that they can teach new ways to improve interpersonal relationships; help students learn to socialize their anger; integrate individuals into the larger school society; offer opportunities to express differences in traditions, ethics, values, tastes, and viewpoints, and help students to appreciate the value of these differences; stimulate cognitive as well as emotional development; resolve immediate conflicts; and, most importantly, provide models for settling future conflicts.

DeCecco and Richards recognize that negotiating might politicize the high school, but "the dangers of politics are minor compared with the dangers of despair and violence which have already transformed many high schools into educational ruins (p. 120)."

IMPROVING THE SCHOOLS: DISCIPLINE MANAGEMENT

During the period 1969–1977, eight of nine Gallup polls (Gallup, 1977) indicated that Americans believe the most important problem in the schools is discipline. In his survey of public school superintendents, Duke (1978) found that the problem of discipline tops their list of concerns, and many of them believe that more time must be spent on its resolution.

If a problem gets attention in the regular curriculum, educators consider it important. Another measure of seriousness is whether educators establish formal objectives related to a problem. To my knowledge, few high schools ever establish school or classroom rules for absenteeism, respect for property, resolving conflicts more democratically, and the like. A final indication of the primacy of an educational concern is whether or not administrators and teachers will spend time after school working on it. The fact that more than half of the administrators reported the use of faculty trouble-shooting sessions (presumably involving staying after school) was encouraging (p. 330).

Most respondents of the Gallup Poll believe that simply using *stricter* discipline is the answer. The proponents of the discipline management approach believe a *variety* of methods should be used to make discipline more positive.

Kindsvatter's Method

Educator Richard Kindsvatter (1978) proposes a method of classroom management that starts with the assumption that

every act of a person is, from his perspective at the time it occurs, the most appropriate response he can make to the stimulus to which he is responding. A student, then, even when misbehaving, is doing what seems to give him, at that moment, the greatest degree of psychological comfort. When a teacher accepts this assumption, managing student behavior can no longer be considered simply forcing the student into compliance or passivity. Rather, a diagnostic component is added to the teacher's role. The teacher attempts to help the student understand his own behavior and guide him to acceptable alternatives (p. 322).

This diagnosis should result in identifying three types of discipline problems: chronic emotional and adjustment problems, students' negative attitudes toward teacher or class, and casual and capricious actions. Kindsvatter urges that teachers make clear the expectations they have for class behavior. Then, when one of these types of misbehavior occurs, the teacher should foster a specific type of behavior adjustment by the use of a specific control technique. These adjustments and techniques are as follows:

Chronic emotional and adjustment problems. The teacher tries to guide students to recognize that they have a problem and to adopt alternative forms of behavior. This is accomplished by a compassionate attitude and possibly a referral to counseling.

Students' negative attitude toward teacher and class. Here the teacher must reconceptualize his or her own role; negative attitudes, whatever the cause, mean the teacher needs to change the classroom climate by changing his or her own approach to teaching.

Casual or capricious actions. This form of misbehavior is usually less serious than the other two. The goal is to help students improve their own self-discipline through reminder, restraint, or reproval where appropriate.

Another suggestion (Kohl, 1960) is that teachers have as few rules as possible. This helps to cut down on the number of infractions and the consequent necessity for dealing with them.

Glasser's Method

Psychologist William Glasser is the author of the well-known book, *Schools Without Failure* (1969). In a *Phi Delta Kappan* article (1978), he suggests that

> disorder in the schools is no different from disorder anywhere else. Any of us has the capacity to break rules under certain conditions, and for too many students these conditions exist in the schools they attend. In school or elsewhere, short of expulsion, there are only two ways to keep order. One is through fear; the other is through having a stake in the situation. It's no longer possible, past the first few years in school, to get students to stay in order because they fear some sort of consequence . . . In fact, it is my opinion that corporal punishment produces fear in very few youngsters, but leads to resentment in almost all who are subjected to it (p. 331).

Glasser believes that the secret of success in discipline management is to make students feel they are cared for and to convince them they cannot fail. In fact, making it impossible for students to fail is one of the most effective ways of making them feel that they are cared for.

Failure in school frequently means failing to learn to read adequately. This happens for several reasons: an initial lack of success that is self-reinforcing, asking students to read material that makes little or no sense to them, and denying students the opportunity to make worthwhile contributions in class and be listened to.

Schools can overcome the problem of early failure by choosing reading materials more relevant to student concerns and by giving them a voice in what they will read. Students should be encouraged to share their ideas and practice their skills through group discussion. This will help students gain confidence, and will show them that no matter how long it takes, the teacher will stay with them until they are successful.

When students misbehave

> [they] are asked to evaluate their behavior and take the responsibility for planning better behavior. If they don't do this and they are out of order, there has to be a consequence; but only if they have a stake in the school do the consequences become meaningful. Basically, we suggest two consequences: (1) the loss of privileges and (2) the loss of freedom (p. 333).

To make this work, Glasser advocates that we increase the number of student privileges so that school is a more enjoyable place, which will increase the impact of losing these privileges. He also employs an **in-school suspension room** where students are forced to go if they refuse to follow their own plan to obey the rules. The room is staffed by a person who is an expert in guidance and is totally nonpunitive. Students stay in the room until they agree to follow the rules. Nothing happens to them there of a negative nature; the purpose of the room is to help students reevaluate their behavior so that they can return to the regular learning situation. The constant emphasis is on avoiding failure, which Glasser believes ultimately produces a great reduction in disciplinary problems.

Johnson's Method

Educational writer Christopher Johnson (1978) has suggested that too much of the responsibility for classroom discipline has been placed in the hands of teachers rather than students, where it belongs.

> *Let a teaching candidate be an effective communicator, a master of his course materials, a creator of original and varied lessons, an envisioner of the concrete attainment of abstract objectives. Fine. But let him also be a mild person who does not establish strict control over his classes, and his future in the profession is shadowed. On the other hand, the strong-armed embodiment of machismo is an immediate success, for he can keep the kids quiet and in their seats. The student learns early in school that the teacher is there to keep him under control. If the teacher fails, then it is O.K. for the kid to throw paper airplanes and write all over desks. Yes, kids learn early, and by the time they get to high school they know that teachers, rather than students, must face the music for an unproductive class atmosphere (p. 339).*

Johnson believes that at the very time when adolescents are struggling toward maturity and need to learn to accept responsibility for their behavior, most high schools make all their decisions for them; the schools actually reinforce irresponsibility. Expectations of responsible behavior are the key to discipline problems.

The mistake of many radical alternative schools has been to underplay discipline in order to encourage individuality and creativity. This leads students to pretend that their behavior has no consequences at all. The consequences of irresponsible behavior should follow logically from its nature. For example, if students destroy property, they should have to fix it. If they miss too many classes, they should be refused academic credit for that course. If they abuse open-campus privileges, they should be restrained to the campus. Consequences should follow quickly so that students see the effect of their behavior. Such punishments as detentions are ineffective because they are too long delayed after the actual infraction.

There is no substitute for creating close, warm relationships among students and teachers. For most students, this is often enough to achieve significant reductions in discipline problems. However, Johnson agrees that there are certain students who are much more difficult to deal with and who require special treatment. These students should be placed in self-contained classrooms run by the best teachers the school can offer. The number of students should be kept low so that the teachers will have ample opportunities to demonstrate the consequences of behavior to students. These teachers should be paid twice as much as regular teachers and should serve only one-year assignments so they do not become hardened to the difficulty of the discipline problems they face. With these two approaches, Johnson believes discipline problems will be reduced to a minimum and the school can get on with its real business: learning.

IMPROVING THE SCHOOLS: COMPREHENSIVE EDUCATION

Recommendations of the National Panel

The recommendations of the National Panel (1976) for improving high schools are far-reaching. The major five recommendations are described below.

1. Replace the **comprehensive high school** with **comprehensive education.** Students should learn through a variety of means and institutional arrangements; much of a teenager's education should occur outside of school.

2. Specific programs should be inaugurated by adolescents themselves and by interested and qualified adults of the community. This **participatory education** is defined by the Panel as "learning by doing what is socially useful, personally satisfying, and supporting for the individual and the community" (p. 10). The goal of participatory education includes the establishment of three kinds of educational centers, closely associated with the high school with which adolescents would be involved for part of their education: a community arts and crafts center, a community career education center, and a center for government at all levels within the community. The Panel believes that only by being involved in the real world of the community can the teenager learn his role as a useful, participating citizen.

3. Small, flexible, short-term, part-time schools should be established and available for all who are qualified and interested.

4. The Panel urges that formal instruction be drastically reduced and participatory education greatly increased by reducing compulsory daily attendance from all-day sessions to two to four hours.

5. The basic requirement of the high school as the primary institution for education of the *intellect* should be reemphasized. In this, the Panel has put itself squarely on the side of the "back to basics" movement. It recommends that all nonacademic goals be eliminated in order to devote full time to the development of a maturing intellect.

Experiential Learning

Many have suggested that what the Panel calls comprehensive education should take place more regularly in nonschool settings. Ivan Illich (1971) has urged that schools are destructive of individual growth; he believes that *all* education should take place in the community through what he calls "learning networks." Caroline

Bird (1975) has made basically the same argument against college education. James Coleman, et al. (1974) think that the school serves a useful function until youth reach the age of 16, after which they should be educated in organizations in the community, such as factories, businesses, hospitals, and orchestras. He suggests that 16-year-olds be given vouchers for the amount of the average four-year college tuition, which they could use to go to college or serve in apprenticeship programs run by vocational schools.

These and other writers have helped to promote a movement known as **experiential learning,** or sometimes **volunteerism.** Largely as a result of growing dissatisfaction with the schools, the experiential learning movement has made great strides in the United States in the past ten years. It is aimed at helping students find work and study assignments in a variety of institutions, as part of their schooling, to better prepare them for life.

There are a number of misunderstandings about learning in nonschool settings. Several of the most substantial are as follows:

1. *Experiential learning assignments are confined to business and industry.* These institutions clearly value having high school students at their establishments on a part-time basis, but so do other institutions such as hospitals, day-care centers, parks, airports, government offices, and in many cases, the schools themselves. It is fair to say, however, that businesses have been one of the primary consumers of the services of experiential learners.

2. *Student volunteerism refers only to the practice of donating one's time in the service of the community.* In addition to community service, volunteerism often serves the goals of career exploration and development, academic enrichment and field training, and psychological and sociological development. Some programs focus on only one of these goals, while others emphasize as many as four. For example, a student may enroll in a psychology course that requires working in a day-care center, an activity touching on all four goals of volunteerism.

3. *Students interested in experiential learning tend to be academically inferior.* Students of varied intellectual abilities increasingly have seen the advantages of spending some of their time in experiential learning; the number of top students who spend some of their time learning outside the classroom has grown rapidly.

4. *Volunteers tend to do only menial and unimportant tasks.* In the past, it was true that volunteers were required to do the most unskilled work, leaving the complicated tasks to full-time employees. This has changed radically since the infusion of federal funds into these programs, which has meant that programs are organized to provide specified training in responsible positions.

5. *Volunteerism tends to attract the lazier students.* It is presumed that doing volunteer work is easier than meeting the demands placed on students by school. Although in the past, the less-motivated student may have sought

experiential learning as a way of avoiding schoolwork, this is no longer the case. Under almost all volunteer contracts now, a student is assigned both a school advisor and a field supervisor. These two individuals insure that the assignment be carried out rigorously. The learning competencies and skills that are to be developed at the volunteer site are spelled out in behavioral terms, and evaluation of each of these competencies and skills is carefully monitored.

The growth of experiential learning in this decade has been phenomenal. For example, Winer and Hochman (1976) found that whereas there were very few volunteer positions in Massachusetts in 1971, five years later there were over 17,000 students in volunteer work experience programs. This growth spurt has been largely due to the action of two federal departments, the National Student Volunteer Program (NSVP) and the National Institute of Education (NIE). NSVP has an extensive catalog of books and pamphlets that has been developed to support school-sponsored volunteer programs. While NSVP has concentrated on the broader interpretation of volunteerism, the goals of NIE have been to promote career development and work experience. It has funded four model programs in various locations across the country, which are now being observed by a multitude of school systems.

A major defect of volunteer programs has been the inability of educators to adequately evaluate their success. Education has traditionally focused on the measurement of cognitive learning, and only recently turned its attention to such affective goals as job satisfaction and self-confidence, which experiential learning programs hope to provide. Cooperative Assessment of Experiential Learning (CAEL) is a group working on methods to measure the impact of experiential learning. CAEL has produced a number of booklets on assessment methods which are now being disseminated to schools across the country. Thus, the volunteer movement has had its tremendous growth not as a result of solid evaluation of its capabilities, but rather because of satisfactory reports from teachers and, most particularly, from students.

IMPROVING THE SCHOOLS: THE OUTWARD BOUND APPROACH

One of the most recent innovations in secondary education has been the adaptation of the **Outward Bound** program for use in the schools. Outward Bound is an organization that has prepared a curriculum of challenging activities to improve self-confidence through the practice of specific skills. Participants may, for example, climb on shaky rope riggings, climb and rappel down mountain cliffs, sail the ocean in open sailboats, learn mountaineering and survival techniques, and spend three days in total isolation on an island. Outward Bound offers training and practice for these events so that the person who successfully completes them will have greater self-knowledge and self-confidence.

Outward Bound has been a useful approach in treating juvenile delinquency. Delinquents who have gone through the program are much less likely to commit further crimes than those who are sent to jail (Dacey, 1976). See Chapter 12.

Recognizing the need of youth for rites of passage, several school systems have recently adopted some of the challenging activities of Outward Bound for use on their campuses. Activities are incorporated as part of the physical education, health, and science programs. An excellent example of this approach is Project Adventure, run by the Hamilton-Wenham School System in Hamilton, Massachusetts.* Students who have gone through Project Adventure say that they learned better how to handle their tensions and anxieties, how to cooperate with other people, and how to develop their own internal resources.

IMPROVING THE SCHOOLS: THE WALKABOUT APPROACH

In the remote regions of Australia, the Aborigines have a rite of passage for all 16-year-old males known as the **walkabout.** In the walkabout, the youth, having received training throughout most of his life in survival skills, must leave the village and live for six months on his own. He is expected not only to stay alive, but to sustain himself with patience, confidence, and courage. During this six-month estrangement from home and family, he learns to strengthen his faith in himself. He returns to the tribe with the pride and certainty that he is now accepted as an adult member.

> *The young native faces an extreme but appropriate trial, one in which he must demonstrate the knowledge and skills necessary to be a contributor to the tribe rather than a drain on its meager resources. By contrast, the young North American is faced with written examinations that test skills very far removed from actual experience he will have in real life (Gibbons, 1974, p. 597).*

Educator Maurice Gibbons suggests that the walkabout be adapted to Western high schools. Phi Delta Kappa, the national education fraternity, set up a task force to study Gibbons's ideas. Their specific suggestions have been incorporated in a pamphlet.† In its introduction, the Task Force (1976) suggests that

> *the American walkabout has to focus the activities of secondary school. It does so by demonstrating the relationship between education and action. It infuses the learning process with an intensity that is lacking in contemporary secondary schools. The walkabout provides youth with the opportunity to*

*A detailed description of Project Adventure can be obtained by writing to Project Adventure, 650 Bay Road, Hamilton, MA 01936.

†This pamphlet is available from PDK, Box 789, Bloomington, IN 47401.

learn what they can do. It constitutes a profound maturing experience through interaction with both older adults and children. The walkabout enriches the relationship between youth and community (p. 3).

There are three phases in this process: prewalkabout, walkabout, and postwalkabout. Each phase calls for learning specific skills. In the prewalkabout the following skill areas are studied: personal, lifelong learning, consumer, citizenship, and career skills. In the walkabout itself, the skills to be mastered are logical inquiry, creativity, volunteer service, adventure, practical skills, world of work, and cognitive development. The task force suggests a great number of activities that would foster learning in each skill. It is conceivable that students would undertake two or three different walkabouts in one school year.

Ideally, each walkabout should contain certain basic elements. It should be initiated by the student, be experiential rather than vicarious, extend the student's capabilities, contain an element of risk, be intense, take place outside the school, involve persons outside the student's age group, strike a balance between individual and group work, be well planned, and, at the same time, promote the occurrence of the unexpected.

The postwalkabout is a ceremony to extend recognition to the student that he or she has engaged in a major rite of passage on the way to adulthood. It is not enough to recognize this experience in a ceremony where members are confirmed en masse, such as the typical graduation. Rather, an individual ceremony involving the graduate's family and friends should be held for each walkabout the student undergoes.

The celebration of transition could take a variety of forms. The ceremonies are varied according to family tastes and imagination, but in each celebration the graduate is the center of the occasion. Parents and guests respond to the graduate's presentation. Teachers drop by to add their comments and congratulations. The graduate talks about his or her achievements, sharing some of the joys and admitting the frustrations (Task Force, 1976, p. 5).

ALTERNATIVE SCHOOLS

The current movement for alternative schools, usually private schools with strongly humanistic values, began in the latter part of the 1960s as a response to the social ferment of the civil rights and antiwar movements. The educational views of the activists of the '60s were widely discussed and debated and were influential in the founding of numerous alternative schools.

Alternative vs. Conventional Schools

Today's alternative schools are certainly not the first **nontraditional schools** in the United States (the most notable were the progressive schools of the 1920s), but they are the most significant. They have provoked a variety of educational strategies and organizations unequaled in the history of American education. Alternative schools are organized chiefly by people who feel that most public schools are bureaucratic, competitive, and dehumanizing; their goal is schools that are humane, personal, and meaningful. Private free schools were the first alternative humanistic schools; during the 1970s nontraditional educational programs have sprung up in the public secondary schools as well. Proponents of alternative schools generally favor the **voucher system,** in which parents are allotted tuition credits by the towns, cities, or states in which they live, which they may spend at public or private schools. This plan is also advocated by basic skills proponents, and this idea is being rejuvenated in the 1980s. The differences between typical conventional and alternative secondary schools are summarized in Table 9–2, developed by Terrence Deal with additions by Arthur Wirth.

Three Alternative Schools

What follows are descriptions of three successful alternative high schools: two in Missouri, the Clayton Alternative School and the Logos School; and one in Massachusetts, the Gloucester Experiment. The Clayton Alternative School, located in a wealthy suburb of St. Louis, is part of the regular public school system. Table 9–2 accurately describes its approach. The Logos School is a private nonprofit institution located in a commercial district of St. Louis. The students are teenagers who have had academic and emotional problems. Table 9–2 does not describe the approach of the Logos School. At this school, there is a traditional emphasis on math and verbal skills and a formal structure, but the school has an informal atmosphere and uses student-centered, nondirective teaching methods. Educational psychologist Deborah Stiles visited these two schools several times and describes them as follows.

The Clayton Alternative School. "My first impression of the Clayton Alternative School was one of serenity. The school is light and airy, artistically painted, and enlivened with plants, mourning doves, and fish. Fifteen students who had stayed after school were quietly engaged in projects and conversations. Three students were skinning a coyote which had been shot by a hunter and found near a stone cabin owned by the school. Each week two students live in that cabin as part of the Camp-a-Week project; they observe area animal and plant life, chop wood, and keep journals. The students skinning the coyote said they hoped to learn about anatomy, preserve the skull of the coyote, and tan the hide. Students spoke with commitment, confidence, and maturity that is rare in high school students. Perhaps it was because they are given so much responsibility in planning their own education. The goals of the Clayton Alternative School have been stated by the students:

To create opportunities for individual growth and respect for differences, to provide skills of questioning, communicating, understanding, and informa-

TABLE 9–2

DIFFERENCES BETWEEN CONVENTIONAL AND ALTERNATIVE SECONDARY SCHOOLS ON IMPORTANT DIMENSIONS OF LEARNING

Learning Dimensions	Conventional Secondary Schools	Alternative Humanistic Secondary Schools
1. *Who* is involved in the learning process (roles)	Certified teachers, counselors, administrators, students. All have relatively well-defined role expectations.	Teachers, administrators, parents, community members, students—anyone who has something to teach. Certification requirements relaxed; role distinctions blurred.
2. *What* is learned (curriculum)	State- or district-prescribed curriculum. Knowledge divided into subject areas. Special programs for noncollege-bound or other "special" students. Emphasis on cognitive learning.	Wide variation in educational substance, dictated largely by interest of students; may encompass areas usually taught in school but also extends into many other areas. Emphasis on affective learning.
3. *Why* it is learned (authority)	Extrinsic motivation; learning to fulfill requirements, to pass tests. Authority vested in teacher: "Do what you are told." Teachers' directive.	Intrinsic motivation; learning because of interest or need to know, to learn a skill or to acquire knowledge. Authority vested in students. Student choice.
4. *How* it is learned (methods)	Emphasis on reading, writing, listening; group presentation; lecture by teacher common; some audiovisual aids; some discussion.	Methods vary as widely as curriculum; reading, writing, listening not excluded, but emphasis on doing and experiencing; all senses involved.
5. *Where* learning takes place (location)	Learning takes place on campus, in classroom. Some field trips, but these are exceptional.	Wide variation in location of learning: private homes, beach, forest, libraries, businesses. Instruction in formal classroom is the exception rather than the rule.
6. *When* learning takes place	Instruction typically between hours of 8 A.M. and 4 P.M.; day segmented into periods or modules.	Learning takes place anytime, depending on nature of learning task; infrequent scheduling, no time segmentation.
7. Basis on which school is selected	Student is assigned to the school specified by the district.	Student with parental permission chooses the alternative.
8. Size of the school	Secondary schools typically from 1000 to 4000 students.	Size of learning center limited to 50 to 150–200 students.
9. Teacher-student relations	Teacher prescribes work, tests, and grades level of achievement. Relations are formal and role-prescribed.	Teacher and student collaborate in formulating goals and means of study in a learning contract. Joint evaluation of results. Relations more informal (first names), less role-prescribed.

Source: Deal, Terence E., "Comparison of Conventional and Alternative Secondary Schools," *Educational Researcher,* April 1975, p. 12. Copyright 1975, American Educational Research Association, Washington, D.C.

tion analyzing, to explore and express our values with assurance, to practice honesty and openness, develop responsibility by making decisions about learning experiences and whole school issues, to recognize current and future needs in preparation for the future, to learn by success as well as failure, and to form a community which values each individual and exists and changes to meet the needs of its members.

"There are forty-three students at the Clayton Alternative School, which is 5 percent of the enrollment of Clayton High School. Prospective students apply to the alternative school and are interviewed by a student-teacher committee.

"Because it is part of a regular high school, its graduation requirements are the same: English, mathematics, science, and history are studied. The school has unusual approaches to traditional subjects which are revealed in course titles such as 'Alternative Energy Forms,' 'History of St. Louis,' 'Ourselves,' and 'Public Relations.' Courses are taught by staff members, district specialists and directors, student teachers from colleges, community volunteers, and occasionally the students themselves. Learning contracts are used; included in the learning contracts are brief descriptions of the courses, student and teacher objectives and responsibilities. No grades are given, but written evaluations of individual performances are used."

The Logos School.   "This school is another successful alternative school, but its educational philosophy, student body, ambience, and appearance are quite different from Clayton. The physical plant of the Logos School is not particularly attractive; the school is housed in a small, dingy converted factory building. The furnishings are worn and secondhand and the carpets are remnants.

"Most of the students look as disheveled as the furniture; one student was wearing a bathrobe over his jeans and T-shirt. Superficial appearances are not important here; the atmosphere is intensely intellectual and stimulating. The students, many of whom had been chronic dropouts, are now very involved in learning. Most of the graduates of Logos later go on to college. The Logos curriculum is academic, not vocational. There is little emphasis on experiential learning, which is the trademark of many alternative schools. Learning experiences are provided by reading and discussion of books, rather than student participation in projects and self-government. Courses are offered in English, math, history, science, and the arts. The purpose of the Logos curriculum is to help students learn skills, not just information. Like Clayton Alternative, the emphasis is on learning how to learn. The course catalog explains the rationale for this approach:

We shift the focus from learning data to learning how to learn because technology, especially cybernation, is generating data so rapidly that half of what one learns today is obsolete in eleven years. This means we must keep learning—unlearning as well as relearning—if we are not to become obsolete ourselves. Thus we want to become learners, not knowers. Logos means "understanding."

"In the school newsletter, Terri Chishom, a student, describes her experience at Logos:"

> When I first came to Logos, I was not very confident about things that I said. I was always afraid that what I said was stupid, and I just couldn't see how anyone could want to hear what I had to say. I wasn't quiet; I always talked. Yet underneath my front of being confident, I felt scared and inadequate. The greatest thing that I have attained from my year at Logos is the ability to communicate with my fellow students in classes. I have not only learned to better express myself to other students, but I have also gained confidence that what I say is being listened to.

The Gloucester Experiment. Accredited through Gloucester (Massachusetts) High School, this alternative school "promotes career-occupational alternatives and organizes community and youth in a partnership for self-renewal." Participants learn basic skills by helping in large community projects. Some projects have been historic site restoration (an eighteenth-century burial ground which was hidden in brush), and building a large educational resource center, a media trailer, and a portable foundry. Students are responsible for planning and carrying out all phases of these projects. In the eight years the Experiment has been operating, 200 students have graduated, most of whom had planned to drop out of school. In a variety of ways, sixteen communities have benefitted from their work.

How Would You Change Your Teachers?

In my conversations with junior and senior high school students, I frequently ask them how they would change their teachers if they had the chance. Below are listed some of their most frequent suggestions.

1. "Be consistent. Some teachers treat you as adults, others as little kids. Some heap on homework, some give none. Most are stricter with some kids than they are with others. Some give many tests, some almost none."

2. "But don't be *too* consistent. 'Honor students' should not necessarily be treated the same as the 'drop-outs.' Some teachers pay no attention to effort, looking only at achievement; but effort should be rewarded sometimes. Some teachers try to be so democratic that they teach all students as though they were exactly alike. Girls have different needs than boys sometimes."

3. "Don't compare us with your times. You know, how in the olden days no one skipped school, teachers were very strict, and all that."

4. "Don't assign tests on Thursday or Friday so we have to study over the weekend."

5. "Try to get to know your students as individuals. When we feel like you know us, we feel we can trust you."

6. "Try not to be prejudiced. Some teachers are prejudiced in favor of whites, but many more are prejudiced in favor of blacks, and give them more freedom than they do the white students."

7. "Don't pick favorites. Even though you think we can't tell, we always can."

8. "Don't punish the majority because the minority is misbehaving."

9. "Coordinate testing so that we don't get all the testing at the same time of the year; space tests out a little more."

10. "Think of other kinds of punishment besides detention; that only makes us hate school more."

11. "Respect our personal rights more. Don't treat us like we were prison convicts."

12. "Notice whether or not we are paying attention to you."

13. "Trust us more. Don't always assume that if we give you an excuse that we're lying."

14. "Don't form opinions of us so early in the year, and be more ready to change them if we change."

15. "Try to understand that we have other things in our lives besides class assignments."

16. "Act more like a salesman and less like a genius."

A PERSONAL POSITION

As you may have noticed, the suggestions to improve the schools described in this chapter lie along a continuum from reactionary to radical. Some urge that we go back to previous goals ("small and simple" education and "back to basics" approaches); others that we improve and institute innovations within the traditional school framework (the discipline management, conflict negotiation, comprehensive education, Outward Bound, and walkabout approaches); and others advocate that we depart from traditional schools altogether or offer students a choice of educational styles (the alternative schools, the voucher system).

I believe that while each of these approaches has merit, those in the center of the continuum offer the best hope of reinvigorating secondary education. In trying to recapture some of our lost effectiveness, the first two approaches would create many new problems because our society has changed so much in the past thirty years.

The main difficulty is that these approaches emphasize cognitive goals so strongly that they tend to neglect students' affective needs. There is considerable evidence, presented in this book and elsewhere (for example, Maslow, 1971) that unless emotional needs are met, little learning can take place. Furthermore, with the declining influence of religion and the family, adolescents have looked to their schools to meet some of these needs. Expecting them to embrace an entirely cognitive curriculum is unrealistic.

While alternative schools do serve to meet the needs of some individuals, most of them attract students who are quite similar to each other. Public schools offer something that is not supplied in private schools: regular, supervised, direct contact with persons *different* in many ways from oneself. Therefore, alternative schools should remain just that: limited alternatives to public schools.

Even most of its severest critics believe that public education in this country can and should be saved. Alvin Toffler (1970) has some suggestions:

> *Why, for example, must teaching be organized around such fixed disciplines as English, economics, mathematics, or biology? Why not around stages of the human life cycle: a course on birth, childhood, adolescence, marriage, career, retirement, death. Or around contemporary social problems? Or around significant technologies of the past and future? Or around countless other imaginable alternatives? (p. 410).*

Toffler argues that people living in tomorrow's industrial societies will need skills in three crucial areas. The first area is *learning:* We must teach people how to classify information, evaluate it, reclassify it when necessary, open-mindedly look for new directions, and to do all this *by themselves.* The illiterate of tomorrow will not be the person who cannot read, but rather the person who has not learned how to learn. The second area is *relating:* There is a great deal of loneliness and inability to "open up" with others. As the rate of change in the world increases, so will our need to learn how to be intimate with others. The third area is *choosing:* Adaptation involves making successive choices. As the number and variety of alternatives in our lives grow, the greater will be our need for a clear-cut sense of values to direct choice. Yet there is considerable evidence that our values, and particularly those of our children, have never been *less* clear (see Chapter 13). Simply taking dogmatic stands on questions will not make problems go away.

Our potential ability to control our lives through knowledge has increased enormously; at the same time, much current change is out of our control. We must teach our youth to deal more effectively with the complicated consequences of their actions. Our secondary schools are a good place to start.

Both the reactionary and the humanistic approaches call for private schools. I believe private schools are usually elitist and always separatist. As such, they promote antidemocratic values. I agree with John Dewey that, by and large, our American society needs the polyglot mix of the public schools to have any hope for national harmony.

SUMMARY

Change has been the predominant theme in America during the latter part of this century, and our schools have been no exception. Students are now remaining in school longer, and more and more adolescents—previously neglected segments of the population—are being served by the educational system.

It has been difficult for schools to keep up with the changes. Thus, the picture we often see is a school filled with angry and frustrated adolescents whose needs are no longer being met. This in turn leads to acting-out behaviors that threaten the well-being of students, teachers, and administrators. Conflict among factions has become prevalent, while education has been sacrificed.

DeCecco and Richards' assessment of the sources of conflict includes: (1) the status difference between students and teachers leading to a power struggle; (2) fear and distrust resulting from the demographic changes; (3) the school's role as custodian of the young; (4) the school's failure to act as a political socializer; and (5) the lack of social contact between the teachers and the students.

The National Panel's study locates the source of conflict in the system and its "technical deficiencies," such as: (1) size; (2) too long a period of schooling; (3) the inefficiency of traditional educational approaches in meeting new needs; (4) unmanageable programs due to diversification; (5) the lack of practical applications of democracy and citizenship; (6) administrators who are unresponsive to the community; and (7) the schools' burden of increasing responsibilities for the total education of the students.

With all these legitimate criticisms of the schools comes the inevitable question, "What do we do now?" Wynne believes that we should return to the pattern of simpler institutions of thirty to forty years ago. Others believe that society itself needs to change.

A third group has suggested a "back to basics" approach based upon the students' skills in reading, writing, and arithmetic. Speaking for a fourth group, DeCecco and Richards recommend a solution to conflict by means of formal negotiation.

A fifth approach is the "discipline management" approach, of which there are several versions. Kindsvatter recommends (1) establishing clear behavioral expectations of the students; (2) identifying the type of discipline problem; and (3) using specific control techniques to produce desired behavior changes. Glasser asserts that feelings of security and success are necessary for the student's positive self-image, and that once this is developed, management is no longer an issue. Finally, Johnson, who agrees that behavioral expectations are crucial, differs by placing the main responsibility on the student, not the school.

The National Panel recommends: (1) replacing the concept of the comprehensive high school by that of comprehensive education, which will be accomplished by (2) establishing educational programs in the community (participatory education); (3) establishing small, flexible, short-term schools; (4) reducing the daily hours of formal education to a compulsory two to four hours; and (5) re-establishing the goal of the schools as education of the intellect.

Movements for education reform based outside of the traditional school systems are four. Experiential learning or volunteerism moves the education of adolescents out of the schools and directly into the community. The Outward Bound program does not necessarily dictate a complete departure from the physical setting of the school, but certainly a philosophical departure. The basis of this approach is the promotion of psychological and educational growth by testing oneself and learning to cope in extreme situations. The walkabout approach is based upon the rite of passage for youth in the Australian Aborigine society. Gibbons has suggested that a similar tradition be initiated in this country in order to test the adolescent's skills in daily living situations. Finally, the alternative school attempts to establish more meaningful, personalized, and less competitive educational systems. This is accomplished through the academic involvement of any individual who has something to teach, deemphasizing purely academic subjects and concentrating on whatever areas seem to interest the students, small classes, using the larger community as an educational setting, and independence of schedules.

Questions

1. What are the main problems of secondary schools? What are their causes?
2. What effect have the modern electronic media had on educating adolescents?
3. What are some of the approaches suggested by current psychologists for improving our schools?
4. What are some suggested alternatives to today's systems of high school education?
5. Does our society need "rites of passage" to accompany high school experience?
6. Should secondary schools be preparation for life? For the world of work? For training the intellect?

References

"The ABC's of school violence." *Time,* January 23, 1978, 73–74.

Arwood, B., Williams, R. L., & Long, J. D. "The effects of behavior contracts and behavior proclamations on social conduct and academic achievement in a ninth grade English class." *Adolescence,* Fall 1974, *9*(35), 425–436.

Bayh, B. "Seeking solutions to school violence and vandalism." *Phi Delta Kappan,* January 1978, *59*(5), 299–301.

Bird, C. "College is a waste of time and money." *Psychology today,* May 1975, *8,* 28.

Coleman, J. S. et al. *Youth: transition to adulthood.* Chicago: University of Chicago Press, 1974.

Coleman, J. "Changing the environment for youth." *Phi Delta Kappan,* January 1978, *58*(5), 318.

Dacey, J. "Where kids swing from the trees." *Learning,* December 1976, *5(4),* 68–73.

Deal, J. "An organizational explanation of the failure of alternative secondary schools." *Educational researcher,* April 1975, *4*(4), 1017.

DeCecco, J. P., & Richards, I. K. "Civil war in the high schools." *Psychology today,* 1975, *9*(6), 51–52; 120.

Duke, D. "How administrators view the crisis in school discipline." *Phi Delta Kappan,* January 1978, *59*(5), 325–330.

Flygare, T. "The Supreme Court approves corporal punishment." *Phi Delta Kappan,* January 1978, *59*(5), 347.

Friedenberg, E. Z. *The vanishing adolescent.* New York: Random House, 1959.

Gallup, G. H. "Ninth annual Gallup poll of the public's attitudes toward the public schools." *Phi Delta Kappan,* September 1977, 33-48.

Gibbons, M. "Walkabout: searching for the right passage from childhood and school." *Phi Delta Kappan,* May 1974, 596-602.

Glasser, W. *Schools without failure.* New York: Harper & Row, 1969.

Glasser, W. "Disorders in our schools: causes and remedies." *Phi Delta Kappan,* January 1978, *59*(5), 331-333.

Goodman, P. *Growing up absurd.* New York: Random House, 1960.

Gorth, W., & Perkins, M.R. *Study of minimum testing programs.* Washington, D.C.: National Institute of Education, 1980.

Hampton, P. J. "Learning needs of academically disadvantaged students." *Adolescence,* Winter 1974, *9*(36), 555-564.

Holt, J. *Escape from childhood.* New York: Dutton, 1974.

Illich, I. *Deschooling society.* New York: Harper & Row, 1971.

Jensen, R. E. "Cooperative relations between secondary teachers and students: some behavioral strategies." *Adolescence,* Winter 1975, *9*(40), 469-482.

Johnson, C. "Secondary schools and student responsibility." *Phi Delta Kappan,* January 1978, *59*(5), 338-341.

Kindsvatter, R. "A new view of the dynamics of discipline." *Phi Delta Kappan,* January 1978, *59*(5), 322-324.

Kobak, D. "Edu-caring—teaching children to care." *Adolescence,* Spring 1977, *12*(45), 97-102.

Kohl, H. *The open classroom.* New York: Doubleday, 1960.

LeUnes, A., & Siemsgluez, S. "Paraprofessional treatment of school phobia in a young adolescent girl." *Adolescence,* Spring 1977, 12(45), 115-122.

Maslow, A. *Farther reaches of human nature.* New York: Viking, 1971.

Massey, T. "Some elements in restoring health." *Phi Delta Kappan,* January 1978, *59*(5), 320.

National Panel on High School and Adolescent Education. *The education of adolescents.* Washington, D.C.: U.S. Dept. of Health, Education, and Welfare, 1976 [HEW No. (OE) 76-00004].

Pacheo, A. "Alienation: a closer look." *Phi Delta Kappan,* January 1978, *59*(5), 317.

Porter, J. "The limits of school power." *Phi Delta Kappan,* January 1978, *59*(5), 319.

Schab, F. "Who wants what minimum competencies?" *Phi Delta Kappan,* January 1978, *59*(5), 350-352.

Sebald, H. *Adolescence: a social psychological analysis* (2nd ed.). Englewood Cliffs, N.J.: Prentice-Hall, 1977.

Snyder, E. E., & Kiblin, J. E. "Perceptions of the sex role among female athletes and nonathletes." *Adolescence,* Spring 1977, *12*(45), 23-30.

Toffler, A. *Future shock.* New York: Random House, 1970.

Tyack, D. "Socialization to what?" *Phi Delta Kappan,* January 1978, *59*(5), 316.

U.S. Department of Health, Education, and Welfare. *Digest of educational statistics: projections of educational statistics to 1982-83.* Washington, D.C.: U.S. Government Printing Office, 1975.

Wagner, B. R., & Brietmeyer, R. G. "Pace: a residential community-oriented behavior modification program for adolescents." *Adolescence,* Summer 1975, *10*(38), 277-286.

Williams, D. "Why public schools fail." *Newsweek,* April 20, 1981, 62 ff.

Williams, R. "Volunteerism." Boston College, unpublished paper, 1978.

Winer, E., & Hochman, R. *Report on Massachusetts secondary school work experience programs.* Boston: Northeastern University, February 1976.

Wynne, E. "Beyond the discipline problem: youth suicide as a measure of alienation." *Phi Delta Kappan,* January 1978, *59*(5), 307-315.

Additional References

Baumrind, D. "From each according to her ability." *School review,* 1972, *80*(2), 161–197.

Baumrind, D. "Coleman II: utopian fantasy and sound social innovation." *School review,* 1974, *83*(1), 69–84.

Behn, W. H., Carney, M., Carter, M. A., Crain, J. C., & Levin, H. M. "School is bad; work is worse." *School review,* 1974, *83*(1), 49–68.

Buser, R. L., Long, R., & Tweedy, H. "The who, what, why, and why not of student activity participation." *Phi Delta Kappan,* 1975, *57*(2), 124–125.

Chand, I. P., Crider, D. M., & Willits, F. K. "Parent-youth disagreement as perceived by youth: a longitudinal study." *Youth and Society,* 1975, *6*(3), 365–375.

Chotiner, M. M., & Forrest, D. V. "Adolescent school phobia: six controlled cases studied retrospectively." *Adolescence,* Winter 1974, *9*(36), 467–480.

Coleman, J. S. *The adolescent society.* New York: Free Press, 1961.

Coleman, J. S. "Comments on responses to youth: transition to adulthood." *School review,* 1974, *83*(1), 139–144.

Coleman, J. S. *Youth: transition to adulthood.* Chicago: University of Chicago Press, 1974.

"Declining SAT scores." *Today's education,* November-December 1977.

Elarbo, R. "Behavior modification in an elementary school: problems and issues." *Phi Delta Kappan,* January 1978, *59*(5), 334–337.

Fisher, R. "Adolescent attitudes to superiors." *Adolescence,* Spring 1976, 87–96.

Friedenberg, E. Z. *Coming of age in America.* New York: Random House, 1965.

Glasser, W. "A new look at discipline." *Learning,* December 1974, 68–75.

Gordon, T. *Teacher effectiveness training.* New York: Wyden, 1975.

Hampton, P. J. "Learning needs of academically disadvantaged students." *Adolescence,* Winter 1974, *9*(36), 555–564.

Horn, P. "How teachers shape students' friendships." *Psychology today,* 1974, *7*(9), 16–18.

Jones, S. "High school social status as historical process." *Adolescence,* Spring 1976, *11*(41).

Keane, S. "The impact of experimental education." *Media and method,* September 1977.

Kline, S. A., & Golomber, H. "The incongruous achiever in adolescence." *Journal of youth and adolescence,* 1974, *3*(2), 153–160.

Kokenes, B. "Grade level differences in factors of self-esteem." *Developmental psychology,* 1974, *10*(6), 954–958.

Kowalski, C. J., & Cangemi, J. P. "High school dropout—a lost resource." *College student journal,* 1974, *8*(4), 71–74.

Lee, P. C., & Gropper, N. B. "Sex-role culture and educational practice." *Harvard educational review,* 1974, *44*(3), 369–410.

Litwak, E., & Meyer, H. J. *School, family, and neighborhood: the theory and practice of school-community relations.* New York: Columbia University Press, 1974.

Michaels, M. "Our nation's teachers are taking a beating." *Parade,* February 1978, 6–7.

Neil, S. "Violence and vandalism: dimensions and correctives." *Phi Delta Kappan,* January 1978, *59*(5), 302–306.

Neill, G. "Women's liberation expected to reach locker room soon." *Phi Delta Kappan,* 1974, *55*(9), 643–644.

"On opening day America's schools ponder some sobering lessons." *U.S. news & world report,* September 12, 1977.

Pine, F., & Olesker, W. "The school failure as a tutor: an exploratory approach." *Journal of youth and adolescence,* 1973, *2*(3), 183–200.

Schillain, "Back to basics backlash—a threat to media." *Media and methods,* September 1976.

Schulman, J. L., Ford, R. C., & Busk, P. A. "Classroom program to improve self-concept." *Psychology in the schools,* 1973, *19*(4), 481–487.

Senna, J., Rathus, S. A., & Siegel, L. "Delinquent behavior and academic investment among suburban youth." *Adolescence,* Winter 1974, *9*(36), 481–494.

Snyder, E. E. "Athletic team involvement, educational plans, and the coach-player relationship." *Adolescence,* Summer 1975, *10*(38), 191–200.

Stanley, J. C. "Accelerating the educational progress of intellectually gifted youths." *Educational psychologist,* 1973, *10*(3), 133–146.

Stein, K. B., Soskin, W. F., & Korchin, S. J. "Interpersonal trust and disaffected high school youth." *Journal of youth and adolescence,* 1974, *3*(4), 281–292.

Trow, M. "Problems of policy in Coleman II." *School review,* 1974, *83*(1), 15–25.

Wilde, J., & Sommers, P. "Teaching disruptive adolescents: a game worth winning." *Phi Delta Kappan,* January 1978, *59*(5), 342–346.

Chapter Ten

Substance Abuse

Chapter Highlights

Some Definitions
   What Do You Know about Drugs?
Soft Drugs
   Marijuana
   Reasons for Using Marijuana
   Cocaine
   Tobacco
   Alcohol
   Talking to Teenagers about Drinking
Hard Drugs
   Hallucinogens—Psychedelics
   Narcotics
   Stimulants
   Sedatives
Stages of Substance Abuse
Drugs and Sex
Ethnic Group and Abuse
Crime and Abuse
Drug Use and Personal Relationships
   Do Your Own Study of Drug Use
Alternatives to Drug Abuse
Summary

Key Terms and Concepts

drug abuse
drug addiction
drug dependence
drug tolerance
drug overdose
victimless crime
controlled drug
soft drugs
hard drugs
physical awareness
sensory awareness
psychological awareness
interpersonal awareness
rites of passage
work as fun
esthetic appreciation
learning
nonrational experience
social and political activism
school climate survey

Perhaps never before in history has there been a period when people turned so readily to drugs as during the years since the early 1960s. From every side the public has been besieged by the wonders that science can perform in relieving physical and psychological aches and pains. One parent takes tranquilizers to "soothe the nerves" and often administers them as well to a hyperactive child to keep him or her reasonably manageable. Another drinks liquor to relax after the stresses and strains of a hard day's work. And the young child, long before he or she learns to read, is given a rudimentary course in physiology and pharmacology by the advertisers who display their wares on television. Small wonder, in this chemical age, that a myth about drugs has developed . . .

—Lambert, et al., 1978, p. 239.

It is unfortunate that one whole chapter in a textbook on adolescent psychology should be devoted to a consideration of substance abuse (sometimes called drug abuse). However, it is clear from national statistics that the use of illegal substances continues to rise. As Table 10–1 indicates, figures on use and abuse in the last half of the 1970s of these kinds of drugs show either no decline or an increase in every category. The use of marijuana, thought by some to be dying out, increased 12 percent. Furthermore, virtually *all* students had used it at least once in their high school years. There is a clearly increasing trend in the use of cocaine, alcohol, and cigarettes, too (although alcohol use cannot get much higher). As we can see in Table 10–2, they are used fairly frequently.

In this chapter, causes and effects of substance abuse are considered, as well as some alternatives to abuse. Before considering these aspects, however, let us look at some definitions of terms which are often misunderstood.

SOME DEFINITIONS

A *drug* is any chemical or vegetable substance that causes a physiological, emotional, or behavioral change.

Drug abuse is use of a drug in such a way that the individual's physical, mental, or emotional well-being is in some way impaired.

Drug addiction historically referred to dependence on narcotics. Today it has so many meanings that experts are now beginning to use the term *drug dependence* instead.

Drug dependence occurs when there is a physical or psychological need, or both, resulting from continuous drug use. Psychological need occurs when the person feels anxious or irritable when he or she doesn't have the drug. Physical dependence, on the other hand, occurs only when negative physical symptoms result from drug withdrawal, such as vomiting, sweating, muscle tremors, delu-

TABLE 10–1
TRENDS IN LIFETIME PREVALENCE OF ELEVEN TYPES OF DRUGS

	Percent ever used			
	Class of 1975 (Number = 9400)	Class of 1976 (15400)	Class of 1977 (17100)	Class of 1978 (17800)
Marijuana	47.3	52.8	56.4	59.2
Inhalants	NA	10.3	11.1	12.0
Hallucinogens	16.3	15.1	13.9	14.3
Cocaine	9.0	9.7	10.8	12.9
Heroin	2.2	1.8	1.8	1.6
Other opiates	9.0	9.6	10.3	9.9
Stimulants	22.3	22.6	23.0	22.9
Sedatives	18.2	17.7	17.4	16.0
Tranquilizers	17.0	16.8	18.0	17.0
Alcohol	90.4	91.9	92.5	93.1
Cigarettes	73.6	75.4	75.7	75.3

NA indicates data not available.
Only drug use which was not under a doctor's orders is included in this survey.
From the National Institute on Drug Abuse.

sions and hallucinations, and almost always a strong sense of anxiety. About 5 percent of all American teenagers are physiologically drug dependent. There is no reliable estimate of how many are psychologically dependent.

Drug tolerance, a condition which develops from continuous use of a drug, occurs when a larger and larger amount is needed to produce the same effect.

Abuse of inhalants such as airplane glue, paint thinners, and gasoline is becoming more common. The most popular new inhalant is amyl nitrite, popularly known as "poppies." These substances are especially dangerous because they can permanently damage the nervous system.

Drug overdose is defined as taking so much of a drug that it causes an acute reaction, usually extreme anxiety which is sometimes followed by stupor, low breathing rate, and in rare cases, coma. Hallucinogens, marijuana, and stimulants can produce an anxiety attack even when taken in small doses; users become agitated, frightened, suspicious, and think that people are "out to get them." While medical attention is always necessary in the case of drug overdose, it is also important that those who are first on the scene remain calm and that they reassure the person he or she will be all right.

Victimless crime is a term often applied to the use of drugs. Some people

TABLE 10–2
TRENDS IN THIRTY-DAY PREVALENCE OF ELEVEN TYPES OF DRUGS

	Percent who used in last thirty days			
	Class of 1975 (Number = 9400)	Class of 1976 (15400)	Class of 1977 (17100)	Class of 1978 (17800)
Marijuana	27.1	32.2	35.4	37.1
Inhalants	NA	0.9	1.3	1.5
Hallucinogens	4.7	3.4	4.1	3.9
Cocaine	1.9	2.0	2.9	3.9
Heroin	0.4	0.2	0.3	0.3
Other opiates	2.1	2.0	2.8	2.1
Stimulants	8.5	7.7	8.8	8.7
Sedatives	5.4	4.5	5.1	4.2
Tranquilizers	4.1	4.0	4.6	3.4
Alcohol	68.2	68.3	71.2	72.1
Cigarettes	36.7	38.8	38.4	36.7

NA indicates data not available.
Only drug use which was not under a doctor's orders is included in this survey.
From the National Institute on Drug Abuse.

feel that abusers are the only ones who suffer from the use of drugs, so they should not be fined or imprisoned for their actions. However, drug abusers tend to be poor financial risks, dangerous drivers, and often resort to theft to support their habit; they are usually dependent on their families and often on society for support. So their acts are seldom victimless.

Controlled drugs are all those that have been limited in their distribution and manufacture under the Controlled Substances Act of 1970. This act empowers the Attorney General of the United States and his designates to punish those who use or sell drugs illegally. There are five levels of punishment under this law. Most of the drugs discussed in this chapter are covered by the Act.

Possession, dealing, and *trafficking* in drug substances are also distinguished legally. Illegal possession refers to obtaining drugs from someone not legally sanctioned to distribute them. Dealing is the sale of drugs on a small scale, usually carried out by a friend of the purchaser. Trafficking involves the sale of much larger amounts of drugs. Each of these violations of the law carries a different penalty.

What Do You Know About Drugs?

Test your knowledge of drugs by answering the following questions.

1. During which time was drug abuse a problem in the United States?

   (a) during the Civil War
   (b) in the 1950s
   (c) in the 1960s
   (d) all of the above

2. In which age group is drug abuse likely to be a problem?
   (a) 12–16
   (b) 16–25
   (c) 25–45
   (d) 45 and over
   (e) All of the above

3. How do most drug users make their first contact with illicit drugs?
   (a) through "pushers" seeking new customers
   (b) through their friends
   (c) accidentally
   (d) through the media

4. Which of the following is the most commonly abused drug in the United States?
   (a) marijuana
   (b) alcohol
   (c) cocaine
   (d) heroin

5. Which of the following is not a narcotic?
   (a) heroin
   (b) marijuana
   (c) morphine
   (d) methadone

6. Which of the following is not a stimulant?
   (a) amphetamine
   (b) caffeine
   (c) mescaline
   (d) methamphetamine

7. Which of the following drugs does not cause physical dependence?
   (a) ethyl alcohol
   (b) morphine
   (c) mescaline
   (d) secobarbital
   (e) codeine

8. Which of the following is not a hallucinogen?
   (a) MDA
   (b) LSD
   (c) STP
   (d) MPA

9. Which of the following has the highest immediate risk to experimenters?
   (a) inhalants
   (b) marijuana
   (c) nicotine
   (d) heroin

10. At what point in time does a person who uses heroin become physically dependent?
    (a) immediately (first time)
    (b) after four or five times
    (c) after prolonged use (twenty times or more)
    (d) different for each person

11. Which ingredient is most commonly found in compounds sold on the street as "mescaline"?
    (a) lysergic acid diethylamide
    (b) morphine
    (c) tetracycline
    (d) naltrexone
    (e) all of the above

12. Why is intravenous injection the most dangerous method of taking drugs?
    (a) because of the rapidity with which the drug enters the system
    (b) because nonsterile equipment and solutions are likely to cause serious medical complications
    (c) because the amount of drug entering the bloodstream is likely to be large
    (d) all of the above

13. When a person becomes physically dependent on drugs, what is the primary reason he continues to take the drug?
    (a) to experience pleasure
    (b) to relieve discomfort
    (c) to escape reality
    (d) to gain acceptance among friends

14. Which of the following drugs has never been used to treat narcotic addiction in the United States?
    (a) cyclazocine
    (b) naloxone
    (c) methadone
    (d) psilocybin
    (e) heroin

15. Which of the following is an effective treatment method for drug abusers?
    (a) maintenance
    (b) detoxification
    (c) abstinence
    (d) psychotherapy
    (e) all of the above

Source: Special Action Office for Drug Abuse Prevention, 1976.

ANSWERS TO "WHAT DO YOU KNOW ABOUT DRUGS?"

1. (d)All of the above. The use of drugs is as old as the history of humankind. In the United States there have been special drug abuse problems in different periods. During the Civil War opium was used medically, and since its addictive properties were not clearly understood, many wounded soldiers became addicted. Following the Civil War, the practice of opium smoking became popular on the West Coast and spread to many urban areas. Throughout the century, there were periodic "drug scares" created by the use of cocaine at the turn of the century, heroin in the 1920s, marijuana in the 1930s, and heroin again in the 1950s. The 1960s saw a social explosion of drug use of all kinds, from LSD to heroin and marijuana.

2. (e)All of the above. Drug abuse is found in all age groups. The recent focus on use of drugs by young people has been out of proportion to the actual age distribution of drug users.

3. (b)Through their friends. With the exception of alcohol, which is usually first used at home, most drug users are introduced to drugs by friends.

4. (b)Alcohol. Estimates are that about nine million Americans are alcoholics.

5. (b)Marijuana. In the past marijuana was legally classified as a narcotic, but it isn't now. Marijuana's psychopharmacological effects are similar to stimulants, sedatives, or hallucinogens, and its actual effects depend on dose, frequency of use, set (personality and expectation of the user), setting (environment), and other factors. Morphine and heroin are legally and pharmacologically classified as narcotics. Methadone is a synthetic narcotic.

6. (c)Mescaline. All are stimulants except mescaline, which is a hallucinogen with effects similar to LSD.

7. (c)Mescaline. Physical dependence on mescaline (the drug derived from the mescal or peyote cactus) and many other hallucinogens has not been verified.

8. (d)MPA. MPA is not an acronym for any known drug. MDA, LSD, and STP are all hallucinogens with similar effects. MDA (Mellow Drug of America) and STP (Serenity, Tranquility, Peace) are street drugs.

9. (a)Inhalants. Sniffing aerosols, glue, or other volatile substances can result in immediate death, although experts disagree on explanations for its rapidity. Although death can result from "mainlining" heroin, most experimentation with heroin takes the form of sniffing or skin-popping (injecting it under the skin but not in a vein).

10. (d)Different for each person. Although the time it takes for a person to become physically dependent on heroin may vary, we know that repeated use of heroin ultimately causes physical dependence, and people can become physically dependent after as few as three or four times.

11. (a)Lysergic acid diethylamide. Street drug analyses indicate that lysergic acid diethylamide (LSD) is often a major ingredient of street "mescaline," although it varies from city to city. Street mescaline may also contain psilocybin, amphetamines, phencyclidine (PCP) or other contaminants, but none of the drugs listed in (b), (c), or (d) have been reported. Street mescaline is rarely pure mescaline and often contains no mescaline at all.

12. (d)All of the above. In particular, nonsterile equipment (b) is a serious hazard often overlooked by the drug user.

13. (b)To relieve discomfort. When a person stops taking a drug that he is physically dependent on, he develops physical withdrawal symptoms (such as muscle spasms, vomiting, sweating, insomnia, and so forth). Taking the drug relieves the discomfort of onset of withdrawal symptoms.

14. (d)Psilocybin. Psilocybin is a hallucinogen which has no accepted medical use. All of the other drugs have at various times been used to treat narcotic addiction. When heroin was introduced in 1898, some people thought it had possibilities for treatment of "morphinism." Methadone, cyclazocine, and naloxine are used currently to block the "high" produced by heroin.

15. (e)All of the above. All these methods have been used successfully to treat drug abusers, and many have been used in combination.

SOFT DRUGS

These drugs are called "soft" because their use does not commonly cause physical dependence. Included are marijuana, cocaine, tobacco, and alcohol.

Marijuana

Since ancient times, marijuana has been widely used, and its short-term effects are well known. We are still uncertain as to its long-term effects. The active substance in marijuana is an ingredient known as *cannabis sativa,* which is obtained from the flowering tops of the mature hemp plant. When the dark brown resin from the flower of this five-leaved plant is processed, a product known as hashish or "hash" is made. Hash is two to ten times more powerful than ordinary cannabis.

The effects of marijuana vary widely; it can be either a depressant or a stimulant. Under certain circumstances, usually among impressionable youth, it can even be a hallucinogen. Although it does not lead to physical dependence, chronic users often become psychologically dependent on it. A recent study completed at the University of California on heavy users (two to four ounces a day for seven years) found no detectable decrease in mental functioning of the subjects (Tessler, 1980). There were only 10 subjects involved, however, and they were all members of a church that used marijuana to symbolize the sacrament of communion. This obviously does not represent the average user. Given clear evidence that marijuana *does* have short-term effects on brain functioning, it seems unwise at this time to conclude that the drug has no harmful long-term effects.

At the present writing, marijuana is an illegal drug. Some urge that it be legalized and sold the same way as alcohol. Others suggest that its possession and use be decriminalized; that is, violation would be considered a civil rather than a criminal offense, punishable only by a fine.

Reasons for Using Marijuana

People give many reasons for their use of marijuana, some of which clearly seem to be rationalizations. Would you like to find out why people you know think they use the drug? Interview as many people of different ages as you can. Then list below under the appropriate age bracket their reasons for using marijuana.

	15–20	20–25	25 and up
1.	_____	_____	_____
2.	_____	_____	_____
3.	_____	_____	_____
4.	_____	_____	_____
5.	_____	_____	_____
6.	_____	_____	_____
7.	_____	_____	_____

8. _____   _____   _____

9. _____   _____   _____

10. _____   _____   _____

Are the reasons more complex with older users? Is the variety of reasons greater? Which group is the most self-centered? Do other patterns emerge? Were these patterns also found by others in your class?

Cocaine

Cocaine is a derivative of the dried leaves of the tropical South American shrub coca. It has been used for centuries as an anesthetic and narcotic. The leaves of the coca bush can be chewed or brewed in tea, and when powdered, can be inhaled. Inhalation frequently damages nasal passages, causing a runny or bleeding nose that may need cauterization. A solution of the powder can also be injected. In any of these uses, cocaine produces hyperstimulation, giving strong feelings of alertness, power, and euphoria.

An early writer stated that the coca leaf "satisfies the hungry, gives new strength to the weary and exhausted, and makes the unhappy forget their sorrows" (Grinspoon and Bakalar, 1977). Sigmund Freud experimented with cocaine in the 1880s and reported that it gave him a feeling of exhilaration and euphoria; it increased his self-control and vigor, and lessened his need for sleep and food; it produced a general sense of well-being and reduced his shyness in social situations.

Cocaine is the fastest growing drug in popularity in the United States. Once considered a hard drug, the fact that it does not appear to cause withdrawal symptoms has led some to argue that it should be considered equivalent to marijuana in its effects. It is expensive ($25 to $100 per half-gram, or "spoon," or $1000 to $25,000 per ounce) and particularly popular with the wealthy young. Cocaine causes psychological dependence in many users. Until considerably more research can be done, its use is being more carefully restricted than marijuana.

Tobacco

The main ingredient in tobacco, nicotine, stimulates the various systems of the body. Tar in the smoke produces carcinogens that may cause lung cancer and, in pipe and cigar smokers, cancer of the lip, mouth, larynx, and esophagus. Due to the effects of smoke on the lung tissue and coronary arteries, even young users may experience such symptoms as shortness of breath, nagging cough, and cardiovascular and nervous difficulties.

Alcohol

Teenagers usually start drinking in imitation of older people for whom alcohol is a key component of social behavior. The pleasures of drinking and the conviviality that surrounds it are promoted by the media. Experimentation with alcohol is natural at this time. Adolescence is a time of trying out behaviors normally reserved for adults; youth are encouraged to do this during the moratorium period so they can learn with safety what behaviors they are capable of and which ones are dangerous. When parents and others place restrictions on drinking, it is often seen by adolescents as a lack of trust. Many teenagers feel forced to engage in drinking just so they can prove their normality. Beginning drinkers often overindulge, not because of any joy in getting drunk, as much as because this is a way of expressing hostility and rebellion toward the adults who would prevent them from doing what they want.

It is also true that adolescents tend to be under considerably greater stress than are younger people. It takes very little drinking to make them realize that alcohol can make them feel more relaxed, more self-confident, and even joyful and ecstatic. A 17-year-old girl recalls,

> *Drinking was just fun. Everyone did it. We couldn't imagine a Friday or Saturday night without drinking. When I'd come home buzzed, my parents would have been drinking too, so they never knew, I don't think. Then we started drinking after school. I remember saying "I'll only drink one day after school," then it went to two, then three, you know? (Chamberlain, 1978, p. 9).*

Talking to Teenagers About Drinking

The Department of Transportation (1976) has made a number of suggestions for talking to teenagers about their drinking behavior:

- Honestly explore your own behavior when drinking before you talk with teenagers.
- Be honest in expressing your feelings and in stating your own values and preferences. Encourage the same from them.
- Be calm, firm, and consistent.
- Remember that you're *sharing* ideas and information about drinking.
- Don't put teenagers on the witness stand or demand a confession.
- Recognize that adolescents are not always able to control the situations they find themselves in.
- Tell teenagers you want to hear what they have to say and to learn what they know about drinking and driving.
- Be a good listener, even when you may not agree.

- Keep to the point. No matter where the discussion leads, and no matter what kind of reaction you may get or may feel, keep forcefully in mind that this discussion concerns only the problem of drinking.

HARD DRUGS

Hard drugs are those that have a powerful ability to alter behavior or cause physical dependence.

Hallucinogens—Psychedelics

Hallucinogens, which are also called psychedelics, are drugs that alter the sensations, emotions, and cognitive patterns of the individual. Their effects commonly include delusions, hallucinations, and changes in time and space perception, which may be mild or bizarre and terrifying. The results cannot be predicted either from the type of drug used or from the amount, because the drugs' actions are so totally individual. Included in this category are LSD, mescaline, psilocybin, and such synthetic chemicals as DMT, DOM (STP), PMA, and MDA.

LSD.   Lysergic acid, the natural derivative of a fungus, was first produced artificially in 1938. Its major effects are changes in sensation and a heightened awareness of the passage of time. Often sensations seem to "cross over"; that is, a person listening to music will think that he can "see" the music or "hear" the color of a painting. While LSD does not alter the body's chemistry to any great extent, it can result in severe anxiety reactions. These disruptions in personality are usually short term, but the drug occasionally causes long spells of anxiety, depression, or disorientation. It is also possible to have a "flashback" even months after using LSD; the same effects that occurred at the time of the drug return spontaneously and unexpectedly. The drug is especially dangerous to emotionally disturbed persons, because it can trigger emotional breakdowns.

Mescaline.   This is a white, alkaloid drug made from the mescal (peyote) cactus and has also been simulated in the laboratory. Some Indians of the Southwest and Mexico chew the buttonlike tops of the mescal during religious ceremonies to produce hallucinogenic effects, which are much like those of LSD.

Psilocybin.   Similar in its effects to LSD and mescaline, psilocybin is made from one of several types of Mexican mushrooms.

Chemical hallucinogens.   Prepared solely in the laboratory, DMT, DOM (STP), PMA, and MDA can all produce hallucinogenic effects. The great danger of these and other hallucinogens is that they are frequently mixed with each other for so-called street purchases, making them unusually volatile. An example of a popular mix is "angel dust." This is a combination of PCP (phencylidine — an animal tranquilizer) and marijuana to give an extra kick. If a person smokes angel dust thinking it is marijuana, the hallucinogenic effects can be so disturbing that they can cause an acute panic reaction.

While flashbacks can occur with any of these drugs, they are most likely to occur with LSD and to heavy users.

Narcotics

Narcotics, also known as opiates, include opium and the drugs derived from opium: morphine, codeine, and heroin. Also included are some chemicals that synthesize the narcotic effect, such as methadone.

Heroin.   Heroin currently accounts for 90 percent of the narcotic dependence in the United States. It is much easier to obtain than opium, morphine, and codeine. Like all narcotics, heroin causes a feeling of relaxation and well-being, a sense that problems have evaporated. Narcotics can quickly cause physical dependence. Another danger is illness or even death from an overdose of the drug or from infections from unsterile needles and other apparatus used in injecting the drug. Withdrawal symptoms, described earlier, are especially painful with narcotics.

Methadone.   Methadone is a synthetic narcotic that has been increasingly used in the treatment of heroin addicts. While addiction to methadone can occur, it does relieve the physical craving for heroin, works longer on the body than heroin, and allows the addict to lead a relatively normal life. Because of danger of methadone addiction, its use is covered by strict government regulation.

Stimulants

Stimulants, which increase alertness and activity, include such drugs as caffeine, cocaine, and amphetamines. In the past, these drugs have been used to treat hyperactivity, epilepsy, Parkinson's disease, narcolepsy, and obesity. Today a variety of other drugs are used for more specific controls of these medical problems.

Amphetamines.   Most people who use amphetamines want an extra "lift" for limited periods of time. They may use them to stay awake while driving, to do better in athletic contests, or to cram for an exam. This seldom leads to serious problems, but some become increasingly dependent on the drug for longer and longer periods. The need for a permanent "high" may lead to drug overdose and sudden death.

Amphetamines do reduce hunger and can improve the performance of a tired person for a period of time. With greater intake, a sense of euphoria results. When the drug wears off, the user feels depressed and sluggish and may take more of the drug in order to overcome these feelings. Long-term use of amphetamines tends to lead to physical exhaustion, shakiness, itching, muscle pains, and tension. Because amphetamines cause increased dilation of blood vessels, increased blood pressure and abnormal heart beats are common. When large amounts have been injected into animals, brain damage has occurred. Other results of regular use of amphetamines are kidney failure, hepatitis, drastic weight loss, malnutrition, and occasional infection from use of the syringes for injecting the drug. Psychologically, heavy amphetamine users may exhibit such reactions as overactivity, irritableness, suspiciousness, and, occasionally, violent behavior, severe delusions of persecution, and hallucinations.

Sedatives

These are drugs that help to reduce anxiety and excitement. They have proven useful for medical purposes, such as reducing high blood pressure and pain from peptic ulcers, and are increasingly used in the treatment of psychiatric disorders. Most sedatives used in the United States today are barbiturates.

Barbiturates.   While barbiturates are prescribed by doctors to treat a variety of symptoms, they can produce both psychological and physical addiction. Users develop a tolerance, demanding higher and higher amounts of the drug. Withdrawal effects are similar to those of narcotics. In an overdose or when combined with other drugs, particularly alcohol, they can cause coma and death.

Methaqualone.   These sedatives, known by the trade name of Quaalude, are somewhat milder than barbiturates, but recent research has shown that users may have the same difficulties as with barbiturates. Quaalude was quite popular on American campuses in the 1970s.

Tranquilizers.   The so-called minor sedatives, Librium, Valium, Miltown, and Equanil, are also used to relieve anxiety. They are weaker than most sedatives and therefore considered to be less dangerous. However, it is possible to overuse them, and they are particularly dangerous in combination with alcohol.

STAGES OF SUBSTANCE ABUSE

As a result of his study of high school students, Nelson (1980) has suggested the stages presented in Table 10–3 as representing the sequence that usually occurs in the use of illegal drugs. This stage theory does not imply that all students go through all the stages, but almost all follow the same sequence up to some end point. It should be noted that in this theory, hallucinogens include PCP, LSD, mescaline, and peyote. Sedatives include barbiturates and methaqualone.

TABLE 10–3
FREQUENTLY SEEN STAGES IN ADOLESCENT CHEMICAL USE

Intake	What the World Sees
1. Experimental Use (Late grade school or early junior high years)	
1. Occasional beer-drinking, pot-smoking, or use of inhalants (glue-sniffing, sniffing aerosols, etc.). Usually done weekends or during the summer, mostly with friends.	Often unplanned, using beer sneaked from home, model glue, etc.
2. Easy to get high (low tolerance).	Little use of "harder" drugs at this stage.
3. Thrill of acting grown up and defying parents is part of the high.	
2. More Regular Use (Late junior high and early senior high years)	
4. Tolerance increases with increased use. More parties involving kegs, pot, possibly pills or hash. Acceptance of the idea that "everyone does it" and wanting to be in on it. Disdain of "local pot" or 3.2 beer. Staying out later, even all night.	More money involved, false ID's used. Alcohol or pot bought and shared with friends.
5. Use of wine or liquor *may* increase, but beer remains the most popular drink. Willing to suffer hangovers.	Parents aware of use. May start a long series of "groundings" for late hours.
6. Consumption increases and pride in being able to "handle it" increases.	Drug-using friends often not introduced to parents.
7. Use on week nights begins, and school skipping may increase.	Lying to parents about the extent of use and use of money for drugs.
8. Blackouts may begin, and talk with friends about "What did I do last night?" occurs.	School activities are dropped, especially sports. Grades will drop. Truancy increases.
9. Solitary use begins—even smoking at home (risk-taking increases). Concentration on fooling parents or teachers when high.	Non-drug-using friends are dropped. Weekend-long parties may start.
10. Preoccupation with use begins. The next high is carefully planned and anticipated. Source of supply is a matter of worry.	
11. Use during the day starts. Smoking before school to "make it through the morning." Use of "dust" may increase, or experiments with acid, speed, or barbs may continue.	
3. Daily Preoccupation	
12. Use of harder drugs increases (speed, acid, barbs, dust).	Possible dealing or fronting for others.

TABLE 10–3
FREQUENTLY SEEN STAGES IN ADOLESCENT CHEMICAL USE
(Continued)

3. Daily Preoccupation

13. Number of times high during the week increases. Amount of money spent for drugs increases (concealing savings withdrawals from parents).

Possible court trouble for minor consumption or possession. May be arrested for driving while intoxicated. Probation may result.

14. "Social use" decreases—getting loaded rather than just high. Being high becomes normal.

May try to cut down or quit to convince self that there is no problem with drugs.

Most straight friends are dropped.

15. Buying more and using more—all activities seem to include drug use or alcohol.

Money owed for drugs may increase. More truancy and fights with parents about drug use.

16. Possible theft to get money to insure a supply. There may be a contact with "bigger" dealers.

17. Solitary use increases. User will isolate self from other using friends.

18. Lying about or hiding the drug supply. Stash may become concealed from friends.

4. Dependency

19. Getting high during school or at work. Difficult to face the day without drugs. Drugs are used to escape self.

Guilt feelings increase. Questioning own use but unable to control the urge.

20. Possible use of injectable drugs. Friends are burnouts (and may take pride in the label).

Low self-image and self-hate. Casual sexual involvement. Continued denial of problem.

21. Can't tell what normal behavior is any more—normal means being stoned nearly constantly.

School dropped. Dealing may increase, along with police involvement. Parents may "give up."

22. Physical condition worsens. Loss of weight, more frequent illnesses, memory suffers. Flashbacks may increase. Thoughts of suicide may increase.

Paranoia increases. Cost of habit increases with most of money going for habit.

Loss of control over use.

©Dennis D. Nelson, CompCare Publications (A division of Comprehensive Care Corporation). 2415 Annapolis Lane, Suite 140, Minneapolis, MN 55441.

DRUGS AND SEX

A number of researchers have looked at the relationship between the use of drugs and sexual functioning (Gay and Sheppard, 1973; Goode, 1969, 1970, 1972a and b; The National Commission on Marihuana and Drug Abuse, 1973; and Wieland and Yunger, 1970). The purpose of these studies was to evaluate the claims of many youth that drugs make them more sexually capable and increase their enjoyment of the sex act. It is alleged that drugs stimulate sexual activity through releasing inhibitions and through direct stimulation of desire.

There is remarkable accord in the findings: only amphetamines actually *enhance* sexual performance, and they do so only for a limited time. Marijuana may stimulate sexual desire under some circumstances because of its disinhibitory effect. Alcohol also has a disinhibitory effect in small doses, but in moderate doses it decreases the ability to function. Barbiturates and psychedelics, the other two drugs investigated in these studies, appear to have no effect on sex whatever.

The studies all conclude that response is mainly dependent on the psychological makeup of the individuals involved and on the setting in which the individual finds himself or herself. Those experienced in the use of drugs with sex say that even when there is a good result, it is only transitory in nature. Most of the participants in these studies say they have decided that they prefer to enjoy sex without the use of drugs.

Another interesting finding of several of the studies was that those who use drugs are much more sexually active than those who don't. Goode (1972a) discovered that drug users are not only sexually more active, but they start their sexual activity at an earlier age and with a more diverse selection of partners. Again, the studies seem to be in accord that the major reason that drugs are helpful in the sex act is because the drug users think they are going to be.

One caution: like all research based on interviews, the data depend on the truth of the testimony of those studied. It may be that drug abusers are more willing to talk about their sexual activity than nonusers, or even that they claim to be more sexually active than they are.

ETHNIC GROUP AND ABUSE

There is not a great deal known about the comparative abuse of substances within ethnic groups. One study looked at the number of arrests per 10,000 members of an ethnic group, with seven groups being considered. Table 10–5 shows the alcohol-related arrests for these seven ethnic groups in 1977.

One of the most interesting questions related to substance abuse has to do with the effects resulting from the family having arrived in this country in the previous generation or two. Tessler (1980) suggests a series of interrelationships between these variables, as presented in Table 10–6. This table shows that conflicts between traditional cultural patterns, immigration factors, and the mores of American society often bring about an increase in the use of drugs, particularly alcohol. Of course, this table is not meant to represent what *always* happens, but in an unfortunately high percentage of the time, this is what occurs.

TABLE 10–4
DRUG CLASSIFICATION SUMMARY

Name	Slang Name	Chemical or Trade Name	Source	Classification	Medical Use	How Taken
Heroin	H., horse, scat, junk, smack, scag, stuff, harry	Diacetyl-morphine	Semisynthetic (from morphine)	Narcotic	Pain relief	⌐mainlined⌐ Injected or sniffed
Morphine	White stuff, M.	Morphine sulphate	Natural (from opium)	Narcotic	Pain relief	Swallowed or injected
Codeine	Schoolboy	Methylmor-phine	Natural (from opium), semi-synthetic (from morphine)	Narcotic	Ease pain and coughing	Swallowed
Methadone	Dolly	Dolophine Amidone	Synthetic	Narcotic	Pain relief	Swallowed or injected
Cocaine	Corrine, gold dust, coke, bernice, flake, star dust, snow	Methylester of benzoylecgonine	Natural (from coca, *not* cacao)	Stimulant, local anesthetic	Local anesthesia	Sniffed, injected, or swallowed
Marijuana	Pot, grass, hashish, tea, gage, reefers, joints, j's	Cannabis sativa	Natural	Relaxant, euphoriant, in high doses hallucinogen	Alleviates nausea from chemother-apy for cancer	Smoked, swallowed, or sniffed
Barbiturates _downer_	Barbs, blue devils, candy, yellow jackets, phennies, peanuts, blue heavens	Phenobarbital nembutal, seconal, amytal	Synthetic	Sedative-hypnotic	Sedation, relieve high blood pressure, epilepsy, hyperthy-roidism	Swallowed or injected
Ampheta-mines _upper_	Bennies, dexies, speed, wakeups, lid proppers, hearts, pep pills	Benzedrine, dexedrine, desoxyn, meth-amphetamine, methedrine	Synthetic	Sympatho-mimetic	Relieve mild depression, control appetite and narcolepsy	Swallowed or injected
LSD	Acid, sugar, big D, cubes, trips	d-lysergic acid diethylamide	Semi-synthetic (from ergot alkaloids)	Hallucinogen	Experimental study of mental function, alcoholism	Swallowed
DMT	AMT, busi-nessman's high	Dimethyl-triptamine	Synthetic	Hallucinogen	None	Injected

Usual Dose	Duration of Effect	Effects Sought	Long-term Symptoms	Physical Dependence Potential	Mental Dependence Potential	Organic Damage Potential
Varies	4 hours	Euphoria, prevent withdrawal discomfort	Addiction, constipation, loss of appetite	Yes	Yes	No
15 milligrams	6 hours	Euphoria, prevent withdrawal discomfort	Addiction, constipation, loss of appetite	Yes	Yes	No
30 milligrams	4 hours	Euphoria, prevent withdrawal discomfort	Addiction, constipation, loss of appetite	Yes	Yes	No
10 milligrams	4 to 6 hours	Prevent withdrawal discomfort	Addiction, constipation, loss of appetite	Yes	Yes	No
Varies	Varies, short	Excitation, talkativeness	Depression, convulsions	No	Yes	Yes?
1 to 2 cigarettes	4 hours	Relaxation, increased euphoria, perceptions, sociability	Usually none	No	Yes?	No
50 to 100 milligrams	4 hours	Anxiety reduction, euphoria	Addiction w/ severe withdrawal symptoms, possible convulsions, toxic psychosis	Yes	Yes	Yes
2.5 to 5 milligrams	4 hours	Alertness, activeness	Loss of appetite, delusions, hallucinations, toxic psychosis	No?	Yes	Yes?
100 to 500 micrograms	10 hours	Insightful experiences, exhilaration, distortion of senses	May intensify existing psychosis, panic reactions	No	No?	No?
1 to 3 milligrams	Less than 1 hour	Insightful experiences, exhilaration, distortion of senses	?	No	No?	No?

TABLE 10–4
DRUG CLASSIFICATION SUMMARY (continued)

Name	Slang Name	Chemical or Trade Name	Source	Classification	Medical Use	How Taken
Mescaline	Mesc.	3,4,5-trimeth-oxyphenethyla-mine	Natural (from peyote)	Hallucinogen	None	Swallowed
Psilocybin		3 (2-dimethylamino) ethylindol-4-oldihydrogen phosphate	Natural (from psilocybe)	Hallucinogen	None	Swallowed
Alcohol	Booze, juice, etc.	Ethanol ethyl alcohol	Natural (from grapes, grains, etc. via fermentation)	Sedative hypnotic	Solvent, antiseptic	Swallowed
Tobacco	Fag, coffin nail, etc.	Nicotinia tabacum	Natural	Stimulant-sedative	Sedative, emetic (nicotine)	Smoked, sniffed, or chewed

Source: U.S. Public Health Service. *Resource Book for Drug Abuse,* Washington, D.C.: U.S. Government Printing Office, 1970, pp. 34–35.

Do Your Own Study of Drug Use

Do the patterns of drug use described in this chapter apply to your friends? Would you find similar statistics if you asked them about their drug use? Below is a guide for making such a mini-study.

There are two parts to the study. First, estimate what percentage of *all* your friends would choose each of the categories in each question, and write the figures in the first column below. Then, interview ten friends, asking them to respond to each of the questions. To make the study more representative, it would be best to choose them through random encounter rather than preselecting them. Keep a tally of their responses in each category. Figuring the percentages for the second part of the study is quite simple: add a zero to the number who said yes in each category and you have the percentage of 100. Put the figures in the second column. The questions are listed below.

Usual Dose	Duration of Effect	Effects Sought	Long-term Symptoms	Physical Dependence Potential	Mental Dependence Potential	Organic Damage Potential
350 micrograms	12 hours	Insightful experiences, exhilaration, distortion of senses	?	No	No?	No?
25 milligrams	6 to 8 hours	Insightful experiences, exhilaration, distortion of senses	?	No	No?	No?
Varies	1 to 4 hours	Sense alteration, anxiety reduction, sociability	Cirrhosis, toxic psychosis, neurologic damage, addiction	Yes	Yes	Yes
Varies	Varies	Calmness, sociability	Lung and heart diseases, cancer	Yes?	Yes	Yes

	Estimated Percent	Actual Percent
1. Do you drink beer?		
A. no	_____	_____
B. once or twice a month	_____	_____
C. once or twice a week	_____	_____
D. practically every day	_____	_____
2. If you do drink beer, how many on one occasion?		
A. one or two	_____	_____
B. three or four	_____	_____
C. five or six	_____	_____
D. more than six	_____	_____
3. Do you drink wine?		
A. no	_____	_____
B. once or twice a month	_____	_____
C. once or twice a week	_____	_____
D. practically every day	_____	_____

4. If you do drink wine, how many glasses per occasion?
   A. one or two
   B. three or four
   C. five or six
   D. more than six

5. Do you drink hard liquor?
   A. no
   B. once or twice a month
   C. once or twice a week
   D. practically every day

6. If you do drink hard liquor, how many ounces on one occasion?
   A. one or two
   B. three or four
   C. five or six
   D. more than six

7. How many times in your life have you been driving when drunk?
   A. never
   B. once or twice
   C. about five times
   D. more than five times

8. How many times have you been in a car when the driver was drunk?
   A. never
   B. once or twice
   C. about five times
   D. more than five times

	Yes	No
9. Do you think marijuana should be legalized?		
10. Do you think cocaine should be legalized?		
11. If you drink, do your parents know about it?		
12. If you use marijuana, do your parents know about it?		
13. If you use hard drugs, do your parents know about it?		
14. Do you think the amount you drink is doing you any harm?		
15. Do you think the amount of drugs you use is doing you any harm?		

CRIME AND ABUSE

Although it is commonly thought that drug users, especially those who use hard drugs, are regularly involved in criminal activities, reliable data on this aspect of drug use is surprisingly limited. FBI statistics indicate that the drug most associated with crime is alcohol. In 40 percent of assaults and 35 percent of rapes, those convicted had been "under the influence."

In one study in California (Tinkleberg, et al., 1974), drug use as a possible cause of assault was investigated. These authors found that of 56 assaults within a one-year period, 36 of the assailants were under the influence of some drug at the time. Alcohol, barbiturates, or alcohol and barbiturates together were reported in use in 31 of the 36 cases; marijuana was involved in six of the assaults; and amphetamines were used in only two of the offenses. Subjects interviewed overwhelmingly reported that secobarbital was most likely to enhance assaultive tendencies.

Research of the relationship between substance abuse and crime (and other undesirable behaviors) was carried out by Santana et al. (1979). This study, which is summarized in Table 10–7, looked at 19 types of undesirable behavior, and compared these behaviors as to occurrence between drug abusers and nonusers. The startling finding of this study was that in every case but one, the users were much more likely to commit undesirable behaviors than nonusers. Even in this single exception, for arson, the behavior was evenly divided. Of course this does not indicate that drug use causes crime, but indicates that there appears to be a strong relationship between the two.

DRUG USE AND PERSONAL RELATIONSHIPS

There has long been a debate as to whether adolescent drug usage is related more to family circumstances than to interactions with peers. Most studies have indicated that the typical drug user has problems with his or her parents (e.g., Babst and Brill, 1973; Bogg and Hughes, 1973; Tec, 1974; Tudor, Petersen and Elifson, 1980). Tudor et al. found that drug users had conflicts with their parents in the following areas: they wanted to be allowed to make their own decisions without having any advice from their parents; they do not believe that they should be limited to only those friends their parents endorse; they are less likely to desire affection from their mothers and fathers, nor do they feel close to them; and in many cases, they do not desire to emulate their parents. One other study (Huba and Bentler, 1979, 1980a, b, and c) found that although relationships with parents do affect substance abuse in younger children, as students get to high school the parental effect drops off:

> The finding that by the ninth grade boys and girls have drug use patterns that are related more to perceived patterns in the peer culture than to perceived patterns in the adult culture suggests that adult models become relatively *less important [emphasis theirs] (p. 464).*

ALTERNATIVES TO DRUG ABUSE

> A major part of the problem Society faces in defending itself against drug abuse is that it is a moving target. We are mobilizing law enforcement re-

**TABLE 10–5
ALCOHOL-RELATED ARRESTS, 1977**

Ethnic Group	Number of Arrests per 10,000 Members of Group
Japanese	18
Chinese	12
Other	59
Black	358
Mexican-American	329
American Indian	385
White	189

Note: "Other" includes Samoans, Koreans, Filipinos, Hawaiians, Vietnamese, Thai, Cambodians, Eskimos, etc. It is estimated that 90 percent or more of this category are Pacific/Asian-peoples.

Figures presented in an Asian-American Drug Abuse Program, Inc. report, Los Angeles, Ca., 1978.

sources to protect us at our borders, but we give little more than lip service to treatment, rehabilitation, research, and education. — Art Linkletter, 1980.

Although better information about drugs may lessen their abuse, it is essential that society promote desirable alternatives to the use of drugs. Dr. Sidney Cohen (1977) describes three types of substitutes for drug use: (1) those that provide a deep feeling of relationship to another person or to humanity; (2) those that contribute to self-knowledge or self-reliance; and (3) those that offer a satisfying experience, either physical, mental, or emotional.

Cohen has suggested ten varieties of alternative experience that meet one or more of these criteria:

Physical awareness. The pleasure of a healthy body in motion through such activities as walking, jogging, dancing, gymnastics, and group sports can promote extremely positive feelings. These activities, as well as physical relaxation exercises, can be effective in overcoming the chronic tension that causes so many people to use drugs, either legally or illegally.

Sensory awareness. Many adolescents use drugs because they heighten their sense of awareness of their surroundings. This enjoyable sensation can be experienced by placing oneself in unfamiliar surroundings (in the out-of-doors, for example) and consciously cultivating one's sensory perceptions.

Psychological awareness. The exploration of "inner space" through reading, self-observation, meditation, therapy, or a self-help group can lead one to a better understanding of oneself, and to an improvement of the negative self-image that is often behind drug abuse. Psychological awareness can "change aggression into assertiveness" and "impulsiveness into spontaneity" (p. 1562).

TABLE 10-6
ASIAN-AMERICAN CULTURAL CLASHES

Traditional Cultural Patterns	vs.	Immigration Factors	vs.	American Society
Close-knit family with strong father.		Father has to hold down more than one job to support family and is unable to provide the strong influence tradition demands.		More democratic approach to family structure. Mothers work. Increase of single-parent families.
High parental expectations.		Language difficulties; inability to make friends; difference in educational systems.		More tolerance of children who are not high achievers.
Shame associated with having a problem.		Immigration brings many adjustment problems.		More openness regarding problems, and more willingness to seek professional help when necessary.
Pride in one's worth and value to himself, the family, and the community.		Inability to communicate, obtain a job, achieve a level of academic excellence.		Prejudice, stereotyping, both old and new; exotic, humble, inscrutable, studious, gang member or participant in Tong Wars.
Women are supposed to stay home and raise the children.		Women may have to enter job market to help support family.		Acceptable for women to enter job market and lead a more independent lifestyle.
Drinking is perceived in many cases as being an acceptable part of family and community life. Alcohol a part of rituals and festivals.		Increased drinking because of pressure may not be considered a problem.		Drinking not perceived as being culturally important.

Interpersonal awareness. Just as self-awareness can eliminate the need for drugs, so can a greater understanding of one's family and friends. As one becomes more self-understanding, honesty and openness with others becomes easier to achieve. Sensitivity training and confrontation sessions can be useful in promoting this awareness.

Rites of passage. A common cause of drug use is the need, especially among teenaged males, to prove one's daring and bravery. If alternatives such as mountain climbing and Outward Bound programs are provided as rites of passage, this need for drug use is diminished.

Work as fun. Competence in such skills as repairing the technological products of today's world can give one a sense of usefulness. Noncompetitive work

TABLE 10–7
INCIDENCE OF ANTISOCIAL BEHAVIORS EXHIBITED BY YOUTHS DURING THE THREE-MONTH PERIOD PRECEDING THE INTERVIEW

Behaviors	Portion of Study Population		Users		Non-users	
	N	%	N	%	N	%
Serious fight	28	10.7	20	71.4	8	28.6
Theft under $50	34	13.0	22	64.7	12	35.3
Theft over $50	6	2.3	5	83.3	1	16.7
Arson	2	0.8	1	50.0	1	50.0
Threaten someone	20	7.6	15	75.0	5	25.0
Runaway	11	4.2	10	90.9	1	9.1
Battery	11	4.2	10	90.9	1	9.1
Vandalism	20	7.6	18	90.0	2	10.0
Shoplifting	27	10.3	22	81.5	5	18.5
Hit instructor	3	1.1	3	100.0	0	0.0
Drinking w/o permission	105	40.1	93	88.6	12	11.4
Hit father	5	2.2	5	100.0	0	0.0
Hit mother	4	1.5	3	75.0	1	25.0
Stolen car	3	1.1	3	100.0	0	0.0
Stolen expensive car parts	1	0.4	1	100.0	0	0.0
Stolen inexpensive car parts	9	3.4	7	77.8	2	22.2
Gang fight	24	9.2	22	91.7	2	8.3
Trespassing	32	12.2	21	65.6	11	34.4
Threaten w/weapon	5	1.9	5	100.0	0	0.0

Source: Santana, et al., 1979.

can also be relaxing. Another type of work that can benefit the ex-heroin addict or alcoholic is helping other addicts.

Esthetic appreciation. Developing appreciation for music, art, and literature can be rewarding not only in itself, but it also can lead to an expansion of creativity of a much more substantial nature than that offered by drugs.

Learning. Although intellectual learning is not high on the list of most teenagers as a leisure-time activity, it can be an exciting pursuit for some. The study of religion, philosophy, or psychology can help illuminate some of the soul-searching questions for which answers are sometimes sought in drug use.

Nonrational experience. The popularity of mystical Christianity, Zen, yoga, mind control, Arica, and est among teenagers is clear evidence of their need for the fulfillment offered by nonrational experience. The mystical and spiritual exercises available through these activities can supplant chemical insights. Technological advances such as biofeedback can also be used to train one for greater relaxation and creative effectiveness.

Social and political activism. It is possible that social activism and increased participation in the political life of the country could direct many away from experiences with drugs.

As Dr. Cohen points out, all of these activities involve active individual participation. While they can help rehabilitate a drug abuser, they are primarily useful in preventing drug abuse in the first place.

IMPROVING SCHOOL CLIMATE

No prevention program is likely to be effective if the climate in the school is conducive to drug abuse. Tessler (1980) argues that to find out what the climate is in any particular school, it is necessary to administer a survey such as the one in the box below. The survey is easy to administer to students, teachers, and administrators alike. It only takes a few minutes to complete. She claims that:

> The results will help everyone get in touch with some of the silent agents responsible for a poor school environment which would make the success of any effective drug education impossible (p. 114).

Questions 1 to 4 relate to situations which can cause antisocial or antiauthority behavior. School and police records can also give information as to whether this kind of problem exists in the school. Questions 5 to 9 concern school services and special programs. Responses here can indicate a lack of school unity. Questions 10 to 12 reveal how members of the school community feel the school fits into the life of the larger community it serves. It also indicates whether or not neighborhood resources are used for the benefit of those attending the school. Questions 13 and 14 deal with whether or not the three main segments of the community—students, faculty, and administrators—are able to communicate effectively with each other. Questions 15 to 20 give an indication of whether or not there are opportunities for students to develop self-respect and self-awareness. Because question 21 is open-ended, it presents an opportunity for all members of the community to express their personal feelings about the school. Responses to each of the questions should be tabulated both in terms of total responses and in terms of the three subtotals for the three segments of the school population. If these data indicate a problem in one of the six areas—antisocial responses, services and programs, community relations, communications, affective areas, and general responses—then committees should be established to improve the situation in the problem area. Tessler says that her

School Climate Survey

Does your school

1. Have racial or ethnic problems?   Yes _____   No _____
2. Have a high truancy rate?   Yes _____   No _____
3. Have cases of vandalism? Violence? Serious fights? Gangs? Drug problem?
   Yes _____   No _____
4. Have many cases of student arrests?   Yes _____   No _____
   (If you don't know the answers to all the above, local law enforcement agencies
   may be able to give you some information.)
5. Plan events which encourage school unity?   Yes _____   No _____
6. Have good recreational and extracurricular activities which are well supported
   by the student body and staff?   Yes _____   No _____
7. Provide good counseling and health services?   Yes _____   No _____
8. Give everyone the opportunity to respect their own heritage and those of
   others?
   Yes _____   No _____
9. Involve parents in important school decisions and events?
   Yes _____   No _____
10. Seek a constructive bond with the community—urban or neighborhood improve-
    ment projects, law enforcement, the handicapped, the elderly, etc.?
    Yes _____   No _____
11. Use community agencies or the expertise of residents to help with school pro-
    grams?   Yes _____   No _____
12. Direct students and parents to community resources which will improve their
    lives?   Yes _____   No _____
13. Provide students with real leadership opportunities (not simply token positions)?
    Yes _____   No _____
14. Have an "emotional climate" in which students, faculty, and administrators feel
    free to express their thoughts and feelings?   Yes _____   No _____
15. Encourage students to be creative and curious?   Yes _____   No _____
16. Help students explore and appreciate their own special talents?
    Yes _____   No _____
17. Allow students to clarify values?   Yes _____   No _____
18. Help students to effectively deal with inner and outer conflicts?
    Yes _____   No _____
19. Provide problem-solving and decision-making experiences for students?
    Yes _____   No _____
20. Help students develop goals for the future?   Yes _____   No _____
21. When you think of your school, what is *the first thing* that comes to mind?

    _____

    _____

Source: Tessler, 1980.

experience with this approach indicates that such changes can go a long way in making the abuse of substances less desirable to students.

SUMMARY

Substance abuse (of so-called soft and hard drugs) has been steadily increasing; this is especially so for soft drugs. There are clear stages in abuse. Soft drugs include marijuana, cocaine, tobacco, and alcohol, and are not known to cause physical dependence.

Marijuana. Only short-term effects are known. Marijuana can be a depressant, a stimulant, or a hallucinogen, depending on the user and the circumstances. It is sometimes psychologically, but not physically, addictive. Some people urge that it should be decriminalized. The use of marijuana has been growing steadily in recent years. There is some evidence that chronic use of marijuana can impair motor performance and can interfere with personality and intellectual development.

Cocaine. Derived from the coca bush, it produces hyperstimulation, giving a feeling of overalertness, great power, and euphoria. No longer considered a hard drug because it does not have withdrawal effects, it clearly causes psychological dependence in a large percentage of cases. It has more legal restrictions than marijuana.

Tobacco. The main ingredient in tobacco is nicotine, which stimulates the various systems of the body. Tobacco is a known carcinogen; smoking is also associated with bronchial and heart disease. There are no known beneficial effects from smoking cigarettes, yet tobacco is one of the most widely used drugs.

Alcohol. The abuse of beer and wine is rapidly increasing among today's youth. Adolescence is a time of trying out behaviors which are normally reserved for adults. Adolescents often feel forced to drink even when they don't care to, just to prove their normality. Also, adolescents tend to be under a considerably greater amount of stress than are people of other ages, and drinking relieves tension.

Hard drugs are those that produce changes in mental functioning. The changes cannot be predicted either from the type of drug used or the amount. Most cause some form of physical as well as psychological dependence.

LSD. Produced naturally from a fungus, but usually made in a laboratory, lysergic acid causes changes in sensation and in awareness of the passage of time. Disruptions in personality are usually short term, although it occasionally causes long spells of anxiety, depression, or disorientation. Therefore, the drug is especially dangerous for those who are emotionally imbalanced.

Mescaline. The effects of this drug, made from peyote cactus, are much like those of LSD.

Psilocybin. Derived from a type of mushroom, its effects are like those of LSD and mescaline.

Chemical hallucinogens. DMT, DOM (STP), PMA, and MDA are prepared in the laboratory and all produce hallucinogenic effects. They are unusually dangerous because the "street" mixtures include highly unpredictable ingredients.

Narcotics. Opium and its derivatives, morphine, codeine, and heroin, are all narcotics. Heroin is especially physically addicting. It accounts for 90 percent of the narcotic dependence in the United States. Methadone is a synthetic narcotic used to relieve the heroin addict of his dependence. Unfortunately there is the chance of the addiction to heroin being transferred to methadone; for this reason its use is strictly regulated by the government.

Stimulants. Included in this category are amphetamines, cocaine, and caffeine. Stimulants increase alertness and activity.

Amphetamines. While the use of amphetamines to give extra energy seldom leads to serious problems, many people become dependent on the drug. Long-term use leads to exhaustion; collapse and death sometimes result. Amphetamines can also cause such psychological reactions as irritability, suspiciousness resembling paranoid schizophrenia, and violent behavior.

Barbiturates. Although often prescribed by doctors, these drugs are dangerous because they can produce both psychological and physical addiction. Like all sedatives, they are especially dangerous when used with other drugs.

Methaqualone. Milder than barbiturates, this drug has most of the same effects.

Tranquilizers. These minor sedatives, such as Librium, Valium, Miltown, and Equanil, are used to relieve anxiety. They are less dangerous, but it is possible to overuse them.

Reliable research on the correlation between drug use and crime is scarce. However, Tinkleberg found that of fifty-six assaults within a one-year period, thirty-six of the assailants were under the influence of some drug. Santana et al. found drug users to be much more criminally active than nonusers.

The research on the relationship between the different drugs and sexual functioning has shown that the major reason that drugs are helpful in the sex act is because the drug user thinks they are going to be. Those who use drugs are more active sexually and start their sexual activity at an earlier age.

Most teenagers are not aware of the drug education resources available to them through schools and community organizations. Greater and more effective efforts must be expended to make teenagers aware of drug use and abuse. Talks by ex-addicts have been found to be exceptionally effective.

Dr. Sidney Cohen has suggested three types of substitutes for drug use: those that provide a deep feeling of relationship to another person or to humanity; those that contribute to self-knowledge or self-reliance; and those that offer a satisfying experience, either physical, mental, or emotional. The alternative experiences Cohen suggests all require active participation. Tessler believes that school climate can effect abuse, and urges that this climate be measured and remedied if necessary.

Questions

1. What are some of the causes of drug abuse among adolescents today?
2. What is the problem with the use of soft drugs?
3. In what ways are hard drugs more dangerous than soft?
4. Why do some adolescents depend on drugs, alcohol, or other stimulants?
5. What is the relationship between drugs and sex?
6. What are some healthy alternatives to drug use?

References

Asian-American Drug Abuse Program. *Pacific Asians and alcohol.* Los Angeles, Ca., 1978.

Abelson, H., Fishburne, P., & Cisin, I. *National survey on drug abuse: 1977. A nationwide study—youth, young adults and older adults, 1: Main findings.* Washington, D.C.: Supt. of Documents, U.S. Government Printing Office, 1977.

American medical association council on scientific affairs. "Health aspects of marijuana use." In *Proceedings of the house of delegates.* Chicago: American medical association. Adopted by the house of delegates, Dec. 6, 1977.

Babst, D., & Brill, L. "Drug abuse patterns among students in upstate N.Y." *Journal of drug issues,* 1973, 348–360.

Bagg, R. A. "Drinking as a precursor to hallucinogenic drug usage." *Drug forum,* 1976, *5*(1), 55–67.

"Barbiturates next on hit list?" *Boston globe,* March 30, 1977, 2.

Barnes, G. "A perspective on drinking among teenagers with special reference to New York state studies." *Journal of school health,* September 1975, *45*(7), 386–389.

Bogg, R., & Hughes, J. "Correlates of marijuana usage." *International journal of addictions,* 1973, *8*, 489–504.

Chamberlain, T. "Teen drinking—rampant and reckless." *Boston globe,* October 13, 1978.

Cohen, S. "Alternatives to adolescent drug abuse." *Journal of the American medical association,* October 1977, *238*(14), 1561–1562.

Doyle, N. *Marijuana and the lungs.* American lung association bulletin, Nov. 1979.

Fox, V. "Alcoholism in adolescence." *Journal of school health,* January 1973, *43*(1), 32–5.

Gay, G. R., & Sheppard, C. W. "Sex-crazed dope fiends! myth or reality?" In E. Harms (Ed.), *Drugs and youth: the challenge of today.* New York: Pergamon, 1973.

Goode, E. "Marijuana and sex." *Evergreen review,* May 1969, *46*, 19–21.

Goode, E. *The marijuana smokers.* New York: Basic books, 1970.

Goode, E. "Drug use and sexual activity on a college campus." *American journal of psychiatry,* April 1972, *128*(10), 1272–76. (a)

Goode, E. "Sex and behavior." *Sexual behavior,* May 1972, *2*(5), 45–51.(b)

Grinspoon, L., & Bakalar, J. B. "Cocaine: a social hstory," and "A kick from cocaine." *Psychology today,* March 1977, 37 ff.

Huba, G., Wingard, J., & Bentler, P. "Beginning adolescent drug use and peer and adult interaction patterns." *Journal of consulting clinical psychology,* 1979, *47*.

Huba, G., Wingard, J., & Bentler, P. "A longitudinal analysis of the role of peer support, adult models, and peer subcultures in beginning adolescent substance use." *Multivariate Behavior Research,* 1980a, *15*, 259–280.

Huba, G., Wingard, J., & Bentler, P. "Framework for an interactive theory of drug use." In Lettieri, D., Sayers, M., & Pearson, H. (Eds). *Theories on drug abuse,* National Institute on Drug Abuse, Rockville, Md. 1980b.

Huba, G., Wingard, J., & Bentler, P. "Applications of a theory of drug use to prevention." *Journal of drug education,* 1980c, *10*, 25–38.

Johnson, L., Bachman, L., & O'Malley, D. "Highlights from drugs and the class of '78." Rockville, Md., National institute on drug abuse, 1979.

Lambert, B. G., Rothschild, B., Altland, R., & Green, L. *Adolescence.* Monterey, Calif.: Brooks/Cole, 1978.

Marijuana and health. Washington, D.C.: Report of the Secretary of HEW to the U.S. Congress, 1976.

National Commission on Marijuana and Drug Abuse. "Drug use in America: problems in perspective." Washington, D.C.: U.S. Government Printing Office, 1973.

New York State Office of Drug Abuse Services. *Drug abuse prevention: the awareness, experience, and opinions of junior and senior high school students in New York state.* Albany, N.Y. NYS Report No. 2, 1976.

Paton, S. M., & Kandel, D. B. "Psychological factors and adolescent illicit drug ethnicity and sex differences." *Adolescence*, Summer 1978, *13*(50).

Santana, G., et al. *Social and familial influences on substance use among youth.* Paper presented to the American Psychological Association, New York, September, 1979.

Schaeffer, J. "Cognition and longterm use of Ganja (cannabis)." *Science, 213* (4506), 465–466.

Smith. G. M., & Fogg, C. P. "Teenage drug use: a search for causes and consequences." *Personality and social psychology bulletin*, 1974, *1*(1), 426–429.

Special Action Office for Drug Abuse Prevention. *Q and A.* Washington, D.C.: Executive Office of the President, 1976 (GPO: 1975 0-576-576).

Swift, P. "Drug stabilization." *Parade*, February 20, 1977.

Tec, N. *Grass is green in suburbia.* Roslyn Heights, N.Y.: Libra, 1974.

Tessler, D. J. *Drugs, kids, and schools.* Santa Monica, Ca.: Goodyear, 1980.

Tinkleberg, J. R., Murphy, P. L., Darley, C. F., Roth, W. T., & Kopell, B. S. "Drug involvement in criminal assaults by adolescents." *Archives of general psychiatry,* May 1974, *30*, 685.

Tobias, J. I., & Wax, J. "Youthful drinking patterns in the suburbs." *Adolescence*, Spring 1973, *7*(29), 113–118.

Tudor, C., Petersen, D., & Elifson, K. "An examination of the relationship between peer and parental influences in adolescent drug use." *Adolescence*, Winter 1980, *60*, 783–798.

U.S. Department of Transportation. "How to talk to your teenager about drinking and driving." Washington, D.C.: National Highway Traffic Safety Administration (GPO 1976 0-625-636), 1976.

U.S. Public Health Service. *Resource book for drug abuse.* Washington, D.C.: U.S. Government Printing Office, 1970.

Wieland, W. F., & Yunger, M. "Sexual effects and side effects of heroin and methadone." *Proceedings, third national conference on methadone treatment.* Washington, D.C.: U.S. Government Printing Office, 1970.

Yankelovich, D. "Drug users vs. drug abusers: how students control their drug crisis." *Psychology today*, October 1975.

Additional References

Aaronson, B., & Osmond, H. *Psychedelics: the uses and implications of hallucinogenic drugs.* Cambridge, Mass.: Schenkman, 1970.

Adelson, J., & O'Neil, R. P. "Growth of political ideas in adolescence: the sense of community." In A.M. Orum (Ed.), *The seeds of politics—youth and politics in America.* Englewood Cliffs, N.J.: Prentice-Hall, 1972.

Annis, H. M., & Smart, R. G. "Adverse reactions and recurrences from marihuana use." *British journal of addiction to alcohol and other drugs*, 1973, *68*, 315–319.

Arnett, H. J., Black, M. W., & McNeary, S. S. "An 11-year study of cigarette smoking habits of students." *American journal of public health*, 1974, *64*(2), 120–123.

Bakalar, J. B. "A kick from cocaine." *Psychology today*, March 1977.

Barber, T. S. *LSD, marihuana, yoga, and hypnosis.* Chicago: Aldine, 1970.

Battegay, R., Mahlemann, R., & Schnider, R. "Comparative investigations of the abuse of alcohol, drugs, and nicotine for a representative group of 4,082 men of age 20." *Comprehensive psychiatry*, May–June 1975, *16*(3), 247–254.

Bayer, A. E., & Dutton, J. E. "Trends in attitudes on political, social, and collegiate issues among college students—mid-1960's to mid-1970's." *Journal of higher education*, 1976, *68*(2), 123–134.

Becker, H. S. "History, culture, and subjective experience: an exploration of the social bases of drug-induced experiences." *Journal of health and social behavior,* 1967, *8,* 163–176.

Blackford, L. "Student drug use surveys, San Mateo County, California, 1968–76." San Mateo, Calif.: Department of Public Health and Welfare, 1976.

Blume, S. B. "A psychiatrist looks at alcoholism." *Intellect,* 1975, *104*(2367), 27–30.

Brickman, W. W. "Adolescents and alcoholic abuse." *Intellect,* 1974, *103*(2361), 165.

Calhoun, J. F. "Attitudes toward the sale and use of drugs—a cross-sectional analysis of those who used drugs." *Journal of youth and adolescence,* 1974, *3*(1), 31–47.

Carlin, A. S., Bakher, C. B., Halpen, L., & Post, R. D. "Social facilitation of marihuana intoxication: impact of social set and pharmacologic activity." *Journal of abnormal psychology,* 1972, *80,* 132–140.

Carroll, J. F. X., & Synogal, M. "Rehabilitating the problem drinker." *Intellect,* 1975, *104*(2367), 31–35.

Cohen, S. "Teenage drinking: the bottle babies." *Drug abuse and alcoholism newsletter,* August 1975, *4*(7), 1–4.

Elinson, J. "Antecedents and consequences of teenage drug behavior." Paper presented at the Conference on Strategies of Longitudinal Research in Drug Use, Puerto Rico, April, 1976.

Flacks, R. "The liberated generation: an exploration of the roots of student protest." In A. M. Orum (Ed.), *The seeds of politics—youth and politics in America,* Englewood Cliffs, N.J., Prentice-Hall, 1972.

Goldstein, J. W. "Drug education worthy of the name." *Impact: the magazine for innovation and change in counseling,* 1972, *1,* 18–24; 64.

Goldstein, J. W. "Students' evaluations of their psychoactive drug use." *Journal of counseling psychology,* 22(4), 333–339.

Goldstein, J. W., Gleason, T. C., & Korn, J. H. "Whither the epidemic? Psychoactive drug use career patterns of college students." *Journal of applied social psychology,* 1975, *5,* 16–33.

Groves, W. E., Rossi, P. H., & Grafstein, D. *Study of life styles and campus communities: preliminary report.* Baltimore, Md.: Johns Hopkins University, Department of Social Relations, 1970.

Haagen, C. H. *Social and psychological characteristics associated with the use of marihuana by college men.* Middletown, Conn.: Wesleyan University, 1970.

Halihas, J. A., Goodwin, D. W., & Guze, S. B. "Marihuana effects: a survey of regular users." *Journal of the American medical association,* 1971, *217,* 692–694.

Hanson, D. J. "College students' reasons for drinking: twenty-year trends." *College student journal,* September–October 1975, *9*(3), 256–257.

Harper, F. D. "Alcohol education: the role of the teacher." *Phi Delta Kappan,* 1975, *57*(4), 259.

Hemminki, E. "Tobacco, alcohol, medicines, and illegal drug taking." *Adolescence,* Fall 1974, *9*(35), 421–424.

Hess, R. D., & Torney, J. V. *The development of political attitudes in children.* Chicago: Aldine, 1967.

Hochman, J. S. *Marihuana and social evolution.* Englewood Cliffs, N. J.: Prentice-Hall, 1972.

Hochman, J. S., & O'Brill, N. "Chronic marihuana use and psychosocial adaptation." *American journal of psychiatry,* 1973, *130,* 132–140.

Jessor, R., Jessor, S., & Finney, J. "A social psychology of marihuana use: longitudinal studies of high school and college youth." *Journal of personality and social psychology,* 1973, *26,* 1–15.

Johnson, B. D. *Marihuana users and drug subcultures.* New York, Wiley, 1973.

Kaiser, F. M., & Lilly, R. J. "Political attitudes among students: a small college experience." *Adolescence,* 1975, 287–293.

Kandel, D., Kessler, R., & Margulien, R.   "Adolescent initiation into stages of drug use: a sequential analysis." Paper at Conference on Strategies of Longitudinal Research in Drug Use, Puerto Rico, April, 1976.

Kaplan, R.   *Drug abuse: perspective on drugs.* Dubuque, Iowa: W. C. Brown, 1970.

Korn, J. H., & Goldstein, J. W.   "Psychoactive drugs: a course evaluation." *Journal of drug education,* 1973, *3,* 353-368.

Krause, M. S.   "School children's attitudes toward public authority figures." *Adolescence,* 1975, *10*(37), 111-122.

Lieberman, J. J.   "The drug addict and the 'cop out' father." *Adolescence,* Spring 1974, *9*(33), 7-14.

McLeaf, J., & Colby, M.   "The effects of students' perceptions of a speaker's role on their recall of drug facts and their opinions and attitudes about drugs." *Journal of educational research,* July 1975, *68,* 382-386.

Milman, D. H., & Su, W. H.   "Patterns of illicit drug and alcohol use among secondary students." *Journal of pediatrics,* 1973, *123,* 314-320.

Moyer, D. H., & Simon, R. K.   "Middle school curriculum change: an action-oriented cooperative drug education pilot project." *Adolescence,* Fall 1975, *10*(39), 313-326.

Muuss, R. E.   "Legal and social aspects of drug abuse in historical perspective. Is the drug abuser a patient or a criminal?" *Adolescence,* Winter 1974, *9*(36), 495-506.

Nowlis, V., & Nowlis, H. H.   "The description and analysis of mood." *Annals of the New York academy of science,* 1956, *65,* 345-355.

Phillipson, Richard.   "Adolescent alcohol abuse." *Drug abuse and alcoholism newsletter,* November 1973, 4.

Proskauer, S., & Rolland, R. S.   "Youth who use drugs." *Journal of the American academy of child psychiatry,* 1973, *12,* 32-34.

Segal, B., & Merenda, P. F. "Locus of control, sensation seeking, and drug and alcohol use in college students." *Drug forum,* 1975, *4*(4), 349–69.

Siegal, R. S., & Brooks, M. H. "Affect for government and its relation to policy output among adolescents." *American journal of political science,* 1977, *21*(1), 111–134.

"Smoking and health." *Children today,* 1972, *1*(1), 37.

Tart, C. T. *On being stoned: a psychological study of marihuana intoxication.* Cupertino, Calif.: Science and Behavior Books, 1971.

Tec, N. "School status and differential involvement with marihuana: a study of suburban teenagers." *Adolescence,* 1972, *7,* 1–28.

Tec, N. "Parent-child drug abuse: generational continuity or adolescent deviancy? *Adolescence,* Fall 1974, *9*(35), 351–364.

"Teenage smoking." *Children today,* 1973, *2*(1), 33.

Valins, S., & Nisbett, R. E. *Attribution processes in the development and treatment of emotional disorders.* Morristown, N.J.: General Learning Press, 1971.

Victor, H., Grossman, J. C., & Eisenman, R. "Openness to experience and marihuana use in high school students." *Journal of consulting and clinical psychology,* 1973, *61,* 78–85.

Weil, A. T. "Adverse reaction to marihuana." *New England journal of medicine,* 1970, *282,* 997–1000.

Wright, J. S. "The rehabilitation of addicts." *Adolescence,* Fall 1974, *9*(35), 437–442.

Ziomkowski, L., Mulder, R., & Williams, D. "Drug use variations between delinquent and non-delinquent youth." *Intellect,* 1975, *104*(2367), 36–38.

Chapter Eleven

Mental Disturbance, Death, and Disease

Chapter Highlights

Mental Disturbance Among Adolescents
   Types of Mental Disorder
   Defense Mechanisms
   The Best Defense—A Good Defense
      Mechanism?
The Crisis of Death
   My Attempts at Suicide
Suicide
   Causes of Suicide
   The Special Case of the College
      Student
   Treatment and Prevention
Disease and Disability
   Incidence
   Community Health Services for
      Adolescents and Their Families
   How Is Your Mental/Physical
      Health?
Summary

Key Terms and Concepts

psychopathology
initiation rites
hypersensitivity
suggestibility
depression
magical thinking
religious fanaticism
death trend
parent-child role reversals
venereal disease
gonorrhea
syphilis
primary prevention
secondary prevention
crisis intervention
tertiary prevention
psychosomatic
self-fulfilling prophecy

Important Person

Elisabeth Kübler-Ross

He always wanted to explain things
But no one cared.
The teacher came and spoke to him.
She told him to wear a tie like all the other boys.
He said it didn't matter.
After that they drew.
And he drew all yellow and it was the way he felt about the morning
And it was beautiful.

The teacher came and smiled at him.
"What's this?" she said. "Why don't you draw something like Ken's drawing?
Isn't that beautiful?"
After that his mother bought him a tie.
And he always drew airplanes and rocket ships like everyone else.
And he threw the old picture away.
And when he lay out alone looking at the sky
It was big and blue and all of everything.
But he wasn't anymore.
He was square inside and brown
And his hands were still
And he was like everyone else.
And the things inside him that needed saying didn't need it anymore.
It had stopped pushing.
It was crushed.
Stiff.
Like everything else.

> —By a 16-year-old boy
> who committed suicide

In my dream I saw the world
   in a frame of imitation gold.
I heard fear pounding in my ears
   And in the white light I could only see black.
Blinded by the sound of darkness
   I saw invisible fingers
And heard nonexistent sounds.
   I was a nonexistent person
In a nonexistent world.

God help me
   As I stab myself with a
      Rubber knife.

> —By a 16-year-old girl
> in a school for "problem girls"

346

Just how serious are problems of mental disturbance and death during adolescence? In their study of 788 psychiatric clinics, Rosen et al. (1965) found that less than one-third of the patients were adolescents. Miller (1975) points out that, with the exception of college students, the suicide rate among adolescents is less than among adults. The overall death rate among adolescents is lower than for any other age group, and death is mostly caused by accidents. Why then devote an entire chapter to such relatively infrequent problems? The main reason is that adolescents *worry* about them so much.

It is only natural that they should. Puberty is an abrupt and dislocating change. It requires taking on unfamiliar roles and responsibilities, which in turn calls for, in an almost literal sense, the death of one's childhood self. The hazing, painful circumcision, and dangerous encounters with actual death arranged in the initiation rites of so-called primitive cultures are designed in part to promote the youth's awareness of human vulnerability and mortality. Although Western cultures consider such rites barbaric, there are ample trials and tribulations related to adolescence in our society. The mental anguish and resentment portrayed in the poems above may be atypical, but there can be little doubt that most teenagers occasionally find life so disturbing as to threaten their mental or physical well-being.

MENTAL DISTURBANCE AMONG ADOLESCENTS

A number of psychologists and psychoanalysts (most notably Freud) have suggested that it is normal in adolescents to have distressing, turbulent, unpredictable thoughts that in the adult would be considered pathological.

> *The fluidity of the adolescent's self-image, his changing aims and aspirations, sex drives, unstable powers of repression, and his struggle to adapt his childhood standards of right and wrong to the needs of maturity, bring into focus every conflict, past and present, that he has failed to solve. Protective covering of the personality is stripped off, and the deeper emotional currents are laid bare (Ackerman, 1958, pp. 227–228).*

This disruptive state is partly characteristic of the identity stages of diffusion and moratorium (see Chapter 2). Identity diffusion shares several characteristics with schizophrenia, a psychotic reaction typified by withdrawal from reality (Erikson, 1956). Among these are a disruption in time perspective and the inability to have intimacy with another. One can also see these characteristics in the moratorium stage, but they tend to be of much shorter duration.

How common and how serious are the disruptions of adolescence? The picture is not clear. In the most comprehensive review available, Weiner (1970) concluded that *true* psychopathology is relatively rare during adolescence. It is impossible to determine the frequency of mental illness, however, because of current disagreements as to its definition. Weiner cites numerous studies, most notably Masterson's, which gives us considerable reason to believe that "adolescent turmoil," while common, does not really constitute **psychopathology.** These studies do indicate that when adolescents become seriously disturbed and do not receive appropriate treatment quickly, the chances of them "growing out" of their problems are dim. Weiner (1970) warns that

> *an indiscriminate application of "adolescent turmoil" and "he'll-grow-out-of-it" notions to symptomatic adolescents runs the grave risk of discouraging the attention that may be necessary to avert serious psychological disturbance (p. 66).*

Types of Mental Disorder

The Rosen et al. study (1965), with its very large numbers of cases, gives us a good idea of the types of mental disorders that adolescents suffer. Approximately 4 percent of the illnesses of both males and females were accounted for by acute and chronic brain disorders (a malfunction of some part of the brain), 10 percent by mental retardation, and 6.5 percent by schizophrenia. Adults (in this hospitalized population) had considerably less mental deficiency and suffered much more (25 percent) from schizophrenia. Differences between male and female adolescents appeared in two categories: 11 percent of the males suffered from neurotic disorders, such as anxiety, depression, and obsessive-compulsive reaction, as compared to 18 percent of the females.

On the other hand, personality disorders such as passive-aggressive personality (having largely unconscious feelings of extreme hostility) and sociopathy (exhibiting no feelings of caring or concern for others), accounted for 30 percent of the cases of males, as compared to 23 percent of the females. Adults had more neurotic disorders (20 percent of the males and 32 percent of the females) as well as personality disorders (41 percent of the males and 25 percent of the females). Interestingly, the highest percentage of mental disorders for adolescents, 36 percent for both males and females, was accounted for by "transient situational personality disorder," meaning a short-term problem directly related to a real difficulty in the person's life. Thus, a significant proportion of adolescent disturbances are considered to be of a temporary nature which will disappear with changing circumstances. This category accounted for only about 5 percent of adults.

Adolescents in college run a greater risk of having emotional problems than others. For example, the suicide rate for college students is 50 percent higher than for the general population. Farnsworth (1966) reports that for *every 10,000 college students*

- 1000 will have serious emotional conflicts.
- 300 to 400 will have periods of depression that impair efficiency.
- 15 or 25 will become ill enough to require treatment.

- 5 to 20 will attempt suicide.
- 1 to 3 will be successful at committing suicide.

The problem of suicide will be discussed in a separate section.

Defense Mechanisms

Although the majority of adolescents do not become mentally disturbed, and their problems usually should not be looked at as pathological, there are still many adolescents in emotional distress. As it is with so many other adolescent problems, the major difficulty is that those most concerned don't talk about it. Each adolescent is left to worry if perhaps he or she is one of the few who is "going nuts." And each adolescent uses defense mechanisms to cope.

Although we are all prone to use defense mechanisms from time to time, adolescence is the peak period for their use (see Chapter 1). Defense mechanisms, as you may recall, are unconscious means that we use to adapt to the outside world. They often serve to shield us from discomforting truths about ourselves.

Some people argue that defense mechanisms are always bad and should be rooted out by making the unconscious conscious, whether in ourselves or in the persons we work with. The drain on psychic energy required to keep up the facade of adjustment, together with the bad judgments that result from the distortion of reality, are too costly to be allowed to continue. Others believe that the vulnerable adolescent often needs defense mechanisms, temporarily at least, to avoid personality disintegration. It is probably true that we can sometimes do more harm than good by forcing a teenager to look his or her defenses in the face.

The Best Defense—A Good Defense Mechanism?

Here is a list of the most common defense mechanisms. Find the definition of each in the right-hand column and mark its letter in the space next to the name of the defense mechanism. The correct answers are given below.

Compensation _____

Introjection _____

Rationalization _____

Projection _____

A. Unconsciously forgetting experiences which are unpleasant to remember.
B. Adopting feelings toward someone which are exactly opposite to one's real feelings.
C. The attempt to make up for a perceived inadequacy by excelling in something else.
D. When unable to fulfill one's sex drives, this need is made up for by being creative in another area (for example, becoming a great artist).

Regression _____

E. Coming to believe that a condition which is contrary to your desires is actually what you wanted all along.

Reaction formation _____

F. Adopting the standards and values of someone with whom you are afraid to disagree.

Identification _____

G. Reverting to behaviors which were previously successful when current behavior is unsuccessful.

Repression _____

H. Ascribing to another the feelings you actually have about him.

Sublimation _____

I. Adopting the standards and values of someone whom you wish you were like.

Displacement _____

J. When unable to express one's emotions to one person (for example, anger at the boss), you express them to someone else (for example, yell at your wife).

Isolation (compartmentalization) _____

K. Holding two mutually exclusive beliefs at the same time.

Answers: 1-C; 2-F; 3-E; 4-H; 5-G; 6-B; 7-I; 8-A; 9-D; 10-J; and 11-K.

THE CRISIS OF DEATH

The death rate is lower among teenagers than in any other group. For example, in Massachusetts in 1976 (see Table 11–1), the death rate for ages 10 through 14 was 30.6 per 100,000 population, and for ages 15 through 19, 91.2. The total population rate was approximately 1000 per 100,000, or 1 in 100. Tables 11–2 and 11–3 show the major cause of death in this population was accidental injuries, which accounted for approximately 40 percent of deaths in ages 10 through 14 and almost half in ages 15 through 19. These data indicate the need for improved accident prevention education, such as driver education, water safety, and first-aid courses.

Teenagers seldom have to deal with their own mortality or the deaths of relatives or friends. How do they become aware of death? Development of children's understanding of death closely parallels other aspects of their cognitive development, as described by Piaget (see Chapter 4). Until about two years of age (the sensorimotor stage), children lack an understanding of death; they become anxious at the absence of a parent or sibling, but this is a temporary state. As children reach the preoperational stage, from 2 to 7 years, they begin to form a concept of death, but they think of it as quite reversible, as a gradual sleeplike state from which the person will probably soon return. Their sense of loss is similar to the feeling that attaches to the loss of a favorite toy, which can be

TABLE 11-1
NUMBER OF DEATHS AND MORTALITY RATE FOR AGES 10-14 AND 15-19 (MASSACHUSETTS, 1976)

Age Group	Number of Deaths, All Causes	Morbidity Rate (deaths per 100,000)
10-14	169	30.6
15-19	470	91.2
Total	56,854	1,000.0

Source: *Health Data Annual,* 1976.

replaced later by another. Towards the end of this stage, death becomes personified, so that it seems to be an invisible being lurking about. For some children, death becomes frightening at this time.

During the years 7 through 11 (the concrete operational stage), death becomes much more of a reality. Children learn that it is not reversible, and become anxious when thinking of the loss of parents or other loved ones. However, they still cannot think of death in terms of themselves. It is only during adolescence (the formal operations stage) that children realize they are mortal and will

TABLE 11-2
NUMBER OF DEATHS AND MORTALITY RATE, AGES 10-14, FOR TEN LEADING CAUSES OF DEATH (MASSACHUSETTS, 1976)

Cause of Death	Number of Deaths	Morbidity Rate (deaths per 100,000)
Motor vehicle accidents	46	8.2
Other accidents	22	3.9
Cancers, lymph and blood	12	2.1
Pneumonia	9	1.6
Congenital anomalies	9	1.6
Accidents, fire and flame	8	1.5
Other cancers	5	.9
Accidental falls	5	.9
Water transport accidents	3	.5
Arthropod-borne viral disease	2	.4

Source: *Health Data Annual,* 1976.

TABLE 11–3
NUMBER OF DEATHS AND MORTALITY RATE, AGES 15–19, FOR FIVE
LEADING CAUSES OF DEATH (MASSACHUSETTS, 1976)

Cause of Death	Number of Deaths	Morbidity Rate (deaths per 100,000)
Motor vehicle accidents	192	37.2
Other accidents	34	6.6
Cancers, lymph and blood	25	4.8
Suicide	23	4.4
Homicide	21	4.1

Source: *Health Data Annual*, 1976.

die someday. Now they have a sense of their own future and a clearer sense of the time dimension itself. As they begin to plan their lives, the inevitability of death becomes real and they develop a new anxiety about death.

> *Many adolescents have a clear feeling of the passing of this life stage with the expectation of a specific ending. This sense of the anticipated end of adolescence might be an important parallel to the concept of the finality of death. . . . I would add that ruminations over suicide and forms of actively promoted death encounters would serve to provide the adolescent with a sense of greater temporal definition in his life (Hankoff, 1975, p. 76).*

Adolescents who have a clear sense of their own values, and who have been helped by their parents to form a set of values, are more likely to have a realistic and less fearful attitude toward death (see Chapter 13). This is not to say that parents can simply give their adolescents an appropriate attitude toward death. Those adolescents in James Marcia's stages of identity diffusion and foreclosure are the most likely to have difficulty with the concept of death because of their unwillingness to confront reality. Kastenbaum (1959) found that youth who are highly religious and who believe in life after death are more likely to show an active concern for the topic and are more likely to conduct their daily lives on the basis of their expectations for the future. They are more apt to have confronted the formal aspects of death.

In her popular book, *On Death and Dying*, Elisabeth Kübler-Ross (1969) points out that in "old country" and "primitive" cultures, children have contact with death from an early age. In technological societies, children are shielded from death because it is considered too upsetting. She suggests that when

> *children are allowed to stay at home where a fatality has stricken, and are included in the talk, discussions, and fears, [it] gives them the feeling that*

*they are not alone in the grief and gives them the comfort of shared respon-
sibility and shared mourning. It prepares them gradually and helps them to
view death as part of life, an experience which may help them grow and
mature (p. 6).*

Kübler-Ross has concluded from her studies that most persons who know
that their death is imminent pass through a sequence of five stages in their
attempts to deal with it: denial and isolation, anger, bargaining, depression, and
acceptance. Reading her description of these stages can be useful to those helping an adolescent who is struggling to handle the dying of a loved one.

Hankoff (1975) has suggested that the absence of **initiation rites** in technological societies is responsible for the deep fear of death common among adolescents. Initiation rites offer youth a meaningful encounter with this most
important aspect of life, which is death:

*In brief, [initiations into] these mysteries involve sexuality, the spirit world,
and death. The mystery of death is brought to the initiand through a ritualized performance in which he is symbolically made to die and be born.
This initiatory ritual thus is a template for the important human spiritual
experience of self-renewal. In traditional cultures the initiatory ritual tangibly
and powerfully provides the youth with knowledge of the spiritual world,
the mysteries and privileges of adult status, and emotional participation in
death and rebirth experiences (p. 379).*

A special form of encounter with death, one which fortunately is still rare, is
the suicide attempt.

SUICIDE

Adolescent and young adult suicide rates have risen sharply over the last twenty
years. As a matter of fact, suicide is now one of the leading causes of death
among teenagers (McAnarney, 1979; Smith, 1980). The rate among 15- to 24-
year-olds almost doubled between 1950 and 1970 (McAnarney, 1979). Of the
approximately 25,000 Americans who commit suicide each year, 6.6 percent are
teenagers. There are nearly twenty times this number of attempts each year
among adolescents (Smith, 1980).

Suicide ranks third in the causes of death in 15- to 19-year-olds and is
roughly one-tenth of the deaths due to accidents, the first cause of death in this
age group. Figure 11–1 shows selected suicide rates for 1925 through 1975.

The means of suicide vary. Males tend to resort to firearms, explosives,
hanging; females are likely to choose less violent means such as sleeping pills.
Girls are three times as likely to attempt suicide as boys, but boys are three times
more likely to die when they do attempt it.

In the last decade, the suicide rate of nonwhite girls, which was twice that

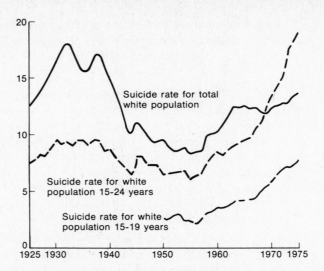

Figure 11–1   Suicide Rate for Selected Groups—United States, 1925–75 (per 100,000 population in specified age groups)*

*In order to portray long-range trends, the above chart displays national suicide rates for three age groups: 1) the total white population, 2) white males aged 15 to 24, and 3) white males aged 15 to 19. Suicide data are not conveniently available for the 15 to 19 age group before 1950, hence the rate for that group has only been graphed for 20 years. Note that increases in rates for the 15 to 19 age group have been an important element in the dramatic upward shift in the long-term pattern of suicide rates for the 15 to 24 age group. (Source: From Edward Wynne, "Desirable School Changes," *Phi Delta Kappan* (January 1978), p. 308.)

for white girls, is now the same. On the other hand, nonwhite male adolescents now have a rate exceeding that of the population as a whole. The incidence of suicide among those who married as teenagers remains at well above the national rates through age 24, at which point it begins to drop and actually becomes lower than the national rate for married adults.

Causes of Suicide

Miller (1975) quotes Albert Camus as having said, "There is but one true philosophical problem and this is suicide: Judging whether life is or is not worth living amounts to answering the fundamental question of philosophy." Apparently many adolescents would agree.

Two major factors figure in the causes of suicide (Corder et al., 1974; Miller, 1975): individual characteristics of the suicide and environmental conditions present at the time of the attempt. A suicide attempt is usually the result of the interaction of these factors.

Individual characteristics.   The most striking characteristics of those who attempt suicide are the following:

Hypersensitivity. All adolescents occasionally overreact to situations, but the hypersensitive will have an extreme reaction to situations that would only mildly disturb most people. The disruptions caused by seemingly trivial events may come together in a suicide attempt.

Suggestibility. Sabbath (1969) has described the "expendable child," who believes that his parent or parents wish him dead. This parental wish may be conscious or unconscious, spoken or unspoken, true or untrue. But to the extent that children are suggestible, they are likely to comply with this perceived wish. The role of the parents in the suicide attempts of highly suggestible children is clear. Lorand and Schneer (1961) have studied parents whose sadistic behavior conveys to children that they are unwanted. Glaser (1965) has studied the emotionally detached parent, who is unwilling or unable to demonstrate love. Such parents may care deeply for their children, but suggestible adolescents tend to take their apparent detachment as a wish for their death. Teicher and Jacobs (1966) found that 88 percent of adolescent suicide attempts occur in the home, quite frequently with one or both parents right in the next room, an indication that parental behavior is a factor.

Depression. A feeling of deep depression almost always accompanies suicide attempts, but is often difficult to spot because adolescents seldom let on that they are feeling depressed. Depression may exhibit itself in boredom, restlessness, and preoccupation with trivia. People's level of "crisis reactivity" is an indication of depression (Hankoff, 1975). When people have a negative self-image, they may well react to a crisis by a lack of emotional feelings and an absence of crisis-solving behavior. Lack of crisis reactivity, together with a sense of disgust at one's inability to feel, is a common factor in suicide attempts (Deutsch, 1937; Hankoff, 1975; Schowalter, 1978).

Magical thinking. Many adolescents have an unrealistic view of death's finality and use suicide as a means to radically transform the world and solve one's problems, or to join a loved one who has already died. These feelings are often aided and abetted by the glorification of suicide that sometimes occurs in the media (Garner, 1975).

Religious fanaticism. Some adolescents, whose faith in the omnipotence and omniscience of God is particularly strong, and who are doubtful about whether they are good enough to continue living, decide to attempt suicide and leave the outcome to God. Just as disagreements were settled in medieval times by jousting matches, extremely religious youths expect God to intervene and save them from death by their own hand if He judges them worthy of life.

Environmental characteristics. The most important environmental characteristics that influence suicide are the following:

The death trend. Quite frequently suicide victims have suffered the death of a person close to them sometime before their attempt. Moss and Hamilton (1956) found that there was a death close to the adolescent in 95 percent of the cases, and in 75 percent of the cases the death had taken place during the suicide's teenage years. Often the adolescents see a loved one's death as abandonment; they may suffer feelings of worthlessness and also anger toward the deceased person, which is often turned inward. These feelings, combined with a sense of identification with the deceased and a desire to rejoin him or her, may lead to the suicide attempt (Dorpat, Jackson, and Ripley, 1969; Paffenbarger and Asnes, 1957).

Stress. In many cases, specific problems in the teenagers' environment challenge their immaturity and sap them of emotional strength. Often stress comes, as you might expect, from the home. For example, Tuckman and Connon (1962) found that in almost one-third of the suicide cases they studied, stress in the home was so serious that the Society for the Prevention of Cruelty to Children had intervened at some time prior to the suicide attempt.

Lack of control over the environment. Corder et al. (1974) cite the suicide's inability to change his or her environment as a frequent cause. This concept was first studied by Rotter (1971); a review of the studies of personal control has appeared elsewhere (Dacey, 1976). People tend to fall into one of two categories in terms of their sense of control over their lives. "Internals" see control as self-derived; they have a sense that they can influence what happens to them by their own actions. "Externals" see control as imposed by outside factors; thus, they see life as a matter of chance or luck. Some externals really do not have much control; others only imagine they do not. In either case, external individuals are far more likely to commit suicide than internals.

Parent-child role reversals. This term "refers to the changing of traditional role behaviors between a parent and child. In the parent-child interaction the child adopts some parent-type behavior (for example, care-taking, supporting, nurturing, advising), and the parent acts more as a child would be expected to act (for example, seeking support, acting helpless, or unable to cope)" (Kreider and Motto, 1974, p. 365).

Role reversal occurs frequently in a home where there is one parent or one child. It tends to produce anxiety, pain, frustration, and hostility in adolescents. They aren't ready to handle such a burden of adult behavior and may blame themselves for their inability. They may seek to alter the family environment, or to escape it, or may collapse under the pressure. They sometimes see suicide as the only way out of the double bind of having to act as both child and adult.

The appearance of not being needed. When we feel that no one needs us, we tend to become lonely and self-centered:

Suicide is not so much the outcome of "pressure," but pressure without social support. Suicide does not automatically mean that a person has not been loved or cared for. It probably does mean that he was not needed by others in an immediate, tangible fashion. "Needed" should be understood in the sense we imply when we say we need the first-string member of an athletic team, the paper delivery boy, the only secretary in a small office, or the only wage earner in a family. The person needed must be obviously relied upon by others, and his absence should create a disruptive and fore-seeable gap. In this light, it is understandable that one of the highest suicide rates is that of middle-aged bachelors and one of the lowest is that of married women with children . . . It is nice to know we are loved, but essential to know we are needed (Wynne, 1978, p. 311).

Another effort to determine the common reasons and causes for suicide among adolescents has been made by McAnarney (1979), who reviewed crosscultural studies. She found that the high suicide rates in the United States appear to be related to the following factors:

The family. In societies where family ties are strong, fewer suicides occur. American adolescents who are experiencing the current changing status of the family may suffer in their achievement of identity. Also, when families are not close, parents may not be able to recognize early warning signs and help their teenagers before suicide becomes an alternative.

Religion. Studies have indicated that in societies where the majority of the people belong to a formal religious organization, suicide attempts are low.

Transition and mobility. Groups in transition tend to have higher suicide rates than stable ones. Examples of such change experienced by American teenagers include life in disorganized urban environments or frequent moves when one or both parents are transferred at work.

Achievement orientation. Cultures such as the United States in which achievement is a major priority have higher suicide rates. Japan and Sweden are other examples of achievement-oriented societies that exhibit high suicide rates.

Aggression. Sometimes suicide is defined as aggression turned inward. In cultures where the expression of aggressive feelings is discouraged or suppressed, suicides are more prevalent.

Abuse. One study hypothesized that children who are exposed to physical abuse may be more likely to exhibit self-destructive behavior, such as suicide attempts. Green (1978) compared abused, neglected, and normal children and found that there was a significantly higher occurrence of self-destructive behavior among the abused children than among the others. The neglected children were also more likely to try to hurt themselves than the normal children.

Green claims that children who are abused come to feel worthless and to hate themselves as a result of their parents' rejections and assaults. These feelings of self-hatred transform into self-destructive behavior. For some children, suicidal behavior is really an attempt to escape from a traumatic situation, while for others it is a cry for help.

My Attempts at Suicide
(Anonymous)

My first psychiatrist told my parents that his testings indicated that I was potentially suicidal. I was 14 then. At 22, I had made five suicide attempts and had been in six mental institutions, which add up to twenty-nine months as a mental patient and five years of intensive therapy. My diagnosis was borderline schizophrenia, chronic depressive, and sadomasochism. Why? How had I become so obsessed with suicide?

When I flash back on my adolescent days, I remember feeling ugly, socially awkward, stuck away in an all-girls' boarding school reading Camus and Hesse, unpopular, and stupid! In fact, I was not quite as dreadful as all that, but in my mind I was. I felt different. I once wrote, "I'm at the bottom of an upside-down garbage can and it's so ugly." The world was horrible, but I was the worst part of it. Suicide was my escape. Unsuccessful suicide attempts put me in the care of others who delicately forced me to confront my feelings of sadness and anger. I had to learn to share with others and sometimes that was what I secretly wanted. Two of my attempts, however, were calculated, purposeful acts. Despite what shrinks may say, I wanted to be dead, not taken care of.

What did death mean to me? One of my earliest memories is sitting on moss-covered ground in a grove of pines, reading *The Prayer for the Dead* with my basset hound curled up beside me. It meant escape from hell on earth. No other purgatory could be worse than this one. Even if I were reincarnated, I would end up being some "lowly animal" with the kind of mind that could not plague me with frightening, lonely, depressing thoughts. I clung to my friends and family, but it only increased my anger and self-contempt. I treated those people as my keepers who temporarily saved me from being left alone with my tormenting mind.

My year in India had the most devastating effect on me. What I saw there was what I felt inside me. All of us were starving for something. The Indians begged for food; I begged for emotional support. We all begged for a chance to survive.

The final blow hit in Boston. I gradually withdrew from the few friends I had as well as my family. Death had grown so close that I no longer felt that I had much time. It was impossible to commit myself to anyone or anything. I was reserved, yet few people could sense how obsessed I was with death. Signs of affection terrified me because I knew I could not let anyone count on me. I needed death if life became too unbearable. It finally did. I had become so passive that I no longer made contact with people. They had to call me. So much time had elapsed since I had felt close to someone that it seemed my "disappearance" would not really upset anyone. In addition to this, I was convinced that I was too stupid to handle academics or even a menial job (even though I had two jobs at the time). On a day when I knew no one would try and reach me, I took three times the lethal dosage of Seconal. I was found twenty-four hours later, and came out of a coma after forty-eight more. My arm was paralyzed. This time, I was placed in a long-term hospital. Another try at life began. With the help of an excellent therapist and the patient love of friends whom I had thus far rejected, I have started once more. It has been two years since I took the pills. I think I know why people bother to live now.

The Special Case of the College Student

As we noted, the suicide rate among college students is considerably higher than for noncollege students. Especially among freshmen, the emotional difficulties of leaving home (often for the first time) create great strains. First-year college students often report feelings of depression and inadequacy. The majority of them agree with the statement "I certainly feel useless at times" (Braaten and Darling, 1962). Temby (1961) found that virtually all college students who have attempted suicide were suffering from depression, and were likely to have obsessive-compulsive tendencies.

Treatment and Prevention

Treatment of adolescents suffering from suicidal tendencies has become considerably more effective in recent years due to two factors. First, we are much more likely these days to take statements of intention of suicide seriously. With increased research on suicide that has resulted from the increase in suicide rates, we have come to realize that virtually anyone is capable of suicide. Second, we have come to realize that the person's family and friends *must* be involved in any attempt at cure. Which techniques are selected depend on the family's and individual's abilities to work at the problem-solving process. They all include helping the individual to cope with the present situation, work out specific changes, ventilate anguish, and remove feelings that suicidal tendencies are necessarily a sign of insanity.

Of course, the best way to treat self-destructiveness is through prevention. Teachers, counselors, and others should recognize the following factors as being precursors to the suicidal crisis:

- Disorganized family life.
- Marital discord between parents.
- Loss or threatened loss of a parent or friend.
- Recent marked changes in behavior, particularly withdrawal or isolation from family and friends.

- History of a previous attempt or threats of attempts.
- Evidence of depression or obsessive-compulsive behavior.
- A change for the worse in academic performance.
- Talking about or actually giving away prized possessions.
- A change toward carelessness, impulsiveness, or accident-proneness.
- Changes in the sleep cycle; insomnia or a great increase in the amount of sleep, especially during the day.

Greuling and DeBlassie (1980) found that many adolescents who had attempted suicide gave no recognizable signals to those around them. Very often an attempt is a sudden, impulsive reaction to a stressful event. But character patterns, such as impulsiveness, depression, and psychotic behavior have been found among attempters. It seems that often when a teenager does give signs and signals they are ignored or misinterpreted as merely part of adolescent behavior or development.

Smith (1980) states that depression, lack of ambition, lack of goals, or a sudden rise in alcohol or drug consumption are all danger signs. School performance is almost always low in suicidal individuals. Often the five years preceding an attempt are marked by personal, medical, social, or family difficulties.

Suicidal adolescents are not likely to consult parents, clergy, or family physicians. School personnel are much more likely to notice when adolescents are sending danger signals (Greuling and DeBlassie, 1980).

These behaviors of themselves do not necessarily indicate that a person has become suicidal. But to the extent that one or more are present, they should serve as a warning.

McCormack (1977) suggests that "teachers (and others working with teenagers) should trust their own feelings in assessing a potentially suicidal young person. Often gut reactions are the most essential yardsticks. [They] may have an uneasy feeling that a child might hurt himself or herself [and] should discuss these feelings with the young person" (p. 13). One should listen for key phrases like "I would like to sleep forever and never get up," "Sometimes I would like to take a gun and blow my damn head off — of course I'm only joking," and "I don't care about tomorrow."

Many crisis intervention services such as agencies and telephone hotlines are available to help suicidal teenagers. But teachers are the most likely adults in an adolescent's life to notice the warning signs. Smith (1980) feels that the study of suicide should be a part of teacher training. Greuling and DeBlassie (1980) claim that school personnel are in an excellent position to provide help. These authors feel that the problem is so widespread that all young people should be checked for suicidal ideation through questionnaires.

Whatever the method of intervention, it is clear that no warning signal should be ignored. Those adults who work with adolescents are in the most strategically advantageous position to detect and hopefully prevent suicidal and self-destructive behavior among teenagers.

Unfortunately, with the trend toward social isolation and "future shock" in our technological, transient society, we can expect suicide attempts to become a greater problem in the future. If we use our greater knowledge of the factors involved in suicide to their fullest advantage we may reverse this trend.

DISEASE AND DISABILITY

Incidence

Venereal disease is the only group of communicable diseases that is currently a major source of illness for the adolescent group. **Gonorrhea** cases have increased more than 30 percent since 1970. In contrast, **syphilis** cases fell 25 percent in the same period (*Health Data Annual,* 1976). However, it is important to note that both diseases are considered to be seriously underreported. These figures are for all age groups, but the high incidence of both diseases among adolescents is widely recognized.

Two other diseases that are also becoming widespread are genital herpes and venereal warts. The latter are treatable, but herpes is especially dangerous because it is resistant to antibiotics, and is at present incurable. The data highlight the need for sex education to prevent infection, plus adequate, available, and accessible treatment facilities and follow-up services.

Information about noncommunicable diseases is not compiled on a routine basis. However, the National Center for Health Statistics (1973) conducted extensive interview and examination surveys of representative population samples. On direct medical examination 25 percent of youths 12 through 17 were found to have one or more significant cardiovascular, neurological, musculoskeletal, or other physical abnormalities. Approximately 3 percent had a history of convulsions, 4 percent reported hearing problems, and 7 percent reported eye trouble. Regional differences were noted, with a higher number of abnormalities in youths in southern states. Despite their greater numbers at the poverty level, black youths were not found to have a higher frequency of abnormalities than whites. This was an exception to the finding concerning the relationship between family income and health of all youth; the proportion found abnormal on examination decreased steadily as family income level increased.

These data indicate a need for better early detection and treatment of disease in school-age children within the school health program. States generally require screening of the total school population in certain grades. This often produces a mass of local reports on known defects, which, nevertheless, remain largely untreated due to inadequate follow-up or inadequate family financial resources. A more effective measure might be assessment and monitoring of high-risk subgroups. One good indicator of disease is children with high absence records (Williams, 1977). Children living in neighborhoods where incomes are low or unemployment is high also constitute another high-risk group that would benefit from aggressive outreach service by school nurses.

Community Health Services for Adolescents and Their Families

Health and social services are provided in American communities by a mixture of public and private agencies in a hit-or-miss pattern. The five criteria of availability, accessibility, acceptability, affordability, and comprehensiveness are seldom met for the total population in need of those services. An additional criterion unmet by the aggregate of existing agencies is provision of the full range of possible interventions from basic or primary prevention (health promotion and problem prevention), through secondary prevention (early problem detection and prompt care), to tertiary prevention (habilitation or rehabilitation) (Kessler and Albee, 1975). Although it is not considered essential or even desirable for each agency to provide this full range of interventions, it is desirable that the full range be available to each person and family and in a reasonably well-coordinated fashion. A list of services typically available in medium- to large-sized towns and cities appears in Appendix C.

Primary prevention.   The most important determinants of the health and social well-being of any age group are found in factors unrelated to the agencies themselves, which include a wide range of sociocultural, politicoeconomic, and other environmental factors. **Primary prevention** refers to these determinants of housing, quality of air and water, adequacy of nutrition, and sociocultural beliefs and attitudes about health and personal life-style choice. Some intervention in the form of health education can ensure that individuals and families make wiser choices in terms of life-style behaviors such as eating, drinking, smoking, and exercise. Only intervention at a societal level can guarantee that all citizens have an equally wide range of choices available to them. At present, existing economic, social, and political constraints prevent a significant number of citizens from being able to select healthy alternatives available to more affluent fellow citizens. Children and youth are overrepresented in this excluded group.

Direct preventive efforts for the adolescent age group are offered by school health education programs and other community health education efforts. Past preventive efforts have achieved reduction or virtual elimination of major childhood diseases through immunization. The current level of public overconfidence and the accompanying drop in immunization levels indicates the need for renewed attention to routine immunization procedures.

Secondary prevention.   Detection and treatment of existing health and social problems — **secondary prevention** — is the major focus of many agencies. Another potential provider of health and social services for the adolescent is the local school system. All states require a minimum health component, mainly aimed at detection and referral of physical health problems. Recent legislation in some states has mandated more extensive evaluation and treatment of a much broader group of conditions, including mental, emotional, and learning disorders. State funds are being made available to pay for some of these evaluation and treatment services. Personnel providing these services are employed either by the school or by other health and social agencies, and include pediatricians, psychiatrists, nurses, psychologists, social workers, vocational and guidance counselors, speech and hearing therapists, physical and occupational therapists, plus teachers and school administrators.

Crisis intervention services are springing up under a variety of local auspices, often operating with limited professional and financial resources. Telephone hot lines, drop-in centers, suicide prevention centers, and rape crisis centers exist in many communities; adolescents often find it easier to relate to the style of these centers than to the more formal operation of traditional agencies. Other community-based social services include voluntary family and children's service agencies, which provide a range of counseling and guidance services and are staffed by social workers, psychologists, human service professionals, and assistants.

An essential feature of many health and social agencies is a commitment to provide services on a family-unit basis rather than to individual adolescents. Health and social problems are usually deeply rooted in family roles and interaction patterns. Successful intervention requires finding and using family strengths. In addition, family members may have undiscovered and untreated problems.

Tertiary prevention.   Children with mental retardation, mental illness, and congenital problems are the bulk of the small proportion of adolescents needing rehabilitation services — referred to as **tertiary prevention.** The former practice of "warehousing" the mentally retarded in institutions has been replaced by a nationwide emphasis on community alternatives. Increasingly, halfway houses and community residences are being developed as a way of returning retarded children and adults to community living. In addition, support systems to assist parents in home care of handicapped and retarded children are being advocated. Special school settings for handicapped, blind, and deaf children are being gradually phased out by including these children in regular classrooms where possible. Called "mainstreaming," it is currently causing much disruption due to a lag in the support and retraining needed to make this innovation work.

In general, it is hard to find any area where the physical and mental health needs of adolescents are well met; by and large, the opposite is true. As Nuttall et al. (1977) concluded in their recent assessment of mental health needs in an eastern state:

> The lesson here is that mental health services should reduce their reliance on traditional modes of providing services if they are to serve the needs of adolescents. More outreach and "off-beat" approaches are needed. Mental health workers should be trained who can assist in alcohol abuse and employment problems as well as emotional problems if the mental health needs of adolescents are to be met (pp. 284–285).

One way of preserving mental health is to recognize its critical dependence on physical health. The relationship between both types of health and the environmental stress can be examined by the Social Readjustment Rating Scale (Holmes and Rahe, 1967) reproduced here.

How Is Your Mental/Physical Health?

Check off the life events which are happening or have happened to you within the last year; then add up your life change units (LCUs).

The authors found that high ratings on this scale were associated with a wide range of physical illnesses, not only the **psychosomatic** disorders usually associated with stress. Colligan (1975) reports that 86 percent of those who had experienced over 300 LCUs in one year came down with some serious health problem. Of course, this does not mean that if you have a lot of LCUs you will certainly get ill. In fact, there is the danger of a **self-fulfilling prophecy** in discovering this relationship. On the other hand, it is clear that if you are under a high level of stress, you should take especially good care of your body and be ready to check with your doctor quickly if you develop physical symptoms.

Life Event	LCUs
Death of spouse	100
Divorce	73
Marital separation	65
Jail term	63
Death of close family member	63
Personal injury or illness	53
Marriage	50
Fired at work	47
Marital reconciliation	45
Retirement	45
Change in health of family member	44
Pregnancy	40
Sex difficulties	39
Gain of new family member	39
Business readjustment	39
Change in financial state	38
Death of a close friend	37
Change to a different line of work	36
Change in number of arguments with spouse	35
Mortgage over $10,000	31
Foreclosure of mortgage or loan	30
Change in responsibilities at work	29
Son or daughter leaving home	29
Trouble with in-laws	29
Outstanding personal achievement	28
Wife begins or stops work	26
Begin or end school	26
Change in living conditions	25

Revision of personal habits	24
Trouble with boss	23
Change in work hours or conditions	20
Change in residence	20
Change in schools	20
Change in recreation	19
Change in church activities	19
Change in social activities	18
Mortgage or loan less than $10,000	17
Change in sleeping habits	16
Change in number of family get-togethers	15
Change in eating habits	15
Vacation	13
Christmas	12
Minor violations of the law	11

Source: From "Social Readjustment Scale," in Holmes and Rahe, *Journal of Psychosomatic Research*, 11 (1967), pp. 213–218.

SUMMARY

Although mental disturbance and suicide are relatively rare among adolescents, thoughts about insanity and death are not at all uncommon. The dramatic physical transformations of puberty and the unfamiliar roles and responsibilities brought on by the transition from childhood to adulthood cause occasional turmoil in the normal adolescent, but this does not constitute mental illness. However, adults should be concerned about adolescents who are experiencing prolonged and intense disturbances, because these teenagers do not "grow out of it."

Adolescents who are most inclined to have emotional conflicts are college students. Adolescents who are trying to separate themselves from their parents and establish their own sense of self may not want to face discomforting truths about themselves. To avoid painful self-realizations the adolescent ego uses what Freud has called defense mechanisms.

The death rate is lower among teenagers than any other age group, but mortality is an important topic for teenagers because they are able to cognitively appreciate the significance of death and dying.

The percentage of deaths by suicide among adolescents has been rising in the last twenty years. A combination of individual personality characteristics and environmental factors cause teenagers to attempt suicide. Teenagers who are hypersensitive, suggestible, depressive, or unrealistic in their view of death are more likely to attempt suicide. Environmental stresses such as family problems or the death of a loved one can precipitate an emotional crisis and, in some individuals, a suicide attempt. All suicide attempts, even expressions of the intent to commit suicide, must be taken very seriously.

Venereal disease is the only communicable disease that is currently a major source of illness for the adolescent group (although information about noncommunicable diseases is not compiled on a routine basis). There is a need for better early detection and treatment of disease in school-age children within the school health program. There are three major approaches to the detection and treatment of physical and mental health problems: primary, secondary, and tertiary prevention. Primary prevention is the removal of the causes before health and psychological problems begin. Secondary prevention attempts to prevent manageable problems from becoming unmanageable; crisis intervention is an example. Tertiary prevention tries to reduce the consequences of psychological disturbances and physical disabilities.

Mental and physical health are interrelated. Psychosomatic illnesses are usually associated with emotional difficulties, but so are a wide range of physical illnesses. Unhappy changes (death, divorce, being fired), and happy changes as well (holidays, marriage, pregnancy) in people's lives can be stressful. Those people who are coping with several major changes in their lives are likely to develop serious physical illnesses.

Questions

1. Why do adolescents worry so much about becoming mentally ill?
2. What types of mental disorder are most common in adolescents?
3. Are defense mechanisms healthy? Why?
4. How does the child's concept of death change as he becomes an adolescent?
5. What makes suicide seem an attractive possibility to the disturbed adolescent?
6. What are the behavior signals in the youth with suicidal tendencies?
7. What are the physical diseases that cause major illness in teenagers? How are these related to mental illness?

References

Ackerman, J. W.   *The psychodynamics of family life.* New York: Basic Books, 1958.

Abraham, Y.   "Patterns of communication and rejection in families of suicidal adolescents." *Dissertation abstracts international*, February 1978, *38*(8-A), 4669.

Braaten, L., & Darling, C. D.   "Suicidal tendencies among college students." *Psychiatric quarterly*, 1962, *35*, 364–391.

Colligan, J. T.   "Achievement and personality characteristics as predictors of observed tutor behavior." *Dissertation abstracts international*, January 1975, *35*(7), 4293–4294.

Corder, B. G., Shorr, W., & Corder, R. F.   "A study of social and psychological characteristics of adolescent suicide attempts in an urban, disadvantaged, area." *Adolescence*, 1974, *9*(33), 1–6.

Dacey, J.   *New ways to learn.* Stamford, Conn.: Greylock, 1976.

Deutsch, H.   "Absence of grief." *Psychoanalytic quarterly*, 1937, *6*, 12–22.

Dorpat, T. L., Jackson, J. K., & Ripley, H. S.   "Broken homes and attempted and completed suicide." *Archives of general psychiatry*, 1969, *12*, 301–304.

Erikson, E. H.   "The problem of ego identity." *Journal of the American psychoanalytic association*, 1956, *4*, 56–121.

Erlich, H.   "Adolescent suicide: maternal longing and cognitive development." *Psychoanalytic study of the child*, 1978, *33*, 261–277.

Farnsworth, D.   "Suicide and student stress." *Moderator,* October 1966, 8–15.

Francis, C.   "Adolescent suicide attempts, experienced rejection and personal constructs." *Dissertation abstracts international,* March 1978, *38*(9-B), 4453.

Garner, H. G.   "An adolescent suicide, the mass media and the educator." *Adolescence,* Summer 1975, *10*(38), 241–246.

Glaser, K.   "Attempted suicide in children and adolescents." *American journal of psychotherapy,* 1965, *19*(2), 220–227.

Glaser, K.   "The treatment of depressed and suicidal adolescents." *American journal of psychotherapy,* April 1978, *32* (2), 252–269.

Green, A.   "Self-destructive behavior in battered children." *American journal of psychiatry,* May 1978, *135*(5), 579–582.

Greuling, J., & DeBlassie, R.   "Adolescent suicide." *Adolescence,* 1980, *15*(50), 589–601.

Hankoff, L. D.   "Adolescence and the crisis of dying." *Adolescence,* Fall 1975, *10*(39), 373–390.

Hawton, K., et al.   "Attempted suicide and suicide among Oxford university students." *British journal of psychiatry,* May 1978, *132,* 506–509.

Health data annual (Vol. 2, No. 1). Boston: Commonwealth of Massachusetts, 1976.

Holinger, P.   "Adolescent suicide: an epidemiological study of recent trends." *American journal of psychiatry.* June 1978, *135*(6), 754–756.

Holmes, J., & Rahe, S.   "A social readjustment scale." *Journal of psychosomatic research,* 1967, *11,* 213–218.

Howze, B.   "A cross-cultural study of certain predisposing characteristics to suicide in a group of urban Detroit youth." *Dissertation abstracts international,* December 1978, *39*(6-B), 2988.

Jacobs, J. *Adolescent suicide.* New York: Wiley, 1971.

Jacobs, J., & Teicher, J. D.   "Broken homes and social isolation in attempted suicide of adolescents." *International journal of social psychiatry,* 1967, *13,* 139–149.

Johnson, R.   "Youth in crisis: dimension of self-destructive conduct among adolescent prisoners." *Adolescence,* Fall 1978, *13*(51), 461–482.

Joint Commission on the Mental Health of Children. *Mental health: from infancy through adolescence.* New York: Harper & Row, 1973.

Kastenbaum, R.   "Time and death in adolescence." In H. Feifel (Ed.), *The meaning of death.* New York: McGraw-Hill, 1959.

Kessler, M., & Albee, G. W.   "Primary prevention." *Annual review of psychology,* 1975, *26,* 557–591.

Klagsbrun, F.   "Preventing teenage suicide." *Family health,* 1977, *9,* 21–24.

Kreider, D. G., & Motto, J. A.   "Parent-child role reversal and suicidal states in adolescence." *Adolescence,* Fall 1974, *10*(35), 365–370.

Kübler-Ross, E.   *On death and dying.* New York: Macmillan, 1969.

Lorand, S., & Schneer, H. I. (Eds.).   *Adolescence: psychoanalytic approaches to problems and theory.* New York: Hoeber, 1961.

McAnarney, E.   "Adolescent and young adult suicide in the U.S.—a reflection of social unrest?" *Adolescence, 14*(56), 1979, 765–774.

McCormack, P. (Ed.).   "The student suicide epidemic." *The patriot ledger,* October 31, 1977, 13.

Miller, J. P.   "Suicide and adolescence." *Adolescence,* Spring 1975, *10*(37), 11–24.

Mitchell, M. E.   *The child's attitude to death.* New York: Schocken, 1967.

Moss, L. M., & Hamilton, D. M.   "The psychotherapy of the suicidal patient." *American journal of psychiatry,* 1956, *112,* 81–82.

National Center for Health Statistics, *Examination and health history findings among children and youth, 6–19 years.* Washington, D.C.: U.S. Department of Health, Education, and Welfare, 1973 (Series 11, 129).

Nuttall, E., Nuttall, R. L., Polit, D., & Clark, K. "Assessing adolescent mental health needs: the views of consumers, providers, and others." *Adolescence*, Summer 1977, *12*(46), 277–285.

Oshman, H., & Manosevitz, M. "Death fantasies of father-absent and father-present late adolescents." *Journal of youth and adolescence*, March 1978, *7*(1), 41–48.

Paffenbarger, R. S., Jr., & Asnes, D. P. "Chronic disease in former college students, III. Precursors of suicide in early and middle life." *American journal of public health*, 1957, 1026–1036.

Peskin, H., & Livson, N. "Pre- and postpubertal personality and adult psychologic functioning." *Seminars in psychiatry*, 1972, *4*(4), 343–353.

Robbins, W. "Youth's suicide may lead to help for other children who are brilliant but troubled." *New York Times*, Sept. 1980, 26.

Rosen, B. M., Bahn, A. K., Shellow, R., & Bower, E. M. "Adolescent patients served in outpatient clinics." *American journal of public health*, 1965, *55,* 1563–1577.

Rosenkrantz, A. "A note on adolescent suicide: incidence, dynamics and some suggestions for treatment." *Adolescence*, Summer 1978, *13*(50), 209–214.

Rotter, J. "External control and internal control." *Psychology today*, June 1971, *5,* 37ff.

Sabbath, J. "The suicidal adolescent: the expendable child." *Journal of the American academy of child psychiatry*, 1969, *8*(2), 272–285.

Schneidman, E., & Swenson, D. "Suicide among youth." *Bulletin of suicidology* (supplement), December 1969.

Schowalter, J. E. "Parent death and child bereavement." In A. Weiner, I. Getber, A. Kutscher, & B. Schoenberg (Eds.), *Bereavement*. New York: Columbia University Press, 1978.

Shenker, I. R., & Schildkraut, M. "Physical and emotional health of youth." In R. J. Havighurst & P. H. Dreyer (Eds.), *Youth*. Chicago: The National Society for the Study of Education, 1975.

Smith, D. "Adolescent suicide." From R. E. Muuss (Ed.), *Adolescent behavior and society: a book of readings*. New York: Random House, 1980, pp. 402–409.

Teicher, D., & Jacobs, J. "Adolescents who attempt suicide: preliminary findings." *American journal of psychiatry*, 1966, *122*(11), 1248–1257.

Temby, W. "Suicide." In G. B. Blaine & C. McArthur (Eds.), *Emotional problems of the student*. New York: Appleton-Century-Crofts, 1961.

Tuckman, J., & Connon, H. E. "Attempted suicide in adolescents." *American journal of psychiatry*, 1962, *119,* 228–232.

Weiner, I. B. *Psychological disturbances in adolescence*. New York: Wiley-Interscience, 1970.

Wenz, F. "Economic status, family anomie, and adolescent suicide potential." *Journal of psychology*, January 1978, *98*(1), 45–47.

White, Reba. "Suicide intent and death attitudes among adolescents: distinguishing suicidal from suidogenic attitudes." *Dissertation abstracts international*, June 1979, *39*(12-B).

Williams, C. A. "Community health nursing—what is it?" *Nursing outlook*, 1977, *25,* 250–254.

Wynne, E. "Beyond the discipline problem: youth suicide as a measure of alienation." *Phi Delta Kappan*, January 1978, *59*(5), 307–315.

Additional References

Bruch, H. *Eating disorders: obesity, anorexia nervosa, and the person within*. New York: Basic Books, 1973.

Chotiner, M., & Forrest, D.   "Adolescent school phobia: six controlled cases studied retrospectively." *Adolescence,* Winter 1974, *9*(36).

Cornuelle, R.   "Society may be kept moving by its misfits." *Psychology today,* 1975, *9*(6), 88.

Corcliero, J.   "Normal and pathological states in adolescence." Revue de neuropsychiatrie infantile et d'hygiene mental de l'enfance (English summary), October–November 1974, *22.*

Demas, R.   "Hysterical personality syndrome in adolescence." *Adolescence,* Fall 1973, *8*(31).

Derenne, R. T., & Tai, S. W.   "Social class, socialization and psychosomatic ailments in adolescents." *Journal of youth and adolescence,* 1975, *4*(3), 271–279.

Gallemore & Wilson.   "Adolescent maladjustment or affective disorder?" *American journal of psychiatry,* 1972, *29*(5).

Hendin, H.   "The new anomie." *Change,* 1975, *7*(9), 24–29.

Hersch, S.   "Suicide: youth's high vulnerability to it, signs to look for, how you can help." *MH,* 1975, *59*(3), 23–25.

Holzman, P. S., & Grinker, R. R.   "Schizophrenia in adolescence." *Journal of youth and adolescence,* 1974, *3*(4), 267–279.

Kelly, J. G., Snowden, L. R., & Munoz, R. F.   "Social and community interventions." *Annual review of psychology,* 1977, *28,* 323–361.

King, M.   "Evaluation and treatment of suicide-prone youth." *MH,* 1971, *55*(3), 344–350.

Kliman, G.   *Psychological emergencies of childhood.* New York: Grune & Stratton, 1971.

Lewis, J. M.   "The development of an inpatient adolescent service." *Adolescence,* *5*(19), 1970.

Lindsey, D.   "Adolescent pathways to residential treatment: the enforced expedition." *Adolescence,* Spring 1974, *9*(33), 135.

Miller, D.   *Adolescence: psychology, psychopathology, and psychotherapy.* New York: Jason Aronson, 1974.

Miller, J. P.   "Schooling and self-alienation: a conceptual view." *Journal of educational thought,* 1973, *7,* 105–120.

Morrison, G., & Collier, J.   "Family treatment approaches to suicidal children and adolescents." *Journal of the American academy of child psychiatry,* 1969, *8*(1), 140–153.

Payne, J.   "Slimming sickness," *Mental health,* Autumn 1970.

Pattee, C.   "Population characteristics and sex-role patterns in a youth-run crisis center." *Journal of youth and adolescence,* 1974, *3*(3), 231–246.

Rosenkrantz, A. L.   "A note on adolescent suicide: incidence, dynamics, and some suggestions for treatment." *Adolescence,* Summer 1978, *13*(50).

Smithson, W. S.   "Emotional maturity." *Mental hygiene,* 1974, *58*(1), 9–11.

Shaffer, D.   "Suicide in childhood and early adolescence." *Journal of child psychology and psychiatry and allied disciplines,* 1974, *15*(4), 275–291.

Stanley, E., & Barter, J.   "Adolescent suicidal behavior." *American journal of orthopsychiatry,* 1970, *40*(1), 87–96.

Toolan, J.   "Suicide in children and adolescents." *American journal of psychotherapy,* 1975, *29*(3), 339–344.

Thomas, G.   "Children in institutions." *Children today,* 1974, *3*(2), 34–35.

Warheit, G. J., Bell, R. A., & Schwab, J. J.   *Planning for change: needs assessment approaches.* National Institute of Mental Health, 1974.

Yusin, A.   "Attempted suicide in an adolescent: the resolution of an anxiety state." *Adolescence,* 1973, *8*(23), 17–28.

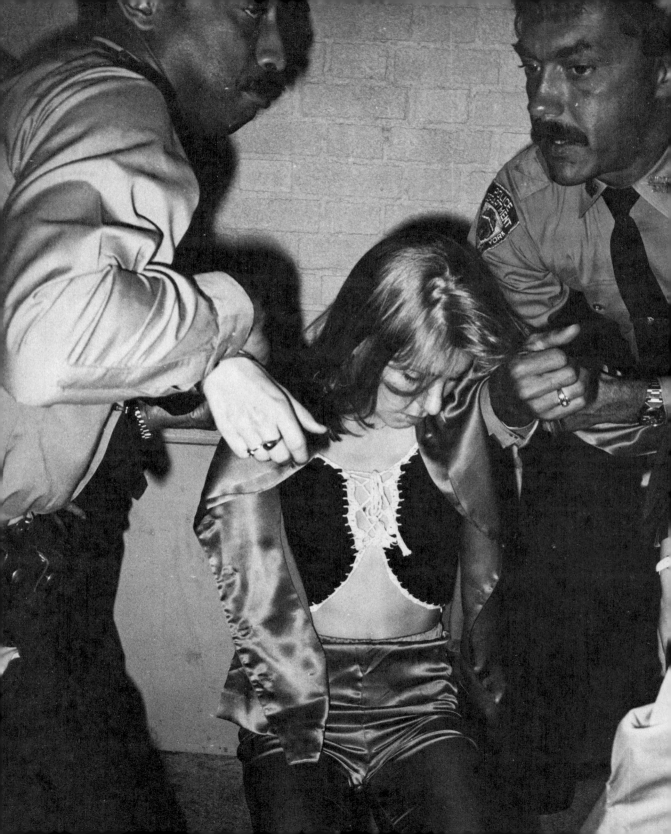

Chapter Twelve

Delinquent Behavior

Chapter Highlights

The Nonaggressive Status Offender
  The Runaway
  The Prostitute
The Juvenile Delinquent
  Juvenile Crime in Your Town
  Social Class and Delinquency
  A Personal Note
  Personality and Delinquency
  The Inadequate Family
  Delinquent Activities of Friends
  Long-Term Implications of
        Delinquent Behavior
Gangs
  Gangs and Social Class
  Characteristics of Gang Joiners
The Treatment of Delinquency
  The Behaviorist Approach
  The Psychotherapeutic Approach
  Halfway Houses
  The Ecological Approach
  Outward Bound
  The Diversion Program
  My Own Crime History
Summary

Key Terms and Concepts

nonaggressive status offender
juvenile delinquent
aggressive gang
juvenile statutes
neurotic delinquency
sociopathic delinquency
psychotic and organic delinquency
behaviorism
psychotherapy
halfway houses
ecological approach
Outward Bound
diversion program
primary reinforcers
secondary reinforcers
token system
residential care center
group therapy
recidivism
life-space interview

Important Person

Fritz Redl

People have always accused kids of getting away with murder. Now that is all too literally true. Across the U.S., a pattern of crime has emerged that is both perplexing and appalling. Many youngsters appear to be robbing and raping, maiming and murdering as casually as they go to a movie or join a pickup baseball game. A new, remorseless, mutant juvenile seems to have been born, and there is no more terrifying figure in America today.

— "Youth Crime Plague," 1977, p. 18.

When malicious damage is done to homes, schools, and other property in an urban ghetto, no one is surprised. But when these same acts start to occur in the quiet neighborhoods of suburbia, that's news. Or at least it was. Such behavior has been spreading in a frightening pattern which also includes rape, robbery, and even murder. More than half of all serious crimes are now committed by youths aged 10 to 17 (Swift, 1977).

Although juvenile delinquency has usually been differentiated from adult criminality only in terms of age (usually 18), this legal distinction is further refined here. In this chapter, adolescent delinquent behavior is distinguished according to three groups: **nonaggressive status offenders,** that is, persons who commit crimes that are mainly harmful to themselves (runaways, prostitutes); the **juvenile delinquent** acting alone, who usually commits theft or destruction to property; and the **aggressive gang,** which engages in a variety of illegal group activities.

THE NONAGGRESSIVE STATUS OFFENDER

Persons in this category are lawbreakers, technically, but they usually do not do physical harm to another person's body or property. Some have suggested that because their crimes are victimless, they should not be prosecuted. Parents of runaways or the wives of husbands who catch venereal disease from a prostitute often disagree. Females constitute the majority of teenagers in this category, although the number of males is growing.

The Runaway

According to the Department of Health, Education, and Welfare (Intradepartmental Committee on Runaway Youth, 1976), the number of children leaving home without permission of their parents has been increasing in recent years. They estimate that one out of ten 12- to 17-year-olds has run away from home at least once. This means that over two million youths have run away in the past ten years, 300,000 in 1975 alone (National Center for Health Statistics, 1975). Senator Birch Bayh (1973) stated in committee testimony:

> *Unlike Mark Twain's era, running away today is a phenomenon of our cities. Most runaways are young, inexperienced kids who run away to major urban areas . . . they often become easy victims of street gangs, drug pushers, and hardened criminals. Without adequate shelter and food, they are prey to a whole range of medical ills from upper respiratory infection to venereal disease.*

Bayh's committee estimates that runaways will soon number one million per year. When caught, most of them are still being jailed in most states. Their own resentment in combination with contact with experienced felons often leads them to become criminals themselves.

Why do children run away from home? The committee cites clashes with family members and the commission of petty crimes as major causes. They also note that 70 percent of the runaways interviewed have low achievement and little, if any, involvement with school. Runaways give as reasons the unfairness of laws which make it necessary to get parental permission for such behaviors as seeing a doctor of their choice or obtaining a job.

Although the problem of the runaway has been almost totally disregarded until recently, a number of services to runaways and their parents have been instituted in the last five years. Among these experiments are special services to runaways by youth agencies; toll-free phone numbers which are open on a twenty-four-hour basis to counsel runaways; school programs which explain the causes and problems of running away to teenagers; and conferences, training sessions, and literature made available to the parents of runaways (Justice and Duncan, 1976).

The Prostitute

> *"It's not so bad, honey," Sherry said. "Flatbackin' ain't the worst thing that can happen to ya." ("Little Ladies of the Night," 1977.)*

Although there are no reliable statistics concerning the number of teenage prostitutes, it is believed that teenage female prostitution has been growing in recent years, and that male teenage prostitution has been growing at an even faster rate (Roberts et al., 1973). There is a definite relationship between the number of runaways and the number of teenagers who turn to prostitution to support themselves. It has been difficult to determine the seriousness of this problem because of the variety of legal definitions of prostitution. "**Juvenile statutes** are phrased in such general terms that virtually any sexual act can be defined as a delinquent offense" (p. 168). Statistics may be distorted by the fact that most police officers are extremely reluctant to charge a female teenager with prostitution, but are much less hesitant to do so with a male.

Psychologists disagree as to the reasons that bring a teenager to prostitution (Kagan, 1969). The psychoanalytic school believes that prostitutes have a highly negative self-image, usually because of rejection by the father. Prostitution is a symbolic way to degrade oneself and a way to defend against the need for love. Prostitution also serves as the defense mechanism of compensation. It can make the teenager feel free of the internal conflicts and anxieties of being unloved. Psychosocial theory explains prostitution as a negative identity. It represents a rejection of society's values in general rather than a rejection of self.

Family problems are common in the prostitute's life. Freudenberger (1973) cites the case of an 11-year-old girl, Maria, who was introduced to prostitution by Dolores, an older girl. A member of a large family, Maria received little love or attention from her parents, but she was expected to be a useful provider for the family. She turned to Dolores, who enjoyed taking care of her. Maria became familiar with the prostitute's life and admired Dolores for it. When Dolores died from an overdose of drugs, Maria's sense of personal isolation and loss drove her to become a prostitute.

Money, drugs, and good times are other attractions of the prostitute's life which seem to be especially appealing to male prostitutes. One male teenage prostitute said that for him, the life offered the appeal of adventure and the risk of danger that is always found in a sexual encounter. He liked the "flashy, fast-paced way you can meet lots of interesting people" (Freudenberger, 1973, p. 11).

The old idea that most prostitutes are nymphomaniacs who simply cannot get enough sex seems to be pretty well discounted among the prostitutes themselves (Kurz, 1977). Kurz interviewed many teenage prostitutes and found that for almost all of them sex is decidedly unpleasant and something that they do only in order to get the money.

THE JUVENILE DELINQUENT

"In his eyes is the fixed stare of the blasted spirit" — *Ned O'Gorman*

Haskell and Yablonsky (1974) point out that the definition of the "delinquent youth" differs from state to state, town to town, and even among neighborhoods within a town. For example, in most areas, the law defines a juvenile offender as someone under 18 years old, but this age can be as low as 16 and as high as 21. The norms for delinquent behavior frequently depend on a youth's social class position. Cavan's criticism of legal definitions (1962) is relevant here:

In defining juvenile delinquency, laws are of little use. Usually laws are spe-

cific only in relation to serious adult offenses such as murder, assault, robbery, burglary, and so forth. Children are found guilty in court if they are found breaking any of the federal, state, or local laws designed to control adult behavior. Delinquency statistics, however, indicate these serious offenses account for only a small proportion of the delinquencies of children. Most of the behavior that gets a child into trouble with the police courts comes under a much less definite part of the law than delinquency. Examples are easy to find. The Illinois law defines as delinquent any child who is incorrigible, who is growing up in idleness, one who wanders about the streets in the nighttime without being on any lawful business, or one who is guilty of indecent or lascivious conduct (p. 38).

When a delinquent act is defined as the violation of legally established codes of conduct, delinquency includes a wide range of illegal behavior from misdemeanors to major crimes against persons and property. Only a small minority of American teenagers have committed major crimes, been arrested, or live a consistently delinquent way of life, but a large majority have committed an illegal act at least once. In their study, Kratcowski and Kratcowski (1975) found that at least three-quarters of male high school students had skipped school, driven without a license, had a fist fight, or gambled for money or objects. Nine-tenths of both males and females had bought or drunk liquor illegally. In this book, however, I will refer to delinquent behavior as the actions of the minority of teenagers who have committed serious crimes or are chronic delinquents. Not that these actions are insignificant; in the period between 1970 and 1975, violent crimes committed by male teenagers went up 24 percent; violent crimes by girls went up 40 percent ("Youth Crime Plague," 1978)!

During 1976, persons under 18 years of age were represented in 43 percent of all the arrests for crime index offenses (see Table 12–1). The arrest rates of persons under eighteen had gone up 1.7 percent between 1975 and 1976, while the arrest rates of persons under fifteen had gone down 1.1 percent. Since the age group 10–17 represents only about 15 percent of the population, the arrest record is disproportionately high and has not changed significantly since 1960.

Juvenile Crime in Your Town

Usually police courts keep records of juvenile offenders by age and class of crime, as shown in Table 12-1. Do you think that the statistics on juvenile crime in your town would compare closely to those given for the nation? You can get these data simply by calling the police force. If the statistics for your town differ greatly from the national ones, can you think of reasons why this would be so?

TABLE 12-1.
TOTAL ARRESTS BY AGE

(11,758 agencies; estimated population 204,622,000)

Offense Charged	Total All Ages	10 and Under	11–12	13–14	15	16	17	18	19
TOTAL	9,506,347	74,652	136,754	450,637	407,152	515,979	558,195	595,798	550,079
Percent distribution	100.0	.8	1.4	4.7	4.3	5.4	5.9	6.3	5.8
Murder and nonnegligent manslaughter	18,264	14	25	167	283	559	659	884	902
Forcible rape	29,164	66	183	832	900	1,213	1,457	1,801	1,701
Robbery	130,753	392	1,837	8,393	8,327	10,480	11,728	11,559	9,955
Aggravated assault	256,597	898	2,173	7,617	7,248	9,866	12,058	13,325	13,145
Burglary	468,085	9,366	17,215	55,122	46,620	50,508	48,849	41,524	32,041
Larceny-theft	1,098,398	23,037	44,947	114,236	81,749	90,788	89,296	78,170	62,013
Motor vehicle theft	143,654	466	2,164	15,569	17,213	18,842	16,422	12,241	9,228
Arson	18,387	1,669	1,289	2,275	1,440	1,276	1,063	959	754
Violent crime	434,778	1,370	4,218	17,009	16,758	22,118	25,902	27,569	25,703
Percent distribution	100.0	.3	1.0	3.9	3.9	5.1	6.0	6.3	5.9
Property crime	1,728,524	34,538	65,615	187,202	147,022	161,414	155,630	132,894	104,036
Percent distribution	100.0	2.0	3.8	10.8	8.5	9.3	9.0	7.7	6.0
Crime Index total[a]	2,163,302	35,908	69,833	204,211	163,780	183,532	181,532	160,463	129,739
Percent distribution	100.0	1.7	3.2	9.4	7.6	8.5	8.4	7.4	6.0
Other assaults	451,475	2,953	6,308	18,847	15,621	18,959	21,570	22,487	22,942

Forgery and counterfeiting	70,977	71	279	1,357	1,718	2,663	3,845	4,331	4,362
Fraud	243,461	105	241	1,224	1,417	1,985	3,400	6,551	9,090
Embezzlement	7,882	6	30	149	124	268	419	405	467
Stolen property; buying, receiving, possessing	107,621	583	1,851	7,744	7,333	8,802	9,317	9,082	7,695
Vandalism	239,246	13,230	16,018	32,712	21,990	23,173	22,480	16,628	12,870
Weapons; carrying, possessing, etc.	152,731	366	1,031	4,450	4,623	6,537	7,984	9,546	8,811
Prostitution and commercialized vice	83,088	24	46	303	487	781	1,678	4,742	7,468
Sex offenses (except forcible rape and prostitution)	62,633	382	839	2,996	2,250	2,290	2,611	2,719	2,762
Drug abuse violations	519,377	502	1,585	14,745	21,157	33,690	42,677	48,880	46,253
Gambling	50,974	15	31	220	357	618	866	1,106	1,293
Offenses against family and children	53,321	599	158	380	412	487	535	2,111	2,102
Driving under the influence	1,231,665	162	38	348	1,077	7,793	20,412	46,310	54,399
Liquor laws	386,957	195	715	9,451	20,009	44,101	64,815	65,282	48,265
Drunkenness	1,090,233	524	383	3,782	6,721	12,810	21,480	42,440	43,673
Disorderly conduct	711,730	3,318	6,839	22,023	22,180	30,508	40,668	51,514	48,425
Vagrancy	34,662	178	203	864	942	1,264	1,505	2,230	2,155
All other offenses (except traffic)	1,595,864	10,728	16,992	59,413	53,909	77,577	77,219	97,427	96,016
Suspicion	18,135	170	260	1,024	952	1,137	1,367	1,544	1,292
Curfew and loitering law violations	78,147	909	3,183	15,584	17,710	23,146	17,615	......	......
Runaways	152,866	3,724	9,891	48,810	42,383	33,858	14,200	......	......

a Crime Index = total of violent and property crimes.

Source: Federal Bureau of Investigation, 1981.

Social Class and Delinquency

Offenders come from all ethnic groups and environments, although many are nonwhite youths whose resentments are nurtured in the slums ("Youth Crime Plague," 1977). Frequently these children are victims of crimes themselves, having been abandoned or beaten by parents. There are indications that less than one-half of the children known to have committed acts classified as delinquent are punished. Social class has an effect on whether or not a behavior is classified as delinquent. Criminal behavior committed by middle-class children, as compared to lower-class children, more often goes undetected or is not recorded by enforcement agencies.

When younger delinquents are caught, the courts usually send them back out to the streets. In most courts, he or she is treated as if still an innocent child. Even if murder has been committed, the jail sentence will probably be no more than a few months. A New York teenager explained, during a radio interview, how he started at 12 years of age to rob old women. "I was young, and I knew I wasn't gonna get no big time. If you're doin' wrong, do it while you're young, because you won't do that much time" ("Youth Crime Plague," 1977, p. 19).

———————————— A PERSONAL NOTE ————————————

With the help of friends who are probation officers, I have often viewed at close hand the workings of a middle-class "kiddie court," as detractors call the juvenile legal system because of its notorious leniency. There are many problems that make it, in my opinion, hopelessly inept.

- Because prosecutors seldom have time or staff to investigate cases, previous arrest records and details of the present case are often not available.

- Long waits in court often make complainants and witnesses give up and leave, causing the case to be dismissed.

- Many complainants are ill-prepared to testify because youthful offenders often choose them as easy targets: the old, the very young, the sick and handicapped, the poor and uneducated.

- Often just the look on the face of the rage-filled defendant so terrifies the complainant that he or she decides not to testify.

- While some judges are amazingly lenient, others are fierce. I saw one 12-year-old sentenced to one month in the disturbed ward of the state mental hospital for "observation"—he had been caught sniffing cleaning fluid. Sobbing, he begged to be jailed. When I later asked the judge the reason for the sentence, he said, "I know the kid is sane, but maybe this will scare some of his rich, smart-aleck friends."

- Many probation officers are ineffective because they are overworked, lazy, or both.

Personality and Delinquency

It has been commonly accepted in psychiatry that symptoms in the adolescent such as bed wetting, fire setting, and cruelty to animals indicate the likelihood that the youth will grow into a violent adult. In a remarkably comprehensive study of this relationship (779 interviews with professionals and the review of 1000 case studies of troubled youth), Justice, Justice, and Kraft (1974) found that these early warning signs are actually rare and that most criminals do not evidence them. They discovered four other behaviors which were much more likely to be associated with later violence: excessive fighting, temper tantrums, inability to get along with others, and school problems and truancy. The authors point out that these behaviors are likely to be exhibited by all children at one time or another; any one does not indicate a violent adult. However, when all four behaviors appear together, there is a strong possibility that the teenager will become a violent adult.

Psychologists and others have identified three personality patterns associated with juvenile delinquency: **neurotic delinquency, sociopathic delinquency,** and **psychotic and organic delinquency.**

Neurotic delinquency. This personality pattern is symptomatic of an underlying personal or intrafamilial conflict. A neurotic delinquent commits illegal acts in order to communicate pressing needs that are being ignored or overlooked by the significant people in his or her environment. Such youths may violate the law because they feel a need to be caught and punished. They often harbor guilt feelings about previous transgressions, real or fantasized. Punishment for illegal acts may relieve the guilt feelings; for example, an adolescent who believes that masturbation is evil and sinful may compulsively steal unneeded things simply in order to be caught and punished. A youngster's ungratified need for affection, the need to be recognized, admired, and accorded status by family and peers, can be communicated through delinquent acts. Richard is an example:

> Richard is a 13-year-old boy who is attending a special school for behaviorally handicapped children in Boston. Sometimes Richard lives with his mother, sometimes he lives with his grandmother, and sometimes he lives on the street. He usually looks neglected and unkempt, he arrives at school with no socks, no coat, and holes in his clothing. He tries to kiss his female teachers and has asked each of them to adopt him. Even though his mother hasn't adequately cared for him, she does not want him to be placed in a foster home. After she learned that his social worker was trying to arrange foster care for Richard, his mother went to the mental health center with a knife, and told the receptionist that she wanted to "cut" the social worker. Recently, his father has involved Richard in drug dealing; his father pays Richard to "run" heroin. At school Richard seems to enjoy doing addition and multiplication problems and learning about fish. He is easily frustrated

and if he makes a mistake, he will stop working and disrupt the class. He has not learned how to read. He enjoys drawing pictures of fish and going fishing with one of his teachers.

Six months ago, when Richard was living on the street, he was caught committing two delinquent acts. He slashed the tires of his favorite teacher, the man who takes him fishing, and he broke into a pet store while attempting to steal tropical fish. He is being sent to a residential treatment center. Richard is a troubled adolescent whose delinquent behavior appears to be primarily psychologically caused. His parents foster his delinquent behavior and Richard seems to be crying out for help. It is evident that when Richard broke into the pet store he was not pulling an ordinary teenage prank, attempting to steal out of necessity, or engaging in motivated goal-oriented behavior learned from experience. Richard's violations of the law seem to be symptomatic of underlying deep personal conflicts.

Sociopathic delinquency. The personality of most sociopathic delinquents is characterized by impulsiveness, low frustration tolerance, and inadequate motivation. They exhibit an inability to accept blame, pathological lying, shallow and impersonal responses to sex, incapacity for love, and lack of guilt or remorse over wrongdoing. Of these personality characteristics, lack of guilt and incapacity for love are considered to be most important in identifying the sociopathic personality. David is an example:

David is a good-looking 14-year-old who attends the same school as Richard. His delinquent acts also appear to be primarily psychologically determined. David was referred to the special school by a public school because of his abusive, aggressive, and disruptive behavior. He was described as having problems relating to peers and adults, as well as wandering around the classroom and having a poor attention span. Prior to attending public school, David lived for two years in a residential treatment center where he was placed because of his delinquent behavior. While in the residential treatment center he received money in exchange for homosexual favors to older boys. While attending the special school David was living at home with his brothers, sisters, and mother. David claimed that his father had been murdered when he was nine years old. His mother claimed that David was lying and that his father was still living but she did not know his whereabouts. During an interview with her social worker, his mother expressed concern and love for her son, but explained that she was unable to control him. As an example she described a recent incident when David attacked one of his younger brothers with a knife and tried to cut off his fingers.

At school David has made a number of gains in all academic subjects. In science, math, and social studies he showed a good understanding of the materials and scored well on examinations. He proved himself to be an excellent athlete. He was both admired and feared by his classmates. Al-

though he was generally cooperative earlier in the year, David's lack of affect and constant smiling made the staff feel uneasy. After a few months it appeared that he was able to express his anger and frustrations in a more appropriate manner and that his relationships with his teachers were improving. There seemed to be a decrease in the amount of verbal and physical abuse in class which was directed toward peers. However, he continued to encourage other students to misbehave by manipulating them in an underhanded way.

These behavioral improvements were deceptive; when one of his teachers walked into the classroom, he found David exposing himself to the other students. David denied that he had done this. David viciously attacked several students in the gym locker room on the same day that he was found in a private shower with another male student. He denied attacking the other students. The next day David vandalized the cars of two staff members apparently without cause. Two days later David's mother withdrew him from the special school.

Psychotic and organic delinquency.   Neurotic and sociopathic personality patterns account for most delinquency, but in a small number of cases, psychotic and organic disturbances appear to be primary causes. Schizophrenic adolescents may use delinquent behavior as a defense against unrealistic fears of anxiety and annihilation. Organic factors that are considered to be of causal significance in some cases of antisocial behavior include mental retardation, minimal brain dysfunction, chromosome abnormality, and certain patterns of epileptic disturbance. Mentally retarded adolescents may fall prey to delinquent gangs that dominate and exploit them.

The personality patterns that characterize delinquent behavior often have their genesis in family relationships.

The Inadequate Family

> *"Our earth is degenerate. . . . children no longer obey their parents"*
> *— carved in stone 6000 years ago by an Egyptian priest.*

The family is, and for millennia has been, the social group that has the most influence on individual behavior. Negative feelings within the family or the sudden alteration of family life can create disturbances that lead to juvenile delinquency.

The function of the family in today's society is changing (see Chapter 6). The peer group is more important to the child as the family becomes less stable. Disturbed family relations play an important role in the causes of delinquency. Craig and Glick (1963) found three factors related to the increase in delinquency in boys: careless or inadequate supervision by the parents, erratic or overly strict discipline, and lack of cohesiveness of the family unit. Bandura and Walters (1959) and Bandura (1973) have reported similar findings. The child's position in the family and family size are also factors. The U.S. Census Bureau reports that the number of children living in single-parent homes has been increasing significantly in recent years. Gordon (1962) found that 30 to 60 percent of children regarded as juvenile delinquents come from broken homes. It may be that many parents are unable alone to raise their children adequately. However, absence of one parent may not affect the child as much as the tensions and fighting that caused the breakdown of the family's relationship. Chilton and Markle (1972) concluded:

> *Our study provides added empirical support for the conclusions of earlier investigators who have suggested that proportionately more children who come into contact with police agencies and with juvenile courts on delinquency charges live in disrupted families than do children in the general population. In addition, the study suggests that children charged with more serious misconduct more often come from incomplete families than children charged with less serious delinquency (p. 99).*

The child's ordinal position in the family has also been shown to affect the possibility of his being delinquent. Lees and Newson (1954) and Glueck and Glueck (1959) have shown that middle children are overrepresented in the delinquent populations. Middle children are most likely to be ignored in the family and therefore have the greatest need for attention and affection. Especially in large families, middle children may get squeezed out of the family and into gangs.

Discipline is important for a child, but only if administered for reasons understandable to the child. McCord and McCord (1963) report that consistency was more important than any particular degree of discipline.

The type of delinquency pattern that a youth will develop is also related to family background. Jenkins (1957, 1966) has distinguished between socialized and unsocialized aggressive patterns in lower-class adolescents. Socialized delinquency is motivated, goal-directed behavior. There is a specific cause for the criminal action taken. Unsocialized delinquency involves random violent acts which are committed for no specifiable reason. Unsocialized delinquents tend to be hostile and vengeful; these are youths who seem constantly to have "a chip on their shoulder." Socialized delinquents usually live in disorganized homes in deteriorated, high-delinquency neighborhoods. They grow up with a lack of parental guidance and supervision during their preadolescent years. They are loved and cared for by their mothers, but in more than one-half of their homes the father is absent. Unsocialized delinquents have a similar type of family background, but differ in that typically they have also experienced maternal rejection from infancy or early childhood.

Delinquent Activities of Friends

Many more delinquent activities go undetected than are discovered. As noted earlier, three-fourths of today's male adolescents have broken the law in some way.

Do you think that three-fourths of your male friends have been lawbreakers in their lives? How about your female friends? Of those who have committed a crime, how many got away with it? Ask your friends to tell you if they have ever broken the law, and make a list of those offenses below. Also note whether their crimes were discovered and whether they were found guilty and punished in some way. It might be interesting to compare your statistics with those of other people who have gathered the same information from their friends.

Laws Broken by My Friends	Undetected	Detected	Arrested	Found Guilty	Punished
_____	_____	_____	_____	_____	_____
_____	_____	_____	_____	_____	_____
_____	_____	_____	_____	_____	_____
_____	_____	_____	_____	_____	_____
_____	_____	_____	_____	_____	_____
_____	_____	_____	_____	_____	_____
_____	_____	_____	_____	_____	_____
_____	_____	_____	_____	_____	_____
_____	_____	_____	_____	_____	_____

Long-Term Implications of Delinquent Behavior

There are two ways to study the relationship between delinquency in children and later criminal behavior in adults: retrospective studies and follow-up studies. Retrospective studies generally look at a sample of adults with antisocial problems and review their childhood behavior through case histories and interviews. Follow-up studies select a population of children who come to the attention of various social agencies and study them years later to determine the relationship between their childhood problems and their adult adjustment.

Follow-up studies have found that it is the aggressive, openly hostile child who is likely to have serious antisocial behavior problems as an adult, rather than the shy, withdrawn child. In a thirty-year follow-up study of 524 child guidance clinic patients, Robins (1966) found that children who were referred to the clinic for speech difficulties, eating and sleeping disturbances, temper tantrums, and tics, and who were diagnosed primarily as *neurotic* resembled closely the one hundred "normal" control subjects as adults. The children who were referred to the clinic for *antisocial* behavior were mostly boys at about age 14 with a history of behavior problems dating back an average of seven years. In addition to juvenile theft, most of these antisocial children had a history of incorrigibility, truancy, running away, "bad" companions, and early sexual activity. Antisocial behavior in the adults could be predicted by the degree of juvenile antisocial behavior. Adults who had been antisocial children showed a high rate of arrests, alcoholism, poor job histories, dependency on social agencies, and psychiatric hospitalization.

GANGS

Gangs often offer youths the fulfillment of normal basic needs. Some of their functions clearly coincide with those of the larger society. Gangs typically provide protection, recognition of the desire to feel wanted, and rites of passage that mark achievement, status, and acceptance, such as the initiation rite of a potential gang member.

According to the New York City Youth Board, urban gangs possess the following characteristics: their behavior is normal for urban youths; they have a high degree of cohesion and organization; roles are clearly defined; they possess a consistent set of norms and expectations, clearly understood by all members; they clearly define leaders; and they have a coherent organization for gang warfare (Haskell and Yablonsky, 1974).

The gang provides many adolescents with a structured life they never had at home, as well as a sense of belongingness, security, and *consistency*. What makes the gang particularly cohesive is its function as a family substitute for adolescents whose strong dependency needs are displaced onto the peer group. The gang becomes a family to its members (Burton, 1978).

Gangs and Social Class

Twenty-five percent of all juvenile crimes are committed by urban gangs. Most of these gangs are highly organized, heavily armed, and decidedly not "queasy about the blood they spill" ("Youth Crime Plague," 1977, p. 23). Suburban gangs, on the other hand, or the few found in rural areas, are more loosely organized temporary alliances. Typically they seem to get their "kicks" from the malicious destruction of property.

Friedman et al. (1976), studying the victimization of youth by urban street gangs, found that "rituals of street gang warfare and the practices of victimizing both gang members and nonmembers by having them commit serious crimes and violent offenses may serve to maintain the continuity of the group, to give it structure, and to symbolize the gang's power of life and death over others." The gang becomes a vehicle for tearing its members away from the main social structures and authorities, in particular the family and school.

According to the President's Commission on Law Enforcement and the Administration of Justice (1967), as well as various reports from law enforcement officials (Ostrow, 1974), the incidence and severity of delinquent behavior is disproportionately high for slum and lower-class youth. Poverty, they find, is a factor contributing to gang crime. However, Haney and Gold (1973) found no strong relationship between social status and delinquent gang behavior. Tobias and LeBlanc (1977) report that the costs of damages caused by affluent male delinquents (typically running in a gang) have escalated tremendously in recent years. Probably social class matters less than it used to.

Characteristics of Gang Joiners

Why don't most adolescents join gangs? Klein (1971) notes several attributes that distinguish gang members from nonmembers. Gang members are much more likely to have divorced parents or parents with a criminal history. They are more likely to do poorly in school and score low on IQ tests. Friedman et al. (1976) reveal that the single most powerful characteristic differentiating the street gang member from the nonmember is the enjoyment of violence. Friedman's findings are in direct support of Klein's, who stressed the importance of "physical and verbal aggression as coping mechanisms on the part of gang members." Gang members also have more unrealistically high expectations of success, yet perceive less opportunity to be successful, than nonmembers (Burton, 1978).

THE TREATMENT OF DELINQUENCY

Until recently, punishment has been the main treatment for delinquency. It hasn't been very successful! Now there are new approaches to the treatment of delinquent behavior that offer some promise. Six of the most important ones are **behaviorism, psychotherapy, halfway houses,** the **ecological approach, Outward Bound,** and the **diversion program.**

The Behaviorist Approach

Behavior therapy or behavior modification is the application of learning theory to the elimination of deviant behavior. Behaviorists are not concerned with the internal feelings of individuals, but with observable behaviors; not with the conflicts that may be underlying juvenile delinquent behavior, but with its undesirable results.

Behaviorists use **primary** and **secondary reinforcers** to change behavior. Primary reinforcers are those that satisfy innate needs, such as for food and love.

Secondary reinforcers are stimuli such as plastic markers, awarded for appropriate behavior. Several markers can be traded for a candy bar. These markers, called tokens by behaviorists, become associated with primary reinforcers and in time acquire reinforcing properties of their own. In a **token system,** the desired behaviors are specified, and when performed, are reinforced with tokens.

Behavior therapy with delinquents began in the early 1960s. Positive reinforcement using the token system proved to be more successful than "do what we say or be punished." There are now several such programs for delinquents. For example, the California Youth Authority has set up several behavior modification programs. A study is being done in that state to compare the effectiveness of the token system used in one institution with the psychotherapeutic approach used in another institution.

A token system is an artificial system that does not conform to the real world. If social approval and self-reinforcement do not substitute for the reinforcing qualities of the tokens after a period of time, changes in behavior may not be maintained when the delinquent is released from an institution. One way to solve this problem may be to use halfway houses where there is a gradual replacement of the token system by natural community controls such as parents, friends, schools, and jobs. Another possible solution is to treat the delinquents within the community in the first place.

The Crossroads Program described here is based on a token system. It uses camping in the out-of-doors as a therapeutic setting. Crossroads was first conducted in the summer of 1977 at the Hale Reservation in Westwood, Massachusetts. Forty-three adolescents ranging in age from 11 to 14 were brought to the reservation in groups of fifteen for two-week intensive programs. Participants were selected on the basis of one or more of the following criteria: low school achievement, stealing, compulsive lying, hyperactivity, dependency on adults, participation in delinquent gangs, withdrawal from peer association, and, most importantly, a low self-image. These teenagers were recruited by school guidance counselors, social workers, and other members of the community. Most of the families in this community are on the lower socioeconomic level.

Activities in the program were based on the combined principles of Outward Bound (described later in this chapter) and the behavior modification token system. Activities included those in any typical camp — canoeing, hiking, and games — and activities especially designed for the program — rock climbing, rappeling, orienteering, and survival training. Participation in these activities, usually enjoyable to the youth, was not rewarded. Tokens were awarded on a daily basis for four other types of behavior: (1) "Run and dip." Everyone climbed out of the sleeping bag early in the morning, ran down to the lake, and jumped in as a group. (2) "Daily tasks." These tasks included gathering wood for the fire, carrying water, food preparation, garbage disposal, and clean-up of the cabin and grounds. (3) "Journal entry." Participants were required to write in their notebook every day their feelings about the events of that day. (4) "Service project." These projects, such as fixing broken fence posts and building a bridge over a stream, were aimed at encouraging group cooperation and at improving the surroundings.

The achievement of these activities was recorded each day and tokens passed out after the evening meal. Participants were allowed to either save their tokens or exchange them each day for items in the "token box," which held attractive articles of varying value.

The token system showed the teenagers that their actions can have immediate consequences. Since many of them come from environments that are disorderly and random, they typically do not expect their behavior to have predictable outcomes. The inability to recognize the connection between behavior and its effects is seen to be a major cause of juvenile delinquency.

In order to understand the extent to which participants increased their recognition of the effects of their behavior, they were administered the Locus of Control Test before and after the two-week sessions. This test measures the extent to which children take credit or blame for their behavior (see Chapter 11). There were clear-cut increases in recognition after each of the sessions. To that extent, the program may be said to have been successful. Investigations are now taking place to determine the long-term effects of this approach to delinquency.

The Psychotherapeutic Approach

Psychotherapy is the usual treatment when the delinquent acts of a teenager are believed to be symptomatic of severe internal conflicts. The aim of psychotherapy is to help the client gain clearer insights into his or her behavior and feelings. Although working through unconscious conflicts is important, psychotherapy with adolescents concentrates on strengthening the ego. "For an adolescent in search of an identity, overcoming the fears and failures of the moment is much more important than knowing the events that led up to them" (Miller, 1959, p. 774). An example of the psychotherapeutic approach, combined with environmental change, is a **residential care center** which I will call Delta House. Delta House represents a relatively new approach to the treatment of delinquency. Adolescent boys chosen for treatment are those who have committed a serious crime but whose attitudes indicate a desire to avoid the usual cycle of arrest, rearrest, and eventual conviction with a long prison term. This treatment is an alternative to "reform school." Residents in the program are nominated by the court system and selected by the staff on the basis of extensive interviews.

Delta House, a large mansion which was donated by a religious organization, is located thirty miles outside an eastern metropolitan area in a large wood adjacent to a lake.

On arriving, residents enter phase one of the program, in which their activities are considerably restricted. They may have only one phone call a week and must stay at the center at all times. If their behavior conforms to house rules, residents in phases two and three may vote that they be promoted to phase two. By the time a participant has reached phase three, he may receive unlimited phone calls, go home on weekends at will, and is gradually reentered into the community, although with frequent returns to the center. The average stay is nine months.

The daily schedule of the program is essential to its success. Life at the House is carefully regimented, with each participant taking part in the maintenance of the facility. The first half of the morning is spent in clean-up and repairs to the house. School occupies the rest of the morning, and in addition to the high school curricula, includes intense individual remedial instruction. Participants frequently make great strides in catching up with their age-mates in learning skills.

The afternoon is spent in **group therapy.** The premise of therapy is that most male delinquents commit crimes because they are trying to prove their masculinity. Most have ineffective or absent fathers. Without a strong male image, they frequently have serious doubts as to their own masculinity. The function of the therapy program is to help them understand that their self-doubts and, in fact, all of their emotions can be more effectively expressed through other than criminal acts.

Delta House has had a phenomenal success rate; less than 15 percent of its graduates have returned to the penal system (this is also known as a **recidivism** rate). Although it is an expensive approach to delinquency, it is ultimately much cheaper in money and human lives than prison. Recently a second house has opened, and plans are being made for others.

Halfway Houses

The halfway house is one way to help the offender who has been jailed to readjust and reconnect to society. Halfway houses serve as a temporary residence for released offenders and are usually located near the penal institution.

In the field of corrections, halfway houses exist for several purposes: for those just out of prison, as an alternative to prison, and as a place for offenders still under confinement (Haskell and Yablonsky, 1974).

The first government-sponsored halfway house was established in 1961. The U.S. Bureau of Prisons now operates fifteen community treatment centers across the country. Most halfway houses serve both males and females and are operated out of homes, apartments, or hotels. Prior to 1970, these facilities were limited only to those people scheduled for release from a correctional institution. Since then, halfway houses have come to be used as a condition of parole or probation in some cases. These community centers can serve several functions: they provide some continuity with education and training programs begun in the correctional institutions; they assist the offender in obtaining adequate employment; they increase use of community resources; and they provide needed support during this difficult period of adjustment.

Gruygier, Nease, and Anderson (1970) studied halfway houses, their methods of operation, and their effectiveness in reducing recidivism. They interviewed house directors and current and former residents to determine attitudes and recidivism rates. The residents had ambivalent feelings toward the staff. They were grateful for the staff's help and support, but on the other hand they often condemned themselves for needing help and projected this hatred on the staff. The study found that small differences exist between the recidivism rates of halfway houses and parole programs. The lower rate for halfway houses is attributed to their more selective screening process. The researchers conclude that halfway houses are expensive to run and their effectiveness questionable.

The Ecological Approach

The ecological approach, borrowing its theory from biology, studies the interaction between individuals and their environments. Ecological intervention tries to improve the shared process that occurs between youths and their family, school, and community.

Psychotherapy focuses on individual psychological processes; interventions within the family and school are peripheral. In the behavior modification approach, the focus is on maladaptive behavior, which is changed through the systematic use of reinforcers. The ecological approach, on the other hand, attempts to influence the quality of the exchange between the teenager's personality, behavior, and environment. An example is the Earn-It program.

The Quincy, Massachusetts Earn-It program attempts to change the interaction between young offenders and their community. The offender pays back the victim or the community for his or her crime through either private employment or public service. Offenders are not merely *given* a second chance—they have to earn it.

Under a program instituted by Judge Albert Kramer, first offenders are made to pay for their crime in a way designed to increase their awareness of their role in society, while they compensate the victim. Funded with a $30,000 Law Enforcement Assistance grant, the program has resulted in thousands of dollars in compensation to specific victims or society at large. At the same time the offender is afforded a chance to earn a responsible place in society. This is facilitated by providing counseling and emotional support. Another benefit of Earn-It is the opportunity for offender and victim to come to know each other as human beings, through meetings that often have a maturing effect on the juvenile and a sobering one on the victim.

In Judge Kramer's words, "Every criminal act is a breach. Unless the person who causes that breach faces the consequences of what he's done and realizes that he has intruded on the rights of other human beings, that breach remains. People are responsible for their actions. If a person is to have self-esteem, he must accept that responsibility."

Another example of the ecological approach is the **life-space interview.** Fritz Redl is a psychologist and educator who has worked primarily with aggressive children. He has founded and directed Pioneer House, the Detroit Group Project, and the Detroit Group Project Summer Camp, and has written three books about working with children. Although he describes himself as a Freudian, his approach has much in common with the ecological model.

Redl and Wineman (1965) emphasize that the environment is a factor contributing to emotional disturbance and therefore is important in treating emotional disturbance. He says that children who hate are those who have been exposed to traumatic events (beatings, divorce, desertion) and for whom several factors were missing from their environment (feelings of being loved, opportunities for making community ties, adequate economic security). In treating delinquency, the environment must be designed or redesigned to fit the child's capacities.

Redl developed the life-space interview as a treatment method. The interview is different from traditional therapy, which is conducted in an office at a designated time by a social worker, psychologist, or psychiatrist. The life-space interview is conducted by someone who sees the youth regularly, such as a group leader or a teacher, and as close in time as possible to the troublesome events in the youth's life, for example, immediately following a youngster's arrest.

There are two goals for a life-space interview: a clinical understanding of the event and emotional first-aid on the spot. The interview is used to help the teenager come to grips with the reasons for the deviant behavior. The adult might help the adolescent articulate such deep and long-standing feelings as physical inadequacy, point out certain recurring behavior such as lying, or may step in to umpire a fight between two youngsters in order to bring it to the level of a discussion.

Anyone who plans to work with juvenile delinquents should read Fritz Redl. His books include many practical suggestions of techniques for working with aggressive delinquent teenagers.

Outward Bound

The Outward Bound program was founded in England in 1941 to increase the possibility of survival of merchant seamen whose ships were torpedoed. It was learned that many sailors died primarily because they became paralyzed with fear when their ship was hit and were incapable of actions that could have saved their lives. A program was designed to prepare the men to handle their fears in dangerous situations, and it was so successful that after the war it was redesigned for much broader use. Its basic premise is that as people learn to deal with their fears by participating in a series of increasingly threatening experiences, their sense of self-worth increases and they feel better able to rely on themselves.

The program teaches the skills necessary to deal with such potentially dangerous experiences as mountain climbing and rappeling and living alone on an island for several days. Some of the experiences in the month-long program also involve cooperation of small groups to meet a challenge (see Chapter 9).

Outward Bound has grown rapidly in recent years and has installations throughout the United States. Each program emphasizes the use of its particular surroundings. For example, the Colorado program plans experiences in rock climbing, rappeling, and mountaineering. The Hurricane Island program in Maine uses sailing on the ocean as its major challenge. The Minnesota program emphasizes reflection and development of appropriate spiritual needs.

Outward Bound has proven its special worth for teenagers (Blake, 1977; Kelly and Baer, 1971). Originally a program for boys, most of its sessions now include equal numbers of girls. The program operates as a basic rite of passage in that it offers a chance to prove one's self-worth and to have this feeling validated by others. The philosophy of the program is that people cannot be told what they are capable of, but must discover it for themselves.

What are the chances that the Outward Bound experience can effectively reduce recidivism rates? Kelly and Baer (1971) have provided the only major study to date. They compared 120 delinquent males who were sent to Outward Bound with another group who were either institutionalized or paroled immediately after having been found guilty. These youths were between 15½ and 17 years old, which seems to be an ideal age for participation in Outward Bound because the teenagers are capable of negotiating these challenging experiences but are not yet old enough to have become hardened criminals. Kelly and Baer found that one year after the experience, 42 percent of the non-Outward Bound group had been found guilty of another crime. Only 20 percent of the teenagers who went to Outward Bound returned to crime.

In a study conducted five years later, however, Kelly and Baer found that the advantages of Outward Bound had decreased considerably. Apparently, it is necessary to follow up on the initial experience in order to maintain the original effectiveness.

These authors also found that different Outward Bound programs had different success rates. The Colorado program had no recidivism, the Hurricane Island program had 11 percent recidivism, and the Minnesota program had a 42 percent rate, the same as for the non-Outward Bound group. Apparently programs that emphasize action are more successful than those with an intellectual approach.

Although there is a lack of evidence on the effects of Outward Bound, there is no scarcity of testimony from the participants themselves. As one short teenager said, "Size really doesn't matter up there. What really counts is determination and self-confidence that you can do it!" Many graduates say that they find life less stressful and feel more confident about their everyday activities as a result of participating in Outward Bound. One of the most positive sides of the program is its effect on women. Many say that they are surprised to discover that they can count on themselves much more than they thought they could before going through the experience.

Although more evidence must be gathered, the potential of the Outward Bound approach to treating juvenile delinquents is very exciting. Comparing the approach to the past successes of the Boy Scouts with suburban youth, one proponent said, "That stuff about 'On my honor, I will do my best' is beautiful, especially if you can make it a reality for inner-city children!"

The Diversion Program

In a number of cities, there is an attempt to make not only the sentence but the entire legal treatment of offenders fit their crime. Under the diversion program, youths who are first offenders and whose crime did not involve bodily harm are not sent to court at all. Instead they are remanded to the care of a specially trained diversion officer.

This officer's responsibility is to try to divert the youth from the common pattern of recurring crime and arrest, through such means as conferences with the family and school officials in an effort to rectify the causes that originally led to the offense, and involving the youth in alternative activities. Often the job calls for acting as a big brother or sister to the teenager.

My Own Crime History

All of us have broken at least some minor law once in our lives, and for most of us, breaking the law makes us feel guilty. When you feel guilty, there is a good chance that you will repress the experience out of your memory, pushing it down into the subconscious. In this exercise, try to remember whether or not you have ever broken the law. In the first column, make a list of the things you have done in your life that were illegal. In the second column, list those things that you almost did, or were tempted to do.

Illegal Activities   Temptations to Break the Law

_____   _____

_____   _____

_____   _____

_____   _____

_____   _____

_____   _____

_____   _____

_____   _____

_____   _____

_____   _____

How do you feel about these activities now? Did you worry about them at the time that you did them? If you feel any regret, was there more then or now? Were these activities things that you only did as a teenager or do you continue to do them? Does breaking the law make you more or less sympathetic with those who do?

SUMMARY

There is no one definition of delinquency, just as there is no one theory of etiology or one treatment approach. Delinquency can be divided into three patterns of behavior: the nonaggressive status offender (mostly runaways and prostitutes); the juvenile delinquent (mainly those who, acting alone, commit crimes of theft and property destruction); and the aggressive gang.

In examining the demographic composition of delinquents, we see an age range of 10 through 17 years and individuals from all social classes and ethnic groups. The critical factor is that adolescents from a lower-class background tend to be caught and prosecuted for their delinquent acts, whereas many of those committed by middle-class youths are overlooked by law enforcement officers. Adult adjustment and behavior patterns are definitely related to early delinquent problems. Robins found that it is "the aggressive, openly hostile child" who is more likely to continue the same behavior pattern as an adult, rather than the withdrawn antisocial child.

In examining the roots of delinquency, three specific personality patterns emerge: (1) neurotic delinquency, in which the acting-out behavior is symptomatic of an underlying personal or intrafamilial conflict; (2) sociopathic delinquency, in which the adolescent, unlike his neurotic counterpart, is incapable of forming interpersonal relationships, acts impulsively, has a low frustration level, a lack of motivation, and a basic inability to accept blame, to show remorse, or to profit from experience; and (3) psychotic and organic delinquency, in which, in the former case, the schizophrenic adolescent uses acting-out behavior as a defense against unrealistic fears, and, in the latter, the occurrence of delinquent behaviors is a result of mental retardation, minimal brain dysfunction, or some type of epilepsy.

Another source of delinquent problems is rooted in the family unit and is influenced by the following: inconsistent discipline, careless or inadequate parental supervision, the child's ordinal position in the family, a breakdown in family communications, and failure of socialization as a result of disorganized homes, exposure to delinquent subcultures, a lack of parental guidance and supervision, and, in more than half the homes, an absent father.

The adolescent's membership in a gang is often an attempt to fulfill frustrated needs. Gangs provide the adolescent with rites of passage, faddism, protection, recognition of the desire to feel wanted, role definition, a clear set of norms and expectations, and leaders. The adolescent within the gang feels a sense of belongingness and security. Acceptance is guaranteed to members who conform to the specified code of behavior.

In view of the ineffective court systems, the high recidivism rate, and the inadequate penal system, it is apparent that more effective interventions need to be made with delinquents. Six treatment approaches to delinquent behavior are the following:

1. The behaviorist approach is the application of learning theory to the elimination of deviant behavior. The main goal is to promote observable behavioral changes. The method used to accomplish this is positive reinforcement, based upon utilizing primary reinforcers (food, praise, and the like) and secondary reinforcers, usually tokens associated with a primary reinforcer, to increase the probability of the recurrence of the desired behavior.

2. Long-term psychotherapy is employed when delinquent acts are believed to be symptomatic of severe underlying conflicts, as with the sociopathic delinquent or the neurotic delinquent. The approach here is to strengthen the adolescent's ego by dealing with the present (as opposed to delving into the past, as one would do with an adult in psychotherapy) and working with the youth to overcome his fears and anxieties.

3. Halfway houses have been established in an attempt to facilitate the offender's transition from jail to society, or as an attempt to provide a real option to incarceration. They provide some continuity with prison educational and training programs, assist in finding jobs and in using community resources, and offer greatly needed support.

4. The ecological approach attempts to influence the quality of the exchange between the child and his regular environment. Here the offender is expected to "own" his behavior, to face the consequences of his acts, and to recompense appropriately.

5. The life-space interview also emphasizes the environment as a therapeutic tool. However, the main therapeutic intervention is the immediate attention provided by an individual who is in regular contact with the youth (unlike in traditional therapy) from the time a troublesome event occurs. The thrust of the intervention is twofold—to provide clinical understanding of the event and to provide emotional first-aid on the spot.

6. Outward Bound is a program designed to increase adolescents' sense of self-worth and development of skills by placing them in survival situations. These situations vary according to the locale of the particular program, but may include living on an island alone, mountain climbing, rappeling, and the like. Outward Bound offers the adolescents a basic rite of passage through which they may prove their self-worth and have it reinforced by others.

Questions

1. What are the basic reasons adolescents turn to delinquency?
2. What four behaviors have been found to indicate the likelihood that a youth is beginning a life of crime?
3. What are the different types of delinquency?
4. What family inadequacies may contribute to delinquent behavior?
5. What are the good and bad effects of gangs?
6. What are some approaches to the treatment of delinquency?

References

Bandura, A. *Aggression: a social learning analysis.* Englewood Cliffs, N.J.: Prentice-Hall, 1973.

Bandura, A., & Walters, R. H. *Adolescent aggression.* New York: Ronald Press, 1959.

Bayh, B. *Runaway youth.* Washington, D.C.: U.S. Government Printing Office, 1973.

Blake, A. "Suburb under siege." *Boston Sunday globe,* May 1, 1977, 11 ff. (a)

Blake, A. "Outward bound: is the experience lasting?" *Boston Sunday globe,* October 2, 1977, 38–39. (b)

Burton, C. A. "Juvenile street gangs: predators and children." Unpublished paper, Boston College, 1978.

Cavan, R. S. *Juvenile delinquency.* New York: Lippincott, 1962.

Chilton, R., & Markle, G. "Family disruption, delinquent conduct, and the effect of subclassification." *American sociological review,* February 1972, *37,* 93–99.

Craig, M., & Glueck, S. J. "Ten years' experience with the *Glueck social prediction scale.*" *Crime and delinquency,* 1963, *24,* 231–242.

Federal Bureau of Investigation. *Uniform crime reports for the U.S.* Washington, D.C.: U.S. Government Printing Office, 1981.

Freudenberger, H. "A patient in need of mothering." *Psychoanalytic review,* Spring 1973, *60*(1), 7–14.

Friedman, C. J., Mann, F., & Friedman, A. "A profile of juvenile street gang members." *Adolescence,* Winter 1975, *10,* 563.

Friedman, C. J., Mann, F., & Adelman, H. "Juvenile street gangs: the victimization of youth." *Adolescence,* Winter 1976, *11,* 527.

Glueck, S., & Glueck, E. *Predicting delinquency and crime.* Cambridge, Mass.: Harvard University Press, 1959.

Gordon, I. J. *Human development: birth to adolescence.* New York: Harper & Row, 1962.

Gruygier, T., Nease, B., & Anderson, C. "An exploratory study of halfway houses." *Crime and delinquency,* July 1970, *16.*

Haney, B., & Gold, M. "Juvenile delinquent knowbody knows." *Psychology today,* September 1973, *7*(4), 48–52; 55.

Haskell, M. R., & Yablonsky, L. *Juvenile delinquency.* Chicago: Rand-McNally, 1974.

Intradepartmental Committee on Runaway Youth. *Runaway youth: a status report and summary of projects.* Washington, D.C.: U.S. Department of Health, Education, and Welfare, 1976.

Jenkins, R. "Motivation and frustration in delinquency." *American journal of orthopsychiatry,* 1957, *27,* 528–537.

Jenkins, R. "Psychiatric syndromes in children and their relation to family backgrounds." *American journal of orthopsychiatry,* 1966, *36,* 450–457.

Justice, B., & Duncan, D. "Running away: an epidemic problem of adolescence." *Adolescence,* 1976, *11*(53), 365–369.

Justice, B., Justice, R., & Kraft, I. "Early-warning signs of violence." *American journal of psychiatry,* April 1974, *131*(4), 457–459.

Kagan, H. "Prostitution and sexual promiscuity among adolescent female offenders." *Dissertation abstracts international,* 1969, *30*(5-B), 2421–2422.

Kelly, F., & Baer, D. "Physical challenges as a treatment for delinquency." *Crime and delinquency,* October 1971, 437–445.

Klein, M. W. *Street gangs and street workers.* Englewood Cliffs, N.J.: Prentice-Hall, 1971.

Kratcowski, P. C., & Kratcowski, J. E. "Changing patterns in the delinquent activities of boys and girls: a self-reported delinquency analysis." *Adolescence,* Spring 1975, *37,* 83–92.

Kurz, S. "Teenage prostitutes." *Equal times,* November 13, 1977, 6.

Lees, J. P., & Newson, L. T. "Family or sibship position and some aspects of juvenile delinquency." *British journal of delinquency,* 1954, *5,* 46–65.

"Little ladies of the night." ABC network television, January 16, 1977.

McCord, J., & McCord, W. "Family interaction as antecedent to the direction of mob aggression." *Journal of abnormal and social psychology,* 1963, *33,* 239–242.

Miller, W. "Short-term therapy with adolescents." *American journal of orthopsychiatry,* 1959, *29,* 772–779.

Miller, W. "The rumble this time." *Psychology today,* May 1977, *10*(12), 52.

National Center for Health Statistics. *Self-reported health behavior and attitude of youth 12–17, United States.* Washington, D.C.: U.S. Government Printing Office, 1975. (PHS 1000, Series 11, No. 8).

Ostrow, R. J. "Soaring crime rate is severe setback: Saxbe warns U.S." *Los Angeles times,* August 28, 1974, Pt. I, 12.

President's Commission on Law Enforcement and the Administration of Justice. *The challenge of crime in a free society.* Washington, D.C.: U.S. Government Printing Office, 1967.

Redl, F., & Wineman, D. *Children who hate.* New York: The Free Press, 1965.

Rice, B. "The new gangs of Chinatown." *Psychology today,* May 1977, *10*(12), 60.

Roberts, R. E., Abrams, L., & Finch, J. R. "Delinquent sexual behavior among adolescents." *Medical aspects of human sexuality,* January 1973, *7*(1), 162–183.

Robins, L. *Deviant children grown up.* New York: Williams & Wilkens, 1966.

Swift, P. "Inner city teens." *Parade,* September 18, 1977, 5.

Stumphauzer, J. "Modifying delinquent behavior: beginnings and current practices." *Adolescence,* Spring 1976, *11*(41).

Tobias, J., & LeBlanc, T. "Malicious destruction of property in the suburbs—1975." *Adolescence,* Spring 1977, *12*(45).

"Youth crime plague." *Time,* July 11, 1977, 18 ff.

Additional References

Adler, F. "The rise of the female crook." *Psychology today,* 1975, *9*(6), 42; 46; 48; 112–114.

Bandura, A., Ross, D., & Ross, S. A. "Transmission of aggression through imitation of aggressive models." *Journal of abnormal and social psychology,* 1961, *63,* 575–582.

Cox, W. B. "Crime and punishment on campus: an inner-city case." *Adolescence,* Summer 1978, *13*(50), 339–348.

Duncan, D. F. "Attitudes toward parents and delinquency in suburban adolescent males." *Adolescence,* Summer 1978, *13*(50), 365–370.

Farley, F. H., & Sewell, T.   "Attribution and achievement motivation differences between delinquent and non-delinquent black adolescents." *Adolescence,* Fall 1975, *10*(39), 391–398.

Gagnon, J. H., & Simon, W.   "They're going to learn in the street anyway." *Psychology today,* 1969, *3*(2), 46–47; 71.

Goldmeier, Harold.   "Vandalism: the effects of unmanageable confrontations." *Adolescence,* Spring 1974, *9*(33), 49–56.

Hanraty, M. A., O'Neal, E., & Sulzer, J. L.   "Effect of frustration upon initiation of aggression." *Journal of personality and social psychology,* 1972, *21,* 30–34.

Harris, J. R.   "A participant observer study: the everyday life of a group of delinquent boys." *Adolescence,* Spring 1974, *9*(33), 31–48.

Howell, M. C., Emmons, E. B., & Frank, D. A.   "Reminiscences of runaway adolescents." *American journal of orthopsychiatry,* 1973, *43*(5), 840–853.

Irwin, T.   "Juvenile delinquency—curing the St. Louis blues." *Psychology today,* 1975, *9*(6), 38–39.

Miller, J.   "Short-term therapy with adolescents." *American journal of orthopsychiatry,* 1959, *29,* 770–772.

"New program to reduce delinquency."   *Intellect,* 1975, *104*(2367), 9–10.

Novotony, E. S., & Burstein, M.   "Public school adjustment of delinquent boys after release from a juvenile corrective institution." *Journal of youth and adolescence,* 1974, *3*(1), 49–60.

Polier, J. W.   "Myths and realities in the search for juvenile justice: a statement by the Honorable Justice Wise Polier." *Harvard educational review,* 1974, *44*(1), 112–124.

Redl, F.   *Understanding children's behavior.* New York: Columbia University, 1954.

Redl, F.   *The aggressive child.* Glencoe, Ill: Free Press, 1957.

Redl, F.   *Mental hygiene in teaching.* 2nd ed. New York: Harcourt, Brace, 1959.

Redl, F.   *When we deal with children.* New York: Free Press, 1967.

Runaway youth: A status report and summary of projects (as of March 1976). Intradepartmental Committee on Runaway Youth, U.S. Department of Health, Education, and Welfare.

"Sharpest spurt ever in violence, theft." *U.S. news and world report,* 1975, *79*(21), 82.

"Violence and culture." *Intellect,* 1975, *104*(2368), 74.

Welsh, R. S.   "Severe parental punishment and delinquency: a developmental theory." *Journal of child clinical psychology,* 1974, *3.*

Wolf, S., & Brandon, J.   "Runaway adolescents' perceptions of parents and self." *Adolescence,* Summer 1977, *12*(46), 175–188.

Chapter Thirteen

Values

Chapter Highlights

Raths's and Simon's Theory of Values
Religious Values
   How Religious Are You?
   Cultural Influences
   Participation and Belief
   The Family's Influence on Religion
   Religious Education
   Stages of Religious Growth
   The Conversion and Confirmation
      Experience
   Religious Revival
The Effect of the Media on Values
   The Media and Aggressiveness
   Television and Other Values
The Effect of Music on Values
The Acquisition of Values
Values Clarification Techniques
   Values Clarification Strategies
   Things I Like to Do
   An Evaluation of Values Clarification
A Comparison of Values Clarification
     and Moral Education
   A Personal Position
Summary

Key Terms and Concepts

learning disabilities
delay of gratification
dogmatism
pluralism
Judeo-Christian dogma
multidimensional
bar/bas mitzvah
confirmation
ritualistic behavior
revival
deprogramming
values clarification

Important People

James Fowler
Louis Raths
Sidney Simon

A lot of older people shake their heads and say kids don't have good values like they did. I don't think we have bad values—I think a lot of kids don't know what their values are, so they just try out being different things. It's not their fault—they just don't know what to do.

—Kevin, age 16

Underlying each person's ethical beliefs and behavior is his or her system of values, that is, the estimation of worth that person puts on all of the various aspects of life. As with morality (see Chapter 5), many educators, psychologists, and sociologists are finding that the values of a majority of today's youth suffer from a lack of clarity and harmony. The first researchers to investigate this problem in depth have been the late Louis Raths and Sidney Simon.

RATHS'S AND SIMON'S THEORY OF VALUES

Values can be likened to guidelines that give direction to life. When a person's guidelines are blurred, he or she is conflicted and has difficulty making decisions. People who have clear values, on the other hand, tend to be positive, purposeful, and enthusiastic about life.

In the 1950s, Raths became convinced that unclear values were causing difficulties for our youth. Schools, he argued, dealt effectively with physical handicaps, emotional disturbance, and **learning disabilities**, but seemed to be helpless in the face of a fourth deterrent to learning, lack of motivation. Raths believed lack of motivation often stems from personal confusion about values. People who are unclear about their values tend to be flighty, inconsistent, apathetic, overconforming or overdissenting, indecisive, and hence less motivated to learn.

Many youth are confused about their values today (Simon et al., 1972). How has this come about? In large measure, it is due to the confusion of choice that afflicts us all from the bombardment of ideas from television, radio, and print, as well as exposure to the myriad human contacts that urban society and modern communication make possible. As Simon and his associates at the University of Massachusetts put it:

The children and youth of today are confronted by many more choices than in previous generations. . . . Modern society has made them less provincial and more sophisticated, but the complexity of these times has made the act of choosing infinitely more difficult (p. 15).

What is meant by the term *value?* Ideally, a complete value is defined by seven processes (Raths et al., 1966):

1. *Prizing and cherishing.* If we truly value something, we have a sense of happiness about it. We are proud to be the kind of person who has such a value.

2. *Publicly affirming, when appropriate.* If we are proud of a value we hold, we readily let others know we feel that way.

3. *Choosing from alternatives.* A value we hold because there are no other alternatives is no value at all.

4. *Choosing after consideration of consequences.* Only when we have given careful thought to the results of our decision can we be said to have a true value.

5. *Choosing freely.* If we are forced by circumstances to take a particular position, it cannot be said to be our own value.

6. *Acting.* Often we hear people say that they hold a particular value, but they are unwilling to act on it. A real value is one on which we are willing to take action.

7. *Acting with pattern, consistency, and repetition.* In the case of a true value, people who know us recognize that this is the way we regularly act.

Clearly, we should not expect each criterion to apply to the entire value system of the adolescent. These seven characteristics serve mainly as a description of the fully formed value. However, the more of these seven criteria that apply to a value, the more deeply and completely that value is a part of the individual's personality.

Raths, Simon, and their associates have suggested several ways in which values may be formed and clarified. Before discussing these, however, let us look at the recent research on several important value areas: religion, the media, and music.

RELIGIOUS VALUES

Though their goals are often confused and inarticulate, they converge on a passionate yearning for openness and immediacy of experience (Keniston, 1968, p. 386).

This statement, written of adolescents at the end of the turbulent '60s, rings true today. It is at the core of the adolescent conflict over religion. Traditional religion emphasizes dogmatic acceptance of principles and **delay of gratification** — even until the afterlife — which contrasts sharply with "openness and immediacy." This clash of values has led to a steady decline in the adolescent's interest and participation in religion (Potvin, et al., 1976).* This decline is a cause for concern, if for no other reason than that religious participation is correlated with (though not necessarily the cause of) personal control and avoidance of deviant behavior (Rohrbaugh and Jessor, 1975).

Adolescents are probably the most religiously devout of all age groups. This period, however, is also a time of questioning, doubt, and increasing alienation. "As the adolescent moves toward independence, he feels compelled to examine and reconstruct the religious beliefs given him by his family" (Knight, 1969). The adolescent struggles to define his or her identity and in so doing recognizes the possibility of conflict between emerging selfhood and the social order. The end result is often a pervasive ambivalence toward both self and society (Keniston, 1970). Religion reflects this ambivalence. "American youth . . . take a 'hedging stance.' There is tremendous diversity in religious interests on the continuum of no religiosity to deep religiosity" (Bealer and Willets, 1967, p. 441).

How Religious Are You?

The statements below deal with religious attitudes. To get a general idea of your own religiosity, put a check in the appropriate column for each statement: SA for Strongly Agree, A for Agree, DK for Don't Know, D for Disagree, or SD for Strongly Disagree.

	SA	A	DK	D	SD
1. Sometimes I feel there is an outside force guiding me.	—	—	—	—	—
2. Science can never unravel all the intricacies of nature.	—	—	—	—	—
3. There are some things you must do whether you want to or not, because God expects it.	—	—	—	—	—
4. I believe death is not the end of everything.	—	—	—	—	—
5. Humankind has the power and the right to control the evolutionary destiny of the human species.	—	—	—	—	—
6. When I long desperately for something beyond my reach, I feel hopelessness.	—	—	—	—	—
7. Tradition should no longer be an important force in our lives.	—	—	—	—	—

*One study ("Survey of College Freshmen," 1974) indicates a slight reversal of this trend.

8. There are no absolute truths; everything is relative.   __ __ __ __ __

9. Everybody and everything is in this world for a reason, known or unknown.   __ __ __ __ __

10. The reaches of the starry universe are unfathomable.   __ __ __ __ __

11. There is good to be found in every person.   __ __ __ __ __

12. Life is an unexplainable gift.   __ __ __ __ __

13. My having lived will not matter in the long run.   __ __ __ __ __

Give yourself 5 points for each statement with which you strongly agreed, 4 for each with which you agreed, 3 for a "don't know," 2 for a "disagree," and 1 for a "strongly disagree." Items 5, 6, 7, 8, and 13 are exceptions; they should be scored just the opposite. Maximum score is 65. Although administration of this scale has been limited, moderate religiosity is probably indicated by a score of around 30. The higher your score, the more religious you are.

Note: The above scoring scale was adapted from Boyle, 1978.

Cultural Influences

The American adolescent develops in a democratic and secular society whose values encourage moral development and inhibit religious **dogmatism** (Kohlberg, 1975). The **pluralism** of religious denominations in the United States means not only the tolerance of religious groups other than one's own, but the acceptance that other groups have a moral right to flourish (Clark and Clark, 1972).

As a result of large-scale immigration, urban neighborhoods in the United States characteristically were segregated by nationality and religion. Contact with opposing views and beliefs of other religious groups was limited and frequently hostile. As schools and neighborhoods became increasingly integrated, children were exposed earlier to religious differences and learned earlier to question and doubt what they were taught. Religious authority was undermined, a situation enhanced by more permissive and evolving social mores.

"What's it all about?" is a recurrent theme of songs popular with adolescents. The teenager questions and ponders the meaning and value of life, relations with others, and God. Friends and peer groups exert a growing influence on thinking and behavior. Lasseigne (1975), in a cleverly designed study of adolescent conformity, found a significant rise in peer influence on religious views from 1964 to 1974. Correspondingly, the influence of adults has lessened. Intellectually, adolescents are developing their ability to think abstractly. Hypothetical questioning, growing disbelief in the unexplainable, and dissatisfaction with previously held dogma increases throughout adolescence.

Participation and Belief

Argyle and Beit-Hallahmi (1975) have suggested that the adolescent years between 12 and 18 are a period of religious awakening, during which people either become converted and devoted participants in formal religion, or decide to abandon their childhood faith, if they had one. The conflict between faith and reason reaches a peak at about age 17 and is generally resolved one way or the other by age 20. A personal crisis, such as the death of a loved one, may hasten a resolution; the absence of a crisis may indefinitely postpone it.

Potvin et al. (1976) conducted a survey of the religious beliefs of 1140 adolescents. Seventy percent believed firmly in a personal God, 20 percent were doubtful but believed in some higher power, and 10 percent held no belief in God. Belief in God has dropped 10 percent since the 1950s, when 99 percent of youths surveyed indicated some belief. Along with the decline in traditional orthodoxy among American adolescents there has been a decline in attendance at religious services. Weekly church attendance dropped precipitously from 70 percent in 1962 to 44 percent in 1975. Of those who do attend church, 45 percent are Catholic, 43 percent Protestant, and 10 percent Jewish.

In a study of adolescents' religious commitment, Bealer and Willets (1967) found that "the individual adolescent may be unwilling to risk social rejection by making public the doubts he has over religion. Consequently his behavior is likely to reflect, for the most part, a ritualistic performance of church attendance and an overt subscription to at least basic **Judeo-Christian dogma**" (p. 62). It would be interesting to repeat this study today. The apparent decline in religious practice may be balanced by an increase in the religious value of concern for others. Potvin et al. (1976) believe that adolescents are showing less concern for property rights and more sensitivity to personal rights; over 75 percent of the 13- to 18-year-olds they studied now say that they believe that treating persons of other races or nationalities as inferiors is always wrong.

The Family's Influence on Religion

There are three major factors that influence religious development: family, personal reflection, and education. The most important is the religious orientation of parents.

Parental influence is **multidimensional.** The quality of parent-child relationships in the child's early stages clearly influences the formation of concepts of God (Spilka, 1975). A child who experiences love and justice and forgiveness projects these attributes onto God; the child who experiences strong parental control and arbitrary authority imagines a punishing God. Potvin et al. (1976) found the association between parental and adolescent religious practice to be very strong: "There appears to be no substitute for a religious home environment and for religious instruction if adolescents are to remain committed to their religious heritage" (p. 173).

Religious Education

Religious textbooks of the major faiths have frequently ignored the developmental needs of their students (Boyle, 1978). In many books, young children are presented abstract concepts long before they have the ability to comprehend them. Preadolescents, whose religious instruction might best be served in discussion group activities and values clarification (described later in this chapter) are encouraged to fix their spiritual growth by the habit of rote prayer. And the searching adolescent who feels the need to question previously accepted beliefs is discouraged. If personal confrontation with religious truth is stifled, a decline in religiousness can be expected. An indication of decreasing interest in religion is the drop-out rate in courses in religion in public schools. Compared to 90 percent of 13- to 18-year-olds who studied religion in 1965, only 44 percent were doing so in 1975 (Potvin et al., 1976).

Stages of Religious Growth

There have been several attempts to map the natural stages of religious development. Harms (1944) identified three stages of religious development of children, the last occurring in early adolescence: the fairy tale stage, the realistic stage, when earlier imaginings are rejected and explanations are given in terms of natural phenomena, and the individualistic stage, in which a person selects from religion that which satisfies his own needs and drives. Goldman (1964) also characterized three stages, calling them prereligious, subreligious, and religious.

Fowler's six stages of faith development.   James Fowler (1974, 1975 a and b) offers a theoretical framework built on the ideas of Piaget, Erikson, and Kohlberg. He believes strongly that cognitive and emotional needs are inseparable, when it comes to the development of spirituality. The spiritual cannot develop faster than the intellectual abilities, which rely on personality development for fulfillment. Thus Fowler's theory of faith development emphasizes the role of the unconscious, of needs, and of personal strivings, as well as cognitive growth.

Fowler sees faith developing in six steps, the same number as in Kohlberg's theory. Fowler's stages do not necessarily parallel Kohlberg's, however. He says that the stages in faith development can be delayed indefinitely, but the person must have reached at least a certain minimal age at each stage in order to move on to a succeeding stage. His six stages are:

1. *Intuitive-projective faith.* Minimal age: 4 years. In this stage, the individual focuses on surface qualities, as portrayed by adult models. This stage depends to a great extent on fantasy — conceptions of God or a supreme being reflect a basic belief in magic.
2. *Mythical-literal faith.* Minimal age: 5 to 6 years. Fantasy ceases to be a primary source of knowledge at this stage, and verification of facts becomes necessary, at least to some extent. Verification comes not from actual experi-

ence, but from such authorities as teachers, parents, books, and traditions. Faith in this stage is mainly concrete, and depends heavily on stories told by highly credible storytellers. For example, the traditional story of Adam and Eve is taken quite literally.

3. *Poetic-conventional faith.* Minimal age: 12 to 13 years. The child is entering Piaget's codification stage. Faith is still conventional, and depends on a consensus of opinion of other, more authoritative persons. Now the person moves away from family influence and into new relationships, however. Faith begins to provide a coherent and meaningful synthesis of these relationships. There is an awareness of symbolism and more than one way of knowing truth. Commensurately, a decreasing dependence on the concrete aspects of spirituality occurs. Learned facts are still taken as the main source of information, but individuals in stage three begin to trust their own judgment and the quality of selected authorities. Nevertheless, they do not yet place full confidence in their own judgment.

4. *Individuating-reflective faith.* Minimal age: 18 to 19 years. Stage three fails to totally synthesize new areas of experience, because depending on others in the community does not always solve problems. Therefore individuals begin to assume responsibility for their own beliefs, attitudes, commitments, and lifestyle. The faith learned in earlier stages is now disregarded, and greater attention is paid to one's own experience. In those few individuals who are unable to relinquish their need for authority figures and charismatic personalities, there is a tendency to join and become completely devoted to clubs and cults.

5. *Paradoxical-consolidation faith.* Minimal age: 30. In this stage the polarity of such elements of faith as symbols, rituals, and beliefs starts to become understood and consolidated. The person begins to realize that articles of faith can be understood on a number of levels of awareness. In recognizing these aspects, individuals increasingly value each. Furthermore, stage five persons come to accept differing cultural traditions. They can recognize that others' approaches to dealing with such complex questions as the supernatural and supreme being can be equally valid. The individual at this stage considers all people to belong to the same universal community and has a true regard for the human race.

6. *Universalizing faith.* Minimal age: 40 years. As with Kohlberg's final stage, very few people ever reach this level. Here the individual lives in the real world, but is not of it. Such persons do not merely recognize the mutuality of existence; they act on the basis of it. People at this stage appear to be truly genuine, and lack the need to "save face" that exists at the lower stages.

Fowler's description of stage seven compares closely to a hypothetical stage seven of morality proposed by Kohlberg (see Chapter 5). Although he has never studied persons at a stage seven level of morality, Kohlberg believes that theoretically there should be a stage for those few persons who rise above the purely cognitive, and achieve a place where they transcend logic. These individuals, who are rare indeed, come to an understanding of why one should be just and ethical in a world that is unjust. A burning love of universal humankind presses them always to act in truly moral ways.

The development of spirituality and morality appears to be parallel all along the sequence, especially in Kohlberg's and Fowler's models. At the early levels, the orientation is basically selfish. Ethical thinking and behavior are virtually nonexistent. The child is "good" only in order to please more powerful persons. At the second two levels, concern for the opinion of the community in general takes over. "What will people think!" is uppermost in religion as well as moral decisions. Only if and when the highest levels are reached do true spirituality and morality emerge. And for a few individuals at the highest level, stage seven, (perhaps, for example, Abraham Lincoln or Eleanor Roosevelt), the distinction between the moral and the spiritual no longer exists.

The Conversion and Confirmation Experience

Today's American adolescents prepare longer for the responsibilities and status of adulthood than any such group in the past and some in the present. Simpler cultures successfully initiate their children into adulthood early in adolescence. American culture, on the other hand, demands continuing education and financial dependence on families for longer periods of time. Laws prohibit voting, conscription, marriage, and other responsibilities of adulthood before the age of 18.

Yet most of the major religions in America expect a firm commitment to religious life at age 13—the Jewish **bar** or **bas mitzvah** at age 13, and Catholic and Protestant confirmation at age 12 or 13. Fundamentalist Protestant sects demand a conversion experience, a "rebirth," to occur between 12 and 17. A National Sunday School Association study of youth who had gone through a conversion showed steady growth through the high school years in their commitment to the conservative, evangelical doctrines of their sect, in contrast to confirmed adolescents, the majority of whom evidenced "backsliding." Clark and Clark (1972) infer from this that sects that demand an unquestioning faith get a less-questioning faithful. Perhaps a more important factor may be that conversion is individual and experiential, as well as generally occurring in older adolescents. In contrast, the **confirmation** process is **ritualistic** and the decision to confirm generally made by the parents or by age attainment rather than by individual decision.

Religious Revival

I had never in my life prayed before, but with help, still sitting on that bench, we held each other's hands and I asked the Light, my Saviour Jesus to come into my heart! What words can express total freedom! I had been dead in my sins but now I was a new person! I was really alive! ("The Love That Came—and Stayed!" *1978, p. 18).*

The suggestion of a religious revival among American adolescents in the mid-'70s is not sustained by data (Potvin et al., 1976). The notion of a **revival** may stem from a small minority's concern with mystical experience and the newer forms of religious expressions that have been widely publicized (such as Jesus freaks, the followers of Hari Krishna, guru Mahara Ji, and Reverend Sun Myung Moon). Such movements are largely concentrated among older youth, often university students and those who were dissatisfied with college life and left (Prince, 1974). Their motive often is a need for group intimacy that is satisfied by belonging to a small community. Most religious groups dictate a dogmatic lifestyle that satisfies the need of many adolescents to be loyal to some person or cause, while disdaining identity with one's former life. Finally, there is the idealistic potential of finding "the answer" and spreading "the word." The evangelical fervor of those who join, and the controversial technique for getting them to leave, called **deprogramming** (Patrick, 1976; Stoner and Parker, 1977, 1978), have served to promote the false impression of a major resurgence in religiousness. Hauser (1981) has criticized deprogramming as a violation of the adolescent's civil rights. He says that although it is designed to reunite families, it frequently does more harm than good. On the basis of his study of religious groups aimed at late adolescents, he states that "If joining a cult can straighten a person out, prevent suicide or harm from drugs, then it may be seen as a viable alternative. Some of their practices may come under suspicion, but many of the cults seem to be serving a positive function for our youth" (p. 317).

The American adolescent of today is not antireligious. His or her religious attitudes and practices seem to reflect the pervasive secularity of the '70s. There is a decline in formal ritualistic practices and a lessened desire for dogmatic information, but a heightened search for interpersonal belongingness. Immediate projections indicate a trend to different kinds of religious association—small, informal groups of people sharing interests and values, loosely connected by dogmatic belief. Given the present needs, attitudes, and values of adolescents, any other approach to increasing their religious participation seems doomed to failure. Whether any of the current religious denominations possess the desire and the ability to move in this direction remains to be seen.

THE EFFECT OF THE MEDIA ON VALUES

People who watch commercial television for any period of time will learn a number of aggressive tactics and countless methods of murder (Bandura, 1973, p. 101).

The Media and Aggressiveness

Is America a "cowboy country"? Do the media make youth value aggression and hostility? Do the media teach children to behave violently? These are questions that have been hotly debated and which have been the subject of considerable research. Several articles (Comstock, 1975; Liebert, Neale, and Davidson, 1973) have reviewed the studies, which give conflicting answers. It seems at this time that no conclusion can be reached with confidence. "As one shifts back and forth, there are few statements about these findings on which there would not be some agreement" (Comstock, 1975, p. 34). There appears to be no recent research on this topic.

Television and Other Values

Since we are unable to decide whether or not the media has any effect on adolescents' attitudes toward aggression, one might conclude that we may as well let our youth watch and read whatever they like, at least until all the evidence is in. This seems to be what the American parent is doing.

> By the time a child is 18, he or she has spent 11,000 hours in school—and 15,000 hours watching television. The average 18-year-old has used up the equivalent of more than two full years of his life mummified in front of the TV set (Torgerson, 1977, p. 4).

The conclusion that television has little effect on children's values in general is certainly *not* supported in the literature. If it does not clearly affect aggressive behavior, there are other areas in an adolescent's value structure that are affected by this heavy involvement with television.

Identification with TV characters. Although most children identify to some extent with their favorite TV characters, there is little evidence that this identification greatly affects their lives. However, as Feilitzen and Linne (1975) discovered, when children have less than an ideal family life, due to death, desertion, divorce, or extreme friction in the family, they tend to seek models in the media; such models have a much greater effect on their lives than would normally be the case. These children are much more likely to watch television to an excessive degree and usually prefer the more violent and bizarre subject matters offered. Other studies by these authors (Feilitzen and Linne, 1969; Feilitzen, 1972) confirm that frequent watchers are more likely to model their behavior after TV characters.

Occupational values. Children learn many of their values about the world of work from television. Dr. Terrel Bell, former U.S. Commissioner of Education, suggests that television is doing a rather poor job in this respect:

I think people ought to learn more about work, and the work that people do, through television. If a young person were to gain his or her impressions of work in this country exclusively from school and television (and some children are near this state today), that person might grow up believing that the only employed people in America are schoolteachers, cops, bus drivers, and Mary Tyler Moore. And sometimes I wonder if the big corporations— through the commercials we see—couldn't help young people in making these decisions. There's a lot you can learn in thirty to sixty seconds (Bell, quoted in Weisman, 1976, p. 13).

Personal relationship values. A fairly recent development is the commitment of teenagers to daytime serials, or "soaps." There has been a considerable increase in the number of teenagers who enjoy these afternoon programs, especially those who are in college. One freshman said, "I wouldn't think of scheduling classes that would conflict with 'Days of Our Lives.' " Some universities are now offering courses on the dramas seen on daytime TV (Collins, 1975).

How accurate a view of adult relationships do teenagers get from watching daytime television? It is hard to say, but it seems likely to be a distorted view. Take, for example, the relationships between the key characters on "Another World":

Iris Harrington has been married three times. Her first husband is now in Alaska working on a pipeline. Their son, Dennis Harrington, has a best friend named Jamie Frame. Jamie's mother, Rachael, is married to Iris' father, Mackinsey Corey. This means that Jamie's stepfather is also Dennis's grandfather. Rachael's second husband, Stephen Frame, Jamie's father, died in a plane crash. However, he did not know that Jamie was his son for quite a while, because Rachael was having an affair with him while she was still married to her first husband, Russ. Both Russ and Stephen assumed that Jamie was Russ's son. Before Stephen died, he divorced Rachael and married Alice. Alice's brother is Russ, Rachael's first husband. So Stephen and Russ, who were both fighting over Rachael's love as well as Jamie's, then became brothers-in-law. And so it goes.

Collins's research indicated that by the time children are in the ninth grade, most are capable of retelling the complicated plots of these stories with amazing accuracy. What is there that makes adolescents willing to devote so much energy to soap operas? Teenagers seem to enjoy dealing with problems and difficulties others have, because it makes them feel less alone in their own problems. As actress Ruth Warrick of "All My Children" explains it, "I think these programs provide an antidote to the alienation which is threatening to take over our lives" (quoted in Furlong, 1977).

Attitudes toward mental illness. A final problem of the effects of television on teenage values has to do with the portrayal of mental illness, primarily on police, detective, and doctor programs. People with emotional problems are often inaccurately portrayed, through both simplification and exaggeration. Adolescents who may have similar reactions to those of mentally ill characters can become confused and even panic-stricken. Many teenagers worry unnecessarily about whether they are developing into pathological murderers, rapists, arsonists, homosexuals, alcoholics, or drug addicts. Wahl (1976) has listed six myths about mental illness reinforced by television and the movies:

"Psychiatrists are omniscient." Psychologists, psychiatrists, and other experts are too often portrayed as being infallible in their diagnoses. Some of these professionals are able to tell the sex, age, motivations, and even childhood histories of criminal offenders from mere scraps of information about the crime itself. Courtrooms employ handwriting experts who are able to deduce with uncanny perfection the characteristics of hostility, depression, and inadequacy in the writer. Wahl states: "This myth of psychiatric omnipotence . . . can be a very harmful one. The false belief that one cannot get near a mental health professional without exposing one's innermost self makes the psychiatrist a very threatening figure" (p. 4).

"Confrontation always equals a cure." Many television physicians insist that if patients are forced to confront the negative results of their behavior, they will automatically gain insight into it and will return to model citizenship. Too bad it doesn't work like that in real life!

"Schizophrenia means a split personality." Films such as *Sybil, The Three Faces of Eve,* and TV programs give people the impression that split personality is relatively common when the truth is that it is really quite rare. Also, it is a neurotic disorder, while schizophrenia is a psychotic disorder characterized by hallucinations, delusions, thought irrationality, incoherence, and withdrawal symptoms.

"Conversion hysteria is about as common as measles." Conversion hysteria refers to the unconscious assumption of a physical disability, such as blindness, deafness, false pregnancy, or paralysis, in order to avoid dealing with an emotional problem. Although a popular plot on television, it is also rare in real life.

"Most murderers are uncontrollable psychopathic killers." Psychopaths are frequently portrayed as tormented individuals who are compelled to kill again and again because of their extremely violent emotional upheavals. In fact, psychopaths suffer from what is termed "moral insanity," which is the absence of feeling, compassion, and love for others. As police reports show, psychopaths are typically involved in burglary, forgeries, and crimes of property, but seldom in murder or rape.

"Mentally disturbed people are all dangerous." As most people find who visit mental hospitals or sanitariums, the people there tend to behave considerably more calmly than the average person (many are heavily tranquilized). Only a small percentage of the mentally disturbed are likely to attack others. This, like the other five myths of mental illness, is a serious distortion of reality and can be very harmful to the adolescent.

In summary, the effects of the media, particularly television, on adolescent values are largely negative. It is true that news documentaries, public service programs, public broadcasting stations, and in particular educational television, present a wide variety of valuable material. But only a tiny percentage of this programming is designed to attract the teenaged viewer, and so the impact is slight. It must be said that by and large, very few media presentations of any kind are successful in fostering positive adolescent values, and very few try.

THE EFFECT OF MUSIC ON VALUES

Although teenagers are interested in a wide variety of music styles, rock is beyond a doubt their favorite. The popularity of rock has its foundation, as do a number of adolescent values, in the black subculture — in particular, in the musical style known as rhythm and blues, which evokes "the simple, lively rhythms of Africa coupled with the sorrow and bitterness of slavery" (Yorke, 1976, p. 17). Rock also has wellsprings in folk music, which in the United States is largely a heritage from poor whites. It appears that adolescents, themselves a relatively powerless minority, have found it easy to identify with the sentiments of these other subordinate groups (Bely, 1972).

These two sources have influenced two separate branches of rock music. Folk music generated what is now called "soft" rock, which emphasizes lyrics. "Hard" rock sprang from rhythm and blues, with its emphasis on the beat. Most teens appear to enjoy both forms, but have some preference for one or the other.

Hard rock.   Pounding, insistent rhythm, overwhelming loudness, repetitious melodic lines, a certain sense of frenzy and abandonment, unintelligible words — these are the hallmarks of hard rock. Its appeal mystifies most adults, which probably enhances its already great appeal to teens. It makes communication almost impossible, discourages physical contact, and may ultimately impair hearing. So why is it so popular?

Williams (1978) suggests the answer lies in its sexual expressiveness. Youth are often starved for respect, intimacy, and love. Not achieving these, many substitute sex. For those who can't get sex, and in between times for those who do, the earthy, driving beat of hard rock is the best available substitute. Farfetched? Picture if you will a *Bee Gees* concert. The audience, especially the females, quickly builds to a screaming hysteria. "I love you!" The demanding stamping of feet adds to the ritual of love/sex. And, perhaps best of all, no commitment or involvement with the ecstatically loved idol is possible.

The emphasis in hard rock is on what one does not *have: love, sex, and self-respect. The music often achieves the same plaintive but frenetic sound as that of the lost child. Much has been made of the interpretation that hard rock is anti-adult, and of course it is. But it is not primarily a vehicle for social criticism. Hard rock is a means for the individual to become introspective, to grieve over the supposed loss of direction, dignity, and love. It is the ultimate expression of what has been called the "Me-generation" (Williams, 1978, pp. 7–8).*

Soft rock. One would expect soft rock, with its focus on ideas rather than raw emotion, to express different values than hard rock. Soft rock is different and it isn't, according to a study by Seltzer (1976). She analyzed the lyrics of the hundred most popular songs written by Joni Mitchell and Paul Simon, two of the most popular soft rock writers during the years 1968–1975. She found that the values expressed in soft rock lyrics are much more clearly stated; however, as with hard rock, these values indicate a definite involvement with self, and in particular with the negative side of life.

Almost no songs speak of fulfillment, mastery, or gratification. Perhaps people of this age have never bought songs that speak of those things. Perhaps they prefer to hear what is not usually discussed or expected of them. Hatred, emptiness, misery, pain, inadequacy, vulnerability, and awkwardness are not easy to articulate. Young people identify with someone else's expression of them. . . . There is no reference in the songs to work, as an activity; nothing to suggest that it might be an engaging, satisfying, or rewarding pursuit (p. 428).

The social concerns of youth in the '60s seem to have given way to more personal concerns in the '70s. Is this due to changing values in our culture in general? Seltzer doesn't think so. She advances the interesting hypothesis that the songwriters themselves are growing up and write lyrics which reflect their own maturation. They simply say well what their slightly younger followers are feeling; hence their popularity. According to this hypothesis, it is natural for youth to trade in the ideological, liberal values of their early teens for the more self-centered moderate values of their late (job-seeking) teens. Seltzer believes the counterculture of the past decade has had little real impact on adolescent values. "It seems that the anguish of 'becoming' is still felt by young people regardless of the cohesiveness of the peer group" (Seltzer, 1976, p. 428).

The only major value she found to have changed in the period studied was the attitude of youth toward their personal freedom.

[It] appears to have undergone a change from freedom "to do" to freedom "from." Value is now placed on freedom from struggle and structure. . . . Education, for example, is an institution that presents the individual with difficult tasks in a highly structured setting. If a value for personal freedom means a devaluing of education, the actual concept of freedom has changed in our society (p. 429).

THE ACQUISITION OF VALUES

There are five basic ways through which adults transmit values to the young.

Moralizing.   This is the most direct way. Children are told they should be "honest, clean, loyal, have self-control, and serve school and community." Kohlberg (1975) calls this the "bag of virtues" approach, and it can only be effective when everyone agrees as to which values are desirable. In former days there was much more of a values consensus; today many different groups and individuals compete with each other to convince our youth of the desirability of particular beliefs. This competition is a major cause of values confusion.

Hidden moral curriculum.   The "curriculum" is not explicitly taught, but through subtle suggestion students learn that it is important for them to be obedient and compliant to their teachers' will. Schools often stress conformity to authority and the status quo, and school management blends fear of punishment with concern for law and order, values that contradict the values of self-direction and democratic participation that are taught in civics and social studies classes.

Laissez-faire attitude.   Some feel that if we just leave children alone, they will acquire "appropriate" attitudes and values on their own. A growing number of parents express this attitude today. However, lack of direction only contributes to the many conflicts and confusions about values that young people feel.

Modeling.   The adolescent is not told what to think, but rather is presented with an attractive model of values (an admirable person) in the hope that imitation will occur. But what model to select? There are so many. The method suffers from the same defect as moralizing.

Values clarification.   Unlike the techniques above, **values clarification** does not aim to instill a particular set of values. Rather, it encourages students to apply the seven values processes (described in the beginning of this chapter) to their daily lives. Values clarification strives to help youth build their *own* value systems; it is based on the belief that unless adolescents struggle to develop their own ideas and attitudes, it is unlikely that they will arrive at solid values they can live by.

This approach is not entirely new; gifted teachers and religious leaders have been using it for a long time. In recent years, however, many new exercises have been designed to promote this process. Simon, et al. (1972) and Howe and Howe (1975) have collected over one hundred practical strategies which help teenagers become clearer about their values. Some of these are described in the next section.

VALUES CLARIFICATION TECHNIQUES

Teachers who practice values clarification are nondirective, that is, they never impose their own point of view on the assertions students make or the discussions that follow, as they believe this would impede the honest expression of values. They rely on the good sense and good will of the discussion group to prevail. They aim to promote (1) critical thinking, because it leads to rationality; (2) divergent thinking, because it leads to creativity; (3) moral judgment, because it leads to just behavior; and (4) free choice, because it leads to personal autonomy.

The topics covered in values clarification are virtually unlimited. They regularly include politics, religion, work, leisure time, school, family, love, sex, material possessions, drugs, culture, sanity, identity, death, health, war and peace, and race.

An example of the difference between traditional approaches to values and values clarification may be seen in the history of drug abuse prevention. Early programs lectured about the evils of drugs; the net effect was that more and more students became interested in trying them. Values clarification begins with the position that people have the right and the responsibility to decide for themselves what to do with their lives. In this approach, drugs and their effects are discussed, but no value position is taken by the instructor. If some students decide that drug usage is for them, no one preaches to them that their position is inappropriate. As you might suspect, the use of the values clarification approach in such areas as abortion, birth control, drugs, politics, and religion is highly controversial.

Things I Like To Do

Things I Like to Do	$	A/P	PL	N5	I	R	M	U	CH	1-5
1.										
2.										
3.										
4.										
5.										
6.										
7.										
8.										
9.										
10.										
11.										
12.										
13.										
14.										
15.										
16.										
17.										
18.										
19.										
20.										

Values Clarification Strategies

The following activities are adopted from Simon et al., 1972.

Things I like to do. For this activity, students complete the form on page 415. First, they fill out the lefthand column listing ten to twenty things they most like to do. Then they follow the instructions below.

1. In the first column, if the item costs more than $5 each time it is done, place a dollar sign after it.

2. If the item is usually done alone, the letter "A" is placed in the next column. If it is usually done with other people, a "P" is placed in this column instead.

3. The letters "PL" are placed after items which require planning ahead.

4. If the choice would not have been listed five years ago, an "N5" is placed in the next column.

5. An "I" is placed next to any item which involves intimacy.

6. An "R" is placed when the item has an element of risk.

7. An "M" is placed next to items you would not mind telling your mother about.

8. Put a "U" next to those activities that other people would say are unconventional.

9. A "CH" is put next to things which you hope your own children will do some day.

10. The numbers 1 through 5 are placed next to the favorite five activities.

After all students in the class have completed the activity, the instructor polls the class to find the average number of responses in each category for each activity. A discussion of the results and their implications then follows.

Values voting. The teacher asks a series of questions of the class, such as "How many of you . . . wish you were an only child?" Those who think the statement is true of them raise their hands; those who don't, point thumbs down; and those who are undecided, fold their arms. The teacher writes the vote for each question on the board according to the three possible responses. When the voting is completed, discussion starts. Some sample questions are: How many of you . . .

- think black people are as valuable as whites?
- would rather live some place else?
- like school?
- get enough sleep at night?
- plan to get married?
- believe in birth control?

Figure 13–1. Forced-Choice Staircase

- think there's much chance of improving the world?
- want to live to be older than 60?

Forced-choice staircase. The teacher suggests four to ten ideas, objects, happenings, facts, names, or the like, and asks the students to make a staircase with the same number of steps. For example, six holidays could be suggested (see Figure 13–1).

The students rank this list, writing their favorite on the top step, their next favorite immediately below, and so on, and the one they like least on the bottom. When everyone has completed the task, each student tells the reasons for his or her choices. Some examples are

- Doctor, lawyer, garbage collector, salesperson, housekeeper, bookie, belly dancer.
- Liar, cheat, bully, borrower, thief, flirt, phony, braggart, slob.
- Mother, father, brother, sister.

Value whips. This is a means by which students can see how others react to various issues. Someone poses a question to the class, then after allowing only a few minutes' thinking time, "whips" around the room calling on students to give their answers, on the assumption that speed of answering tends to promote honesty. Sample questions are:

- What is something you're proud of?
- What is a choice you made today?
- What is a favorite thing to do?
- What is something you're afraid of?
- What is something you hate?
- What is something you are ashamed of?

"I wonder" statements. This method is designed to stimulate probing, critical attitudes. Best used after some other value clarification exercise, it begins by asking the students to complete such sentences as these:

- I wonder if . . .
- I wonder about . . .
- I wonder why . . .
- I wonder when . . .

Brainstorming. The goal of this exercise is for the group to generate as many imaginative solutions to a problem as possible. Students are encouraged to respond quickly, avoiding criticism of their own ideas or those of the others; to respond often, because quantity tends to breed quality; to make humorous and even impractical suggestions, because even if such ideas are not useful, they often spark ones that are. Everyone should be urged to contribute; timid students frequently have excellent ideas. Some questions might be:

- How can we make this class a happier place to be?
- What would be an interesting topic for discussion?
- Who are the finest people in the world today?
- What are the worst things people do to each other?
- What is the best thing to do when you're bored? When you're scared?

Unfinished sentences. Students are asked to complete unfinished sentences, such as:

- If I had my own car, I would . . .
- I like it best when people . . .
- If I had a thousand dollars . . .
- Secretly I wish . . .
- It makes me cry when . . .
- The most exciting thing I can think of is . . .

Students then tell the class their responses, and comparisons among them are made.

Who comes to your house? Students list all the people they can remember who have come to their house during the past year. Next to the list of names, they make six columns, labeled R/F/O, M, *, X, S/D, and SR/DR. In the first column, students put an R if the person is a relative, an F if he is a friend, and O for others. In column two, they put an M if the person's manners bother them. In column three, they place a star next to the names of the persons they were really glad to see. In column four, they put an X next to names of persons they don't want to come back. In column five, they put an S or a D if the person's religion is the same or different from theirs. In column six, they put an SR or DR if the person's race is the same or different from theirs. The responses are analyzed to see what factors (relationship, manner, religion, race) are associated with one's likes and dislikes of people.

Baker's dozen. The teacher says, "Make a list of thirteen things you use around your house that run on electricity. If you can't think of thirteen, make a list of as many as you can. Draw lines through the things you don't really need. Now draw a circle around the three things you'd be lost without." A discussion, as usual, follows.

An Evaluation of Values Clarification

Values clarification has received a great deal of favorable interest in recent years, but it is not without its critics. The major criticism is that whereas teachers must never evaluate the values expressed by the students, nevertheless some students will espouse "unacceptable" values. For example, a student may say he thinks Hitler was right to order the murder of millions of Jews because Jews belong to an inferior race. Many feel that teachers should take a stand when our culture is so clearly opposed to such a value. Simon argues strongly that teachers must allow such value statements to stand, relying on group pressure to change the student's mind.

Another criticism is that values clarification allows teachers a subtle means to condition the students to choose particular values. Experience seems to indicate, however, that teachers try to influence values anyway, and that values clarification training makes them more likely to be aware of their own biases.

Educator John Stewart (1975) has added his own list of criticisms: (1) Values clarification is too shallow. It gets at the context (the what), but not the structure (the why) of values. (2) It pushes all members of the group toward acceptance of the average position. (3) The discussion of certain values, such as premarital sex, can be very embarrassing for some students. (4) Frequently the only students who really tell the truth about their values are the most popular ones who are most secure in the esteem of their peers. Often the others merely acquiesce. (5) When people, particularly teenagers, publicly agree to a value that they have not carefully thought out, they often rigidly refuse to change their minds even when faced with contrary evidence. (6) Raths's and Simon's criteria of values are extremely stringent. It would appear that according to their criteria, only saints have values. (7) Some of the activities betray a value bias of the designers.

A COMPARISON OF VALUES CLARIFICATION AND MORAL EDUCATION

Values clarification and moral education (see Chapter 5) are philosophically incompatible methods of education. Lawrence Kohlberg, the major proponent of moral education, strongly criticizes the values clarification approach. In values clarification, becoming more aware of one's values is an end in itself; teachers stress that values are different, rather than that one value is more adequate than another. Kohlberg believes that certain values are intrinsically more adequate. There is a hierarchy in moral reasoning, the highest stage of which is based on the universal principle of justice. Decisions based on this principle are better, because they are decisions on which all moral people would agree. The goal of this approach is not the clarification of values, but the stimulation of movement to the next higher stage of moral reasoning.

There are similarities between values clarification and the Kohlberg approach to moral education. Both methods oppose an indoctrination of moral beliefs. Teachers do not preach or impose their own values; adult "right answers" are not stressed. Students are not told that virtue is always rewarded. Teachers do not lecture; they guide peer discussions of moral dilemmas toward better understanding of moral judgment.

However, the values clarification method assumes that discussion itself will produce more highly principled values. The Kohlberg approach assumes that more highly principled values are only produced by changes in reasoning, which result from adults pointing out what these higher levels are.

A PERSONAL POSITION

I have used values clarification under many circumstances (in classrooms, around campfires, in informal conversations), and I am convinced it is an extremely valuable technique. Most of the time, teenagers can understand how it works and can benefit from participating in it.

But I agree with Kohlberg that some values simply should be discouraged; racial superiority is an example. Also, it should be remembered that while moral education does suggest what a higher level (than the students' present level) would be, no force is applied. Students can disagree. I feel that in some isolated situations it is neither realistic nor believable for teachers to act as though they have no ethical stand; this is a serious weakness of values clarification.

SUMMARY

There is considerable evidence that, in general, our values—the estimation of worth we place on the various aspects of life—are less clear than they used to be. Psychologists Raths and Simon have warned of the seriousness of values confusion among youths, which they suggest is primarily caused by the distracting assortment of ideas that come to them through the ever-expanding media. Raths stresses that lack of clarity regarding values causes youths to be "flighty, inconsistent . . . and hence less motivated to learn."

They define seven elements involved in the process of forming any given value. They are: prizing and cherishing; publicly affirming when appropriate;

choosing from alternatives; choosing after consideration of consequences; choosing freely; acting; and acting with pattern, consistency, and repetition. The more of these elements involved in the formation of a value, the more deeply held the value is.

Although adolescence is a period of questioning, religions traditionally have emphasized dogmatic acceptance of principles. This is a source of confusion in the formation of values. Declining church attendance among adolescents in this country is a reflection of their growing doubt that religion is helpful to them. While the much discussed "religious revival" of the past few years has actually been limited to a small percentage of youth, the American adolescent of today is not antireligious. There is a decline in religious formalism among youth, but "a heightened search for interpersonal belongingness."

Television, which constitutes 15,000 hours of the average 18-year-old's life experience, influences value formation through role models offered in plot characterizations, emphasis on sex and violence, treatment of social problems such as mental illness, and the coverage given news stories.

Popular music is also an important factor in the value development of most young people. There are two major forms of pop music — "soft rock," emphasizing lyrics; and "hard rock," which emphasizes a rhythmic beat. Much of the interest in hard rock has its basis in its driving sensuality — which may even provide a safe form of surrogate sex for adolescents. Whereas hard rock gives vent to physical feelings, soft rock is a form of intellectual and emotional release.

There are at least five basic ways in which values are acquired: through moralizing, a hidden moral curriculum, a laissez-faire attitude, modeling, and values clarification. The last of these, values clarification, does not instill values so much as it seeks to lend coherence to values as perceived and defined by the individual.

The values clarification techniques that parents or educators can use with youngsters attempt to promote critical thinking, because it leads to rationality; divergent thinking, because it leads to creativity; moral judgment, because it leads to just behavior; and free choice, because it leads to personal autonomy.

Kohlberg, a proponent of moral education, disagrees with the nonjudgmental approach of values clarification. He argues that some values should be discouraged, and that parents and educators should identify their ethical posture, especially when the values questioned are complex and difficult.

Questions

1. What are the processes by which values are chosen?
2. What are the models by which children acquire values?
3. What aspects of religion are adolescents interested in?
4. What effects has the influence of Eastern religions had on American culture today?
5. What impact have the media had on the adolescent's values?
6. According to values clarification techniques, how can teachers best help teenagers identify their values?
7. What are the differences between values clarification and moral education?

References

Adelson, J., & O'Neil, R. P. "Growth of political ideas in adolescence: the sense of community." In A. M. Orum (Ed.), *The seeds of politics.* Englewood Cliffs, N.J.: Prentice-Hall, 1972.

Ames, L. B. "Don't complain about t.v.—use it." *TV guide,* May 1-7, 1977, 2-4.

Argyle, M., & Beit-Hallahmi, B. *The social psychology of religion.* London: Routledge & Kegan Paul, 1975.

Balswick, J. O. "The Jesus people movement: a generational interpretation." *Journal of social issues,* 1974, *30*(3), 23-42.

Bandura, H. *Aggression: a social learning analysis.* Englewood Cliffs, N.J.: Prentice-Hall, 1973.

Bayer, A. E., & Dutton, J. E. "Trends in attitudes on political, social, and collegiate issues among college students: mid-1960's to mid-1970's." *Journal of higher education,* 1976, *68*(2), 123-134.

Bealer, R. C., & Willets, F. K. "The religious interests of American high school youth." *Religious education,* 1967, 62.

Berson, R. "The educational situation and the realm of values." *Educational theory,* 1975, *25,* 125-130.

Bely, C. *The story of rock* (2nd ed.). New York: Oxford University Press, 1972.

Boyle, J. "Religious attitudes in adolescence." Unpublished paper, Boston College, 1978.

Clark, S. M., & Clark, J. P. *Youth in modern society.* New York: Holt, Rinehart, & Winston, 1972.

Collins, W. A. "The developing child as viewer." *Journal of communication,* Autumn 1975, 35-44.

Comstock, G. "The evidence so far." *Journal of communication,* Autumn 1975, 25-34.

Feilitzen, C. "On the function of the broadcast media: radio and TV meet its audience." Stockholm, 1972, Sveriges Radio Forlag.

Feilitzen, C., & Linne, O. "A survey of 8-16-year-olds' media consumption and an intensive study of the functions of pop music and television." Stockholm, 1969, Sveriges Radio Forlag.

Feilitzen, C., & Linne, O. "Identifications with television characters." *Journal of communication,* Autumn 1975, 51-55.

Flacks, R. "The liberated generation: an exploration of the roots of student protest." In A. M. Orum (Ed.), *The seeds of politics.* Englewood Cliffs, N.J.: Prentice-Hall, 1972.

Fowler, J., Keen, S., & Berryman, J. *Life maps: the human journey of faith.* Needham, Mass.: Humanities Press, 1976.

Furlong, W. "You have to give the soaps credit." *TV guide,* May 14-20, 1977, 20-23.

Goldman, R. *Religious thinking from childhood to adolescence.* New York: Seabury, 1964.

Harms, E. "The development of religious experience in children." *American journal of sociology,* 1944, *50,* 112-122.

Hauser, J. "Adolescents and religion." *Adolescence,* Summer 1981, *16*(62), 309-320.

Hess, R. D., & Torney, J. V. *The development of political attitudes in children.* Chicago: Aldine, 1967.

Holloway, S. M., & Hornstein, H. A. "Good news makes us good." *Psychology today,* December 1976, 76-78; 106-108.

Howe, L. W., & Howe, M. M. *Personalizing education.* New York: Hart, 1975.

Kaiser, F. M., & Lilly, R. J. "Political attitudes among students: a small college experience." *Adolescence,* Summer 1975, *38,* 287–296.

Keniston, K. *The uncommitted.* New York: Harcourt, Brace & World, 1965.

Keniston, K. *Young radicals.* New York: Harcourt, Brace, Jovanovich, 1968.

Keniston, K. "Student activism, moral development, and morality." *American journal of orthopsychiatry,* 1970, *40*(4), 577–592.

Knight, J. A. "Adolescent development and religious values." *Pastoral psychology,* 1969, *20,* 39–43.

Kohlberg, L. "The cognitive-developmental approach to moral education." *Phi Delta Kappan,* 1975, *56*(10), 610–677.

Kraus, M. S. "School children's attitudes toward public authority figures." *Adolescence,* 1975, *10*(37), 111–122.

Lasseigne, M. "A study of peer and adult influence on moral beliefs in adolescence." *Adolescence,* Summer 1975, *38,* 227–230.

Leonard, G. "Beyond 'getting better'." *The graduate review (EST),* March 1977, 1–5.

Liebert, R. M., Neale, J. M., & Davidson, E. S. *"The early window": effects of television on children and youth.* Elmsford, New York: Pergamon Press, 1973.

"The love that came—and stayed!" *New nation news,* 1978, *1*(1), 17–20.

Maslow, A. *Toward a psychology of being.* New York: Van Nostrand, 1962.

Maslow, A. *Farther reaches of human nature.* New York: Viking, 1971.

New York Academic, 1971. *The control of aggression and violence,* Ginger, J. L. (Ed). Elmsford, N.Y.: Pergamon, 1973.

Patrick, T. *Let our children go.* New York: Dutton, 1976.

Potvin, R., Hoge, D., & Nelson, H. *Religion and American youth.* Washington, D.C.: Catholic University of America, the Boys Town Center for the Study of Youth Development, 1976.

Prince, R. "Cocoon work: an interpretation of the concern of contemporary youth with the mystical." In I. Zaretsky & M. Leone (Eds.), *Religious movements in contemporary America.* Princeton, N.J.: Princeton University Press, 1974.

Raths, L., Merrill, R., & Simon, S. *Values and teaching.* Columbus, Ohio: Merrill, 1966.

Rohrbaugh, J., & Jessor, R. "Religiosity in youth: a personal control against deviant behavior." *Journal of personality,* 1975, *43,* 136–155.

Ryals, K. "Classroom climate and value teaching." *Education, 94,* 1975, 354–359.

Seltzer, S. "Changing adolescent values as the lyrics of popular music." *Adolescence,* 1976, *11,* 419–429.

Siegal, R. S., & Brookes, M. H. "Affect for government and its relation to policy output among adolescents." *American journal of political science,* 1977, *21*(1), 111–134.

Simon, S., Howe, L. W., & Kirschenbaum, H. *Values clarification.* New York: Hart, 1972.

Spilka, A., & Rosencohn, H. "Parents, self and God: a test of competing theories of individual-religion relationships." *Review of religious research,* Spring 1975, *16,* 154–165.

Stewart, J. "Clarifying values clarification: a critique." *Phi Delta Kappan,* June 1975, 684–688.

Stoner, C., & Parker, J. H. *Reprogramming.* New York: Chilton, 1977.

Stoner, C., & Parker, J. H. "How to rescue your child from a cult." *Parade,* January 1, 1978.

"Survey of college freshmen." *Intellect,* 1974, *102*(2358), 482.

Swift, P. "Citizen dropout." *Parade,* September 4, 1977.

Torgerson, E. "What teenagers watch and why." *TV guide,* April 23–29, 1977, 4–7.

Wahl, O. "Six myths about mental illness." *TV guide,* March 13–19, 1976, 4–8.

Weisman, J.   "The test television is flunking." *TV guide,* May 15-21, 1976, 12-13.

Williams, F. R.   "Hard rock music and adolescent values." Unpublished paper, Boston College, 1978.

Yorke, R.   *The history of rock'n'roll.* Toronto: Metheun, 1976.

Additional References

Bellah, R. N.   "The new religious consciousness and the secular university." *Daedalus,* 1971, *1*(4), 110-115.

Bodemann, Y. M.   "Mystical, satanic, and chiliastic forces in countercultural movements. Changing the world—or reconciling it." *Youth and society,* 1974, *5*(4), 433-446.

Braungart, R. G., & Braungart, M. M.   "Protest attitudes and behavior among college youth. A U.S. case study." *Youth and society,* 1974, *6*(2), 219-248.

Drabman, R. S., & Thompson, M. H.   "Does violence breed indifference?" *Journal of communications,* Autumn 1975, 86-89.

Goranson, R. E.   "Media violence and aggressive behavior: a review of experimental research." In L. Berkowitz (Ed.), *Advances in social psychology* (Vol. 5). New York: Academic Press, 1970.

Harmon, J.   "The new music and counterculture values." *Youth and society,* 1976, *4*(1), 61-83.

Hoop, K.   "Why student apathy?" *American mercury,* 1974, *110*(514), 5-15.

Jeffries, V.   "Political generations and the acceptance or rejection of nuclear warfare." *Journal of social issues,* 1974, *30*(3), 119-136.

Keniston, K.   *Youth and dissent.* New York: Harcourt, Brace, Jovanovich, 1970.

Knox, Ian.   "Religion and the expectations of modern society toward the adolescent." *Religious education,* 1975, *70,* 649-660.

Kohlberg, L.   "Education, moral development, and faith." *Journal of moral education,* 1974, *4*(1), 5-16.

LaVoie, J. C., & Collins, B. R.   "Effect of youth culture music on high school students' academic performance." *Journal of youth and adolescence,* 1975, *4*(1), 57-65.

Leifer, A. D., Gordon, N. J., & Graves, E. B.   "Children's television more than mere entertainment." *Harvard educational review,* 1974, *44*(2), 213-245.

McMahon, M. B.   "Religion, scientific naturalism, and the myth of neutrality." *Intellect,* 1974, *102*(2357), 430-432.

Maller, A. S.   "Religious pluralism, political values and American teenagers." *Religious education,* 1974, *49*(4), 446-450.

Manaster, G. J.   *Adolescent development and the life tasks.* Boston: Allyn & Bacon, 1977.

Murray, J. P.   "Television in inner city homes: viewing behavior of young boys." In E. A. Rubenstein, G. A. Comstock, and J. P. Murray (Eds.), *Television and social behavior* (Vol. 4). Washington, D.C.: U.S. Government Printing Office, 1972.

Niebuhr, H.   *Experiential religion.* New York: Harper & Row, 1972.

Norton, D. L.   "The rites of passage from dependency to autonomy." *School review,* 1970, *79*(1), 19-41.

O'Kane, J. M.   "Student activists, downward mobility and social change." *Youth and society,* 1975, *6*(3), 376-392.

Olmo, B.   "The threat of new ideas: a values clarification lesson." *Adolescence,* Fall 1975, *10*(39), 456.

Quarter, J.   "Shifting ideologies among youth in Canada." *Youth and society,* 1974, *5*(4), 448-474.

Rohwer, W. D., Jr.   "Prime time for education: early childhood or adolescence?" *Harvard educational review,* 1971, *41*(3), 316–341.

Rutherford, J. A.   "Violence in the media." *Language arts,* October 1976, *53*(7), 793–794.

Scully, M. G.   "The job generation." *Intellectual digest,* 1974, *4*(10), 37.

Starr, J. M.   "The peace and love generation: changing attitudes toward sex and violence among college youth." *Journal of social issues,* 1974, *30*(2), 73–106.

Strauss, G. H.   "Two perspectives on high school student politics: political objects versus political actors." *Youth and society,* 1974, *5*(3), 360–376.

"Student apathy and cynicism."   *Intellect,* 1974, *102*(2358), 483.

"Today's high school kids are turned off by politics."   *Compact,* 1975, *9*(1), 27–28.

Vandermyn, G.   "Assessing students' political IQ." *American education,* 1974, *10*(5), 23–25.

Wagner, H.   "The adolescent and his religion." *Adolescence,* Summer 1978, *13*(50).

Weinberg, J., & Hiltz, T.   "Effects of independent religious study on religious interests of high school sophomores." *Religious education,* 1975, *70,* 416–477.

Wright, J. D.   "The socio-political attitudes of white, college-educated youth." *Youth and society,* 1975, *6*(3), 251–296.

Wuthnow, R., & Glock, C. Y.   "Religious loyalty defection and experimentation among college youth." *Journal for the scientific study of religion,* 1973, *12*(2), 157–180.

Wuthnow, R., & Glock, C. Y.   "The shifting focus of faith: a survey report, God in the gut." *Psychology today,* 1974, *8*(6), 131–136.

Yankelovich, D., & Clark, R.   "College and noncollege youth values." *Change,* 1974, *6*(7), 45–46.

"Youth's attitudes."   *Children today,* 1975, *4*(6), 14–15.

Chapter Fourteen

Adolescence Past, Present, and Future

Chapter Highlights

Adolescence Past
Adolescence Present
Adolescence Future
  New Ways of Dealing with
    Adolescents
  New Ways of Understanding
    Adolescents
Advice of Experts to Beginners
  Honesty
  Sense of Humor
  Tolerance

Clarity in Setting Limits
Paying Attention to the Withdrawn
  Child
Clarifying Values—Yours and Theirs
Communications Skills
Summary
  A Personal Note

Important People

Robert Grinder
George Leonard
Abraham Maslow

Each youth must forge for himself [and herself] some central perspective and direction, some working unity, out of the effective remnants of childhood and the hopes of an anticipated adulthood.
—Erikson, 1958, p. 14.

Growing up is no easy task, and today's adolescents certainly do not think it is. But, to repeat the question asked in the first chapter, is growing up in the last quarter-century all that different from before?

One of the best ways to see how adolescence today differs from past years is to compare the ways in which it has been described by writers then and now. In the next section, a description of adolescence past is compared with the present.

ADOLESCENCE PAST

In 1944, the Forty-third Yearbook of the National Society for the Study of Education was published (Jones, 1944). Entitled *Adolescence,* it assembled articles written by the major experts on the subject in that decade. In 1975, the Society published its Seventy-fourth Yearbook (Havighurst and Dreyer, 1975) on the same general topic. It is entitled *Youth,* and is a collection of the ideas of the major experts of this decade. As psychologist Robert Grinder (1975) documents in his epilogue to this latter book, there have been several highly significant changes in our thinking in this area over the thirty-one years that have intervened between these two publications. He particularly notes the following five:

Developmental age. In the earlier yearbook, the experts identified ages 10 to 22 as adolescent on the basis that this was the range within which the growth spurt occurred. They believed that coping with the psychological stress that results from puberty constituted the main teenage problem, and perhaps for that time, they were right. The 1975 writers divided the period into two sections: adolescence, 10–18; and youth, 19–25. This division was made primarily on the basis of the types of societal pressures with which young people must cope. Thus, the period of striving for maturity is now seen as taking longer and as resulting more from social than of biological factors. Grinder suggests that both groups of experts have accurately portrayed development as it occurred in the decade during which they were writing.

Consciousness of self. In the 1940s, teenagers viewed themselves strictly in comparison to other teenagers. They were "victims of the tyranny of the norm." They still make comparisons today, but now there is more concern over the role expectations they have for themselves as adults. "Anxiety, crisis, tension, and other aspects of personality discomfort are [currently] viewed as everyday inconveniences of coping in a highly complex, often obstructive society" (p. 439).

Alienation. Teenaged antagonism toward the world around them is seen as a serious problem in both yearbooks. However, in 1944, such feelings were believed to be limited primarily to lower-class families. Middle-class youth were pictured as having such a monopoly on privilege as to have little to be angry about. Alienation in 1975 is portrayed as much more widespread and as the result of depersonalization of society and institutional racism.

Outlook toward careers and work. The world of work was seen by most writers in the 1940s as fixed and predictable. Virtually any youth who had ambition could become a success by climbing the available ladder in any career. Youth in the 1970s face a far less stable situation. In addition, the goals of productivity, status, and achievement which were espoused so widely in the 1940s are seen as less desirable today. For about a third of modern youth, self-expression, challenge, and making a contribution to society matter more than simple material success.

Cultural limitations. Writers in the 1940s were far more ready to accept the necessity for curtailment of civil liberties and other life options than are theorists today.

ADOLESCENCE PRESENT

Apparently the answer to the question "Are adolescents today really different?" is "In some ways, yes, and in some ways, no." That has been the overall conclusion of this book, too.

In an effort to get at the very latest information about adolescents and the changes they are undergoing, my graduate students and I sent a fifty-item questionnaire to over one hundred people currently working closely with adolescents. We selected our respondents as carefully as possible so that they would be representative to a large extent of the thousands of persons working with teenagers in the United States today. Results were analyzed on the basis of four categories: male/female; metropolitan/nonmetropolitan; younger (11–14)/older (15–19); and typical/atypical. Those in the atypical category were, for example, in jail or in intensive therapy. This study, completed as this book was nearing completion, is described in detail in Appendix A (page 440). (In the update for this edition, almost no significant changes were found.) In most ways, our survey confirmed the results reported in the various chapters of this book. Some of these findings are described briefly below.

- Most teens are trying to make occupational choices earlier than was the case a few years ago.
- Conformity in dress, speech, and other behaviors has increased significantly.
- The great majority of youth today, male as well as female, anticipate getting married and having a family. (Such behavior was less popular in the 1960s.)
- The majority expect to marry without previously having lived with their spouse.
- The same percentage of girls (25 percent) now participate in athletics, and with as great enthusiasm as boys.
- More typical youth express a concern that they might commit suicide than atypical youth.
- The number of typical youth who exhibit risky, daredevil behavior is quite high (over half), and among atypical older youth, the practice is nearly unanimous.
- Virtually all atypical males, including the younger ones, drink, smoke, and use drugs heavily.
- More nonmetropolitan youth have stolen property worth more than $50 than have metropolitan youth. Differences between males and females are slight.
- The most important factor (of those offered) in adolescent popularity is physical appearance. Style of dress is second.
- The major reason (of those offered) teenagers *say* they take drugs is "to be popular with my friends."

A major question this survey was designed to answer was "Which of these four categories makes the most difference in terms of the forty-nine questions asked: younger/older; typical/atypical; male/female; metropolitan/nonmetropolitan?" Before reading on, try to guess which one it is. I have asked many of my colleagues, none of whom had seen the survey results, and none guessed correctly.

The answer is: typical/atypical. This category accounted for major distinctions on 45 of the 49 items in the survey. Some will say this is not surprising; after all, atypicals by definition are different from typicals. But so are the members of the other groups — apparently less so than one might have thought.

What is disturbing is that these youth are seen as being *so* different. It would be useful in our attempts to help them if we knew why. The survey seems to point to at least one major cause: atypicals are especially poor at *interpersonal communication*. They conform more than typicals, but it does them little good — they have great trouble joining groups. They very much want to marry, but have serious problems relating to their own parents and siblings. They are much more likely to give up on these relationships and run away from home.

This may have some implications for treatment: perhaps we should spend more time teaching these youngsters the communications skills and attitudes they seem to have missed out on and concentrate less on their specific symptoms — whether they are emotionally disturbed, physically or mentally handicapped, extremely intelligent or creative, or the aggressive member of a gang.

In the next section, a number of other suggestions for improving the adolescent condition are offered.

ADOLESCENCE FUTURE

The future of adolescence is not bright. The best prediction we can make is that unless action is taken quickly, it will become even dimmer. Such monumental problems as the breakup of the family, the loss of control in schools, and the disintegration of adult value systems are not likely to remedy themselves.

A number of suggestions have been made in this book as to what our society can do to improve the quality of adolescent life. In this section, a summary of those suggestions and their relationships is presented. The suggestions are of two types: new ways of dealing with adolescents, and new ways of understanding them.

New Ways of Dealing with Adolescents

Among the many ideas that have been advanced, five seem to be of major importance:

Rites of passage. As educator George Leonard (1977) puts it:

Young people in many old and wise cultures have been offered ordeals, rites of passage, at some age between 12 and 16 — something to give them a chance to go up against a challenge, to give up childhood. After the ordeal they have their lives reconstituted as an adult in a meaningful society. If we don't provide that kind of risk in socially sanctioned ways that bring young people back into the matrix of society, . . . they'll find their risks in socially destructive ways (p. 4).

Outward Bound and the walkabout are recommended as ways to achieve the rite of passage in our society.

Improving the educational system. Four major changes need to be made in our educational system. We should strike a better balance between teaching basic skills and providing youth with a liberalizing education; develop a continuing education system, so that education can proceed as a lifelong right and responsibility; provide opportunities for adults and adolescents to learn new skills together; and develop new curricula in several areas.

The areas in which new curricula are needed are the following: (1) Marriage and the family, including greatly improved courses in sex education. (2) Career education, which involves *all* courses throughout all of the grades in schools, and which places the responsibility for decision making in the hands of teenagers themselves. This effort may include the creation of new jobs specifically designed to meet the needs of adolescents. The apprenticeship model should be useful here. (3) Law and economics. (4) The psychology of adulthood, including an improved understanding of the prerequisites of mental health. (5) Communication skills, including a better understanding of the sociology of human interaction.

A revamped penal system. It can be said categorically that our penal system is an almost complete failure with adolescents. Several suggestions for revamping the criminal system are represented in Chapter 12. However, it is imperative that more innovations in this area be developed.

Encouraging family life. We need to encourage the success of the nuclear family and, as much as possible, the return of the extended family. Some of the forces that have contributed to the breakdown of the American family, such as the large percentage of mothers going to work full time, should not, and probably cannot, be discouraged. However, the following changes would be beneficial: (1) Families should be persuaded to stay in the same location during the childcaring years. Perhaps governmental reinforcements are needed here. (2) New working arrangements, so that fathers can be more involved in the raising of the family and mothers can work without penalizing their families, should be fostered by American industry. (3) More cooperation among families, and between families and social agencies, should be encouraged in the raising of children.

Values clarification and moral education. These activities have been described in Chapters 5 and 13. They should be an active concern of school, church, and most importantly, the family.

New Ways of Understanding Adolescents

New approaches for dealing with adolescents means that we need to understand this period of life in new ways. The attitudes of adults, especially adults who work closely with adolescents, must change if we are to improve the quality of adolescent life. Among the necessary changes are the following.

A new psychology of adolescence. There are three ways to perceive the nature of human beings: they are basically bad; they are basically good; or, they are basically neutral.

The view that human beings are basically bad was popular with educators in earlier centuries; it required that children be regularly beaten and disciplined in order to help them overcome their evil nature. The more widely accepted belief today is that human nature is basically neutral. This view is held by the two major schools of psychology in America today, psychoanalysis and behaviorism.

Let us examine how each of these schools would analyze the case of Richard, the disturbed 13-year-old described in Chapter 12 whose teacher often took him fishing in an attempt to help him improve his behavior. Subsequently, Richard slashed the teacher's tires and threw a rock through the side of an aquarium in a pet shop.

The psychoanalytic school would suggest that Richard is not responsible for his behavior; these aggressions stem from problems in his early childhood. Richard, it would seem, is fixated in the phallic stage. That is why he thrusts hostilely at those who would help him. The knife and rock are symbolic penises. Richard cannot help himself; he needs psychoanalysis so he can be freed from his earlier fixation and reach maturity.

Behaviorists would say that Richard is doing these hostile acts because he is being reinforced for them. In the past, when Richard was bad, his teacher took him fishing. Therefore, in hopes of getting more special treatment, Richard is behaving even worse. Treatment of Richard would involve taking away reinforcements for bad behavior and substituting reinforcements for appropriate behavior. In this case, too, Richard is not to blame for his behavior; he does what he does as a reaction to his environment.

A relatively new school of psychology, humanism, would analyze this situation quite differently. The humanist would hold that Richard is by nature a good person, but because his basic needs are not being taken care of, he is in conflict with his nature. If he is helped to meet these needs, Richard will react responsibly and warmly to others.

The late humanistic psychologist Abraham Maslow (1962, 1971) suggests that there is a hierarchy of six basic needs. Until the lower needs are met, it is impossible to meet higher-level ones. Listed in the order in which they are essential, they are (1) *physiological needs,* such as food, water, and air; (2) *safety needs,* such as shelter, clothing, and freedom from fear of personal danger; (3) *belongingness and love needs,* the feeling that at least one other person feels loving and caring toward you; (4) *esteem needs,* the sense of being worthwhile and capable of making a contribution to society; (5) *self-actualization needs,* in which one enjoys the experience of creativity and the joy of personal success; and (6) *aesthetic needs,* in which one finally comes to a deep understanding of the world and the purpose of life and feels a part of the cosmos.

We need to achieve a better understanding of how these needs can be fulfilled in adolescents. Humanistic psychology, which assumes that people are basically good so long as their basic needs are met, has a better chance of doing so. Those of us who would be helpful to teenagers should become more aware of the teachings of this newest school of psychology.

Clearer values.   Because adults have become less certain of their own values, their normal influence on adolescents has been weakened. Not knowing what to say to them, we have frequently said nothing. As a consequence of this permissiveness, teenaged behavior has become increasingly immoral or, often, amoral. On the other hand, lack of guidance has frequently made adolescents overly self-analytical. Erikson speaks of self-absorption being the chief danger of middle age. It appears that self-absorption is also a danger for the teenager. The way to help adolescents avoid self-absorption is to help them become more productive, to be more responsible and self-controlled. First, adults must become clear about their own values for productivity; they must then encourage youth to take responsible roles. Shortening the current period of adolescent moratorium is therefore essential.

Tolerance of ambiguity.   That the world is becoming more ambiguous and unstable has been clearly demonstrated (Toffler, 1970; Havighurst and Dreyer, 1975). Dealing with this instability and high rate of change is particularly difficult for adolescents. They need help to tolerate the ambiguity they are likely to face in the future. This means that we are going to have to spend more effort teaching them *how* to learn and less on *what* to learn. More importantly, it means that we have to foster their creative abilities (see Chapter 4), to give them ample opportunity to make decisions on their own and the chance to fail under the safety of our protection.

Searching for meaning.   The most important gift that adults can give to adolescents is the sense that life is meaningful. Leonard (1977) suggests that many youth feel "nothing I do makes any difference. No matter how good I am, or how bad I am, I am still going to be graduated. Even if I'm a zero, it doesn't count. I am afraid all the time. The walls around me seem to be made of rubber" (p. 4).

Changing this all too prevalent attitude will mean making important transformations within our society itself. As Leonard says,

> *Real risk is often involved. There is also a fear of change when there isn't much real risk. Right now it seems the country is in a sort of holding pattern. We've been infected with a sense of helplessness, as if our problems have gotten too big for us. If we're going to get past these feelings of helplessness, we're going to have to be willing to take personal responsibility (p. 4).*

The suggestions presented here *will* take a great deal of effort and personal risk, because the task itself is enormous. If implemented, they may improve the quality of adolescence sometime in the future. What about the person who wants to be useful to teenagers now? The next section offers some down-to-earth advice.

ADVICE OF EXPERTS TO BEGINNERS

The final part of the survey sent out to practitioners working with adolescents requested that they suggest five pieces of advice that would be helpful to those beginning in their occupation. Since 101 respondents did make suggestions, there were a great many. It was at first planned to present these pieces of advice grouped in the category of the person responding; for example, a teacher working with normal, 15–18-year-old, metropolitan males and females. In reading over these suggestions, it became clear that there was really little difference between the various categories of practitioners; the advice applied to all categories almost equally. Therefore, all of their suggestions have been summarized below.

There appeared to be seven basic categories of suggestions: honesty, sense of humor, tolerance, clarity in setting limits, paying attention to the withdrawn child, clarifying rules, and communications skills. The most representative quotations are presented within these categories.

Honesty

- "Honesty with adolescents is absolutely essential. They deeply resent double standards."
- "You should make it clear from the beginning what your relationship with the kids will be."
- "Teenagers are especially sensitive to dishonesty, phoniness, and manipulation."
- "You should try to be a model for genuine caring through your own truthfulness."
- "Never cover up your true feelings."
- "Always tell them if you don't agree with them, but give your reasons why."
- "Remember that adolescents can spot a phony a mile away."
- "Be honest at all times about what you think — don't talk down to them about sex, drugs, life in general."
- "There's no need to be afraid to state your honest feelings."
- "Never say what you don't mean; you'll pay for it in the end."
- "Never use psychological warfare — they can always tell when you are trying to."

Sense of Humor

- "Try to have a sense of humor. The things they do are really funny."
- "A sense of humor is essential if only to get you through the rough days."
- "Outlaw ethnic jokes, at least in your presence. They need to know that some types of humor are not appropriate."
- "Be able to laugh at yourself."

Tolerance

- "Don't be surprised at erratic behavior."
- "Don't get angry at kids who misbehave—get mad at their behaviors."
- "Adolescents need flexible adults who can accept their moods and who allow them a reasonable amount of freedom and thought."
- "Try to remember that many kids are very lonely. This will help you tolerate their moodiness."
- "Listen hard to what they're really trying to tell you."
- "Adolescents have a need and a right to make decisions, and you should respect this right."
- "You are going to need a tremendous amount of patience."
- "Flexibility is essential in working with adolescents."
- "Their defiance and antagonism usually masks their fear."
- "Adults who stick with adolescents usually develop their trust."
- "Much of what the adolescent is doing is caused by his need to grow out from under the family umbrella. Try to understand this need."
- "Try to serve as a model, but never moralize."

Clarity in Setting Limits

- "Adolescents need clear-cut limits."
- "Be fair, but firm."
- "Listen to them, but don't allow yourself to be manipulated."
- "Realistic goal setting must involve both the student and the teacher."
- "Don't 'stretch' rules. Be assertive enough to say no when necessary."
- "It is imperative to establish right off the fact that you are in charge."
- "A counselor needs to know the balance between being a professional and being a friend. That isn't always easy to discern."
- "Kids need and want to know their parameters."
- "Be consistent in the standards that you set."
- "Most students really respect you for setting boundaries."
- "Don't try to be a pal—just be yourself and don't make deals."
- "Limits are appreciated even when they are protested against. Stopping unacceptable behavior indicates your concern and is usually appreciated by all."
- "After you have set your standards, don't start bending them."
- "Learn to make the distinction between a deliberate violation of your rules and an inadvertent stumble."

- "Because adolescents need structure, your role is to exercise control in the most democratic way you can. They respect you for it if you succeed."
- "Respect for young people means not only understanding and empathy; it also means having strength and firmness."
- "Although it is important to have clear rules, it is even more important to apologize when you overreact."

Paying Attention to the Withdrawn Child

- "So-called 'good kids' (those who give you no trouble) may need more of your attention than the troublemakers."
- "Because a kid is not disturbing the class doesn't mean that he is in good shape."
- "Often the quietest teenagers are deeply depressed. You should look carefully for suicidal tendencies."
- "Try to get to know all of the teenagers you work with. Avoid paying too much attention to the rabble rousers."

Clarifying Values—Yours and Theirs

- "The instability of the adolescent stems mostly from his own values about himself. For this he needs a stable and compassionate adult."
- "Within reasonable limits, be as accepting of their values and priorities as you can."
- "Don't judge adolescents by your own standards."
- "Adolescents need to feel useful and valued. Society does not often provide them with the opportunity to get these feelings."
- "Be open-minded to their attitudes and values."
- "Sometimes the opinions they express are more the result of strong peer pressures than because they really believe in those opinions."
- "Don't place yourself so far above the kids that you are out of their reach, but don't descend to their level either. For example, I never make fun of what they wear, but I would never wear blue jeans, gym shoes, and a sweatshirt to class myself."
- "Clarifying one's values is the most important thing teenagers can do. Knowledge is only a secondary goal."
- "It is important to respect an adolescent's views no matter how alien to your own way of thinking they may be."
- "The basic thing for anyone working with adolescents is to help them learn to enjoy life."

Communications Skills

- "Always keep your lines of communication open."

- "You should listen more than you talk. Try to give the kids *time* to think of and express their feelings."

- "Be aware that each kid is an individual and has his or her own individual way of expressing things."

- "Try to make time each day to listen to what they have to say."

- "Keep in touch with their parents if you possibly can. Their backgrounds and their home lives play a very important part in their behavior."

- "Be a good listener. Many of these children have no one that they truly trust and who will listen to them."

- "*Never* betray a confidentiality. Trust is vital to everything you do with them."

- "Don't always expect to get positive feedback from them."

- "Always avoid using diagnostic labels. These labels tend to turn into self-fulfilling prophecies."

- "Be prepared to hear their hostility as well as their praise. Don't expect to be loved just for your good intentions."

- "Never accept a confidence which you cannot honestly keep."

SUMMARY

As you probably have already decided, following all this advice is far from easy. For one thing, the suggestions reflect a wide range of attitudes—from the extreme of telling you to be quite strict and concerned with limits to telling you to be open and flexible with adolescent needs and moods. One counselor even went so far as to say "If you have other job alternatives, take them!"

However, it is most encouraging to note that almost all of the respondents had positive regard for their work with adolescents and seemed optimistic in their advice to the beginner. Despite the many suggestions that you be on your guard, most felt that flexibility, openness, and trust were the major keys to working well with adolescents. As one person who has worked with adolescents for twenty-seven years said, "Idealism turns to cynicism unless you are constantly monitoring and adjusting your responses. You need to grow in the understanding of your teenage friends, as well as in the understanding of yourself."

—————————— **A PERSONAL NOTE** ——————————

It is my sincerest hope that this book will have helped you attain these two most admirable goals!

Questions

1. In what significant ways have adolescents changed recently?
2. What can be done to aid adolescents in the future?
3. What are some important suggestions for beginners working with adolescents?

References

Erikson, E.   *Young man Luther.* New York: Norton, 1958.

Gibbons, M.   "Walkabout: searching for the right passage from childhood and school." *Phi Delta Kappan,* 1974, *55*(9), 596–602.

Gill, B. D.   "Kappans respond to the walkabout idea." *Phi Delta Kappan,* 1974, *56*(1), 63–64.

Grinder, R. E.   "Epilogue: two models for the study of youth—1944 versus 1975." In R. J. Havighurst & P. H. Dreyer (Eds.), *Youth.* Chicago: National Society for the Study of Education, 1975, 435–442.

Havighurst, R. J., & Dreyer, P. H.   *Youth.* Chicago: National Society for the Study of Education, 1975.

Jones, R. (Ed.).   *Adolescence.* Chicago: National Society for the Study of Education, 1944.

Leonard, G.   "Interview." *The graduate,* 1977, 3–7.

Maslow, A. H.   *Toward a psychology of being.* New York: Van Nostrand, 1962.

Maslow, A. H.   *Further reaches of human nature.* New York: Viking Press, 1971.

Toffler, A.   *Future shock.* New York: Bantam, 1970.

Appendix A

The Survey

As part of the effort to make this text as up-to-date as possible, a forty-nine-item survey on many aspects of adolescent life was devised. It was mailed to 150 persons who are known to be working closely and effectively with various types of adolescents. The mailing list was compiled by people (college faculty, teachers, and the like) who personally knew the practitioners. A personal letter from one of these people was mailed with each questionnaire, requesting the practitioner's participation. This method undoubtedly accounts for the number of returns, 101, which is considered an exceptionally high rate for surveys, especially in these days of survey saturation.

In a follow-up study of 62% of these same respondents, only three areas were found to have changed significantly. These areas are time of occupational choice, attitude toward school, and church attendance.

CHARACTERISTICS OF THE ADOLESCENTS CONSIDERED

The respondents were deliberately selected so their viewpoints would reflect five factors: area of the country (Northeast, Midwest, West, and South); type of adolescent worked with (typical, atypical); size of town (metropolitan, nonmetropolitan); age group (11–14, 15–19); and sex (male, female). It was explained that although no teenager is really "typical," that term was meant to include those in such an ordinary setting as a school. Most of the respondents in this category were teachers. "Atypical" referred to those youth being dealt with in such settings as therapy, hospitals, or jails. Most of these respondents were probation officers and mental health professionals. These two distinctions are quite broad, but finer ones were not numerically possible.

In terms of section of the country, the distribution of respondents was as follows: Northeast, 46; Midwest, 18; West, 22, and South, 15. Responses came from thirty-one states; therefore, the study is not based on a representative sample of the entire United States. However, when responses were looked at by region, no clear patterns emerged; to the extent that these data *are* representative, we may conclude that adolescents are seen in roughly the same way across the country.

Respondents who work with typical youngsters numbered 78; 23 work with atypical youth. This is not necessarily a reflection of the actual numbers of these two types of adolescents in society as a whole; the respondents were chosen to give this balance.

The same is true for size of town. There were 49 responses from metropolitan areas, and 52 responses from nonmetropolitan areas.

In terms of age groups, 31 respondents usually work with 11–14-year-olds, and 70 work with 15–19-year-olds. Of the 101 responses, 96 work with both males and females, and responded on separate answer sheets for each. Of the remainder, 3 answered only for females and 2 answered only for males.

CHARACTERISTICS OF THE RESPONDENTS

Three questions were asked of the respondents: How long had they been working with adolescents? What size group did they usually work with? and Were they or were they not teachers?

Those with four or less years of experience numbered 32; there were 69 with five or more years in practice. Almost all deal with adolescents in groups of 11 or more; only 9 work with less, and most of these are mental health specialists. Two-thirds of the respondents are teachers.

THE QUESTIONNAIRE

From two to seven questions were asked about the topics covered in Chapters 2 through 13 in this book. Because the results consist largely of the conclusions of professionals in the field about the various attitudes and values of adolescents, and because morality itself is so hard to define, no separate questions were asked for Chapter 5 *(Moral Judgment)*.

For each question, respondents were asked: What percentage of the teenagers with whom you work (for example) "are making occupational choices earlier than teenagers did a few years ago"?

0–25%	25–50%	50–75%	75–100%	Don't Know
A	B	C	D	E

Answers for each question were marked on separate IBM mark-sense sheets for males and females. A summary of the answers to each question, presented by chapter, follows.

RESULTS

Chapter 2: Identity

"What percentage are having serious trouble developing their own identity?" Responses to this question were not very surprising. The group that is suffering the most in the identity crisis stage is the atypical, older adolescent. Over 65 percent of both male and female atypical adolescents from the ages of 15 to 18 years in both the metropolitan and nonmetropolitan areas are viewed as having identity problems. The group experiencing the most problems is the atypical older males in the metropolitan areas.

The rest of the adolescent population experiences little identity difficulty. This finding corroborates viewpoints expressed by many adolescent psychologists. The experts who responded to the survey viewed less than 25 percent of the *typical* adolescents of either sex or age groupings to be having serious identity problems.

"What percentage have a paying job during the school year?" In the area of vocational identity, the groups most likely to have a paying job during the school year were the typical male and female nonmetropolitan adolescents and the older typical males of the metropolitan area. The group that was least likely to have a job was the younger metropolitan typical or atypical adolescent. With current high unemployment figures for metropolitan youths, this finding is not surprising either.

"What percentage are making their occupational choices earlier than teenagers did a few years ago?" In the first survey, this same group (least likely to have a paying job) was also seen as the group that was making occupational choices earlier. In the followup survey for this second edition, *all* groups are seen as making occupational choices earlier. This is probably due mostly to the job shortages caused by world economics or the baby boom.

Chapter 3: The Onset of Puberty

"What percentage are early maturers who have a negative attitude toward their own body (as shown by slouching, deprecating remarks, and the like)?" Our survey indicates that of those adolescents who are *early* maturers, a slightly larger percentage of the nonmetropolitan, atypical youths experience a negative body image. This is true for both males and females, regardless of the age group studied.

"What percentage are late maturers who express a negative attitude toward their own bodies?" The pattern hardly changes when we look at those adoles-

cents who are *late* maturers. Here we find it is again the atypical, non-metropolitan youth who seems more prone to a negative body image. It should be noted that, in most cases, less than 25 percent of the early- or late-maturing youth appear to suffer a negative body image; nowhere does it exceed 50 percent.

It was expected that all types of early-maturing females would have more problems than males, but our respondents do not see it this way. Perhaps the women's movement has finally managed to downplay the chauvinistic tendency of males to take advantage of females whose bodies mature earlier. Also, perhaps other females are no longer so jealous of them.

It is difficult to hypothesize on why there should be a more negative body image among nonmetropolitan atypical youth. Possibly being delinquent or emotionally disturbed in a nonmetropolitan area makes one stand out and feel a negative self-image in general.

Chapter 4: Thinking Style

"What percentage think creativity is a valuable asset to have?" No more than one-third of adolescents in any category think being creative is an asset. This is in line with other studies reported in this chapter, which indicate that most youth fear and dislike others who tend to think differently from them. Interestingly, typical teenagers are more likely to value creativity than atypicals. This is surprising, in that many atypicals are more creative than average. Perhaps because they often suffer the contempt of their less imaginative peers, they do not have respect for their own creative abilities. The only other significant difference was that females hold creativity in somewhat higher regard than males.

"What percentage think of themselves as creative?" Less than 20 percent of all youth currently view themselves as creative. Although one-half of all youth are above average for their age level, by definition, it is a reflection of their attitude toward creativity that so few teens think of themselves that way. As with the question above, the atypicals are viewed by respondents as much less likely to view themselves as creative than are typicals. In fact, atypicals were rated as close to zero percent on this attitude, probably a further indication of the atypical adolescent's attempt to avoid seeming different. There were no other significant differences.

"What percentage would have trouble answering questions calling for hypothetical thinking?" In most cases, atypical youth have more trouble with hypothetical thinking—an average of about 25 percent, as compared to 15 percent of typical teens. This is not surprising, since many of the difficulties of atypical adolescents seem to occur because they often cannot foresee the consequences of their actions. In fact, a higher percentage was expected. Interestingly, metropolitan youth have less trouble with hypothetical thinking. Typical youth are actually seen as having greater difficulty than atypicals when they live in non-

metropolitan areas. It is not clear why—perhaps living in the city presents a greater stimulus to the imagination.

Chapter 6: The Family

"What percentage usually have pleasant interactions with the other members of their families?" According to the respondents, the adolescents they work with are quite like those described in Chapter 6. Atypical youth of all types are seen as having few pleasant interactions with other members of their families; only one-sixth of them do. Over 50 percent of all typical adolescents are seen as experiencing pleasant interactions with members of their families. These findings support the notion that most adolescents have fairly good interactions with other members of the family, and that it is the atypical adolescent whose family interactions are a serious problem.

"What percentage have serious problems with their parents?" As seen by those who responded, over three-fourths of all atypical adolescents have serious problems with their parents, compared to approximately 25 percent of all typical adolescents. The findings are significant in that they support what most professionals have always assumed about the relationship between adolescents and their parents. One may conclude that having good relationships with one's parents decreases the potential for deviance and increases the potential of being seen as typical.

"What percentage have a close and happy relationship with their fathers?" Almost 75 percent of all typical adolescents between 11 and 14 have a close and happy relationship with their father, as compared to less than 25 percent of atypical adolescents of the same age group. Of the typical adolescents between 15 and 18, just under 50 percent are seen as having close and happy relationships with their fathers; this is compared to 15 percent of atypical older youth.

There was no significant difference between the males and females, although typical females in both the 11–14 and 15–18 age group were seen as having slightly closer relationships with their fathers.

"What percentage have a close and happy relationship with their mothers?" The survey again supports the conclusions in Chapter 6 with regard to the importance of the relationship between adolescent and mother. According to the respondents, over 75 percent of all typical 11–14-year-old adolescents have close and happy relationships with their mothers, compared to less than 25 percent of atypical adolescents of the same age group. Of those typical adolescents between the ages of 15 and 18, almost 50 percent have close and happy relationships with their mothers, compared to less than 25 percent of atypical adolescents of the same age group.

In summary, one may conclude that those who have good relationships with parents and other members of their families will generally be seen as typical and doing well with their struggle through adolescence. Not having a close and happy relationship with one's parents may lead to other difficulties. Surprisingly, these relations are seen as worsening somewhat as the individual reaches the later teen years. It has been suggested that this may often be due to the need of parents and youth to get some psychological distance from each other, preparatory to the latter's leaving home.

Chapter 7: Peer Groups

"What percentage are having serious trouble joining any group?" Being accepted and validated by some group is a crucial part of forming an identity. To be rejected for whatever reason is an assault on the integration of one's personality. It comes as no surprise, then, that the major group difference here is between typical and atypical students.

Almost none of the typical adolescents are seen as having a problem with acceptance by peers. An average of 40 percent of the atypical youth do. It is not possible to tell from this survey, but it seems likely that it is the emotionally troubled, rather than the delinquent, atypical youth who has most of the difficulty here. This points to the importance of improving the communications skills of these youngsters.

"What percentage conform more to the others in dress, speech, and other behaviors than teenagers did a few years ago?" About half of the teenagers in this study are seen as more conformist than those a few years ago. Unfortunately, due to the wording of this question, we cannot say whether the other half is the same as or less conforming. Interestingly, there were no significant differences between any groups.

These findings appear to agree with the general picture of adolescents being more homogeneous in dress, speech, and other behaviors than teens in the turbulent 1960s. Clearly the support derived from being like the others is as important as it ever was.

"What makes adolescents popular with each other?" The characteristics were physical appearance, extracurricular activities, style of dress, academic ability, and athletic ability. The respondents were asked to select the most important, second most important, and third most important of these characteristics. Results of this part of the survey are striking. First, there are very few differences between the way the various characteristics are seen, for any of the three choices. This is surprising in that some differences were expected at least for age and sex.

There was considerable agreement as to the most important popularity factor: physical appearance won, hands down. The stereotype of the female being more interested in the whole person than the male is challenged here. Females were seen as being even more concerned with physical characteristics than males. There was less agreement on second choice, but the majority of the respondents chose style of dress. Next most chosen trait for second place was physical appearance, an indication of how really important it is. Choices for third place were almost exactly split between the last four options in this question.

However, high academic performance comes in last, just as it did in James Coleman's 1961 study of these variables. He found athletic performance to be first then; it is not even a clear third now.

It appears likely that these choices are made in imitation of adult values. To the extent that beauty, youth, and good clothes are extolled in the media, we can expect youth to value them above all else.

Chapter 8: Love and Sex

"What percentage think it's important that they themselves be a virgin when they are married?" Approximately three times as many 11–14-year-olds think it is important to be a virgin than do 15–19-year-olds. Slightly more nonmetropolitan youths think it's important to be a virgin when married. Slightly more females also think so. However, the percentages are not high; most adolescents don't think it's important to be a virgin.

"What percentage feel that what people do sexually is their own business?" The majority of respondents believe that most adolescents have a laissez-faire attitude about sex—people should do what they want to. Interestingly, there were no significant differences among the various groups on this question. There was more unanimity here than on any other question.

"What percentage are planning to get married sometime?" The great majority of teens are seen as planning to marry. A difference between males and females was expected here but did not occur. The one difference that did occur is an interesting one. For younger adolescents, more typicals plan to marry than atypicals; this difference is reversed for older teens. It is hard to be certain why. Perhaps the insecurity of being atypical makes one more likely to want the help of a married partner when one is older.

"What percentage are planning never to get married?" In the late 1960s, many youth were proclaiming that marriage was no longer necessary. The number of couples who lived together unmarried is still increasing. However, our respondents feel that very few adolescents today think they will never wed. The percentage is even lower for atypical youth than for typical. This adds to the picture of atypical: rather than daring radicals who resist socialization, they are seen as persons hoping for a loving relationship with the opposite sex.

"What percentage are planning to live with a partner prior to getting married to that partner?" There is wide variation in responses to this question; either the practitioners disagree in their views or (more likely) teens have widely different attitudes about this. Because differences are not uniform according to groups, it is hard to say what attitudes are.

"What percentage want to have children?" The answers here are not surprising. Most adolescents plan to have children. The percentages are slightly higher for female, typical, nonmetropolitan younger adolescents.

"What percentage want to have no children?" Most adolescents are not seen as being opposed to having children. Group differences were slight.

Caution must be taken with the interpretation of responses to the last three questions. In each case, about one-fifth of the respondents answered "don't know." This was unusually high.

"What percentage date at least once each month?" The study found a wide variation in dating patterns, from none to a great deal. This fits the picture given by other research: dating patterns are in a definite state of flux at present. On the average, about one-third date at least once a month. Notable exceptions were younger atypical youths, who almost never date, and older atypical youths, two-thirds of whom are seen as dating regularly. This corroborates the pattern seen in marriage expectations. It is an interesting reversal which is not easy to explain.

Chapter 9: The Schools

"What percentage feel that school is really a waste of time?" The responses of the first repondents indicated that about 35 percent of youth feel that school is really a waste of time. In the second survey, this figure had dropped to 25 percent, probably as a result of greater concern for getting a good job. It should be noted that for the typical population, respondents felt that less than a quarter of the youth viewed school as a waste of time. On the other hand, over half of the atypical group thought so. Generally, the percentages showed no change between younger and older or nonmetropolitan and metropolitan groups.

"What percentage actively work to improve their school?" The experts saw very few students as actively trying to improve their school. Atypicals in the nonmetropolitan systems are rated consistently higher here than the others, regardless of age or sex. Although the difference is not great, this finding is difficult to explain.

"What percentage participate in athletics with great enthusiasm?" Generally, about one-fourth of the students are seen as participating in athletics with great enthusiasm. The highest mean, again not by much, was for atypical, metropolitan boys. This seems to fit with some of the studies done on delinquent boys, which indicates that the male delinquent tends to be athletic and have a good self-image in terms of his body. This may also be part of the reason why new delinquency prevention programs rely on using physical ability and interest in trying to give boys what they need to function in society.

Only about half as many females as males are seen to be enthusiastically athletic, with the exception of typical, young, nonmetropolitan girls, who equal boys. Perhaps they are the most liberated female group, or perhaps their schools are doing more for them in athletics.

"What percentage expect to complete high school?" The responses for the typicals are consistent. In general, our respondents saw about 70 percent of the youth expecting to complete high school, which seems low. For atypicals, it was less than half.

"What percentage expect to continue their education after high school?"

Respondents believe about one-third to one-half of the typical students would continue their education after high school. This is less than now go on to college, and may reflect the higher costs and lower regard for college which an increasing number of youth seem to feel. Atypicals are uniformly alike in the practitioners' views: less than one quarter are seen as college-bound.

Chapter 10: Substance Abuse

"What percentage smoke cigarettes?" The respondents are evenly divided in this category. Estimates indicate that from one-third to seven-eighths of adolescents smoke. A safe estimate seems to be 60 percent. Within metropolitan areas, twice as many 15–18-year-olds smoke as 11–14-year-olds. Although girls lag far behind boys at ages 11–14, they seem to catch up by ages 15–18. Atypical males predictably smoke in greater numbers than atypical females. Within nonmetropolitan areas the 11–14 and 15–18 age groups smoke at about the same rate—40 percent. The same is true across sex groups. Although in general metropolitan and nonmetropolitan areas seem to have the same percentage of smokers, those in nonmetropolitan areas appear to smoke more at an earlier age. Atypicals always have a higher percentage of smokers.

"What percentage use alcohol?" The respondents are widely divided on this issue. Every category has a substantial percentage. A majority do believe, however, that at least 60 percent of youth use alcohol. Nevertheless, in relation to other studies, the survey was expected to have obtained results with more unanimity.

Two-thirds of metropolitan adolescents drink. A majority are between 15 and 18. Somewhat surprisingly, in both age groups males and females drink at the same percentages. More predictable was the finding that atypicals tend to drink more than typicals. Our practitioners were unanimous in saying that almost all atypical males drink. In nonmetropolitan areas both age groups have a similar rate of use. Although older males drink more than older females, in the 11–14 group the use rate was equal. Again atypicals drank more than typicals. Metropolitan adolescents use alcohol more than nonmetropolitan adolescents, especially in the 15–18 group.

"What percentage smoke marijuana?" It seems the respondents do not know or are just guessing. The percentages are almost evenly divided among all five categories. Perhaps this is one of the questions where asking the students would have been more profitable.

In the metropolitan area all 11–14-year-olds seem to use marijuana at the same rate—33 percent. The same is true for the 15–18-year-old group. The 15–18-year-olds' use rate is slightly higher across the board. The nonmetropolitan area is exactly the same as the metropolitan area, except for 11–14-year-old typicals, whose use rate seems very high (66 percent). Between metropolitan and nonmetropolitan areas, average use is approximately equal—50 percent. The only consistent difference is the 15–18-year-old group, whose use seems slightly higher in metropolitan areas. These figures are somewhat higher than in studies of adolescents' responses. It seems likely that the practitioners may be somewhat overestimating use.

"What percentage use stronger drugs, such as LSD, heroin, cocaine, speed, or barbiturates?" Most agree that usage is low, probably less than 15 percent. Surprisingly, they see no differences between metropolitan and nonmetropolitan groups. With the exception of younger metropolitans, atypicals are more likely to use strong drugs than typicals. A fairly high number of the respondents, 12 percent, admitted that they had no knowledge of how much of this behavior takes place.

"The major reason the kids I know *say* they take drugs is . . ." Choices were to be popular with friends, to increase self-awareness and creativity, to escape an unpleasant reality, to relax, to satisfy their curiosity. Respondents were asked to choose the most important, second most important, and third most important reasons.

In metropolitan areas more than 50 percent of all adolescents take drugs to be popular with their friends. There is no difference between age groups or sex. In nonmetropolitan regions, the only meaningful difference is between 11–14-year-old females and the others. Only about 20 percent of the former seem to take drugs to be popular. Across age and sex, nonmetropolitan adolescents seem to take drugs to be popular with friends less than metropolitan adolescents. Atypicals, especially females, are judged to exhibit drug-taking behavior to be popular more than any other group. For second- and third-place reasons for using drugs, no pattern emerged. The five options given were chosen about equally for each of the groups. These findings are generally in accord with other studies of this question.

Chapter 11: Mental Disturbance, Death, and Disease

"What percentage have expressed a concern that they might commit suicide?" The responses here are surprising. It was found that *typical* boys and girls in both metropolitan and nonmetropolitan areas were more likely to express a concern about committing suicide. The atypical adolescents of both age groups were much less likely to express this concern. Little difference was observed between the sexes over this question. The trend is for 11–14-year-old typical adolescents to express this concern more than the 15–18-year-old adolescents, but the idea of suicide in the latter group is far more prevalent than in atypical adolescents.

Perhaps one way of defining whether an adolescent is atypical, then, is the degree to which he or she does *not* express concern about committing suicide. It may well be that atypicals, who are more likely to attempt suicide, are less willing to discuss it with others, especially older people, than typical teenagers.

"What percentage seem to have a fascination with death?" Over half said fascination with death occurs in up to 25 percent of the adolescents; a further 16

percent said that it occurs in a quarter to a half of the adolescents they see, while 19 percent said they don't know. The fascination seems to change slightly during adolescence. The metropolitan 11–14-year-old girls seem to have this fascination earliest, yet it does not decline much with age. Youngsters in nonmetropolitan areas have somewhat less fascination with the subject, but adolescent females in the 15–18-year-old group in nonmetropolitan areas demonstrate the most fascination. Differences between sexes or ages are less striking than between these typical females and their atypical female counterparts, who are thought to have less fascination with death.

"What percentage have ever attempted suicide?" This was a poor question. Most respondents think the occurrence is low (and of course it is), but so many answered "don't know" as to make this item of little value.

"What percentage exhibit risky, daredevil behavior?" Almost half of the respondents thought that up to one-quarter of the adolescents exhibit this behavior. Over one-quarter of the respondents thought that as many as half the adolescents did, and a further 17 percent felt three-quarters did. This pattern of behavior is popular with at least a fourth and possibly as many as half the adolescents seen by respondents.

Predictably, risky, daredevil behavior occurs most frequently in older boys. There was one exception: atypical nonmetropolitan boys of 11–14 years were seen as exhibiting this type of behavior far more than typical nonmetropolitan boys of 15–18. Mainly, however, the two age groups revealed the most clear-cut differences. Those older adolescents in metropolitan areas were more likely to engage in this behavior than their age mates in the nonmetropolitan areas, and those boys in the 15–18 age range identified as atypical were even more likely to exhibit this behavior than typical boys in both metropolitan and nonmetropolitan areas.

These findings are generally in accord with other studies, and indicate our great need for adequate rites of passage. Without them, there is far too much risk taking on the part of youth.

Chapter 12: Delinquent Behavior

"What percentage have stolen property worth less than $50?" Our survey generally supports other research in this area: the majority of adolescents have stolen something sometime. If they live in an urban environment, are boys, and are older, it is extremely likely that they will steal. Although most groups of younger adolescents tended to steal less, the highest frequency for this age occurred with the atypical boys from metropolitan homes, which is not surprising. What it does point out is an obvious need to provide services or programs for disadvantaged youth, in particular, boys. This should be done at an early age and with a good deal of consistency.

"What percentage have stolen property worth more than $50?" Survey results continue to point to overt reactions by urban atypical youth, particularly

males. Their frequency was significantly higher on this question than any other group. However, of great interest is the finding that in general more non-metropolitan than metropolitan adolescents had stolen property worth more than $50. An average of one-third are believed by respondents to have done so. Apparently, many adolescents in suburbia are able to steal items of higher value. Yet their record of arrest, as indicated in other research, is lower than for the urban adolescent. This implies a double standard. Youth offenders brought before suburban courts receive reprimands or probation for crimes that are punished more severely in the cities.

"What percentage have run away from home?" Running away is a less frequent problem than stealing. Girls tend to run away slightly more than boys, but the reaction is rare in adolescents, with three striking exceptions: atypical, younger, metropolitan males and females; and atypical older, nonmetropolitan females. About 60 percent of these teens have run away at least once. It would be interesting to discover whether this behavior is caused by similar or dissimilar motivations.

"What percentage have taken part in a gang fight?" Results were generally consistent with other data: atypical males from urban situations are involved in gang fights far more often than other groups. However, since a fairly high percentage of respondents "don't know" (21 percent), further generalizations are not warranted.

"What percentage have sold drugs?" The respondents see drug selling as quite rare, but as with the above question, the number of those who "don't know" (19 percent) is fairly high and generalizations cannot be made. By and large, the findings from the survey about drugs fit well with other studies reported in Chapter 10.

Chapter 13: Values

"What percentage tend to behave in a more moral way because they are actively religious?" The typical adolescent is viewed as behaving in a more moral manner as a result of active religious participation, whereas the atypical youth does not. Apparently the latter see little relationship between religious activity and morality. It may also be that so few atypical youth *are* actively religious that there can be no relationship. Probably this question should have been asked as two separate questions. More younger teenagers feel that being actively religious had an effect on their morality than did older teenagers. This is also somewhat truer of females than males. These findings are in line with those of earlier studies.

"What percentage attend church regularly?" Our first respondents believed that about one-third of the teenage population attend church on a regular basis. This estimate is now up to 50 percent.

Regular church attendance increases to some extent with age. This may reflect the trend that as adolescents reach the age of 16, they become either more or less committed to religious life. Adolescents in metropolitan areas attend church more regularly than do teenagers in nonmetropolitan areas. There is no evidence in this study which could tell us the reason for this. Attending church on a regular basis may provide some needed solace and structure to those young people living in metropolitan areas where the pressures of living and growing up are much greater. The sophisticated transportation networks in metropolitan areas (particularly in inclement weather) may make city churches more accessible. Catholics and Orthodox Jews, who consider nonattendance a sin, tend to reside in urban areas. There is no significant difference between male and female church attendance. One of the most curious findings in this survey is that more younger atypical youth attend church than the average, and many fewer atypical older youth. Perhaps being atypical makes one hope that being religious will be helpful when one is young, but as the youth grows older, that hope is lost.

"What percentage express a belief in God?" With only one exception, about one-half of all groups express a belief in God. This is lower than most studies show, but in accord with the drop in attendance in religious education programs. The exception is metropolitan, younger, atypical males, most of whom are seen as not believing in God. Although values other than religious values are considered in Chapter 13, they were not anticipated when the survey was designed.

A summary of the major findings of this survey appears on page 430.

Appendix B

An Evaluation of Birth Control Techniques

Only about 30 percent of sexually active teenagers use birth control. Over 80 percent of all teenage pregnancies are unwanted. Although some of the major religions are opposed to birth control, most notably the Catholic Church, it is clear that no one is in favor of the conception of unwanted children. Therefore birth control in the broadest sense, avoiding the birth of unwanted children, is favored by everyone. It is the means that are controversial.

Why don't adolescents use birth control more regularly? Certainly for some of them it is because of lack of knowledge. Although birth control information is far more accessible to teenagers than it used to be, the use of birth control has increased only slightly.

It seems that a confusion over values and attitudes towards birth control is mainly at fault. Adolescents, told by many adults that birth control is wrong, are not sure how they feel. It becomes easier to avoid their conflict by not thinking about it. It is essential that those working with adolescents help them face the issue and clarify their values on the subject. To be successful these persons must be clear as to their own feelings about birth control.

Birth control methods can be placed on a continuum from no sexual activity at one end of the scale to infanticide on the other, as shown in the list below. The continuum represents points at which intervention can occur. All other birth control techniques exist somewhere along the continuum. Each individual, then, must decide where he or she stands along that continuum according to personal values. Other considerations in choice of technique are effectiveness (probability of preventing pregnancy) and safety (the possibility of dangerous side effects). A teenager who decided that all of the techniques on the continuum up through (3) withdrawal are *morally* acceptable to him or her should also consider that withdrawal is not an *effective* method of birth control. Likewise the adolescent should

Your Position on Birth Control

Below is the continuum of birth control techniques. Put an X at the place along the line that represents the most extreme position which you would consider using yourself. Then compare your choice with those of your friends.

1. Chastity
2. Rhythm
3. Withdrawal
4. Condom
5. Diaphragm
6. Foam, jelly, etc.
7. The pill
8. Sterilization
9. Intrauterine device
10. "Morning after" pill
11. Abortion—embryo
12. Abortion—unviable fetus
13. Abortion—viable fetus
14. Infanticide

recognize that certain techniques (the pill, the IUD, the morning-after pill, abortion) may have harmful side effects.

Below are the fourteen techniques for achieving control over birth that fall along the continuum described, along with an indication of their effectiveness and side effects.

1. *Chastity, abstinence.* Although freely admitting to sexual desires, persons using this technique completely avoid sexual intercourse, either permanently or for periods of their lives. Effectiveness: 100 percent. Possible side effects: unclear.

2. *The rhythm system.* Natural family planning is the only type of birth control allowed by the Catholic Church and other religious groups. The rhythm system attempts to determine the woman's "safe" period during the menstrual cycle during which ovulation, and hence conception, will not take place. The techniques include (1) the ovulation method (the woman studies changes in her cervical mucus), (2) the temperature method (the woman takes her temperature daily with a special basal body temperature thermometer), and (3) the symptothermic method (methods one and two are combined with calendar chart-keeping), all of which are used to mark the time of ovulation. Effectiveness: depends on the woman's motivation to monitor these body signs; 65–85 percent effective. Possible side effects: none.

3. *Withdrawal (coitus interruptus).* By withdrawing his penis before ejaculation, the male tries to prevent his semen from entering the vagina. Effectiveness:

because preseminal fluid contains sperm 25 percent of the time and is ejaculated prior to the male's awareness of ejaculation, this method is considered unreliable; 75–85 percent effective. Possible side effects: none.

4. *Condom ("rubber," "safe")*. A condom is a plastic or latex rubber sheath which covers the penis. It prevents semen from being released into the vagina. Effectiveness: 97 percent effective with good quality condoms used properly. Condoms are more effective than IUD's. Possible side effects: none.

5. *Diaphragm*. A soft rubber dome attached to a flexible spring which is fitted into the vagina and over the cervix. Sperm entering the vagina are prevented by this physical barrier from going into the uterus. The diaphragm is best used in conjunction with a spermicidal jelly spread over the dome and around the edges. Effectiveness: 97 percent with consistent and careful use. Possible side effects: certain creams or jellies may be irritating to some vaginas and penises.

6. *Foam, cream, jelly*. These are chemical preparations which are injected into the vagina with a special applicator. They too kill sperm as they try to enter the uterus. Effectiveness: 97 percent when used carefully. Possible side effects: these preparations may irritate the vagina or penis.

7. *The pill*. The best known of current birth control techniques, the pill is taken daily and consists of the hormones estrogen and progesterone. By administering these hormones, the woman's system is artificially persuaded that she is pregnant, and therefore no eggs are released to be impregnated by sperm. Effectiveness: 99+ percent when taken conscientiously. Possible side effects: increased risk of developing blood clots, heart attack, gall bladder disease, hypertension, diabetes, and other diseases; greater susceptibility to venereal disease and urinary tract infections; may cause liver tumors, depression, weight gain, skin problems; may have long-range effects on infants.

8. *Sterilization*. Both males and females can be sterilized by surgical techniques. The technique for male sterilization is to sever the vas deferens, the tube leading from the scrotum to the prostate gland, thus preventing sperm from mixing with semen. In the female, the fallopian tubes leading from the ovaries to the uterus are severed, thus preventing sperm from reaching eggs or eggs from reaching the uterus. Effectiveness: 99+ percent. Possible side effects: unclear.

9. *Intrauterine device* (IUD). This is a small coil-shaped piece of plastic which is inserted into the uterus. It creates an irritant to the uterus which has the effect of preventing a fertilized egg from attaching itself to the uterine wall. Thus, although conception may occur, pregnancy is not allowed to continue. Effectiveness: 93–99 percent effectiveness when in place (there is a 4–19 percent expulsion rate). Possible side effects: perforation of the uterus, increased risk of infection, bleeding and cramping, tubal pregnancies. Polyethylene, the material of most IUD's, is known to be a weak carcinogen.

10. *The morning-after pill*. This pill may be taken up to three days after intercourse and is usually capable of ending pregnancy. It contains a series of a very high dose of synthetic estrogens (usually DES). Effectiveness: not determined. Possible side effects: common side effects are severe nausea and vomit-

ing, headache, menstrual irregularities, breast tenderness; other side effects are severe headaches, blurring or loss of vision, severe leg pains, chest pain, shortness of breath. DES is linked with vaginal and cervical cancer in female offspring.

11. *Abortion: embryo stage (0–8 weeks).* The embryo is a fertilized egg at the prefetal stage. Abortion in this period is considerably simpler than it is in later pregnancy. Two techniques are commonly used: (a) vacuum suction, a technique in which the amniotic sac containing the tiny embryo is sucked out of the uterus by the use of a vacuum curettage, an instrument inserted into the uterus; and (b) dilation and curettage, a technique in which the cervix is dilated and an instrument used to scrape the uterine walls, thus removing the embryo. Effectiveness: 100 percent. Possible side effects: bleeding, discomfort, infection, perforation, hemorrhage.

12. *Abortion: unviable fetus (9–28 weeks).* When the embryo reaches eight weeks, it is referred to as a fetus. From nine to about twenty-eight weeks of the fetal period, it is "unviable," that is, it cannot live outside its mother's body. Most doctors, and in many states the law, use "viability" as a criterion for permitting abortion. The two abortion techniques described above can be used in the early parts of this period. There are two other techniques that are used later: (a) saline-induced labor, a technique in which a needle is inserted through the abdomen into the amniotic sac, a small percentage of the amniotic fluid is withdrawn, and is replaced with a saline or salt solution. This results in contraction of the uterus, which causes the woman to go into labor and give birth to the fetus which cannot live outside of the uterine environment; and (b) hepterotomy, a small incision made in the abdomen, permitting removal of the amniotic sac and fetus. Effectiveness: 100 percent. Possible side effects: bleeding, discomfort, infection, perforation, hemorrhage.

13. *Abortion: viable fetus (28–36 weeks).* The two techniques mentioned above can be used. It is illegal in most countries and considered to be murder by most people, since the fetus at this stage could live on its own outside the mother's body.

14. *Infanticide.* Killing a child upon or shortly after its birth is not strictly a birth control technique, but rather a means of population control that was employed in a number of cultures in the past. It is almost unknown today.

A major result of the widespread ignorance of birth control techniques has been, and still is, the large number of unwed teenage parents in this country. Appendix C lists several services that provide counseling for teenagers on birth control.

Appendix C

Services Available to Youth in Most Medium-to-Large Cities

This is a sample list of youth services that are available in most cities of 50,000 or more people. Some of these services are offered by nationwide organizations; others are offered by local groups in most communities.

Most cities have teen centers. To find the name of a teen center in your community, try the yellow pages of the telephone directory under "Youth" or "Teen," or call the city hall or a local high school.

GENERAL YOUTH ORGANIZATIONS

Big Brother Association. Provides male companions for boys aged 7 to 16 years who have lost their fathers through divorce, death, or separation. In order to qualify for the program, boys must not have had recent contact with their fathers. The adult "big brother" spends three hours a week for a period of one year or more with the boy.

Big Sister Association. A counterpart of Big Brother.

Boy Scouts of America. Consists of three groups: Cub Scouts, Scouts, and Explorer Scouts. Builds character, good citizenship, and develops physical fitness through educational and recreational activities.

Campfire Girls. Provides creative experience in living; develops individuality and life skills; operates resident and day camps.

Girl Scouts of America. Provides educational and recreational events for small groups of girls. Seeks to develop individuality, a system of values, leadership, and service.

Salvation Army. A variety of services are offered. Contact the Salvation Army in your community.

Teen Center Alliance, Inc. Variety of activities.

The Beginnings. Provides the following services and activities for junior high and high school age youth: theater, vocational counseling, sports, arts, crafts, social programs, individual counseling.

Young Men's Christian Association. Sponsors social and athletic activities.

Young Women's Christian Association. Sponsors social and athletic activities. Also provides youth with assistance in receiving high school diploma by part-time study.

457

EMPLOYMENT

Rent-a-Kid. Runs an odd-jobs service for adolescents aged 14 to 18.

Y.E.S. Youth Employment Services. Seeks full-time jobs for older youth.

ETHNIC AND RACIAL GROUPS

Afro-American Cultural Center. Provides activities for black youth.

Boston Chinese. Provides activities for Chinese youth.

RELIGIOUS ORGANIZATIONS

Associated Jewish Charities. Variety of services for Jewish teens.

Catholic Youth Organization. An organization sponsored by the Catholic Church that provides social and athletic activities for teens; also religious counseling.

Church Home Society. An Episcopalian organization that provides a variety of services.

Interfaith, Inc. Runs activities designed to promote cooperation and understanding between faiths.

COUNSELING AND MEDICAL SERVICES

Adolescent and Family Counseling Center. Provides crisis counseling for teens and their families.

Adolescent Rehabilitation Program. In-patient program for emotionally disturbed youth who have severe acting-out problems and impulse control problems. The program provides schooling, counseling, and psychiatric services.

The Crittendon Clinic. Abortion counseling and medical services.

The Florence Crittendon League. Provides a residence and service program for the young pregnant woman who seeks a temporary community geared to her special needs.

Legal Aid Bureau. Law offices serving the community with free legal advice and representation in civil legal matters for persons unable to pay.

Planned Parenthood League. Provides open counseling about birth control and sex.

Preterm. Services include gynecological clinic, abortion clinic, and birth control counseling.

Project "Place." Hot-line counseling; runaway house provides temporary shelter.

Rape Crisis Center. Provides emotional support, legal, medical information to rape victims.

Single Parents. Advises unwed teen parents as well as older single parents.

Travelers' Aid Society. Provides social services to travelers and a protective travel service for children and the handicapped.

SPECIAL EDUCATION

Center for Blind Children. Provides social and educational services for the blind and partially blind.

Special Education Products, Inc. Promotes physical education and cultural activities for children with physical and mental handicaps.

OUTDOOR EDUCATION AND RECREATION

American Youth Hostels, Inc. Provides inexpensive overnight lodging for teens and adults. Also sponsors organized trips for groups.

Appalachian Mountain Club. Sponsors hikes, camping trips, and other outdoor activities. Adolescents under 18 can participate only if they come with an adult.

Community Boating. Provides inexpensive sailing training (both in the classroom and on water) for teens. Youth membership is subsidized by adult membership fees.

Fresh Air Society. Provides ten-day camping experiences for young teens.

Outward Bound. Operates various programs aimed at increasing self-confidence (see Chapter 12).

Glossary

Abstract thought: Considering something apart from the particular instance; thinking about concepts and ideas; theoretical thought.

Accommodation: Piaget's term for acquiring new schemas to meet the demands of new information or experiences.

Acquiesor: Someone who usually accepts or complies with the will of others.

Adaptation: The process by which living things adjust to their environment.

Aggressive gang: A club, usually comprised of males, organized expressly to commit such antisocial acts as theft and property damage. It is often organized to allow members to prove their masculinity.

Anaclitic identification: Freud's theory that both boys and girls identify with their mother in the first two years; when boys later learn to identify with their fathers, one result is that they feel insecure about their gender.

Androgyny: Being able to engage in situationally effective behavior without regard for its stereotype as male or female.

Anthropoid: An animal that resembles man; one of the higher apes.

Appropriateness: Jackson and Messick's second criterion for judging creative products. The product must fill some need or desire to a great degree.

Assimilation: Piaget's term for the mental process in which a person perceives new experiences and information because of their similarity to previous experiences and information.

Associationism: The theory that creative people associate various parts of problems together into new, imaginative solutions.

Authority figures: Adults who are "in charge." Those adults (especially teachers, police officers) who are perceived by adolescents as people who have power and are in command.

Autonomy: Independence of thought and behavior; self-ruling.

Autosexuality: Love of oneself; first stage in sexual development.

Bar or bas mitzvah: Ceremony in which a Jewish child becomes responsible for his or her moral and religious duties and so becomes an adult.

Behavior modification: A systematic attempt to change or manage behavior through reinforcement, punishment, or extinction of behavior.

Behavior therapy: A behavior modification approach to psychological problems. Behavior therapy deals with observable responses and not with intrapsychic conflicts or underlying motivations.

Behaviorism: A school of psychological theory and practice that is concerned with observable behavior and the effects of conditioning on that behavior.

Behavioristic theory of the formation of subcultures: Subcultures develop as a result of a series of trial-and-error behaviors, which are rewarded by society and become part of a group's repertoire.

Birth order: The order of birth of siblings. Some psychologists believe that this factor is a significant determinant of adult personality characteristics.

Career education: The attempt of the school to improve the validity of the vocational choices of its students.

Case studies: In-depth descriptions of the lives of individuals.

Catharsis: Emotional release of pent-up feelings.

Center-of-the-world status: Because first-born children and only children do not have to compete with other siblings when they are infants, they experience a center-of-the-world status; their environment is totally centered around them.

Chauvinist: Devotion to and glorification of one's own sex, nationality, age group, and the like.

Chromosomes: The structures of the cell nucleus composed of genetic material responsible for the determination and transmission of hereditary characteristics.

Cliques: Small groups of three to eight individuals who more or less consciously exclude others from their tight friendship.

Clubs: Clubs are cliques with a more formal organization. Membership has specific goals which are stated explicitly.

Codification: Reducing behaviors to a code: systematizing; the process of developing new laws; Piaget's term for the adolescent stage of moral development.

Cofigurative culture: A culture in which the main models for the young are their own contemporaries rather than adults.

Commitment: A value or belief to which a person has become devoted as the result of experiencing some crisis.

Commune: A group of people who live together in a relationship of mutual social and economic interests.

Companionship marriage: A marriage in which the partners work for a relationship of equity, flexibility, and intimacy.

Compensation: When unable to express feelings to one person, they are shown to another; in cognitive theory, refers to balanced approaches to problem solving.

Comprehensive education: A total plan for education that responds to the intellectual and developmental needs of students and includes the mastery of learning skills as well as subject material.

Comprehensive high school: A high school that offers courses in all the basic subject areas and provides programs of college preparation and vocational training.

Concrete operational stage: Piaget's third stage of cognitive development, which takes place approximately during the elementary school years.

Condensation: Jackson and Messick's fourth criterion for judging creative products; it refers to the simplicity and summary power of the product.

Conditioning: Manipulation or training to habitually respond in a certain manner.

Confirmation: A Christian rite through which a person becomes a full member in his or her church.

Conservation: Piaget's term for the intellectual understanding of the invariance of quantity.

Consolidation: The use of newly learned problem-solving skills in more and more inclusive ways.

Constitutional rights: The rights guaranteed to a citizen by the United States Constitution, especially those guaranteed by the first ten amendments to the Constitution (the Bill of Rights) such as freedom of speech and religion, and protection against double jeopardy and unreasonable searches and seizures.

Controlled drug: Any drug which is covered by the rules of the Food and Drug Administration.

Conventional morality: The second two levels in Kohlberg's theory of moral development where individuals are mostly concerned with what others think of them.

Corporal punishment: Bodily punishment; physical punishment.

Crisis: A period of physical or psychological turmoil, at the end of which the person tends to change for worse or better.

Crisis intervention: Assistance given at the time that a particular crisis is occurring.

Critical period: That time of a person's life when a particular issue or growth process is most important; for example, the second critical period for creativity is adolescence.

Cross-sectional studies: The measurement of change in groups of individuals of different ages to determine the effects of age.

Crowds: Crowds are loosely knit organizations, made up of several cliques.

Cultural mores: Accepted traditional customs; moral attitudes held by a particular social group.

Culture transmission: A theory that new subcultures begin as imitations of those of the previous generation.

Custodial function: A school situation in which the school "babysits" the students; the school provides students with a place to spend the day rather than providing them with true learning experiences.

Death trend: The increased likelihood of a suicide being committed in a family in which a death has recently occurred.

Deductive reasoning: The conclusion follows from the stated premises; reasoning from general to particular ideas. Example: (1) All humans eventually die. (2) Alice is a human. (3) Therefore Alice is going to die some day.

Defense mechanisms: Unconscious techniques used to avoid confronting some unpleasant truth about ourselves.

Delay of gratification: Waiting for a pleasurable experience or reward until a prior condition is met or a behavior is performed.

Depression: Low spirits, despondency, dejection.

Deprogramming: Forceful technique for persuading youth to end their membership in esoteric religious groups.

Descriptive studies: Those in which information is gathered on one characteristic of a large number of individuals.

Developmental tasks: Skills, knowledge, functions, and attitudes which are needed in order to succeed at the various stages of life.

Dogmatism: Strong expression of belief; the inability to imagine that one might be wrong in any way.

Dominant role: A pattern of behavior indicating that the person is seen as superior to his or her peers.

Diversion program: An early intervention program for potential juvenile delinquents.

Drug: Any chemical or vegetable substance which causes a physiological, emotional, or behavioral change in a person.

Drug abuse: Use of a drug in such a way that the individual's physical, mental, emotional well-being is in some way impaired.

Drug abuse alternatives: Activities that are suggested as helping youth avoid drug abuse. Included are: physical, psychological, and sensory awareness; work is fun; esthetic appreciation; learning; nonrational experience, and social and political activism.

Drug addiction: A term that has so many meanings that experts in this field are now beginning to use the term *drug dependence* instead.

Drug dependence: Occurs when there is a physical or psychological need, or both, resulting from the continuous use of a drug. Psychological need occurs when the person feels anxious or irritable when he is unable to obtain the drug. Physical dependence, on the other hand, only occurs when strong physical symptoms result from the use of the drug, such as vomiting, sweating, muscle tremors, delusions and hallucinations.

Drug overdose: The situation in which taking a drug has abnormal or severe reactions, not planned.

Drug tolerance: A condition that develops from continuous use of a drug, when a larger and larger amount is needed to produce the same effect.

Dualism: The belief that something is either true or false, right or wrong; the acceptance of absolute dichotomies.

Duplication theory: Tolman's theory that the kinds of persons one chooses as a spouse, friend, partner, and so on will be determined partially by old intimate relationships.

Early maturer: Person for whom puberty starts significantly earlier than average.

Ecological approach: A therapeutic approach that studies the relationship of individuals to their environment and advocates helping troubled people in their own environment rather than in an office or institution.

Ego: Freud's term for that aspect of personality that negotiates conflicts between id and superego.

Emancipated minor: A teenager who is under the legal age but who is self-supporting.

Empirico-induction: To look at available facts and attempt to induce some generalization from them.

Equilibrium: A state of balance. Piaget said that humans strive for a state of balance between themselves and the world.

Erogenous zones: Areas of the body that produce sexual pleasure; primarily the mouth, the anus, and the genitals.

Esthetic appreciation: Developing an appreciation for music, art, or literature as a way of overcoming drug dependence.

Ethical development: Growth in the understanding of the principles of right or good conduct.

Evolution: The theory that higher organisms (such as man and other primates) are descended from more primitive organisms.

Experiential learning: An educational approach that is the trademark of alternative schools and programs; experiential learning takes place in nonclassroom settings and through volunteer and paid jobs rather than textbooks.

Extended family: Parents, children, grandparents, aunts, uncles, and other relatives and associates all living under the same roof.

Feedback: Information about the result of a process.

Fixated: To become stuck or held up at one stage of development, usually permanently. Only outside intervention such as therapy is likely to change the condition.

Focal theory: Coleman's theory that adolescents tend to deal with a series of personal crises, which are dealt with one at a time.

Formal operational stage: Piaget's fourth stage of cognitive development which often begins at puberty.

Future shock: Toffler's term for the uncomfortable and disorienting condition that results from the technological change and the "premature arrival of the future."

Gangs: Like a club, the gang has a specified membership, but tends to disdain the specific organization of rules, relying more on the day-to-day leadership to decide what the members will do.

Generation gap: Psychological, attitudinal, and ideological differences between younger and older people created by a difference of experiences in a rapidly changing world.

Genetics: The branch of biology that deals with heredity; determines traits that children inherit from their parents.

Gonorrhea: An infectious disease transmitted by sexual contact and caused by a bacterium called gonococcus. Untreated gonorrhea can lead to sterility and blindness in the eyes of a newborn infant of an infected mother.

Group therapy: Treatment of emotional problems, particularly those affecting social interaction, within a group situation.

Halfway houses: Transitional, therapeutic homes for ex-convicts and former mental patients.

Hard drugs: Drugs that cause physical as well as psychological dependence.

Hermaphrodites: A true hermaphrodite has the primary sex organs (testes and ovaries) of both the male and female. A false hermaphrodite has the primary sex organs of one sex in undeveloped form and the secondary sex characteristics of the other.

Heterosexuality: Love of a member of the opposite sex; third stage in sexual development.

Homosexuality: Love of a member of one's own sex; second stage in sexual development.

Hormonal balance: The relationships among chemical substances such as estrogen, progesterone, and testosterone, which regulate bodily functions.

Hormone therapy: Regulating sex characteristics or other metabolic functions through the use of hormones.

Hypersensitivity: Excessive or abnormal sensitivity.

Hypothetical deductive reasoning: The form of abstract thinking that is reflective and which considers imaginary possibilities; usually starts during adolescence.

"I" message: Thomas Gordon's term for stating a personal problem as one's own problem rather than defining it as someone else's.

Id: Freud's term for the innate drives with which we are born.

Identity: Sense of self; the knowledge of who and what one is; the state of being at one with oneself; having a well-integrated personality.

Identity achievement: A state in which numerous crises have been experienced, resolved, and enriched, and the relatively permanent commitments to an identity have been made.

Identity confusion: A state in which no crisis has been experienced by the individual and no commitments have been made as yet.

Identity crisis: A major turning point, or situation, arising in the process of determining what and who one is.

Identity foreclosure: A state in which no crisis has been experienced, one in which the person has been made to make a commitment on his identity, usually forced on him by his parents.

Identity moratorium: A state in which considerable crisis has been experienced, but one in which no commitments have yet been made to an identity.

Identity status: While adolescents are growing toward adulthood, their state of identity, that is, sense of self, can be described by one of four terms: identity confusion, identity foreclosure, identity moratorium, or identity achievement.

Inconsistent conditioning: Mixed messages having contradictory expectations and rewards.

Incorrigible: Incapable of being made to obey the law.

Individualization: Designing an educational program for the specific needs of an individual student.

Inductive reasoning: Drawing a conclusion about all the members of a class from the examination of a few members of the class; reasoning from the particular to the general. For example: (1) Every day at dawn it has gotten brighter. (2) Tomorrow there will be a dawn. (3) Tomorrow at dawn it will probably get brighter.

Information processing: The use of clear-cut plans to solve new types of problems.

Innate: Inborn; those traits and characteristics that are genetic.

Initiation rite: A program carried out, usually in preindustrial cultures, to induct youth into adulthood. Such rites usually include hazing, tests of strength and self-control, and circumcision. In virtually all cases, the initiates are males between the ages of 13 and 16.

In-school suspension room: A place for children with behavior problems who need to be temporarily removed from the classroom.

Instructional modes: Ways of organizing educational experiences for students; teaching strategies.

Intellect: That aspect of the mind capable of intelligent thought, such as problem solving and association.

Intelligence: The ability to learn and understand.

Intelligence quotient: Derived from test scores, IQ equals mental age divided by chronological age multiplied by 100; a measure of ability to perform well in middle-class American schools.

Interpersonal awareness: A state in which one's self-understanding, honesty, and openness with others is increased; often used as an approach in dealing with drug dependence.

Inversion: The attempt to solve a problem by returning a situation to its original state.

Isolates: Persons who do not form relationships with others.

Judeo-Christian dogma: A set of religious beliefs derived from the Old and New Testaments of the Bible.

Just Community School: A school in Cambridge, Massachusetts designed to facilitate growth along the lines of Kohlberg's theory of moral development.

Juvenile delinquent: A person usually under 18 who has committed a crime; the most common crimes are theft and vandalism.

Juvenile statutes: Laws governing the conduct of young people.

Language of acceptance: A communication technique developed by Thomas Gordon through which adults show their acceptance of a youngster's feelings or desires.

Late maturer: A person for whom puberty starts significantly later than average.

Latency: Period of childhood, usually from ages 5 to 10, when sexual interests appear to be dormant.

Learning: Any relatively permanent change in behavior which cannot be attributed to states such as anxiety, exhaustion, drug use, and the like.

Learning disabilities: An inability to learn at a normal rate, which is not due to a known physical defect.

Learning theory: Based on the idea that people's behavior, not their thoughts, is the best predictor of their future behavior; rests on the belief that people act the way they do because of what they have been taught by their environment.

Libido: Freud's term for the source of psychic energy. It usually has sexual connotations.

Life-space interview: A child counseling approach developed by Fritz Redl. Unlike traditional psychotherapy which takes place in a therapist's office, a life-space interview takes place "on site" and is conducted by an adult who is a regular part of the child's daily life.

Linear thinking: McLuhan's term for the logical, sequential thought processes that are influenced by the phonetic alphabet and print.

Longitudinal studies: The measurement of change in a group of individuals over time to determine the effects of age.

Magical thinking: Irrational, wishful thinking; the belief that one's thoughts can actually affect events.

Manipulative experiments: Research in which the experimenter manipulates a variable such as an instructional technique in order to discover the effects on some group of individuals.

Maturation: The process of growing and developing.

Maturity: The state of being fully developed physically, socially, and psychologically.

Maximum growth spurt: The period when growth is at its fastest rate.

Melancholy: Depression; low spirits, sadness.

Menarche: The establishment or beginning of menstruation.

Mental structures: Piaget's term to describe the tools of adaptation that exist in the mind.

Milgram electric shock obedience test: An experiment that investigated the willingness of persons to inflict pain on others.

Mini-generation gap: A small generation gap that can exist between persons who are separated in age by only a few years, caused by rapid and dramatic social change.

Moral maturity score: The score that is derived from responses to hypothetical dilemmas on Kohlberg's scale for rating a person's level of moral development.

Moratorium of youth: That period in our society during which young people are allowed to postpone adult commitments and delay life choices in order to experiment with different ways of being.

Motor development: Growth of coordination and strength.

Multidimensional: Any situation which has more than one dimension in force.

Naturalistic experiments: Research in which the investigator measures the effects on some group of persons of some change in their environment caused naturally, e.g., crises caused by a flood.

Negative identity: A sense of self and pattern of behavior that is adopted by adolescents who are rebelling against demands that they follow an opposite pattern.

Negative reinforcement: A stimulus that stops when a behavior begins and makes that behavior more likely to occur again in the future, for example, a threat that ends when the desired act is performed.

Neotribal people: McLuhan's idea that electronic media and instant communication have bound the world together into a single modern tribe (the prefix *neo* means "new").

Networks: An association among several clubs, gangs, or crowds. Usually formed to promote communication between people of similar interests.

Neurotic delinquency: Illegal behavior that is caused by youngsters' desires to communicate their unfulfilled needs to significant adults.

New convergence: Boorstin's term for the diminishing differences among peoples of the world because of modern technology.

New obsolescence: Boorstin's term for rapid societal changes brought about by technology that produce a lack of continuity in people's lives.

Nocturnal emissions: Also known as "wet dreams"; ejaculation of semen during sleep.

No-lose method: Thomas Gordon's term for a six-step communication technique that helps people work out conflicts.

Nonaggressive status offender: One whose crime usually does not cause harm to the property or body of another, e.g., running away, prostitution.

Nondirective approach (to teaching and counseling): An approach developed by Carl Rogers in which the client or student assumes responsibility for the direction of discussions with the therapist or teacher reflecting feelings rather than interpreting behavior.

Nonlinear thinking: McLuhan's term for the thought processes that have evolved as a result of the change from printed to electronic media.

Nonrational experience: Any experience of a mystical or spiritual nature. Often used to combat drug dependence.

Nontraditional schools: Schools that have unusual and unconventional approaches to education.

Normal range of development: Growth that progresses in normal stages; the ages within which development is considered to be occurring normally.

Nuclear family: Parents and their children.

Numerical descriptive studies: Research that studies the number or percentage of a particular trait to be found in a specified population.

Object constancy: An infant's awareness that objects exist independent of his perception.

Oedipal conflict: Sigmund Freud's term for the discomfort children feel when they experience sexual attraction to the parent of the opposite sex, but are not allowed to fulfill this desire because of societal mores.

Open campus: A school program in which students receive school credit for work or educational experiences that take place in the community.

Open marriage: A marriage in which the partners agree they will allow each other the freedom of having sexual relations with others.

Operations: Piaget's term for the mental manipulation of the environment; an action that takes place in the imagination.

Organic delinquency: Illegal behavior of juveniles that can be attributed to brain damage or mental deficiency in the offenders.

Organization: Piaget's term for the inborn tendency of people to mentally organize schema.

Outward Bound: An organized outdoor education program that teaches survival skills, cooperation, nature appreciation, and personal development through the meeting of physical challenges.

Paraprofessionals: School aides, often adults from the local community, who assist professionally trained personnel such as teachers and administrators. Paraprofessionals are often hired to facilitate community and parental involvement in the schools.

Parent-child role reversal: A situation in which the parents are incapable of fulfilling their role and the children are forced to take on the responsibilities of the parents both for themselves and their parents.

Peer groups: Groups of people who are of the same age, class, or social standing.

Physical awareness: The awareness one achieves of one's own body through such activities as walking, jogging, dancing, gymnastics, and group sports.

Pluralism: The coexistence of distinct ethnic, religious, or cultural groups within a geographic area.

Political activism: Involvement in activities of a political nature; greater than average effort to promote some candidate or cause.

Positive reinforcement: Any event that makes a response more likely to occur again in the future, for example, rewarding an animal with food when it performs a trick.

Postconventional morality: The third two levels, based on the principle of justice, in Kohlberg's theory of moral development wherein individuals use their own moral principles rather than blindly conforming to conventional morality.

Preconventional morality: The first two levels in Kohlberg's theory of moral development wherein moral behavior is largely based on self-concern.

Premarriage relationships: Sexual relationships taking place before marriage.

Premature foreclosure: Ending the moratorium period and choosing an identity too early; a situation in which young persons do not allow themselves sufficient time to consider what kind of adult they want to become.

Preoperational stage: Piaget's second stage of cognitive development which roughly corresponds with the preschool ages.

Primary group: A group whose members have intimate face-to-face interaction and spontaneous cooperation.

Primary prevention: A community mental health concept that refers to the removal of the cause of problems before they begin.

Primary reinforcers: Food, drink, praise, or privileges that are used as rewards for desirable behavior.

Principle of justice: According to Kohlberg, the principle of justice comes from a universal understanding of fairness and is the fundamental issue of morality.

Print-oriented people: McLuhan's term for the general personality and intellectual characteristics that result from learning about events by reading.

Psychogenic: Originating in the mind.

Psychological awareness: The exploration and greater understanding of one's inner resources through reading, self-observation, meditation, therapy, or participation in a self-help group.

Psychopathology: Disorders or illness resulting from problems in the mind.

Psychosocial dwarfism: A condition in which puberty is so delayed by parental mistreatment that the teenager looks like a much younger child.

Psychosomatic (disorder): Physical symptoms caused in part by psychological problems such as extreme anxiety.

Psychotherapy: An intervention approach to the psychological treatment of emotional disorders in which the patient and the therapist discuss the emotional problems of the patient, and the therapist attempts to help the patient resolve intrapsychic conflicts and become better adjusted to his or her daily life.

Psychotic delinquency: The illegal behavior of juveniles that can be attributed to mental illnesses such as schizophrenia.

Puberty: The period during which the individual's reproductive organs become functional and secondary sex characteristics develop.

Racial composition: Refers to the number of Caucasian, Negro, Asian, Hispanic, Native American, and so on, members in a particular group.

Recapitulation: G. Stanley Hall's theory that the development of the life of each human is a telescoped repetition of the development of our species as a whole.

Recidivism: Relapsing into criminal behavior; being convicted a second time.

Reflexes: An automatic response to a specific event; for example, the knee-jerk response to the knee being tapped in a certain place.

Reinforcer: Anything that makes behavior more likely to occur again.

Relativism: The belief that all facts depend for their truth on the circumstances; the belief that all positions are relative, and may be equally true.

Religious fanaticism: Extreme belief that one's religion is the only possible right one.

Religious revival: The strong rebirth of interest in a religious way of life.

Remote associations: Seemingly unrelated words or ideas that occur during creative thought.

Repudiation: Disavowal; rejection. Adolescents need to reject numerous possibilities in life in order to choose an identity.

Residential care center: A treatment center that houses patients who need counseling or adult supervision.

Reversibility: Piaget's term for the intellectual understanding that an action can be retraced by an opposite equal action.

Revival: Refers to the increased interest in the country in religious activities.

Rites of passage: Ceremonies and tests that mark the transition from childhood to adult status.

Ritualistic behavior: Acting according to a prescribed ceremony.

Schema: Piaget's term for basic mental forms of action that interact with the environment; a well-defined sequence of physical or mental actions.

School phobia: Abnormal, irrational fear of attending school.

Secondary group: A group whose members have less permanent and more casual contacts.

Secondary prevention: A community mental health concept that refers to slowing down the progress of problems that have already begun.

Secondary reinforcers: Tokens, points, or other acknowledgements of desirable behavior that can be exchanged for food, privileges, or money.

Self-fulfilling prophecy: An event that occurs because the person *thought* it would; for example, you fail an exam because you are convinced that you are going to.

Sensory awareness: Experiences that make one aware of one's senses, such as camping in the outdoors.

Sensorimotor skills: Movement involving interaction of the muscular system and the senses; how infants discover the world around them.

Sensorimotor stage: Piaget's first stage of cognitive development which extends from birth until the appearance of language.

Sex education: Learning programs to help children understand human reproduction and sexual behavior.

Sex identity: All the physical characteristics and behaviors associated with being male or female that are determined by genetic inheritance.

Sex role: Those behaviors identified with gender that are both biologically and culturally determined.

Sex role adaptation: How one adapts to behavior expectations associated with one's sex.

Sex role orientation: How comfortable a person feels about his or her biologically determined sex identity (being born male or female).

Sex role preference: The preference a person shows for the behavior traits that society has assigned to the feminine or masculine sex role.

Sexual revolution: Changes in attitudes about sexual behavior that have resulted largely from the availability of new forms of birth control.

Skeletal growth: Development or growth of the bony or cartilaginous framework supporting the soft tissues and protecting the internal organs.

Social activism: Greater than normal involvement in social causes.

Socioeconomic status: An index of a person's social status based on his or her own or family's level of education and income.

Sociogram: A schematic drawing that shows the social groupings in a classroom at any particular time.

Sociopathic delinquency: Illegal behavior of juveniles that can be attributed to character disorders in which the offenders have an incapacity for love and an absence of guilt.

Soft drugs: Drugs which may or may not cause psychological dependence and which do not cause physical dependence.

Solidification: New problem-solving skills gradually become used with greater confidence and applicability.

Stereotypes: Conforming to a general pattern; conventional, oversimplified beliefs.

Stimulation: Excitation, activation, arousal.

Storm and stress: "Sturm und drang"; emotional turbulence and instability thought to occur primarily during adolescence.

Structuralism: School of thought that believes creative solutions are obtained by changing one's point of reference.

Subcultures: Groups having social, economic, ethnic, or age characteristics and corresponding behaviors distinctive enough to distinguish them from others within the same culture or society.

Submissive role: A pattern of behavior indicating that the person is seen as inferior to his or her peers.

Suggestibility: Easily influenced by others; susceptible to suggestion.

Superego: Freud's term for the individual's conscience; one of the three structures of personality in his theory.

Swinging: An approach to sexual relationships in which couples exchange sexual partners.

Syphilis: An infectious disease transmitted by sexual contact and caused by a microorganism called a spirochete. Untreated syphilis can lead to paralysis and insanity.

Tertiary prevention: A community mental health concept that refers to the rehabilitation of the patient after damage has been done, so that the spread of the problem within the community is reduced.

Thinking style: The way people perceive and interpret the world around them.

Token system: Secondary reinforcers that may be exchanged for food, money, or privileges are used to reinforce desirable behaviors.

Transformation: Jackson and Messick's third criterion for judging creative products; judging a product in terms of the constraints within which the creator is working.

Transsexual: A person who has had an operation to alter his or her primary sex characteristics.

Traumatic (experience): An emotional shock that creates lasting damage to psychological development.

Trial marriage: A relationship in which teenagers are allowed to live together and to have sexual intercourse with the use of birth control.

Unusualness: Jackson and Messick's first criterion for judging creative products; the product must be unique or at least statistically rare.

Validate: To verify, accept, and value another's thoughts and feelings.

Values clarification: A set of techniques used to help youth determine their own values.

Vandalism: Willful or malicious destruction of property.

Venereal disease: Contagious diseases such as syphilis or gonorrhea that are transmitted by sexual contact.

Victimless crime: The belief that those who commit crimes having no victims should not be fined or imprisoned for their actions, for example the drug abuser who is the only one who suffers from the use of drugs.

Vocational identity: People's way of thinking about themselves in relation to the kind of job they seek or the job they have.

Volunteerism: Another term for experiential learning. Education takes place through the direct involvement in "real life" work situations, but on a volunteer basis.

Voucher system: An alternative educational funding system in which parents are given vouchers they can use to send their children to the school of their choice.

Walkabout: A planned program of life experiences for adolescents designed to prepare them for adulthood; the concept comes from an Aborigine rite of passage.

Work as fun: The concept that when work is engaged in as an enjoyable and fulfilling activity, it can help to combat drug dependence.

Name Index

Aaronson, B., *340*
Abelson, H., *339*
Abernathy, T. I., 251, *269*
Abbott, L. T., 29, *35*
Abbott, S., 29, *35*, 245, *269*
Abney, C., *151*
Abraham, Y., *366*
Abrams, L., *396*
Abt, L. E., *202*
Ackerman, J. W., 347, *366*
Adamak, R. J., *199*
Adams, B., *271*
Adams, D., *202*
Adelman, H., *395*
Adelson, J., 59, 77, 206, *232*, *340*
Adeniran, T., *234*
Adilman, P. H., *201*
Adler, A., 135
Adler, F., *396*
Afrow, M., 142, *148*
Albee, G. W., 362, *367*
Aldous, J., Jr., 206, *233*
Allen, C. D., *109*
Altland, R., 310, *339*
Ames, L. B., *422*
Anderson, C., 388, *395*
Angrist, S. S., *110*
Annis, H. M., *340*
Anspaugh, D., 250, *269*
Antorousky, H., *269*
Argyle, M., 404, *422*
Aries, P., 199
Aristotle, 57
Arlin, P. K., 120, 124, *148*
Armstrong, S., *270*
Arnett, H. J., *340*
Arnold, S., *272*
Arword, B., 283, *304*
Askov, W. H., *273*
Asnes, D. P., 356, *368*

Babikian, H., *273*
Babst, D., 331, *339*
Bachman, J. G., 40, *76*
Bachman, L., *339*
Baden, M. A., 206, *233*
Baer, D., 391, *396*
Bagg, R. A., *339*
Bahn, A. K., *368*
Baizerman, M., *234*
Bakalar, J. B., 318, *339, 340*
Bakher, C. B., *340*

Balswick, J. O., 251, *269, 422*
Baltes, P. B., *109, 151*
Bandura, A., 206, *232*, 381, *395*, 396
Bandura, H., 408, *422*
Baran, A., *201*
Barber, T. S., *340*
Barinbaum, L., 79
Barker, R. G., 221, *232*
Barnes, G., *339*
Barnlund, D. C., *269*
Barter, J., *369*
Battegay, R., *340*
Battistone, D. L., 182, *200*
Baumrinel, D., 182, *200*, 306
Bauer, R., *76*
Baumrinel, D., 182, *200, 306*
Beethoven, L., 128
Bayer, A. E., *422*
Bayh, B., 276, *304*, 373, *394*
Bayley, M. M., 59, *78*
Bealer, R. C., 402, *422*
Beauty, S., 93
Becker, H. S., *340*
Beever, A., 256, *271*
Behn, W. H., *306*
Beit-Hallahmi, B., 404, *422*
Bell, M., 53, *77*
Bell, R. A., *369*
Bell, T., 409
Bellah, R. N., *424*
Bely, C., 412, *422*
Bem, S. L., 65, *76, 201*
Benedict, R., 19-20, *35, 151*
Bengston, V. L., 32, *35, 201*
Benjamin, L., 258, *272*
Bennett, S., 64, *79*
Benson, R., 264, *270*
Bentler, P., 331, *339*
Berdie, R. F., 79
Berg, M., *269*
Berger, A. S., 61, *76*
Berger, B., *201*
Berger, S. E., *79*
Berkov, B., *271*
Berman, M., 41, *76*
Berson, R., *422*
Berzonsky, M., *151*
Best, D., *79*
Bettelheim, B., 93, *109, 182, 200*
Bickham, S., *151*
Bieliauskas, B., 64, *76*
Bierman, B., 256, *269*

Bierman, J., 256, *269*
Binet, A., 139
Bird, C., *304*
Black, M. W., *340*
Blackford, L., *340*
Blake, A., 391, *395*
Blake, L., 126, *148*
Blatt, M., 169-174
Block, R., 208, *232*
Blocker, T., 251, *270*
Blume, J., *84*
Blume, S. B., *341*
Blumer, H., *341*
Boas, F., 86, *109*
Bodemann, Y., *424*
Bogg, R., 331, *339*
Boorstin, D., 72-74, *77*
Bourne, R. S., 84, 100, *109*
Bower, E. M., *368*
Boyle, J., 403, *422*
Boyle, H. P., 220, *232*
Boyd, D., 126, *148*
Braaten, L., 359, *366*
Brabeck, M., 126, *148*
Brake, M., *273*
Brandon, J., *397*
Braungart, M. M., *424*
Braungart, R. G., *424*
Broughton, J., 126, *148*
Bricker, D. C., *175*
Brickman, W. W., *340*
Brietmeyer, R. G., 283, *305*
Brill, L., 331, *339*
Brim, O. G., 59, *77*
Bronfenbrenner, W., 181, 186-187, *200*
Brookes, M. H., *423*
Broverman, D., *77*
Broverman, I., 60-77
Brown, M., 251, *269*
Brown, J. W., *273*
Brown, P. E., *109*
Bruce, J., 256, 259, *269*
Bruch, H., *368*
Buff, S., *273*
Burnham, W. H., 84, *109*
Burstein, M., *397*
Burton, C. A., 385, *395*
Buser, R. L., *306*
Bush, S., *201*
Busk, P. A., *307*

Calhoun, J. F., *340*

Campbell, B. K., *269*
Camus, A., 354
Cangemi, J. P., *306*
Carlin, A. S., *340*
Carney, M., *306*
Carroll, J. F. X., *341*
Carroll, J. W., *234*
Carroll, L., 40
Carter, M. A., *306*
Cavan, R. S., 374, *394*
Chamberlain, T., 319, *339*
Chance, P., 244, *270*
Chand, I. P., *306*
Charnay, E., *271*
Chilman, C., *269*
Chilton, R., 382, *395*
Chotiner, M. M., *369*
Cisin, I., *339*
Clark, J. P., 403, *422*
Clark, K., *368*
Clark, R., *424*
Clark, S. M., 403, *422*
Clarkson, F., *77*
Clemens, S., *148*
Clifford, E., 100, 102, *109*
Cline, D. W., *273*
Cohen, S., 332, *339, 340*
Colby, M., *342*
Coleman, J. C., 27-29, *35*, 61, *77*
Coleman, J. S., 184, *200*, 207, *232*, 284, *304*
Coles, R., *201*
Colletta, N., 256, *269*
Collier, J., *369*
Colligan, J. T., 364, *366*
Collins, B. R., *424*
Collins, J. K., *271*
Collins, W. A., 410, *422*
Colston, D. H., *234*
Comstock, G., 409, *422*
Conger, J., 220, *232*
Connell, D. M., 65, 77
Connon, H., 356, *368*
Constantinople, A., 48, *77*
Corder, B. G., 354, *366*
Corder, R. F., 354, *366*
Cornuelle, R., *369*
Corcliero, J., *369*
Cottle, T. J., *37, 201*
Coulter, M., *270*
Cowing, D. E., *269*
Cox, W. B., *396*
Craig, M., 381, *395*

Crain, J. C., *306*
Crider, D. M., *306*
Culkin, J., *148*
Curtis, R. L., Jr., *307*
Cvetkovich, G., 79

Dacey, J. S., *35*, 133, 135, 138, *148, 150, 269*, 295, *304*, 356, *366*
Damico, S. B., 220, *232*
Dali, S., 127
Darling, C. D., 359, *366*
Darwin, C. R., 11, *37*
Davidson, E. S., 408, *423*
Davis, G. A., 206, *232*
Davis, J., *175*
Davis, K. E., *273*
Deal, T. E., 298, *304*
De Blassie, R. R., 360, *367*
De Cecco, J. P., 277, *304*
Dellas, M., 79
Demas, R. *369*
Dembo, M., 263, *269*
Derenne, R. T., *369*
Deutsch, H., 355, *366*
Dezelsky, T., *271*
Dickenson, G., 262, *269*
Diepold, J., 249, *269*
Digman, M., 250, *269*
Donovan, J., 79
Dorpat, T. L., 356, 366
Douglas, J. W. B., 100, *109*
Douvan, E., 59, *77*, 206, *232*
Doyle, N., *339*
Drabman, R. S., *424*
Dranoff, M., 242, *269*
Dresen, S., 260, *269*
Dreyer, P. H., 428, *439*
Duke, D., 288, *304*
Duncan, D. F., 373, *396*
Dunn, P., 264, *271*
Dunphy, D. C., 215, *232*
Duska, R., 172, *174*
Dutton, J. E., *422*

Eagan, A. B., 182, *200*
Edwards, L., *269*
Ehrhardt, A., 58, *78,* 101, *109*
Eicher, J. B., 109
Eichorn, D. H., 100, 109
Eiduson, B. T., 195, *200*
Einstein, A., 128
Eisenman, R., *342*

Elarbo, R., *306*
Elias, J., 241, *269*
Elifson, K. W., 331, *340*
Elinson, J., *341*
Elkin, F., 206, *232*
Emerick, R., *273*
Emmons, E. B., *397*
English, H. B., 209, *233*
Epstein, A., 258, *269*
Erikson, E., 21-27, *35*, 40, 74, *77, 174, 366*, 428, *439*
Etzioni, A., *175*
Evans, R., *35*, 77
Ewer, P. A., *307*

Fagot, B. I., 60, *77*
Farley, F. H., *396*
Farnsworth, D., 348, *367*
Farris, J. A., *202*
Faust, M. S., 100, 102, *109*
Feilitzen, C., 409, *422*
Feldman, D., 132-133, *148*
Feldman, S., *269*
Fendrich, J. M., *234*
Finch, R., *396*
Finney, J., *341*
Fiore, Q., 282
Fischman, S. H., *272*
Fishburne, P., *339*
Fisher, R., *306*
Fitzgerald, J. M., *151*
Flacks, R., *341*
Flavell, J., 120-124, *148, 151*
Flomenhaft, K., 30, *35, 269*
Floyd, H. H., Jr., 219, *233*
Flygare, T., 279, *304*
Fogg, P., *340*
Foner, A., 219, *233*
Forbush, J., *270*
Ford, R. C., *307*
Foreman, J., *269*
Forrest, D. V., *369*
Fortes, M., 193, *200*
Fowler, J., 405-406, *422*
Fox, G., 262, *270*
Francis, C. *367*
Frank, D. K., *397*
Frank, I., *201*
Freedman, M. L., 48, *78*
Freud, A., 16-17, *35*
Freud, S., 12-16, *35,* 58, 135, *174*
Freudenberger, H., 374, *395*

Friedenberg, E. Z., 240, *270,* 277, *304*
Friedman, C. J., 384, *395*
Frisk, M., 100, *109*
Fromm, E., 238, *270*
Furlong, W., 410, *422*

Gagnon, J. H., 60, *76,* 242, *270, 271*
Gaier, E. L., 79, *201*
Gaite, A. J. H., 120, *149*
Galbraith, R., *175*
Gall, M., *151*
Gallagher, B. J., *201*
Gallemore, B., 369
Gallup, G., 244, *270,* 288, *305*
Gandi, M., 167–168
Gardener, J., 195, *200*
Garner, H. G., 355, *367*
Gartner, A., 80
Gay, G. R., 324, *339*
Gebhardt, P., 241, *269*
Gerson, A., *272*
Gibbons, M., 295, *305*
Gibbs, J. O., *272*
Gifford, V. D., *234*
Gill, B. D., *439*
Gilligan, C., 166–168, *174*
Ginott, H. G., 194–195, *200, 201*
Ginsburg, H., *151*
Glaser, K., 355, *367*
Glasser, W., 290–291, *305*
Gleason, T. C., *341*
Gliek, S. J., 381, *395*
Glock, C. Y., *424*
Glueck, E., 382, *395*
Glueck, S., 382, *395*
Godenne, 241, *270*
Goethals, G. W., 40, *77*
Gold, H., 206, *232*
Gold, M., 385, *395*
Goldman, A., *273*
Goldman, R., 405, *422*
Goldmeier, H., *396*
Goldsmith, S., *273*
Goldstein, J. W., *341*
Golomber, H., *306*
Goode, E., 324, *339*
Goodenough, D. R., *153*
Goodman, P., 277, *305*
Goodwin, D. W., *341*
Goranson, R. E., *424*
Gordon, I. J., 382, *395*

Gordon, N. J., *424*
Gordon, T., 228, *233*
Gorth, W., 286, *305*
Gottlieb, D., 53, *77,* 220, *233*
Gowan, D., *151*
Grafstein, D., *341*
Graves, E. B., *424*
Gray, D. F., *201*
Green, A. W., 357, *367*
Green, L., 310, *339*
Green, R., 207, *233, 273*
Greenberger, E., 80
Grinder, R. E., 30–35, 428, *439*
Grinker, R. R., *369*
Grinspoon, L., 318, *339*
Griswold, B., *151*
Gropper, N. B., *306*
Gross, B., *270*
Grossman, J., *342*
Groves, W. E., *341*
Gruygier, T., 360, *367,* 388, *395*
Guilford, J. P., 135, *149*
Gump, P., 221, *232*
Gunter, B. G., 183, *200*
Gutmann, D., *234*
Guze, S. B., *341*

Haagen, C. H., *341*
Hackett, B., *201*
Hakansa, E., *269*
Halihas, J. A., *341*
Hall, G. S., 11–12, *35,* 29, 239, *270*
Hall, R., *175*
Hallman, R., 135, *149*
Halpen, L., *340*
Hamilton, D., 356, *367*
Hampton, P. J., 283, 305
Handel, G. F., 128
Haney, B., 385, *395*
Hankoff, L. D., 352, *367*
Hanraty, M. A., *396*
Hanson, D. J., *341*
Hansson, R., 251, *270*
Harmon, J., *424*
Harmon, L. W., *77*
Harms, E., 405, *422*
Harper, F. D., *341*
Harper, L. V., 80
Harris, J. R., *397*
Harris, L., *270*
Harrison, C. W., *234*
Hartshorne, H., 169, *174*
Harvey, D., 125, *149*

Haskell, M. R., 374, *394*
Hatcher, S. L. M., *273*
Hauser, J., *422*
Havighurst, R. J., 20–21, *35,* 160–161, *175,* 428, *439*
Hawton, L., *367*
Healey, G. W., 80
Heffernan, J., 126, *149*
Hemminiki, E., *341*
Henderson, E. H., 182, *200*
Hendin, H., *369*
Hendricks, L., 259, *270*
Henle, M., 124, *149*
Herold, E. S., 251, *270*
Herriott, R. W., 220, *233*
Hersch, S., *369*
Hess, R. D., *422*
Hetherington, E. M., 59, *77*
Higgins-Trenk, A., 120, *149*
Hill, R., 206, *233*
Hiltz, T., *424*
Hochman, J. S., *341*
Hochman, R., *305*
Hoffman, A., *272*
Hoffman, L. W., 181, *200*
Hoge, D., *423*
Hoolinger, P., *367*
Holden, C., 251, *271*
Holloway, S. M., *422*
Holmes, J., 364, *367*
Holt, S., 262, *271*
Holtz, J. A., *273*
Holzman, P. S., *369*
Hooker, E., 244, *270*
Hoop, K., *424*
Horn, P., *109, 306*
Hornstein, H. A., *422*
Hortling, H., 100, *109*
Howe, F., 62, *77*
Howe, L. W., *422*
Howe, M. M., 414, *422*
Howell, M. C., *397*
Howze, B., *367*
Hout, K., 55
Huba, G., 331, *339*
Hughes, J., 331, *339*
Hunt, D., 126, *149*
Hunt, C. 126, *150*

Iaconetta, R. G., *234*
Illich, I., *305*
Inazu, J., 262, *270*
Inhelder, B., *151*

Irwin, T., *397*

Jacklin, C., 63, *78*
Jackson, D. W., *273*
Jackson, J. K., 356, *366*
Jackson, P. W., 31, *36,* 127, *149*
Jacobs, J., 355, *368*
Jeffries, V., *424*
Jekel, J., *270*
Jencks, C., 180, *200*
Jenkins, R., 188, *200,* 382, *395*
Jensen, A., 141, *151*
Jensen, R. E., 283, *305*
Jersild, A. T., *270*
Jesser, C. J., 64, *77*
Jessor, R., 402, *423*
Jessor, S., *341*
Jofferth, S., *271*
Johnson, B. D., *341*
Johnson, C., *271,* 290–291, *305*
Johnson, D. W., *234*
Johnson, J. E., 65, *77*
Johnson, L., *339*
Johnson, M. M., 59, *77*
Johnson, R. T., *367*
Johnson, V., 242, *271*
Johnston, J., 40, *76*
Johnson-Laird, P. N., 124, *150*
Jones, M. C., 100, *109*
Jones, R., 428, *439*
Jones, S., *306*
Jones, T. M., *175*
Jones, W., 251, *270*
Josselyn, I. M., *270*
Jouard, S., 45, *77*
Juhasz, A., 256, 260, *270*
Jurich, A., 249, *270*
Justice, B., 373, *396*
Justice, R., 379, *396*

Kagan, H., 374, 396
Kaiser, F. M., *423*
Kandel, D. B., 51, *77,* 340
Kantner, J. E., 250, *270,* 272
Kaplan, H., *270*
Kaplan, R., *342*
Karabenick, S. A., *109*
Karp, S. A., *153*
Kash, C., *271*
Kastenbaum, R., 352, *367*
Kavenaki, S., *269*
Keane, S., *306*

Keillor, J., *151*
Kellogg, R., 60, *77*
Kelly, F., 391, *396*
Kelly, J. G., *369*
Kendall, N., *273*
Keniston, K., *35,* 183, *200,* 401, *423*
Kessler, M., 362, *367*
Kessler, R., *342*
Kiblin, J. E., 283, *305*
Kilpatrick, W. K., 59, *77,* 209, *233,* 265, *270*
Kindsvatter, R., 289, *305*
King, I., 89, *109*
King, K., 251, *269*
King, M., *369*
King, P., 126, *149*
Kinsey, A., *202*
Kirp, D., *202*
Kirschenbaum, H., *423*
Kitchener, K., 126, *149*
Klagsbrun, F., *367*
Klein, M. W., *396*
Kliman, G., *369*
Kline, D., 31, *36,* 271
Kline, S. A., *306*
Klos, D. S., 40, *77*
Knapp, J., 109, *202*
Knefelkamp, L., 126, *149*
Knight, J. A., *423*
Knox, I., *424*
Kobak, D., 283, *305*
Kogan, N., *153*
Kohl, H., 289, *305*
Kohlberg, L., 161–172, 403, *423*
Kokenes, B., *306*
Komarovsky, M., 61, 64, 69, *78*
Konner, M., 255, *270*
Korchein, S. J., 206, *234*
Korn, J. M., 342
Korn, S. J., *110*
Kotter, T., *202*
Kounanay, R., *270*
Kowalski, C. J., *306*
Kraft, I., 379, *396*
Kratcowski, J. E., 375, *396*
Kratcowski, P. C., 375, *396*
Krause, M. S., *423*
Krebs, R., 164, *174*
Kreider, D. G., 356, *367*
Krupor, K., *233*
Kubie, L. S., *37*
Kubler-Ross, E., 352, *367*

Kuhmerker, L., *175*
Kung, P. R., *202*
Kurfiss, J., 126, *149*
Kurz, S., 374, *396*

Lambert, B. G., 310, *339*
Lambert, T. A., *201*
Langman, L., 209, *232, 234*
Lancet, M., *269*
Larson, L. E., *202*
Larson, L. G., 206, *233*
Lasseigne, M. W., 403, 423
Laufer, R. S., *202*
LaVoie, J. C., *424*
LeBlanc, T., 385, *396*
Lee, P. C., *306*
Lees, J. P., 382, 396
Lefrancois, G., 181, *200,* 207, *233*
Leifer, A. D., *424*
LeMasters, E. E., *202*
Leming, J. S., *175*
Lenney, E., 68
Leona, M., 211, *233*
Leonard, G., 423, 431, *434*
Lerner, R., *110, 202*

Lesser, G., 51, *77*
Le Unes, A., 283, *305*
Levin, H. M., *306*
Levine, J., 181, *200*
Lewis, J. M., *369*
Lewis, R. W., *151*
Liberman, D., *77*
Lickona, T., 171, *174, 175*
Liddle, G. P., 220, *233*
Lieberman, J. J., *342*
Liebert, R. M., 409, *423*
Lilly, R. J., *423*
Lincoln, A., 407
Lindsey, D., *369*
Linkletter, A., *332*
Linne, O., 409, *422*
Lipitz, M. E., *273*
Litwak, E., *306*
Livson, N., 100, *109, 368*
Long, B. H., 182, *200*
Long, J. D., 283, *304*
Long, R., *306*
Lorand, S., 355, *367*
Love, B., 245, *269*
Lorenz, K., *110*
Lowery, P., *270*

Ludford, J., *111*
Lundell, B., 263, *269*
Lurie, E. E., *202*
Luther, M., 44
Lyness, J. L., *273*

Maccoby, E. E., 59, 63, *78*
MacDonald, G. W., 80
Mace, D. R., 198, *200*
Mace, V. C., 198, *200*
Macklin, E. D., 198, *200*, 270
Macredes, C., *201*
Magid, T., *270*
Mahlemann, R., *340*
Malinovich, M., 245, *270*
Maller, A. S., *424*
Manaster, G., 40, 53, *78*, 207, *233*
Mann, F., *395*
Manosevitz, M., *368*
Mantle, D., 251, *270*
Marcia, J. E., 45-48, *78*, 252
Marcus, I., 242, *270*
Margulien, R., *342*
Markle, G., 382, *395*
Marotz-Badan, R., *201*
Marsland, D., *234*
Marshall, W. A., 101
Martin, J., *270*
Martindale, C., *151*
Martorano, S. C., 124, *149*
Marx, B. S., 221, *233*
Maslow, A. H., 301, *305, 423, 433, 439*
Massey, R. H., *202*
Massey, T., 284, *305*
Masters, W., 242, *271*
Matis, J., 109
May, M. A., 169, *174*
May, R., 266, *270*
McAmarny, E. *271*, 353, 357, *367*
McBride, A. B., *202*
McCord, J., 382, *396*
McCord, W., 382, *396*
McCormack, P., 360, *367*
McCracken, J. H., 60, *78*
McIntire, W. G., 182, *200*
McKenry, P., 256, *271, 272*
McLeaf, J., *342*
McLuhan, M., 282
McMahon, M. B., *424*

McMorris, R., *151*
McNeary, S. S., *340*
Mead, M., 19-20, *37*, 186, *200*, 240, *271*
Mednick, M., *150*
Mednick, S., 129, *150*
Mendelsohn, G., *151*
Menken, J., *273*
Merenda, P., *342*
Merrill, R., 401, 423
Mertin, D., 211, *233*
Messick, S., 127, *149*
Meyer, H. J., *306*
Meyers, J. H., *202*
Meyer, P., 126, *150*
Michaels, M., *306*
Milgram, S., 164, *174*
Millar, R. M., *201*
Miller, D., 369
Miller, J. P., 347, 354, 367, *369, 396*
Miller, L., 30, *36*
Miller, W., 387, *396*
Millett, K., 64
Milman, D., *342*
Mines, R., 126, *150*
Minuchin, P., 60, *78*
Mischel, W., 59, *78*
Mitchell, J. J., 220, *233*
Mitchell, M. E., *367*
Modan, B., *269*
Moerk, E. L., *273*
Mondale, W. F., *200, 202*
Money, J., 57, *78*, 101, *109*
Moore, B., 186, *200*
Moore, H. A., 183, *200*
Moore, K., 256, 271
Morris, J., 57, *78*
Morris, W., *36*
Morrison, G., *369*
Moss, L. M., 356, *367*
Motto, J. A., 356, *367*
Moyer, D. H., *342*
Mulder, R., *342*
Munoz, R. F., *369*
Murphy, R., *273*
Murray, J. P., *424*
Mustein, B., 251, *271*
Mussen, P. H., 59, *78*, 100, *109*
Muuss, R. E., *36*, 46-47, *78, 342*
Myrick, R., 221, *233*

Naffziger, C. C., *77*

Naffziger, K., 60, *77*
Nash, S., *269*
Nass, G. D., 182, *200*
Neale, J. M., 408, *423*
Nease, B., 387, *395*
Neil, S., *306*
Neill, A. S., 170, *175*
Neill, G., *78, 306*
Nelsen, H., *423*
Nelson, E. A., 59, *78*
Nesselroade, J., *111, 151*
Nettleton, C., 31, *36, 273*
Newman, B. M., *78, 209, 233*
Newman, P. R., *78, 209, 233*
Newson, E. T., 382, *396*
Niebuhr, H. R., *424*
Niemark, E. D., 124, *150*
Nisbett, R. E., *342*
Noe, R. P., *234*
Norton, D. L., *424*
Novotony, E. S., *396*
Nowlis, H. H., *342*
Nowlis, V., *342*
Nutall, E., 362, *368*
Nuttall, R. L., 362, *368*

O'Brill, N., *341*
O'Conner, N., 251, *270*
Offer, D., *273*
O'Gorman, N., 348
O'Hair, M. M., 156
Ohnmacht, F., *151*
O'Kane, J. M., *424*
Olesker, W., *306*
Oliver, S., 80
Olmo, B., *424*
O'Malley, B. M., 40, *76*
O'Malley, D., *339*
O'Neal, E., *396*
O'Neil, R. P., *340*
Opper, S., *151*
Orloff, H., *202*
Orlos, J., *111*
Oshman, H., *368*
Osofsky, J. D., *273*
Osofsky, H. J., *273*
Osmond, H., *369*
Ostrow, R. J., 385, *396*

Pacheo, A., 284, *305*
Paffenbarger, R. S., Jr., 356, *368*
Pankove, R., *153*
Pannor, R., *201*

Parker, C., 126, *151*
Parker, J. H., 408, *423*
Parsons, T., 65, *78*
Paton, S. M., *340*
Patrick, T., 408, *423*
Pattee, C., *369*
Patterson, G. R., 60, *77*
Payne, E. E., 59, *78*
Payne, I. R., *202*
Payne, J., *369*
Peck, R. H., 160-161, *175*
Perkins, M. R., 286, *305*
Perry, M., *234*
Perry, W., 124-126, *150*
Peskin, H., 100, *109, 368*
Petersen, A., *271*, 331, *340*
Peterson, E. T., *202*
Phillipson, R., 342
Piaget, J., 114ff, 157-160, *175,*
    350
Pine, F., *306*
Place, D. M., *273*
Platt, L., 182, *200*
Plume, M., *271*
Pokorny, A., *270*
Polit, D., 360
Polsby, G. K., *271*
Pomeroy, W. B., 241, *271*
Ponzo, Z., 64, *78*
Poppleton, P. K., 98, *109*
Porter, J., 284, *305*
Post, R. D., *340, 341*
Potvin, R., 402, *423*
Presser, H. B., *273*
Prince, Raymond, 408, 423
Pringle, M. K., *152*
Proskauer, S., *342*
Protinsky, H. O., Jr., *81*

Quarter, J., *424*

Rajan, R., *273*
Rahe, S., 364, *367*
Ramsdell, E. A., *81*
Rank, J. L. 84, *109*
Rank, O., 17-18, *36,* 135
Raths, L., 400, *423*
Rathus, S. A., *307*
Rawls, D., *234*
Rawls, J., *234*
Redl, F., 389, *396*
Repin, T. A., 157, *175*
Reimer, J., 171, *175*
Rice, B., *396*

Rice, F. P., 49, *78,* 184, *200*
Richards, I. K., 277, *304*
Riesman, D., 181
Riessman, F., 180, *200*
Ripple, R. E., 135, *150*
Ripley, H. S., 356, *366*
Roazen, P., *36,* 41, *78*
Robbins, W., *368*
Roberts, E., 261, *270*
Roberts, J., *111*
Roberts, R., 373, *396*
Robins, L., 383, *396*
Robinson, J., 251, *269*
Roe, A., *78*
Rogel, M., *271*
Rogers, D., 53, *78,* 207, 218,
    233
Roghmann, K., *271*
Rohrbaugh, J., 60, *78,* 402, *423*
Rohwer, W. D., Jr., *424*
Roll, S., 30, *36*
Rolland, R., *342*
Romar, N., *111*
Roosevelt, E., 407
Rosen, B. M., *271,* 347, *368*
Rosenberg, B. G., 60, *79*
Rosenberg, F., *273*
Rosenblatt, P. C., *202*
Rosencohn, H., *423*
Rosenkrantz, A., *368,* 369
Rosenkrantz, P., 64, *77, 79*
Ross, D., *396*
Ross, J. N., 100, *109*
Ross, S. A., *396*
Ross, R. J., *152*
Rossi, P. H., *341*
Rothschild, B., 310, *339*
Rotter, J., 356, *368*
Rubin, I., 254, *271*
Rubin, K. H., *175*
Rubenstein, H., *271*
Rubenstein, J., 264, *271*
Rutherford, J. A., *424*
Russ-Eft, D., 256, *271*
Rutter, M., *202*
Ryals, K., *423*
Ryan, I., 264, *271*
Ryor, John, *200*

Sabbath, J., 355, *368*
Salzman, L., 183, *200*
Sanders, K. M., 80
Santana, G., 331, *340*

Santrock, J. W., *79*
Satchell, M., *340*
Savin-Williams, R. C., 32, *36*
Saybrook, E. L., 180, *200*
Schab, F., 286, *305*
Schaeffer, J., *340*
Scheck, D. C., *273*
Schenkel, S., *79*
Schildkraut, M., *271*
Schillain, D., *307*
Schneer, H. I., 355, *367*
Schneider, F. W., *175*
Schnider, R., *340*
Schooler, J. C., 193, *200*
Schowalter, J. E., 355, *368*
Schroder, H., 126, *149*
Schulman, J. L., *307*
Schumsky, D. A., *109*
Schwab, J., *369*
Schwartz, G., 211, *233*
Schwartz, M., 206, *233*
Scully, M. G., *424*
Sears, R. R., 65, *79*
Sebald, H., 181, 184, *200,* 207,
    233, 253, *271,* 276, *305*
Segal, B., *343*
Seltzer, S., 413, *423*
Senna, J., *307*
Serson, J., (Mrs. E. Erikson), 41
Sewell, T., *396*
Sexton, P., 219, 233
Shaffer, D., *369*
Shakespeare, W., 128
Shearer, L., *271*
Shellow, R., *368*
Shenker, I. R., *271*
Sheppard, C. W., 324, *339*
Shoham, I., *269*
Shorr, W., 354, *366*
Shuman, B., *270*
Siegal, L., *343*
Siegal, R. S., *423*
Siegler, R. S., *152*
Siemsgluez, S., 283, *305*
Silber, T., 256, *271*
Simmons, R. G., *273*
Simon, R. K., *342*
Simon, S., 400, *423*
Simon, W., *76,* 242, *270*
Sklar, J., *271, 273*
Skoogberg, E., *202*
Sleptiza, R., 126, *149*
Smart, M. S., 209, *233*
Smart, R. C., 209, *233*

Smedley, F. W., 84, *110*
Smith, D., 353, 360, *368*
Smith, G. M., *340*
Smith, P., *270*
Smithson, W. S., *369*
Snowden, L. R., *369*
Snyder, E. E., 283, *385*
Sommers, P., *307*
Socrates, 4
Sorensen, A. B., *80*
Sorosky, A. D., 187, *200, 201*
Soskin, W. F., 206, *234*
South, D. R., *201*, 219, *233*
Spanier, G. B., 264, *271*
Spencer, W. A., 283
Spilka, A., 404, *423*
Springer, M., 256, *271*
Stanley, E., *369*
Stanley, J. C., *307*
Starr, J. M., 32, *35, 424*
Stattieri, J. R., *111*
Stein, A. H., 59, 61, 65, *79*
Stein, K. B., 206, *234*
Steinbeck, J., 186, *201*
Steinem, G., 64
Stempfel, R. S., *111*
Stephenson, B., 126, *150*
Stinnett, N., *202*
St. John, N. H., 220, *233*
Stoner, C., 408, *423*
Strauss, A. H., *424*
South, D. A., 219, *233*
Strowig, R., 64, *78*
Stuart, I. R., 419, *423*
Stumphauzer, J., *396*
Su, W. H., *342*
Sudia, C. E., 181, 201
Sugar, M., *273*
Sullivan, E., *175*
Sulzer, J. L., *397*
Sutton-Smith, B., 60, *79*
Swanson, R. B., *202*
Swift, P., 157, *175, 340,* 372, *396*
Synogal, M., *341*

Tai, S. W., *369*
Tallman, I., *202*
Tanner, J. M., 85, 101, *110*
Tapp, J. L., *175*
Tart, C. J., *343*
Tatelbaum, R., *271*
Tavris, C., 60, *79*
Taylor, B., *269*

Taylor, R., 80
Tec, N., 331, *340, 343*
Teicher, D., 355, *368*
Teilhard de Chardin, P., *150*
Temby, W., 359, *368*
Tenhouten, W., 220, *233*
Tenhunen, T., *109*
Terman, L. M., 103, 132
Tessler, D. J., 325, 335–337, *340*
Thomas, G., *369*
Thomas, L. E., 206, *234*
Thompson, K., 257, *272*
Thompson, M. H., *424*
Thompson, V. D., 193, 201
Tietze, M., 256, *272*
Tinkleberg, J. R., 331, *340*
Tissot, M., 242
Tobias, J. I., *340, 385, 396*
Tobin-Richards, M., *271*
Toffler, A., 71–72, *79,* 302, 305, *434, 439*
Toolan, J., *369*
Toman, W., 191, *201*
Torgerson, E., 409, *423*
Torney, J. V., *422*
Torrance, E. P., 135, *150*
Trow, M., *307*
Tuckman, Jacob, 356, *368*
Tudor, C., 331, *340*
Turiel, E., 164, *175*
Twain, Mark, 139
Tweedy, H., *306*
Tyack, D., 284, *305*

Updike, J., *150*

Valins, S., *343*
Vandermyn, G., *424*
Varma, V. P., *152*
Vener, A. M., *272*
Verville, E., *272*
Victor, H., *343*
Vincent, C. E., 183, *201*
Vogel, S., *77*

Wagner, B. R., 283, *305*
Wagner, C., 252, *272*
Wagner, H., *424*
Wahl, O., 411, *423*
Walter, W., 202
Walters, J., 262, *272*
Walters, L., 256, *271, 272*
Walters, R. H., 361, *395*

Waltz, G., 258, *272*
Ward, W. C., *153*
Warheit, G. J., *369*
Warshaw, M., 4, *36*
Warwick, R., 410
Washington, B., 157, *175*
Wason, P. C., 124, *150*
Wasserman, E., 170, *175*
Watson, F., *271*
Wax, J., *340*
Webb, A., 65, *79*
Wechsler, D., 140, *150*
Weil, A. T., *343*
Weinberg, J. T., *424*
Weiner, I. B., 347, *368*
Weinrich, H., *175*
Weinstock, A., *202*
Weisman, J., 410, *424*
Welfel, E., 126, *150*
Welles, O., 71
Welsh, R. S., *397*
Wenz, F., *367*
Wertheimer, I., *271*
Wertheimer, M., 131
Wenz, F., *367*
Westley, W. A., *232*
Whelan, M., 172, *175*
White, R., *367*
Whitehurst, R. N., *202*
Widholm, O., *109*
Widick, C., 126, *150*
Wieder, D. L., 219, 234
Wieland, W. F., 324, *340*
Wilde, J., *307*
Williams, C. A., 362, *368*
Williams, D., 276, *305, 342*
Williams, F. R., 412, *424*
Williams, J., 64, *79*
Williams, R. L., 283, *384*
Williams, R. M., Jr., 207, *234*
Willits, F. K., 402, *422*
Wilson, H., *369*
Wineman, D., 390, *396*
Winer, E., *305*
Witkin, H. A., *153*
Witt, M. T., *109*
Wohlford, P., 60, *79*
Wolf, S., *397*
Wolff, G., 102, *109*
Woodward, K., 181, *201*
Wright, J. D., *424*
Wright, J. S., *343*
Wuerger, M. K., *272*
Wuthnow, R., *424*

Wylie, P., 167, *175,* 181, *200*
Wynne, E., 283, *305,* 354, 357, *368*

Yablonsky, L., 374, *395*
Yankelvitch, D., *339, 424*
Yarber, W., 263, *272*

Yorke, R., 412, *424*
Yost, E. D., *203*
Young, R., 249, *269*
Yunger, M., 324, *340*
Ysin, A., *369*

Zegans, L., *202*

Zellermayer, J., *203*
Zelnick, M., 250, *272*
Zemitis, O., 251, *270*
Zimmerman, D. A., 219, *234*
Ziomkowski, L., *343*
Zuehike, M., *271*

Subject Index

Abstract thought, 114
Accommodation, 116
Adaptation, 115
Adolescence, definition, 5, 28
Adolescence, future of, 428ff
  new ways of dealing with, 431
  new ways of understanding, 432
Advice of experts to beginners, 434
Age-related activities, 187
Aggressive gang, 372
Alcohol, 319
  talking to teenagers about, 319
Alternative schools, 296–300
Amphetamines, 321
Anaclitic identification, 58
Androgyny, 65–70
Argot, 211
Assimilation, 116
Associates, 214
Autosexual behavior, 241–243
Aversive stimuli, 208

Barbiturates, 322
Bar-mitzvah, Bas-mitzvah, 407
Basic skills, competency in, 284–286
Behaviorism, 207
Behavior therapy, 208
Birth order, 191–194
Body, attitudes toward, 102ff
Body image, 103
Brainstorming, 388

Catharsis, 11
Career education, 55–57
Chemical hallucinogens, 321
Chromosome failure, 58
Cliques, 214
Clubs, 215
Cocaine, 318
Codification, 159
Cofigurative culture, 186
Cognitive development, stages of, 117ff
  the concrete operational stage, 118–119
  the formal operational stage, 119–120
  the preoperational stage, 118
  the sensory-motor stage, 117
Communes, 195
Communications, 229, 438

active listening, 229
games, 224–228
"I" messages, 229
language of acceptance, 228–230
"no-lose" method, 229
peer group, 223–230
Community health services, 362–364
  primary prevention, 362
  secondary prevention, 362
  tertiary prevention, 363
Compensation, 122
Comprehensive high school, 292
Comprehensive education, 292–294
Conditioning, 157
Confirmation, 407
Conservation, 119
Consolidation, 123
Constitutional rights, 279
Controlled drugs, 312
Conventional morality, 162
Corporal punishment, 279
Courts and the family, 182
Creative development, 127ff
Creativity
  appropriateness in, 127
  condensation in, 127
  critical period (hypothesis), 135
  guidelines for, 138
  intelligence and, 139–140
  mental process, 128–132
  obstacles to, 135
  personality traits, 133–134
  product, 127, 128
  transformation in, 127
  unusualness in, 127
Crisis intervention, 363
Crossroads Program, 386
Crowds, 215
Cultural lag, 189
Cultural mores, 168

Dating, 240
Death
  awareness of, 350
  crisis of, 350–353
Death rate, 350–351
Death trend, 356
Defense mechanisms, 13, 349–350
Delay of gratification, 402

Delinquency, 371ff
  follow-up studies on, 375
  and the inadequate family, 380
  long-term implications of, 380
  neurotic, 379
  and personality, 379
  psychotic and organic, 380
  retrospective studies, 381
  and social class, 380
  socialized, 373
  sociopathic, 380
  unsocialized, 382
Delinquency, treatment of, 385
  behaviorist approach, 385
  diversion program, 392
  the ecological approach, 389
  halfway houses, 388
  Outward Bound, 390
  psychotherapeutic approach, 387
Dependency needs, 193
Depression, 355
Deprogramming, 408
Disease and disability, 360
  incidence of, 360
Divorce, and the family, 181
Dogmatism, 403
Drug abuse, 310ff
  alternatives to, 331
  definitions, 310
  ethnic group, 325
  prevention of, 332
Drug addiction, 310
Drug dependence, 310
Drug overdose, 311
Drug tolerance, 311
Drug use, and behavior, 328
  and crime, 330
  patterns of relationships between, 331
  and school climate, 335
  and sex, 324
Duplication theory, 193

Emancipated minor, 183
Empirico-inductive reasoning, 121
Equilibrium, 120
Ethical development, 156ff
  autonomy of, 158
  sex role in, 162
  the awareness of rules, 158
  the practice of rules, 157
Extended family, 180–181

Family
  alternatives to the traditional,
    195–198
  the changing status of, 180ff
  inappropriate patterns, 188
  loss of function, 184
Family tree, 196
Fanaticism, 355
Fathers, new role of, 181
Feedback, 238
Fixation, 161
Focal theory, 27–29
Foreclosure, premature, 45
Friends, 214
Future shock, 71–78

Gangs, 215, 384–385
  characteristics of joiners, 385
  and social class, 384
Generation gap, 189
Giftedness, 132–133
Gonorrhea, 361
Group identity versus alienation,
    209
Group therapy, 388
Gynecomastia, 58

Hallucinogens, 320
Hard drugs, 320
Hermaphrodite, 57
Heroin, 321
Heterosexuality, 249ff
Hirsutism, 58
Homosexuality, 243ff
  causes of 244–245
  myths about, 243
  societal attitudes toward, 245–
    246
Honesty, 434
Hormonal balance, 94
Hormone therapy, 101
Humor, sense of, 435
Hypothetical deductive reasoning,
    120, 121

Identity, 24–26
  achievement, 45, 71–74
  confusion, 25, 45
  crisis, 41ff
  foreclosure, 44, 45
  individual, versus role diffusion,
    208
  moratorium, 44, 45

search for, 393ffp
status, 45ff
Inconsistent conditioning, 208
Incorrigible child, 183
Individualization of instruction,
    279
Initiation rites, 352
In-school suspension room, 290
Instructional modes, 279
Intellectual development, 114ff,
    124–126
Intelligence, 115ff
  measurement of, 139–140
  the intelligence quotient, 139–
    140
  genetic influences, 140–141
Intergenerational dissonance, 190
Inversion, 122
Isolate, social, 219

Jargon, 211
Just Community School, 170–
    171

Kibbutz, 181

Language of acceptance, 228–
    230
Learning disability, 142
Life change units, 364
Living together, 198
Love, 265–267
  demythologizing of, 265
L.S.D., 321

Magical thinking, 355
Marijuana, 316
Marriage
  companionship, 198
  experiments within, 195
  open, 196
Masturbation, 241–243
Maturation, 94ff
Maximum growth spurt, 94ff
Meaning, the search for, 434
Menarche, 92
Menstruation, 92
Mental disturbance, 346ff
  types of, 348
Mental operations, 116
Mental process
  associationism, 128
  structuralism, 131

Mental structures, 115
Mescaline, 320
Methadone, 321
Methaqualone, 322
Milgram electric shock obedience
    test, 164
Mini-generation gap, 190
Minimal competency
    requirements, 286
Momism, 188–189
Moral development, 155ff
  Piaget's theory of, 157–160
  Peck and Havighurst's theory
    of, 160–161
  Kohlberg's theory of, 160,
    161–162
Moral education, 168
Moral judgment, 155ff
Moral maturity scores, 169
Moratorium, 44
Motor development, 94
Musical values, 265

Narcotics, 321
Negative identity, 44, 219
Negative reinforcement, 208
Networks, 215
New individualism, 78
Nocturnal emissions, 92
Nonaggressive status offender,
    372
Nonlinear thinking, 143
  print-oriented people, 144
  neotribal people, 145
Nonrational experience, 335
Nontraditional schools, 296–300
Normal range of development,
    94
Nuclear family, 181

Object constancy, 118
Obsolescence, new, 78
Oedipal conflict, 15
Open campus, 279
Open marriage, 195–198
Organization, mental, 116
Other-borns, 191
Outward Bound, 294–295

Paraprofessionals, 279
Parental attitudes, 183
Parent-child role reversals, 356

Parenthood, unwed teenage, 255–261
Parents, advice to, 194–195
Parole, 385
Participatory education, 292
Peer groups
  developmental patterns of, 214–218
  failure of, 219–220
  purposes of, 218–219
  sex role of, 63
  stages of development, 215
  types of associations, 214–215
Peer interactions, 220
  effects of the school on, 221
  evaluating the classroom, 221–222
Peer relations, failure of, 219
Pluralism, 403
Postconventional morality, 162
Positive reinforcement, 208
Preconventional morality, 162
Prevention and treatment of suicide, 359
Primary group status, 184
Primary reinforcers, 385
Principle of justice, 165
Probation, 381
Prostitution, 373
Psilocybin, 321
Psychoanalysis, 387
Psychodelics, 321
Psychopathology, 348
Psychosocial dwarfism, 101
Psychosomatic disorders, 364
Psychotherapeutic approach, 387
Puberty, 84ff
  beginnings of, 91
  inappropriate physical growth, 101
  normal age ranges, 94, 101
  timing of, 94ff

Race, sex differences in, 257–258
Recidivism rate, 388
Reflexes, 115
Religiosity scale, 402
Religious values, 401ff
  conversion and confirmation, 407
  family's influence on, 404
  participation and belief, 404

revival, 407
  stages of growth, 405–406
Reproduction, 85
Republic of technology, 72–73
Research techniques, 30–33
Residential care center, 387
Reversibility, 119
Rites of passage, 407
Ritual, 407
Runaways, 372

Schema, 115
Schizophrenia, 347
School phobia, 283
Schools, 276ff
  academic effectiveness of, 281–284
  comprehensive education in, 291
  crisis in, 277ff
  discipline management in, 288–292
  experiential learning in, 292
  improvements to, 284ff
  negotiation in, 287–288
  numbers served, 276
  peer interactions, 220
  technical deficiencies in, 279
  violence in, 277
  vocational, 280
Scholastic Aptitude Test, 283
Secondary group status, 184
Secondary reinforcers, 385
Sedatives, 322
Self-fulfilling prophecy, 364
Sex identity, 57ff
Sex role, 57ff
  sex-role orientation, 57
  sex-role preference, 57
  sex-role adaptation, 57
  morality and, 166–168
Sex-role stereotype, 62–64
Sexuality, 238ff
  education of, 85, 261–264
  motivations for, 253–254
  stages of, 241
  values, 254–255
Sexual revolution, 239–241
Skeletal growth, 91
Slang, 211
Social role, 62
Social stability, 186
Socioeconomic status, 220

Sociograms, 221, 223
Soft drugs, 316
Soft rock, 413
Solidification, 123
Soviet education, 157
Stages of life, 42–43
Status achievement, 184
Status ascription, 184
Stimulants, 321
Stress, 355
Subcultures, 205ff
  elements of, 208ff
  origin of
    behaviorist model, 207
    culture transition model, 207
    psychogenic model, 207–208
Suggestibility, 355
Suicide, 353–361
  among college students, 359
  causes of, 354–358
  means of, 353
  treatment and, 359
  prevention of, 361
Swinging, 198
Syphilis, 361

Thinking style, 113ff
Tobacco, 318
Token system, 386
Tolerance, 436
Tranquilizers, 321
Transductive logic, 118
Transsexual, 57
Two-string test, 134

Universal ethics, 162
Universal justice, 165

Validation, 239
Values, 400ff
  acquisition of, 414
  clarification of, 414ff, 433
    compared with moral education, 419
  clarification techniques, 415
  hidden moral curriculum, 414
  laissez-faire attitude, 414
  and the media, 408
    aggressiveness, 409
    attitudes toward mental illness, 410
    occupational, 409

personal relationships, 410
moralizing, 414
and music, 412–413
Venereal disease, 361
Victimless crime, 311

Vocational identity, 49ff
influence of sex on, 53
parental influence on, 51
Vocational instruction, 185
Volunteerism, 293

Voucher system, 297

Walkabout, 295–296
Withdrawn child, 437
Working mothers, 181